PENGUIN BOOKS

THE PENGUIN HISTORY OF THE CHURCH

Volume Six

Stephen Neill spent twenty years as a missionary in southern India, where he eventually became Bishop of Tinnevelly. In 1944 he returned to Europe because of ill health and subsequently became Professor of Missions and Ecumenical Theology at the University of Hamburg (1962–9) and then Professor of Philosophy and Religious Studies at the new University of Nairobi, a post which he held until 1973. From 1979 until his death in 1984 he was Assistant Bishop in the Diocese of Oxford. Professor Neill wrote much on the history of Christianity, especially on the New Testament, the history of Christianity in India, and the Ecumenical Movement.

STEPHEN NEILL

A History of Christian Missions

REVISED FOR THE SECOND EDITION
BY OWEN CHADWICK

PENGUIN BOOKS

PENGUIN BOOKS

Published by the Penguin Group
Penguin Books Ltd, 27 Wrights Lane, London W8 5TZ, England
Penguin Books USA Inc., 375 Hudson Street, New York, New York 10014, USA
Penguin Books Australia Ltd, Ringwood, Victoria, Australia
Penguin Books Canada Ltd, 10 Alcorn Avenue, Toronto, Ontario, Canada M4V 3B2
Penguin Books (NZ) Ltd, 182–190 Wairau Road, Auckland 10, New Zealand

Penguin Books Ltd, Registered Offices: Harmondsworth, Middlesex, England

First published in Pelican Books 1964
Second edition 1986
Reprinted in Penguin Books 1990
7 9 10 8

Printed in England by Clays Ltd, St Ives plc
Filmset in Linotron Baskerville

The Penguin History of the Church
(formerly The Pelican History of the Church)

GENERAL EDITOR: OWEN CHADWICK

1. *The Early Church*. By Sir Henry Chadwick, Honorary Fellow and former Master of Peterhouse, Cambridge, and Regius Professor Emeritus of Divinity, Cambridge University.
2. *Western Society and the Church in the Middle Ages*. By Sir Richard Southern, formerly President of St John's College, Oxford.
3. *The Reformation*. By Owen Chadwick, formerly Chancellor of the University of East Anglia and Regius Professor of Modern History, Cambridge University.
4. *The Church and the Age of Reason, 1648–1789*. By Gerald R. Cragg, formerly Professor of Church History at Andover Newton Theological School, Boston, Mass.
5. *The Church in an Age of Revolution*. By Alec R. Vidler, formerly Fellow and Dean of King's College, Cambridge.
6. *A History of Christian Missions*. By Stephen Neill, formerly Profesor of Philosophy and Religious Studies at the University of Nairobi and Assistant Bishop in the Diocese of Oxford.
7. *The Christian Church in the Cold War*. By Owen Chadwick, formerly Chancellor of the University of East Anglia and Regius Professor of Modern History, Cambridge University.

Contents

Preface

To write the whole history of Christian Expansion in one volume is a difficult task. A number of excellent books have been written on the subject, but almost all of them suffer from the attempt at completeness. If every country in the world has to be separately treated, every single missionary society commended, every outstanding missionary and convert listed, the result is almost bound to be an arid catalogue of dates, events, and names. Some of these books are very valuable as works of reference and indispensable to the student, but they are not easily readable. Against this tendency there is only one safeguard – a resolute determination to omit. In this book, I have tried to keep the main lines of Christian advance steadily before my eyes, and to use the notable event and the outstanding career as illustrations of the main theme. I hope that I may be successful in conveying to the reader a sense of movement, not always movement in a straight line of progress, often aberrant, sometimes retarded or diverted, at times seeming to come altogether to a standstill, but always in the end acquiring new impetus and so leading to the point of history at which we now find ourselves.

Once again I am greatly indebted to Miss G. I. Mather, who typed the whole book from a rather illegible manuscript; her wide knowledge, missionary experience, and minute accuracy have saved me from many errors. In the correction of the proofs, I have received valuable help from three distinguished missionaries of the younger generation, Dr G. H. Anderson of Manila, and Dr Lothar Schreiner and the Rev. Edward Nyhus, both of Siantar, Sumatra. The book was written in my room on the twelfth floor of the new University building in Hamburg; I hope that my colleagues of the Theological Faculty will feel that the time taken off from other duties for the writing of it has been well spent. The proofs have been read under the hospitable roofs of Trinity Theological College, Singapore and McMaster University, Hamilton, Ontario.

S.N.

Publisher's Note

The author died in 1984. Just before he died, he sent to the publisher instructions on how he wished to revise the book for its next edition. The Editor of the series therefore carried out for this Edition a revision which he believed to be in accordance with the mind of Dr Neill. It was clear that he wished the last two chapters to be rewritten in the light of recent developments. And the opportunity has been taken to include a few minor corrections in the earlier chapters.

PART ONE

1

A Faith for the World

Most of the religions of mankind have been local, and even tribal, in their character. 'For all the peoples walk each in the name of its god, but we will walk in the name of the Lord our God for ever and ever.'[1] As in old days every city had its temple and its god, so to this day among simple peoples every tribe and every clan has its spirits, many of whom are ancestors, but some of whom represent the hostile and terrifying powers of nature. You cannot worship my spirits, since you have neither connection with them nor claim upon them; neither can I worship yours, for the same reason. Nor can these gods be worshipped outside the territory which is theirs in the sense that it lies under their protection. These ancient ideas are found in almost every part of the Old Testament. When David is driven out from the land of Palestine, he can no longer worship Israel's God: 'They have driven me out this day that I should have no share in the heritage of the Lord, saying, "Go, serve other gods".'[2] When Ruth decides to follow her mother-in-law from the land of Moab to Judah, and says, 'Your people shall be my people, and your God my God'[3], this noble utterance is an expression not so much of religious faith as of social solidarity. Coming to a strange land, she must renounce the god of the Moabites, Chemosh, and as part of her new inheritance she must accept also the worship of Israel's God.

It is true that, through the researches of anthropologists, we now know that almost all the races of men, the most primitive among them included, have some knowledge of and belief in one Supreme God. But this Supreme God is in most cases a dim and distant figure, to whom sacrifice and worship are not offered, and who is not supposed to concern himself very much with the affairs of men. Some tribes have the story that in ancient days the sky was so near to the earth that a man could touch it with his hand; then there was real contact between God and man; but later men offended

1. Micah 4:5.
2. 1 Sam. 26:19.
3. Ruth 1:16.

God, who being angry withdrew himself to the present immense distance, and since that remote time nothing more has been heard of him. He is not effectively a living principle of unity among men. Even higher religions, such as Hinduism, which have kept the idea of the unity of all things and therefore of God himself, have shown little disposition to go out and convert others, or to assert that theirs is the only kind of worship that will be acceptable to God.

Three religions alone seem to form the exception, and to have been missionary and universal in their outlook from the beginning – Buddhism, Christianity, and Islam. It is notable that these are among the few religions of mankind which it is possible to trace to a definite beginning in time and the origin of which can be attributed to an indentifiable founder. Each of the three great teachers believed himself to have received a revelation which is of universal significance for mankind; each commissioned disciples to go out and proclaim the message as widely as they could. Buddhism, till our own day, has always been an eastern religion; having died out in its homeland, India, it has spread to north and east and south, only in recent years to the west. Islam was and is a religion of the desert and the Middle East, with outliers in all directions; it stretches today from Morocco to western China, from Albania to Indonesia, and is making ever increasingly successful inroads into tropical Africa. With modern emigration it reached Europe and America. Christianity alone has succeeded in making itself a universal religion. This does not, of course, mean that everyone in the world has become Christian. Yet it is a fact that this Levantine form of religion, stamped with the marks of its origin in the eastern Mediterranean, has now found a home in almost every country in the world; it has adherents among all the races of men, from the most sophisticated of westerners to the aborigines of the in-hospitable deserts of Australia; and there is no religion of the world which has not yielded a certain number of converts to it.

This is something that has never happened before in the history of the world. In a famous phrase in the sermon at his enthrone-ment as Archbishop of Canterbury in 1942, William Temple (1881–1944) referred to the existence of this great world-wide Christendom, the result in the main of the Christian missionary work of the last two and a half centuries, as 'the great new fact of our time'.[4] How has all this come about? How is it that a religion of

4. It is sometimes imagined that the Archbishop was referring to the so-called

the Middle East radically changed its character by becoming the dominant religion of Europe, and is now changing its character again through becoming a universal religion, increasingly free from the bounds of geography and of Western civilization? This is the theme of this book.

It must be admitted that at the start the nature of the Christian Gospel and the circumstances of its origin were anything but favourable to such a world-wide expansion. In the time of Jesus, the Jews, always a source of perplexity and sometimes of indignation to their non-Jewish neighbours, had so withdrawn behind their intellectual and spiritual defences that, apart from the special influence of the synagogue to which we shall come later, there was little contact between them and the world which surrounded them. The Roman poet Juvenal speaks of them as a race so morose and surly that, if you ask one of them your way in the street, he will not answer unless you are one of his own conventicle.[5] The consequences of this attitude of alienation from the world reached their highest point in the Jewish war of A.D. 67–70, when Jerusalem fell before the Roman armies amid irreparable disaster, but this was only the culmination of a process that had been going on for a long time.

Jesus was born a Jew, and never pretended to be anything else. In adult years he never travelled beyond the narrow limits of Palestine.[6] His native language was Aramaic. It is almost certain that he could read the Old Testament in Hebrew. It is likely that he knew a little Greek, perhaps some words of Latin, but the whole cast of his thought is Semitic. He speaks with unparalleled originality and poetic power, but his language is that of the Psalms, and his style is that of classical Hebrew poetry.

This means that a great part of what Jesus said could not have been readily intelligible to an ordinary hearer who was not a Jew. He had taken up and made his own the apocalyptic language of the Jewish people. An oppressed and unhappy people had found

'ecumenical movement', or even to the World Council of Churches. Reference to the text shows that this is a misunderstanding.

5. Satire XIV: l. 103. In this, says Juvenal, they are obeying the law handed down to them by Moses.

6. Apparently as a child he was for a time a refugee in Egypt (Matt. 2:13–23). Tales of his having spent some of his earlier years in India or elsewhere rest on no historical foundation whatsoever.

compensation for its miseries in brilliant and hopeful pictures of the time of the end. God will not for ever leave his people comfortless. He will in the end intervene in judgement. Then, all the present framework of the world and of human society will be dissolved, the sovereignty of God will be established, and under his direct guidance his people will live in happiness and prosperity. Some schools associated this hope for the days of the end with the figure of the Anointed of the Lord, the Messiah, who would rule in the name of God. Central in all these pictures is the rehabilitation of the people of Israel, who will be exalted to be chief of nations over their enemies.

It is still a matter of dispute among scholars whether Jesus ever identified himself with the Messiah of popular expectation. Certainly he rejected the immediate and violent aims of the people, and their hopes of early liberation through a successful rising against the Roman power. Yet his thought and speech are apocalyptic through and through: the kingdom of God is at hand, the last days are upon us; therefore an urgent call goes out to all men to repent and accept this good news of which Jesus is himself the mouthpiece and the content. The message is for Jews: they are the people of God to whom the word of proclamation must be addressed. If Gentiles are admitted, it is only grudgingly, and on the basis of a faith as great as, or even greater than, that manifested by the sons of Israel.[7]

It is hardly possible to imagine a setting or a doctrine less likely to serve as the starting-point for a religion that was to become the faith of all mankind. Yet closer consideration may suggest that this picture is one-sided, and that the Jewish background and form of the Gospel message do not exhaust its significance.

The Jews had constituted themselves 'the second race', a people with laws and customs that separated them from the whole of the rest of mankind. But, in so doing, they were acting in defiance of one part of that revelation which had called them into being as a nation. A strain of universalism, of a sense of world-wide responsibility, runs through the whole of the Old Testament. The Jews believed themselves to be, and claimed to be, the people of God – a claim on the face of it so absurd that no one could be expected to pay it any attention, unless it happened to be true. And, after all, the Jews were right. The Old Testament, akin though it may be in certain details to other ancient Scriptures, is in reality not in the

7. Luke 7:9.

least like the sacred book of any other religion. It alone can be read aloud today to a modern audience, and be felt to be, on page after page, luminous, contemporary, and challenging. Like other ancient books it is marred by certain crudities, but among them all it alone can establish a claim to be a permanently valid message for the whole of mankind. And of this the Jews were not unaware; at the highest and best levels of their thought they were conscious that the treasure of the knowledge of God was given to them not for their personal exaltation, but in trust for the benefit of the whole world:

It is too light a thing that you should be my servant to raise up the tribes of Jacob and to restore the preserved of Israel; I will give you as a light to the nations, that my salvation may reach to the end of the earth.[8]

It is here in the Second Isaiah, the great prophecies of chapters 40–55, which seem to have been written towards the end of the captivity of Israel in Babylon, that such thoughts find their clearest and most splendid expression. The people are in exile, poor and oppressed; what have they to oppose to Babylonian idolatry, the gigantic monuments of which surround them on every side, when it seems so plain that the power of the God of Israel has gone down before the greater power of the gods of the heathen? In this situation the mind of the prophet goes back again and again to the doctrine of creation. Lift up your eyes to the heavens, he seems to say, and you will see something far greater than the Babylonian gods:

Have you not known? Have you not heard? The Lord is the everlasting God, the Creator of the ends of the earth. He does not faint or grow weary, his understanding is unsearchable . . . Behold, the nations are like a drop from a bucket, and are accounted as the dust on the scales; behold, he takes up the isles like fine dust.[9]

The doctrine of creation is not, in the Bible, a philosophical or cosmological theory; it is simply the background to the human story, God's love story with the human race, which follows. If the God of Israel really is the Creator of the whole universe, if he carries all the nations in his hand, then the unity of the world of nature and of men is guaranteed, and it seems to follow, as part of the divine purpose, that sooner or later all men should find their way to the God who has made them. Unity in religion is the natural corollary of the doctrine that all men are already one under God.

8. Isaiah 49:6.
9. Isaiah 40:28, 15.

After the period of the prophets, the people of Israel had signally failed to realize the generosity of God's purpose and the nature of its own vocation. Jesus, however, with an imaginative understanding of the Old Testament singularly different from the arid and scholastic methods of his contemporaries, reverted to the best and deepest teaching of the prophets. The universalism which had been lost is in him to make its reappearance. Yet this affirmation is at once contradicted by the apparent limitation of the mission of Jesus to Israel only. 'I was sent only to the lost sheep of the house of Israel.'[10] 'Go nowhere among the Gentiles, and enter no town of the Samaritans, but go rather to the lost sheep of the house of Israel.'[11] Earlier readers of the Gospels (and readers today who take uncritically everything that is recorded in them) could at once balance such expressions of limitation with the words that indicate a universal destiny for the faith of Jesus: 'And the gospel must first be preached to all nations'[12]; 'Go therefore and make disciples of all nations.'[13]

Even if the authenticity of all the words of Jesus were questioned, there is one action of his which is so thoroughly attested that hardly a doubt can be entertained as to its historical reality – the triumphal entry into Jerusalem. It is clear that this was carefully planned by Jesus, both in order to make clear the nature of the kingdom which he came to bring, and in order to appeal to the people of the capital to accept him. In all this he was carefully following the prophecy of Zechariah which reads:

Rejoice greatly, O daughter of Zion! Shout aloud, O daughter of Jerusalem! Lo, your king comes to you; triumphant and victorious is he, humble and riding on an ass, on a colt the foal of an ass.[14]

Of a hundred who are familiar with this passage, hardly one, perhaps, has taken the trouble to read the verse that follows:

He shall command peace to the nations; his dominion shall be from sea to sea, and from the River to the ends of the earth.

This verse, no less than the other, must have been in the mind of Jesus on this solemn occasion. And he cannot have been unaware that these phrases occur also in Psalm 72, the clearest picture in the

10. Matt. 15:24.
11. Matt. 10:5–6.
12. Mark 13:10.
13. Matt. 28:19.
14. Zechariah 9:9.

Old Testament of the kingdom as God intended it to be. The vision of Jesus reached out far beyond Jerusalem and his immediate problems; he is thinking in terms of a kingdom that has become coextensive with the inhabited world.

The death of Jesus, and the resurrection which followed it, determined the whole future destiny of the people of God. Jesus alone, by his obedience to God to the uttermost, fulfilled the destiny of Israel. The old Israel, the people of God's choice, could as such have no further part in it. The purpose of God was now to go forward through a new Israel, called into being through faith in Jesus Christ, the chief characteristic of which was to be its willingness to die and to rise again with him. The day of the Gentiles had come. The door was still open to all Israelites who would accept and believe; but, for Jew and Gentile alike, the only entry now was through faith in Jesus Christ.

All this, of course, was not immediately evident to the little group of Jews who gradually became convinced of the truth of the resurrection, and met in Jerusalem to constitute what, by a slight anachronism, we may call the first Church. Jerusalem was still to them the centre of the world: this was where the Lord had died and risen; this was where he would shortly descend again from heaven, to proclaim his sovereignty and to accomplish what was still unfulfilled in the purposes of God.

This does not necessarily imply that they were thinking of the good news in Jesus Christ as a revelation intended only for the Jews. The picture of the end given in various passages of the Old Testament is that of the nations coming up to Jerusalem to receive at the hands of the Jews the revelation of God:

And many peoples shall come, and say: 'Come, let us go up to the mountain of the Lord, to the house of the God of Jacob; that he may teach us his ways and that we may walk in his paths.' For out of Zion shall go forth the law, and the word of the Lord from Jerusalem.[15]

or again:

In those days ten men from the nations of every tongue shall take hold of the robe of a Jew, saying, 'Let us go with you, for we have heard that God is with you.'[16]

15. Isaiah 2:3.
16. Zechariah 8:23.

It seemed to the believers that on the day of Pentecost they had seen the fulfilment of this prophecy. Men from many climes and many nations had come to Jerusalem to worship, and had heard the words of the new proclamation. Some had believed and would carry the good tidings to their own people. These, of course, were Jews by religion, but some, it is expressly stated, were proselytes, Gentiles who through the acceptance of the Jewish Law had become members of the nation of Israel, and this to the first believers seemed to be the natural order of events – Gentiles would accept the law of the Lord and be circumcised, and then to this old revelation they would add the conviction that the law had found an unexpected fulfilment and extension in Christ.

If this was really the idea which the apostles entertained, subsequent events were not to confirm their expectations. Three radical changes were to take place, and gradually the whole pattern of Christian thinking and Christian action was to be modified.

In the first place, as days passed and Christ did not return in glory, the believers were compelled to recognize that an unspecified time, much longer than had originally been supposed, would intervene between the first and the second coming of Christ. The first person fully to apprehend what this meant was that great historian and theologian St Luke, to whose merits perhaps insufficient justice has as yet been done in the Church. It was he who first saw that the new Israel, like the old, was destined to have its history, and recognized that sacred history must be related to the history of the world.[17] The life of the Church is to be not a frenzied proclamation because the time is short, but a steady programme of expansion throughout the world, yet with an unfailing sense of urgency because for each man any and every moment may prove to be the crucial time of decision.

Secondly, it became clear that the movement of the Church was to be not from the circumference inwards to Jerusalem, but outwards from Jerusalem to the circumference. This change of outlook came very gradually, but it is primarily associated with the mind and work of Saul of Tarsus, later called Paul. To him the preaching of the Gospel to the Gentiles is an essential part of the plan of God. Brought up a strict Jew, he had discovered with amazement that the way of salvation is open to the Gentile no less than to the Jew. Particularism, national limitation, in religion is

17. Luke 3:1–2.

abolished, through the simple fact that Jesus Christ has died for all. This opening of the door to the Gentiles is one of the signs that we are really living in the last age; Paul thinks that he himself may live to see the grand consummation, but it is clear to him that this cannot take place until the fulness of the Gentiles has come in. So with unwearied pace he moves throughout the Roman Empire, until as a prisoner he comes to Rome, and so by divine providence is able to bear witness to the Gospel in the very presence of the emperor himself.

The third great change came about when Jerusalem was destroyed by the Romans in A.D. 70. Until that date Jerusalem had been without question the mother Church of the whole Christian world. James the brother of Jesus had presided over its fortunes, and there seems to have been a feeling in the minds of some Christians that a kind of caliphate ought to be developed in the family of the Lord. The disastrous result of the war changed all that.[18] Since A.D. 70 the Christian Church has never had one local centre; it has learned to look only to the living presence of the Lord within itself. Rome has never been a local centre for all, such as Jerusalem was in the early days. And even if Rome were to become the centre of organization for all Christians, it could never become for the Christian what Mecca is for the Muslim. The devout Muslim turns to Mecca to say his prayers; he dreams that one day he may be able to make the pilgrimage, and see it with his own eyes. The Christian does not share these ideas; he is aware that he belongs to the wandering people of God, who here have no continuing city. If the opportunity to visit Jerusalem or Rome comes, he will gladly take it; but the doctrine of the Holy Spirit forbids him to suppose that if the opportunity comes, he will gain anything of spiritual value that is not available to him in his ordinary daily life.

The Church of the first Christian generation was a genuinely missionary Church. There were, of course, the whole-time workers, such as Saul and Barnabas, specially set apart with prayer for the prosecution of missionary endeavour.[19] Paul had his helpers, whom he trained and sent out in their turn to be the founders of Churches (Epaphras for Colossae,[20] etc.). It was laid down as a

18. On consequences of the destruction of Jerusalem, see W. Telfer, *The Office of a Bishop* (1962), pp. 68–73.

19. Acts 13:1–4.

20. 1 Corinthians 9:13–14.

clear principle that those who served the Gospel with all their time
and strength had a right to be maintained from the Gospel, and
that therefore responsibility for their support rested on the
Church.[21]

Apart, however, from these special workers, the Church could
count on the anonymous and unchronicled witness of all the
faithful. Our first mention of this comes in Acts 8:4, where we are
told that those who were scattered as a result of the persecution
that followed on the death of Stephen went about preaching the
word; some of them, more venturous than the leadership of the
Church, seem to have made Christian history at Antioch by
preaching directly to Gentiles, without the intervention of any
preliminary preparation through the law.[22] But these were far from
being the only volunteer missionaries. When Paul came to Rome,
he was welcomed by believers; how they had got there we are not
told. Doubtless there was much coming and going on the great
trade routes and the wonderful Roman roads of the Mediterranean
world. Some of the Christians were slaves, as we know from Paul's
epistles; such would naturally be carried hither and thither in the
retinues of their masters. Some Christians were probably merchants and travelled in the interests of their trade. Over all this,
time has cast the mantle of obscurity.

What is clear is that every Christian was a witness. Where there
were Christians, there there would be a living, burning faith, and
before long an expanding Christian community. In later times
great Churches were much set on claiming apostolic origin – to
have an apostle as founder was a recognized certificate of respect-
ability. But in point of fact few, if any, of the great Churches were
really founded by apostles. Nothing is more notable than the
anonymity of these early missionaries. In the second century there
were three outstanding centres of Christian life in the Mediterranean – Antioch, Rome, and Alexandria. Of the foundation of the
Church of Antioch we have just recorded all that is known; Luke
does not turn aside to mention the name of a single one of those
pioneers who laid the foundation. Peter and Paul may have
organized the Church in Rome. They certainly did not found it. And
of the foundation of the Church of Alexandria we know nothing for
certain – neither when nor whence nor by whom.[23]

21. Colossians 1:7.
22. Acts 11:19–21.
23. The later evidence of Eusebius and Jerome (fourth century) says that St
Mark was sent into Egypt and created the see of Alexandria.

That was the greatest glory of the Church of those days. The Church was the body of Christ, indwelt by his Spirit; and what Christ had begun to do, that the Church would continue to do, through all the days and unto the uttermost parts of the earth until his unpredictable but certain coming again.

2

The Conquest of the Roman World, A.D. 100–500

The world to which the early Christians came was in many respects not unfavourable to the preaching of the Gospel.

The Roman Empire had imposed on a large area of the world such a massive unity as it had never known before. Peace was never perfect. There were always threats on the frontiers; revolt in this province or that was endemic; the overthrow of one emperor or another continually threatened, though it did not till a much later date manage to disrupt, the intricately balanced organization of the empire. Yet peace was a great reality. Where the Romans went, there they built roads, paved, well-engineered, running undeviatingly forward over hill and dale. Later, when the Roman order had collapsed and the roads were neglected, a great part of mankind lived in isolated villages, which during the long northern winters were cut off from every sort of communication with their kind. But in the Roman days it was not so; travel was safer and more rapid than at any later time till the nineteenth century.[1] Nothing about the early Christians is more striking than the extent to which they managed to get about the world.

The Church in its earliest days spoke Aramaic, the common language of Palestine; in the course of time it found it necessary to use a whole array of languages for the expression of its faith. But almost from the start and in the main it was a Greek-speaking Church. The Roman Empire had accepted Greek both as the language of trade and as the medium of familiar intercourse between all educated men. One who knew Greek could go anywhere and find friends to whom he could talk; when the Churches of Lyons and Vienne in the south of France about A.D. 177 wished to communicate to the rest of the Christian world tidings of the terrible persecution which they had suffered, it was in Greek that they set forth the tale. Not only so. The conquests of Alexander in the fourth century B.C. had spread Greek civilization and the Greek language far into the heart of Asia. A Greek kingdom

---

1. The classic exposition of this is the article by Sir William Ramsay, 'Roads and Travel (in N.T.)', in Hastings's *Dictionary of the Bible, Additional Volume*, pp. 375–402. Although published in 1904, this is still the best survey available in English.

maintained itself for more than two centuries on the Indian frontier, indeed for a time in India itself, with notable effects on Indian art.[2]

Perhaps more important than either of the two factors we have so far mentioned was the presence of Jews in large numbers in every part of the Roman Empire. It is impossible to reckon how many they were, but some good authorities have placed the number as high as 7 per cent of the total population. These Jews were a vigorous, active, and at times turbulent people. For all their morose unfriendliness, they had come to exercise a remarkable influence on their neighbours, and to attract a considerable number of them to the Jewish faith. The quest for wisdom was an ancient passion with the Greeks, always in search of something new; the synagogue offered a profound and moving wisdom apparently more ancient even than that of Homer. Monotheism was in the air; the Old Testament set forth a monotheism purer, more radical, and more personal than that of any other system known to the ancient world. Some Gentiles submitted to the rite of circumcision, and so became part of the people of the Jews; the majority remained in that category of 'God-fearers', interested spectators, who meet us so constantly in the pages of the Acts of the Apostles.[3]

It was in this group that the preaching of the Gospel found its most ready and its most immediate response. When it was made plain to these folk that, without undergoing the rite of circumcision, which both Greeks and Romans regarded as degrading and repulsive, they could win all that Judaism could offer them and a good deal else besides, it was not hard for them to take one further step and to accept the faith of Jesus Christ. It was the presence of this prepared élite that differentiated the missions of the apostolic age from those of every subsequent time, and makes comparison almost impossible. These people, or the best of them, had been well trained in the Old Testament; they had accepted its moral as well as its theological ideas. Many of them brought to their Christian faith a basis of understanding and of disciplined character which made it natural for them to step into positions of leadership in the nascent Christian congregations, and, as it appears, in certain

2. For centuries after his death the Buddha was never depicted in art, his place being taken by symbols like the wheel. It was only under the influence of the Graeco-Indian tradition that the pictorial representation of the Buddha, so familiar in all Buddhist countries and beyond, began to take shape.

3. e.g. Acts 13:16.

cases they became pioneers in the development of the Church's thought.

The second century was an anxious and troubled age. Man was once again in search of a soul, and was open to the approaches of various types of religion. In some recent writings great stress has been laid on the 'mystery religions' of the decaying Roman Empire as parallel to, and perhaps sources of, Christian doctrine. It is beyond doubt that some of these mysteries were concerned with dying and rising gods, that they had solemn ceremonies of initiation and sacred meals, the purpose of which seems to have been some kind of participation of the worshipper in the life of the god. Careful research has suggested that there are few signs of direct influence of the mysteries on Christian faith and practice, and that the similarities are the result rather of parallel developments in similar situations than of direct borrowing. In point of fact, Christian thinkers seem to have felt themselves to be far more directly in conflict with the mysteries, which they regarded as diabolical travesties of the true revelation of God, than in any kind of alliance with them. Nevertheless, the mystery religions and their developments in the early centuries of our era are valid as evidences of the unquenchable desire of man for certainty about God and his own destiny, and in that sense if in no other they may be said to have served as a preparation for the Gospel.

If Luke had never written the Acts of the Apostles, or if that great work, like so much of early Christian literature, had been lost to us, we should have known nothing of the development of the early Church, except for such stray hints as are available to us in the Epistles. And, owing to Luke's predilection for Paul, we know a great deal more about Paul than we know about anyone else. He tends to dominate the scene, and we are inclined to think of him as the typical missionary. In point of fact the picture is far more complex than that. We have to think of a great many full-time missionaries moving rapidly in many directions, and also of that mass of unprofessional missionaries, already alluded to, through whose witness churches were coming into being all over the place, unorganized, independent, yet acutely aware of their status as the new Israel and of their fellowship with all other believers in the world.

But Luke, after all, is right: Paul was the greatest, and probably the most systematic, of all the early missionaries. It was his aim to work rapidly through all the Gentile countries to the utmost ends of the world. Rome was not his goal; he planned to spend only a brief time with the Roman Christians, and then to move on to Spain[4] – Spain, the pillars of Herakles, which to an age that knew nothing of new worlds in the further west was literally the end of the inhabited earth. It was Paul's custom to settle for a time in one of the great cities of the empire, and through his younger helpers to radiate out from that centre to the smaller cities of the region. It is pardonable exaggeration on the part of Luke, when he tells us that 'all the residents of Asia heard the word of the Lord, both Jews and Greeks'.[5] As soon as a church had taken root and showed signs of being able to stand on its own feet under its local leaders, Paul felt free to move onward towards a further fulfilment of his plan, that all the Gentiles might hear the word of the Lord and so the end might come.

Paul was correct in his strategy. In contrast to modern India, for example, in which the movement is still from the villages to the towns, the Roman Empire was a world of cities, each of which dominated the thought as well as the economic life of the surrounding country. The Christian Church began as a city Church; it was only slowly and gradually that it moved out into the country, and in general the country folk were the last to yield to its influence.

It is greatly to be regretted that we know so little of the activity of the other apostles, and of the spread of the Church in other directions. Jews were strongly established in large numbers in the eastern provinces of the Roman Empire. It is recorded that on the day of Pentecost Parthians and Medes and Elamites from the eastern limits of the empire and beyond were there to hear Peter's first sermon.[6] It may be supposed, though we have no evidence, that some of the preachers of the Gospel followed them to their homes, and that what was happening in the western world was balanced by what was happening in the eastern. We have just one palpable hint. The first Epistle of Peter ends with the greeting: 'She who is at Babylon . . . sends you greetings.'[7] Most expositors take it that the Epistle here anticipates that identification of Babylon with Rome which is clearly expressed in the Book of Revelation; but there are good scholars who think that Babylon means Babylon, and that what meets us here is a voice from the Church that was taking root in Mesopotamia.

4. Romans 15:24.
5. Acts 19:10.
6. Acts 2:9.
7. 1 Peter 5:13.

The first large body of evidence outside the New Testament, the Epistles of Ignatius,[8] confirms both the validity and the continuance of the Pauline pattern. Ignatius, the Bishop of the busy metropolis of Antioch in Syria, is on his way to martyrdom in Rome somewhere about the year A.D. 110. He finds time on his journey to write seven letters – five to the Churches in Asia, some of them Churches in small cities, of which outside these letters we have little knowledge, one to Rome, and one to Polycarp (c. 69–155), the Bishop of Smyrna. These Churches are already threatened by division and false doctrine, but it is clear that they are already settling down to that pattern of close-knit fellowship organized around the local bishop which was to become classic in the Christian world.

Our next piece of evidence, the famous letter of the younger Pliny to the Emperor Trajan in about the year 112, gives us a very different picture. Pliny, an intelligent, humane, and not unsympathetic observer, was dismayed by the rapid spread of Christian faith in the rather remote and mainly rural province of Bithynia in north-west Asia Minor which he had been sent to govern. He speaks of 'many in every period of life, on every level of society, of both sexes . . . in towns and villages and scattered throughout the countryside'. What was he to do with them? All the handbooks quote the illogical answer of the emperor that Christians were not to be sought out, but that if they were brought before the governor they were to be punished. We are interested at this point not in the legal question, but simply in the growth of the Church. The evidence of Pliny is unimpeachable; we seem to encounter here one of the first mass movements in Christian history. The growth of the Church was so rapid that Pliny had cause to fear that the shrines of the pagan gods would come to be wholly deserted.[9]

On a survey of the course of events in the Roman Empire, as far as we are able to gather them, in the first three centuries of our era, the general impression is of rapid, though uneven, progress.

In *Palestine* the destruction of Jerusalem did not bring the Christian Church to an end. It did put an end to the national existence of the Jews for a period of more than 1,800 years, and this was probably one of the factors that exacerbated the relations

8. English translation by K. Lake in *Apostolic Fathers*, Vol. 1, pp. 166–277, in the Loeb Classical Library.

9. Pliny, *Epistles* x, 96, 97. For the full text, see J. Stevenson, *A New Eusebius* (1957), pp. 13–16.

between the synagogue and the Church.[10] For a considerable period after the Resurrection of Jesus the Church continued to preach to the Jews in the hope that Israel might turn and be saved. But few Jews had been converted, and relations had deteriorated to the point at which, in the Fourth Gospel, the words 'the Jews' tend to mean simply the enemies of Jesus – a fact which has led some Jews in modern times to accuse the author of that Gospel of being the author and chief architect of anti-Semitism. Jewish Christendom waned and dwindled and finally died away in heresy. The policy of the emperors after A.D. 70 was to develop the non-Jewish elements in Palestine; the churches and bishoprics of that area appear to have been of the ordinary Graeco-Roman type.

Antioch in Syria was the second home of the Church. It was here that the disciples had first been called Christians.[11] In the capital of the East, Christian faith took deep root and grew; under a succession of notable bishops this Church exercised widespread influence throughout the whole province of Syria. It is from Antioch that we receive one of our scanty pieces of information regarding population and the growth of the Church, and, though this comes from a considerably later date than that of which we are treating, it is worth recording here. It is stated that in the time of John Chrysostom, towards the end of the fourth century, the population of Antioch was not less than half a million, and that half of the inhabitants at that time were Christian.

Asia Minor had been from the time of Paul one of the most promising fields for Christian work. The Roman province of Asia, particularly, with its high civilization and its intelligent and volatile people, proved readily receptive of the Gospel. But what was true of the Greek-speaking city-dwellers was not true of the more backward peoples who kept to their own barbarian speech and their more primitive ways. As late as the sixth century the Emperor Justinian was organizing campaigns for the final extirpation of paganism from the inland regions.

After Jerusalem and Antioch, *Rome* was the third great centre of the Christian world. Only in the fourth century did the Church of

10. As Professor C. F. D. Moule points out, the radical division had already come about; the destruction of the city only made evident what was already implicit in the teaching of Paul. He quotes from Eduard Meyer the remark that 'the break away from the Jerusalem moorings had already been achieved by Paul' (*The Birth of the New Testament*, 1962, pp. 45–6).

11. Acts 11:26.

Rome begin to put forward those claims to universal dominion which have been a cause of controversy and a source of division in the Christian world until the present day. But from the beginning its status as the Church of the capital, its more than legendary association with the names of both Peter and Paul, and the heroism of the believers in the days of persecution under Nero in 64 and 65, combined to ensure for this Church the respect and admiration of the whole of the rest of Christendom. It seemed natural that, on the occasion of division and strife in the Church at Corinth in or about the year 96, Clement should write on behalf of the Roman Church to bring the Corinthians to a better mind.[12]

It is clear that at first the Roman Church drew its members from the poorer classes. For more than a hundred years it was a Greek-speaking Church – this fact at once settles the question of its social origins. True Romans of the upper classes spoke and wrote Latin; Greek was the language of the poorer classes and of slaves. Victor, who was Bishop of Rome from about 189 to 199, is the first Roman Christian whom we know to have expressed himself in writing in Latin. But from an early date some had been brought in from the higher classes. We learn that in the persecution under the Emperor Domitian about A.D. 96, the emperor's cousin Titus Flavius Clemens was put to death, and his wife Domitilla banished to the island of Pandataria, on the ground of 'sacrilege'. What this sacrilege may have been is not absolutely certain, but many good authorities believe that it consisted in adherence to the Christian faith. If so, before the end of the first Christian century the Gospel had already touched some in the highest circles of society in the capital of the empire.[13]

The Roman Church grew by conversion, but also by the convergence on the city of Christians from many lands. Rome was a magnet, which steadily drew the peoples to itself. Of the rapid growth of the Church we have one or two notable indications. About A.D. 166, Bishop Soter remarks in passing that the number of Christians had already surpassed that of the Jews. And from about the year 251 we have the most precise statistics that have come down to us from any time or area of the early Church. Bishop Cornelius of Rome writes to his colleague Fabius of Antioch:

12. There is little doubt that Clement was Bishop of Rome; but he writes 'the first Epistle of Clement', one of the oldest Christian works outside the New Testament, not in his own name but on behalf of the whole Church at Rome. English translation by K. Lake in *Apostolic Fathers*, Vol. 1, in the Loeb Classical Library, p. 3.

13. See J. Stevenson, *A New Eusebius*, p. 8.

This vindicator of the Gospel [the schismatic Novatian] then, did not know that there should be but one bishop in a Catholic Church; yet he was not ignorant (for how could he be?) that in it there were forty-six presbyters, seven deacons, seven sub-deacons, forty-two acolytes, fifty-two exorcists, readers and door-keepers, over 1500 widows and persons in distress, all of whom the grace and loving kindness of the Master nourish.[14]

Harnack has calculated that this represents a Christian population of at least 30,000. What was the population of Rome at that date? We have no means of telling, but it is clear that the Christian Church formed a considerable and influential part of it.

In *Gaul* and *Spain* progress seems to have been rather slow. Irenaeus (*c.* 130–*c.* 200), who was Bishop of Lyons in the last quarter of the second century, speaks of using the Celtic no less than the Latin tongue. This makes it clear that the Church had gone out beyond the Romanized people of the cities to the less educated tribal peoples. But Christian influence seems to have been almost wholly limited to the south of what is now France, perhaps because communications with the northern regions were still very difficult, perhaps because the northern tribes proved more resistant to the Gospel than their southern brethren. By the end of the third century many churches and bishoprics had been established in Spain; but the canons of the Council of Elvira, held at some point during the first ten years of the fourth century, at which thirty-six dioceses seem to have been represented, suggest that the Spanish Churches had not been more than partially successful in bringing the disorders of both personal and social life in the pagan world under the control of the new law revealed in Jesus Christ.

As to the first entry of Christianity into *Britain* we have no certain information. Legend associates it with the Apostle Paul or at least with one of his companions;[15] but here certainly the wish was father to the thought, and to such stories no credence can be given. Tertullian, the ex-lawyer and Church father of North Africa (*adv. Judaeos* 7: written about A.D. 208), tells us that Christ had followers on the far side of the Roman wall in Britain, where the legions had

14. Quoted by Eusebius, *Eccles. Hist.* VI, 43, 11; see J. Stevenson, *A New Eusebius*, pp. 284–5. Note also the interesting use of the term 'Master', which in the later translation of Rufinus becomes simply 'God' (No. 145, p. 194). We recognize here the *seven* orders of the ministry, as these have been retained in the Roman Catholic Church.

15. Joseph of Arimathea, whose legendary connection is with Glastonbury, is another candidate.

never yet penetrated; but this may be no more than the imaginative flight of a not always very accurate writer. The story of the martyrdom of Alban in the persecution under Diocletian (284–305) does not belong to established history, but may be related to real historical happenings. It is certain that in 314 Britain was represented at the Council of Arles in southern France by the Bishops of York, London, and a third see. Of this British Christianity we know little or nothing; but we may suppose (and the supposition is confirmed by archaeological discovery) that it was the Romano-British dwellers in the villas, and not the less civilized Celtic inhabitants, who first felt the attraction of the new religion.

It is certain that the Gospel came very early to *Egypt*, and especially to the busy and thriving port of Alexandria; but of this area, as of so many others, we have to admit frankly that we do not know how or when the earliest Church came into existence.

From its foundation in the days of Alexander the Great in 332 B.C. Alexandria had been a thriving commercial metropolis, a centre for trade with both East and West. Its people were diligent, intelligent, and mercurial, eager to understand new ideas, but all too liable to outbursts of frenzied violence. And the city had a very large Jewish population. About these Jews we know a great deal, since we have the works of the philosopher Philo, a contemporary of St Paul, who was sent by his people on an embassy to Rome in the days of the Emperor Caligula (Gaius, A.D. 37–41). Philo had set himself to be an interpreter between the world of the Greeks and the world of the Jews, and has left behind an imposing series of works in which this labour of synthesis was steadily carried forward.

It was natural that thoughtful Alexandrian Christians should tread in the footsteps of Philo, and should be the pioneers in facing the problem of the relation of Christian faith to the non-Christian world of Greece and Rome. In one direction, the bold speculations of the Gnostics were prepared to take so much from the Greek and oriental traditions as to imperil the true quality of Christianity as historical revelation. In another direction, the great Alexandrian Christian thinkers and teachers Clement (*c.* 150–215) and Origen (*c.* 185–254), while standing firm in the orthodox doctrine of the revelation of the Father through the Son who is also the divine Word, were able to accord generous recognition to Greek philosophy as a true preparation for the Gospel of Christ, and to believe that the God who guided the destinies of Israel was active also in the history of the Greeks. The writings of these Fathers have a contemporary ring in the twentieth century, when so many younger Churches in Asia and Africa are faced by the same problems as confronted their predecessors in the third.

Christianity in Egypt was not limited to those who spoke Greek. Translation of the Scriptures into various dialects of the speech which we now know as Coptic began not later than the middle of the third century. About that time, or a little later, the deserts began to be filled by companies of monks and hermits. The majority of these desert-dwellers spoke Coptic and knew little, if any, Greek. The fanaticism which they at times displayed goes some distance to justify the astringent remark of Edward Gibbon about the triumph of barbarism and religion. But this darker side must be held in balance with the charming simplicity and devoutness manifested on almost every page of the lives of the Desert Fathers.[16]

Cyrene, west of Egypt, is mentioned in four crucial passages of the New Testament. Simon of Cyrene carried the cross of Jesus; it is almost certain that he became a believer, since his sons Alexander and Rufus appear to have been well known to that circle of Christians for which the Gospel according to St Mark was written.[17] Cyrenians were present when Peter delivered his first sermon on the day of Pentecost,[18] and were among those who disputed with Stephen.[19] Cyrenians took part in that decisive step which carried the Gospel out of the field of Israel directly into the Gentile world.[20] At a later date we learn a good deal about Cyrene from the pen of that delightful country squire Synesius, who in the year 410 was persuaded, albeit unwillingly, to become bishop of his native city.[21] At that time there were half a dozen bishoprics in the area.

16. An admirable selection from the full *Vitae Patrum*, first published in Antwerp in 1615, has been made by Helen Waddell, in an enchanting volume called *The Desert Fathers* (1936).

17. Mark 15:21; see also Romans 16:13.

18. Acts 2:10.

19. Acts 6:9.

20. Acts 11:20.

21. A good many of the letters of Synesius have been preserved. English translation by A. Fitzgerald (London, 1926). In letter 105 he tells us of his dismay at being elected bishop: 'Though I am fond of amusements – for from my childhood I have been accused of being mad after arms and horses – still I will consent to give them up – though I shall regret to see my darling dogs no longer allowed to hunt, and my bows moth-eaten!'

It was, however, further west, in the parts of *North Africa* that are today called Tunis and Algeria that the Gospel most rapidly took hold. There are reasons for thinking that the Christian faith travelled both westwards from Egypt and southwards from Rome. What is important is that the Churches in this area were the first Latin-speaking Churches of the world. It is probable that the first translations of the Scriptures into Latin were made in North Africa. Latin Christian literature here made its splendid first appearance with the ex-lawyers Tertullian (*c.* 160–220) and Cyprian (d. 258); their by no means inconsiderable gifts were later to be overshadowed by the towering achievements of Augustine of Hippo (354–430).

The Church of North Africa was a Church of bishops. Every town, almost every village, had its bishop. As early as the middle of the third century a provincial council summoned by Cyprian of Carthage might be attended by anything up to eighty bishops. This was in contrast to the rest of the Western world, where bishops were located only in the cities, and were comparatively few in number.

This Church, like that of Egypt, had to wrestle with the problem of race and language. All the North African Christians whom we know well – the great writers, the martyred Perpetua and her companions – belong to the Romanized section of the community, and this means in general the upper classes. Augustine refers at times to the Punic language, which the Carthaginian settlers had long ago brought in from Phoenicia; it seems that there were areas where a knowledge of Punic was a necessary qualification for a priest. Below the Punic level were the village and desert dwellers of Berber stock and language. It is uncertain to what extent the Church had taken this language seriously, and adapted its message to the needs of this more primitive level of the population. It seems clear that linguistic and racial feeling were among the many factors that underlay the Donatist schism,[22] which racked the Church in North Africa generation after generation and left it hopelessly weakened in the face of its enemies when the day of judgement came upon it.

22. This schism broke out in the fourth century, as a result of grave differences as to the treatment to be accorded to those who had failed in their Christian duty in time of persecution, and rapidly spread through the whole of north-west Africa. Many other factors – racial, social, and economic – contributed to the schism and helped to make it extraordinarily difficult to heal.

To sum up this rapid survey, we may say that by the end of the third century there was no area in the Roman Empire which had not been penetrated to some extent by the Gospel. But distribution was very uneven. The areas of strongest development were Syria, Asia Minor, Egypt, and North Africa, with some other notable centres such as Rome, and Lyons in the south of France. The Church for the most part spoke Greek and Latin, and the village people were as yet to a large extent untouched.

When every allowance has been made – for legendary exaggeration, and for the grave imperfections of the work – even sober historical realism must recognize in this rapid spread of the Gospel a notable phenomenon. How did it come about?

First and foremost we must reckon with the burning conviction by which a great number of the earliest Christians were possessed. A great event had burst upon them in creative power. They knew that the world had been redeemed, and they could not keep to themselves tidings of such incomparable significance for the whole of the human race. It would be hard to find better expression for this spirit than the words of the first great ecclesiastical historian, Eusebius of Caesarea (*c.* 260–340):

> At that time [about the beginning of the second century] many Christians felt their souls inspired by the holy word with a passionate desire for perfection. Their first action, in obedience to the instructions of the Saviour, was to sell their goods and to distribute them to the poor. Then, leaving their homes, they set out to fulfil the work of an evangelist, making it their ambition to preach the word of the faith to those who as yet had heard nothing of it, and to commit to them the books of the divine Gospels. They were content simply to lay the foundations of the faith among these foreign peoples: they then appointed other pastors, and committed to them the responsibility for building up those whom they had merely brought to the faith. Then they passed on to other countries and nations with the grace and help of God.[23]

This broad generalization says little of the work of the non-professional missionaries to which we have referred earlier. It does, however, well represent that unshakeable assurance that in face of every obstacle men can be won and must be won for Christ, which was the mainspring of the whole enterprise.

The tidings which they had to bring were in many ways welcome to their hearers. The age was perplexed by the transitoriness of all things and by the desire for immortality. The philosophers, from

23. Eusebius, *Eccles. Hist.* III, 37, 2–3.

Plato on, had not managed to give more than an uncertain answer to men's anxious questionings. The mystery religions did rather better. But the trouble was that there were too many of them, and this very multiplicity made it plain to the thoughtful mind that the mysteries still moved in the twilight of mythological imagination and not in the broad daylight of established fact. And now came these other preachers, speaking with the confidence of eye-witnesses or of men utterly convinced, concerning one who had lived in quite recent times and died and risen from the dead, no mythological figure of the corn or the grape, but a living reality who would give himself to those who trusted in him, in such a way that they too could share in his everlasting life. This could be understood rather too mechanically, as when Ignatius speaks of the Holy Communion as 'the medicine of immortality'. But, from the time of the first apostles onwards, the message by which the Church brought conviction to its hearers concerned Jesus, the resurrection, and the forgiveness of sins.

Thirdly, the new Christian communities commended themselves by the evident purity of their lives. We wrong these early Christians if we idealize them. They were ordinary men and women like ourselves, living in the midst of a corrupt society and exposed to all its temptations. The First Epistle to the Corinthians shows us plainly how hard they found it to live up to their new aspirations. But in those days to be a Christian meant something. Doubtless among the pagans there were many who lived upright and even noble lives. Yet all our evidence goes to show that in that decaying world sexual laxity had gone almost to the limits of the possible, and that slavery had brought with it the inevitable accompaniments of cruelty and the cheapening of the value of human life. Christians were taught to regard their bodies as temples of the Holy Spirit. The Church did not attempt to forbid or abolish slavery; it drew the sting out of it by reminding masters and slaves alike that they had a common Master to whom their allegiance was due, and that they were brothers in the faith.[24]

In the earlier days of the Roman world the sense of community and of mutual loyalty had been very strong. The break-up of society had resulted in the weakening of the bonds of local loyalty,

24. One of the earliest and noblest expressions of this attitude is the letter of Paul to Philemon. Philemon is to receive back his runaway slave Onesimus 'no longer as a slave, but more than a slave, as a beloved brother, especially to me but how much more to you, both in the flesh and in the Lord' (Philemon 16).

and, though the Stoics had tried to replace this by a wider loyalty in their doctrine of man as a citizen of the world magnificently expressed by the Stoic Emperor Marcus Aurelius, this had proved too remote and theoretical to have much effect on the mind of the ordinary man. What the Stoics had aimed at, the Christians seemed to have produced: here was a society in which all were welcome without distinction, from which the age-long discrimination between Jew and Gentile, bond and free, Greek and barbarian, man and woman seemed to have been banished. The Christian, wherever he was, knew that he belonged to a society which was potentially world-wide, and which was bound together by the principles 'One Lord, one faith, one baptism'.[25] This was a real world, in which the aristocrat Perpetua and the slave-girl Felicitas, with equal mutual tenderness and equal courage, could go to face the wild beasts in the amphitheatre of Carthage (7 March 203).

One notable feature of this common life was the elaborate development of charitable service, especially to those within the fellowship. Harnack discusses at length no less than ten such forms of service – care of orphans and of widows, of prisoners and of travellers, and so forth.[26] It seems that the churches first obtained legal recognition as burial clubs; they were still sufficiently men of their time to feel that deprivation of honourable burial was a terrible thing. So Lactantius (*c.* 240–320) writes:

We will not allow the image and creation of God to be thrown out to the wild beasts and the birds as their prey; it must be given back to the earth from which it was taken.[27]

The evidence of enemies is frequently reliable. Some of our best evidence for the effect of this Christian philanthropy comes, at a rather later date than that of which we are now writing, from the apostate Emperor Julian (332–63). Julian was finding it more difficult than he had expected to put new life into the ancient religion, which he wished to bring back into honour. He saw clearly that what was drawing many to the Christian faith was this manifest exhibition of love in practice:

Atheism [i.e. Christian faith] has been specially advanced through the loving service rendered to strangers, and through their care for the burial

25. Ephesians 4:5.
26. *The Mission and Expansion of Christianity* (Eng. trans., Vol. I), p. 153.
27. Lactantius, *Instit.* VI, 12.

of the dead. It is a scandal that there is not a single Jew who is a beggar, and that the godless Galilaeans care not only for their own poor but for ours as well; while those who belong to us look in vain for the help that we should render them.

There could be no hope of the re-establishment of the older faith unless it too could show itself to be equally fruitful in good works.

Finally, we must consider the effect of the persecution of the Christians on popular opinion about them. Here again it is important not to be led away into mythological exaggeration. Undoubtedly, Christians under the Roman Empire had no legal right to existence, and were liable to the utmost stringency of the law. But, equally, it is clear that on the whole the magistrates were not anxious to proceed to severities – often they did their utmost to persuade Christians to save themselves by conformity to the simple demands of the law – and that (until the systematic persecution ordered by the Emperor Decius in the middle of the third century) when persecution broke out it was in answer to popular clamour rather than as the result of a planned campaign on the part of the authorities. It was a vicious circle. Because of their dangerous situation *vis-à-vis* the law, Christians were almost bound to meet in secret; because they met in secret, the most horrible tales of iniquity were spread abroad about them, and so the popular clamour grew. But, for the most part, persecution was spasmodic. Every Christian knew that sooner or later he might have to testify to his faith at the cost of his life, but no church was subjected to relentless and continuous persecution over a long period of time, and the number of martyrs was much smaller than the piety of later ages imagined it to be.

When persecution did break out, martyrdom could be attended by the utmost possible publicity. The Roman public was hard and cruel, but it was not altogether without compassion, and there is no doubt that the attitude of the martyrs, and particularly of the young women who suffered along with the men, made a deep impression. In later times, the long continuance of strain produced a certain element of hysteria, and the Church had to lay it down that those who broke idols or insulted the gods, and thus deliber-ately provoked their own death, were not to be reckoned among the Church's martyrs. But in the earlier records what we find is calm, dignified, decorous behaviour, cool courage in the face of torment, courtesy towards enemies, and a joyful acceptance of suffering as the way appointed by the Lord to lead to his heavenly kingdom.

There are a number of well-authenticated cases of conversion of pagans in the very moment of witnessing the condemnation and death of Christians; there must have been far more who received impressions that in the course of time would be turned into a living faith.[28]

In the first twenty years of the fourth century the whole situation changed, as the Emperor Constantine (274–337) progressively showed himself favourable to the new religion, accepted it as the religion of the state, and as the last act of his life accepted Christian baptism at the hands of his friend Eusebius of Nicomedia. Christians were able finally to come out of the catacombs (in which as a matter of fact they had spent very little of their existence) and to sun themselves in the light of imperial favour.

We may pause for a moment to consider the situation of the Christian mission at this time of the greatest revolution in its history.

Endless attempts have been made to calculate the number of Christians in the Roman Empire in the year 313. But, as has been made plain, accurate evidence is almost wholly lacking. It is thought that the population of the Roman Empire at that time may have amounted to about 50 million. It would not be unreasonable to suppose that perhaps 10 per cent of these were Christian by the end of the third century. It must, however, be repeated that distribution was very uneven. There were some areas, such as parts of Asia Minor, where half of the population was already Christian, others, such as the inland parts of Greece, where the Gospel seems hardly to have penetrated.

More important than numbers was the character and quality of the Christians.

Throughout this period the majority of the believers were simple and humble people – slaves, women, petty traders, some soldiers, though service in the army was not generally approved by the Church because of the necessary implication of soldiers at times in heathen ceremonies. Here again some of our best testimony comes from the enemy. Towards the end of the second century the intelligent Alexandrian Celsus wrote a book against the Christians. Part of his complaint against them is as follows:

28. On all this, see E. R. Hardy, *Faithful Witnesses* (World Christian Books No. 31, 1960), an admirable selection from the original contemporary documents relating to the persecutions.

Far from us, say the Christians, be any man possessed of any culture or wisdom or judgement; their aim is to convince only worthless and contemptible people, idiots, slaves, poor women, and children. They behave like mountebanks and beggars; they would not dare to address an audience of intelligent men . . . but if they see a group of young people or slaves or rough folk, there they push themselves in and seek to win the admiration of the crowd. It is the same in private houses. We see wool-carders, cobblers, washermen, people of the utmost ignorance and lack of education. They are careful not to open their mouths in the presence of their masters, who are of full age and able to judge for themselves. But if they manage to get children alone, or women as senseless as themselves, then they set to work to put forth their wondrous tales. These are the only ones whom they manage to turn into believers.[29]

We need not doubt that Celsus is in the main telling the truth, and it is the glory of the Church that it was so. But this is only one side of the picture. Before the Church had been in existence very long, educated men and intellectuals had begun to find in its message the answer to their quest. Justin Martyr (c. 100–165) is typical of this class. Born in the ancient Shechem, he had, as he himself tells us, wandered far and wide in search of the true wisdom and had dabbled in almost all the schools of Greek philosophy. It was not until he met a Christian teacher at Ephesus that he found in the Gospel the solution to his problems. The majority of Christians were then, as always, poor and simple, but there was a minority representing every level of social prestige and intellectual excellence.

Nothing, indeed, is more striking about this early Church than the way in which it managed to gather into itself almost all that was vital in the thought and creativity of the last phase of the life of the ancient world. After the massive and sombre genius of Tacitus, Roman literature tended to descend into triviality. Later, it produced only one great writer, the historian Ammianus Marcellinus (c. 325–91). The Greeks could claim one witty and entertaining author, Lucian (c. 120–80), and one outstanding philosopher, Plotinus (204–70). In these first three centuries, the small Church could put in the balance against the pagans the gentle wisdom of Clement, the learning of Origen, the sometimes turbid vigour of Tertullian, the legal lucidity of Cyprian, and a host of other writers of real and varied distinction. What created Christian literature was the fact that these Christians had something of vital importance to say. As the ancient world descended nearer to its ruin, the

29. Origen, *Against Celsus* III, 49–55.

historic Greek art of oratory was reduced to the level of merely artificial rhetoric. The last of the famous Greek orators, Libanius, really had nothing to say, and said it interminably with consummate skill. His friend and pupil John Chrysostom (*c.* 347–407) had a great deal to say, and said it, also at great length, with an admirable mastery of good and idiomatic, though not altogether classical, Greek.

As we have said, the favourable attitude of the emperor produced a complete change in the situation of the Christian Church. From obscurity it emerged into brilliance, from obloquy to the height of popularity. Crowds pressed into it, and the Church was in danger of being submerged under the flood of new believers. Pockets of resistance were still to be found, as among the ancient aristocracy of Rome, whose representative Symmachus (d. about 405) protested strongly against the removal of the altar of victory, the great traditional symbol of the ancient power of Rome, and among the philosophers of Athens whose schools were formally closed by the Emperor Justinian in A.D. 529. But Christianity was fashionable, and the majority of men, then as now, found it convenient to follow the fashion. It seems likely that the number of Christians in the empire at least quadrupled itself in the century that followed Constantine.

In all this there were great dangers. Faith became superficial, and was identified with the acceptance of dogmatic teachings rather than with a radical change of inner being. As the Church became rich, bishoprics became objects of contention rather than instruments of humble service. With a new freedom, the Church was able to go out into the world; at the same time, in a new and dangerous fashion, the world entered into the Church.

Yet all was not for the worst. Apart from the patient work of doctrinal definition, which was the achievement of the Church Councils from Nicaea (325) to Chalcedon (451), in two directions the Church showed great and creative vitality.

In these years the synthesis between Christian faith and the ancient languages and culture was brought to completion. Clement and Origen had been pioneers, with all the freshness and also the uncertainties of the pioneer. The Cappadocian Fathers – Basil (*c.* 330–79), Gregory of Nazianzus (329–89), and Gregory of Nyssa (*c.* 330–95) – had received the best education that the times offered, the two former having been, in fact, fellow-students of the future Emperor Julian in the University of Athens. Perfectly familiar with Homer and Plato and Demosthenes, these fathers wrote in a Greek which, though not classical, is clear and idiomatic and admirably adapted to the purposes for which they used it. Purists, and defenders of Hebrew as the only tongue in which theology can really be expressed, may criticize the Hellenization of the Gospel as necessarily deformation. But, if the Word of God was to make itself at home in a world in which Greek was the universal medium, it could do so in no other way than by teaching itself to think and speak in Greek.[30]

Secondly, the fourth century was the period of the development of the great classical liturgies. Most of our ecclesiastical histories deal with the outstanding leaders and the great controversies of the times. In all this side of Church history there is much that is grievous and discreditable – the rivalries of the great sees and their incumbents, political chicanery, personal malevolence, and even bribery and corruption. But the Church lived in its humble and faithful members, and in the ceaseless life of prayer and worship in which the true apostolic succession was to be found. As the Church emerged from the twilight, its public worship increased in splendour and impressiveness; but this was only the outward expression of a marvellous development of liturgical sense and understanding. All the classical liturgies are anonymous; we do not know who the writers were. All are somewhat closely interrelated, and all give evidence of coming as the culmination of a long process of development. It seems probable that Antioch was the centre in which the development was most rapid, and most firmly based on a theological understanding of the true nature of worship. But such great creative achievements do not just grow: behind them stand individuals. A Church which could produce the unknown men of genius who have left to the Church a legacy of such incomparable value was not lacking in the fire of the Spirit.[31]

So far, for convenience, we have been thinking of the Church within the Roman Empire. We must now take account of the fact that, even before the great change which took place in the Constantinian era, the Church had spread far beyond the imperial frontiers.

Our first glance must be in the direction of *Edessa*, and the little country of *Osrhoene* in the northern part of Mesopotamia. From this

30. Essential now for the study of this process is W. Jaeger, *Early Christian and Greek Paideia* (1961).

31. All the liturgies in use in the Eastern Churches today are derived from these classical liturgies of the fourth and fifth centuries.

quarter comes to us one of the most charming of early Christian legends, the letter of King Abgar to Jesus. Abgar has heard of the cures wrought by Jesus, and being himself sick he writes to Jesus, inviting him to come to Edessa:

Having heard all this of thee, I had determined one of two things, either that thou art a God come down from heaven, and so doest these things, or art a Son of God that doest these things. Therefore have I now written and entreated thee to trouble thyself to come to me and heal the affliction which I have. For indeed I have heard that the Jews even murmur against thee and wish to do thee hurt. And I have a very little city but comely, which is sufficient for us both.

To this the Lord deigned to reply that he must fulfil his destiny in Palestine, and therefore could not come to Edessa; but that after his ascension he would send one of his disciples to heal the king 'and give life to thee and them that are with thee'.[32]

We owe this little narrative to Eusebius of Caesarea, who says that he drew it from a Syrian document preserved in the archives at Edessa. The whole story is, of course, purely legendary, and we do not know when it grew up. But it does point us to three important facts – that the Gospel early spread eastwards from Palestine into the region of Mesopotamia; that Edessa was one of the great Christian centres in that region; and that the language of that area was Syriac.

Syriac is a Semitic language akin to Hebrew and Aramaic. The Churches of that region which still use Syriac in their liturgy boast that they alone among the Churches have kept the original and authentic speech of our Lord himself. This can hardly be made out, but Syriac is certainly not very far removed from the Aramaic which was spoken in Palestine in the time of Christ. Syriac-speaking Christianity had a character of its own. Its adherents were sharply critical of the Greeks, whom they called 'disputers' – always asking complex theological questions, and obscuring the simplicity of the Gospel by human imagination. The Syrians were simple, more direct, inward-looking, and with a certain mystical quality in their faith. Much less original than the Greeks, they yet produced what is in some ways the most remarkable of all early Christian documents, the *Hymn of the Soul*. This is a kind of early *Pilgrim's Progress*. The soul is sent forth into the world to find and bring back a very precious pearl; in spite of much forgetfulness and

32. See M. R. James, *The Apocryphal New Testament* (revised ed. 1955), pp. 466–7.

many perils the pearl is recovered from the land of Egypt, and brought back to the heavenly dwelling. We set down here the opening and closing verses of the poem:

When I was an infant child in the palace of my Father,
And resting in the wealth and luxury of my nurturers,
Out of the East our native country, my parents provisioned me and
    sent me
And of the wealth of those their treasures they put together a load both
    great and light that I might carry it alone . ... and said:
If thou go down to Egypt, and bring back thence the one pearl
Which is there in the midst of the sea girt about by the devouring
    serpent,
Thou shalt put on again the garment set with gems, and that robe
    whereupon it resteth . . .
In my royal robe excelling in beauty I arrayed myself wholly,
And when I had put it on, I was lifted up into the place of peace and
    homage
And I bowed my head and worshipped the brightness of the Father
    which had sent it unto me,
For I had performed his commandments, and he likewise that which
    he had promised. . . .
And he rejoiced over me and received me with him into his palace
    and all his servants do praise him with sweet voices.
And he promised me that with him I shall be sent unto the gates of the
    king,
That with my gifts and my pearl we may appear together before the
    king.[33]

This striking poem is found in a third-century romance known as the *Acts of Thomas*, a work important because it connects the name of the Apostle Thomas with the beginnings of missionary work in *India*.

This, too, is a charming tale. It tells how the Lord wished to send Thomas to India, but Thomas was unwilling to go. 'I am a Hebrew man; how can I go among the Indians and preach the truth?' So the Lord arranged that Thomas should be sold as a slave to an Indian merchant named Abbanes, who was at that time in Jerusalem seeking a skilled carpenter. Thomas is then brought to India in the days of King Gundaphorus, and is bidden to build a palace for the king. But the Apostle decides to build the king not a visible and carnal palace but a spiritual home in heaven, by distributing as alms to the poor and afflicted the great provision that the king has

33. M. R. James, *The Apocryphal New Testament*, pp. 413–15.

made. When at length the king demands to see the palace, the Apostle calmly answers: 'Thou canst not see it now, but when thou departest this life, then shalt thou see it.' Naturally the king is incensed, and has the Apostle shut up in jail. But through miraculous intervention all is put right, and the story ends happily with the baptism of the king.

Naturally, sober persons treated this rigmarole as mere fancy – until archaeology firmly established the fact that Gundobar was a real person, and reigned in north-western India in the first century A.D. On his coins the name appears in the Greek form Hyndopheres. Is it possible that the *Acts of Thomas* contains a little more than mere legend?

In south-west India the very ancient Church of the 'Thomas Christians' still exists. Among them it is the first article of the faith that their Church was founded by the Apostle Thomas himself, and that through the intrigues of the Brahmans he was betrayed to death and was buried at St Thomas's Mount not far from Madras. Is it possible that they are right?

Two things we can affirm with certainty.

First, we know that this Church has existed from very early times. This is proved by the existence of inscribed copper plates, which confirm to the Christian merchants the privileges which had been granted to them by the local king; these merchants are spoken of not as newcomers, but as a well-known and well-established community. And there are ancient crosses, the oldest of which may date from the seventh century, with an inscription in Pahlavi or Middle Persian.[34]

Secondly we can say that a voyage by St Thomas to South India in the first century would have been perfectly possible. The monsoon was discovered in the first century B.C. Seamen realized that if in certain months of the year instead of making the long coastal voyage round Arabia and Baluchistan, they spread their sails to the open sea, the wind would carry them directly to the shores of India, where their most probable landfall would be the

34. Scholars have given a number of fanciful and mutually inconsistent interpretations of the inscription. In 1929 Mr Winckworth of Cambridge showed that it really says exactly what one would expect: 'My Lord Christ, have mercy on Afras, son of Chaharbucht the Syrian, who carved this'! See L. W. Brown, *The Indian Christians of St Thomas* (1956), p. 80, facing which is a good photograph of one of the crosses. Mr Winckworth's article is in the *Journal of Theological Studies* (1929), pp. 237–44.

port which medieval writers infuriatingly call Columbum (it has nothing to do with Colombo), and which is found on modern maps as Quilon. When the wind changed they could be blown safely back to the mouth of the Red Sea. Discoveries of Roman coins in South India have shown clearly that in the first three centuries of our era, trade was vigorous and active between India and the Roman Empire. They suggest that the traders, instead of taking the dangerous sea route round Ceylon, took the land route through the low and easily accessible Palghat gap to the east coast. This probability was turned into almost certainty by the discovery, twenty years ago, of a Roman commercial settlement at Arikamedu near Pondicherry. Unfortunately this settlement has yielded no written or literary remains.[35]

This is as far as the evidence takes us at present. Simple faith will no doubt continue, to the end of time, to affirm the directly apostolic origin of the Indian Church. More sceptical people will suspend judgement, and will not confuse a possibility with that kind of historical certainty that depends on reliable and unshakeable evidence.

We have already taken note of the strength of Christianity in Egypt in the third century A.D. We have what seems to be reliable evidence as to the extension of the faith southwards into *Ethiopia*, where the Church still lives after sixteen centuries of unbroken tradition. Here is the story. Early in the fourth century two young Christian men of Tyre, Aedesius and Frumentius, were travelling down the Red Sea with the uncle of the former, when they were shipwrecked on the coast. The sailors were killed, but the young men were spared and taken as slaves to the court of the king at Axum. There they succeeded in winning the favour of the king, were later appointed to high office, and had full liberty to preach the Gospel. Converts were won, and the Christian cause was strengthened by the bringing in of other Christians from Egypt. After some years Aedesius returned to Tyre, but Frumentius went to Alexandria, where the great Athanasius (c. 296–373) was reigning in glory as patriarch. Frumentius asked that priests might be sent to help him in the work, to which Athanasius replied, 'Who could be found more suitable than yourself?' and consecrated him

35. On all this see Sir Mortimer Wheeler's *Rome Beyond the Imperial Frontiers* (Penguin Books, 1955), pp. 153–7 and 164–82.

as bishop. This is a notable example of lay witness to the Gospel, and, as the more famous example of Ambrose of Milan (*c.* 339–97) reminds us, the transition from lay status directly to the episcopate was far from being unknown in the ancient Church. The date seems to have been 341. Frumentius returned to Ethiopia and served until his death as the head of the Ethiopian Church, with the title Abba Salāma, father of peace.[36]

Returning now to Edessa, we travel in a north-westerly direction. If Osrhoene was the first Christian kingdom, the second was undoubtedly *Armenia*.

The Gospel spread to Armenia from Cappadocia, where the most notable evangelist was Gregory, known as Thaumaturgus, the wonder-worker. Gregory, who was born about 213, had been a student under Origen in Caesarea, and has left to us a noble oration in praise of his great teacher. Soon after his return to Cappadocia he was consecrated bishop of the city where he was born. Tradition says that when he became bishop there were only seventeen Christians in the city, but that when he died thirty years later there were only seventeen pagans.

It was from Cappadocia that the Gospel spread to Armenia. The founder of the Armenian Church was Gregory the Enlightener or Illuminator (*c.* 240–332). When Armenia passed for a time under Persian rule, Gregory fled to Roman territory, and there received a thorough Christian education. Upon the liberation of Armenia, he returned to his own country and was called to take part in a reorganization of that country's life, which included the restoration of its ancient religion. At the great festival of the goddess Anahit, Gregory as a Christian refused to lay garlands on her altar, and was in consequence cruelly tortured and shut up in prison. At length the situation changed: the king Tiridates was willing to be baptized, and from that time on king and Christian leader worked hand in hand for the Christianization of the country. In the face of violent resistance by the priests, the great temple of Anahit in the ancient capital Artaxatar was levelled with the ground. After some years, at the desire of the king, Gregory went down to Caesarea in

36. A careful study of the beginning of Christianity in Ethiopia, based on Ethiopic as well as other sources, is E. Hammerschmidt: 'Die Anfänge des Christentums in Äthiopien' in *Zeitschrift für Missionswissenschaft und Religionswissenschaft*, Vol. 38 (1954), pp. 281–94. Our earliest authority for Frumentius is the *Ecclesiastical History* of Rufinus, who wrote about A.D. 400.

Cappadocia, and was consecrated by Bishop Leontius as Bishop and 'Catholicos' for the Armenian Church.[37]

The Church of Armenia is remarkable in a number of ways. This is the first clear case known to us in which the conversion of a king was the first step in the conversion of a whole country. Tiridates accepted Christianity as the religion of his state; willy-nilly the aristocracy had to follow him, and then the Gospel spread among the common people. Secondly, from the start the Church was associated with the language and the thought of the people. Gregory had preached in Armenian. In A.D. 406 the scholar (later patriarch) Mesrob invented a new alphabet for the Armenian language, and took part in the translation of the New Testament, which was completed in 410. The close identification of race, language, culture, religion, and political organization has given to Armenian Christianity an extraordinary resilience and pertinacity. In the face of endless wars and persecutions the Armenians have held on, and can rightly claim that theirs is one of the most ancient Churches in the Christian world.

Travelling still further westwards, we come to the barbarian nations north of the Danube, which from the middle of the third century onwards were an increasing threat to the stability of the Roman Empire. In one of their many wars the *Goths* had captured a number of Cappadocian prisoners; these remained faithful to their Christian profession, and through them the Goths acquired their first acquaintance with the Gospel. But widespread evangelization began only with the coming of Ulfilas (*c.* 311–83), one of the most notable missionaries of whom we have record in any period of the history of the Church.

Ulfilas seems to have been the son of a Cappadocian mother and a Gothic father. On a visit to Constantinople he made the acquaintance of Bishop Eusebius of Nicomedia, who consecrated him bishop for the Gothic race, and sent him back, about A.D. 341, to begin work among his own people. For forty years Ulfilas carried on his work patiently and successfully, beyond the frontier of the empire and later within it, among his wild and undisciplined charges. The greatest service that he rendered them was that he reduced the Gothic language to writing and translated the Bible

---

37. It is interesting to notice that for some generations the Catholicate was hereditary in the family of Gregory, who himself was closely related to the royal family. It is clear that many of the ancient customs survived in Armenia, even after the people had become Christian.

into it. This was the first time that a language of northern Europe became a literary language. It is not certain whether the Gothic New Testament as we now have it is the work of Ulfilas himself or of later revisers; it remains, in either case, one of the great monuments of courageous and vigorous Christian expansion.[38]

Of the peoples between the Danube and the North Sea there is at this period hardly anything to relate. The next step in our imaginary journey carries us to the farthest westward limits of the then known world. *Ireland* had never formed part of the Roman Empire. But during the fifth century this remote island was called to begin its Christian career as the island of the saints.

Patrick was born, somewhere in Britain, about A.D. 389. When he was sixteen years old a band of Irish marauders descended upon England and carried off a crowd of captives, Patrick among them. Six years were spent as a shepherd among the barbarians on the wild mountains of Ireland. At the end of that time Patrick escaped, and crossed to France. But he never forgot the land of his captivity, as he himself said:

I heard calling me the voices of those who dwelt beside the wood of Foclut which is nigh to the western sea, and thus they cried: 'We beseech thee, holy youth, to come and walk again amongst us as before.'

Patrick decided to return to Ireland. Much in his life history is obscure, and later legend has confused still more the scanty data which we have from Patrick's own pen. It is likely that he returned to Ireland about A.D. 432 and continued to labour there until his death in 461. It is certain that he was a bishop, but it is not known exactly when and where and by whom he was consecrated. It is possible that he came to Armagh about 442, and made that the centre of his work. Ireland at that time was almost wholly, if not entirely, a heathen country; Patrick writes of his journeys to regions 'where never any one had come to baptize, or to ordain

38. It has been to the prejudice of the work of Ulfilas in the eyes of later writers that he was an Arian. Arianism is a simplification of the faith that must in the end be regarded as un-Christian, since it reduces the Son of God to the level of the highest of the creatures. But to simple people it may have presented itself as a rather attractive simplification, since it set them free from the knotty controversies about the nature and person of Christ, to follow him as a leader and to concentrate on the already sufficiently difficult task of learning to live a sober, righteous, and godly life. It is said that Ulfilas did not translate the warlike Books of Kings in the Old Testament, on the ground that the Goths knew quite enough about fighting anyway.

clergy, or to confirm the people'. He encountered much opposition – from the representatives of the old religion, from the kings whom he tried to convert, from British raiders who disrupted his work and massacred his converts. But he outlived his enemies and wore down the opposition and at the time of his death Ireland was largely a Christian country.

In his writings Patrick gives the impression of being a man wholly possessed by the love of Christ, simple, and not highly educated – he seems to have been painfully conscious of his lack of theological competence and fitness for the office of a bishop.[39] Dreams played a large part in his experience, and he lived at all times conscious of a supernatural world, both of good and evil. 'The Breastplate of St Patrick', which tradition has long associated with his name, is itself of the nature of a charm – the name of the Trinity is stronger than the spells and machinations of evil, and can guard against peril the one who binds it to himself.

Celtic Christianity was in some respects unique. The centre of life was not the diocese but the monastery; like all other Churches, the Irish Church was episcopal, but the chief place in the monastery belonged not to the bishop but to the abbot. From very early times the monasteries of Killiney, Clonard, Bangor, and Clonmacnoise were famous; famous also the austerities of the monks. The ancient beehive dwellings in the Skelligs off the coast of Cork give evidence of a poverty such as modern men would find intolerable; and tales of the monks, who would recite the whole Psalter while plunged in icy water, or stand so long in prayer with arms crossed that the birds had time to build nests in their hair, suggest an element of fanaticism. But these things were only the extravagances. What made the greatness of the Irish monks, as we shall see in the next chapter, was the development of an admirable Christian culture, and an equally admirable missionary passion.

Our tour of the horizon brings us next to *France*. As we have seen, progress beyond the southern regions was slow and difficult. The hero of Christian expansion was St Martin, Bishop of Tours (*c.* 316–97)[40], a soldier turned monk who was unwilling to leave his

39. From his own *Confession*, it seems that this was a charge made against him by his enemies; and the poverty of his later style shows that there were grounds for the accusation. See J. B. Bury, *The Life of St Patrick and his Place in History* (1905).

40. There is considerable doubt about the dates of St Martin's life. Some authorities think that he may have been born as late as 335.

cell in order to become a bishop; a wise, gentle, but courageous man – he refused to hold communion with the bishops who brought about the death of the Spanish heretic Priscillian in A.D. 385 – a true evangelist, who travelled far and wide, combating paganism at every step, and bringing the Gospel to bear on the life of the country folk in regions in which previously it had been limited to the cities.

The end of the fifth century saw in France an event which has rightly been recognized as one of the turning points of Christian history, the baptism of Clovis, king of the Franks. As the old Roman power broke down, western Europe became increasingly the prey of the barbarous peoples who streamed in from the German forests and the plains of central Europe. Though the Franks have given their name to France, they were a Germanic people, and at this time they were still pagans. In 493 Clovis their king married a Christian princess, Clotilda of Burgundy, who did her best to convert him, but without success; when their first child died, Clovis remarked: 'My gods would have saved him; yours has let him die.' But, if later writers can be trusted, the crisis came not long after, when Clovis was threatened with overthrow in battle by the Alemanni, the most German of all the German peoples. In the moment of peril Clovis swore that, if victory was his, he would become the servant of the God of the Christians. He kept his vow: on Christmas Day 496 he was baptized with three thousand of his warriors.

This event was significant in two ways. Of the barbarians who had become Christian the majority were Arians; Clovis had been baptized by a Catholic[41] bishop, and had accepted, as far as he understood it, the Catholic form of the Christian faith. The adhesion of the Franks was one of the factors that turned the scale against the Arians and in favour of the faith as it was understood at Rome. We need not take literally the story that, at their baptism, the warriors of Clovis held their right arms above their heads – the God of the Christians could have all else, but they would maintain the independence of the warrior's arm. But the story tells us something that is really significant. When the barbarians entered

41. The word does not, of course, mean Roman Catholic. It distinguishes those bishops who accepted the decisions of the great Councils from Nicaea (325) to Chalcedon (451) from the various heretics – Arian, Apollinarian, Monophysite, Nestorian, and others – who at one point or another departed from or refused to accept the teaching of the Councils. A study of the conversion of Clovis is K. Aland, *Über den Glaubenswechsel in der Geschichte des Christentums* (1961), pp. 48–55.

the Church, they did not bring into it the virtuous simplicity of untutored peoples; as we learn plainly from the historians of the next century, what they brought in was fierce untempered natures, with an inveterate tendency to brutality and excess.

In the year 500 the Church could look back on five centuries of miraculous success. As yet it knew almost nothing of the ancient and stable civilizations of India and China, but it had constituted itself the greatest civilizing force in the Western world. It had drawn into itself the best of the ancient Greek and Roman civilizations. It had shown its ability to survive the collapse of the Western Roman Empire. It had manifested a versatility that could adapt itself to the needs of peoples on very different levels of civilization.

Inwardly, the Church had gone far to consolidate its life and to perfect its organization. It had defined the limits of the Scriptures, and had given to the New Testament equal canonical status with the Old. Through the work of the great Councils it had settled many questions of doctrine, and had laid down the limits within which Christian thought has moved ever since. It had developed a system of worship which laid its hand on the day and the week and the month and the year, and which claimed to sanctify every part of the life of man. In the great Councils it had developed a marvellous instrument for the expression and the maintenance of Christian unity. In spite of troublesome disputes as to the relative status and authority of patriarchs – Antioch against Alexandria, and at times Rome against all the rest – Christians in every part of the world felt themselves to be one with all other Christians.

It might seem that the Church could look forward to unhindered and continuous progress, until it should become literally coextensive with the inhabited world and with the human race. In reality, in the year 500 it was about to enter on a period of bitter and disheartening conflict. It was to be called to engage in desperate struggles on two quite different fronts. On one, after more than five hundred years of effort, it was to emerge almost wholly victorious; on the other, it was to endure fearful losses, and for much more than five hundred years to do little more than hold its own. The year 500 marks the beginning of what Professor K. S. Latourette called 'The Thousand Years of Uncertainty'.[42]

---

42. The title of Volume 11 of his great *History of the Expansion of Christianity*.

3

The Dark Age, 500–1000

At the end of the last chapter we spoke of the two conflicts which the Church found on its hands in the years following A.D. 500 – the struggle with the barbarians, and the unending battle with Islam.

From the beginning of human history, the Central European plain, with its vast extension through Russia to the steppes and deserts of Central Asia, has been what a Roman historian called it, *officina gentium*, a factory of nations. The movements of peoples within that area are mysterious to us, since they have no recorded history. But from time to time, for causes that may be equally mysterious to us, these peoples begin to spill outwards over the edge of their own proper territory towards other and perhaps more fortunate lands; one race or tribe presses another, and the ripples spread onwards till they reach the utmost oceans, and then they can spread no more. When this happens, written history becomes aware of the movements, and begins to concern itself with the barbarians. From the middle of the third century onwards the Roman Empire was gravely troubled by the northern peoples beyond its borders, and found the work of defence increasingly difficult. The pressure continued until the old civilization of the Western Roman Empire had been almost completely destroyed, and the long period of movement and counter-movement, destruction and chaos, commonly known as the Dark Ages, followed.

Some of the invaders, like the Huns, seem to have been animated by a senseless passion for destruction; they passed and left a wilderness behind them, having created nothing. Others, such as Alaric the Goth who captured and sacked Rome in A.D. 410, had had long contact with the Romans and had acquired a considerable measure of civilization. Some of the invaders had become Christian before they entered the Roman Empire, though more of them professed the Arian than the Catholic form of the Christian faith. But the vast majority were pagan and hardly touched by civilization. For five hundred years the major task of the Western Church was that of wrestling with the barbarians and with barbarism in the effort to make their conversion something more than nominal; in the process, it found itself transformed from an imperial into a feudal Church. By A.D. 1000 the greater part of this task had been at least outwardly accomplished, though, as we shall see, it was still very far from being completed.

Far more difficult, dangerous, and disastrous was the Church's warfare on its other front. In A.D. 622 inspired, as he believed, to be a prophet of the living God, Muhammad moved from Mecca to Medina. Before his death ten years later, he had gathered together a not very large group of converts on the basis of his new monotheistic message that 'there is no God but God, and Muhammad is the prophet of God', had imposed a unity hitherto unknown on the warring tribes of Arabia, and had given them a sense of mission that sent them out conquering and to conquer to the four winds of heaven, with an *élan* that even in the twentieth century has not wholly died away. Islam, surrender, was their new religion; the Muslim was the man dedicated to the carrying out of the will of God as he understood it. Under certain aspects the Muslim aggression is part of the long history of the conflict between the desert and the sown – the desire of the desert-dweller for the richer and softer lands which he finds in the possession of others; but it is very much more than that – it is the expression of a profound religious faith, of the dynamic and creative power of a civilization which has its own special characteristics and is unlike any other that has existed on the earth.

Once the Arabs had begun to emerge from the fastnesses of their deserts, their progress was astonishingly rapid. By 650 the ancient empire of Persia had been destroyed. Jerusalem fell in 638, Caesarea in 640, and with them Palestine and Syria came under Muslim domination. In 642 Alexandria was captured; it was not long before the whole of Egypt was added to the Muslim domain. The advance westward along the coast of Africa continued, and in 697 Carthage was seized. By 715 the greater part of Spain was in Muslim hands. Then came the first great check: in 732 a Muslim army was encountered by Charles Martel at Tours in the very heart of France, and was utterly defeated. Islam was never successful in establishing itself north of the Pyrenees. Elsewhere, however, advance continued. In 846 Rome itself was invested and plundered. By 902 Sicily was a Muslim country, and strongholds had been established on the South Italian coast. In Asia Minor the Muslim armies had begun that relentless pressure on the Eastern

Roman Empire which they were to maintain with fitful energies and varying fortunes, and which the Christian forces were doggedly to resist, until at last in 1453 Constantinople fell to the Turks, and the Eastern Roman Empire, the bulwark of Christendom for a thousand years, was at an end.

Christian tradition has drawn a tragic picture of the fate of the Christians in face of the Islamic advance, in terms of the alternative – death or apostasy. Naturally, conquest is an unpleasant business for those who are on the receiving end of it. There were occasional massacres, and no doubt much casual loss of life. There were steady losses of Christians through conversion to Islam. But the most surprising thing about these invasions is that the loss of life was so small and the collapse of the Christian civilization so rapid. A great many Christians lived on as Christians. They suffered certain hardships, and had to endure loss of equality and privilege. They were second-class citizens and tax-payers, and could never hope to rank with the Muslim overlords. But the last thing the Muslims wished was to exterminate or to convert them all. The Arabs were not farmers: they needed peasants to cultivate the land. They were not administrators, and they needed educated Christians to serve as clerks and translators and to carry out all the minor obligations of government. A number of Christians rose comparatively high in government service, though there was ceaseless pressure on them to improve their position by turning Muslim, and a great many of them yielded to this pressure.

Nevertheless, though less violent than has often been represented, the Muslim conquest was a major disaster for the Christian world. The ancient Eastern Churches lost their dominant position in government and in the world of thought. They were constantly drained of their resources through the defection of so many of their young men. The Muslim sense of superiority naturally found itself reflected in a Christian sense of inferiority. That these Churches have survived at all in such unfavourable circumstances is in itself a miracle. They maintained their worshipping tradition with courage.

We cannot but ask why it was that the Churches from Babylon to Morocco opposed so feeble a resistance to the onrush of the Muslim armies. The causes were in part political, in part quasinational. Some Eastern Christians were in part technically heretical, having followed the Monophysite or Nestorian way in the period of the close definition of the relation between the divine and human in Jesus Christ.[1] They had been harried and oppressed by what they felt to be a foreign government in Byzantium. Taxes were heavy and administration was often corrupt. To them it often seemed that a change of masters might be no bad thing, and that a life under the Muslim, though necessarily in an inferior station, might be more tolerable than life under the alien Christian. The acceptance of this status brought with it, of course, the abandonment of any attempt to convert the Muslim master. A few cases of conversion to Christianity are on record, but they are very few. The Muslim law, which punishes apostasy with death, may not in every case have been put into execution; yet it was there as a constant deterrent, and has remained so till the present day. The cynical remark that perfect religious freedom exists in the Muslim dominions – any Christian can at any time become a Muslim – is not without its point; there has always been traffic, but almost always in one direction only.

The Muslim conquests, and their control of many of the great trade routes of the ancient world both by land and sea – a control which in large measure the Arab countries still exercise, and which they extended in modern times by the control of oil from Iran to Libya – involved a notable shift in the whole perspective of the Christian world. Christianity became an almost completely European religion. It is true that in those days the concepts 'Europe' and 'Asia' were less clearly defined than they later became; the narrow waterway of the Bosporus was in no sense felt to be a sharp dividing line. It is perhaps truer to say that Christianity, with its two great centres in Constantinople and Rome, became a religion of the Mediterranean world, and, with the steady weakening of the Eastern Empire through the aggressions of the Muslims, increasingly a religion of the northern and western Mediterranean. This it continued to be, till the great discoveries of the fifteenth century brought about another shift. All roads till then led to Rome.

The problem which confronted the Church in its dealings with the barbarians was entirely different from that which it had to face

1. To put it pictorially, the Monophysites followed the tradition of 'wine and water' – that in the incarnate Lord the divine and the human merged into one single and unique nature; the Nestorians that of 'oil and water' – in Jesus the divine and the human remain distinct, so distinct that the Nestorians were accused of teaching the doctrine of 'two sons'. The Council of Chalcedon (451) tried to avoid both these aberrations.

with the Muslims. Except for the Scandinavians, the barbarian nations which entered the Roman Empire, or lived on or just beyond its frontiers, had no organized culture of their own. They had, of course, their own way of life, their ancient traditions, their primitive religion, their ancestral laws. But there was nothing that could carry on such a resistance to the Christian Gospel as that maintained by the philosophers of Greece or the aristocratic families of Rome. Rome was a name to conjure with, almost to the furthest limit of the barbarian world; it struck awe into the minds even of the invaders who came to destroy it. Civilization meant Roman civilization, and hand in hand with civilization went the Church, which was the heir of the ancient world. As in many parts of Africa today, any man who wished to be regarded as civilized was almost bound to become a Christian.

The task of bringing these people into the Church took a long time to accomplish, and was not complete, even in externals, till nearly the end of the fourteenth century. Distances were great, and communications slow. Successful Christian work was again and again interrupted, or disrupted, by some new wandering of the peoples. And far more difficult than the task of first bringing these peoples into the Church was that of making Christian faith effective in their lives, of bringing proud, undisciplined, and illiterate natures under the yoke of the Gospel. That it was accomplished at all was due in the main to three continuing factors, which we shall encounter in almost every one of the countries that will come under our scrutiny – royal favour, martyrdom, and monasticism.

Our survey may start with *Britain*, the furthest of the isles. Here we are fortunate in having extensive and reliable information. The Venerable Bede (*c.* 673–735) is the one great historian of the Dark Ages. This wise, gentle, and extensively learned man lived almost the whole of his life in the remote monastery of Jarrow in Northumbria. The story that at the very moment of his death he was engaged in completing his translation of the Gospel according to St John into his beloved Anglo-Saxon is well known, and is almost certainly true. Bede is not a critical historian in the later sense of the term. In his pages we encounter tales of marvels and miracles that critical study is bound to discount as legendary. But he understands the use of original sources. He is deeply concerned about the truth of events. He has a real sense for human character and for the depiction of it. If he had not written, or if his work had failed to survive, we would have known little of the entry of the Gospel into Britain and of the early progress of the Church in these islands.

We have noted the existence of Christian Churches in Britain not later than the third century. But this ancient Christianity had been overthrown two centuries later by the invasions of the Angles and Saxons; Christianity had withdrawn into the fastnesses of Wales, and there carried on a remote and precarious existence. Hatred of the invaders was such that the Britons seem to have felt that it was almost certainly impossible and quite certainly undesirable to attempt to convert them.

Britain first re-entered the full tide of European history when Pope Gregory the Great personally initiated the mission to England and in 596 despatched Augustine and his party of monks to Canterbury. Gregory would have been a notable figure in any age. He stands out as the first great medieval man. Called from a monastery to be Bishop of Rome in 590, he did more than any other man to strengthen the hold of the papacy on the Church, and to establish the Church on the ruins of the vanishing Roman Empire as the one great power that had survived in the western world. It may be that he did not actually say on seeing British slave-boys in the market, '*Angli sunt, angeli fiant*' – 'They are Angles, let them become angels'; perhaps he already knew too much about the English to fall into any such confusion. But his action was fresh and remarkable, since, in contrast to the haphazard way in which Churches had generally grown up, this was almost the first example since the days of Paul of a carefully planned and calculated mission. Gregory, himself a monk, had seen the vital part that the monk and the cloister could play in missionary work among the new nations. And Augustine's first task was to set himself to the conversion of the kings and rulers.

Augustine and his companions, on their way through Gaul, seem to have lost heart at the thought of going so far and working among people of whom they knew nothing; they asked to be relieved of their task. Gregory was inexorable. In point of fact Augustine and his friends had exaggerated the dangers of their way. England was divided up into a number of small kingdoms constantly at war with one another – many years were to pass before the land again found its unity under Egbert, king of Wessex (802–39) – but it was far from being a wholly barbarous land. King Ethelbert of Kent (*c.* 560–616), in whose territory the missionaries landed, had wedded Bertha, a Christian princess from Gaul. The monks were well received. The king was, indeed, a little anxious, and would not receive them in any house 'lest, if they were skilful in sorcery, they might the rather by surprise deceive him and prevail against him'. But in the end he allowed them to settle in Canterbury, his capital; so they came in, with the holy Cross and the picture of Jesus Christ carried before them, singing one of the antiphons for the Rogation Days: 'We beseech thee, Lord, in all thy mercy, that thy fury and anger may be taken from this city, and from thy holy house, because we have sinned. Alleluia.' Their virtuous life and their preaching made such a deep impression that the king was before long converted, and by the end of the year Augustine was able to baptize 10,000 Saxons.

The missionaries were faced with many problems, not least that of knowing how to treat the ancient habits and customs of the people. One of the later letters of Gregory, which is dated 18 July 601, is a notable example of that principle of accommodation which we shall encounter again in our narrative:

The heathen temples of these people need not be destroyed, only the idols which are to be found in them. . . . If the temples are well built, it is a good idea to detach them from the service of the devil, and to adapt them for the worship of the true God . . . And since the people are accustomed, when they assemble for sacrifice, to kill many oxen in sacrifice to the devils, it seems reasonable to appoint a festival for the people by way of exchange. The people must learn to slay their cattle not in honour of the devil, but in honour of God and for their own food; when they have eaten and are full, then they must render thanks to the giver of all good things. If we allow them these outward joys, they are more likely to find their way to the true inner joy. . . . It is doubtless impossible to cut off all abuses at once from rough hearts, just as the man who sets out to climb a high mountain does not advance by leaps and bounds, but goes upward step by step and pace by pace.[2]

The direct connection of Augustine's mission with Rome gives it primary importance. But it is important to remember that in Britain three streams of Christianity meet – the British, the Celtic, and the Roman. Northern Britain owed its Christianity to the Irish; the starting-point of this great adventure was the holy island of Iona off the west coast of Scotland.

We have already mentioned the missionary zeal which sprang

2. Bede, *Ecclesiastical History of the English Nation*, Bk 1: 30. This letter was addressed not directly to Augustine but to the abbot Mellitus, who was on his way to Britain and was instructed to convey the contents to Augustine.

from Irish monasticism. The most notable figure of our period is St Columba, the Apostle of Scotland. Born about A.D. 521 of a noble Irish family, Columba had already founded the two monasteries of Durrow in King's County, and Londonderry, when in 563 he decided to cross the narrow seas with twelve companions and to found a new monastery on the island called Hy or Iona. The purpose of this foundation was evangelistic; the Gospel was to be preached to the still heathen Picts. Columba was not strictly a pioneer in the sense of entering entirely unevangelized country. In the south of Galloway, St Ninian (*c.* 360–430) had worked at an earlier period, and had founded his famous church called Candida Casa (the White House) in Wigtownshire. But the greater part of Scotland was still utterly wild and pagan until Columba came to Iona. Before his death in 597 a number of monasteries had been founded, all remaining under the control of the central foundation at Iona. Columba left behind him a tradition of real and simple sanctity. It is written of him that 'in the midst of all his cares he showed himself open and friendly to everyone; he bore the joy of the Holy Spirit in the inmost places of his heart'.[3]

It was after Columba's death that the work from Iona received its greatest extension. Oswald, king of Northumbria, like Constantine and Clovis before him, decided in time of battle in 633 or 634 that he would become a Christian and sent to Iona to ask for teachers. After an unsuccessful start, Aidan was sent to pull things together, and was given a dwelling at Lindisfarne. Aidan brought with him the gentleness that we have noted in Columba, and also the ascetic traditions of Irish monasticism; it is recorded that he made his journeys on foot after the manner of the *peregrini*, the wanderers for the sake of Christ. The death of Oswald in battle in 642 did not stay the process of conversion. Oswald found a worthy successor in his brother Oswin (642–51), just as Aidan found a successor in Cuthbert (d. 687), most lovable of saints, who was wont

to resort most commonly unto those places and preach in those hamlets lying afar off in steep and craggy hills, which other men had dreaded to

3. There is a new edition of *Adomnan's Life of Columba*, with Latin text and English translation, by A. O. and M. O. Anderson (1961). There is a touching story that on the last day of his life a white horse, knowing that Columba's departure was near, laid its head on his bosom and began to mourn; the attendant tried to drive the horse away, but Columba forbade him, and blessed his servant the horse, as it sadly turned away from him (*Life*, pp. 522–5).

visit, and which from their poverty as well as uplandish rudeness teachers shunned to approach; tarrying in the hilly part, he would call the poor folk of the country to heavenly things with the word of preaching as well as work of virtuous example.[4]

To a slightly earlier period belongs the most famous of all the stories of the early preaching of the Gospel in north-western Europe. When King Edwin (d. 633) and his warriors were assembled in his hall and Bishop Paulinus had urged them to accept the new teaching, a bird flew through the hall and out into the darkness. Whereupon one of the nobles present commented and said:

The life of man is as if a sparrow should come to the house and very swiftly flit through. So the life of man here appeareth for a little season, but what followeth or what has gone before, that surely we know not. Wherefore if this new learning hath brought us any better tidings, surely methinks it is worthy to be followed.[5]

As we have seen, there were differences between Roman and Celtic Christianity. These might seem to us insignificant. They related to such matters as the date on which Easter ought to be kept, and the manner in which the tonsure of the clergy ought to be carried out. Trivialities – but behind them lay a vast and many-sided question: when such differences arise, who is to decide? Has the Bishop of Rome in fact the last word? Rome found its champion in the northerner Wilfrid (634–709), a vigorous, high-handed, not altogether scrupulous man, who for a time was Bishop of York. The issue was tried at the Synod of Whitby in 663–4; after hearing both sides, the king of Northumbria decided in favour of Rome. It is important not to overestimate the independence of the Celtic Churches. They never imagined that there could be more than one Church, and they never doubted that the Bishop of Rome was the successor of Peter; they were standing simply for their right to be faithful to ancient traditions which had grown up in a remote and inaccessible part of the world. It was now decided that the writ of Rome ran everywhere, and that even Britain was to conform to the instructions that came from the centre. This was one step in that process of the imposition of a uniform pattern with which Rome was to exercise itself for more than a thousand years.

In later years (686–7) Wilfrid was himself to carry out notable

4. Bede, *History* IV:27.
5. Bede, *History* II:13.

evangelistic work among the still heathen Saxons in Sussex. With this, the conversion of England was held in principle to have been completed. Its organization as a regular ecclesiastical province was the work of Theodore of Tarsus, who, coming to Canterbury in 668 at the age of sixty-six, in twenty-two years fashioned England into the regular ways of ecclesiastical life, as these were understood by the Rome of that day. Regular dioceses with fixed boundaries were created. Great Synods were held (673, 680). Progress was made with the development of the parochial system. The authority of the Archbishop of Canterbury was effectively extended over the whole country.

We have already seen something of the missionary activity of the Irish monks in Scotland. But this was far from being the limit of their field. Roman culture, which had been almost wholly driven out from the ancient Latin lands, was to know a late and unexpected flowering in the furthest of the Western Isles, and from there to flow back to the continent of Europe. The best-known monument of this wonderful Christian culture, later to be tragically destroyed by the invasions of the Northmen, is the Book of Kells, an illuminated Gospel manuscript of the eighth century still preserved in the library of Trinity College, Dublin. But this great manuscript is only one of many, and the peculiar Irish script – neat, legible, and artistic – meets us in ancient libraries all over Western Europe. When the monks went out as missionaries, this culture was one of the great gifts that they carried with them.

One of the most notable of these 'wanderers for Christ' was the younger Columba, often called Columban to distinguish him from his more famous namesake (550–615). Columban was already forty years old when he set out on his travels. His first scene of labour was eastern *France*, where he founded the monastery of Luxeuil. Twenty years later Columban incurred the hostility of the Burgundian court because of the boldness with which he rebuked the immorality of the ruler. Expelled from Luxeuil with his Celtic monks, he set out again to preach the Gospel to the still pagan people whom he found in the neighbourhood of Lake Constance. Driven out yet once more by the spread of the Burgundian power, he retired to die in another of his foundations, the monastery of Bobbio in northern Italy.

One of those who had accompanied Columban from Ireland was St Gall. Gall became the Apostle of north-eastern *Switzerland*. The bear which came out of the woods and kindly helped him to build his hermitage is still to be seen in the arms of the city of St Gallen;

and the library of the cathedral appropriately houses what is perhaps the finest collection of Irish manuscripts in the world.

The Irish enthusiasm spread to the Church in England, which for the next four centuries was, and then ceased to be, a great missionary Church.

The first of whom we have to take note was Willibrord (*c.* 658–739), a monk of Wilfrid's foundation at Ripon, who became the Apostle of the Frisians in what is now *Holland* and part of *Belgium*. Christianity had been extending in this direction through France, Bishop Caesarius of Arles (470–542) having rendered notable service. And throughout his career Willibrord was much indebted to Pepin of Heristal, mayor of the palace and later king of the Franks. We have a brief note, written in the margin of a calendar in Willibrord's own hand, which tells us that 'in the name of the Lord came Clement[6] Willibrord, in the year 690 after the Incarnation of Christ, across the sea into the land of the Franks'. Pepin at all times supported him against the Frisian ruler Radbod, with whom his relationships seem never to have been good. Willibrord and his eleven companions started work at what is now Utrecht. After some years of good success, it was clear that the mission must have a bishop. After one unsuccessful appointment, the choice of Pepin fell upon Willibrord. This was confirmed by his companions, and in 695 Willibrord went to Rome to receive consecration from the Bishop of Rome himself. The consecration took place on 22 November 695; Pope Sergius gave Willibrord the status of an archbishop in order that he might be independent of the Frankish bishops, and sent him back to continue his work among the Frisians. With many ups and downs the work went on until the death of Willibrord forty years later.

Our sources give us little detail by which to judge of the methods followed in his work, and nothing at all on which a statistical reckoning can be based. It is clear that the monastery was the centre of the whole work; Willibrord was able during his lifetime to found monasteries – Utrecht and Epternach. There the steady work of prayer and discipline went forward; there a home was provided, from which the monks went out on missionary journeys, and to which they returned for rest and renewal. There were some cases of actual violence or persecution but the principal difficulties were the inconstancy of the people, and the endless political

6. At the request of the Pope, Willibrord took the additional name of Clement at the time of his consecration as bishop.

tensions between Frisians and Franks, with the latter of whom the missionaries were naturally associated in the minds of the people. But, for all the setbacks and failures in parts of the area, the work went forward, and by the time of the death of Willibrord, Frisia had a well-established Church which was able to survive through all the later vicissitudes of political change.

We turn now to the work of the greatest of all the missionaries of the Dark Ages, Wynfrith of Crediton, later known as Boniface (*c.* 680–754), the Apostle of *Germany*, and in the words of Mr Christopher Dawson 'a man who had a deeper influence on the history of Europe than any Englishman who has ever lived'.[7]

Until the age of forty Wynfrith had been a monk, living after the godly tradition of Wessex in the monasteries of Exeter and Nursling or Nutshalling, near Winchester. His missionary efforts, and those of many of his contemporaries, were not the adventures of hot-headed youths; they were planned and calculated efforts on the part of mature men, based on a sober conviction that the Gospel of Christ must be preached to those who from their point of view were still barbarous peoples.

The forty years' activity of Boniface falls into five main periods.

First came some years of service in Frisia with and under Willibrord; of this period there is little to record.

The great turning-point came when Boniface was summoned to Rome, and on 30 November 722 consecrated by Pope Gregory II as bishop for the German frontier without a fixed see. On this occasion Boniface took the same oath of direct submission and allegiance to the Pope as was taken by the bishops of the dioceses in the neighbourhood of Rome. Boniface had realized that the extended missions could attain permanence only if the new Churches were well and strictly organized, and only if they could be assured of the direct support and help of the centre at Rome. This was to a large extent a new principle; it was long before the Popes could make it really effective, but it was of cardinal importance for the later evangelization of Europe.

Shortly after his return from Rome (724), Boniface won fame for himself and repute for the Christian cause by his courageous act in felling the sacred oak of Thor at Geismar in Hesse, the chief object of the superstitious reverence of the non-Christians and of the half-Christianized peoples of that area. Such acts are rather

7. *The Making of Europe* (9th impression, 1953), p. 166.

frequently recorded of the missionaries of the time; thus we read that one of the first acts of St Gall when he arrived in north-eastern Switzerland was to destroy the local pagan sanctuary. The act was akin to the trial by ordeal, which was part of the tradition of the northern nations; it was, in fact, a conflict not between men but between the gods. The Germans were convinced that anyone who infringed the sacredness of the sanctuary would be destroyed by the gods; Boniface affirmed that he would be unscathed. The oak was felled; nothing happened. The watchers were at once convinced that Boniface was right, and that the God he proclaimed was really stronger than the gods of their fathers. With the wood of the tree Boniface built a chapel in honour of St Peter.

After another visit to Rome in 737–8, Boniface returned with authority to settle the affairs of the Church in Bavaria and beyond. He organized the bishoprics of Freising, Passau, Ratisbon, and Salzburg, to which were later added Eichstätt and Würzburg. In 744 he founded the great monastery of Fulda, which up to the present day has played a special part in the Roman Catholic Christianity of central Germany.

In 741 Boniface was called to execute a great reform of the Frankish Church. The mayors of the palace, who exercised the real rule under the decadent Merovingian kings, had taken the Church under their protection, but they had done little to build it up and nothing to reform it. Bishoprics and abbeys were given away as rewards to those who had rendered some service to the court, without regard to their spiritual competence. It naturally followed, as Boniface wrote in his complaint to the Pope, that

religion is trodden under foot. Benefices are given to greedy laymen, or to unchaste and publican clerks. All their crimes do not prevent their attaining the priesthood; at last, rising in rank as they increase in sin, they become bishops, and those of them who can boast that they are not adulterers or fornicators are drunkards, given up to the chase, and soldiers who do not shrink from shedding Christian blood.[8]

Boniface was not successful in carrying out all his purposes of reform; but in a series of Councils between 742 and 747 he was able to impose a measure of discipline on the Frankish Church, to eliminate the worst of the abuses, and to bind the Frankish Church closely in allegiance to Rome. When in 751 Pepin, the mayor of the palace, took over the kingship, Boniface made it clear that the Pope

8. *Epistle* XLIX.

approved of this transference of sovereignty from one house to another and according to later evidence crowned the new king.

As Boniface grew older, he withdrew more and more from the field of administration; at the end, the spirit of the missionary prevailed, and drove him out again into the lands where Christ had not been named. In 753 with a party of companions he moved northward to the area on the far side of the Zuider Zee, where the Frisians were still pagan. The work met with marked success, but at the same time stirred up a violent pagan reaction. On 5 June 754 Boniface and his companions were waiting in the neighbourhood of Dokkum for the arrival of a number of newly-converted Christians, who were to be confirmed. They were suddenly attacked by a group of angry pagans; Boniface attempted to protect himself by holding to his head a book containing random Christian writings, but to no purpose; the old man and his fifty companions were all killed.

We know more of Boniface than of any other of the missionaries of this period, through the survival of a number of letters and treatises from his hand; from these we can learn a good deal about his missionary methods. When a group, often under the influence of a chieftain or ruler, had decided to become Christian, it was customary to baptize the catechumens without any long delay. But these great baptisms were ordinarily held only at the canonical seasons of Easter and Whitsun. Then followed the long and patient process of trying to make Christians in deed of those who had become Christians in name. To the age of Boniface and his successors belongs the development of the rules and practice of penitential discipline.

We have referred more than once to the part played by the monasteries – in the time of Boniface for the first time extended to include houses for women – in the conversion of Europe. The service rendered by the monks was twofold.

These pioneer houses were for the most part placed in remote and uncultured regions. In order to live, the monks had to carry out the ideal of St Benedict by cultivating the land with their own hands, as well as carrying out the regular *opus dei*, the ceaseless round of prayer and praise. This brought them very near to the peasants among whom they dwelt, and from whose ranks in later times many of the members of the community were drawn. They understood the country folk. Instead of attempting to destroy or uproot all their beliefs, they set to work to transform them by bringing sacred spots and seasons and festivals into relationship to the liturgy and the Christian year. There was danger in this; old superstition could, and did, and does, linger on under the mask of new piety. Yet the principle was right, and we still overhear at places in the liturgy the echoes of this time when the faith and the soil were brought very close together. 'Seedtime and harvest shall not fail.' So in the Liturgy for the Ember Days in Advent the Church is reminded of the sowing of the seed:

The Divine seed descends, and whereas the fruits of the field support our earthly life, this seed from on high gives our soul the Food of Immortality. The earth has yielded its corn and wine and oil, and now the ineffable Birth approaches of Him who through His mercy bestows the Bread of Life upon the Sons of God.

Secondly, the northern monks brought with them the idea of a vernacular culture, which was part of the Anglo-Saxon and Irish tradition. Those of the Latin races tended to regard the tongues of the barbarians as so uncouth that nothing could be done with them; thus it has come about that the ancient Celtic speech of France has entirely disappeared, except in parts of Brittany, and has been replaced by a Romance language. In the north, the monks were tied to Latin for the liturgy, but from the start they believed that the local languages could be preserved, reduced to writing, and used for literary purposes. Thus they prepared the way not only for the medieval unity of Europe, of which Latin was the vehicle, but also for that rich variety of national languages which is the mark of later European civilization.

The next stage in the conversion of Europe presents many less attractive features.

Charlemagne is without question one of the greatest figures in the history both of the Church and of the world. From 771 until his death in 814 he was the sole ruler of the kingdom of the Franks. When, on Christmas Day 800, Pope Leo III crowned him in Rome as emperor, that strange archaeological fiction the Holy Roman Empire came into being, and was destined to last for just over a thousand years.

Charlemagne was a wise and powerfully effective ruler. He had a real interest in theology and in learning; by gathering round him such scholars as Alcuin of York (*c.* 735–804), he set in motion that Carolingian Renaissance which is one of the brightest spots in the long night of the Dark Ages. Yet he was a man of his own times, and later in this chapter we shall have to record acts of violence and cruelty in which are reflected the savagery of a hard and merciless epoch.

Here we are concerned mainly with the extension of the Christian realm through the campaigns of Charlemagne against the *Saxons*. Kings in those days were always troubled about their frontiers: wave upon wave of barbarians welled up from the apparently inexhaustible 'factory of nations', and constant watchfulness was the price of survival. In Charlemagne's day the Saxons were the menace; the emperor decided that they must be brought and kept under his control by a mixture of armed force and religion. From 772 till 798 we read of a constant succession of campaigns, conversions, conspiracies, and repressions. The whole unedifying story has been well summed up by Professor K. S. Latourette:

> The narrative is a repetition, with variations, of campaigns resulting in outward submission and followed by the peaceful efforts of missionaries, of revolts, of fresh campaigns, of more or less sullen acquiescence, of fresh revolts, and of eventual victory.[9]

Once a German tribe had been conquered, its conversion was included in the terms of peace, as the price to be paid for enjoying the protection of the emperor and the good government that his arms ensured. But this meant an association of the new religion with the conquering power that could only be dangerous. Any spark of patriotism, any movement of resistance to the dominant race, could only take the form of equally violent opposition to the Christian faith. So every uprising of the people was accompanied by a resurgence of paganism, and the long tale of martyrdoms and massacres sheds a lurid light on the process by which the Saxons were finally converted.

Violence on the one side led to violence on the other. It is recorded that on one occasion Charlemagne put to death 4,500 Saxons in a single day. The *Capitulatio de partibus Saxoniae* lays down savage penalties for the infringement of a whole variety of Christian rules:

Anyone who kills a bishop, a priest, or a deacon, shall be put to death.

Anyone who burns the body of a dead person, as is the pagan fashion, shall be put to death.

Any unbaptized Saxon who attempts to hide himself among his own people and refuses to accept baptism shall be put to death.

Anyone who plots with the pagans against the Christians shall be put to death.

It is not to be supposed that all these atrocious regulations were carried into effect all the time. But the fact that they were there on the statute book, and could at any moment be put into effect, made it dangerous to be both a Saxon and a pagan.

It would be a mistake, however, to concentrate too much attention on the political aspect and on the element of coercion in the proceedings. It is the remarkable fact that, whenever the Saxons rose in arms and went out hunting for missionaries, priests and monks were always there to be martyred. In an age of the Church which was not on the whole distinguished by heroic sanctity, apparently men and women were always found to take the place of those who had fallen. With the process of time, the missionaries won their way. Resistance to the Gospel grew weaker, and by the time of the death of Charlemagne the pacification and the conversion of the Saxons were reckoned to be complete.

The newly conquered territory was organized in six dioceses, of which the most notable were Bremen (787) and Minden (*c.* 780). The diocese of Hamburg was created in 801. The vision which prompted the foundation of this great Christian centre leads us on to the next stage in the conversion of Europe – the first attempts to enter the *Scandinavian countries*.

The Scandinavian nations alone among the 'barbarians' had a distinctive civilization and culture of their own. The conquest of the Saxon territories by Charlemagne had naturally aroused great apprehension in the territories to the north; the Danes, being nearest to the danger, took the most active steps to counteract it. In 810 they built an immense wall, the Danevirke, across the isthmus of Schleswig, and seemed ready to shut out all influences, secular and religious, which might approach them from the south.

The first attempts of the Church to break through this barrier were hardly auspicious. The Emperor Louis the Pious had thoughts of taking the work in hand. His first point of contact was an exiled prince, Harald Klak, who in 826 was persuaded to receive baptism with 400 of his followers at Mainz. Harald then set out to regain his kingdom, and it was decided that he should be accompanied by a missionary. The choice fell on Anskar (801–65), a native of Picardy who had become a monk at Corbie. The first attempts met with no success; Harald did not regain his kingdom, and no footing for the Church could be found in Denmark. A second venture was more successful. Merchants at Birka in Sweden, who had connections with the south, asked that a mission should be sent to them. Anskar was once again despatched to the north. King Björn received the missionaries kindly, and gave them permission to preach and to build a church, the very first in Scandinavia. A few Swedes were baptized, but the majority of the faithful seem to have been slaves of Christian origin. After eighteen months in the heart of Scandinavia, Anskar returned to Frankish soil.

Well pleased with his success, the emperor appointed Anskar Archbishop of Hamburg (about 832), with the idea that this should be the Christian outpost in the direction of Scandinavia, and that Anskar should await opportunities of entering it. The omens were not favourable. In 845 Hamburg was burned by the Vikings. Appointed Archbishop of Bremen in 848, Anskar by patient diplomacy managed at last to win the confidence of the king of Denmark, and was able to build a church in Schleswig, and later another at Ribe on the west coast. But this was a day of very small things. After the death of Anskar, on 3 February 865, practically everything that he had achieved was lost, and his successors gave little attention to Scandinavia. Anskar is a memorable and prophetic figure, not because of what he achieved, but because of the patience and devotion with which he pushed against a door which was not yet ready to open, and because he is the first of a great succession of bishops who worked outwards from a well-established Christian centre into the regions beyond which were still pagan.[10]

We must now turn our attention to a very different part of the world. Christian history has so constantly been written from the Western, and specifically from the Roman, point of view that readers in the West are liable to forget the continued existence of the Eastern Roman Empire with its centre at Constantinople, the

---

10. Rimbert's *Life of Anskar* (Eng. trans. by C. H. Robinson, 1921) is one of the best of early missionary biographies. Our most extensive authority for the northern Christianity of the early period is the *Gesta Hammaburgensis Ecclesiae Pontificum*, written by Adam of Bremen about A.D. 1075.

ancient Byzantium.[11] That empire lasted so long that it is only by an effort of imagination that we can grasp the centuries that flowed over it. From the foundation of Constantinople by Constantine as a Christian city to its final overthrow by the Turks in 1453 eleven centuries elapsed. To think backwards, eleven centuries would carry us far beyond the Norman Conquest, back to the days of Alfred the Great. Byzantine history is longer than the whole course of recognizably English history till the present day. And for eight centuries out of the eleven the Eastern Empire was the great bulwark of Christendom against the encroachments of the Muslim power.

Constantinople had undergone a number of vicissitudes. From the beginning of the eighth century the empire had begun to feel seriously the Muslim threat. At the same time its inner unity was threatened by the bitter tensions of the iconoclastic struggle. May the Church use pictures and images in its life and worship? The traditionally-minded answered yes. A more puritanically inclined group, headed by the Emperor Leo III the Isaurian (*c.* 675–741), answered no. It is permissible perhaps to see here the influence on the emperor's mind of the Islamic puritanism with which he must have been in contact in his early days on the eastern frontier. For more than a century (725–843) Church and state alike were convulsed by this dispute, and resources which ought to have been deployed in the defence of the Christian world and the propagation of the faith were squandered in futile recrimination and mutual persecution.

But Constantinople had amazing powers of recovery. The ninth and tenth centuries, in which the West reached its lowest depth of squalid barbarism, were for Constantinople a time of renaissance, military, political, cultural, and in a measure religious. In 863 the university of Constantinople was founded by Bardas. There was a rediscovery of the ancient Greek classics, such as heralded the renaissance in the West; from that time on Constantinople was the home of a vigorous, though slightly artificial, literary culture which lasted almost till the day of its destruction. And, even in its worst days, Constantinople was by far the greatest and most civilized city in the Christian world. It had trade connections which spread out

11. English readers have tended to follow too exactly the judgement of the historian Edward Gibbon, who wrote of Byzantium that its history represented 'a dead uniformity of abject vices which are neither softened by the weakness of humanity nor animated by the vigour of memorable crimes'. *Decline and Fall of the Roman Empire*, chap. 48.

in every direction, and eastwards reached as far as China. Its people were alert and intelligent, volatile and inclined to violence, passionately religious, or perhaps we should rather say passionately inclined to theological disputation. The Church had become so far subservient to the state, in the person of the divinely appointed Christian prince, as to have lost a great deal of its independence, but it was still the representative of a great authentic Christian tradition, and intensely proud, as it is today, of that unbroken line of continuity by which it was directly linked to the Church of the Apostles.

From the missionary point of view, there seems little to record of the disturbed seventh and eighth centuries. Leo III, aiming at the unity of his empire, set to work to convert the Jews by force, but this can hardly be regarded as missionary work. Then, with the recovery of vigour in other directions, a renewal of missionary effort is also to be observed. In the ninth century, interest was concentrated on the *Slavonic* peoples, whose power was steadily growing in north and west. Would they become Christians? And if so, in what Church would they find their home?

The first great mission to the Slavs is associated with the names of two brothers, Constantine (later Cyril, 826–69) and Methodius (*c.* 815–85). So many legends have gathered about the work of the two brothers that it is not always easy to distinguish fact from fiction; but the main lines of what happened are reasonably clear. As so often, politics and religion were mixed up in the beginnings of the mission. Boris of Bulgaria had approached the Franks in the West, had asked for missionaries, and had undertaken to be baptized. This was serious news for Constantinople. The Pope always claimed that Bulgaria formed part of the patriarchate of the West, but Leo III had managed to extend his influence over the country and to deny the Pope the exercise of any rights in it. It now seemed that Bulgaria was on the way to rejoining the West politically, and to accepting a place in the Western Church. At this juncture Rastislav, the prince of Moravia in what is now Slovakia, felt it wise to turn eastwards, and to ask the Eastern emperor for missionaries.

The emperor selected Constantine and Methodius, the two scions of a noble family employed in Thessalonica. Each had received a fine education and was theologically competent; each had had some experience of government and diplomatic work. And apparently the brothers had been familiar from childhood with some form of Slavonic speech. Even before leaving Constantinople

Constantine had decided that Slavonic was to be the medium through which the Gospel was to be preached to the Slavs.

The first step was to create an alphabet in which the Slavonic languages could be written. Constantine set to work and produced the so-called Glagolitic Script, the basis of the alphabets in which almost all the Slavonic languages are written to this day.[12] Certain readings from the Scriptures were at once translated. On reaching Moravia, Constantine set to work on the translation of the liturgy as a whole. This was introduced only gradually, as the previous contacts of the Moravians had been with Western Christians who used only Latin as their liturgical language, and it seems that Constantine, out of prudence, did not introduce the entire Byzantine liturgy but at certain important points followed the Latin tradition of the Mass. Later on, if the tradition is to be trusted, he followed up this work with the translation of the whole Bible into Slavonic.

There were numerous causes for dispute between Eastern and Western Christians in this area, but the storm centre was the Slavonic liturgy. For here Constantine had launched out on what in the eyes of the West was a revolutionary procedure.

Rome had throughout insisted on Latin as the sole liturgical language of the West. The languages of the barbarians were uncouth, uncultured, and unwritten, and were judged to be ill-adapted to the dignity of liturgy; Latin came with all the prestige of antiquity and of the civilizing power. The advantage gained by this method was the creation of a real unity of the Western world, in which Latin was the common language until the end of the eighteenth century and a great unifying force. The weakness was that worshippers understood little, if anything, of what was going on in Church. The sense of mystery was increased; intelligent participation was at a minimum.

The attitude of Constantinope was entirely different. Orthodox Christians were familiar with Armenians and Syrians, who had a different alphabet and their own liturgical traditions. The desire for ecclesiastical centralization did not extend to language; and it always seemed natural to Byzantine churchmen that as new peoples were brought within the Church they should be encouraged to build up their Church and their national culture on the basis of their local language. The Greek influence was always

---

12. The exceptions are Polish, Czech, and Croatian, which are written in Roman letters.

profound. Yet this measure of tolerance for local usage, and the at least partial recognition of the independence of the local Churches, has been one of the strong factors in fostering Orthodox unity. The daughter Churches have not felt themselves to be dominated or oppressed; tensions have not been lacking, but underlying them has been a real feeling of affection for the mother Church in Constantinople.

The question of the boundary between the Eastern and Western worlds could not but be the cause of endless friction. There was no doubt at all that the jurisdiction of the Archbishop of Salzburg extended over areas which were inhabited by Slavonic tribes. Had Constantine and Methodius, as emissaries of the Byzantine Church, any right to be in Moravia at all? It became clear to the brothers that, unless their relationship with Rome could be regularized, their work was likely to be in vain. The journey to Rome was undertaken. Pope Nicholas I had died (13 November 867) just before Constantine and Methodius arrived in the city, but his successor Hadrian II took up their case. In general his attitude was entirely favourable. The orthodoxy and sanctity of the brothers were generally recognized. The work in Moravia was approved. The use of the Slavonic liturgy was permitted, and, if tradition is to be trusted, the Eucharist was celebrated according to this rite in St Peter's and three other basilicas in Rome.

Just at this crisis Constantine died (14 February 869). But the Pope revived the ancient see of Sirmium, and appointed Methodius as archbishop and as his special legate with wide powers over the great Slavonic areas of Pannonia and Moravia. Armed with these powers, Methodius was able for the most part to hold his own in the ceaseless guerrilla warfare that had to be carried on with the Frankish bishops. But the affray was not without wounds. In the early days of his episcopate, Methodius was arrested, charged with infringement of the jurisdiction of the Archbishop of Salzburg, and thrown into prison, where he remained for three years until liberated by the direct intervention of Pope John VIII. Apart from such setbacks the work prospered. Svatopluk, the successor of Rastislav, was able to extend his dominion over a large part of what is now called Galicia, Silesia, and Saxony. Svatopluk was more in favour of the Franks and Methodius had a difficult time. Archaeological discovery in recent times has provided evidence of the high quality of Moravian civilization, with its unusual combination of Byzantine and Latin elements.

But with the death of Methodius everything changed. His Swabian and hostile suffragan Wiching had ready access to Pope Stephen V. The use of the Slavonic liturgy was forbidden. The chief disciples of Methodius were driven out, and with the most distinguished of them, Clement, at their head, moved over into Bulgaria. The fortunes of the Church in Moravia declined, until in the tenth century the invasions of the Magyars presented the Church with a problem other than that of the conversion of the Slavs.

Like Anskar, Constantine and Methodius are memorable for their vision and endurance rather than for the permanence of their actual achievements. Yet in this case much more survived than might be supposed from the collapse of the work in Moravia itself. At the end of the ninth century Bulgaria provided the most favourable soil for the propagation of an indigenous Slavonic Christian culture. The Tsar Boris had been baptized in 864. After endless backing and filling between East and West, Bulgaria had at length decided to throw in its fortunes with the East. The greatest of its rulers, Simon (893–927), gave to the country a brief period of independence and imperial splendour. During his reign, a Slavonic Christian literature was created by translation from the Greek, and a new Slavonic culture, based on that of Byzantium but in many ways different from it, came into being. It was from Bulgaria that this Slavonic culture spread to what is now Yugoslavia, to Russia, and in part to Romania. The Bulgarian Empire did not last long; the last vestige of independence was stamped out by the Emperor Basil of Constantinople in 1018. But its work was done, and through it the seed sown by Constantine and Methodius grew into a great tree. They can be regarded without question as the first authors of the great Slavonic Christian culture which still persists in the world today.

The vast area that we now call *Russia* had been for centuries the home of many tribes of varying racial origins, without unity and without a developed culture of their own. The creation of the Russian nation was the work of Scandinavian traders in search of wealth. The Scandinavians discovered two new trade routes – one south-eastwards down the Volga to the Caspian and so to Baghdad, the other down the Dnieper to the Black Sea. Their first central colony was Novgorod; in 860 they delivered the Slavs of Kiev from the dominion of the Khazars, and from that time on Kiev was the centre of their operations. It appears that about this time the Patriarch Photius of Constantinople had sent a mission and a bishop to Kiev, but Kiev was overwhelmed by the prince of Novgorod, who was still a pagan, and this first attempt at the Christianization of the northern Slavs ended in nothing. Russia had to wait another century for the establishment of a Church.

The great step forward was taken by the Princess Olga, who after the death of her husband Igor ruled Kiev from 945 to 964. The Russian sources are loud in their commendation of the justice and equity of her rule. In 957 Olga decided to go herself to Constantinople, and to seek baptism at the hands of the patriarch; the baptism was solemnized in a scene of prodigious splendour. All did not go well, however, with the plans of the princess, and on her return she found that her nobles were in no way inclined to follow her into the Church. It is typical of the confusions of the time that Olga, wishing to strengthen her hand, sent an embassy to the Western Emperor Otto asking him to supply her with a bishop. Otto replied with alacrity, but before his messenger could reach Kiev the situation had changed – Olga's son Sviatoslav had taken over the government from his mother, and had thrown himself heart and soul into the anti-Christian reaction.

There was a moment at which it seemed possible that Sviatoslav and his whole court might turn Muslim. He had conquered a race of Turks on the Volga who had accepted Islam, and, while staying among them, had been much attracted by their way of life. If Russia had turned Muslim, the whole history of the Western world would have been notably different. Byzantine diplomacy averted this danger, and the Muslim peril never again seriously raised its head.

It was under Vladimir (980–1015), the son of Sviatoslav, that Russia became deeply and for so long Christian. Our oldest Russian source, *The Chronicle of Nestor*, tells us an interesting story of the manner in which Vladimir sent deputations in various directions to investigate the religions professed by his neighbours, in order that he might adopt on behalf of his subjects that which should prove the most sublime. Islam did not attract the messengers. They turned then to the Khazars, the only example of a people which in the Christian era has on a large scale accepted the Jewish faith, and did not find that Judaism was well adapted to the Russians. The ceremonies of the Western Church, as encountered in Germany, appeared to them too simple, but when they reached Constantinople, they found what they had been seeking:

We did not know whether we were in heaven or on the earth. It would be impossible to find on earth any splendour greater than this, and it is vain that we attempt to describe it. . . . Never shall we be able to forget so great a beauty.

This is no doubt legend, but it does for us exactly what legend ought to do; it sets forth in picturesque form the various influences which at that time were actually at work on the court of Kiev, and that decision of the ruler to throw in his lot with Constantinople which was of such lasting significance for the history of the world.

The world owes a great debt of gratitude to those missionaries who from A.D. 1000 onwards spread Christian culture throughout Russia. All the bishops, and most of the clergy, were Greeks, though many of the Greeks were from the Crimean region, that ancient home of Greek colonization which was not so very far away from Russia. The last Greek Metropolitan of Kiev held office as late as the fifteenth century. The work spread outwards from Kiev – northward to Novgorod, north-east to that region of Moscow which later was to be the very centre of Russian life. This culture was Byzantine through and through, yet with that plastic flexibility, so characteristic of Byzantium, which made it possible for that which was essentially an alien importation to be felt as native, and to take on gradually the qualities of the area into which it had been transplanted.

We have noted from time to time the clash of interests between East and West, as each attempted to extend its field of influence among the nations. In the end the line of division between what we now call Roman Catholic and Orthodox came to be rather erratically drawn across the heart of Europe, through the Slav lands and not on their western frontier.

The progress of Western Christianity eastwards across Central Europe can be traced in the foundation of a number of notable bishoprics, some of which remain to this day as powerful centres of Christian faith. Thus, for instance, the great see of Magdeburg was founded in A.D. 968 by the Emperor Otto to serve – as Salzburg had served at an earlier date – as the jumping-off place for work in the Eastern lands. The record in place after place tends to be much the same. The first bishop is martyred by the savage tribes; his blood then appropriately forms the seed of the Church. Initial successes are followed by pagan reactions, but the Church comes in again under the aegis of a deeply converted ruler, with whom one or more outstanding bishops are able to work in harmony. The initial

Christianization is inevitably very superficial, but this is in each case followed by a long period of building, in which the faith becomes part of the inheritance of the people. Political alliances, frequently cemented by marriages, form a large part of the picture; and, as in the cases of Clovis and of Ethelbert of Kent, the influence of Christian queens seems to have played a notable part in the work of conversion.

Three great areas come under our consideration: Bohemia (the western part of Czechoslovakia), Poland, where the people were Slavs, and Hungary, where they were the rather recently arrived Magyars.

Christianity seems first to have entered *Bohemia* from Moravia; it is said that a number of Bohemian chiefs and their retainers were baptized at Ratisbon in 845. But by the end of the ninth century the links of Bohemia were firmly with the West and with what is now Germany. Vratislav, who ruled at the end of the century, was nominally a Christian, but his death was followed by a pagan reaction, and it was only under his son, the pious Václav (the Good King Wenceslas of the carol), who had been reared from childhood as a Christian, that the faith began to make progress. But in 929 Václav, while on his way to Mass, was murdered by his own brother Boleslav; he cannot have been more than twenty-four at the time of his death. Boleslav succeeded his murdered brother, apparently without protest on the part of the Czechs, and another period hostile to Christianity set in. It was not until the time of the son, namesake, and successor of Boleslav, who reigned from 967 to 999, that the evangelization of the country in outline was completed. Boleslav II is said to have built twenty churches and to have enriched the monasteries in his dominions. Like all the other princes, Boleslav wished to have a church organization of his own, with an independent bishop at its head – independent, that is, in the sense that the bishop would be dependent only on the good will of his prince. In this he was not successful; when the bishopric of Prague was created in 975, it was dependent on the archbishopric of Mainz.

The first Bishop of Prague was German, the second was a genuine Slav. Vojtech had been brought up in the great Christian centre of Magdeburg, where he had received his better known German name Adalbert.[13] Member of a noble family, and con-

---

13. Adalbert of Prague is to be distinguished from the more famous Adalbert of Bremen (*c.* 1000–1072).

nected by relationship with other noble families, distinguished by his stern and austere piety, Adalbert became Bishop of Prague in 983. It was his purpose to use his position to extend missionary work among the Poles and the Magyars. But almost from the first he had difficulties with his half-heathen flock, who did not appreciate the severe methods that he used in his attempts to raise the standard of their Christian living. Later he had troubles with his prince, Boleslav. Twice he left the ungrateful task, and twice returned. When he left for the third time, to return no more, he went to open up missionary work among the heathen Prussians, almost the last people in Europe to receive the Gospel, and there in 997 met a martyr's death at the hands of the wild inhabitants.

His work in Prague appeared to have been a failure, but in point of fact from A.D. 1000 onwards Bohemia could be reckoned as among the Christian lands.

The Christian history of *Poland* begins with Duke Mieszka, who in 963 had been compelled to recognize the overlordship of the Emperor Otto I. Mieszka married a Christian lady, Dobrawa, the sister of Boleslav II of Bohemia; it was probably under her influence that in 966 or 967 he agreed to be baptized. This event was followed in 968 by the creation of an episcopal see for Poland, Poznan, which was probably under the jurisdiction of Magdeburg.

Under Mieszka's son, yet another Boleslav – Chrobry, the Brave – who ruled from 992 to 1025, Poland made great progress both in political power and in ecclesiastical stability. Boleslav had greatly extended his dominions, and had made Poland the largest kingdom in eastern Europe. In 1024 he received from the Pope the title of king, and a royal crown to go with it. Boleslav had been a great admirer of Bishop Adalbert of Prague. After the martyrdom of the saint in Prussia, his body was solemnly brought to Poland, and placed not at Poznan, the centre of the bishopric, but at Gniezno (Gnesen). Three years later Gniezno was made the ecclesiastical centre of the realm; the brother of Adalbert was made archbishop, and had under him suffragan bishops at Kolberg in Pomerania, Breslau, and Cracow.

Affairs in Poland have always been notoriously unstable. After the death of Boleslav, everything for a period fell apart, and it was only after a century of confusion and reorganization that the Christianization of Poland could be held to be complete.

The Magyars of *Hungary*, a people of Mongolian origin, whose language and customs mark them out as being akin to the Finns and the Turks, began to appear in Europe about the end of the ninth century. They were a ruthless and destructive people, whose raids, accompanied by the murder of priests and the desecration of churches, made them very widely feared. In 955 they suffered an overwhelming defeat at the hands of the Emperor Otto I in the neighbourhood of Augsburg; this set the limit to their westward expansion, and also brought them within the sphere of influence of the Western and Christian powers.

What followed is not very clear. Bishop Pilgrim of Passau sent priests into the country, and later himself visited it. He reported to the Pope that 5,000 Magyars had been baptized, and that there were Christian prisoners of war who were strenuously holding to their faith. In 973 Geisa, the prince of Hungary, married a Christian princess, Adelheid of Poland, as his second wife; two years later he was baptized, together with his young son Vajk, who received the name Stephen. From then on, Geisa set himself to make his country Christian; where persuasion did not prove effective, he had recourse to other and less agreeable methods. Converts multiplied rapidly. In 995 Stephen was married to Gisela, sister of Duke Henry II of Bavaria, and was thus brought within the orbit of the Western world.

It was during the reign of Stephen (997–1038) that Hungary really became a Christian country. Stephen, who in 1000 received from the Pope the title of king and a royal crown (that still preserved is of later date), proved himself to be the ideal Christian prince. Devout, wise, but uncompromising, he showed his people the way into the kingdom of God, and like his father rather more than gently indicated that they should follow the good way pointed out to them. The king himself was not too proud to preach to his subjects. A hierarchy was established, with two archbishoprics and eight bishoprics, the ecclesiastical centre being at Esztergom (Gran). Under the new Christian laws, bishops and abbots of the Benedictine monasteries were given a privileged status among the aristocracy, the bishops being also judges in certain types of legal case.

The death of Stephen was naturally followed by a pagan reaction. But his work was never really undone; Christianity survived the various threats to its existence, and by the end of the eleventh century had found general acceptance as the national religion of the Hungarian people.

The successes of the Muslims had cut the world in two. Having taken to the sea, they had made the Mediterranean unsafe for Christian traffic, and in Indian waters they were the dominant power. This state of things continued unchanged until at the end of the fifteenth century Bartholomew Diaz rounded the Cape of Good Hope, and so turned the flank of the Muslim powers. By land most of the familiar trade routes were in their hands, though some of the northern routes through Central Asia were still open to Christians, and Byzantium was not wholly deprived of its trade relations with Cathay.[14]

Western Europe as a whole, however, was almost completely cut off from Asia, and it is hardly likely that anyone at the time was aware of one of the most remarkable of Christian adventures, the penetration of China by Nestorian Christians in the seventh century.

We have seen that from an early date Christianity was well established in Mesopotamia and Persia. In Persia, indeed, the Church was exposed to the vicissitudes of prosperity and persecution, according to the changes in the political climate, and, as long as the Roman Empire lasted, Christians were liable to be suspected of disloyalty because of their religious affinity to the empire of the West. Probably to no other Christian group in the world did the Muslim conquests bring such advantages. Under the Abbasid Caliphs (eighth to thirteenth centuries) who were setting themselves to bring into existence the brilliant Muslim civilization of Baghdad, and who had need of their educated Christian subjects to help them in their projects, Christians were protected and favoured, and some attained to high place under the Muslim rulers. Most of these Christians were attached to the Nestorian heresy. This partly accounts for the failure of the rest of Christendom to take an interest in these remote and isolated Christians.

It was Nestorian Christianity which spread itself out along the trade routes of Central Asia, and by A.D. 635 had reached the heart of China. China at that time was under the rule of the T'ang dynasty (618–907), a race of vigorous and able rulers, under whom the unity of the empire had been restored and peace and order established. Trade flourished, and visitors were many. Under T'ai

14. Early and medieval Europe had rather vague ideas as to the geographical location of Cathay. At a much later date we shall note the circumstances in which the identity of Cathay with China was conclusively proved.

Tsung, China was probably the wealthiest and most civilized empire in the world.

We should have known little or nothing of the entry of Christianity into China in those days, but for the accident of the discovery of 'the Nestorian monument' at Hsianfu somewhere about the year 1623. The tidings conveyed by it were so extraordinary that at first its genuineness was widely doubted. But confirmatory evidence has been found in the shape of a hymn to the Trinity, the Chinese *Gloria in Excelsis*, together with a list of Christian books in Chinese, discovered in 1908 in the grottoes of Tun-huang in north-west China, and through references to Nestorian Christianity in imperial edicts of the years 683, 745, and 845. All doubt has now been set at rest, and the monument is universally accepted as genuine. It dates from the year 781.

It tells us that in the year A.D. 635 A-lo-pên arrived in the capital of the great T'ai Tsung, bringing with him 'the luminous Religion of Ta-ch'in' (Syria). He was well received by the emperor, who himself studied the religion, approved it, and gave orders for its dissemination. Naturally there were anti-Christian reactions on the part of the Buddhists; but the Church, such as it was, managed to survive, and had a history of more than two centuries. We hear, too, of a Metropolitan David, who had been consecrated for China somewhere before the year 823.

The Christianity of China seems to have been in the main monastic – a characteristic by no means detrimental in a country so familiar with the traditions of Buddhist monasticism. The list of translations of Christian books in Chinese suggests that the monks took the trouble to learn the language and to make themselves at home in the land in which they had settled. But it is permissible to wonder to what extent they really made their presence felt, and how far their influence extended beyond the monastery walls. Their task was completely different from that of their fellow monks in the wastes and forests of Central Europe. There the monk was the only literate man, bringing knowledge, and also better methods of agriculture, to an essentially simple population. Here he dwelt in the midst of a highly civilized people, in constant rivalry with other religious systems which were perhaps more congenial to the inhabitants of the land.

In 845 trouble fell upon the Church. The Emperor Wu Tsung, who was an ardent Taoist and opposed to monasticism in all its forms, issued a decree proscribing Buddhism, dissolving the monasteries, and ordering the monks to return to private life.

Nestorians were monks; the decree was held to apply to them as well. Here are the emperor's words:

As for the foreign Bonzes [monks] who come here, to make known the Law which is current in their kingdom, there are about 3,000 of them, both from Ta-ch'in and from Mu-hu-po. My command is that they also return to the world, so that in the customs of our Empire there be no mixture. Alas! It is only too long that people have delayed to put things back on their ancient footing! Why delay any longer? The thing is finished and done. In view of the present command, let it be put into execution. Such is our will.[15]

We do not know what happened. It is unlikely that the Christian Church was exterminated. But it is probable that its power was broken, and that from that time onwards it dwindled rapidly. In 987, a monk who had been sent with five others to inquire into the state of the Church in China returned to report that he and his companions had found no trace of Christians in the Empire.[16]

The day of Asia had not yet dawned. In the Middle East the Churches survived, but did little more than survive. But in the area which we now call Europe the Churches had shown astonishing vitality, and in the face of countless obstacles had managed to spread out in all directions and to make the Gospel an effective power in the life of people after people. As we have emphasized again and again, the work was often superficial and imperfect; half-converted peoples brought their superstitions and their evil practices with them into the Church. And the conversion of Europe was as yet far from complete; in the next chapter we shall have to write of those peoples in the north and east who by the year 1000 had hardly been reached or touched. But, all in all, it is a notable picture of achievement; and the conquest of Europe from the Bay of Biscay to the Volga, and from the north of Scotland to the Danube, might be held to compensate for the loss of many great and famous provinces to the Muslims.

By the year 1000, the Dark Ages were beginning to pass away. The lowest depths had been reached in the early years of the tenth century, when (in 909) clerics in France could write:

---

15. Quoted in C. Cary-Elwes, OSB, *China and the Cross* (1957), p. 32.
16. On all this the classic work is A. C. Moule, *Christians in China before the Year 1550* (1930). More popular, John Foster, *The Church of the T'ang Dynasty* (1939).

The cities are depopulated, the monasteries ruined and burned, the country reduced to solitude. . . . As the first men lived without law or fear of God, abandoned to their passions, so now every man does what seems good in his own eyes, despising laws human and divine and the commands of the Church. The strong oppress the weak; the world is full of violence against the poor and of the plunder of the goods of the Church . . . Men devour one another like the fishes in the sea.

In the year before these despairing words were written, the great monastery of Cluny had been founded, and was destined to be one important source of a great and beneficent reform in the life of the Church. In 1000 the new day is just beginning to dawn upon Europe, but we are not far from the world of Lanfranc and Anselm, of Abelard and his adversary Bernard. Europe is again becoming a reality, and beginning to prepare itself for a great new age of Western civilization and of the Western Church.

4

Early European Expansion, 1000–1500

The year 1000 was marked by widespread fear and anxiety throughout almost every part of the Christian world. It was extensively believed that the period of the Church was to last just one thousand years, and that, according to the calculations of Dionysius Exiguus in the sixth century, which we now know to have been inaccurate,[1] this period was just about to come to a close. The end would be announced by fearful calamities, and then the last and terrifying judgement would begin. In point of fact nothing very much happened, and the history of the world seemed set to continue for an indefinite number of years. Yet, for all that, the year 1000 may be taken as something of a watershed. A Europe which was at last in outline Christian was turning its back on the worst horrors of the Dark Ages, and was gathering that store of inner resilience which would show itself in the course of the next four centuries in travel, trade, military adventure, art and architecture, in the development of great new vernacular languages, and finally in the towering edifice of theological thought.

The first task, however, for Europe was to extend the Christian world to its own limits. We begin this chapter with a survey of the lands on the frontiers of the Church which in 1000 did not form part of the Christian realm.

Scandinavia had for centuries lived in almost complete isolation from the rest of the world, and in its isolation had developed a tradition and a culture very different from anything else to be found in the world of a thousand years ago. The centre of this culture was the art of war, to which everything else was subordinate. There was no right of primogeniture, and leadership among the people depended on a man's strong right arm and his capacity to gather round him a group of armed and faithful followers. Any man could make himself a leader: the qualities most admired were

---

1. We owe to Dionysius the 'Christian era' under which we still live. We do not know for certain the year of the birth of Christ. Probably the date where Dionysius put it is not quite accurate.

courage and liberality. But these northerners were not mere barbarians: they had their own tradition of art and song. Their greatest achievements were to come after the period in which they had become Christian, yet many of these later writings reflect with remarkable faithfulness the thoughts and ideas of an earlier time. Above all, the northerners had their religion and their mythology. Over all broods a sense of fate and disaster. From this not even the gods are exempt; the day of their doom also will come, though 'it is not surely to be known when the grey wolf shall come upon the seat of the gods'. Defeat rather than victory is the mark of the true hero; the warrior goes out to meet his inevitable fate with open eyes.

For centuries the northerners had remained in their distant homelands, fighting among themselves but causing little disturbance to anyone else. Then suddenly in the eighth century, for causes that are obscure to us but may be associated with the increasing over-population of their desolate valleys, they began to overflow, and to become the terror of the civilized, and in particular the Christian, world. The range of their depredations is astonishing, and the destruction which they caused was almost without limit.

England was one of the first victims. Lindisfarne was sacked in 793, Jarrow in 794. A new series of attacks began in 835. The Saxon kingdom of Northumbria went down in flames in 867, and it seemed for a time that the whole of England might become a Danish colony. It was Ireland, however, that suffered most bitterly from the attacks of the Vikings. Here the great and beautiful Christian civilization, the source of so much missionary effort, was completely destroyed. Raid followed raid throughout the whole of the first half of the ninth century, churches and monasteries proving the easiest, and also the richest, object of attack in that still largely primitive country. The great monastery of Clonmacnoise was destroyed, and the Norwegian leader enthroned his wife, a heathen prophetess, on the altar of the desecrated church. In 851 the Norwegian Olaf the White set up in Dublin a pagan kingdom that was to endure for about three centuries.

On the continent of Europe it was the Danes rather than the Norwegians who took the lead. Year after year great expeditions were organized, and the whole of western Europe was systematically ravaged. In northern France and the Netherlands wide areas reverted to desert, and Christians, wherever they could, fled from the destroying storm. Beyond the Alps, the Normans eventually made themselves at home in southern Italy and Sicily, and their kingdom gradually flowered into that high civilization which reached its culminating point under the Emperor Frederick II (1194–1250), and drew together elements from Greece, from the Muslim world, from the Latin tradition, and from the far north.

Not all was defeat. The noble work of King Alfred (849–99) set a limit to the advance of the Danes in England, and eventually they were absorbed into the unity of the restored kingdom. In northern France the treaty between Charles the Simple and the Viking leader Rollo, signed at St Clair-sur-Epte in 911, drew the Norsemen into the regular feudal order in the establishment of that Duchy of Normandy from which fresh influences were to flow back to England in the famous invasion of 1066.

It is hard to imagine a people less likely than the Norsemen to respond to the advances of a gentle faith such as that of the Gospel. The more settled peoples of Europe were so horrified by the savage destruction wrought by the invaders that they seem neither to have hoped for their conversion nor very much to have desired it. In point of fact, the conversion of the Scandinavian peoples was a long and slow process, accompanied by many setbacks. At an earlier point in our story we left Anskar looking out longingly in the direction of those northern lands for the conversion of which his great bishopric of Hamburg had been called into being. Three centuries were to pass before his dreams were fully realized.

Denmark was more closely in contact with Germany, and therefore with the Christian world, than any other part of Scandinavia. It was there, naturally, that Christianity made its first hopeful entries.

We have seen that Anskar had been able to found a certain number of churches in Denmark. But the pressure of evangelization could not be maintained, and the life of the Church was fitful and uncertain. At the beginning of the tenth century a powerful king named Gorm decided to exclude Christianity completely from his kingdoms, and set himself to the familiar pastime of destroying churches and assassinating priests. His son and successor Harald Bluetooth swung in the other direction. He claimed to have 'made the Danes Christians', and it is in his days that we first hear of bishops among them (948). But it was only with the reign of Knut, familiar to all schoolchildren as the King Canute who pointed out to his flattering courtiers that he could not prevent the tide from rising, that Christianity became an effective part of the life of the Danish people.

This remarkable man appears to have been brought up a

Christian. In 1013 he was fighting in England together with his father Sweyn, and by 1016 he had conquered a large part of the country. In that year, on the death of Edmund Ironside, he was elected king of the whole country. Two years later the death of his brother made him king of Denmark. At one time he was master also of Norway, and till his death in 1035 was ruler of a great empire on both sides of the North Sea. As he grew older he grew more pious, and devoted himself with intense earnestness to making of his realms a Christian kingdom. The laws of the Christian world were the basis for the laws which he introduced, and the tradition which he established was one of an almost Byzantine unity of Church and state.

In 1026 Knut made a pilgrimage to Rome; his visit happened to coincide with the coronation of the Emperor Conrad. This is one of those symbolic events in which a great deal of history is summed up. The ancient Mediterranean civilization was present in the person of the Pope. Conrad represented those Germanic races which, originally coming in as barbarians, had long been domesticated within the empire, and, in fact, through their creation of the Holy Roman Empire, had come to regard themselves as the successors of old Rome and as protectors of its legacy. The presence of Knut indicated that the distant and vigorous races of the north also recognized the principle of the spiritual unity of the Western world and were prepared to take their place within the fellowship of the Christian peoples.

Knut made England the centre of his realm. It was, therefore, quite natural that, when in 1022 he wanted to provide his Danish dominions with bishops, he sent them to the Archbishop of Canterbury to be consecrated. This at once brought him into conflict with the see of Hamburg, the bishop of which claimed to be the metropolitan for all the northern nations. This controversy, unimportant in itself, draws attention to two points which are of considerable interest. In the first place, although the first Christian approaches to Scandinavia had come by way of Germany, from the eleventh century on the development of missionary work was undertaken from England. Secondly, in the north we see the emergence of what can properly be called nations. As a natural result of the close association between sovereign and Church to which we have referred, every king wished to have his own church organization, headed by an archbishop who would be under the direction of a king, except in so far as the Pope was able to exercise a shadowy suzerainty. Denmark was the first country in which this clash between national and ecclesiastical ideas of organization was resolved, in the main in favour of the crown.

From 1045 till 1072 Hamburg was in the hands of a notable prelate, Adalbert of Bremen, who was at the same time aristocratic, able, and ambitious. Adalbert's mind was filled with the idea of a 'patriarchate' of the north,[2] centred in Hamburg. Bishops and archbishops would alike be under the patriarch, who would himself be subject to no one but the Pope. This idea came to nothing. There were no precedents for the creation of new patriarchates – the last had been Constantinople in the fourth century, and this had not passed without criticism. And political and other jealousies stood in Adalbert's way. In the end the king of Denmark got his wish. In 1104 Lund in what is now Sweden, at that time the principal city of the Danish dominions, was made an archiepiscopal see, and a Dane was appointed to be its archbishop. The Danish Church was now a corporate body, independent of any neighbouring prelate.

In *Norway*, as in Denmark, royal power played a large part in the introduction of the Christian faith.

The first notable hero of the Christian campaign, if hero he can be called, was that typical Viking swashbuckler Olaf Tryggvessön (969–1000), who had been brought up in one of the Scandinavian settlements in Russia and had there begun his career as a Viking warrior. Somewhere about 990 Olaf was in the Scilly Islands, which at this point make their entry into European history, and was so deeply impressed by a hermit whom he encountered there that he accepted baptism at his hands. In 995 Olaf returned to Norway, and shortly afterwards was elected king of the whole country.

No sooner was Olaf elected than he set to work to make his religion the religion of the Norwegians. But sovereignty was not unlimited in Norway, and the various local assemblies, the *things*,[3] had to be consulted. Democracy, however, was not unlimited

2. The West had its single patriarchate, Rome; the East had four – Constantinople, Jerusalem, Antioch, and Alexandria. No new patriarchate was created until the sixteenth century (Moscow, 1589). The patriarch was head over a large area of the Church, with precedence over all archbishops and bishops in that area.

3. This sense of the word is found also in Anglo-Saxon. The Oxford Dictionary gives as the meaning in Old Saxon 'assembly for judicial or deliberative purposes, conference, transaction, matter, affair, thing, object', a definition which is in itself a brief history of the process of development in language.

either. Olaf made use of every weapon – flattery, guile, persuasion, and, when all else failed, sheer naked coercion. In most cases, when the members of the *thing* saw that the king was prepared, if necessary, to thrust his religion down their throats at the point of the sword, they saw reason; a happily democratic solution was arrived at, and all agreed to substitute the new religion for the old.

Olaf Tryggvessön was killed in battle in A.D. 1000. His work was carried on by another Olaf – Olaf Haraldssön (995–1030), to be known to later ages as St Olaf; the canonization may be held to have been due to the notable services that Olaf rendered to the Christian cause rather than to any endowment of personal and heroic virtue. Winning the kingdom from his enemies in battle in 1016, Olaf then set himself, like his predecessor, to make the hold of the Gospel on his people deep and permanent. He seems to have taken a less personal, and certainly less violent, part in the proceedings than Olaf Tryggvessön, and relied more on the bishops and priests whom he had brought in from England. When Olaf in his turn was overthrown by his enemies, the work of Christianizing Norway was still far from complete. Many were as yet unbaptized, and Scandinavian paganism, though never again a serious rival to the Gospel, showed a recalcitrant power of persistence and of lurking on in secret places till well into the Middle Ages. What finally emerged was Christianity a good deal modified in the light of the ancient ways and traditions of the Norsemen.

Norway, like Denmark, was perplexed by problems of ecclesiastical order. Olaf's successor, Harald Hardrada, was accustomed to getting his bishops consecrated in France or England. To this the masterful Adalbert naturally objected – to be met with fierce royal objections to his objections. For a time Norway was under the Archbishop of Lund, but in 1152 the kings of Norway got their way, with a hierarchy of their own which was not subject to any other control, except the remote direction of the Pope.

On the furthest rim of the known world, Iceland had developed a vigorous and individual culture of its own. The original settlers were Vikings who wished to escape from even such restraints as were imposed by the disorderly society of Norway. It might have been expected that, in their remote isolation, they would have produced an even more lawless state of affairs; instead, they built up a society which was aristocratic, dignified, passionate, and in its own way democratic.

The truth is that these rebels and their commonwealth were more self-possessed, more clearly conscious of their own aims, more critical of their own achievements, than any commonwealth on earth since the fall of Athens.[4]

The Icelander of today proudly recalls that his Parliament is the oldest in the world, with its history of more than a thousand years since it first met in the romantic basaltic valley of Thingvellir; and he is proud that he has kept his own complex language so pure across the centuries, that schoolchildren today have little difficulty in understanding the classical language of the Edda.

Appropriately, Iceland is the one country of those times in which Christianity was accepted by genuinely democratic process. Olaf Tryggvessön interested himself in the island, but the work of his emissaries seemed likely to lead to civil war between those who were prepared to accept the new religion and those who opposed it. To avoid this catastrophe, it was agreed that the matter should be referred for settlement to one of the wisest men of the land, and that all should follow his decision. The wise man pondered long and deeply, and in the end reported that the new religion was good. His decision was accepted by all, but with certain reservations; infanticide, and the eating of horseflesh, ritually connected with the old pagan religion, were still to be permitted, and only a minor penalty was to be exacted for sacrifices to the ancient gods. In 1016 even these reservations were withdrawn; the island settled down to the ordinary pattern of medieval Christian life, with the two bishoprics of Skálholt and Hólar. The island Church was subject in 1104 to Lund and from 1154 onwards to Trondhjem in Norway.

It might seem that this acceptance of Christianity was a rather calculating and lifeless thing. That it was more than this – a real weighing of two different ways of life and genuine acceptance of the higher – is shown by the utterance of Hialte on behalf of the Christians at the Althing of 1004:

The heathen men summoned a great gathering, and there they agreed to sacrifice two men out of each Quarter and call upon the heathen gods that they would not suffer Christendom to spread over the land. But Hialte and Gizor had another meeting of Christian men, and agreed that they too would have human sacrifices as many as the heathen. They spoke thus: 'The heathen sacrifice the worst men and cast them over the rocks or cliffs, but we will choose the best of men and call it a gift of victory to our Lord Jesus Christ, and we will bind ourselves to live better and more sinlessly

4. W. P. Ker, *The Dark Ages* (1904), p. 314.

than before, and Gizor and I will offer ourselves as the gift of victory of our Quarter.'[5]

Even in remote *Greenland* the Vikings found themselves a home. Erik the Red, twice outlawed – from Norway and from Iceland – had settled on the west coast, and gradually others had gathered around him. Erik's son Leif had been baptized in Norway in the time of Olaf Tryggvessön, and brought back a priest with him.[6] There is no evidence that Erik, who died in 1002, was ever baptized; it is interesting, however, to note that he is recorded as having said: 'There is an evil custom in Greenland to bury the dead in unconsecrated ground, and hardly as much as to sing the burial hymns over them. I wish that you should bring me and any others who may die here to the Church.' In 1123 the first bishop was sent from Norway. In this small and distant colony, it seems to have been found that the bishop was the only person capable of exercising authority; before long he became the civil as well as the religious head of the community, and this arrangement was continued during the three centuries of the existence of the colony.

Sweden was slower even than the other Scandinavian lands in accepting Christianity. The first Christian king seems to have been one Olof Skotkonung, at the beginning of the eleventh century, who arranged for a bishop to be consecrated in Hamburg and located in Skara. His attempts to make his people Christian met with obstinate resistance. His intention of destroying the famous temple at Uppsala was frustrated; the temple stood, and its sacrifices were continued until nearly a century after his time.[7]

Nearly a hundred years after Olof, Inge became king, and again tried to abolish sacrifice and to insist that his subjects be baptized. But once again pagan reaction set in, and it was only in the reign of Sverker (1130–55) that Christianity finally got the upper hand.

5. Quoted in C. Dawson, *The Making of Europe*, pp. 280–1, from *Origines Islandicae* I, pp. 400–1.

6. At the time of writing, a well-equipped archaeological expedition has been excavating ancient sites and has found what must certainly be the original church of Leif, at Brattalid in the neighbourhood of Julianshaab. The church was tiny – it cannot have been more than 20 feet long by 12 wide. About 100 burials seem to have taken place in the yard.

7. Adam of Bremen in the *Bishops' Chronicle* (1072–6) gives a lurid description of these sacrifices: 'Nine heads are offered from every living creature of the male sex. By the blood of these the gods are appeased. The bodies are hung up in a grove not far from the temple. Dogs and horses may be seen hanging close by human beings; a Christian told me that he had seen seventy-two bodies hanging together.'

The notable thing about this stage of the Christianization of Sweden is that Sverker and his wife called in the Cistercians from southern Europe. This, like the visit of Knut to Rome, was an indication that northern Christianity was determined to play its part in the Christianity of the world. Cistercian monasticism, one of the most austere manifestations of that spirit of renewal which had shown itself first at Cluny, was to come as a sharp challenge to the more easygoing style of Christian life which had come in from Germany and England. When Sweden also was given its hierarchy, the seat of the archbishopric was placed at Uppsala, which for centuries had been the heart and centre of Swedish paganism, and the first Archbishop, Stephen, appointed in 1164, was a Cistercian. But it is easier to destroy temples than to uproot old and long-established patterns of thought. Long after Sweden was technically Christian, the presence of the old superstitions could constantly be felt not far below the surface.

The greater part of the population of *Finland* belonged to an entirely different race from the Scandinavian, and the difference is marked by a language which is unrelated to the other northern languages but has its affinities with Turkish and Hungarian. We hear of some early contacts of Finland with the Christianity of Hamburg-Bremen; but effective penetration began only when Sweden was strong enough to bring large parts of Finland under Swedish control. In 1155 Erik IX of Sweden carried out a crusade on a major scale against Finland, and in addition to establishing military control demanded of the inhabitants that they should be baptized. Erik was accompanied by Bishop Henry of Uppsala, an Englishman, who seems to have remained there after the King returned to his own country, in order to settle the Christian order of Finland. In the usual pagan reaction Henry was martyred, and has since been venerated as the founder of the Finnish Church. Swedes resident in Finland were no doubt Christians (to this day the Church of Finland has one bishopric of Swedish speech); but progress among the real Finnish people was extremely slow. It is only with the appointment of the first indigenous Bishop of Åbo, Magnus, in 1291, that the outward Christianization of the country can really be said to have reached its end.

By 1200 almost the whole of Europe was in a measure Christian. One corner, a large corner, of intensely obstinate paganism remained. To the south and east of the Baltic lived Wends,

Prussians, Lithuanians, and a mass of other races, united only in one thing – their determination never to be Christians. Nowhere did the Gospel make slower or more laborious progress than here. Christian forces could advance from four different directions. German Christianity was always pressing eastwards from its great metropolis Hamburg. Denmark managed to establish a brief dominion to the south of the Baltic. Poland then, as much later, was pressing for an outlet to the sea. And the more recent Christianity of Russia was spreading north-westwards, and could naturally establish a claim to interest in the Slavonic-speaking sections of the population. But the price paid for any advance was heavy. We have already seen that Adalbert of Prague had died as a martyr in Prussia in 997. A few years later (1009) Bruno of Querfurt, who had been educated at Magdeburg and consecrated as bishop for those parts, met with the same fate. Martyrs, known and unknown, were many on this frontier of the Christian world.

Whatever we may think of the method finally used, history cannot deny that the addition of these regions to the Christian world was brought about by the campaigns of the Order of Teutonic Knights. The Teutonic Knights of St Mary's Hospital at Jerusalem, organized in 1198–9 by merchants of Bremen and Lübeck in order to give help to the sick and wounded at the siege of Acre, and living under much the same statutes as the Templars, had gradually been drawn into the service of the Church on its Prussian frontier. The understanding was that the Order was entitled to annex to its dominions any lands of the pagans that it might conquer, on condition that Christian instruction was given to the conquered people in compensation for the ownership of their lands which was taken from them. (Later, when bishops were appointed for this area, the Pope varied the gift – two-thirds to the conquerors, and one-third to the bishops.) The newly founded Dominican Order was called in to help the Knights with that religious side of the work for which they could hardly be held to be well fitted.

The pagans, valiant though they were, could not stand before the disciplined chivalry of the Empire. Fifty years were spent in the conquest; at the end of that time resistance was over, and *Prussia* had been added to the Christian realm. One of the treaties between the conquerors and the conquered laid down that

all who were not baptized must receive the rite within a month, that those who declined to comply should be banished from the company of Christians, that any who relapsed into paganism should be reduced to slavery, that pagan worship was to cease, that such Christian practices as monogamy were to be adopted, that churches were to be built, that the neophytes must attend church on Sundays and feast days, that provision must be made for the support of the clergy, and that the converts must observe the Lenten fast, make their confessions to a priest at least once a year, and partake of the Communion at Easter.[8]

Here was the whole apparatus of medieval Christianity brought in as an accompaniment to military conquest. And the terms of the treaty were very far from being polite and kind advice. All this was couched in terms of command, and the highly efficient and watch-ful forces of both Church and state were there to see that the commands were punctiliously obeyed. How far inner conviction followed upon outward observance may be questioned, but this is an anxious question that has pursued us ever since Charlemagne first took the sword to help forward the conversion of the Saxons, indeed, since the time of the mass baptism of Clovis and his warriors in 496.

Only one European people remained in the heathen world – the Lithuanians. *Lithuania*, like Poland, never had clearly defined boundaries; its rulers were warlike, and at times extended their dominion almost as far as the Black Sea. Seven hundred years ago the name covered a far larger territory than that of the small state of Lithuania which enjoyed a brief independence in the period after the First World War. As early as 1244 we hear of Christians in Lithuania. A King Mindowe seems to have been baptized about 1251, and in his day provision was made for the consecration of a bishop of Lithuania. But by 1268 Mindowe was dead, having according to some reports been assassinated. For the time being every trace of Christian influence seems to have been eliminated from Lithuania.

In the fourteenth century the struggle recommenced, but the century was nearly at an end before the Christian cause tri-umphed. Jagiello, king of the Lithuanians, was carrying on the hereditary warfare of his people against the Teutonic Knights. Looking round for allies, he turned to the Poles who had long been Christians. As so often, war, politics, matrimony, and a genuine Christian concern combined to bring about a memorable event. The Poles agreed to an alliance, on condition that Jagiello should be baptized and should marry the Christian princess who was first

8. K. S. Latourette, *A History of the Expansion of Christianity*, Vol. II (1938), pp. 205–6.

in succession to the Polish crown. Jagiello agreed, and was baptized on 15 February 1386. He was accompanied back to his realm by numerous clergy, one of whom became bishop of the newly founded see of Vilna. It was thus that Lithuania came to be allied not with the Eastern but with the Western Church, and with the Slavonic rather than the Germanic portion of that Church.

Historians are generally agreed that the baptism of Jagiello marks the end of European paganism as an organized body, though not, certainly, of its influence as a subterranean force. Conversion had been a long, slow business, in which every kind of quality and action had played their part, from pure and heroic sanctity down to the basest chicanery and violence. And it is well that at this point we should remind ourselves of the stage that had been reached in general Church history. In 1386 two rival popes claimed the allegiance of Europe in the Great Schism. Dante had already been sixty-five years in his grave. Geoffrey Chaucer, member of the Parliament of this very year 1386, was already launched on the writing of his *Canterbury Tales*. Byzantium had only another sixty-seven years to live, and less than a century was to pass before the birth of a miner's son named Martin Luther.

It has been convenient to pursue in one continuous narrative the progress of the Gospel in northern and eastern Europe. We must now turn back to ask what had been happening in the south, and in Asia and Africa.

We have suggested that by the year 1000 Europe was beginning to emerge from its Dark Ages, to become aware in a new way of its unity – a Christian unity with its centre in Rome – and to be possessed of that daemonic energy which in the course of six centuries was to lead it to world hegemony.

The first great enterprise of reawakened Western Europe was the Crusades.

The idea of the deliverance of the Christian holy places from the hands of the unbelievers was not in itself an ignoble one – men have fought for baser causes than this. It was a shrewd stroke on the part of the popes to turn the restless vigour of the knightly class away from the futility of the internecine wars that endlessly devastated western Europe. For those who fell in the Holy Land, the halo of martyrdom was set upon death in an ostensibly Christian cause. For those who survived, there was the hope of considerable material rewards for spiritual endeavours – new lands to be conquered, far away from a Europe which was not a generous mother to younger sons. Unquestionably the Crusades educated the early Middle Ages; Christians became aware of another world and of a civilization in many ways more advanced than their own.

But, when all has been said that can be said on the favourable side, the Christian is driven to the judgement that the Crusades were an almost irreparable disaster for the Christian cause. They have been romanticized in legend, and doubtless there were among the Crusaders some righteous and high-minded men, such as Godfrey of Bouillon, the first Christian king of Jerusalem. But to the majority of the Christian warriors Muslims were simply unbelievers, who had no right to existence, with whom no faith need be kept, and who might be slaughtered without ruth or pity to the glory of the Christian God. It is true, of course, that hate breeds hate, bitterness bitterness. The Saracens were just as happy, and in their own judgement equally well justified, when they had the opportunity of slaughtering Christian unbelievers. And so, for the two centuries that elapsed between the first conquest of Jerusalem in 1099, and the loss of the last Crusader stronghold at Acre in 1291, the Mediterranean world was darkened by an ever more sombre cloud of hatred, all the more disastrous because this hate was conjured up in the name of Christ.

In three ways the Crusades have left an almost indelible stain on Christian history.

They permanently injured the relations between the Western and the Eastern branches of Christendom. The Crusaders, Westerners, were guests in the Eastern world, which still lay under the jurisdiction of the Eastern patriarchates. At first, they recognized their proper status, but it was not long before they set up Latin bishoprics subject to the Western Patriarch in Rome – and not unnaturally all Eastern Churchmen were bitterly resentful. Ill-feeling reached its horrible climax when the Fourth Crusade turned aside from its proper object, sacked Constantinople in 1204, and set up a precarious Latin Empire on the ruins of the Eastern Empire that had been destroyed. After sixty years the Byzantines reacted, expelled the foreigners, and set up again their own Eastern Empire. But it was only a shadow of its former self, permanently weakened in its unending struggle against the Muslims. When Constantinople fell to the Turks in 1453, the full extent of the guilt of the Crusaders was revealed.

The Crusades left a trail of bitterness across the relations between Christians and Muslims that remains as a living factor in the world situation to the present day. To Muslims the West is the great aggressor. Nearly 900 years ago it deliberately entered into that role in the name of Christ, and today it finds it extremely difficult to change the image of itself that still remains in the Muslim mind. It is not, of course, the case that the Muslims have always been mild and gentle – they have been aggressive enough, wherever they have had the strength and the opportunity. But in any case Muslims do not pretend to be followers of the Prince of Peace. To Westerners it may appear that the Crusades happened a very long time ago; the Crusaders have slept well in their tombs in quiet English churches. The East has a different time scale; to every Muslim in the Mediterranean lands the Crusades are an event of yesterday, and the wounds are ready at any moment to break out afresh.

Thirdly, the Crusades involved a lowering of the whole moral temperature of Christendom. We have anticipated, by showing what a 'Crusade' might mean when directed against the pagan barbarism of the north. It was not long before Innocent III showed that the same principle could be used for the suppression of Christian heretics, and the savageries which devastated Provence in the days of Simon de Montfort and after were simply a repetition, in a different setting, of the savageries that had attended on the Christian recovery of Jerusalem.[9] It is impossible to dissent from the sober judgement of a historian of the Crusades in our own day:

Seen in the perspective of history the whole Crusading Movement was a vast fiasco . . . The triumphs of the Crusades were the triumphs of faith. But faith without wisdom is a dangerous thing . . . The historian, as he gazes back across the centuries at their gallant story, must find his admiration overcast by sorrow at the witness that it bears to the limitations of human nature. There was so much courage and so little honour, so much devotion and so little understanding. High ideals were besmirched by cruelty and greed, enterprise and endurance by a blind and narrow self-righteousness; and the Holy War itself was nothing more than a long act of intolerance in the name of God, which is the sin against the Holy Ghost.[10]

9. 'The Lateran Council 1215 took the moral defeat of the Church, sanctified it, and erected it into a law. The Pope had not been unaware of the atrocities committed by the Crusaders; the day after Béziers was taken, the Abbot of Cîteaux had written to him, with appalling frankness: "Nearly twenty thousand of these people were put to the sword, *without regard for age or sex*."' – Z. Oldenbourg, *Massacre at Montségur: A History of the Albigensian Crusade* (1959: Eng. trans. 1961), p. 183.

10. S. Runciman, *A History of the Crusades*, Vol. III (1954), pp. 469, 480.

Most of the Crusaders seem to have held the view that nothing could be done with the infidels except to exterminate them, or to reduce them to permanent slavery. As unbelievers they were destined for hell anyway; and, if they were allowed to live, this could only be because of the services that they might be able to render to faithful Christians. A few voices were heard in protest. Roger Bacon maintained that the Crusades were an expensive and futile folly. Thomas Aquinas held that even the infidel has certain natural rights which must be respected. Almost the first Christian, however, to attempt to act on these more liberal principles was Francis of Assisi. Convinced that, if the Paynims had not been converted, this was because the Gospel had not been presented to them in its simplicity and beauty, he himself made three attempts to reach them. The first two, to Morocco in 1212 and to Spain in 1214, came to nothing, but in 1219, when the soldiers of the Fifth Crusade were encamped in Egypt, Francis joined them, and was successful in making his way into the presence of the Sultan of Egypt. It is unlikely that the Sultan was able to understand much of what the strange little man from Italy was trying to convey to him, but a holy man is always respected in the East, and the Sultan seems to have shown marked deference to Francis.

This trip made by Francis to Egypt was more than an expression of personal interest or missionary zeal. It meant that a new spirit had come into the Christian world, and that a notable shift was about to take place in the missionary methods of the Christian Churches. For five centuries, at the heart of the missionary enterprise had stood the monastery, that element of unchanging perpetuity in a constantly changing world. From now on and for two centuries the central place will be held by the two great Orders of Friars: the Franciscans and the Dominicans. Until the foundation of the Jesuit Order in the middle of the sixteenth and seventeenth century, we shall hear more of Franciscans and Dominicans than of anyone else. There was, of course, a great difference between the aims and purposes of the two Orders. Francis (1181–1226) lived to bring back simplicity and joy into the Christian world, and to release new forces for the service of the very poor. In the work of Dominic (1170–1221) there were from the beginning harsher traits. His Order was to be intellectually competent, devoted to the conversion of heretics particularly through the work of preaching, as its official title the 'Order of Preachers' indicates. But in each lived a genuine missionary impulse. Before the thirteenth century is out, we shall find Franciscans at the ends of the known earth. And about 1300 the Dominicans formed the *Societas Fratrum peregrinantium propter Christum inter gentes*, 'the company of brethren dwelling in foreign parts among the heathen for the sake of Christ'.

The first field that seemed to open up was in what is now called the *Ukraine*. A people of Turkish origin, the Cumans, had settled in this area. At times they threatened their neighbours to the west, the Hungarians; at times they tended to be allied to them. Today the Ukraine is part of Russia, and we should naturally regard it as belonging to the world of the Eastern Church. But at that time Constantinople was far too closely occupied in repelling the Muslim threat on its eastern borders to have much time for missionary work, and the Russian Church was engaged in consolidating itself in the northern and eastern regions. The Ukraine was ecclesiastically a no-man's-land, and here, in 1221, the Dominicans entered in. The beginnings of the work were extremely difficult; a number of brothers were killed or sold into slavery. But in 1227 a prince named Bort was converted and baptized, and in the following year a bishopric was created, the first bishop being a Hungarian Dominican. These converts were placed directly under the control of the Holy See, in order to make it plain that missionary work was not intended to result in an expansion of Hungarian political power.

Beyond the Ukraine, the Hungarians had heard of a mysterious realm 'Greater Hungary', the original home of their Magyar ancestors before the invasions. They naturally wished to see to the conversion of those who had been left behind in this ancient home, somewhere in the region between the Volga and the Ural Mountains. In 1235 a group of four missionaries was sent out to look for the original Magyars; the journey was terrible, and only one of the four reached journey's end. Of a second expedition, not a single member reached his destination. Nothing came of this mission, which was swallowed up in the next great disaster that fell upon the Christian world; it remains as a monument to the vision, courage, and pertinacity of the medieval missionary.

Central Asia was preparing once again to spill forth upon the world some of its apparently inexhaustible treasure of human lives. When the western world first heard of the Mongol movements, the news was received with some cheerfulness. The neighbour always tends to be the enemy; if that is so, the neighbour's neighbour may well prove to be a friend. If it were possible for the Christians to ally themselves with this new power, and so to take the Muslims in the rear, then the world might be done with the Muslim menace for good and all. If, better still, the two enemies could be caused to fall upon one another, the Christian Church could well be the *tertius gaudens*, the man who profits from the misfortunes of everyone else. This was the view cynically put forward by the Bishop of Winchester to Henry III of England in 1238:

> Let these dogs destroy one another and be utterly exterminated, and then we shall see the universal Catholic Church founded on their ruins and there will be one fold and one shepherd.

It was not long before the Christian world discovered the gravity of the new menace which was overshadowing it. The first to suffer were the Russians, and their southern neighbours the Cumans, in whose territories an unknown horde of barbarians suddenly appeared in the spring of 1222:

> For our sins, unknown tribes came, none knows who they are or whence they came – nor what their language is, nor of what race they are nor what their faith is – God alone knows who they are and whence they came out.

So writes a Russian chronicler.[11] After one great victory the barbarians disappeared, and for fifteen years the land had peace. But in 1236–7 they were back again, this time to stay. The Russian cities were besieged and destroyed one after the other, and the Mongol methods of extermination recalled the Huns in the worst days of the earlier barbarian invasions.[12] This was not the end. In December 1240 Kiev was captured and destroyed. The Mongol right wing passed through Poland and entered what is now Silesia; the Poles and Germans were defeated on 9 April 1241 at Liegnitz. Two days later the main body met and destroyed the Hungarian army at Mohi near Budapest. The whole West lay open to the destroying locust; a year later one group reached Cattaro on the Adriatic and another penetrated Austria. Then, confused by the death of the Great Khan Ugedey (Ogdai), and by internal quarrels, the Mongols withdrew. Europe and Christendom were allowed to breathe again.

What Europe did not know was that behind these farflung

11. *The Chronicle of Novgorod* (Eng. trans. 1914), p. 64, quoted by C. Dawson in *The Mongol Mission* (1955), p. xii.

12. 'No eye was left open to weep for the dead' is the sorrowful summary of the chronicler; quoted in *Encycl. Brit.* under 'Mongols'.

movements lay the personality of one of the world's most remarkable conquerors, Genghis Khan. Raising himself by his own efforts from comparatively obscure origins, in 1211 Genghis set himself to the conquest of northern China. Within twelve years from this time his armies had reached the Pacific Ocean, the Indus, and the Black Sea. The Mongols, on their wide open steppes, had brought to perfection the art of moving cavalry with great rapidity. The lumbering heavy armies of the other nations were no match for them. Genghis died in 1227. Kubilay, Kublai Khan (famed in Coleridge's poem), who reigned from 1267 onwards in Peking and died in 1294, was his grandson.

Genghis Khan was himself a barbarian, who had inherited nothing but the primitive shamanism of the Mongolian steppes.[13] But he was aware of the importance of religion. He laid it down that all religions were to be respected, and that priests and holy men were to be shown all deference. The Great Khans, more enlightened than many Western rulers, faithfully observed this principle; Christopher Dawson refers to the approving comment of Gibbon that 'a singular conformity may be found between the religious laws of Zingis Khan and of Mr Locke'.

The Western dream of co-operation with the Mongols against the Muslims was not quite so absurd as some later generations have imagined. After the obliteration of the earlier Nestorian missions, Christianity had again spread through Central Asia through means which are obscure to us, but probably in the main through the pilgrimages of traders on those endless routes. Except for brief periods of utter chaos, trade never ceased to move. War and slavery meant the disappearance of considerable numbers of Christian captives into the far wastes. All the most intelligent peoples of these regions were by the thirteenth century at least in part Christian. The Uighur Turks in the great oases of Turkestan were partly Buddhist and partly Christian. In Mongolia the Keraits, and on the northern frontier of China the Ongut Turks, were deeply influenced by Christianity. In the story of the Mongol Khans, it is notable that many of the princesses were Christians; if they did not succeed in converting their husbands, they were there to exercise their great influence in favour of the Christians or at

13. The Oxford Dictionary defines shamanism as 'the primitive religion of the Ural-Altaic peoples of Siberia, in which all the good and evil of life are thought to be brought about by spirits, who can be influenced only by Shamans'. The shaman is the priest or priest-doctor of the tribe, impolitely called by a writer in 1756 a 'diabolical artist'.

least in favour of religious toleration. A number of the leading officials at the courts of the successive Khans were also Christians. To the Mongol the principal enemy, the principal obstacle to the establishment of universal dominion, was the Muslim. So an alliance of the Mongol with the West was not wholly beyond the reach of human possibilities.

It is in the light of these hopes and desires that we should understand the embassies despatched by the Pope to the Great Khan. Though these can hardly be regarded as part of Christian missionary work, they are so important, in relation to the growing Western understanding of the Asian world and to the sense of responsibility for sending the Gospel to it, that they cannot be passed over in silence.

The first messenger was Fr John of Plano Carpini, a Franciscan who had been born about 1180, and had been very vigorous in spreading the Franciscan Order in many parts of Europe. On 2 February 1246 John left Kiev and plunged into the heart of Central Asia as the bearer of letters to the Great Khan from Pope Innocent IV, who protested against the attacks of the Mongols on Christians, gave a brief account of the Christian faith, and urged the Great Khan that 'following their salutary instructions, you may acknowledge Jesus Christ the very Son of God and worship his glorious name by practising the Christian religion'. Making contact with Batu, the ruler on the lower Volga, the travellers were despatched by him with all speed to the camp of Güyük, then about to be elected Great Khan, in the very heart of Mongolia:

And so we started at dawn and journeyed until night without a meal, and many a time we arrived so late that we did not eat that night but were given in the morning the food that we should have eaten the previous evening. We went as fast as the horses could trot, for the horses were in no way spared, since we had fresh ones several times a day, and those which fell out returned as has already been described, and so we rode swiftly without a break.[14]

John and his companions reached the camp of Güyük on 22 July and left it on 17 November. They were present at the solemn ceremony of the installation of the Great Khan, and were kindly and respectfully treated by him. At the court were a number of Christians, of whose faith and morals the Western Christians did not have a very high opinion. These were free to perform their own

14. The whole of the 'History of the Mongols' by John of Plano Carpini is given in English in C. Dawson, *The Mongol Mission* (1955), pp. 3–76.

religious ceremonies, and had high hopes that the Great Khan would declare himself a Christian:

> The present Emperor may be forty or forty-five years old or more; he is of medium height, very intelligent and extremely shrewd, and most serious and grave in his manner. . . . The Christians of his household also told us that they firmly believed he was about to become a Christian, and they have clear evidence of this, for he maintains Christian clerics and provides them with supplies of Christian things; in addition he always has a chapel before his chief tent, and they sing openly and in public and beat the board for services, after the Greek fashion, like other Christians, however big a crowd of Tartars or other men be there.

The Christians were over-optimistic as to the attitude of Güyük. He sent the messengers back with a letter to the Pope, in which he rejected the idea of baptism, and instead called upon the Pope to head the Western princes in submitting to the divinely appointed ruler of all things:

> Now you should say with a sincere heart: 'I will submit and serve you.' Thou thyself, at the head of all the Princes, come at once to serve and wait upon us! At that time I shall recognize your submission. If you do not observe God's command, and if you ignore my command, I shall know you as my enemy. Likewise I shall make you understand. If you do otherwise, God knows what I know.

The messengers reached Kiev safely on 9 June 1247, after an absence of rather more than a year.

A second embassy, that of the Dominicans Ascelius and André of Longjumeau, proved even less fruitful than that of John of Plano Carpini.

The third, and in many ways the most remarkable, was that of the Flemish William of Rubruck. Word had reached St Louis, king of France, that Sartak (Sortach), the son of Batu, was himself a Christian. St Louis decided to send a purely religious embassy to Sartak, to make contact with the Christians of Central Asia and to encourage them in their faith. William left Constantinople on 7 May 1253, and made his first contact with the Tartars on 1 June. He made his way to the camp of Batu on the Volga, and by him was sent on, like John of Plano Carpini, to the Great Khan himself in the heart of Mongolia.[15]

It did not take long for Brother William to discover that Sartak was not a Christian, but he did encounter a great many Christians

15. The Great Khan now was not Güyük but the usurper Mongka.

of the most various kinds. He heard of the city of Talas, in which was a group of German slaves. At the court of the Khan was a woman from Metz in Lorraine named Paquette, who had been captured in Hungary; she had suffered much, but now was reasonably prosperous, as she had a young Russian husband and three lovely little boys by him. She told him also of a master goldsmith named William, a Parisian by birth. As in so many other cases, among the wives of the Great Khan and his chieftains were Christian women. And there were many Nestorian priests, who celebrated their mysteries with considerable solemnity, but were gravely addicted to the Tartar vice of drunkenness, and this seems to have passed among them without any censure.

William had access to the Great Khan a number of times, and was able to carry on theological discussions in his presence, but without apparently making any deep impression on his mind. After eight months he came away bearing a letter expressed in much the same terms as that given by Güyük to Fr John: the Great Khan regards himself as the divinely appointed sovereign of all the world; all that the Pope and the Western princes have to do is to submit to him, and all will be well:

> If, when you hear and understand the decree of the eternal God, you are unwilling to pay attention and believe it, saying 'Our country is far away, our mountains are mighty, our sea is vast', and in this confidence you bring an army against us – we know what we can do; He who made what was difficult easy, and what was far away near, the eternal God, He knows.

Brother William passed safely through all the hazards of the return journey, and eventually arrived at Tripoli in Syria, where the chapter of his Order was held on 15 August 1255.

These embassies seemed to have little value. Yet they were not ill-timed. For just at this period the Mongols had decided to attack next the Muslim world, and came almost to the point of destroying it. Baghdad was captured and destroyed in 1258, Damascus in 1260. The fate of Islam hung by a thread, only Egypt remaining as an independent and vigorous centre of Islamic power. The Christian world rejoiced at the overthrow, and celebrated it in terms worthy of an Old Testament prophet – for five centuries. Baghdad had ruled all the nations and sucked the blood and treasure of the world; now at length the judgement of God had gone out against her, and she had been punished for her evil deeds and for the blood that she had shed. A Christian reconquest of the ancient Christian lands seemed by no means improbable. As a first instalment, the Nestorian Church attained to a prosperity and extent that it had never known before; its hierarchy was re-established throughout Central Asia, and in 1275 an archbishopric was established at Khanbalik (Peking), the new capital of Kublai Khan.

It was by no means impossible that an alliance should be formed between the Il Khan, who ruled at Tabriz in Persia, and the western world. In point of fact the Il Khan Abaga (1265–82) did in 1274 send envoys to the Council of Lyons, and these were present when a temporary union was patched up between the Eastern and Western Churches. Unhappily the West was at this time sorely divided against itself, and only one Western prince, the wise and statesmanlike Edward I of England, was able to understand the bearing and the possibilities for Christendom of such a far-eastern alliance.

It is in this connection that we encounter one of the most astonishing episodes of Church history, and the eastern counterpart to the heroic journey of William of Rubruck. Rabban Sauma, an Ongut Turk, or perhaps a Uighur, was born of a Christian family in Peking a little before or after A.D. 1250. About the year 1278, Sauma, with a friend named Mark, decided to travel westwards to visit the holy places. A long and adventurous journey eventually carried the pair to Baghdad; while they were there, the patriarch died, and Mark (commended no doubt in part by his kinship with the ruling Mongolian race) was elected patriarch under the title Mar Yaballaha III. When the new Il Khan, Argun, decided once again to send an embassy to the West, the choice fell upon Rabban Sauma, who arrived in Rome somewhere during the year 1287.

Pope Honorius IV had just died, but Rabban Sauma was warmly welcomed by the cardinals. Sauma, who was a man of some theological education, was apparently unaware that in the West he might be considered a heretic, and when the cardinals proceeded to put him through his theological paces he showed a good deal of not unnatural irritation. It was inconceivable to them that any orthodox Christian could live without conscious fellowship with the Bishop of Rome. To this Sauma tartly replied: 'No man has come to us Orientals from the Pope. The Holy Apostles, whose names I have mentioned, taught us the Gospel, and to what they have delivered us we have clung until this present day.' When the cardinals wished to press him further, he said: 'I have not come from remote countries to discuss or instruct any in matters of faith, but to get the blessing of the Pope and from the shrines of the saints, and to make known the words of King Argun and the Catholicos.' He seems to have been able adequately to convince the Roman authorities. It is recorded that he celebrated the Eucharist at Bordeaux in the presence of Edward I of England, and there the king of the north-western island received the Holy Communion at the hands of the Turk from far Cathay.

Ecclesiastically, the pilgrimage of Rabban Sauma had been successful and valuable in its results. But little attention was paid to its diplomatic possibilities, except by King Edward, and the moment of opportunity was lost. Argun died. The Saracens in 1291 captured Acre, the last Christian stronghold in the Levant. Rabban Sauma died in 1294. The son of Argun, Oljaitu, whom Sauma himself had baptized by the name Nicholas, turned Muslim. Gradually the whole of the Mongol world – in Russia, in Persia, in Turkestan – became absorbed in the spreading Muslim culture, and the Turks, instead of becoming allies of the Christian West, became the spearhead of the new and most threatening Islamic advance.

For the moment, however, this was not clear. The coming of Rabban Sauma had reawakened the interest of Rome in the Far East, an interest stimulated also by the astonishing journeys of Marco Polo and his uncles, who were in China from 1275 to 1291. If Marco Polo is to be trusted, the uncles, on their return from their first journey in 1266, brought with them a message to the Pope from Kublai Khan, asking for the despatch of a hundred men of learning, devoted to the Christian faith, who would be able to prove 'to the learned of his dominions, by just and fair argument, that the faith professed by Christians is superior to and founded on more evident truth than any other'. If attention had been paid to this request at the time, the results might have been considerable. But twenty years passed, and when Pope Nicholas IV decided, in 1289, to resume the practice of embassies, he sent two men, one of whom died on the way.

His choice fell on John of Monte Corvino, a Franciscan, who had already had experience in the East. As the land route was closed, John took the then unusual course of going by sea. On the way he spent thirteen months in India, and is our best witness for the condition of Christianity in that country in the Middle Ages. He found Nestorians in a number of places, notably at St Thomas's Mount near Madras, the traditional site of the martyrdom of the Apostle. Like all the other remote fragments of the Church, these groups were suffering from their isolation from the great centres of Christian life and thought, but they had sturdily resisted all the tendencies of Hinduism to absorb other religious systems into itself, and had maintained themselves firmly as unassimilated Christians.

John of Monte Corvino reached Khanbalik (Peking), probably in 1294, and was warmly received by Timur, the successor of Kublai Khan. He hoped to convert the Khan, but in this he was unsuccessful, as the Emperor had 'grown too old in idolatry'. But he was able to build a church, and to establish himself in face of the opposition of pagans, Nestorians, and some European travellers who had also found their way to Peking. By 1305 he claimed to have baptized 6,000 persons; he had also gathered a group of about 150 boys, whom he was teaching Greek and Latin, and training to sing the service after the Western manner.[16]

When the Pope, now Clement V, heard of this notable achievement, he decided to establish a Western hierarchy for China, with John as Archbishop. As John could not come to Europe, there was nothing for it but to arrange for him to be consecrated in China. Seven Franciscan brothers, zealous and learned in the Holy Scriptures, were consecrated bishops, and sent off on the hazardous journey, in order that at the end of it they might consecrate their own metropolitan. One of the seven failed to start, three died on the way, but three arrived, and in 1308 John became canonically the first *Archiepiscopus Cambalensis* of the Latin Church in the Far East. The presence of the other bishops made expansion possible, and a second centre was opened at Zaitun (Ch'uan-Chou) in 1313.

John of Monte Corvino died in 1328. John di Cona, who wrote a book *On the Estate of the great Caan*, gives us some details of his funeral:

To his obsequies and burial there came a very great multitude of people, both Christian and pagan. And those pagans rent their mourning garments as their manner is; and both Christians and pagans devoutly laid hold of pieces of the clothing of the Archbishop and carried them off as relics with great reverence. . . . And they still visit the place of his interment with very great devotion.

---

16. John of Monte Corvino himself states that he had translated the New Testament and the Psalter into the Ongut language, and even that he celebrated Mass in Ongut. A. Mulders, *Missionsgeschichte* (1960), p. 172.

After the death of the Archbishop, the mission gradually declined. Various expeditions were sent out, but not infrequently these failed to reach China. At last, in response to an appeal from the Great Khan and his Alan chiefs, one more great embassy was despatched. In December 1335 John of Marignolli, with a company of no less than fifty friars, left Avignon for China. After a journey overland which lasted more than three years, thirty-two of the travellers at last reached Peking, and once again were favourably received by the Great Khan, Timur:

> The Grand Khan . . . when he saw us, rejoiced greatly . . . and treated us with greatest honour. And when I entered the Khan's presence, it was in full vestments, with a very fine cross carried before me, and candles and incense, whilst *Credo in unum Deum* was chanted in that glorious place where he dwells. And when the chant was ended I bestowed a full benediction, which he received with all humility.

But this, once again, was an embassy, and not permanent reinforcements. In 1346 John of Marignolli left China. During his journey homewards he spent a year in Quilon in South India, and is thus our second notable authority on that period of Christianity in India. He reached Avignon in 1353.[17] It is said that the last Latin Bishop of Zaitun, James of Florence, was martyred when the Chinese recovered the city from the Mongols in 1362, and that the Latins were finally expelled from Peking in 1369. That was the end of Western missionary enterprise in China for two hundred years.

We have seen that the attempts of the Western Church to advance into the Ukraine and the steppes of the Caspian beyond it had been broken up by the depredations of the Mongols in their first destructive fury. As soon as more settled conditions returned, the attempt was renewed, from the year 1300 on, by both Franciscans and Dominicans. In order to make missionary work possible, a number of unusual privileges had to be granted to the friars of both Orders; in addition to certain ecclesiastical authorizations – to give dispensations and so forth – they were permitted, contrary to their rule, to carry money, to wear clothes other than their habit, and to grow beards. The Mongols were nomads; if they were to be evangelized, the missionaries must also adopt the nomad way

17. In later years John became Bishop of Bisignano, and was commanded by the Emperor to write the chronicles of Bohemia – a task which he found so tedious that he inserted into his book an irrelevant and not wholly accurate account of his adventures in the East.

of life. About the year 1335 we have word of small groups of Franciscans who wore Mongol dress, followed the Mongol 'hordes', and carried their portable altars and vessels on wagons very much like those of the pastoral people to whom they ministered. It was said that those who worked through these 'mobile convents' were far more successful than others in winning converts.

It was in the territory of the 'Golden Horde', in the eastern part of Russia,[18] that the most notable success of the missionaries was won. Toqtai, who had become Khan of this whole region in 1290, was brought to the faith by the Franciscans in 1311, and received baptism together with his wife, his three sons, and a number of other Mongol chiefs. This gave great hopes of further success, but as so often, the conversion of one chief proved to be only a false dawn. Toqtai, 'brother John', died in 1312. His two elder sons immediately reverted to Islam, and his successor, Ozbeg (1312–40), was a convinced Muslim. Nevertheless, Ozbeg remained on friendly terms with the missionaries and did not interfere with their work; it was only in 1342 that it became evident that the future of the Mongol people was to be in the hands of Islam and not of Christianity. As early as 1320, the city of Sarai, on the Volga not far from the point at which it flows into the Caspian Sea, had been provided with a Latin bishop; in 1362 this was raised to be an archbishopric, with oversight of all the missions in the territory of the Golden Horde.

The missionaries were not the only westerners in the regions around the Black Sea and the Caspian Sea. Europe was reviving as a trading power. The great rival cities of Venice and Genoa had made themselves rich by transporting, feeding, and not infrequently swindling the Crusaders. Now that the Crusades were over, they were busy expanding their commercial empire beyond the limits of the Christian world. Venice had a commercial colony on the shores of the Sea of Azov. Genoa had established something like a commercial empire all round the Black Sea. It has to be admitted with shame that the staple of trade was slaves; slaves from Russia were apparently regarded as highly desirable in Egypt, and were not unknown in the West. In spite of the protests of the Pope and the Great Khan, the traffic went on.

---

18. Golden Horde: 'name for a tribe who possessed the Khanate of Kipchak, in eastern Russia and western and central Asia, from the thirteenth century till 1480'. *Oxford Dictionary*, under 'Horde'.

In 1333 two Dominicans, Francis of Camerino and William the Englishman, won a notable success with the conversion of the Alan prince of Vospro in the Crimea, who ruled under Mongol suzerainty over a large area between the Black Sea and the Caspian. The Pope accordingly decided to create a new ecclesiastical province for the Black Sea area, with its metropolitical see in Vospro. This was a miscalculation: before long the Mongols resumed direct control of the Crimea; the Latin bishoprics continued to exist, but became increasingly chaplaincies to the westerners in the area, rather than centres for missionary work among the as yet unevangelized peoples of the interior.

We have seen earlier that the situation of the Christians under the Mongol Il Khans in Persia was by no means unfavourable. A large part of the population was Christian and the Mongols had not yet decided to embrace the faith of Islam. As in Russia, groups of western traders had gradually spread through Asia Minor, across Armenia, and into Persia, where their chief centre was Tabriz. In 1318 the Pope decided to create a new mission with its centre at Sultaniyet, the capital of the Khanate of Persia, partly in order to care for Western Christians in the region, partly to work for the conversion of Muslims, but mainly to aim at the 'return' of Eastern Christians to the Roman fold. The Dominicans, to whom this mission was entrusted, spread themselves out through Azerbaijan and Georgia. Conversions from among the Muslims were few, but they were successful in producing in Armenia a rather strong move of dissidence from the ancient Armenian Church. As always happens in Armenia, a violent nationalist reaction set in, and after 1380 little if anything is heard of this particular movement for Christian unity.

From Persia it was not a long journey to India. We have already noted the brief sojourn in India of Christian travellers on their way to or from China. From the fourteenth century we have one note of an attempt to introduce Latin Christianity into India on a more permanent basis. A group of three Franciscan friars and a lay brother had arrived in India, and were at Tana near Bombay. There a dispute broke out. Brother Thomas of Tolentino, being challenged directly to say what he thought of Muhammad, unwisely replied:

Muhammad is the son of perdition, and hath his place in hell with the devil his father, and not only he but all such as follow and keep his Law, false as it is, and pestilent and accursed, hostile to God and the salvation of souls.

Not unnaturally three of the visitors were seized and put to death. The survivor, Brother Jordan of Severac, gathered up the remains and buried them. He determined to give his life for the evangelization of India. In the north he found little success. A wider door was open to him in the south; he settled at Columbum (Quilon) in Travancore, among the Nestorian Christians, then as through so many centuries suffering from their isolation, and among them seems to have found a measure of success. It appears that in 1329 the Pope appointed him Bishop of Columbum,[19] but it is not clear that he was ever consecrated. A few years later John of Marignolli found some traces of his labours; but thereafter night descends again on the remote and isolated Christian groups in India.

It has been necessary to note *seriatim* these various enterprises of the Church; only so is it possible to make clear the strong missionary vigour that was at work, and the restless probing that went on all through the Middle Ages, in the attempt to find a thoroughfare for the Gospel in the most diverse regions of the world. But at the end of the narrative we are driven to ask why, after all, this immense expenditure of effort and adventure remained on the whole so fruitless. At the end of the fifteenth century Christianity was almost wholly a European religion. It had not completely died out in Asia, but everywhere it was on the wane. In certain areas it had been completely exterminated. Even where it survived, the Christian groups were for the most part isolated, backward, and lacking both in holiness and in dynamic power. They were so much occupied in the effort of survival as to have little strength left over for witness, and apparently in many cases had little hope that their neighbours, who were often also their masters, could be converted.

Various reasons for this failure can be enumerated. The first and the most obvious is the great distances that had to be covered, and the difficulties of travel. Missionaries remained unvisited for years on end. When reinforcements could be sent, it was by no means certain that they would ever reach their destination. The loss of life was high, both through the violence of the barbarous tribes and through the natural hazards of travel in unknown regions and of

19. Even the careful Mulders is misled by this medieval spelling, and places the bishopric of Columbum in Ceylon (op. cit., p. 174). It is, however, unquestionably Quilon in South India.

exposure to unfamiliar climates. Conversion of the Turkish tribes seems to have been fairly easy; but lapse to Islam or to some other form of religion was equally easy and frequent; there was little permanence and stability in the Christianity of these regions. It seems to be untrue that the missionaries failed to learn the languages of the regions where they worked and to give the people at least the New Testament in their own tongue. But critics of these medieval missionaries seem to have forgotten that at this time the printing press had not yet been invented; if the New Testament was to circulate in Uighur, every single copy had to be written out by hand – and where were the skilled copyists, who could give their time to such a multiplication of books? The Latin missionaries were slow to work for an indigenous priesthood and episcopate, but this was not true of the Nestorians, who seem at least in part to have had priests and bishops from among the local peoples. It is true that the Christianity of those times does not give the impression of having been a dynamic conviction producing both holiness of life and the inspiration to witness. Yet, when all is said and done, when we take into account the setbacks that later and far better supported missions have encountered and all the difficulties that had to be faced in this earlier period, we may feel that the medieval missionaries made as good use as was possible of their opportunities and of the material that they had to hand.

Yet, for all their labours and devotion, they did not bring into being stable and enduring Churches in the distant lands which they evangelized. For this there was one overmastering cause, and one which they could do nothing to control – the tragic unsettlement of the times, and the recurrent calamities caused by one invasion of the barbarians after another. We have noted the universal panic caused by the first incursions of the Mongols in the years leading up to 1241, and the widespread annihilation of the missions for which they were responsible. Gradually the Mongols were brought under the influence of civilization, and both the land and sea routes to the far east were again opened. But hardly had the missionaries had time to enter in and consolidate their position, when the last and worst of all the medieval disasters broke upon them like a flood. Tamerlane (Timur-i-Leng) was not, like the first Mongols, a primitive and illiterate barbarian; he was a civilized sovereign, who maintained a splendid court and had a wide knowledge of the world. Yet he was the most cruel and destructive of all the medieval conquerors. His conquests began in 1358. Within twelve years his armies, like those of Genghis Khan, had poured out in every direction – to the Volga and to northern India, to China and almost to the Mediterranean Sea. By the time of his death at Samarkand in 1405, the work of destruction had been completed. Everything of Western and Christian civilization had been swept away. East and West were more completely separated than they had ever been before, and, when travel again became possible, from the Christian point of view everything had to be begun afresh.

In the early days Christianity had profited by the Roman peace, as later it was to profit by the limited and uncertain peace of the colonial era. Once the Gospel has taken firm root and Churches have been established, they are able to survive through a considerable period of persecution. If there is no period of tranquillity and stability, it seems almost impossible for them to be established and to take root. This, basically, is the history of the medieval period in the lands from the Dnieper to the Pacific Ocean. It seemed as though the time for Asia had not yet come. Only the great revolution which was to make of Europe the dominating power in the world for four succeeding centuries would usher in the next great period of Christian expansion.

The Crusades were the first sign of the recovery of Europe, and of a new capacity on the part of the European peoples to work together as a Christian whole. But they were not the only sign. From the twelfth century onwards, Christian pressure in Spain and Portugal was driving the Muslims back. The last Muslim stronghold, Granada, fell as late as 1492. But from the middle of the thirteenth century Portugal had been wholly free, and it was clear that in Spain it was only a matter of time – the Christians already had the upper hand. The Muslims were to leave behind countless traces of the effects of their occupation on the life of the Iberian Peninsula, but Spain and Portugal were again to be Christian countries. In the process of reconversion there were some things that were noble, others that were discreditable; it was perhaps inevitable that violence and the pressure exercised by Christian rulers should be more noticeable than the loving preaching of the Gospel.

But, if some Christians held that the only good Saracen was a dead Saracen, there were others who thought otherwise, and believed that through clear and faithful preaching of the Gospel even Saracens could be won to faith in Christ.

Ramón Lull must rank as one of the greatest missionaries in the history of the Church. Others were filled with an equally ardent desire to preach the Gospel to the unbelievers, and if necessary to suffer for it; it was left to Lull to be the first to develop a theory of missions – not merely to wish to preach the Gospel, but to work out in careful detail how it was to be done.

Ramón Lull[20] was born in the island of Majorca, probably in 1235, only five years after the Catalans (under the leadership of their king, James the Conqueror) had recovered the island from the Saracens. Until he had reached the age of thirty, Lull was a young man about the court, gallant, frivolous, a poet with no particular thought of religion. Then suddenly one day a thrice-repeated vision of Christ recalled him to himself, and called him to the service of the Saviour. The conversion was complete; for the next fifty years Lull was tireless in the service of his Lord; the central theme of all his desires and purposes was the conversion of the infidels to the faith of Christ. At first he was attracted by the Dominicans; not finding much sympathy among them for his plans, he transferred his affections to the Franciscans, and later became a tertiary of that Order. At one time or another we find him everywhere in the Christian world of that day – at the universities of Paris and of Montpellier; at the court of the kings of Aragon, of France, of Sicily, even of Cyprus; in the presence of every Pope who reigned between 1265 and 1320; in the republics of Genoa, Pisa, and Venice, which, as we have seen, had notable connections with the Muslim world; and finally at the General Council which met at Vienne in 1311.

Lull was a profound scholar, well acquainted with all the philosophical and theological systems of the day. His own religion was mystical in character; and in a steady stream of books and poems in his beloved Catalan, as well as in Latin, he strove to set forth the relations between the Lover and the Beloved.[21] But in his

20. The best English work on Lull is still that by E. Allison Peers, *Ramón Lull* (1929). Peers has also translated into English a number of the principal works of Lull.

21. The best known of his mystical works is the *Book of the Lover and the Beloved*. Two short quotations may serve as an indication of the simple and penetrating quality of his thought.

'Said the Lover to his Beloved: "Thou art all, and through all, and in all, and with all. I would give thee all of myself that I may have all of Thee, and Thou all of me." The Beloved answered: "Thou canst not have me wholly, unless thou art wholly mine." And the Lover said: "Let me be wholly thine, and Thou wholly mine."'

'The Lover and the Beloved met, and the Beloved said to the Lover: "Thou needest not to speak me. Sign to me only within thine eyes – for they are words to my heart – that I may give thee that for which thou dost ask."'

case, as in that of St Teresa of Avila and of many others of the Latin race, a mystical propensity was combined with a shrewd realism which expressed itself in attention to the minutest details of his schemes. All that was lacking to him was that executive effectiveness which clothes a well-constructed scheme with flesh and blood and makes of it a living reality.

Lull was of the opinion that for the evangelization of the Saracens three things were necessary:

The first is a comprehensive and accurate knowledge of their language. As early as 1276 he had received royal authorization to establish at Miramar in Majorca a college for the study of oriental languages. The college existed for some twenty years but it is not known how many well-qualified missionaries went forth from it. In 1311–12 the Council of Vienne, yielding to the urgent importunities of Master Ramón, decided on the formation of five colleges in association with the most famous universities of the world – Rome (or Avignon), Bologna, Paris, Oxford, and Salamanca – for the study of the languages of the Muslim world. Lull indicated as the indispensable tongues Hebrew, Arabic, Syriac, and Greek. He added the extraordinarily modern and enlightened suggestion that learned men from different parts of the world should be invited to come to these colleges, and to obtain there a thorough theological education.

Lull was not the first Christian to be interested in Semitic languages. There had been notable linguists in Spain, and it was through their translation of Arabic books into Latin that the knowledge of Aristotle began to seep back into the ignorant West. But Lull was almost certainly the first to relate the study of languages directly to the work of evangelism; he was not interested so much in the languages for themselves as in that to which they should lead – a competent understanding of the thought and the doctrines of the Saracens, and the possibility of elevated and charitable discourse with them on matters of religion.

The second of Lull's requirements was the composition of a book in which the truth of the Christian religion should be demonstrated by necessary reasons. We may doubt whether the composition of such a book is possible, and in fact the views of Lull were for a long time the subject of animated debate in the Roman Catholic world. But Lull was impelled in this direction by his own encounters with learned Muslims, and by what he had understood of their point of view. Muslim theology had developed its own scholasticism; it was confident that it could demonstrate the truth of its doctrines beyond the possibility of error. This was the challenge launched at Lull by the Grand Mufti of Bugia in Tunis, the 'Saracen bishop' as the ancient biography of Lull pleasantly calls him:

'If you hold that the law of Christ is true and that of Muhammad false, you must prove it by necessary reasons.'

Was this not a challenge that must necessarily be taken up?

The third requirement is the willingness to be a faithful and courageous witness among the Saracens, even at the cost of life itself. It was certainly a perilous affair to undertake the preaching of the Gospel in Islamic countries, where such preaching was, under Islamic law, an offence punishable with death. As Lull himself wrote:

Missionaries will convert the world by preaching, but also through the shedding of tears and blood and with great labour, and through a bitter death.

He himself was never the man to entertain thoughts which he was not prepared to translate into action. He seems to have paid four visits to North Africa in order to preach to the Muslims and to dispute with them in person. On the fourth of these visits, to Bugia in 1315, he was so roughly handled that he died of his injuries.

The liberation of Spain and Portugal was followed by an expansive period, during which the Christian forces pursued the Muslims into Africa, and set in motion a process which only the twentieth century has been able to reverse.

The Straits of Gibraltar were crossed in 1415, and Ceuta was captured. Other places followed, notably Tangier in 1471. A bishopric was created in Ceuta in 1421, another for Tangier in 1468.[22] But it cannot be said that these dioceses were in any way missionary: they were outposts of Portugal, and no more. This was not true of another early outpost of Portugal, the Canary Islands. The original inhabitants of these islands were probably of Berber stock, and in process of time have been almost completely assimilated to the immigrants from Europe. The bishopric established here in 1404 (transferred to Las Palmas in 1483) was one of the oldest Latin bishoprics outside Europe. The process of evangelization was slow; we have the names of at least two Dominican missionaries martyred by the inhabitants. But by the end of the

22. Naturally the bishop did not reside in Tangier, which in 1468 was still in Muslim hands.

century the Christianization of the islands was regarded as being complete.

Much more interesting, as a sign of European expansion and of far greater things to come, were the voyages of discovery organized by Prince Henry the Navigator (1394–1460) from about 1420 onwards. Prince Henry never left his own country and never went himself on any voyage of discovery. He was the guide, the director, and the inspirer of the explorers. Madeira and the Azores had been discovered, or rediscovered, by 1430. But far more important than these island voyages were the patient advances through which the western coasts of Africa gradually became known to Europe. In 1434 Cape Bojador was turned. In 1444 the first contacts were made with the Negro races of tropical Africa. In 1482 the mouth of the Congo was reached. In 1487 Bartholomew Diaz discovered the Cape of Good Hope.

In those days, when new races were discovered by European explorers, it was taken for granted that an attempt would be made to bring them to the Christian faith. The first Portuguese mission to the Congo set forth in 1490. Considerable doubt exists as to its composition, and as to the Orders which were represented among its members. Some success was attained: a local king and queen were baptized, and took the names of John and Eleonora. Towards the end of the century, their eldest son, who bore the Christian name of Don Affonso, sent a number of young men of good family, including one of his sons, Don Henrique, to Lisbon to study; he appealed for new missionaries to replace those who had died, and continued to send young Congolese to Portugal to study. It was the desire of the king of Portugal that Don Henrique should be raised to the episcopate. At last this was accomplished; in 1518 this African prince was consecrated as titular Bishop of Utica, and in 1521, after more than twenty years' absence, returned to his country as the first Vicar Apostolic for West Africa. But high hopes, as so often before, were frustrated. The African Bishop seems to have accomplished very little.[23] Missionaries were not replaced; Don Affonso died. By the middle of the sixteenth century the mission had died out, leaving hardly a trace of its existence.

But the story of this first African mission has carried us beyond the limits of this chapter. We are already in the world of the great

23. It is not absolutely certain that he ever returned to the Congo. On this episode, see C. P. Groves, *The Planting of Christianity in Africa*, Vol. 1 (1948), pp. 128–9.

discoveries, and of that revolution as a result of which Christianity became a world-wide and no longer a primarily Mediterranean religion.

5

The Age of Discovery, 1500–1600

In 1492 Christopher Columbus crossed the Atlantic, touched at the little island of Guanahari (San Salvador) in the Bahamas, believed himself to have reached the coast of India, and gave to the islands the name which they have wrongly borne ever since – the West Indies. In 1497 Vasco da Gama, following in the steps of Bartholomew Diaz, rounded the Cape of Good Hope, struck out across the open ocean, and reached the west coast of the true India at Calicut. Like almost all other Portuguese expeditions, the fleet of Vasco da Gama carried with it a number of priests.

It is impossible to exaggerate the enlargement of views which these discoveries brought both to the European mind and to the outlook of the Christian Church. New worlds, hitherto wholly unknown, were opened up to Western exploration. At last the back door into Asia had been found, behind the Muslims and the control that they had been able to exercise over the trade routes by land and sea which connected the West with Asia. It is clear from all the early records that the bold and hardy men who made the great voyages, and the rulers and others who stood behind them, had two great purposes in view: first, to bring the light of the true Gospel to hitherto unknown nations who had lived in darkness; secondly, and from the point of view of that age even more important, to enter into contact with the Christian Churches which were believed to be in existence in those lands, and so to make a great world alliance of the faithful, through which at last the power of the Muslims would be brought to the ground. The legend of Prester John, the Christian king who was believed to rule over a great empire somewhere in the hidden lands, was always present in men's minds. What exactly lay behind the legend it is difficult to say. Some have thought that Ethiopia, the Christian kingdom which really did exist in Africa, was the source of the legends; others that it is to be attributed to recollections, dimly diffused by travellers, of the Christian peoples – Onguts, Uighurs, and others – in the steppes of Russia and Mongolia, which had in course of time disintegrated or adopted the Muslim faith. Whatever the source of the stories, Prester John was for centuries a potent magnet, drawing Western Christians on the never-failing hope that somewhere, somehow, his kingdom would be found.

In the thirteenth and fourteenth centuries Venice and Genoa had been the great navigating powers. From the middle of the fifteenth century this role was taken over by Portugal, to which Spain not long after began to appear as a powerful competitor. This meant, inevitably, rivalries between the two powers, and an umpire was called in to arbitrate. The Pope had already recognized the discoveries of Portugal in Africa; the Bull *Romanus Pontifex* of Pope Nicholas V in 1454 had affirmed the right of the Portuguese to the peaceful occupation of all lands of the unbelievers that might be discovered along the west coast of Africa. In 1456 Pope Calixtus III gave to the Great Prior of the Order of Christ in Portugal (of which Henry the Navigator himself was administrator) spiritual oversight over all the existing dominions of the Crown of Portugal, and over any that might in the future be added to them. These were very extensive privileges. But the voyages of Columbus had been undertaken under the patronage of the Crown of Spain. How were the rights of the two expansionist powers to be related to one another?

In 1493, Pope Alexander VI set forth three Bulls, in which the matter was definitively settled. He recognized the exclusive right of the Spanish crown to trade with lands that had been or might be discovered to the west of the Atlantic, and at the same time laid on the king the injunction 'to bring to Christian faith the peoples who inhabit these islands and the mainland . . . and to send to the said islands and to the mainland wise, upright, God-fearing, and virtuous men who will be capable of instructing the indigenous peoples in good morals and in the Catholic faith'. To avoid rivalry between the powers, the Pope drew a line on the map from the North Pole to the South, west of the Azores; that which lay to the west was to belong to Spain, and that which lay to the east to Portugal. (By an agreement of 1494 the line was moved 370 leagues to the west, and thus Brazil – which in the year 1500 was discovered by the Portuguese explorer Pedro Alvares Cabral – was included in the Portuguese zone.) All rights and privileges which had been accorded to the king of Portugal in his area were to be equally enjoyed by the king of Spain in his.

Students have differed in their interpretation of the significance of the Pope's action. For the moment it was a useful and practical decision; it could not then be foreseen that within a few years Englishmen, Frenchmen, Dutchmen, and Danes would enter into these realms so cheerfully allocated by the Pope to two Roman Catholic sovereigns, and would dispute the privileges and monopolies which he had accorded. Nor did it occur to the Pope that, if he drew a line of division through the Atlantic, a similar line would have to be drawn through the Pacific, for at that time the latter ocean still lay hidden in the world of the unknown. For the moment all parties were very well satisfied. The Pope had emphasized the Christian element in these discoveries and conquests, and had laid upon the Christian powers the responsibility to find and support missionaries, and at a later date to found and endow bishoprics. The kings had secured the highest possible recognition of their ecclesiastical as well as political sovereignty over their new dominions, and could go ahead with a good conscience to make conquest a reality. It was only later on that Rome was to discover how many problems had, in fact, not been solved by the Bulls which set up the system of the 'Padroado', that system of royal patronage which seemed for the moment so admirably to meet the needs of the day.

The Portuguese had not been long in India before they discovered the existence of the 'Christians of St Thomas' in the far south. In 1500 Cabral landed at the small port of Cranganore, and there encountered a number of these Christians. He took back with him to Europe one of them named Joseph, supposedly the author of a book called *The Travels of Joseph the Indian*, through which a good deal of highly imaginative and inaccurate knowledge of Indian Christianity penetrated the western world.[1]

We have had occasional glimpses of this Indian Church through the eyes of medieval travellers; now they emerge into the full light of history. At the time of their first contacts with the Portuguese, the Christian community, which numbered 100,000, had been so long established in the country as not to be regarded as in any way foreign. In many respects it had become assimilated in manners and customs to the surrounding peoples. Yet this was undoubtedly a Christian people. Some authorities have stated that the Thomas Christians had lost contact with the Patriarch in Babylon, who was their spiritual head, and had long been without a bishop; this can hardly be true; it is probable that they had managed to maintain a

1. This book, first published in Latin under the title *Novus Orbis*, was translated by Simon Grynaeus and published at Basel in 1532. Later criticism has made it doubtful whether any of the material contained in it really goes back to Joseph the Indian at all. See L. W. Brown, *The Indian Christians of St Thomas* (1956), pp. 12–13.

measure of contact, and had had a succession of bishops all of whom came from Mesopotamia. No member of the community in Kērala[2] was raised to the episcopate until the seventeenth century. This external contact, and the use of the Syriac language in the liturgy, were safeguards without which this isolated community might well have been entirely absorbed into the ocean of Hinduism by which it was surrounded. These Christians were, without doubt, technically Nestorians; but they had little knowledge of theology, and like Rabban Sauma at an earlier date, were confident that they had loyally maintained the faith as it had come down to them from their founder the apostle Thomas.

The Portuguese were charmed by the simple dignity of these Christians. The 'Syrians'[3] were at first delighted with the Portuguese, and warmly welcomed the possibility of having such strong allies against local tyranny and Muslim aggression. It was only gradually that theological difficulties began to appear. The Syrians had never heard of the Pope; the Portuguese naturally regarded it as inconceivable that any Christians should exist in independence of the Bishop of Rome, whom they regarded as the sole Vicar of Christ on earth. The history that follows is tortuous and complex. Two parties were contending for supremacy in the Chaldaean Church in Mesopotamia; two rival patriarchs, one of whom had made his submission to Rome, were trying to oust one another; each was naturally desirous of attaching to himself the strong outlying part of his Church that lived in South India. But among the Portuguese a strong feeling was growing up that the Thomas Christians should come directly under the Pope, naturally through the Portuguese who represented him, and that the control of the patriarch over them should be eliminated. Goa, the centre of Portuguese dominion in India, had been raised to be a bishopric, the bishop being a suffragan of the Bishop of Funchal in Madeira. In 1557, Goa became an archbishopric, with suffragan sees in Malacca and Cochin, to which were later added Macao in China (1576), Cranganore (1600), and Mylapore (1606). The Archbishop of Goa was thus the representative of the authority of the

2. This is the name by which south-west India, the area in which Malayalam is spoken, is now known; it includes the former Indian states of Travancore and Cochin, and the former British district of South Malabar.

3. This common designation of the 'Thomas Christians' is misleading. It refers only to their ecclesiastical connection with Mesopotamia. No doubt many of the earliest Christians had been foreigners, but for centuries the 'Syrians' had been an essentially Indian community.

Western Church throughout the whole of East Asia.[4] This being so, was it not right and necessary that all Christians in the East should come directly under his jurisdiction?

A number of bishops from Mesopotamia were active in South India in the sixteenth century. Of two of them we have somewhat extensive information. Mar[5] Joseph, with one Mar Elias, had been consecrated by the pro-Roman patriarch Abdiso in about 1556 and sent to India. The Portuguese were not well pleased by the arrival of a bishop of this line, and kept Mar Joseph under strict observation in a monastery for eighteen months. At last, in 1558, he was allowed to go south, and took possession of his diocese in the 'Serra', the hill country of what was later the state of Travancore. Then followed an extraordinary series of accusations and persecutions. Joseph was accused of heresy – it is quite possible that he had slipped back from Roman to Nestorian ways of thinking – and was packed off to Lisbon. Cleared of all the charges against him, he was sent back to India, and arrived in 1565. The charges of heresy were renewed; he was condemned by the first Council of Goa in 1567. Again sent to Europe, he was again declared completely innocent; but he died in 1569, before he had had time to return for the third time to India.

One Mar Abraham had been sent from Mesopotamia by the rival patriarch, in response to a request from the Indian Christians, and had been enthusiastically received by them. Warned by the experiences of Mar Joseph, Mar Abraham managed for a time to keep clear of the Portuguese, but it was not long before he too was arrested and sent off to Rome. On the way, Abraham managed to escape and to make his way to the Romanizing patriarch, by whom he was approved, reconsecrated to the office of bishop, and sent on to Rome with commendatory letters. Here he won the favour of the Pope, was consecrated to the episcopate yet a third time,[6] and sent off again to Travancore, where he arrived in 1568. It is clear that he never trusted the Western missionaries and that they never trusted him; but apart from various rubs and

---

4. At a much later date (1886), the title of Patriarch of the Indies was added to the other dignities of the holder of the primatial see of the East. The Archbishop of Goa still retains the title, but it does not mean much in the modern world.

5. The title Mar (= lord) is commonly given to bishops in the Syriac-speaking Eastern Churches.

6. It is curious that Mar Abraham found it necessary for various reasons to ordain all his priests in Travancore three times over – to make sure that they really had been ordained!

accusations he managed fairly well to maintain his independent position until his death in 1597.

During the reign of Mar Abraham an event of great importance in the life of the Church took place. The Jesuits entered Kērala, and founded at Vaipicotta a seminary for the training of the clergy. In the past, training for the ministry had been minimal in the Syrian Church. Here, as elsewhere, what the Jesuits offered was very much better than anything else, and not surprisingly young men streamed in to take advantage of the instruction, which was given in Syriac as well as in Latin. This greatly helped forward the tendency of many in the ancient Church at that time to make the best terms they could with the Portuguese and with Rome.

The fate of the Syrian Church was sealed by the arrival in Goa of a new Archbishop, Aleixo da Menezes. Only thirty-five years old, of an aristocratic family, vigorous and devout, de Menezes had already held high office in Portugal, and was to hold even higher – after his return from India in 1609 – as Archbishop of Braga and viceroy of Portugal. Once arrived in India, Menezes had no doubt at all as to what was to happen: all Christians in India must come under his jurisdiction, all must adopt the Roman orthodoxy of the sixteenth century as defined by the Council of Trent, and there must be no nonsense about any independence.

The death of Mar Abraham gave Menezes the opportunity to act. In the autumn of 1598 he came down to the Serra, and carefully laid his plans. Having noted the deep reverence in which the people held their priests, and knowing also of the deep reverence of the priests for the bishop who had ordained them, he gave notice that he would hold ordinations.[7] The number of those ordained is not exactly known, but it cannot have been less than a hundred. Then the representatives of the ancient Church, clerical and lay, were summoned to meet the Archbishop at Udiyampērūr. What is commonly known as the Synod of Diamper opened on 20 June 1599. When it is observed that, together with 660 lay representatives, there were present only 153 priests, of whom certainly a good deal more than half had been ordained by Menezes within the last few months, it is clear that he had laid his plans well, and could be certain of a majority. In point of fact, very little was left to chance. Day after day decrees already prepared in

7. Some accounts maintain that Menezes had promised not to hold any ordinations in the Serra, and it is in fact doubtful how far he was canonically justified in doing so.

advance were read out in Portuguese; not much trouble was taken to make sure that the Syrians understood what was being read – it was taken for granted that they would consent. On 26 June everyone, beginning from the Archbishop, signed the decrees, and the Synod came to an end.

The actions of Menezes have been diversely judged by historians. To most of his contemporaries the Synod of Diamper seemed to be a glorious achievement; a great act of Church union had been carried through with a minimum of expense. Others have felt that Menezes was high-handed rather than high-minded, and that he had no business to rob an ancient Church of its independence in the name of an allegiance which they had never known and which they were not much interested to recognize. There are signs that Rome itself is today prepared to take a somewhat critical attitude to these proceedings.[8] But for the moment the triumph of Menezes was complete: the Church of St Thomas lay at his mercy. Syriac was not replaced by Latin as the liturgical language, and some harmless local customs were permitted, but in almost every detail Roman order and Roman practice prevailed. The wise and conciliatory Francis Roz, a Jesuit of the Seminary at Vaipicotta and a competent Syriac scholar, became Bishop of Angamālli. When the Syrians learned that he was not to be an independent archbishop but a suffragan of Goa, their resentment was considerable; but for the moment they could do nothing about it. For the time being the Church of the Thomas Christians, as an independent part of the family of Christ, had simply ceased to be.[9]

The story of the Syrian Christians has carried us some way forward in history, and a passing reference to the Jesuits in Travancore recalls us to what is perhaps the most important event in the missionary history of the Roman Catholic Church, the foundation of the Jesuit Order. On 15 August 1534, Ignatius Loyola had gathered round him in Paris the little group of six friends who were to form the kernel of the new militia of Christ –

8. In a book published at Rome in 1958 and dedicated to Cardinal Tisserant, Fr Jonas Thaliath (*The Synod of Diamper*, 1958) takes the view that Menezes had no canonical right to hold a synod in the Serra, that canonical requirements for a Synod were not met, that his actions were a characteristic piece of Western arrogance, and that the harm done by them began to be remedied only when Leo XIII in 1896 provided the ancient Church with its own independent Syrian hierarchy.

9. The history of the ancient Syrian Church is taken up again on pp. 228–31.

this strange new body of men who were to be neither secular priests nor religious, who were to be bound by the most rigid vows of obedience, were to be utterly subject to the Pope, and were to be devoted to the reconversion of heretics, and the conversion of pagans, to the Catholic faith. In 1540, by the Bull *Regimini militantis*, Paul III confirmed the existence of the new Order; within the next hundred years Jesuits were to lay their bones in almost every country of the known world and on the shores of almost every sea.

One of the first companions of Ignatius was the Basque Francis Xavier (1506–52), who was to become the most famous of all Roman Catholic missionaries, and one of the greatest missionaries in the whole history of the Church. To a passionate but disciplined nature, profound devotion, and an eager longing for the salvation of souls, Xavier added the wide outlook of the statesman and the capacity of the strategist for organization on a large scale. He went to India in 1542, not as an ordinary missionary but as the representative of the king of Portugal, armed with considerable powers, and with the right to correspond directly with the king. At the same time, as Apostolic Nuncio, he was furnished with extensive authority by the Pope.

His first port of call was Goa. Goa had grown into a great city, with as many churches and monasteries as could be found in a southern European city. But the moral condition of the inhabitants was deplorable. Wealth was flamboyant and irresponsible. The Europeans, coming without women, had naturally formed alliances with Indian women; the children, though nominally Christian, were left for the most part without any care or instruction, and tended to manifest the worst characteristics of both races. Considerable pressure had been brought to bear on the Hindu population to conform at least outwardly to Christianity, since idolatry could not be tolerated in the territory of a Christian sovereign. But not much progress had been achieved in making the conformity more than external. Goa was in a bad way. Xavier spent some months in the work of reforming it, but it was not his business to settle down as parish priest of Goa, and he was soon called away to a much larger task in South India.

In 1536 the entire caste of the Bharathas (Paravas), the fisher-folk of the Coromandel Coast, perhaps 10,000 of them, was baptized. They had been suffering grievously from the depredations of Muslim raiders from the north. Poor, wholly illiterate, and helpless, they turned to the Portuguese for protection;

protection was granted, the price to be paid for it being baptism. So all were baptized *en masse* – and then left for six years without instruction or pastoral care. This was Xavier's new field of work.

He came down to find a rough, hardy, undisciplined, but good-hearted folk, physically strong and admirably dextrous in the management of their catamarans – their only source of livelihood – living scattered in small villages along 200 miles of coast. The movement which had brought them into the Church had not touched one single other caste; they lived as scattered islands in the midst of a solidly Hindu population. They could not read or write, and they knew nothing whatever of the Christian faith which they were supposed to profess. The real greatness of Xavier's work, as of his character, is obscured for us by the haze of sentimental legend which has collected around it. In spite of his own firm rejection of the claim, later ages believed that he had a miraculous gift of tongues; the evidence of his letters shows that, in the three years that he spent on the coast, he never acquired more than a rudimentary knowledge of Tamil, that most difficult form of human speech. But the method that he followed was perhaps the best that could possibly have been devised. First, with the help of very imperfect interpreters, he hammered out a rough translation of the Lord's Prayer, the Creed, and the Ten Commandments, which was highly defective, as later investigation proved. Then, in each village he would gather the boys around him – he seems always to have had a wonderful capacity for attracting the young – taught them these Christian elements by heart, and then set them to instruct the older people. The Sunday service consisted of repeating the things that had been learned in a kind of litany:

On Sundays I assemble all the people, men and women, young and old, and get them to repeat the prayers in their language. They take much pleasure in doing so, and come to the meetings gladly . . . I give out the First Commandment, which they repeat, and then we say all together, Jesus Christ, Son of God, grant us grace to love thee above all things. When we have asked for this grace, we recite the Pater Noster together, and then cry with one accord, Holy Mary, Mother of Jesus Christ, obtain for us grace from thy Son to enable us to keep the First Commandment. Next we say an Ave Maria, and proceed in the same manner through each of the remaining nine Commandments. And just as we say twelve Paters and Aves in honour of the twelve articles of the Creed, so we say ten Paters and Aves in honour of the ten Commandments, asking God to give us grace to keep them well.

Xavier had to suffer bitterly from the incompetence of his assistants, from the evil lives and violence of the Portuguese on the coast, from the ignorance of the Paravas and their unwillingness to change. But he had laid a good foundation; he arrived to find an untutored mob, he left behind him a Church in being. By the end of the century, the Jesuits had gathered the Paravas into sixteen large villages, in each of which a Jesuit father was resident. Discipline was stern; on Sunday no catamaran might go out to fish, and a part of every Friday's catch had to be contributed to the Church. Not much was done for education; but the work has endured. The visitor who crosses the sandhills to Manappādu today, expecting to enter a village of huts, is astonished to find himself in a city of palaces, dominated by two gigantic churches.

Before we follow Xavier to the Far East, we must pause to consider briefly the second of the outstanding ventures of the early Jesuits in India.

The arrival of the Portuguese in India coincided with the development of the Mogul power. In 1526 Babur had descended from the fastnesses of Afghanistan, and defeated the rival powers in a great battle at Panipat. This was the beginning of that Mogul dominion in India which lasted until 1858, though in increasingly shadowy form during the last century of its existence. The Moguls were foreigners in India, no less than the British. Babur in his *Memoirs* describes the India which he had come to rule in no flattering terms:

Hindustan is a country that has few pleasures to recommend it. The people are not handsome. They have no idea of the charms of friendly society, of frankly mixing together, or of familiar intercourse. They have no genius, no comprehension of mind, no politeness of manner, no kindness or fellow-feeling, no ingenuity or mechanical invention in planning or executing their handicraft works, no skill or knowledge in design or architecture; they have no horses, no good flesh, no grapes or musk-melons, no good fruits, no ice or cold water, no good food or bread in their bazaars, no baths or colleges, no candles, no torches, not a candlestick.

The Moguls never forgot their alien origin, and their connection with that Persian culture which they made fashionable in India. But they managed, much more than the British, to make themselves at home; and, though Muslims, they accorded a considerable measure of toleration to their Hindu subjects.

Akbar, who ruled from 1556 till 1605, was one of the greatest monarchs of whom we have record in history. In his day India more nearly attained unity than at any time up to the final completion of the British supremacy in the middle of the nineteenth century. Peace was maintained throughout this wide realm; administration reached a high level of efficiency, and, as always under the Moguls, attention was directed to the development of art and culture. In addition, Akbar had a deep and sincere interest in religion, and was disturbed by the divisive effects that it tended to have on his subjects. He decided to investigate the claims of Christianity, and sent a message to Goa to the effect that he would welcome the presence of some Jesuit fathers at his court.

Such an invitation was bound to meet with immediate response. In Europe the Jesuits had extended their influence largely through their successful approach to rulers and to the aristocratic classes. If opportunities were given in India for a similar approach, the results might be beyond calculation. Father Rudolf Aquaviva was despatched, with a number of companions, and reached the court of Akbar in 1580. The reception accorded to the missionaries lacked nothing in cordiality. A number of public disputations on religion were held in the presence of the emperor himself. The missionaries had access to all classes of the population, and to members of the emperor's family, including even the ladies of the harem. For a time hopes ran high of the conversion of Akbar himself, and of other members of the court in high places.

But, in fact, the mission was based on a miscalculation. Akbar, whose critical intellect had begun, about 1575, to be dissatisfied with orthodox Islam as interpreted by the learned men of his entourage, was not at all inclined to commit himself to another of the disputing faiths. His mind was already reaching out in the direction of a new religion, which should combine the merits of them all, and of which he himself should be the prophet and the centre. In 1580, just at the time of the arrival of the Jesuit fathers, the *Din Illāhi*, the divine faith, was proclaimed. The new faith was rigidly monotheistic, but generous in the extreme in its borrowings from existing religions:

In ceremonies the *hōm* or fire sacrifice was borrowed from Hinduism, the worship of fire from the Parsis, prostration from Islam, and baptism from Christianity. The cult was in fact highly syncretistic as well as aristocratic. It can be loosely described as a royal theosophy.[10]

10. Percival Spear, *India* (1961), p. 135.

The *Din Illāhi* never really caught on, and after the death of Akbar it rapidly faded away. Its importance was that it closed the mind of Akbar to any serious consideration of the Christian faith. He remained on excellent terms with the missionaries; a second mission was sent in 1591, and a third in 1595.[11] The missionaries lived in an alternation of hope and frustration, until it became clear that Akbar would never attach himself to their party. Even after his death, Jesuits continued to reside at the court of the Moguls, and the mission was maintained, though in a rather fitful and spasmodic fashion, till the dissolution of the Jesuit Order two centuries later. But the missionaries became increasingly chaplains to the Armenians and other foreigners who frequented the court, and hope of penetrating the highest circles in the land was gradually abandoned.

The Portuguese had early extended their voyages of discovery beyond India to South-east Asia. *Malacca* had been occupied in 1511, and became the centre of Portuguese operations in the spice islands, until in the seventeenth century the Dutch became the dominant power in this region and the Portuguese were driven out.

Xavier, whose commission from king and Pope extended to the whole of the East, spent some months in this region in 1546 and 1547. But his eager mind was already ranging onwards, and was filled with thoughts of *Japan*.

Japan had for some centuries been known to the West only through the somewhat imaginative eyes of Marco Polo, who had never been there:

Chipangu is an Island towards the east in the high seas, 1,500 miles distant from the continent; and a very great Island it is. The people are white, civilized, and well-favoured. They are Idolaters and are dependent on nobody. And I can tell you the quantity of gold they have is endless. . . . Moreover all the pavement of the Palace, and the floors of its chambers, are entirely of gold, in plates like slabs of stone, a good two fingers thick; and the windows also are of gold, so that altogether the richness of this Palace is past all bounds and belief.[12]

It seems that the first contact in historical times was made by a group of Portuguese mariners, who in 1542 were driven far out of

---

11. The head of this third mission was Fr Jerome Xavier, a great-nephew of Francis Xavier, who was at the Mogul court almost continuously from 1595 till 1615. On all this, see Sir Edward Maclagan, *The Jesuits and the Great Mogul* (1932).
12. H. Yule, *The Book of Ser Marco Polo*, Vol. II (1903), pp. 199–200.

their course by a storm and found themselves on the shores of the unknown land.

A certain Anjiro (Yajiro), who had killed a man in Japan, had escaped from justice and by devious ways had made his way to Goa. There Xavier met him in 1548, and learned from him something of the ways of his country:

I asked him whether, if I went back with him to his country, the Japanese would become Christians, and he said that they would not do so, until they had first asked me many questions and seen how I answered and how much I knew. Above all they would want to observe if I lived in conformity with what I said and believed. If I did those two things, answered the questions to their satisfaction and so demeaned myself that they could not find anything to blame in my conduct, then, after knowing me for six months, the king, the nobility, and all other people of discretion would become Christians, for the Japanese, he said, are entirely guided by the law of reason.

It is not surprising that the soul of Xavier became inflamed by the desire to preach the Gospel to this superior people. It was with high hopes that at last, on 15 August 1549, after many perils passed, he landed – together with two Jesuits and Yajiro and his Japanese attendants – at the port of Kagoshima, Yajiro's native town. Yajiro proved indeed to be a broken reed: he had very little knowledge of his own country; he was not a highly educated man; his efforts at the translation of Christian terms into Japanese was to lead the missionaries into errors, which they were later sorely to rue, and his character was far from being altogether admirable. But the moment of the arrival of the missionaries was on the whole propitious. Japan was passing through a period of grave political disorder; there was no central authority, and the land was divided up among 250 *daimyos*, local rulers, each of whom claimed full authority in his own dominions. The country was open to the foreigner. The Japanese were eager for trade, and were especially interested in guns, which, once acquired, they set to work to copy in their own arsenals, with the remarkable Japanese capacity for imitation. Buddhism was in discredit; there was no strongly established form of national religion to resist the preaching of the Gospel, and there was a genuine openness to new ideas.

The missionaries suffered severely from the cold – they had no idea in advance of what a Japanese winter could be like. They had difficulty in getting enough to eat. They wrestled with the daunting difficulties of the language:

Now we are like so many statues amongst them, for they speak and talk to us about many things, whilst we, not understanding the language, hold our peace. And now we have to be as little children learning the language.

They gradually became aware of the imperfections of Yajiro's translations, in particular of the harm wrought by his choice of the wholly inappropriate Buddhist term *Dainichi* to represent 'God' – a difficulty the missionaries then dodged by simply introducing Portuguese terms into Japanese to represent the Christian ideas. And yet friendship and understanding did develop, and in spite of all disappointments Xavier never lost his feelings of respect for the Japanese. In a letter of 5 November 1549 he writes:

Firstly the people whom we have met so far are the best who have as yet been discovered, and it seems to me that we shall never find among heathens another race to equal the Japanese. They are a people of very good manners, good in general, and not malicious; they are men of honour to a marvel, and prize honour above all else in the world. . . . They are a people of very good will, very sociable and very desirous of knowledge; they are very fond of hearing about the things of God, chiefly when they understand them. . . . They like to hear things propounded according to reason; and, granted that there are sins and vices among them, when one reasons with them, pointing out that what they do is evil, they are convinced by this reasoning.

These early contacts with the Japanese produced a change in Xavier's understanding of the nature of Christian missionary work which was to be of the greatest significance for the whole future of the enterprise. In earlier years he had been inclined to accept uncritically the doctrine of the *tabula rasa* – the view that in non-Christian life and systems there is nothing on which the missionary can build, and that everything must simply be levelled to the ground before anything Christian can be built up. This was the general view of the Spanish missionaries in Latin America and the West Indies; in his dealings with the simple and illiterate fishers in South India, Xavier had seen no reason to modify it. But now that he was confronted by a civilization with so many elements of nobility in it, he saw that, while the Gospel must transform and refine and recreate, it need not necessarily reject as worthless everything that has come before. This new idea was to be fruitful in results – and also in controversies.

Xavier stayed twenty-seven months in Japan. He left behind him three little groups of converts; how much they understood of the Gospel is questionable – they probably imagined themselves to have accepted a new and superior kind of Buddhism. The great

thing, however, was that a beginning had been made and the way
had been shown. A French scholar, Claude Maître, has summed
up in the following terms what Xavier had achieved:

With remarkable penetration he had grasped the social and political
situation in Japan, and had settled on the methods which could ensure
success. He had realized that it was both impossible and useless to gain
access to the emperor or to the Shogûn (Mayor of the Palace); and that on
the other hand conversions among the lower classes would never be able to
produce a great movement towards the Faith. The only way to secure
permanent results was to win over the local rulers with their almost
complete independence – this is what the *daimyos* were at that time –
nothing, therefore, must be neglected which might help to win their
favour, their confidence, and, if possible, their conversion. He had understood that, if this proud, intelligent, logical people, with its passion for
disputation, was ever to be won, it would be necessary to send missionaries
of the highest quality, flexible enough to adapt themselves to the customs
of the country to the limit of what was permitted by their faith, but strong
enough in character to fashion their conduct according to the most rigid
requirements of the faith which they taught.[13]

Until 1593 the evangelization of Japan was entirely in the hands
of the Jesuits. The number of missionaries increased rapidly, and
their work was crowned with notable success. The first converts
had been from among the poorer classes. In 1563 began the
conversion of the *daimyos*; the first to receive baptism was Omura
Sumitada, who remained faithful and active to the end of his life.
His example was rapidly followed by others, and in many cases the
conversion of the *daimyo* was followed by that of the majority of his
subjects. This did not always take place immediately; in 1571
Sumitada had only 5,600 Christian subjects, but then the mass
movement set in, and by 1575 the whole population of the region –
amounting in all to more than 50,000 – had become Christian. Of
the depth and sincerity of these conversions it is hard to judge. As
in the case of other mass movements there were no doubt many
weaknesses and shadows, but unquestionably there was in Japan
an élite of convinced and devoted Christians.

In 1579 Japan was visited by Alessandro Valignano (1539–
1606), an Italian Jesuit who had been appointed Visitor of all the
eastern regions. He left his impress on the Japan mission in three
remarkable ways.

He held very strongly the view that in all possible ways,
especially in external matters, missionaries and Christians must

13. Quoted in Delacroix, *Histoire universelle*, Vol. I, pp. 284–5.

adapt themselves to local custom and prejudice. The then Superior of the Mission, Francis Cabral, did not see eye to eye with the Visitor on every point; the crucial issue – one that may seem utterly trivial to the Western reader, unfamiliar with the importance that may attach to such details in an Eastern country – related to the dress of the missionary: should this be of cotton or of silk? Cabral held that cotton was more in accordance with evangelical poverty; Valignano decided in favour of silk, and there can be little doubt that in the circumstances of the time he was right, since a missionary dressed in cotton was inevitably associated in local opinion with the poorer classes and denied access to the wealthy and the influential.

Secondly, Valignano decided that the time had come when selected Japanese should see for themselves the glories of the Christian world of which they had heard from the missionaries. Four young men of noble family in Kyushu were selected to make the hazardous journey to Europe, and set out in 1582 under the care of Valignano and of a Jesuit Father who travelled with them as their tutor. It was not until the year 1590 that they returned to Japan. In the course of their travels they were received by King Philip of Spain and by Pope Gregory XIII; such an unusual group of travellers attracted great attention throughout the Christian world.

In the third place Valignano held the view that the time had come for Japanese to be admitted to the priesthood. In this, needless to say, he was opposed by the redoubtable Cabral. The Japanese, affirmed Cabral, are naturally proud; if they are put on the same level as the Europeans through admission to the priesthood, they will be swept away with intolerable arrogance. But Valignano had his way. A seminary was opened; the statistics for the year 1593 show that in that year fifty-six European priests and eleven lay brothers were active in the mission, and that the seminary had eighty-seven students together with five novices. Most of those who had attached themselves to the Jesuit Order served as *dojuku*, catechists of a higher order; only those were admitted to this rank who had taken the vow of celibacy and had pledged themselves to serve the mission till the end of their lives. In 1601 there were no less than 250 *dojuku*, but none had yet been ordained to the priesthood, for the simple reason that there was no bishop in Japan. A Jesuit had been appointed Bishop of Funai in 1587, but had died on the way. His successor, Pedro Martinez, arrived in Nagasaki on 14 August 1596, but found the mission in such confusion, through rivalries between the Portuguese and the Spaniards who had recently come in from Manila, that he decided to return to Rome to seek guidance, and died on the voyage. Fortunately he had been provided with a suffragan bishop, Luiz de Cerquiera, and it was he who on 22 September 1601 carried out the first ordination of Japanese priests. One was a secular; two were Jesuits – Sebastian Chimura, and Aloysius Niabara from Nagasaki; of these the former died as a martyr on 10 September 1622.[14]

For in the meantime a complete change had taken place in the political situation of Japan, and also in the situation of the Christian Church, which by the end of the century was reckoned to have 300,000 baptized believers. The chaos of the period of the *daimyos* was about to pass away. By about 1590 the first of the new centralizing rulers, Hideyoshi, had managed to subject the whole of Japan to his control, and was thus the first ruler for 500 years to bring the country once again to unity. He was followed after the brief reign of his son Hiyadori, by Ieyasu (1542–1616) and Iemitsu (1603–51), under whom persecution of the Christians reached such a level of ferocity that the flourishing work of half a century was demolished and the Christian problem solved by the death or apostasy of almost all the believers.

The exact motives of the persecution of the Christians are a little difficult to fathom. In part, the position of the Jesuits had been weakened by the arrival of the Franciscans and Dominicans from Manila, and by the manifest lack of unity among the missionaries themselves, still more by the arrival of the 'red-heads', the Dutch and British, who lost no opportunity of carrying forward in Japan the feuds which divided their nations in Europe. The most remarkable of the British, Will Adams, who arrived in 1600, lived for many years in Japan and was employed by the *shogûn* as the builder of his fleet. The Jesuits roundly blamed the Spanish Franciscans for the violent reaction against Christianity, and there is reason to think that the rash talk of the latter did suggest to the sensitive Japanese that they were there as forerunners of an army of conquest, and that Christian infiltration would be followed by

14. The original authorities differ somewhat from one another. C. R. Boxer states that two Japanese Jesuits were ordained in 1602, and the first of the secular priests two years later; *The Christian Century in Japan* (1951), p. 226. H. Cieslick, sj, also, in his extremely important study 'Die Geschichte der kirchlichen Hierarchie in der alten Japanesischen Mission' (*Neue Zeitschrift für Missionswissenschaft*, April 1962, pp. 81–107), speaks only of the two Jesuits, but adds that in 1605 the first Japanese secular priest took over the charge of a parish in Nagasaki.

political occupation. But, when all is said and done, Christians were persecuted because they were Christians and had introduced into Japan a law which turned the world upside down.

In 1587 Hideyoshi had issued an order of expulsion against the foreigners:

Japan is a country of the *Kami* [the gods of Japan] and for the padres to come hither and preach a devilish law is a most reprehensible and evil thing. . . . Since such a thing is intolerable, I am resolved that the padres should not stay on Japanese soil. I therefore order that having settled their affairs within twenty days, they must return to their own country.

This edict was not strictly put into execution. It was not until 1614 that persecution set in in earnest; it then continued, with ups and downs of fury, till 1630, by which time the Christianity of Japan had been destroyed. The decree of 1614 affirmed that:

The Kirishitan band have come to Japan, not only sending their merchant vessels to exchange commodities, but also longing to disseminate an evil law, to overthrow true doctrine, so that they may change the government of the country and obtain possession of the land. This is the germ of great disaster, and must be crushed.

A number of missionaries left Japan:

All the Fathers did desire to remayne hid and diguised in Japan, to help the Christians and be partakers of their sufferings; but it could not be, by reason of the strict order that was taken against their stay, and the extreme difficulty in finding means to keep them secret.

Yet twenty-seven Jesuits, fifteen friars, and five secular clergy did manage to evade the order of banishment. It was not until April 1617 that the first martyrdoms of Europeans took place, a Jesuit and a Franciscan being beheaded at Omura at that time, and a Dominican and an Augustinian a little later in the same area.

Every kind of cruelty was practised on the pitiable victims of the persecution. Crucifixion was the method usually employed in the case of Japanese Christians; on one occasion seventy Japanese at Yedo were crucified upside down at low water, and were drowned as the tide came in. For Europeans the penalty was generally burning alive:

Bits were put in their mouths to hinder them from speaking; and their heads being pulled backwards, with halters put about their necks and tied behind them, they were compelled to hold their faces directly upwards; and thus sitting upon a lean horse they were carried to the place designed for their martyrdom.

As the persecution moved forward, what the authorities wanted was not death but apostasy. The torments were carried to the point at which resistance was almost impossible; again and again victims were brought back from the point of death, and then again put to the torture. Apostasies among the Japanese were very numerous, and we have the records of seven missionaries, all as it appears Jesuits, who gave way and apostatized. The first case was in 1633. Most of these almost immediately afterwards recalled their apostasy and died; but one lived on in Japan till 1685, apparently at the end declaring that he was still a Christian.

As usual, legend has greatly exaggerated the numbers of the martyrs. Careful calculation has shown that the number of those put to death was about 1,900 in twenty-four years, of whom sixty-two were European missionaries. To these must be added the far larger number of those who died from the hardships of imprisonment and malnutrition. There were, no doubt, cases of timidity and too ready repudiation of the faith. But the great Japanese persecution has added a memorable chapter to the long record of Christian endurance and faithfulness unto death. More than two centuries were to pass before Japan was again open to Christian preaching, but, as later discovery was to show, even the bitterest persecution had not been able entirely to destroy the seed of the Gospel.

China proved for a long time far less accessible to the Gospel than Japan.[15] The well-known Chinese xenophobia kept the doors entirely closed, except as the Chinese themselves expressed it, 'to members of subject races who come to pay tribute, to Muhammadan merchants who come to trade under the guise of paying tribute, and to foreigners who wish to settle in the empire, being lured by the good fame of Chinese virtues'. In spite of the prohibition, the Portuguese had managed in 1557 to install themselves in the tiny settlement of Macao at the mouth of the Canton river, which is still Portuguese territory.

Macao, like other Portuguese settlements in the East, soon became a curious blend of East and West, with churches and monasteries, trading centres, a considerable half-caste population, and the maritime riff-raff of half the nations of the earth. It was also to be the jumping-off place of many missionary enterprises. There,

15. Francis Xavier died on 3 December 1552 on the island of Sancian, close to the coast of China, looking out on the land which it had proved impossible for him to enter. See J. Brodrick, *St Francis Xavier* (1952), p. 526.

in 1579, came the Visitor Valignano. A well-known anecdote records how, looking out on the not distant mainland, he cried out: 'Rock, rock, oh when wilt thou open, rock?' He found no encouragement in Macao for his plans for the evangelization of China; the priests who were resident there told him that the conversion of a Chinese was completely impossible.

Valignano bethought him of a thirty-year-old Italian who was then teaching in the seminary in Goa, and brought to Macao the man who was to become, after Xavier, the most famous of all Roman Catholic missionaries in the East – Matthew Ricci (1552–1610). Ricci's first task was to settle in Macao, to learn the Chinese language and Chinese customs – and to wait for the Rock to open.[16]

Success was easier than might have been expected. In 1583 Ricci and a companion received from the viceroy of the province permission to settle in Chaoch'ing, the provincial capital. Step by step Ricci moved towards the imperial capital, and at last in 1600 received permission to enter it. The Chinese of that period regarded theirs as the only true civilization in the world, and could not imagine that any foreigner could have come to China for any reason but to do homage to the Son of Heaven. It was in this guise that Ricci presented his plea at the imperial court of Wan-li:

Li Ma-ton, your Majesty's servant, come from the Far West, addresses himself to your Majesty with respect, in order to offer gifts from his country. Your Majesty's servant comes from a far distant land which has never exchanged presents with the Middle Kingdom. Despite the distance, fame told me of the remarkable teaching and fine institutions with which the imperial court has endowed all its peoples. I desired to share these advantages and live out my life as one of your Majesty's subjects, hoping in return to be of some small use.

The point at which he was able to be of use was the repairing of clocks. Two clocks were among the presents which he had brought with him; when they ran down, the Chinese experts had no idea how to start them again. The emperor, who never saw the face of any living person except his eunuchs and the women of his harem, had been particularly pleased with the clocks; the skill of Ricci in keeping them in order gained his warm approval, further built up by Ricci's skill as a maker of maps. This imperial favour made it

16. G. H. Dunne, sj, *Generation of Giants: the First Jesuits in China* (London, 1962), though full and well-informed, has been rather sharply criticized as giving only the point of view of the Jesuits, and doing less than justice to the work of the other Orders.

possible for Ricci to remain in the capital for ten years, and gradually to bring into being the nucleus of a Christian Church, and of Chinese Christian literature.

Like all pioneers, Ricci was faced with the thorny problem of finding Chinese equivalents for Christian terms, and of deciding how far ancient Chinese custom was reconcilable with Christian principle. From the start he had inclined to the later view of Francis Xavier – that in dealing with a great and ancient civilization it is necessary to proceed with great circumspection and respect. His travels had made him well acquainted with the Chinese suspicion of everything foreign; if Christianity was to be acceptable to the Chinese, it must be made as little foreign as possible. It was easy to announce the principle – to apply it in detail was difficult beyond imagination.

The first question related to the translation of the word 'God' – always a tangled problem for the missionary. Ricci generally used the expression *T'ien Chu*, Lord of Heaven; in one of his earliest Catechisms he had written that 'those who adore Heaven instead of the Lord of Heaven are like a man who, desiring to pay the Emperor homage, prostrates himself before the imperial palace at Peking and venerates its beauty'. But he had convinced himself that the ancient Chinese terms *Shang-Ti* and *T'ien* (simply 'Heaven') have a theistic significance and can rightly be used by Christians. Similarly, he held that the Chinese word *Sheng*, usually translated 'holy', was used in a wide sense of anything venerable, so that there was nothing improper in Christians using it of Confucius – good ground for the later cavil of his enemies that he had added the Chinese teacher to the Christian pantheon as 'St Confucius'.

In China the whole of society rests on the cohesion of the family, of which the reverence paid to ancestors is symbolic. Is this pagan in character, or has it only the character of civic and family respect?

Ricci, after prolonged study, took the moderate position, deciding that the rites in honour of Confucius and family had only a civil significance and that Christians could engage in them in so far as the laws of the Empire required. He would trust the Chinese Christians to decide eventually what they could and could not do, and he hoped that the Catholic practices concerning burial and honouring the dead would gradually supplant those of the older China.[17]

17. K. S. Latourette, *A History of Christian Missions in China* (1929), p. 134.

Under Ricci's wise guidance, both as missionary in Peking and as Jesuit superior for the whole of China, the mission continued to flourish. A number of converts, among them members of notable families and scholars of considerable distinction,[18] had been baptized. At the time of Ricci's death, on 10 May 1610, it was reckoned that the Church had about 2,000 members. Yet the presence of the missionaries and the lives of the converts were dependent on the ever-shifting winds of imperial favour, as was seen in the occurrence of persecutions, severe while they lasted but not of long duration, in 1616 and again in 1622. As usual, part of the accusation was that the missionaries were seditious; but it seems that no lives were lost, and it was not very long before the missionaries were back at their work.

The opening years of the seventeenth century were marked by one of the most venturesome and heroic missionary journeys ever undertaken. On 29 October 1602 Benedict de Goes, a lay brother of the Society of Jesus who had been born in the Azores in 1562, set out from Agra in disguise, to settle finally the questions of the identity of Cathay, and of the existence of the Great Christian realm of Prester John. The journey across Central Asia, now everywhere in the hands of the Muslims, was perilous and slow. It was only at Christmas 1605, more than three years after leaving Agra, that de Goes arrived in the city of Suchow in Szechwan, and realized beyond all possibility of doubt that Cathay was in reality China. In Suchow he was compelled reluctantly to dwell practically as a prisoner in the Muslim quarter. On Easter Day 1606 he wrote to the missionaries at Peking:

I am a member of the Society. I was sent by my superiors to discover Cathay, but I now believe that no such country exists, for I have traversed Asia without finding it, and this country which we in Europe call China is known to the people of Central Asia as Cathay. I have found no Christians, despite the tales of so many Muhammadans. I beg you, Fathers, or any other Portuguese Christians in Peking, to help me escape from the hands of the infidels.

This letter is evidence of the decline in Western knowledge of Central Asia since the days of Rabban Sauma and of John of Monte Corvino. The journey which proved at last the identity of Cathay with China was of the greatest scientific value, though,

18. The most outstanding of all was Hsü Kuang-ch'i, baptized under the name of Paul, who was a native of Zikawei in the neighbourhood of Shanghai.

now that the sea route was open and largely controlled by Christians, the land route had less significance for missionary work. The letter of de Goes took eight months to reach Peking. Help was at once sent, but the messenger could not arrive in Suchow till March 1607. By that time de Goes was dying; in fact he died ten days after the arrival of the lay brother from Peking, and was not able to carry out his purpose of returning to Europe by the sea route.[19]

So many things were happening at once in this vigorous sixteenth century that it is impossible to keep the happenings in different areas entirely separate from one another. A reference to the arrival in Japan of Spanish missionaries from Manila has indicated that the *Philippines* had already become a mission field. In 1579, when the Pope created the bishopric of Manila (raised to be an archbishopric in 1595), it ranked as a suffragan see of Mexico! This made it plain that the islands were regarded as belonging to the Spanish field of authority; the natural route of approach to them was across the Pacific from Mexico, and not by the sea route through the Indian Ocean.

The first missionaries, the Augustinians, seem to have landed in 1565[20]; by the end of the century a number of other Orders, including the Spanish Jesuits, had come in, and the islands were well stocked with Christian teachers. Here there was no powerful and ancient civilization to oppose the progress of the Gospel; nor was there potential wealth to attract the demoralizing influences of the Western traders. The tribes were simple, disunited, and easily accessible. As in the new world, Spanish discovery was followed by Spanish occupation; by the end of the century the islands as a whole had passed under Spanish control. The inhabitants were treated kindly; there are few tales of massacre or atrocity.

The missionary method followed by all the Orders was the same – the creation of strong Christian villages, in which church, school, hospital, and orphanage all played their part. In large measure the people were allowed to retain their old manners and customs, and their own languages. In 1601, the Jesuits opened to Filipinos the schools which had been founded for the education of Spanish children. In 1611, the Dominicans founded in Manila the college which was later to become a university. The tribes living in the

19. For de Goes, see C. Wessels, *Early Jesuit Travellers in Central Asia, 1603–1721* (The Hague, 1924), where some of the early documents are printed in full.

20. Mass had been celebrated in the Philippines as early as 1521 by priests accompanying the expedition of Magellan.

remote mountains, and the rough Muhammadan Moros, were hardly touched. Otherwise within a century the whole population had been after a fashion Christianized. Two dangers affected the progress of the work. First, the Church was in possession of considerable riches; a great deal of time was spent on the management and administration of estates, to the detriment of spiritual work. The accusations of commercial involvement and inordinate wealth, later made (especially against the Jesuits), were not altogether without foundation. And, as is always the case with mass movements, much of the Christianization remained very superficial. Yet to this day the Philippines remain unique in the world as the one Christian nation in the East; Filipinos have no background of an ancient non-Christian culture – the only culture that they knew till the end of the nineteenth century was that form of Christianity which came to them with the Spaniards in the sixteenth century.

We must now turn to the other side of the world, to consider the success of the Spaniards and the Portuguese in *Central* and *South America*.

The approach of these two powers to the New World of the West was always marked by three considerations – conquest, settlement, and evangelization. The peoples of these unknown lands were to be brought permanently under the dominion of the Christian kings, to whom God through the Pope had given sovereignty. This dominion was to be maintained through the presence of a considerable number of Europeans as permanent settlers and residents – an expedition of 1502 to Hispaniola brought with it 2,500 prospective colonists. The purpose of this Christian rule was to create Christian peoples out of those who were regarded by their conquerors as members of barbarous and pagan races. So the instructions given by the king of Spain to his early governors included the requirements that they should care for the Indians without the use of violence, that they should settle them in villages, and that they should build churches and schools.

Nothing is more astonishing than the rapidity with which the Spanish and Portuguese conquests were accomplished. The first voyage of Columbus took place in 1492. By 1515 the occupation of the West Indies was complete. Cortés made his first contacts with the Aztecs in 1519; by 1521 this proud and notably civilized people had finally lost its independence. Ten years later Pizarro entered the realm of the Incas in Peru; within five years he was master of the whole country. Brazil had been discovered by Cabral in 1500. The Portuguese never penetrated far beyond the coastal regions of this vast country, but by 1550 they had stations at intervals along the whole coast-line. São Paulo, now the largest city in South America, was founded in 1553–4. The regions of La Plata, now Argentina and Paraguay, were occupied rather later by the Spaniards, but before the end of the century the Jesuits had begun that notable missionary enterprise which carried them far into the desolate regions of the Chaco.

With every expedition for exploration or conquest came priests and friars. The major part of the work was undertaken by Franciscans and Dominicans, with the Jesuits following a little later. The dates of the creation of bishoprics will serve as a useful indication of the speed and direction of Christian occupation and organization. The first bishopric west of the Atlantic, that of Santo Domingo, was set up in 1511; by 1522 the ecclesiastical organization of the Antilles, with eight bishoprics, was complete. The first diocese in Mexico was Tlaxcala (1525); to this Mexico City was added in the following year. In 1548 Mexico became the metropolitical see, with seven dioceses under it. In South America, Caracas was the first diocese. Lima followed in 1541, and by 1575 was the metropolitical see of an enormous province, extending over the countries that are now called Ecuador, Bolivia, Peru, and Chile. In the La Plata region, four bishoprics were founded – the first Asuncion in 1547, the fourth Buenos Aires in 1582. Brazil received its first bishop in 1551, for the diocese of San Salvador de Bahia.

Neither Spaniards nor Portuguese had to face long and arduous campaigns in their easy and rapid conquest of this new world. The Aztecs, through their cruelty, had made themselves hated by the neighbouring peoples, among whom the Spaniards found ready allies. The rigid hierarchical rule of the Inca civilization had robbed the people of independence and initiative; their resistance was brief and ineffective. Similarly, when the Gospel was introduced as an accompaniment of Spanish civilization, the peoples seem to have shown little unwillingness to receive it. Peter of Ghent, one of the early Franciscan missionaries in Mexico, wrote in a letter of 27 June 1529:

I and the brother who was with me baptized in this province of Mexico upwards of 200,000 persons – so many in fact that I cannot give an accurate estimate of the number. Often we baptized in a single day 14,000 people, sometimes 10,000, sometimes 8,000.

All did not always go well with the Christian teachers. There were frequent uprisings of the Indians, and these were almost invariably accompanied by the massacre of a number of the missionaries. In what is now the state of New Mexico, for instance, the first two Franciscans who in 1540 attempted to make a settlement in the area were murdered by the natives. Exactly the same thing happened forty years later, when another group of three Franciscans were able to begin work among the wild Indians of those parts; violent death put a sudden end to the promising beginnings of a mission. It was only in the seventeenth century that stable and regular occupation of this area became possible.

The principal obstacle to the evangelization of the western peoples was the cruelty with which they were treated by the Spanish colonists. Under the system of *encomienda*, recommendation, a certain number of Indians were given over to a colonist, with the right to exact tribute or labour from them, on the understanding that in return they would be given protection and instruction in the Christian faith. The system was well intended; it broke down completely in face of the cupidity and harshness of the men into whose hands the helpless Indians had been given over. It is recorded that, when a cleric urged Pizarro, the conqueror of Peru, to put a stop to the spoliation of the Indians and to see that Christian instruction was given to them, he replied: 'I have not come for any such reasons; I have come to take away from them their gold.' In the harsh conditions under which they were condemned to live, whole populations began to die out; it may well be that their principal sickness was despair.

The Indians did not however lack their champions. On the Sunday before Christmas Day 1511, in the island of Hispaniola, a Dominican named Antonio de Montesinos preached a sermon on the text 'I am a voice crying in the wilderness', and raised a tumult which has not yet quite died away. In no measured terms, he denounced the sins of the white man against the brown:

Tell me, by what right or justice do you keep these Indians in such cruel and horrible servitude? . . . Why do you keep them so oppressed and weary, not giving them enough to eat, nor taking care of them in their illnesses? For with the excessive work you demand of them, they fall ill and die, or rather you kill them with your desire to extract and acquire gold every day. . . . Are these not men? Have they not rational souls? Are you not bound to love them as you love yourselves? Be certain that in such a state as this, you can no more be saved than the Moors or Turks.

The work of Montesinos was taken up by a much more famous man, Bartholomew de Las Casas (1484–1566). Las Casas arrived in the new world in 1502, and even after his ordination as priest had lived as a gentleman cleric, much as other colonists lived, profiting by the servitude into which the Indians had been brought. It was not until 1514 that he experienced the conversion that led him to the conviction that 'everything done to the Indians thus far was wrong and tryrannical', and to fifty years of service in their cause.

The views of sixteenth-century Spaniards on the Indians were forcibly, if coarsely, expressed by the historian Gonzalo de Oviedo y Valdés:

They are naturally lazy and vicious, melancholic, cowardly, and in general a lying, shiftless people. Their marriages are not a sacrament but a sacrilege. They are idolatrous, libidinous, and commit sodomy. Their chief desire is to eat, drink, worship heathen idols, and commit bestial obscenities.

Las Casas naturally comes in with a strongly-worded plea on the other side:

God created these simple people without evil and without guile. They are most obedient and faithful to their natural lords, and to the Christians whom they serve. They are most submissive, patient, peaceful, and virtuous. Nor are they quarrelsome, rancorous, querulous, or vengeful. They neither possess nor desire to possess worldly wealth. Surely these people would be the most blessed in the world if only they worshipped the true God.

In passionate hostility to those who maintained, on the authority of Aristotle, that certain peoples are by nature slaves, and thus justified the Spanish oppression of the Indians,[21] Las Casas affirmed that

we clearly see by examples ancient and modern that no nation exists, no matter how rude, uncultivated, barbarous, gross, or almost brutal its people may be, which may not be persuaded and brought to a good order and way of life, and made domestic, mild and tractable, provided the method that is proper and natural to men is used; namely love, gentleness, and kindness.

21. A great debate on this subject was held in Valladolid in 1550 and 1551 between Las Casas and the scholar Juan Ginés de Sepúlveda, who maintained the Aristotelian view.

It is easy to criticize Las Casas, and to point out the sentimental exaggerations of which he was guilty. As a modern writer has pointed out, to speak generally of 'Indians' was to conceal under one term a vast variety of peoples of the most diverse qualities and traditions:

> Indians were the Tekestas and Tahinos ... mild and hospitable; Indians the cannibalistic Caribs; Indians the primitive Otomi, who lived in caves. ... Indians the artistic Maya stone-cutters; and the Chibcha jewellery craftsmen, and the wise Inca legislators. ... Their intelligence, cruelty, and meekness varied as did the colour of their skins, their languages, their rites, their theogonies. ... Neither in their juridical position, in their physical aspect, in their language, in their tastes, in their morality, nor in their creative capacities were they alike.[22]

But, when all allowance has been made for ignorance and hasty judgement, Las Casas was on the side of the angels; through him the voice of Christian conscience genuinely spoke. It was largely through his influence that on 20 November 1542 the Emperor Charles V promulgated the New Laws, under which the *encomienda* system was brought to an end, or at least severely limited. It is true that in face of the violent reactions of the colonists the Crown went back on some of its decisions, and revoked some of the laws which had been most vigorously criticized; but the principle that Indians too have human rights had once for all been conceded, and in this, though the battle was long and fierce, the eventual victory was already guaranteed.

In 1544, when already seventy years old, Las Casas accepted the bishopric of Chiapa. But he held this office for little more than three years, and then returned to Spain, to carry on his great campaign in speech and writing for nearly twenty years until his death in 1566.

The work of the missionaries throughout Latin America followed certain generally accepted lines. A serious attempt was made to learn the local languages, and to provide the beginnings of a Christian literature in them. Schools were founded, though higher education seems to have been limited to those of Spanish or mixed origin. An attempt was made in many regions to gather the Indians into villages, and so to bring them under strict discipline (to be

22. Roberto Levillier, *Don Francisco de Toledo I* (1935), p. 178, quoted in L. Hanke, *Bartolomé de las Casas* (1951), pp. 85–6.

exercised by the priests or their representatives) and under more regular religious instruction. Interpreters were used for sacraments, with precautions. Rome gave leave in 1570 but revoked it because of abuse in 1658.

Two grave defects are to be noted in the rapidly developing Christianity of these regions.

In the first place, the Churches of the Indians were almost entirely non-communicating Churches. The first council held at Lima in 1552 discussed in detail the question as to which sacraments may be administered to the Indians; it was held that, until they were better instructed and strengthened in the faith, it would be wise to admit them only to baptism, matrimony, and penance. It was permitted to the bishops, if it seemed right and wise to them, to communicate to them the sacrament of confirmation, and, only under the licence of the bishop himself, to admit to the most holy sacrament of the Eucharist those who seemed to understand what they would be receiving through it. As late as 1573 a Dominican in Mexico felt it necessary to publish a work dealing with the admission of the Indians to Communion. Gradually in many areas the custom grew up of admitting the most regular of the faithful to Communion once a year, at Easter.

No serious attempt was made to build up an indigenous ministry. It was often maintained that there was a sufficiency, indeed an excess, of priests in the New World. At certain points this was true. Not long after its foundation Lima was like a Spanish city, with cathedrals, churches, and convents. But in most of these the priests and brothers had settled down to what has been described as the life of a 'select bachelor club', with plenty of Indians and other servants to wait upon their needs, and showed no enthusiasm for the evangelization of the Indians of the interior – perhaps not surprisingly in view of the steady tale of massacre and martyrdom of priests and religious resident among the Indian peoples. The missions, properly so called, suffered throughout Latin America from that penury of priests, which has never been fully remedied up to the present day.

The matter had often been discussed. In 1525 the Contador Rodrigo de Albornez in Mexico had written to the king of Spain urging the foundation of a higher school for the sons of Indian chiefs and leaders, with a view to the formation of Indian priests:

If out of these Indians one priest can be produced, he could be of more use, and bring more Indians to the faith, than fifty European priests.

From this and other initiatives came the foundation by Bishop Zumárraga of Mexico[23] of the College of Tlatelolco. It is certain that the Bishop had in mind the two purposes of creating an Indian élite, which could in time do good service in the state, and of producing an indigenous clergy. With the first of the two projects good success was attained – the teachers were astonished by the aptitude of the young Indians for learning Latin; but as early as 1540 the Bishop was expressing doubt whether the latter plan was really feasible; the difficulty of celibacy, here as elsewhere, proved almost insurmountable:

> We are not sure whether it will be possible to maintain the College at Tlatelolco; the best students among the Indians are more inclined to marriage than to continence.

In 1555, the first Council of Mexico explicitly forbade the admission to Orders of anyone of 'Moorish' race; and this was taken to cover Indians, 'mestizos', those partly of Spanish and partly of Indian blood, and mulattos, those partly of Negro origin. One or two exceptions seem to have been made – we hear of one Indian who had been ordained, some time between 1560 and 1573, by Bishop Novales of Michoacán. And the second Council, held in 1585, did not repeat the prohibition in quite such stringent terms. Yet in practice the rule was kept, and all the religious Orders seem to have had equally strict rules closing the door of their membership to all those who were not of pure European stock.

In 1576 Gregory XIII in the Bull *Nuper ad Nos* drew attention to the grave lack of priests who knew the languages of the Indians; his Bull permitted the ordination of half-castes, and gave dispensation from the ban of illegitimacy – 'illegitimate sons of Spaniards and Indian women may be ordained . . . provided that they know the Indian languages and meet the requirements of character laid down by the Council of Trent'. This aroused a good deal of opposition, and in 1578 the king of Spain wrote to the Bishop of Lima that in no circumstances was he to confer Holy Orders on mestizos – it was held that they had not shown such qualities as would fit them for the dignity of the priesthood.

The Council of Lima in 1585 did not take quite so strictly

23. This most unusual prelate carried on the liberal traditions of Erasmus, and maintained views as to the translation and wide diffusion of the Scriptures in the Indian languages, as a necessary accompaniment of missionary work, such as were not often heard again in the Roman Catholic world until the middle of the twentieth century.

conservative a view as the Council of Mexico in 1555. It merely laid great stress on the qualities essential for the priesthood as laid down by the Council of Trent, and left it to the bishops to decide in each individual case. It seems that the bishops took a negative view of the possibilities; very few mestizos were ordained, and no Indians. The ban which thus existed in practice was not removed till the third Council of Lima, held in 1772; this was followed by the ordination of the first three Indian priests in 1794.

When mere numbers are considered, the spiritual conquests of Spain and Portugal in the New World are deeply impressive. More than 40 per cent of all the Roman Catholics in the world live in those great regions. But to what depth has the new religion penetrated? Modern Roman Catholic writers are inclined to the view that all through the centuries Roman Catholicism has been felt by the ancient peoples and their descendants to be still a foreign religion. Did the fathers of the sixteenth century miscalculate? Would the history of the Church in Latin America have been different, and more edifying, if they had from the start shown greater courage, and greater belief in the power of the Holy Spirit to raise up a national Christian leadership from among the peoples of South and Central America?

If we compare the Christian situation in 1600 with that in 1500, we are aware at once of an immense difference. Europe has burst its bonds. Its military, political, and economic powers are about to impose themselves upon the whole inhabited world. Europeans are beginning to think that their civilization is the only civilization in the world that is worthy of the name, and to develop the strange complex of the superior people. With the expansion of Europe, and often in advance of it, has gone the expansion of the Church. Now, as never before, the Church has to face the challenge of the great religious systems of the world in the Far East, in India, and in the Muslim world. It has to decide whether its relationship to simple peoples is to be one of destruction or of conservation, of the elimination of all that had gone before or the transformation of the old under the influence of Christ. Now there can be no going back. The stage has been set. The questions have been asked. The study of Christian missions outside Europe up to 1500 is of little more than archaeological interest. In 1600 we are already in the modern world.

6

The Roman Catholic Missions, 1600–1787

The seventeenth century, like the sixteenth, was for the Roman Catholic world a time of great and notable enterprises, though these cannot quite equal in interest the essentially pioneering efforts of the earlier time. What, however, most deeply distinguishes the two centuries is a radical change in the organization of the missions, and in their relationship to the centre in Europe.

As we have seen, in the sixteenth century the initiative had been taken by the kings of Spain and Portugal, and by the great religious Orders, the Jesuits playing perhaps the leading role but with the Franciscans and the Dominicans not far behind. There were at the time great advantages in this method of work. Missionaries enjoyed royal protection and had no difficulty in securing passages in Spanish and Portuguese ships. Financial help in many cases, though not in all, was generous. And the godly rivalry between the Orders tended to promote vigorous and independent action. There were, on the other hand, grave drawbacks. The political connection meant that missionaries were liable to be too much engaged in secular concerns and even in trade. The rivalry between the Orders was often very much less than godly; in Japan, even under the shadow of the cross, Franciscans bitterly criticized the Jesuits for fawning on the great and the lordly in the land, and the Jesuits in reply mocked at the Franciscan pool of Bethesda at which the poor, the lame, the halt, and the blind gathered, to the discredit of the Christian name among the Japanese. The association of the missions with Spain and Portugal meant that, in reality, only a small part of the Christian world was being drawn on for support. Missionaries from northern Europe were not unknown; even an occasional Englishman was to be found, such as the Jesuit Thomas Stephens (1549–1619), who during his many years in Western India wrote a grammar of the Konkani dialect, and also an immensely long Christian *purāna* (quasi-historical, quasi-legendary poem) in the same tongue.[1] But the vast majority of the missionaries were from the Latin races. As the missions grew, the

1. See V. Cronin, *A Pearl to India* (1959), pp. 173–6. Cronin gives the length of the *purāna* as 10,962 strophes!

burden became too heavy to be borne. Portugal had at this time a population of probably not much more than a million; its power was growing less, and it simply could not carry out the duties which, under the Padroado[2] scheme, it had undertaken. Bishoprics had been created – all too few – but often they were left for many years without bishops. Even in the case of the great archbishopric of Goa, the periods during which it was occupied were shorter than the periods during which it was left vacant.[3]

Clearly the time had come when Rome must take a hand, and all the missions must be brought under the guidance and direction of the central authority.

In 1622 Pope Gregory XV took action and brought into being the Sacred Congregation for the Propagation of the Faith, often conveniently known for short as the Propaganda:

In the Name of Christ. In the year 1622 after his birth, on January 6, our Holy Father in Christ, Gregory XV by divine providence Pope, in the conviction that the most notable duty of his pastoral office is the dissemination of the Christian faith, through which men may be brought to the knowledge and adoration of the true God, constituted a congregation of thirteen cardinals and two prelates, with a secretary, to whom he entrusted and commanded the care for the propagation of the faith.

Francesco Ingoli, who held office as the first secretary of the Propaganda until his death in 1649, was one of the most remarkable missionary statesmen of whom we have record. Determined that action should be taken only on the basis of accurate knowledge, he first set himself to acquire the fullest possible information about the state of the missions in every part of the world. Then he decided on certain lines of action. Missionary work must be freed from the stranglehold that Spain and Portugal had been able to maintain upon it. Many more bishoprics must be created, and bishops must stand in a much closer relationship to Rome. Far more secular clergy must be employed, in order to keep the balance with the religious Orders. An indigenous clergy must be developed as rapidly as possible in every part of the world. The Christian faith must be delivered from those colonial associations which condemned it to be everywhere and in permanence a foreign religion.

The prophetic quality of the mind of Propaganda in its early

2. This convenient term is used to denote that division of spheres of influence between Spain and Portugal which had been made by the Pope in the fifteenth century. See pp. 121–2.

3. For details see *The Catholic Encyclopaedia*, under 'Goa'.

days is to be seen most notably in the instructions which it sent out in 1659, ten years after the death of Ingoli, to its vicars apostolic:

> Do not regard it as your task, and do not bring any pressure to bear on the peoples, to change their manners, customs, and uses, unless they are evidently contrary to religion and sound morals. What could be more absurd than to transport France, Spain, Italy, or some other European country to China? Do not introduce all that to them, but only the faith, which does not despise or destroy the manners and customs of any people, always supposing that they are not evil, but rather wishes to see them preserved unharmed. It is the nature of men to love and treasure above everything else their own country and that which belongs to it; in consequence there is no stronger cause for alienation and hate than an attack on local customs, especially when these go back to a venerable antiquity. This is more especially the case, when an attempt is made to introduce the customs of another people in the place of those which have been abolished. Do not draw invidious contrasts between the customs of the peoples and those of Europe; do your utmost to adapt yourselves to them.

Even when customs are bad and have to be changed, so run the instructions, it is better to do this gradually, and by helping the people themselves to see what is perverse in them rather than by any direct attack or condemnation in words.

The second great triumph of the new movement that had been set on foot in Rome was the inauguration in 1663 of the seminary of the *Société des Missions Étrangères* at Paris. With the decline of Spain and Portugal, France came more and more to the fore as the great Roman Catholic missionary nation; with the suppression of the Jesuit Order, which will be recorded in its place, the role of the secular clergy in the missions gained overwhelming importance. Here again we are conscious of an unexpectedly modern note in the proceedings. The first of the articles of association of the new society informs us that the primary intention was

> to hasten the conversion of the heathen, not only by proclaiming the Gospel to them, but above all by preparing . . . and raising to ecclesiastical orders those of the new Christians or of their children who are considered best suited to that holy state; in order to create in each country a clerical order and a hierarchy such as Jesus Christ and the apostles have appointed in the Church. They realized that that is the only way in which true religion can be established on a permanent footing; and that, moreover, it will be difficult for Europe to go on for ever supplying priests, who take a long time to learn the language, and in the time of persecution are easily recognized, arrested, driven out, or put to death, while priests of

the country are able more easily to remain in concealment, and in the end will be able to bring their countries to the point at which they will no longer need help from abroad.[4]

The third plan of the Propaganda was to increase the number of bishoprics overseas. Already the creation of the Propaganda had met with criticism on the part of Spain and Portugal, and was far from being welcome to all the missionaries overseas. The proposal to create new bishoprics brought matters to a head, since under the arrangements entered into by the popes in the fifteenth century it seemed clear that only the kings of Spain and Portugal could create bishoprics in their respective halves of the world, and appoint bishops to them. The legal and canonical difficulty was overcome by the appointment of vicars apostolic – a distinction almost without a difference, since the vicar apostolic could exercise all episcopal functions within an assigned area. It was, however, the case that on the strict interpretation of canon law he acted as direct representative of the Pope and did not carry any territorial title for the area in which he worked.[5] The legal and canonical position might be unassailable; nevertheless, the appointment of vicars apostolic was deeply resented by the rulers of Spain and Portugal as an infringement of the rights to which they had an equally unassailable claim.

The first vicars apostolic were appointed on 16 November 1637 – Franciscus Antonius de Santo Felice, Archbishop of Myra, for Japan; and Matthew de Castro, Bishop of Chrysopolis, for 'Idalcan', the interior parts of India, in which in point of fact the Portuguese missions were not at work. These were followed in 1659 by François Pallu, Bishop of Heliopolis, for Tongking; Pierre Lambert de la Motte, Bishop of Berytus, for Cochin-China; and in 1660 by Ignazio Cotolendi, Bishop of Metellopolis, for Nanking. The early days of this experiment were far from propitious. The vicar apostolic for Japan never reached the area for which he was designated. The others all had to experience ferocious opposition from both secular authorities and missionaries on the spot. As representatives of the Pope, the vicars apostolic required an oath of canonical obedience to themselves; if the missionaries refused, they would find themselves forbidden to carry out any priestly or sacramental acts; if they obeyed, they were likely to find them-

---

4. This statement was actually drawn up in 1700; but it correctly represents the views of those who had prepared the way for the seminary half a century before.

5. Vicars apostolic bore the titles of nominal sees *in partibus infidelium*.

selves deprived of the financial support from the political authorities on which they depended for their very existence. The endless and squalid squabbles arising out of this divergence of points of view need not further concern us in this history; but they cannot be altogether forgotten as part of the background of the expansion of Roman Catholic missions. It was not till 1950 that the ghost of the Padroado was finally and successfully laid, through a comprehensive agreement between the Vatican and the Portuguese authorities, in which all the remaining points of controversy were definitively settled.

What is really important is that one of the first two vicars apostolic was, in spite of his name, an Indian. Matthew de Castro was a young Brahman convert from the neighbourhood of Goa. He had been refused ordination by the Archbishop of Goa, perhaps, as was alleged, on account of Portuguese prejudice against the Brahmans. He succeeded in making his way to Rome, and after some years of study was ordained priest in 1630 and sent back to India to work among his own people. His enemies made so many difficulties for him that in 1636 he made his way back to Rome by the land route. Propaganda had the bright idea of securing his secret consecration as bishop, and of sending him off – to Japan if possible, and, if Japan proved unattainable, to the interior parts of India. From the moment of his arrival in India, difficulties multiplied; the Archbishop of Goa refused to recognize him as bishop, or to admit the validity of ordinations which he had carried out. Matthew was by no means a conciliatory figure, and did less than nothing to appease his opponents. Eventually he had to return to Rome to state his own case in person. After an abortive effort to pack him off to Ethiopia, in 1651 he was back in India, breathing threats against all Portuguese and all Jesuits. The Jesuits retaliated in kind, on one occasion referring to him less than politely in an Annual Letter as *aper exterminator*, 'the wild boar out of the wood' (Psalm 80:13 B.C.P.); after he had left for his own field they remarked that 'the wind ceased, and there was a great calm'.

Complaints followed one another thick and fast to Rome. On investigation it proved that many of the accusations launched by Matthew against the Portuguese and the state of the Church in Goa were at least in part true. But it seemed wiser to remove the main source of the trouble; in 1658 Matthew was deprived of his title and relieved of his functions. He died in 1677, still apparently enjoying the esteem and regard of the cardinals at Rome. The experiment of an Indian episcopate had not for the moment worked out well; apart from provision for the special field of the Thomas Christians in Travancore, it was not repeated for a long time. The next Indian Roman Catholic bishop of the Latin rite was consecrated in 1923.[6]

It is time to turn from these administrative details to the progress of the missions in various parts of the world.

We may begin with *India*. In 1605 a young Italian Jesuit of good family, Roberto Nobili (1577–1656), arrived in India. After a few months spent on the Fisher Coast learning Tamil, Nobili was sent to Madurai. He was to remain in South India for fifty years, and to prove himself a pioneer of extraordinary dexterity in working out new methods of approach to the Indian world. Madurai was the great centre of Tamil culture. Tamil, the most ancient of the four great Dravidian languages, is the only form of Indian speech which has developed a classical literature of its own in independence of Sanskrit. Modern Tamil includes a great many Sanskrit words, but its grammatical structure, its prosody, and its literary style are all its own. Moreover, South India has developed forms of Hindu philosophy and religion, such as the *Saiva Siddhānta* and the hymns of the Ālvārs, which are markedly different from the classical traditions of northern India. At the time of Nobili's arrival, there was little that was original or creative in Tamil thought and literature, but there was deep interest in religion and a willingness to hear.

There was already a mission in Madurai, under the charge of a Portuguese Jesuit, Father Fernandez. But the adherents of the faith were almost all immigrants from the Fisher Coast and elsewhere; and Father Fernandez followed the method, familiar to him from Goa, of turning the converts as nearly as possible into Portuguese. The higher Indian castes had an invincible repugnance for the manners and customs of the 'Parangi' (Franks); and this close association of the faith with abhorrent customs made it practically impossible for any man of standing or respectable position even to consider becoming a Christian. Nobili had no doubt heard of the methods followed by Matthew Ricci in China; he decided to experiment on the same lines and to carry them even further. To win the Indians he would become an Indian. He made a careful study of Brahman custom and prejudice, and abandoned

6. The life of de Castro has been written by Dom T. Ghesquière, OSB, *Mathieu de Castro, Premier Vicaire Apostolique aux Indes* (Bruges, 1937).

everything that could offend, such as the eating of meat and the wearing of leather shoes. He adopted the ochre (*kāvi*) robe of the holy man, and as far as could be converted himself into a *sannyāsi guru*, a teacher who has renounced every form of attachment to the world. He mastered classical Tamil. To this he was later able to add Telugu and Sanskrit; he was, it is believed, the first European ever to study the ancient classical language of India.[7] In order to avoid what in Indian eyes was contaminating, he cut himself off entirely from contact with the existing Christian Church.

Nobili's bold experiment was at once crowned with success. Word of the new teacher spread around. His method was to hold public discussions on religious subjects, in particular such subjects as the unity of God and the doctrine of creation. The scholastic method of argument which he had learned as a theological student, recast in Indian form and with apt illustrations from the Indian classics, proved remarkably convincing. Within a year or two of coming to Madurai, Nobili was able to baptize ten young men of good caste. In 1609 the number of converts rose to sixty-three, a few Brahmans being included among them. The converts were not required to break their caste rules, except in so far as these were actually idolatrous. The Brahman could continue to grow the *kudumi*, the hair tuft at the back of the otherwise shaven head. Members of the 'twice-born' castes could continue to wear the sacred thread, the distinguishing mark of their rank – though a special thread, blessed with Christian payers, was provided.

We have very few testimonies from converts of the period, and it is hard to judge what they imagined themselves to have accepted in the act of baptism. New *gurus*, with reforming teachings, have appeared periodically in Hinduism. Undoubtedly Nobili's intellectual nimbleness, the charm of his manner, his ascetic way of life, and his intense earnestness made a deep impression. But it is not clear that the converts had fully understood the radical nature of the step that they had taken.

Nobili had, as far as possible, separated himself from Father Fernandez and all his works. But the secret could not be indefinitely kept. A Parava Christian told some of the converts that Nobili was really a Parangi, and that by baptizing them he had irrevocably incorporated them into the caste of the Parangis. The resulting storm was violent in the extreme, and the whole work of Nobili was at stake. In order to defend himself, he wrote a

7. The celebrated philologist Max Müller refers to him as 'our first Sanskrit scholar'.

declaration in Tamil on *ōlais*, the strips of palm-leaf locally used in place of paper, and had it nailed to a tree in front of his house:

> I am not a Parangi, I was not born in the land of the Parangis nor was I ever connected with their race . . . I came from Rome, where my family hold the same rank as respectable Rajas hold in this country . . . The law which I preach is the law of the true God, which from ancient times was by his command proclaimed in these countries by *sannyāsis* and saints. Whoever says that it is the law of the Parangis, fit only for low castes, commits a very great sin, for the true God is not the God of one race but the God of all . . . [8]

This writing of Nobili has been very diversely judged by different readers. Much turns on the meaning of the word 'Parangi'. Nobili emphatically maintained that, in local use, it meant Portuguese, and Portuguese only, and that in declaring himself not to be a Parangi, he was speaking the strict truth. But were the people of Madurai at that time so wholly ignorant of the existence of a number of different countries in Europe? And is it possible for an Indian Christian to maintain caste distinction in all its rigidity and still to be a Christian? Nobili, coming from a still hierarchically organized Europe, regarded caste as involving no more than social distinction; others maintained, then as now, that caste and religion are inseparably involved with one another. The Indian Church is far from having solved the problem of caste, and Nobili cannot be blamed for having held one particular view of it; but later history suggests that he had overlooked elements that are really present in the system.

Local feeling was not Nobili's only problem. Reports had gone to his bishop, to Goa, and to Rome to the effect that he was tolerating Hindu superstition, that he was deceiving the people, and that by segregating his converts he was creating a schism in the Church. To these charges Nobili wrote in 1610 a full and dignified answer, explaining his method and defending it against misunderstandings – *A reply to the objections raised against the method used in the new Mission of Madurai for the conversion of Gentiles to Christ*.[9] The controversy raged back and forth, until at length a reply was received from Rome which exonerated Nobili from all the graver charges and in the main approved his methods: Hindu converts might retain their traditional usages, but only on condition that everything specifically pagan attaching to them was abandoned.

8. Full text in V. Cronin, *A Pearl to India* (1959), pp. 137–8.
9. The full text of this has been published by Fr Dahmen, sj (Paris 1931).

In later years Nobili was able to extend his mission to Trichinopoly and Salem. Then, as members of the lower castes began to press into the Church, he ingeniously divided the mission into two, and arranged for an order of missionaries, the *Pandāraswāmis*, who would work among the lower orders without prejudice to the work which he and the smaller group of *Brāhmanasannyāsis* would carry on among the higher castes. In 1645 Nobili was withdrawn from the Madurai mission; the last years of his life were spent in poverty and almost total blindness at Mylapore near Madras, the traditional site of the martyrdom of St Thomas. He died on 16 January 1656.

Legend, unfortunately, has greatly exaggerated the success of Nobili's work. The true facts seem to be more or less as follows: between 1607 and 1620, 178 persons of good caste had been baptized, but this includes children and those baptized on their death-beds. In 1623 hardly a hundred Christians were left in the mission in Madurai, many having apostatized and others having followed the court to Trichinopoly. In 1643 the Jesuit *Annual Letter* reckons that not more than 600 of the higher castes had been baptized in thirty-seven years; and two years later it is recorded that not more than twenty-six Brahmans remain. It was only with the extension of the work to the lower castes that something like a mass movement started, and that the baptisms began to be reckoned in thousands. The achievement of Nobili was splendid, and such a measure of success among the higher castes is almost unparalleled; legendary exaggeration has done nothing to add to the glory of the historic reality.

It is impossible, however, to exaggerate the price paid in human devotion and suffering for this success. To live, year after year, under Indian conditions in that torrid climate demands a super-human measure of self-sacrifice. Many of the missionaries broke down in health; often there were not more than six or seven Jesuits in the whole large area; and, as the mission failed to develop an Indian ministry, they had no more than the help of catechists in their work. Few of the missionaries attained to special distinction, but of two of these particular mention must be made.

John de Britto, of a noble Portuguese family, came to India in 1673. His name is specially associated with the Marava country – the district of Rāmnād and the state of Pudukottah. Here the mission had enjoyed considerable success, but a time of persecution followed, and no Jesuit had been able to visit the flock between 1679 and 1686. De Britto's first visit, in 1686, ended in arrest and torture, but he and his party were finally set free by the rajah of

Rāmnād. On another visit matters did not turn out so well; de Britto, who had made a deep impression on Christians and Hindus alike by his devotion and gentleness, was again arrested and was publicly beheaded on 4 February 1693 outside the little town of Uraiyur – one of the few missionary martyrs of whom the Church in India can boast.

Constant Joseph Beschi served in the mission from 1711 to 1742. Beschi's principal claim to fame is his extraordinary mastery of the Tamil language. His grammars may be said to have laid the foundation for all subsequent scientific study of Tamil. He composed spiritual writings in prose for his catechists; an amusing romance, *The Story of Guru Simple*; and a long Christian epic, the *Tēmbāvani*, the life of St Joseph with a great many digressions, a work which is very tedious to western taste, but manifests such a perfect mastery of the elaborate diction characteristic of later Tamil poetry that it has always been regarded by the Indians themselves as a minor classic of Tamil literature.

We turn to *China*. At the death of Ricci the mission of the Jesuits was in a flourishing condition. The fathers were firmly established in Peking. Their three most distinguished converts had left them, to found missions, each in his own home area – Paul Hsü in Shanghai, Michael Yang in Chekiang, and Leo Li in Hangchow. Persecution was troublesome but intermittent, and on the whole the next fifty years were a time of steady and hopeful progress. Ricci had found a worthy successor in the German Johann Adam Schall von Bell (1591–1666). Schall, who arrived in Peking in 1622, was a highly competent astronomer. In 1623 and 1624 he prophesied eclipses which his Chinese rivals had failed to foresee; this greatly enhanced his reputation, and in 1630 he was appointed to the board which regulated the calendar. The number of baptisms rapidly increased,[10] and it is said that one of the wives of the emperor, with her child, was included among the number.

The Ming dynasty was now trembling to its fall. Peking was captured in 1644; the remaining traces of the old dynasty were wiped out with the death of the last emperor, Kuei Wang, in 1662. Surprisingly enough, the change of dynasty did not affect the

10. It is said that in 1650 there were 150,000 Christians in the empire, and 254,980 in 1664 (Latourette, *Expansion*, Vol. III, p. 344). There is no means of checking these figures, but it seems likely that they comprise all Christians baptized since the beginning of the mission, including the enormous numbers of children baptized by the missionaries at the moment of death.

fortunes of the mission. Schall was able to convince the new rulers that he was indispensable, and in 1645 he was actually appointed president of the board for the control of the calendar. Such a position could not be held without jealousy. In 1664 the old charge that the missionaries were emissaries preparing the way for a Portuguese occupation of the country was revived, and Schall von Bell, already seventy-three years old, was condemned to death with five of his assistants. Schall was reprieved and died a natural death in the following year. But in the meantime the five Chinese had been executed, and all the priests in China, at that time thirty-eight in number, were collected in Canton with a view to their expulsion from the country. An exception was made in favour of four Jesuits, who were able to remain in Peking.

Once again the wind changed. In 1667 the great Emperor K'ang-Hsi, then aged fourteen, began to take a hand in the affairs of government. It was not long before he made friends with Schall's colleague and successor the Fleming Ferdinand Verbiest (1617–88), who shared the same astronomical and scientific interests. Measures taken against the Christians were rescinded and the position of the Fathers seemed secure. At last in 1692 an edict of toleration was put out by the emperor:

> The Europeans are very quiet; they do not excite any disturbances in the provinces, they do no harm to anyone, they commit no crimes, and their doctrine has nothing in common with that of the false sects in the empire, nor has it any tendency to excite sedition . . . We decide therefore that all temples dedicated to the Lord of heaven, in whatever place they may be found, ought to be preserved, and that it may be permitted to all who wish to worship this God to enter these temples, offer him incense, and perform the ceremonies practised according to ancient custom by the Christians. Therefore let no one henceforth offer them any opposition.

The triumph of the Jesuits seemed to be complete. And their victory also provided security for the missionaries of other Orders, mainly Franciscan and Dominican, who had in the meantime entered China and worked with a considerable measure of success. Yet the situation for foreigners throughout the Far East remained uncertain and precarious.

It was this that led Rome to the remarkable step of appointing a Chinese bishop. Lô Wen-Tsao had been born in 1611 to a family of peasants in the province of Fukien. In 1633 he was won to the faith by a Spanish Franciscan; after a number of years of study in Manila he was raised to the priesthood. As usual, his European friends gave him a European name, and Lô appears in all the later records as Fray Gregorio López. It was on this experienced man that the choice of the Propaganda fell: on 4 January 1674 he was appointed titular Bishop of Basilinopolis in Bithynia and Vicar Apostolic for the northern part of China. It is at this point that we are able to trace in their clearest form the difficulties caused by the tensions between the governments and Rome; it was only on 8 April 1685 that Lô was able to secure consecration, at the hands of Bernardino della Chiesa, the newly arrived Italian Vicar Apostolic.[11] He was able to exercise his episcopal ministry for no more than six years, as he died in February 1691; but the reports of his work suggest that he was a wise, humble, and competent man, though perhaps, from the point of view of the stricter school of European missionaries, too much inclined to favour the retention by Christians of old Chinese habits and customs. Yet, till the twentieth century, Lô had no successor as a Chinese Roman Catholic bishop.

Closely connected with the consecration of Lô was the question of the liturgical language for China. In 1615 Pope Paul V had given permission for Chinese priests to say Mass in Chinese, subject to the direction of the local bishops. By 1666 all the liturgical books had been translated by the Jesuits; it appears that Bishop Lô made use of the papal permission and used Chinese for the liturgy. But there was a good deal of uncertainty in the matter, and no clear decision had been reached, when Lô ordained three elderly Chinese as priests. What language were they to use? By this time a reaction in favour of Latin had set in, and it is probable that the Chinese felt it a point of honour to use the same language as their Jesuit friends, in order that no stigma of inferiority might rest on their priesthood. They decided to use Latin. But, as one of the Jesuits wrote on 9 October 1688:

I have assisted at Mass said by one of these. He sweated, was in an agony of mind, and those present were equally put out and irritated. God knows how many faults and mistakes he made, all hot and bothered as he was, reciting parrot-like what he could not understand.[12]

Latin, however, won the day. Candidates were sent to the seminary established at Ayuthia in Siam, where the only common language was Latin. During the eighteenth century a number of Chinese students were sent to the College of the Holy Family at

11. No Spanish or Portuguese bishop dared or was willing to consecrate him, for fear of the consequences of this infringement of the Padroado tradition.

12. Quoted by C. Cary-Elwes, *China and the Cross* (1956), p. 136.

Naples, which trained 100 Chinese priests in the 150 years of its existence.

What we have written has at various points revealed the existence of grave differences of opinion between the missionaries of various groups and Orders. It is easy to see how these had come about. New missionaries were horrified to find among the converts of the Jesuits what they regarded as a semi-pagan Christianity; they felt that the Jesuits, out of a base desire to stand well with the nobility and to avoid persecution, had sold out on essentials of the Christian faith. The Jesuits looked with great disfavour on these newcomers, who would not take the trouble to understand the Chinese mind, and by their reckless disregard of the feelings of the people of the country were likely to bring disaster not only on their own work but on that of those who had laboured much longer than they, and with a much greater understanding of what the situation required. The three burning points of difference related to the customs to be observed at funerals, the reverence to be paid to ancestors – was this civil difference, or did it involve an element of religious worship? – and the terms to be used in translating the name of God. We need not concern ourselves with the details of this squalid and endless controversy; one or two of the main stages in its development have to be noted.

In 1656 Rome had ruled in not very precise terms that, in so far as the honours rendered to Confucius and other departed ancestors had only a civil character, they were not offensive and could be permitted. The Jesuits took this as at least a provisional approval of their point of view and their methods. In 1693, the French Vicar Apostolic Charles Maigrot (1652–1730), who had been in China since 1683, holding that the Jesuits had not rightly understood what they were doing, issued peremptory orders that the terms *T'ien* and *Shang-ti* were not to be used of God, and that the customary honours to the departed were not to be paid. This judgement he forwarded to Rome.

The Jesuits had in their hands what they believed to be a trump card. They asked the emperor himself to give a ruling as to the exact significance of the disputed terms and rites. K'ang-Hsi obliged with a statement to the effect that honours were paid to Confucius only as a legislator, that the honours paid to ancestors were a demonstration of love and commemoration of the good that the dead had done during their lives, and that sacrifices to *T'ien* were not paid to the visible heavens but to the Supreme Lord, the creator and preserver of heaven and earth. This letter the Jesuits forwarded to Rome.

The scholars at Rome seem to have regarded themselves as better qualified to make decisions on matters of theology, in so far as these affected the Chinese, than any Chinese, emperor or no. Their decision was almost wholly unfavourable to the Jesuit position. Only the term *T'ien Chu*, Lord of Heaven, might be used for God. Honours might not be paid to Confucius on any occasion, nor to departed ancestors; ancestral tablets might be kept, provided that they had nothing on them except the monogram of the deceased. Such was the decree of 20 November 1704.

In the meantime, in 1701, the Pope had despatched to the East a special legate, Charles Maillard de Tournon, a young aristocrat at that time thirty-three years of age, who was appointed titular Patriarch of Antioch and later raised to the cardinalate. Tournon seems to have been a sincere and well-intentioned man; but he lacked both the knowledge and the tact to deal with the complex problems committed to him. And, to make things worse, Rome had failed to notify Portugal of his mission.

Tournon arrived at Pondicherry in November 1703 and spent nine months there. Shortly before his departure, he issued a decree in sixteen points, wholly unfavourable to the methods and practices of Nobili and his Jesuit followers. Ceremonies which had been suppressed as offensive to Indian ideas were to be restored in detail. Caste differences were not to be observed, as they had been in the past. Practices regarded as too nearly allied to Hindu superstitions were to be suppressed. The dismay of the Jesuits was great, and their attempts to obtain some modification of this, to them, so grievous decision were many.

Tournon then went on to China, and reached Peking in December 1705. Here he completely misread the situation; the emperor had been quite pleased to have 'his' Jesuits in his capital; he was much perturbed to find that they owed some allegiance to a distant sovereign, the Pope, of whom he knew nothing, and he was gravely affronted that this sovereign should send him an envoy on terms which appeared to claim at least equality between the Pope and the emperor of China. Tournon was sent back, first to Nanking, and then to Macao, where his relations with the local Portuguese archbishop were, if anything, slightly worse than his relations with the emperor in Peking. From Nanking the legate issued orders, even stricter than the decree of 1704, forbidding everything in Jesuit custom in China that did not seem to him to square perfectly with the demands of Roman custom. He died in Macao on 8 June 1710.

The emperor vented his anger on Tournon and his colleagues in the form of an imperial decree; only those missionaries would be allowed to remain in China who swore to accept the rules laid down by Father Ricci; on doing so they would receive a *p'iao*, or imperial document, entitling them to the toleration accorded by the decree of 1692. All others would be expelled. Four of the bishops then in China, and many missionaries, applied for and received the *p'iao*; all others were driven out.

In China, as in India, the missionaries made many attempts to have the decision of 1704 and the rulings of Tournon changed. A temporary success was achieved when the legate Mezzabarba in 1720 granted a number of concessions in the form of permissions. But Rome proved adamant. On 11 July 1742 Pope Benedict XIV, in the Bull *Ex quo singulari*, listed the eight permissions granted by Mezzabarba, and swept them completely away:

We define and declare that these permissions must be considered as though they had never existed, and we condemn and detest their practice as superstitious. And thus, in virtue of our present constitution to be in force for ever, we revoke, annul, abrogate, and wish to be deprived of all force and all effect, all and each of those permissions, and say and announce that they must be considered for ever to be annulled, null, invalid, and without any force or power.

Two years later, Rome took similar action in the matter of the so-called 'Malabarian' rites in South India. In the Bull *Omnium Sollicitudinum*, Pope Benedict XIV supported in every detail the decisions of Tournon, except that permission was given to omit for a further ten years those ceremonies which were felt to be particularly disagreeable to the Indian Christians.

The first great attempt at 'accommodation' had failed. Rome had ruled that Roman practice, nearly as it was at Rome, was to be in every detail the law for the missions. This was to govern Roman Catholic missionary practice for the next two hundred years.

It is pleasant to turn from this painful history to another and very different scene. South-east Asia has always proved a difficult area for missionary work. In *Siam*, all the efforts of the Jesuits did little to make an impression on the Buddhist population. In *Vietnam* the work met with remarkable success.

The hero of this epic of conversion was Alexander de Rhodes, who was born at Avignon in 1591 and arrived in Macao, destined for Japan, in 1623. As Japan was closed to missionaries, Rhodes was sent off to South Vietnam, where Jesuits had been working for eight years, and immediately manifested exceptional ability to master the Vietnamese language. His stay was short; the missionaries were expelled in 1625. The next attempt was made in North Vietnam in 1627. Here for a time all went well; but before long the animosity of the local ruler led to the ejection of all the missionaries, and in 1630 Rhodes was back in Macao, where he was to spend ten rather dreary years. But it is said that in these three years in North Vietnam he had baptized 6,700 converts; others were able before long to enter in and carry on the great work.

The third opportunity for Rhodes came in 1640, when he was able once more to effect an entry in South Vietnam; and this time he was able to make a beginning in the capital, Sinoa, now called Hué. But opposition was fierce, and the missionaries were constantly on the run between Hué and Macao. In 1645 the attitude of the ruler became so violent that it was no longer possible to hold on. Rhodes was banished in perpetuity, and it was specifically stated in the decree that any captain of a Portuguese ship who brought him back to Vietnam would be beheaded. To show that this was no empty threat, two of the catechists were arrested and put to death. Rhodes left for Macao, and then for Europe, where he was to be engaged in important but very different work in the cause of missions.

It was, perhaps, the very uncertainty of his position, the only missionary in a hostile environment, which led Rhodes to his most notable discovery in missionary method – the formation of the 'company of catechists'. Rhodes was one of the first to realize to the full the gravity of the lack of priests; a group of well-qualified catechists could not entirely make up for this lack, but it could go far to maintain the life and faith of isolated Christian communities. Catechists were not unknown in the missions, but these were generally married men living with their families. It was the genius of Rhodes which brought into being what was in effect a celibate lay brotherhood, living in community and under rule. The catechists were carefully trained and were given elementary instruction in medicine, a qualification which secured them ready access to all classes of the people. After passing successfully through two lower grades, they were permitted publicly to take three vows – that they would remain unmarried, that they would pay into the common fund whatever they received by way of alms or gifts, and that they would obey the member of their group who was appointed by the missionary as their superior.

Growth was astonishingly rapid. In 1658 it was claimed that there were 300,000 Christians in the two parts of Vietnam taken together. Without doubt these figures were greatly exaggerated, and they were inflated by the common practice of death-bed baptisms[13]; but it cannot be doubted that the number was large. When not more than two priests were in the country, and these two living a hunted and precarious existence, the work of the catechists proved itself invaluable.

The second great gift of Rhodes to the Church was the reduction of the Vietnamese language to writing in the Latin alphabet. He must have had, in addition to a great gift for languages, a remarkably accurate ear; for Vietnamese is a tonal language, and the accurate representation of these tones is extraordinarily difficult. Furthermore, Rhodes rejected the tendency of the scholars to a high style of writing, with many words and phrases borrowed from Chinese and written in Chinese characters; he set himself to develop the *quōc-ngu*, the ordinary language of the people, and to make of it a fit instrument for the expression of Christian truth. He thus anticipated by a century and a half the work that William Carey was to do in India for Bengali.

We have seen how medieval missions in *Africa* gave rise to good hopes through the consecration of the first African bishop. Such hopes were periodically renewed at intervals through the next three centuries, but all ended in frustration.

Again and again Portugal made attempts to establish permanent missionary settlements on the west coast of Africa. In this region the chosen missionaries were the Capuchins. A number of bishoprics was established, though it is not clear that bishops were regularly sent out to fill them. In almost every case the history was the same. One or other of the local rulers would show interest in the Gospel, and perhaps be baptized; but, if one ruler became a Christian, it was almost certain that his successor would be a stalwart pagan, and that the Christian tendencies of the one would be neutralized by the anti-Christian vigour of the other. Thus we read of the conversion in 1656 of a princess of Matamba in Angola

13. This was carried on to such an extent that one of the accusations laid against the missionaries by their enemies was that they possessed a 'death-water', by means of which they would proceed rapidly to the depopulation of the country.

named Jinga; the desire of the princess to bring her people to the Christian faith apparently made a deep impression on the neighbouring potentates. In 1663 Jinga wrote to the Pope and the Propaganda, urging that more missionaries be sent. But a few years later she died, and no more was heard of this promising movement.[14]

In spite of these uncertainties, it is affirmed that between 1645 and 1700 the Capuchins had baptized 600,000 people in the Congo, Angola, and neighbouring regions, and that from 1700 on the number of baptisms remained in the neighbourhood of 12,000 a year. We may suppose that the level of instruction given was extremely low – though some catechisms had been prepared in the African languages – and that few steps were taken of a kind that could lead to the building up of stable and permanent Churches. A report from the year 1648 informs us that the Africans complained about the delay that the missionaries wished to impose upon them before granting baptism:

> Why so much bother? Why so much circumspection, so many enquiries as to the firmness of our purpose in asking for baptism? . . . We are here, like all the other white men, to eat all the salt that you are willing to give us. Why then do you keep us at arm's length?

It is clear that the Africans believed the giving of a pinch of salt, in the rites of the catechumenate which precede baptism, to be the essential element in the sacrament! In 1650, a missive was sent to Rome asking whether very ignorant and stupid people might be baptized simply on the profession of their willingness to believe all that the Church believes. The answer of the Propaganda was that such people might be baptized *in fide ecclesiae*, like small children and those who are not in their right mind.[15] This does not suggest a very high ideal of missionary work. To add to the difficulties of the Portuguese, from about 1643 onwards the Dutch had a trading-station in Luanda, and as usual were far from favourable to Roman Catholic missionary work.

On the other side of Africa, Mozambique had been constituted a vicariate in 1612, and in 1624 the Jesuits reported that they had

14. Jinga had been baptized in 1622, but had then relapsed and had attached herself to the cannibal sect of the Jaggas. As a result of her late repentance, thirty years later, 8,000 people became Christians between 1655 and 1663.

15. L. Kilger, 'Die Taufpraxis in der alten Kapuzinermission am Kongo und in Angola', in *Neue Zeitschrift für Missionswissenschaft*, Vol. v, 1949, pp. 30–40, 203–16. From these two very important articles it is clear that the vast majority of the baptisms in this part of Africa were of infants.

eight stations and about twenty missionaries in the region of the Zambezi. The Dominicans and the Augustinians also had places of residence on this coast. But here the involvement of missionaries and Christians in local wars gravely compromised the mission, and strengthened the impression that already existed among the Africans that to accept baptism meant also to accept the sovereignty of Portugal. Thus we read that in the year 1628 King Kaprazine of Monomotapa murdered the representatives of the king of Portugal and declared war against the Portuguese and the Christians. The Christians took up arms under the leadership of a certain Dominican; their counter-attack was successful, whereupon the new king, Mavura, whom they installed, promised allegiance to the king of Portugal and protection to the Christians. Another king was baptized in this region in 1652; but in no case does the attachment to the Christian faith appear to have been more than nominal. A document of 1751 states that at that time only a few, and some of these slaves, were baptized in Mozambique; and this is confirmed by the statement of the vicar-general of the Dominicans that adults were baptized only as adults for fear that they might apostatize from the faith.

In 1642 the Compagnie Française des Indes Orientales planned to found a French colony on the great island of *Madagascar*. Lazarists were sent to care for their welfare, and to begin missionary work among the inhabitants. In 1657 Madagascar was again without a priest. A new attempt to start the mission came to a tragic end when in 1674 the local inhabitants murdered seventy-five of the colonists, and the remainder had to withdraw. In the eighteenth century the Lazarists made two further attempts to settle in Madagascar, but the French Revolution put an end to all such work, and at the beginning of the nineteenth century no trace seems to have been left of the earlier missions.

Such was the sad history of early Roman Catholic efforts in Africa. The terrible climate and the high mortality among the missionaries, the extreme instability of the political situation among the Africans, and the erratic granting and withholding of support from Europe, to a large extent account for the impermanence of what at times gave promise of being a considerable achievement. But the real cause of failure was deeper. No serious attempt seems anywhere to have been made to face all that is involved in a mission to quite primitive peoples – the need for a deep and accurate knowledge of the language, understanding of their customs and mentality, the long and patient instruction that must precede baptism, the endlessly patient pastoral care that must follow it. Africa had no Xavier, and no Alexander de Rhodes; where the foundations were so unstable, it was certain that sooner or later the building would fall.

We must now turn to the Western world, and to the progress of missions in the American continent.

At the beginning of the seventeenth century *Canada* was still almost an unknown country. In 1534 the traveller Jacques Cartier claimed possession of the country. A great cross was erected; the party knelt down, and, as Cartier recorded, 'we folded our hands and venerated the Cross in the presence of a large number of savages, in order to show them – by the lifting up of our hands to heaven – that our salvation depended on the Cross.' But these encouraging beginnings were not followed up. It was only with the discoveries of Champlain that France really became engaged in the occupation of Canada; on 24 June 1615 Mass was celebrated for the first time on the island which is now the site of the city of Montreal.[16]

At that time the population consisted of three groups of Indians – the Hurons, the Algonquins, and the Iroquois – probably not more than 150,000 in number and all constantly at war with one another. The French at once set themselves to the evangelization of these peoples; many Orders took part, but once again the Jesuits claimed the lion's share. Recruits were never lacking, and within a few years the Society had sent no less than fifty French Jesuits to this new field. The first of the new groups of missionaries arrived in Canada in 1632.

At just the same time, a remarkable movement among Christian women in France was preparing the way for a new departure – the participation of women on a large scale in missionary work. An Ursuline nun, Mary of the Incarnation, who was living in the convent at Tours, saw during a night in December 1633 a vision relating to Canada, from which she dated her vocation to work in that country. In 1635 she received a second vision, which assured her that it was the will of God that she should go personally to that

16. Many of the English expeditions were accompanied by Anglican chaplains, e.g. that of Frobisher to find the North-West Passage in 1578. It is probable that Anglican celebration of the Holy Communion in this region preceded Roman Catholic by a number of years. The first recorded service according to the Anglican rite in what is now the United States was held in June 1579 in the neighbourhood of San Francisco, during Sir Francis Drake's voyage around the world.

country and found a convent there. It was not until 1639 that the plans were complete, and that three Ursulines and three nursing sisters were able to set out for the new continent. Their work in Montreal, their sufferings, and their patient endurance have been brilliantly delineated by the historian Francis Parkman.[17]

A veil of romance has concealed from the world what life among the Indians was really like. With noble courage they combined unbelievable squalor, treachery, and bestial cruelty. Conditions of life for the missionaries were miserable; communications were so difficult that at one time the rule had to be made that no more than three drops of wine could be allowed for each Mass. The constant wars between the Indians threatened the peace of the mission. In 1642 Father Isaac Jogues was captured by the Iroquois and brutally tortured. He managed to escape, but in 1646 returned among them, saying *Ibo et non redibo*, 'I shall go but not return'. His prophecy was true; on 18 October 1646 he was murdered, to be followed the next day by the young layman, Jean de la Lande, who was his companion. Worse was to follow. In 1649–50 the Iroquois fell on the Hurons and practically exterminated them; the three Jesuit missionaries Brébeuf, Lalemant, and Garnier were tortured and burned alive. This was practically the end of the mission.

Various further attempts at missionary work were made throughout the area which is now Canada and the United States, but with little lasting success. The missionaries were, in fact, watching the tragedy of the red man. Neither Britain, France, nor Holland comes well out of this. The inhuman cynicism with which the white man engaged the Indian in his own quarrels, setting Indian against Indian and Indian against European, makes one of the most shameful passages of colonial history. To make things worse, 'drink and the devil had done for the rest'; the Indian could not resist the temptation of the white man's fire-water, and here as elsewhere the supply of alcohol to a primitive people was almost tantamount to deliberate murder.

In *South America*, the most notable enterprise was the Jesuit mission in Paraguay,[18] the Republic of the Guaranís. We have already mentioned the custom of drawing the inhabitants of these countries into Christian villages, for protection and for the sake of

17. *The Jesuits in North America* (Centenary Edition, 1925).
18. It is to be noted that a large part of the area covered by this mission was in what is now Argentina.

better Christian instruction. This method was carried to its highest point by the Jesuits in Paraguay. The first settlement, Loreto, was founded in 1610; by 1623 there were no less than twenty-three settlements in La Guayra, with a population that was reckoned at roughly 100,000. The majority of these people were still pagans, and had come in for the sake of the peace and protection from enslavement guaranteed to them by the Fathers. The Jesuits, who were few in number, often no more than a single missionary in each 'reduction', were faced by a Herculean task in bringing order, discipline, and a measure of Christian belief to these large groups of simple though not altogether uncivilized people. The work suffered gravely in early years from the hostility of the colonists, who did not wish to see so large a proportion of the population withdrawn from their control, and also from the attacks of the 'Mamelukes', wild bands of Portuguese-Indian half-castes, who descended on the villages and carried away large numbers of the inhabitants into slavery. This was not remedied until 1641, when the king of Portugal strictly forbade his subjects all access to the Jesuit region, and permitted the fathers to arm the Indians for their own defence.

The plan of all the 'reductions' was much the same. In the centre stood the church; in many cases this was a really noble and splendid edifice, as is attested by the ruins which still stand amid the encroaching jungle. The people were lodged in houses neatly arranged in rows. A large part of the cultivable land belonged to the Church, and here the people had to work for an appointed number of hours each week, but they had also their own gardens in which they could work at their pleasure. A considerable number of industries were introduced. Elementary education was given, and literature, though not in any very large quantities, was produced in the Guaraní language. The Christian festivals were celebrated with great splendour, and much attention was given to music, sacred and secular.

Life was peaceful, happy, and well ordered. Discipline was strict and harsh, but not cruel. Indians were appointed as overseers and headmen, but they had little authority. In reality the Jesuit was master of all he surveyed.

The weakness of all this great enterprise was that the Jesuits did so little to develop a sense of initiative and independence among their flock. They seemed to wish rather to have around them docile children than to train adults for self-government. They had complete control of the situation for more than a century; in that time they never brought forward a single candidate for the priesthood, and developed no order of religious women or nuns. The Jesuits maintained that the time for such things had not yet come – among simple people progress is slow, and the Indians had not yet manifested that stability of character which would justify their admission to the priesthood. The nemesis of this policy came when the Jesuits were expelled; the Indians had not the necessary self-discipline and power of leadership to maintain themselves in a hostile world. Everything crumbled, and by the end of the eighteenth century hardly anything was left. The jungle had claimed its own.

The second half of the eighteenth century was a period of tragic collapse for the Roman Catholic missions.

The first cause of this collapse was undoubtedly the change in the whole international situation. Spain and Portugal were now no longer the leading powers in the world; the Pope's Bulls dividing the world between them were no longer worth the paper on which they were written. From 1600 onwards, the Protestant powers – England, Holland, and Denmark – began to enter what the Roman Catholic nations had regarded as their exclusive demesne. French Canada was separated from French Louisiana by a whole belt of English colonies. Jamaica, captured by the British in the days of Oliver Cromwell, had not been given back. In 1624 the Dutch occupied Formosa. In 1633 they captured Cochin; in 1641 Malacca; in 1658 Colombo; in 1660 Macassar. By the middle of the eighteenth century it was clear that England, not France, would be the dominant power in India, and Portugal had almost ceased to count.

The two hostile camps into which Christendom had been divided by the wars of religion extended their quarrels overseas. Cromwell's 'western plan' (1654–8) was uncompromisingly directed towards the expansion of Protestantism and its consolidation through the weakening of the Catholic powers. In later times Britain was less openly hostile to the work of Roman Catholic missions, and maintained an attitude of neutrality towards them. Holland was throughout mercilessly opposed, and intent on destroying what the Roman Catholics had built up. In Ceylon, where Roman Catholics numbered perhaps 300,000, lack of priests, political pressure, and the favour shown to Protestants resulted in a landslide of converts into the Dutch Church – a process which was reversed when the British restored religious liberty in 1795.

Missions in Asia depended very largely on the favour of the local rulers. From this point of view also the eighteenth century was an unfavourable time. We have seen how Japanese Christianity was almost completely destroyed by persecution. Similar experiences were to follow in other parts of the world also.

In China, as the Jesuits had feared, Roman interference and the imprudence of some of their brethren led to wave upon wave of persecution. In 1724 a decree of the new emperor Yung-chêng declared that the Jesuits who were in Peking might be permitted to remain, as they were useful to the court, but that all missionaries in the provinces must be rounded up and deported to Macao. The Jesuits did manage to maintain themselves in Peking almost till the end of the century; but, though persecution was intermittent and a number of missionaries were able to escape the net, numbers were always few, martyrdoms were many, the Chinese priests were not sufficient to maintain the work, and everywhere the tale was of diminishing congregations, of ruined churches, and of steadily deepening shadows.

In 1747 a Dominican, Bishop Sanz, with four other Dominicans, was arrested and tortured in Fukien. The bishop was beheaded in the following year, and somewhat later his companions. The Jesuit Bishop of Nanking, Laimbeckhoven, however, managed to maintain himself, almost always in hiding, from 1760 till 1787, when he died at T'ang-ka-laong, not far from Shanghai. One of the most notable of the Chinese priests, Andrew Ly (1693–1774), who had been trained at the seminary in Ayuthia and ordained in 1725, lived for forty years in Szechwan. He is our best authority for this period, since his diary for the years 1746 to 1763, written in fluent Latin, has been preserved.[19] His constant complaints are of the lack of Chinese priests and of the low level of life among the Chinese Christians. It is a sad picture.

In 1784 two bishops and sixteen European priests were rounded up; six of these died in chains. Something of Chinese Christianity survived; it is not surprising that it was not very much, and that in the nineteenth century almost everything had to be done afresh from the start.

A similar situation prevailed in Siam and in North Vietnam. Only in South Vietnam were the prospects brighter; a Christian community of, it is said, 200,000 members, with twenty-eight

19. The Latin text of this diary has been printed by A. Launay, *Journal d'André Ly, prêtre chinois, missionaire et notaire apostolique, 1746–1763* (2nd ed. Hong Kong, 1924).

European and forty-seven local priests, lived in comparative peace, and was able not merely to maintain itself but to grow.

In this period, in which the missionary work of the Church had run into grave difficulties, a final blow was struck by the dissolution of the Jesuit Order. From the beginning, as we have seen, both secular clergy and religious Orders had been hostile to the Jesuits. Complaints of their arrogance, their improper missionary methods, their interference in political affairs, and the vast wealth accumulated through their commercial speculations, had been endless. Rome waited long, but in the end decided to strike. On 21 July 1773, in the Brief *Dominus ac Redemptor*, Pope Clement XIV dissolved the Society of Jesus, sequestrated all its property, and declared that no pope in the future should ever recall it into being. At that time the Society numbered 22,589 members, of whom 11,293 were priests. As a result of the dissolution at least 3,000 missionaries were withdrawn from their fields. A certain number gave up the name of Jesuit and remained at their posts; the great majority were given no choice – they were put on board ship like cattle and carried off to their country of origin. They were literally irreplaceable; the Pope had condemned Roman Catholic missions to temporary eclipse.

In many places, as in Paraguay, disaster was complete. In South India, the Paris Society rather reluctantly took over the Jesuit work, and was able to supply about six Frenchmen where there had been forty Jesuits. Xavier's Fisher Coast was supplied with a number of Goanese priests, who (if their enemies are to be believed) were not altogether admirable, and hardly cared to maintain even a nominal celibacy. The Malabar coast was rather better provided for, as the number of Indian priests was greater. But everywhere there was the same feeling of desertion, desolation, and almost despair.

This finds a poignant expression in the *Letters on the State of Christianity in India* of the Abbé J. A. Dubois, one of the French missionaries sent in to replace the missing Jesuits. For him the great time of missionary work was the seventeenth century and the age of Roberto Nobili. Around him he could see nothing but decay and poverty. Possessed of a precisely accurate acquaintance with the country and its people,[20] he took a low view of the Indian character and of the quality of Indian Christians. To read Dubois

20. He was also the author of the famous *Hindu Manners, Customs and Ceremonies*, a classic of patient and accurate observation.

is to wonder whether in Asia there could be any second spring for the Church.

Our survey of two centuries has shown us a number of men who would have been outstanding in any age or country, and a number of notable experiments. Almost every possible form of missionary work had been tried – accommodation and the fierce refusal of accommodation; individual conversion in China and group conversion in South India; the ordination of priests in Goa and the refusal of ordination in other areas; the appeal of the Jesuits to the rulers and the appeal of the Franciscans to the poor and outcast. Every method had had its at least partial successes; none escaped from the general disaster and collapse. At the end of two centuries there was remarkably little to show for so much heroism, labour, and self-sacrifice.

Some of the causes of these disasters have come before us. It is necessary to look a little further before closing this chapter.

Missionary activity is always a sign of vitality in the Church. The sixteenth and seventeenth centuries had been times of great spiritual renewal, ready to pour itself out in labour for the world's benefit. The eighteenth century, in all the Churches, was a time of lassitude and retreat. The Roman Catholic Church had been internally weakened by the endless controversies over Jansenism; neither the Jansenists nor their opponents the Jesuits could really claim to be victorious. And, with this inner weakness, the Churches in Europe were unable to meet the crying demands of the missions for reinforcement and support.

The number of those engaged in the work was in reality very small and totally inadequate. In two hundred years the Jesuit Order had only 456 members in China, of whom nearly one fifth were Chinese. Mortality through disease and persecution was heavy. Every journey was an adventure. Of 376 Jesuits sent to China between 1581 and 1712, 127 were lost on the voyage through disease or shipwreck. It is amazing that so small a company of men achieved so much.

The Propaganda did its utmost to achieve central direction of the work, but at point after point its work was frustrated by the difficulty of communication, by the rapidly changing circumstances of the times, and by the opposition of the rulers. The inflamed disputes between the various Orders, which have come before us again and again, must bear a heavy weight of responsibility for the limited success of the work. We have seen the brethren in the faith prepared to fight one another tooth and nail on the very edge of the pit; energy which ought to have gone into extending the frontiers of the Church was constantly dissipated in the trivial battle of maintaining canonical rights over a narrow area.

Two further comments may be made, in the light of later knowledge and especially of the experience of Protestant missions.

The heavy preponderance of foreigners over indigenous priests was a grave disadvantage to the cause. The reasons are easily understandable, and the results of some hasty experiments in the ordination of converts were enough to make prudent men hesitate. But the gravest obstacles were the insistence of the Roman Church on making local rules of its own – the celibacy of the clergy and the use of Latin for the liturgy – into principles for universal acceptance throughout the younger Churches. We have seen some rather weak attempts to modify the latter of the two rules; the former was never even questioned. It was not until the twentieth century that the indigenous priesthood in the Roman Churches overseas began to overtake the foreign element, and the process is still far from having been completed.

The first principle of Protestant missions has been that Christians should have the Bible in their hands in their own language at the earliest possible date. The Roman Catholic method has been different. It is not true to say that nothing had been done; we have heard of some translations of Scripture. But for the most part such literature as had been produced was made up of catechisms and books of devotion. It is a fact that, though the Roman Catholics had been on the Fisher Coast in South India since 1534, the first translation of the New Testament into Tamil was that completed by the Protestant Ziegenbalg in 1714. The first Roman Catholic missionaries arrived in the Philippines in 1565. In three centuries almost the whole population had become Christian, yet it appears that the first translation of any part of the Scriptures into any language of the Philippines, the Gospel of Luke in the Pangasinan language, was made only in 1873. Is it possible that the translation of Scripture is not a Protestant fad, but a Catholic principle of universal obligation, which any missionary enterprise will neglect at its peril?

Much had been destroyed. But not all had been lost. In almost every country the Church had a bridgehead. Languages had been learned and grammars written. The great memories of the past remained. The revival of Roman Catholic missions in the nineteenth century was not an absolutely new beginning: the dry bones lived again. What seemed to be a dry tree revived through the scent of water. Through tragedy and disaster there was still a continuity of faith.

7

New Beginnings in East and West, 1600–1800

So far we have recorded the work of only one part of Western Christendom. It could not be otherwise. The active participation of Christendom as a whole in the work of the Christian mission belongs to the nineteenth century. In this chapter we shall record beginnings in the Orthodox and Protestant worlds, but these are only beginnings, and glaringly weak in comparison with the efforts put forth by the Roman Catholic Church.

It is easy to see why this was so.

The Eastern Churches had been paralysed by the double blow of the advance of Islam through Asia Minor almost to the heart of Christian Europe, and of the advance of the pagan Tartars into Russia. The capture of Constantinople marked the end of the Eastern Empire and of the great missionary history of the Greek-speaking Churches. The southern Orthodox Churches of the great patriarchates of Constantinople, Antioch, Jerusalem, and Alexandria lived on sufferance and under duress in the successive periods of Arab and Turkish domination. There can be no doubt that they could and did exercise a profound influence on their Muslim masters – this is clear from the utterances of many of the Sūfīs, the mystics of the Muslim world. But direct evangelization was impossible. In the nineteenth century many of these Churches regained their freedom, together with the political emancipation of their countries, but the work of Christian missions had not yet been resumed. It was long before Russia was able to pull itself together, to reassert its independence, and to take its place as an aggressive and expansive Christian power.

One effect of the Tartar invasion was to create a real unity of the Russian nation. All the various stocks – Slavs, Scandinavians, Finns – of which it was made up had suffered so much together that opposition to a common foe had brought them into a unity such as they had not previously known. And it is not to be supposed that no attempt was made in these troubled days to preach the Gospel to the still pagan peoples. The most notable of the missionaries of this period was Stefan Charp (1340–96), who in 1383 was consecrated as Bishop of the missionary diocese of Perm, in which he had been active for a number of years. Stefan followed the excellent tradition of the missions of the Eastern Church – the use of the local language, the maintenance of the customs and manners of his Syrian flock, as far as this was possible, and the avoidance of doubtful methods of winning converts. It is the judgement of a modern scholar that his work

was marked by wisdom and breadth of outlook . . . It was entirely free from political involvements . . . His whole missionary activity was solid and prudent. He was careful to guard against merely outward success, and devoted himself to the strengthening and deepening of Christian faith among his converts.[1]

Stefan's actual success was small, and his efforts were not adequately followed up, but his example remained as a memory and as an inspiration to those who came after.

Three new factors changed the whole attitude of the Russian state towards missionary work.

The first was a sharpening of the sense of opposition to Islam. When the Tartars first entered Russia, they were not Muslims. When, a century later, they accepted Islam, the form in which they accepted it was entirely free from fanaticism or persecuting zeal. Christians and Muslims lived together in amity. This made possible a great deal of interpenetration, and kept the eastern steppes open to Russian infiltration. On the other hand, such friendly coexistence is not easily compatible with converting zeal. This situation was altered when the new Khanates on the Volga took up a more rigid attitude, and turned the Volga into a boundary which the Christian could no longer easily pass.

This sharper attitude of Islam towards Russia, and Russia towards Islam, was strengthened by the fall of Constantinople in 1453. The last great bastion in the south has fallen. Moscow is now the heir and champion of the Byzantine world. From now on the rulers of Moscow begin to refer to their city as 'the third Rome'. The first Rome has fallen into heresy. (Russia never accepted the temporary union of the Eastern and Western Churches achieved at the Council of Florence in 1438, and signalized its independence by refusing to receive back Isaac of Kiev, the last of the Greek metropolitans of Russia.) The second Rome, Constantinople, has fallen under the dominion of the Turk. Moscow alone is left, called into existence by God to be the centre of the world in these later times.

1. K. Lübeck, *Die Christianisierung Russlands* (1922), p. 23.

Ivan III (1462–1505) married as his second wife the niece of the last emperor of Constantinople, John Palaeologus. From that time on he adopted the title emperor and regarded himself as the legitimate successor of the Byzantine line. He is the second Constantine, God's representative upon earth, to resist whom is rebellion against God. So when Ivan IV the Terrible (1533–84) set out in 1552 to reduce the Tartar Khanate of Kazan to subjection, the campaign took on in his eyes the character of a holy war. His first official document after the capture of the city of Kazan related to the foundation of a Christian church; the inhabitants of the city were either baptized or driven out and replaced by Russians. It was only a logical step when in 1589 the Oecumenical Patriarch of Constantinople rather unwillingly raised Moscow to the dignity of a patriarchal see. The Russian state and the Russian Church were both ready to expand.

Once the expansive process had begun, the geographical extension of the Russian world was astonishingly rapid. The city of Tobolsk was founded in 1586. In 1619 the river Yenisei was crossed. In 1632 the Lena was reached, in the neighbourhood of what is now Yakutsk. In 1648 Russians stood for the first time on the shores of the Pacific Ocean, and Dezhnev rounded the East Cape and discovered the Bering Sea. Such rapid discovery did not, of course, mean a regular occupation of this vast and sparsely populated area, still less the assimilation and Christianization of its many peoples. That is a process which has been going on over three centuries, and in many ways is not complete even today.

The first activity of the Russian Church was no more than a skeleton provision for the needs of Russian Christians as they streamed over into the newly opened lands. It was recognized that the missionary task was difficult. Three forms of religion were already competing for the souls of the people. The majority were simple animists whose religion, commonly called shamanism, had perhaps more in common with magic than with what we call religion. But lamaism – Buddhism in its Tibetan form – had crept in from the south, and in certain regions Islam was a force to be reckoned with. The beginnings of a serious attempt to Christianize Siberia are to be traced only in the reign of Peter the Great.

On 18 June 1700 Peter set forth a *ukase*, in which it is laid down that:

for the strengthening and extension of the Orthodox Christian faith and for the proclamation of the Christian faith among the idolatrous peoples; also in order to bring the tributary peoples of the neighbourhood of Tobolsk and the other towns of Siberia to Christian faith and holy baptism, his highness . . . decided to write to the Metropolitan of Kiev in the following terms: he should . . . seek out a virtuous and learned man of good and blameless life; this man shall become Metropolitan of Tobolsk, and with God's help shall gradually bring those peoples in Siberia and China who live in the blindness of idolatry, and generally in ignorance, to the knowledge, the service, and the worship of the true and living God.

There can be no doubt that the sceptical intelligence of Peter was concerned as much with political as with religious aims, and it is characteristic of Russian missions, almost without exception, that the connection between Church and state has been so close that it is almost impossible to separate the work into its constituent elements.

The work went gradually forward, and seven phases can be distinguished in its progress.

1. *The Mission in West Siberia.* On 4 January 1702 Filofey (Philotheos) Leschinski (Leszczynski) was consecrated Bishop of Tobolsk, and set off at once for his vast and desolate diocese. With much discouragement he laboured intermittently till 1727 for the conversion of the Ostiaks, Voguls, Yakuts, and others of the region. Filofey was without doubt a zealous and devoted missionary, and his work was not without result; in his time the number of churches increased from 160 to 448, and he is said to have baptized 40,000 converts. One sinister feature of his work is the permission he obtained from the emperor to declare that those who became Christians would be free from arrears of taxes.

After the death of Filofey, the mission, already sadly lacking in personnel, fell into grave disarray. A period of renewal set in with the coming of Bishop Silvester Golovacky (1746–55); 462 baptisms are recorded for 1753, and 311 for 1754. But it was only after the lapse of a century that the work in this area was taken up with the needed vigour.

2. *The Mission to China.* From the end of the seventeenth century onwards, a number of Russians, some of whom seem to have been deserters from the army, were resident in Peking. When this became known in Russia, attempts were made to send priests to care for them, but this was so obviously a step in the direction of a Russian diplomatic mission that the Chinese, still faithful to their policy of the closed door against foreigners, steadily refused per-

mission for the residence of a Russian priest. It was only through the treaty of Kiachta (1727), in which the Russian emperor recognized the *de jure* sovereignty of China over Mongolia, that by way of compensation permission was granted for Russian clerics to dwell in Peking. The number of priests was limited to four.

The Russian mission managed to maintain itself throughout the eighteenth century. On the whole good relations were maintained with the Jesuits and their successors; so much so that when the last Roman Catholic bishop of the old mission, the Lazarist Pirès, died in 1838, he bequeathed the entire property of his mission to the Russian archimandrite. But the Russians could not but sadly contrast their own poverty and lack of influence with the position enjoyed by the Roman Catholics and the security guaranteed to them by the favour of the emperor. A small number of baptisms took place. One of the missionaries reported in 1732 that he had baptized nine Chinese, and between 1755 and 1772 there was a small but steady number of adhesions. Furthermore, the mission did serve as a centre for study, and even in the eighteenth century produced a number of notable orientalists. But this was very much a day of small things; in 1795 it was reported that there were only twenty-five Russian and ten Chinese Christians in the Church of Peking.

3. *The Mission to the Kalmucks.* The Kalmucks were a wandering people in the steppes to the south-east of the Ural mountains. Christian work among them was fatally compromised from the start by the involvement of the Russians in disputes as to the succession to the chieftainship among them. One of the candidates, Baksadai Dordjhi, thinking that he would be more sure of Russian aid if he became a Christian, was baptized and took the name of Peter Tayshin. Attempts were made to provide him with a priest, to follow him around in his nomadic life, but these were spasmodic, and little could be done to instruct these nominal Christians.

The leader in the work was a monk, Nicodim Lenkeevich (born 1673). At a somewhat later date, an attempt was made to give the Kalmuck Christians a settled home within Russia, but it was found impossible to wean them from the nomadic life which they preferred; few accepted the offer, many of them withdrawing again into their own inaccessible steppes. The incorporation of the Kalmucks into the Russian way of life did, however, make gradual progress; but this was not accompanied by any marked progress in Christian virtue; as late as 1780 the archpriest Chubovsky reported that the Kalmucks were living a completely double life, and that they were still much more Lamaists than Christians.

4. *The Mission on the Middle Volga*. The work in this region enjoyed far more notable outward success than any of the others which we have so far studied, but this was due not so much to greater apostolic zeal as to more steady application of the principle of rewards and favours to those who became Christians. Peter the Great confirmed the promises of his predecessors, and further added the privilege of exemption from the hated military service for those who would accept baptism. It is not surprising that these offers proved welcome to the inhabitants. It is recorded that, in the years 1701 to 1705, 3,683 pagan Tschermisses accepted baptism.

In later years, however, it was found that this method had not worked out entirely satisfactorily. A number of those who had been baptized years before knew hardly a single Christian prayer, and could barely make the sign of the Cross. It was explained that these converts knew no Russian, and that teaching had not been provided for them in their own language. Steps were taken to put things right, but without much success. In the 1730s it was discovered that no proper lists of the baptized were being kept, and that a number of people were being baptized two or three times over in order to secure the presents which were provided on the occasion.

The glorious time of this mission came in the period of the vigorous Metropolitan of Kazan, Luke Konashevich (1738–55), who set up a 'counting house of the newly baptized', organized on the strict lines of a business concern. The old privileges were renewed. The people, if not compelled – indeed in the *Instructions* set out by the bishop compulsion was forbidden – were at least warmly invited to come in. The 'counting house' showed that, in the twenty years from 1741 to 1762, 430,550 Chuvashes, Tschermisses, Ostiaks, and members of other tribes, had been brought into the Church. Not a single pagan was left in the area.

The Muslim Tartars resisted blandishments and threats alike. Only 8,310 were baptized. In 1750 the mullahs protested to the synod against the high-handed methods of the metropolitan. The synod did not accept their complaints as justified, but when, a little later, open revolt broke out among the Tartars, the government found it prudent to remove the over-zealous prelate to the purely Russian area of Belgorod.

5. *The Mission of East Siberia*. As early as 1682 a group of thirteen missionaries had been sent to 'the remote cities on the Lena and in

Dauria'. Their method of work was simple. Accepting the custom, imposed by the Cossacks, of buying and selling human beings as though they were cattle, they purchased numbers of the tribes-people, baptized them, and set them to work as serfs on the monastery lands. Thus a number of churches came into being. But the missionaries were not replaced, and in 1733 this first mission came completely to an end.

In 1727 Irkutsk became an independent diocese. The first bishop, Innocenty Kulchicky, who ruled for only four years, made such a deep impression of holiness that in 1805 he was officially recognized by the Church as a saint. But the organization of this wide area presented insuperable difficulties, and the work of evangelization, such as it was, was rather left to the initiative of individual missionaries than carried out according to any centrally directed plan.

Most notable among these individuals was Cyril Vasilyevich Suchanov (1741–1814). This layman devoted his whole life to the conversion of the Tungus people of Dauria. Believing that mission-ary work depended more on quality of life than on the spoken word, he reduced his personal possessions to what he could carry about in a travelling-bag, moved ceaselessly among the nomads, and won their whole-hearted affection. In 1776 he was able to build his first church. He gathered the Christians together to a more settled existence around the church, and taught them not only the Christian faith but also their first lessons in agriculture and handicraft. Now finding his ministry incomplete, he travelled to Irkutsk to be ordained by the Bishop Michael Mitkevitch, and then returned to devote himself again to his self-chosen toil.

6. *The Mission to Kamschatka*. This distant peninsula is largely made up of volcanoes, which rise at their highest point to 17,000 feet. The climate is hard, the mean temperature for the year in the southern and more genial part of the land being only 3°C. Almost from the time of its discovery Kamschatka was used by the Russians as both a military station and a penal colony. Its inhabitants, who belonged to three quite separate races, were just emerging from the stone age when they were brought into contact with Russian civilization.

The first Christian witness on the peninsula was the archiman-drite Martinian, who arrived in 1705. He was able to baptize a number of converts, but was murdered in 1717. In spite of this unpromising beginning, the work went forward, and it was re-ported that, between 1733 and 1744, 878 baptisms had taken place.

The real apostle of Kamschatka, however, was Ioasaf Chotun-shevsky, who had been preacher in the Moscow Academy, and arrived in the peninsula in 1745, accompanied by two monks, a deacon, and six students who had travelled with him from Moscow, and no less than seven clerics whom he had picked up in Tobolsk. Chotunshevsky first directed his attention to the Russian population, which was scandalous both in its conduct and in its neglect of the rites of the Church. Stern measures were taken to bring things back to order. Then, dividing his company into two, he set to work on a careful visitation of the whole peninsula. Baptisms were numerous, and Church life was regulated; two years later, Chotunshevsky was able to report that the moral life of the indigenous Christians was on a higher level than that of the Russian settlers. The mission was not carried through without loss; a monk, a student, and two acolytes were murdered in a revolt of the inhabitants. But in 1748 Chotunshevsky was able to report a Christian population of 11,574 and to state that special missionary work was no longer necessary in what could now be regarded as a settled Christian area.

At a later date disaster fell on the peninsula. In the winter of 1766–7 a fearful epidemic of smallpox broke out. More than half the population died, including four out of the seven priests. Eight of the ten schools were closed. This was a blow from which the Church did not recover till well on in the nineteenth century.

7. *The 'American' Mission.* The Aleutian islands spread out in a semi-circle between Asia and America, and are now divided between Russia and the United States. In 1728 Vitus Bering, a Dane in Russian service, rightly recognized that the land which Dezhnev had seen to the east was the American continent, and crossed the sea which still bears his name. The Aleutians were discovered in 1743 and annexed to Russia in 1766. In 1770 a Russian merchant Shelekhov sent a trading vessel to the islands; it was through the enterprise of this layman that Christian missionary work was begun.

Shelekhov had noticed that the local people used to gather round the camps and listened eagerly while the exiled Russians sang the Christian songs that reminded them of their homeland. In 1787 he wrote to the senate and the synod to suggest that missionaries should be sent. The request was heard, and the archimandrite Ioasaf Bolotov was appointed head of the mission. He took with him four monks, two deacons, and two lay brothers. We possess a lively record of his journey which opens with the words, 'I started off from Moscow on 22 January 1794.'

On arrival, the missionaries found that the inhabitants, whose own religion amounted to little more than the fear of evil spirits, and who regarded the Creator God *Aguguk* as being so distant that they offered him no worship, were extraordinarily ready to accept baptism. They believed the explanation for this to be that the people had already had long and friendly relations with the Russian settlers. In one winter 6,000 people were baptized in the island of Kodiak alone, 'and they accepted baptism with such conviction that they broke and burned all the objects of their shamanistic worship'. In 1796 a Christian population of nearly 10,000 was reported, and the work had been extended to the American mainland.

Such good news suggested that Ioasaf should be raised to the episcopate, in order to care more fully for this growing church. On 10 April 1797 he was consecrated at Irkutsk. But these high hopes were not to be fulfilled; not far from its destination, the ship in which he was returning foundered, and was lost with all hands. In the years that followed, vodka and disease wrought havoc with the simple people of the Aleutians. We shall have to record one later period of successful missionary work; today only a pathetic fragment remains of what at one time was a promising younger Church.

The history of Russian expansion, which we have been following, is strangely mixed – statecraft, coercion, bribery, heroic zeal, apostolic simplicity, willingness to suffer and to die. And looking back over two centuries of effort it is hard to judge what the results may really have been. The final impression, perhaps, is that the Russian Church was still living in the Middle Ages or even earlier. We often feel that we are in the eighth and not the eighteenth century. Yet out of the chaos and darkness of that confusing time were to spring some of the most notable achievements of the nineteenth century. The winds of spring were cold and nipping, but they too may have made their contribution to the harvest that was to follow.

In the Protestant world, during the period of the Reformation, there was little time for thought of missions. Until 1648 the Protestants were fighting for their lives; only the Peace of Westphalia in that year made it certain that Protestantism would survive – and in France its survival was precarious, as was made clear by the revocation of the Edict of Nantes by Louis XIV in 1685. Instead of standing together and waiting for better times to clear their theological differences, Protestants everywhere wasted their strength, with honourable but blind and reckless zeal, in endless divisions and controversies – strict Lutherans against 'Philippists', Lutherans against Reformed, Calvinist predestinarians against Armenians, Anglicans against Puritans and Independents.

Apart from this inner weakness, in the sixteenth century the Protestant powers were not in touch with the wider world outside Europe. Spain and Portugal controlled the sea routes, and combined a certain religious imperialism with the political imperialism of their rulers. The Germans mostly stayed at home. And the geographical limitations were strongly reinforced by the psychological limitations of the concept of the regional Church, the *Landeskirche. Cuius regio, eius religio* – in each area the ruler is responsible for the spiritual welfare of his people; he will decide how they will worship, and in his dominions he will exercise supreme authority over the Church as well as in the state. *In his dominions.* He has no responsibility for anything outside; other rulers will care for the people of their own dominions. It is hardly possible for a Church so confined within the boundaries of a given geographical area ever to become missionary in any real sense of the term. The whole situation underwent radical alteration in the seventeenth century, when Holland and England became great maritime powers, but the theological climate was very slow to change.

At the end of the sixteenth century the famous Roman Catholic controversialist Robert Bellarmine included among the eighteen marks of the true Church its missionary activity, and made it a subject of reproach to the Protestants that they had no comparable missionary activity. His actual words should be quoted:

C 12: The effectiveness of its teaching. Heretics are never said to have converted either pagans or Jews to the faith, but only to have perverted Christians. But in this one century the Catholics have converted many thousands of heathens in the new world. Every year a certain number of Jews are converted and baptized at Rome by Catholics who adhere in loyalty to the Bishop of Rome; and there are also some Turks who are converted by the Catholics both at Rome and elsewhere. The Lutherans compare themselves to the apostles and the evangelists; yet though they have among them a very large number of Jews, and in Poland and

Hungary have the Turks as their near neighbours, they have hardly converted even so much as a handful.[2]

This was a damaging charge, and it cannot be said that the Protestants were happy in their attempts to answer it. We are all much given to rationalization, to finding good reasons for what we do, when the real reasons may in fact be less creditable. Instead of saying 'We ought to have missions, and we will have them, as soon as the Lord opens the door', the Protestants tended to say 'Missions are neither obligatory nor desirable, and our lack of them cannot be held against us as blindness or unfaithfulness'.

Naturally the Reformers were not unaware of the non-Christian world around them. Luther has many things, and sometimes surprisingly kind things, to say about both Jews and Turks.[3] It is clear that the idea of the steady progress of the preaching of the Gospel through the world is not foreign to his thought. Yet, when everything favourable has been said that can be said, and when all possible evidences from the writings of the Reformers have been collected, it all amounts to exceedingly little.[4]

In the seventeenth century the negative view was set forth – in controversy with Adrian Saravia (1531–1613), a Dutchman who had come to England and become canon of Westminster – by Johann Gerhard (d. 1637). Gerhard's point of view was that the command of Christ to preach the Gospel to all the world ceased with the apostles. In their day the offer of salvation had been made to all the nations; there was no need for the offer to be made a second time to those who had already refused it. This kind of judgement was frequently repeated, and when the independent thinker Justinian von Welz (1621–68), in a series of notable writings, and later in a missionary enterprise to the Dutch colony of Surinam in which he lost his own life, tried to swim against the

2. R. Bellarminus, *Controversiae*, Book IV; quoted in C. Mirbt, *Quellen zur Geschichte des Papsttums und des Römischen Katholizismus* (3rd ed. 1911).

3. Not always so kind. The remark that 'the faith of Jews, Turks, and Papists is all one thing' was not likely to be particularly welcome to any one of the three parties. But it is noteworthy that when the town council of Basel in 1542 forbade the publication of Theodore Bibliander's translation of the Qur'ān, it was the appeal of Luther, supported by the Strasbourg theologians, that led the town council to change its mind. Luther wished Christendom to know 'what an accursed, shameful, and desperate book it is'. See E. Kellerhals, *Der Islam* (1956), pp. 319–25.

4. Everything that can be said is carefully set out by H. W. Gensichen in his *Missionsgeschichte der neueren Zeit* (1961), pp. 5–7.

current, he was met by the shocked disapproval of the authorities of the Church.

At three points in the sixteenth century we can see faint beginnings of missionary enterprise. King Gustavus Vasa of Sweden, from 1526 on, encouraged work among the still pagan Lapps in the furthest north of his dominions; after a period of little success, largely due to the failure of the missionaries to learn the local language, and an interval in which nothing seems to have been done, the work was resumed years later with better effect under Charles IX (1604–11). A group of which the centre was the German nobleman Hans Ungnad von Sonneck set itself to propagate the principles of the Reformation by the circulation of books in the South Slavonic languages, and hoped by this means to enter the world of Islam. They never got to the point of sending out Christian books in Turkish, but lived in the hope that it might one day be possible in this way to 'bring the Turks to true Christian faith'[5] – an interesting early example of evangelism through Christian literature. Wenzel Budowetz von Budow (Václav Budovec), who was in Constantinople from 1577 to 1581, produced in 1614 a refutation of the Qur'ān in the Czech language, and is reported to have converted one single Turk.

In reality, it is only when the Dutch and the English begin to push their commercial ventures to the ends of the earth that Protestantism begins to breathe a freer missionary air.

The universal genius Hugo Grotius (1583–1645) wrote an outline of the Christian faith, *De Veritate Religionis Christianae* (1627). Its first short version in Dutch is meant for the use of Dutch sailors travelling to the Far East.[6] Under the influence of the pressure exercised by some in the Churches, the Dutch East India Company (founded 1602) set up a seminary in Leyden, which between 1622 and 1633 trained twelve ministers for service in what were by that time the Dutch possessions in *Indonesia* and *Ceylon*. Dutch missionary work here followed very closely the Roman Catholic model. The ministers were civil servants, whose primary responsibility was the spiritual care of Dutchmen in the East. But at the same time they were to work for the conversion of the natives. The minister received a cash bonus for each person baptized.

5. E. Benz, *Wittenberg und Byzanz*, p. 194.
6. Latourette affirms, on the authority of G. Warneck, that this work was translated into Malay (*Expansion*, Vol. III, p. 304). The orientalist Edward Pocock translated it into Arabic in 1660.

Special privileges were given to Christians, and the political motive played as large a part as the religious. It is not surprising that the number of converts was large; by the end of the seventeenth century the Dutch claimed 100,000 Christians in Java and 40,000 in Ambon. But the sincerity of the converts left much to be desired. Not all, however, was dross; the New Testament was translated into Malay (1668), a notable achievement, and the first Bible translation into any language of South-east Asia.[7] The Church in Ambon has maintained a vigorous existence until the present day. But on the whole the work was lamentably superficial. In 1776 there were only twenty-two ministers in the whole of Indonesia, and of these only five could speak the language. Of the thousands baptized, not so many as one in ten was ever admitted to Holy Communion.[8]

In *Taiwan* (Formosa), which the Dutch partly took over from the Spaniards in 1624, they seem to have made a better showing; a real attempt was made to plant the Church of Christ. But the Dutch were driven out in 1661 by Chinese pirates, under the lead of Chêng Ch'êng-kung, 'Koxinga', who is now regarded as a national hero, and this first attempt at the evangelization of that most beautiful country ended in nothing.[9]

The discovery of America and the beginning of European colonization let loose in England, as elsewhere, a flood of interest in the primitive peoples who had there been brought to light. Whatever might be thought about the other nations, it was quite clear that the American Indians had not been evangelized by the apostles; by the late discovery of this new world God was calling his Church to new and apostolic venture. The charter granted to Sir Humphrey Gilbert in 1578 referred to the compassion of God 'for poor infidels, it seeming probable that God hath reserved these Gentiles to be introduced into Christian civility by the English nation'. Similarly, when Charles I granted a charter to the colony of Massachusetts, he included the statement that the principal end of the plantation was that the colonists might 'win and incite the

---

7. It should be added that the entire Bible appeared in Malay in Roman letters in 1733 and in the Arabic script in 1758; but this was subsequent to the appearance of Ziegenbalg's Tamil New Testament in 1714.

8. Note here the close parallel to Roman Catholic practice in Latin America.

9. It appears that most of the converts were won from among the primitive and aboriginal peoples and not from among the Chinese.

natives of the country to the knowledge of the only true God and Saviour of mankind and the Christian faith'.

Anglicans were not on the whole very good at spreading Christian civility among their Indian neighbours. The first sustained attempt to carry out this pious purpose was the work of the Presbyterian John Eliot (1604–90). In 1632 Eliot became pastor of Roxbury in Massachusetts, and almost immediately set himself to learn the language of the Pequot tribe of the Iroquois. In 1651 the first baptisms took place. Finding that it was almost impossible for the converted Indian to live a Christian life, if he remained within his tribe, Eliot took a leaf out of the Roman Catholic book, and began to form 'Praying Towns' of which Natick was the first. By 1671 he had gathered about 3,600 Christian Indians into fourteen settlements, and had begun the training of Indian preachers, who numbered twenty-four at the time of his death. Indians who came to dwell in the settlements made a covenant in the following terms:

> The grace of Christ helping us, we do give ourselves and our children to God to be his people. He shall rule us in all our affairs, not only in our religion and the affairs of the Church, but also in all our works and affairs in this world.

The work for which Eliot is most widely remembered is the translation of the Bible into the 'Moheecan' language. The New Testament was published in 1661, and the Old Testament in 1663. At the end of his Indian grammar, Eliot appended the motto which sums up his life, and that of many other missionaries: 'Prayer and pains, through faith in Christ Jesus will do anything.'[10]

The most famous, after Eliot, of those who laboured among the Indians, was David Brainerd (1718–47). When he died, worn out by his labours, in the house of his friend Jonathan Edwards, he left behind one notable treasure, his diary, a classic of the devotional life in which the true Protestant aspiration after utmost holiness of life finds faithful expression. Brainerd died, but lived on in the lives of those, like William Carey and Henry Martyn, who found inspiration in his impassioned words.

In 1701 the Anglican Society for the Propagation of the Gospel in Foreign Parts was founded as an incorporated society with a royal charter. During the eighteenth century the main work of the Society was in caring for the needs of the Anglicans in America and

10. Carleton Beals, *John Eliot, The Man who Loved the Indians* (New York, 1957), has not been accessible to me.

the West Indies, who had been gravely neglected by the mother
Church, and for two centuries were left without episcopal care.
Three hundred and fifty missionaries were sent out, many of them
men of sterling worth and devotion. It must not, however, be
forgotten that missionary work among the non-Christians also
stood high on the list of the Society's purposes. On 20 April 1710
the Society carried two resolutions:

1. That the design of propagating the Gospel in foreign parts does chiefly
and principally relate to the conversion of heathens and infidels, and
therefore that branch of it ought to be prosecuted preferably to all
others.

2. That, in consequence thereof, immediate care be taken to send
itinerant missionaries to preach the Gospel among the Six Nations of the
Indians according to the primary intentions of the late King William of
glorious memory.

In pursuance of this plan, the missionaries of the Society in
many parts of America devoted themselves to work among the
Indians and Negroes, apparently with no small success, judging by
the report of the officer in command of the garrison of Fort Hunter,
New York State, in 1735:

I have found the Mohawk Indians very much civilized, which I take to be
owing to the industry and pains taken by the Rev. Mr John Miln in
teaching and instructing them in the Christian religion. The number
of communicants increases daily. . . . They are very observing of the
Sabbath, convening by themselves and singing Psalms on that day,
and frequently applying to me that Mr Miln may be oftener among
them.

Many other Churches, including the Roman Catholic, joined in
the work, which still goes on at the present day.[11] But over all the
work among the Indians hangs the shadow of tragedy. Long before
his death John Eliot had seen his work almost completely destroyed by the war between the Indians and the English. Whole
tribes have died out; it is the sad fact that today there is no one
living who can read Eliot's 'Moheecan' Bible. It is the tragic
history of the clash of two peoples at different stages of civilization;
almost inevitably that which is weaker in economic resources loses
the will to live. In recent years the Indian peoples in the United
States and Canada have at last begun to increase again in

11. Shortly before this chapter was written the writer had the privilege of
confirming a number of Onondaga Indians in the neighbourhood of Syracuse, NY.

numbers; but the problem of their integration into the life of the nation is very far from having been solved.

The history of missions supported by Churches on the European continent begins only with the emergence of the movement called pietism. Movements of the Spirit are always mysterious. The 'Spiritualism' of the sixteenth century, Roman Catholic mysticism, English Puritanism with its emphasis on individual conversion – all these things seem to have played their part in the origins of pietism. The first recognizable manifestation of what grew to be a world-wide movement was the book by Philipp Jakob Spener entitled *Pia Desideria* (1675). The aim of Spener, as of all his true followers, was not to create a sect or to separate from the Church, but to gather those within the Church who were most deeply concerned for their own salvation and that of others into groups for mutual edification and encouragement. The principles of pietism are the demand for personal conversion and for holiness, close fellowship in the Society, and responsibility for witness. The expectation that the return of Christ, which cannot be much longer delayed, will be preceded by a great outpouring of the Spirit of God on Jews and heathen led by a natural gradation of thought to a sense of responsibility for 'foreign' missions.

Just at the time at which pietism was becoming a power in the Churches, King Frederick IV of Denmark made up his mind to emulate the Roman Catholic rulers, and to concern himself for the well-being of his Indian subjects in the tiny Danish settlement of Tranquebar on the Coromandel Coast of south-east India. No missionaries could be found in Denmark, so the king turned to Halle in Germany, where the great pietist leader August Hermann Francke (1663–1727) was building up a complex of diverse good works, centring in the famous orphanage. Francke was at once able to supply two young men, Bartholomew Ziegenbalg and Henry Plütschau. They sailed from Europe at the end of 1705, and arrived at Tranquebar on 9 July 1706, the first non-Roman-Catholic missionaries to reach India from Europe.

Ziegenbalg was only twenty-three when he set out on his missionary career, and he died after only thirteen years in the field. But Francke knew his man, and could not have made a better choice. At point after point, with hardly any precedent to guide him, Ziegenbalg made the right decision, and showed the way that has been followed ever since by the best and most successful among the Protestant missions. And Ziegenbalg was an exhaustive and inexhaustible correspondent; in consequence, we know a great deal about what happened in the early and formative period of the Royal Danish Mission.[12]

Like most pioneers, Ziegenbalg and Plütschau were faced with endless difficulties – the hostility of the local Danish community, ceaseless harassment from the surly and unpleasant governor, the ill-will of the Danish clerics sent out to care for the spiritual well-being of the European population, misunderstandings and prejudices in Copenhagen, the dislike of the higher castes, the lack of interest on the part of the lower castes, the contemptuous hostility of the Roman Catholics. They had the utmost difficulty in finding any place in which to live, and in meeting anyone who would be willing to teach them Tamil. But gradually patience wore down the difficulties, and the pattern of the mission began to emerge. Five principles stand out clearly from the beginning:

1. Church and school are to go together. Christians must be able to read the Word of God, and therefore all Christian children must be educated.

Some years ago twenty-two coats of whitewash were removed from a very old building in the compound which the missionaries were able after some years to acquire; over the door were found the words *Dharmappallikūdam*, 'charity school'.

2. If Christians are to read the Word of God, that word must be available to them in their own language.

As soon as he was able, Ziegenbalg set to work to translate the New Testament. Fortunately, he had an excellent gift for languages; and, not content with being able to speak colloquial Tamil, set himself to master the extremely difficult classical form of the language. As we have seen, the Roman Catholics had made no attempt to translate the Scriptures; but they had gone a long way towards creating a Tamil Christian vocabulary, and of this Ziegenbalg was able to make use. The completed New Testament appeared in 1714.

Before his death, Ziegenbalg had advanced as far as the book of Ruth in the Old Testament; the work was completed by others, but these translators unfortunately lacked his careful scholarship, and the work had to be done all over again. This was the achievement of Johann Philipp Fabricius, whose Bible appeared in 1796, and is still in use, in a revised form, in some Churches. Fabricius was

12. Professor Arno Lehmann, of the University of Halle, published a large selection from the hitherto unpublished correspondence of Ziegenbalg, under the title *Alte Briefe aus Indien* (1957).

perhaps the greatest of all missionary translators of Christian hymns.

3. The preaching of the Gospel must be based on an accurate knowledge of the mind of the people.

To this end Ziegenbalg made a careful study of the actual religious beliefs of the people of South India and sent the results of his researches home to Europe. He received the tart reply that his business was to root out Hinduism in India, and not to propagate heathen superstition in Europe. His book remained unpublished for a century and a half; it was at last published in 1867 under the title *The Genealogy of the Malabar Gods*, through the efforts of his biographer Wilhelm Germann in Halle.[13]

4. The aim must be definite and personal conversion.

The Tranquebar missionaries were not faced by the problems of a group movement; they did, however, experience the difficulties arising from the attraction of missionary money for the very poor. It is unlikely that they were always well advised in their acceptance of candidates for baptism, and in their reception of discontented Roman Catholic candidates; at least they tried to keep their standards high.

5. At as early a date as possible an Indian Church, with its own Indian ministry, must come into being.

It has often been maintained that the missionaries, being pietists, were so concerned about rescuing individual brands from the burning as to have little sense of Church and community. This may or may not be true of later missionaries; it is wholly untrue of the pioneers in Tranquebar. In 1709, only three years after the foundation of the mission, Ziegenbalg wrote that one member of the mission ought to be given the *potestas ordinandi*, in order that the organization of the Church might be complete. In point of fact, the first ordination of an Indian pastor, Aaron, took place as early as 1733. A convert from Hinduism, he had already served for fifteen years as a catechist when he was brought forward for ordination; he served faithfully in the area of Māyāvaram until his death in 1745.

Only fourteen pastors were ordained in the mission in a hundred years. Great care was taken in the selection, and missionaries were so few that a pastor, once ordained, had to work in almost complete

13. *Genealogie der Malabarischen Götter* (Madras, 1867). Another work of Ziegenbalg on a similar subject, *Malabarisches Heidentum*, was discovered in the archives at Halle and published by W. Caland at Amsterdam (1926).

independence. There were few failures, and some of these men did quite outstanding service.

When Ziegenbalg died there was in Tranquebar a Christian community of about 350 persons. Some of these were slaves of European masters, some were children adopted as orphans; some, as we have seen, had come over – for good or bad reasons – from the Roman Catholics. But a considerable number were genuine converts. The Lutheran Church was beginning to take root in South India.

Nowhere had the work in Tranquebar been followed with greater interest than in England. The *Annual Letters* of the missionaries had been translated. Ziegenbalg, during his one leave in Europe, had been received both by the king and by William Wake, Archbishop of Canterbury. The press on which the Tamil New Testament had been printed, in its clumsy amateurish characters, had been presented by the Anglican Society for Promoting Christian Knowledge. This interest was of the greatest importance for the future of the work. It was not long before the missionaries grew tired of evangelizing the little world of Tranquebar, and extended their journeys into areas which were already British territory and into the still independent kingdom of Tanjore under its foreign Marātha ruler. The king of Denmark made it clear that money contributed by him could be used for the work in Tranquebar and nowhere else; the principle of *cuius regio* was sacrosanct. At this point the SPCK stepped in, and agreed to support the missionaries who worked in Madras, Cuddalore and other centres in what came to be known as 'the English mission'.

The East India Company had been formed in 1600. Its first ambassador (1616–18) at the court of the Great Mogul, the notable Sir Thomas Roe, was accompanied by his chaplain, and from that time on the Company did its best to provide religious ministrations for its servants in India and beyond. Some of the chaplains were faithful and even outstanding men. But chaplains were ill-paid, and all too many of them fell into the temptation of breaking the rules and engaging in the trade from which by law they were rigidly excluded. And in any case the workers were at all times too few for the work to be done. From time to time the Company issued firm regulations to the effect that the chaplains were to learn the local language, in order that they might better make known to the 'Gentoos' the truths of the Christian faith, but this seems at all times to have remained a dead letter. Only one baptism of an Indian in the Church of England is recorded in the seventeenth century. In 1614 a Bengali boy was brought home to England and instructed by Patrick Copeland, one of the Company's chaplains. He was baptized on 22 December 1616 in St Dionis, Backchurch, King James I himself choosing for him the baptismal name of Peter, to which he later oddly added the surname 'Pope'.[14] The event aroused great interest at the time, but it was not followed up.

It is, therefore, not altogether surprising that the British authorities in India turned to the German missionaries for help in the pastoral care of the troops and other British subjects who were to be found in increasing numbers in all parts of India. In general the East India Company was hostile to missionary effort, not so much on principle as because it had lived on the basis of non-interference with the customs of the country, and feared that religious propaganda might provoke the resentment of the inhabitants and so prove harmful to the development of commerce, but in South India it seemed to recognize no difficulty in the employment of missionaries as chaplains.

The missionaries of 'the English mission', then, in this remarkable ecumenical experiment, in many cases found themselves serving in a dual capacity. They were Germans sent out originally by the king of Denmark, taken over by the High Church Anglican Society for Promoting Christian Knowledge, and financially supported with a view to their preaching the Gospel to the non-Christians, and at the same time, they were chaplains to British regiments and communities. They used the Book of Common Prayer, and indeed translated it into Tamil; they baptized and celebrated the Lord's Supper according to the Anglican rite. All the details have not yet been worked out, but, strange as it may seem, the episcopal Church of England from 1728 to 1861 employed in South India missionaries who had never received episcopal ordination according to the Anglican rite. And when at last (1814) a bishop was appointed to Calcutta, he did not raise the question of Anglican ordination, and felt no difficulty in licensing those missionaries who were by that time in charge of settled congregations.

By far the most famous of all the missionaries who have worked in South India was Christian Friedrich Schwartz (1726–98), who

14. It is interesting to note that at that time the Book of Common Prayer contained no service for the baptism of adults; this was added only in 1662.

served in India for forty-eight years without a break. After ten years in Tranquebar and sixteen in Trichinopoly, where he served also as chaplain to the British community, he moved to Tanjore, which was his residence from 1778 till his death in 1798. Here he quickly gained the confidence of all classes, from the rajah down, and at one time was actually Diwān (prime minister) of the still independent kingdom, and special emissary of the British to the court of Haidar Ali the tyrant of Mysore. His uprightness and probity were such that, as a British officer wrote: 'The knowledge and integrity of this irreproachable missionary have retrieved the character of Europeans from imputations of general depravity.' Even at the height of his power, Schwartz never forgot that his character was first that of a Christian missionary; he preached, catechized and taught the young. The Tanjore Church under his care grew to a membership of 2,000 Christians. With his knowledge of the Indian character, Schwartz was always on his guard against the merely self-seeking convert; yet it has to be admitted that some found their way into the fold who would better have been kept out, and that after his death the congregations founded by him fell into a sad state of decay and collapse.

It is a little difficult to account for the extraordinary power exercised by Schwartz over the minds of the men of his day and for long afterwards. Something must be attributed to his wide knowledge – in addition to Portuguese, English, and Tamil, he had mastered Persian, which was then the language of the court, and Hindustani; to the charm which enabled him to move easily in all classes of society; to the extreme simplicity of his life – Schwartz spent nothing on himself and died a rich man, leaving considerable sums as endowment for the work that he had started; and to his reputation for utter self-forgetfulness and integrity. But central to everything was a simple and stalwart faith, and a total dependence on the merits of the Redeemer. Men who met Schwartz knew that they had seen a man of God. It is strange that the East India Company, at that time engaged in strenuous efforts to keep missionaries out of the other parts of India, set up at their own expense a memorial to Schwartz in the Fort Church at Madras. And the young Rajah Saraboji, who had been for years under Schwartz's care, also set up a marble monument, with the epitaph that he had himself composed:

> Firm wast thou, humble and wise,
> Honest and pure, free from disguise;

Father of orphans, the widow's support;
Comfort in sorrow of every sort.
To the benighted, dispenser of light,
Doing, and pointing to, that which is right.
Blessing to princes, to people, to me,
May I, my Father, be worthy of thee,
Wisheth and prayeth thy Sarabojee.

The later years of Schwartz were saddened by the decline of missionary zeal in Europe, and by the failure of the Churches adequately to support the missions. But before his death two great events had happened – William Carey had arrived in Bengal, and the first Protestant mass movement in India had begun. In 1771 Schwartz had visited Palamcottah and found Christians there. Some years later he baptized a Brahman lady, Clorinda, who had been previously living irregularly with a British officer; Clorinda built the first church, which was dedicated in 1785.[15] Some years later, in circumstances that are very far from clear, a large movement broke out among the hardy and vigorous, but almost wholly illiterate Nādār (Shānār) community in the neighbourhood of Cape Comorin. Between 1795 and 1805, the Tanjore missionaries and their Indian colleagues baptized upwards of 5,000 people. The foundation had been laid for the Tinnevelly Church, which a little more than a hundred years later was to produce the first Indian bishop of the Anglican Communion.

From the ever-warm we must turn to the ever-cold. One of the fruits of the Missionary College at Copenhagen was the mission of Hans Egede to *Greenland*.[16] Egede set out, with wife and family, in 1722, and lived in Greenland till 1736. A hardy northerner,[17] he did not find the climate of Greenland unduly harsh, and rejoiced in the beauty of both the Arctic winter and the Arctic spring. But in his work he experienced to the full the frustrations and hardships of the pioneer. He had the utmost difficulty in mastering the Eskimo language, and found it seemingly deficient in terms that could be

15. This small and undistinguished building is still in existence, and is occasionally used for Christian worship.

16. For his life and work, see O. G. Myklebust (ed.), *Hans Egede, 1686–1758* (1958), a series of essays in Norwegian, prepared for the bicentenary of Egede's death (5 November 1758); and L. Bobé, *Hans Egede: Colonizer and Missionary of Greenland* (Copenhagen, 1952; in English).

17. He had been born on 31 January 1686, at Harrestad, north of the Arctic Circle in Norway.

used for the expression of Christian truth. And the superstition of the Greenlanders seemed to him impenetrable; they were under the domination of the belief in evil spirits, and of their soothsayers (*angakut*), whose words were implicitly believed. It was long before Egede was willing to baptize a single adult Greenlander, contenting himself with the baptism of infants in the hope that the younger generation would be more deeply penetrated by Christian truth than their elders.

Egede was often harsh and overbearing in his dealings with the people, especially with the *angakut*, in spite of a genuine inner love for them. It was the terrible smallpox epidemic of 1733 which enabled him to overcome his natural hauteur, and really to win the love of his people. He and his devoted wife wore themselves out in caring for the sick – in her case literally, since she never recovered her health and died in 1734. But the value of her sacrifice is seen in the words of a dying Greenlander:

> You have been more kind to us than we have been to one another; you have fed us when we were famished; you have buried our dead, who would else have been a prey to dogs, foxes, and ravens; and in particular you have told us of God and how to become blessed, so that we may now die gladly, in expectation of a better life hereafter.

In 1734 Egede was greatly encouraged by the return from Denmark of his son Paul, who had been ordained as his helper in the mission. Paul had grown up with the Greenlanders, and could speak their language as his father was never able to do. When the settlement at Christianshaab was established in 1734, the people came from far and near to hear him preach in their own tongue; many sought baptism, and something like a religious revival came into being around Disko Bay. Paul had to return to Denmark because of failing eyesight; but to the end of his long life (he died in 1784) he never ceased to serve the cause of Christ in Greenland. In 1744 he produced a translation of the four Gospels in the Eskimo dialect spoken in Greenland, in 1760 a grammar, and in 1766 the whole of the New Testament.

Egede's mission was to lead to something greater than itself. In 1731 Count Nicolaus Ludwig von Zinzendorf was in Copenhagen. He heard that there was a likelihood that the Greenland mission would be abandoned; at once he decided to call his Brethren at Herrnhut to step into the breach, and 21 August 1732 is celebrated by the Moravian Churches as the beginning of their missionary work.

Some years earlier Zinzendorf had received the exiled brethren from Moravia on his estate at Herrnhut, and had organized them into a Church. Later he became an ordained minister, and finally in 1737 Bishop of the Church of the Brethren. Herrnhut developed its own form of pietism, with a deep devotion to the crucified Redeemer and an intense and strenuous demand for total surrender and consecration to his will. Under the leadership of Zinzendorf this small Church was seized with a missionary passion which has never left it. The Moravians have tended to go to the most remote, unfavourable, and neglected parts of the surface of the earth. Many of the missionaries have been quite simple people, peasants and artisans; their aim has been to live the Gospel, and so to commend it to those who have never heard it.

The Moravian missionaries arrived in Greenland in May 1733. Their leader was a layman, Christian David, a carpenter whose 'dauntless preaching and apostolically universal spirit' were praised by Zinzendorf, but who at the same time was self-willed and intolerant of the opinions of others. Denmark had had, in fact, no intention of abandoning the Lutheran mission, and the first task of the new missionaries was to determine their relationship to Hans Egede and his work. What followed is typical of what almost always happens when a second mission enters a territory where an older mission is already established. The newcomers pick on the weaknesses of the old, with little regard for what the pioneers have endured. The Moravians were very critical of Egede as a 'colonializer', a stiff orthodox churchman, possessed (in their judgement) of very little real Gospel light; while Egede found that the Moravians preached an intolerably sentimental Gospel, and had little idea of the moral conflict involved in the attempt to change the whole way of life of the Greenlanders.

Yet the Moravians, too, were faithful men, and built up in Greenland a Church which has endured. One of them has recorded a notable change in missionary method which was made in 1740, and the results which followed from it:

The method hitherto pursued by them consisted principally in speaking to the heathen of the existence, the attributes, and perfection of God, and enforcing obedience to the divine law ... abstractly considered, this method appears the most rational; but when reduced to practice, it was found wholly ineffectual. ... Now, therefore, they determined in the literal sense of the word to preach Christ and him crucified, without laying first 'the foundation of repentance from dead works, and faith towards God'. ... This reached the hearts of the audience, and produced the most astonishing effects. . . . They remained no longer the stupid and brutish creatures that they had been. . . . A sure foundation being thus laid in the knowledge of a crucified Redeemer, our missionaries soon found that this supplied the young converts with a powerful motive to the abhorrence of sin and the performance of every moral duty towards God and their neighbour.

Moravian work in the west began with the sending of two brethren to the island of St Thomas in the West Indies. In 1738 the work was extended to *Surinam* or Dutch Guiana. Results were long in coming. One of the early missionaries, George Dähne, lived for two years alone in a hut in the forest, surrounded by wild beasts and wilder men. Six years passed before the first convert, an old woman, was baptized. From that time on the work spread and grew, and, unlike so many of the efforts of earlier times, has continued till the present day.

One single isolated attempt at missionary work in Africa has to be recorded. In 1751 the Reverend Thomas Thompson, who had for five years been a missionary of the SPG in New Jersey, offered to go to the *Gold Coast* (now Ghana) to work among the Negroes – whom he had come to know in America – in their original home. Thompson was able to spend less than five years on the coast, and the results of his work were few. But he had sent three African boys under the age of twelve to England for education. Two died, but one, Philip Quaque, survived. Philip was baptized on 7 January 1759, and in 1765 was ordained as the first African to receive Holy Orders in the Church of England. He died in 1816 in Cape Coast, having served more than fifty years as 'missionary, schoolmaster, and catechist to the Negroes on the Gold Coast'.

America was at this stage of its development a mission field rather than an exporter of missionaries. Yet in America, too, the sense of the nearness of Christ's return, and the spirit of revival, awakened the sense of missionary obligation. The noted Congregationalist minister Cotton Mather (1663–1728) in Boston corresponded with Francke in Halle and with the missionaries in Tranquebar, and agreed with them that a world-wide preaching of the eternal Gospel, free from confessional limitations, would help to usher in that great outpouring of the Spirit which would be one of the signs of the end of the age. Jonathan Edwards (1703–58), theologian and revivalist and later president of Princeton, put mission in the centre of his programme, and associated it with the idea of a world-wide 'Concert of Prayer' for missionary work. This idea, originating in Scotland, caught the imagination of Edwards, who set out the programme at length in *A Humble Attempt to Promote Explicit Agreement and Visible Union of God's People in Extraordinary Prayer for the Revival of Religion and the Advancement of Christ's Kingdom on Earth, Pursuant to Scripture Promises, and Prophecies Concerning the Last Time*. This book, first published in 1747, was reprinted again and again until well on in the nineteenth century. It, and the wave of individual and united prayer which arose from it, was a potent instrument in extending the spiritual horizons of many Christians, and making them aware of another world for which also Christ had died.[18]

Why did our fathers, and especially President Edwards, pray for the expansion of the kingdom, but fail to act? So asked the Reverend Francis Brown, preaching before the Maine Missionary Society in 1814. Certain it is that the eighteenth century was a time of renewed awareness, and of small and tentative beginnings; it was the nineteenth that was destined to be the great century for the Christian world.

18. A very full and careful account of this aspect of the work of Edwards and his colleagues is given by P. Kawerau, *Amerika und die Orientalischen Kirchen: Ursprung und Anfang der amerikanischen Mission unter den nationalen Kirchen Westasiens* (Berlin, 1958).

PART TWO

8

Introduction

As a matter of pure chronology the nineteenth century should presumably extend exactly from 1800 to 1900, but in practice most working historians have found it convenient to treat it as having begun in 1789 with the outbreak of the French Revolution, and as having lasted till 1914, the beginning of the First World War. This was pre-eminently the European century in world history, the period in which Europe was able to impose its will and its ideas on the whole of the inhabited world. Whatever the unfaithfulness of Europe to the Christian faith, it is a matter of historical fact that Christianity and the Christian ideal have been inseparably connected with the growth of European civilization, and form no small part of its contribution to the life of the world.

In 1800 it was still by no means certain that Christianity would be successful in turning itself into a universal religion. It was, it is true, no longer a purely European phenomenon. In the three centuries since 1500 the Church had managed to project itself outwards with varying success in every direction. It was clear that the New World was destined to be a Christian world. The original inhabitants in the north had been wholly unable to stand against the successive waves of immigration from Europe, and were in process of becoming a segregated and diminishing minority. In the south, those of pure European stock were, and are, a minority. But political authority, social prestige, cultural eminence, and religious influence were concentrated in the hands of the white man. It may be held that Christian penetration has been much less deep in South America than in North; but there also, in so far as civilization exists, it is European and Christian civilization. There is no rival system and no rival religion.

America, together with the West Indies, had become a world led by men from Europe. The dominance of their religion and civilization in those areas provided no answer to the question whether Christianity could make itself permanently at home in the lands of the great and ancient non-Christian civilizations. At the end of the eighteenth century the omens might be regarded as being distinctly unfavourable. Christianity had been violently thrown out of one Far Eastern country, and almost paralysed by persecution in another. In India it had hardly touched the higher castes which were the trustees of the old civilization, and its hold even on its converts from the lower castes had been shown to be anything but secure. The Gospel had made no impression worth mentioning on the Islamic lands. In tropical Africa, the power of Islam, together with the desperately unfavourable climate, had confined Western man to the coast, and his few and ailing Christian settlements were less than promising bases for triumphant conquest. Christianity was still mainly the European's religion.

Why had so much Christian enterprise resulted in such limited success?

We are so used to the concept of a strong, rich, thickly populated, expanding Europe that it is hard for us to reach and to accept the obvious explanation that, until the end of the eighteenth century, Europe was weak. The great increase in population began only in the last third of that eighteenth century. Europe was divided, and recurrently bled itself white in its absurd and apparently endemic civil wars. The Wars of Religion in the seventeenth century, which ended with the peace of Westphalia in 1648, left many of the fairest regions of Germany devastated almost beyond repair and extensively depopulated, and put back the march of civilization by a couple of centuries. In the eighteenth century, the wars of the Austrian and the Spanish Successions kept the nations at one another's throats, and for the first time engaged the non-European peoples on a large scale in European conflicts. The nineteenth century was an oasis of peace in comparison with the evil that had gone before and the worse evil that was to follow. Partly because of these endless wars Europe was economically weak, and was hardly able to feed its own population. There was great wealth for some. But unseasonable weather, causing the failure of the crops, could lead to widespread famine; as late as the reign of King William III, Scotland suffered from a devastating famine in which it is reckoned that from a fifth to a quarter of the population died. The progress of the Gospel is not tied to the political or economic fortunes of any one part of the human race, but as long as men live in human and very physical bodies, it will not be possible completely to separate the religious from other aspects of the human situation.

Two great changes made possible the beginning of a new era. The first change was psychological. Early European settlers in the

East never dreamed of establishing dominion in the lands in which they had made their home. They were visitors on bare sufferance, like the Dutch merchants on their island in the bay of Nagasaki or in the tiny tolerated settlement of Canton. If they managed to establish themselves in certain territories, like the Portuguese in Goa or the British in Fort St George (which is now Madras), they claimed the right to defend their possessions, if necessary by force of arms. But their area was limited, and basically they were still traders, who became soldiers of necessity and not by choice.[1] The man who changed all this was the Frenchman Joseph François Dupleix (1697–1763). He was the first to realize the weakness that lay behind the still splendid exterior of the Indian kingdoms. Other adventurers had found fame and fortune by training the armies of the Indian princes, and in certain cases had set up as princes on their own. Dupleix saw that it should be possible to set up an empire in perpetuity, and was resolved that, when the Mogul empire finally collapsed, it should be to the profit of France. By the irony of history, it was Clive and the British who were the heirs of the splendid dreams of Dupleix. But the vision, once seen, did not fade; what we now know as colonialism was on the way.

The second change was scientific and economic. Europe set itself to the mastery of speed, and to the mastery of power.

It is strange to reflect that the Emperor Napoleon could travel no more speedily than the Emperor Augustus. The most rapid form of motion known to men was that of the galloping horse or camel. At the end of the eighteenth century, the voyage to India still frequently took six months. The great cities of India were separated from one another by more than a month's journey on land. The rapidity of communication which set in with the invention of the steam-engine and the steamship did more than anything else to make possible the birth of the new world in which we live.

When all manufacture was carried out by hand, there was no great disparity between the civilizations of East and West. The craftsmen of India and China were incomparable in the spheres that they had made their own. It was taken for granted everywhere that at all times a few would be rich and many would be poor; universal plenty was not even a dream. It was only the industrial

1. The interest of the Dutch in what is now Indonesia was primarily and mainly commercial; but perhaps they had gone further than other Europeans in the seventeenth century in developing the imperial idea.

revolution, and the application of mechanical power to manufacture, that made the disparity between Europe and Asia extreme. The use of power had not previously been unknown: those most ingenious inventions for the use of natural power, the windmill and the watermill, go very far back in human history. It was the coming of steam, and later electricity, that made all the difference. The world was found to be far richer than had ever been imagined – though at first the riches would accrue only to those who had made the inventions and controlled the sources of power.

The acquisition of the new resources, and the breakdown of the old order in the French Revolution, sent Europe out conquering with a new self-confidence, and increasingly, as the century advanced, with a new sense of mission to the world.

One aspect of this new spirit was the passion for exploration. This was not in itself new. But, with larger ships and more scientific methods of navigation, it acquired new dimensions in the period that we have now to consider. Few things did as much to prepare the minds of men for the new world that was on the way as the voyages of Captain James Cook and the admirable volumes in which they were recorded. Christians, no less than others, shared in the sense of enlarged horizons that came with the discovery of so many hitherto unknown lands. By the end of our period, almost all the great geographical puzzles of the world had been solved. Livingstone and Stanley had crossed and recrossed Africa. Both the Poles had been reached. The highest mountains had not yet been climbed, but they had been charted and surveyed.

Exploration was followed, or accompanied, by exploitation. The European still came to trade, but he nearly always stayed to rule.

In the course of the century, Britain established its dominion, direct or indirect, over the whole of India, Burma, and Ceylon, and gave to the sub-continent a unity which it had never known even in the famous days of Asoka and of Akbar. France, perhaps unwisely and certainly too late, and in the face of considerable opposition at home, used alleged persecution of Christians as the ground for the annexation of Indo-China. Holland completed its occupation of Indonesia, and gradually converted what had been a great trading estate into a great empire. Japan saved itself from the fate of other countries by the astonishing feat of transforming itself almost overnight from a sleepy medieval kingdom into a modern military power, annexed Korea, and prepared the way for further military adventures on the mainland. If China was not wholly colonized, this was rather because the colonial powers, like a crowd of quarrelsome vultures, could not agree on the division of the spoils, than for any other reason.

After a thousand years of dominion, Islam began at last definitively to recede. The liberation of Greece in 1821 was followed progressively by the emancipation of the other Balkan peoples, until in 1913 Turkey was left with nothing but a tiny strip of territory in Europe. In 1830 France occupied Algeria, and followed this up with the acquisition of Tunis. Later, Morocco was divided between France and Spain. Britain established almost complete control in Egypt. Italy in 1911 took over Tripoli and Libya as the result of a successful war. The Mediterranean was well on the way to becoming – what it had been in the early days – a Christian lake.

Africa's turn came rather later. Britain, like Portugal, had had trading interests on the west coast from an early date, but showed steadily persistent unwillingness and hesitancy in turning trading stations into colonies, zones of influence into areas of imperial control. Yet, through the vision of Cecil Rhodes and the concern of missionaries for the abolition of the slave trade and other factors, by 1914 a large part of Africa had been added to the British Empire. The French advance was far more deliberate and purposeful; a profound sense of colonizing mission drove the French forces onward through the Sahara and the Sudan, until some of the British territories were cut off from their natural hinterlands. Germany came in later. It was not till after 1870 and the unification of Germany under Prussia that the German demand for a place in the sun became clamant. Most of the best joints had already been cut from the carcass, but with Togoland, the Cameroons, South-West Africa, and Tanganyika, Germany did not come off too badly. Last of all, Belgium, taking over the independent Congo state from King Leopold, who had run it for nearly thirty years as his private property, found itself responsible for an area of a million square miles. The whole of Africa had ceased to be independent, except for the ancient kingdom of Ethiopia, which, assailed by Italy, had succeeded at the Battle of Adowa (1896) in throwing out the enemy, and maintaining itself in the remote fastnesses of its mountains.[2]

The innumerable islands of the Pacific had to a large extent fallen a prey to ruthless exploitation by traders, and their peoples seemed to be on the way to extermination. Western governments

2. Liberia was technically independent but financially and in other ways dependent on the United States.

stepped in, France, Britain, and Germany taking the lead, and disorder was followed by orderly government. The greater part of New Guinea was unexplored, but this vast island also was neatly divided up into its Australian, Dutch, and German sections. And even the penguins were not left in peace: the colonizing powers set up their rival flags on the desolate shores of Antarctica. The domination of the European seemed to be complete.

Many years must pass before the balance of colonialism can be correctly struck. On the one hand, it is easy to see the destructive forces that were let loose; on the other, in every part of the world there is also a record of high-minded devotion and desire to serve the interests of the people who had come under alien rule. It has to be remembered that in the nineteenth century the alternatives for many peoples were not independence and enslavement, but total destruction (by unscrupulous exploiters or through the slave trade) and the possibility of survival in a state of colonial dependence. In many areas the European powers found the peoples divided, poor, and barbarous, and left them united, prosperous, and well on their way to taking their place in the councils of the nations of the world.

For the time being, however, the world outside Europe and America finds it hard to interpret the relation of the West to the East, during the period Mr K. M. Panikkar taught us to call the Vasco da Gama era, in terms of anything but aggression. Political aggression destroyed the ancient kingdoms, and the ancient political orders; in Africa the system of chieftainship seems as certainly on its way out as the rule of the princes in India. Economic aggression tore in pieces the old way of life and production; the formerly subject peoples are convinced, often in the face of all the facts, that this revolution is the one and only cause of the grave poverty that still rules in many of their countries. Social aggression disrupted the minutely balanced order of society in such matters as the relationship between the sexes, or between the different orders within the community. Intellectual aggression, disregarding the ancient wisdom, imposed Western forms of thought and education which, however useful as passports to acceptance in the modern world, were alien to the mental make-up and psychology of the people concerned. And finally comes religious aggression. For, say what we will, Christian missionary work is frequently understood by the peoples of Africa and the East not as the sharing of an inestimable treasure, but as an unwanted imposition from without, inseparably associated with the progress of the colonial powers. How far this unfavourable judgement is justified we shall have later to consider; it needs to be stated at the outset as part of the history, and part of the tragedy, of Christian missions in the great century of Europe.

For the economic and imperial upsurge of Europe was accompanied by an unforeseen religious awakening which affected almost every Christian denomination in every country of the West.

The opening of the nineteenth century saw the Roman Catholic Church in a sad state of disarray. But, in point of fact, the phoenix was just about to arise again from its ashes. The sufferings of the Pope at the hands of Napoleon won both sympathy and respect for the institution which he represented. A series of outstanding popes succeeded in effecting that centralization of the life of the Church in Rome after which earlier pontiffs had striven in vain. Currents of new life and thought flowed in many countries, and, as always happens, new life in the Church found its outlet in renewed missionary activity. It was in this century that the missionary work of the Roman Catholic Church became fully international. Already in the eighteenth century France had begun to replace Spain and Portugal as the main source of missionary personnel. Throughout the nineteenth century France continued to contribute more than her share, but Belgium came in at her side with steadily increasing representation, to be followed by Holland and Ireland, and later by America and Britain.

The Orthodox Church became again a force in the Christian world, as it had not been for centuries. The breaking of the Turkish yoke brought new life to Greece and the Balkans. The Russian Church shook off the undue weight of western and Roman Catholic influences which had long constricted its freedom, and set to work to recover its own treasures of patristic thought and Byzantine devotion. There was a danger that the interest in western Europe and its culture, which had been growing since the time of Peter the Great, might inhibit this natural development, but the great poets and novelists of the century showed that it was possible to be at the same time fully western in culture and fully Russian in spirit. This new life in the Orthodox Churches only in part found expression in renewed missionary zeal.

The Protestant Churches owe an immeasurable debt to the Evangelical Revival in the broad sense of that term. Many forces – high Anglican piety, the mystical tradition, the pietism both of Halle and of Herrnhut – combined to produce John Wesley and the

Methodist movement in Britain. The Calvinist wing of the Evangelical movement stayed within the Church of England. Sharing with Wesley the demand for personal conversion and holiness of life, it added to these basic requirements an intense sense of civic responsibility, and this naturally found its expression both in such movements of reform as the campaign for the abolition of slavery and in zeal for missionary endeavour. Various areas in Germany in the nineteenth century were swept by revival movements of great power. The *Réveil* of the 1830s in Geneva spread to French Protestantism, and in France as in Switzerland led to the beginning of missionary work overseas. Norway had its own special process of revival through the work of Hans Nielsen Hauge (1771–1824); this movement, like that of the Anglican Evangelicals, stayed within the national Church, though often acting in considerable independence of it. At a time when all these movements were showing signs of dying down, the Second Evangelical Awakening crossed the Atlantic from America to Britain in 1858. This was undenominational in character, and produced that new phenomenon of the nineteenth century, the interdenominational or undenominational missionary society.

For this was the great age of societies. In many cases the Protestant Churches as such were unable or unwilling themselves to take up the cause of missions. This was left to the voluntary societies, dependent on the initiative of consecrated individuals, and relying for financial support on the voluntary gifts of interested Christians. The first of the new missionary societies was that of the English Baptists (1792). This was followed by the London Missionary Society (1795), which started with the laudable aim of preaching the eternal Gospel to the heathen without being tied to any particular form of Church order or government, but in fact became before long the organ of the English Congregational body; and by the Anglican Evangelical Church Missionary Society (1799). In 1804 the British and Foreign Bible Society gave a notable example of inter-Church co-operation, having a committee which was made up half of Anglicans and half of Free Churchmen. America entered the lists in 1810 with the American Board of Commissioners for Foreign Missions, mainly Congregational, and in 1814 with the American Baptist Missionary Board. Germany had its first missionary society in 1824, the Berlin Society. Switzerland, with the Basel Mission (1815), was a little earlier. Denmark (1821), France (1822), Sweden (1835), and Norway (1842) followed in due course. And then the list becomes so long that in a book of this size it is no longer possible to follow it. By the end of the century every nominally Christian country and almost every denomination had begun to take its share in the support of the missionary cause.

The immediately obvious result of this release of new Christian energy was the rapid geographical expansion of the work. William Carey had proposed that a general missionary conference should be held in 1810 at the Cape of Good Hope.[3] It is interesting to reflect what would have been the representation if 'Carey's Pleasing Dream' had been realized. From Japan and Korea there would have been no one, and hardly a soul from China or South-east Asia, except for a few from Indonesia; a small group from the islands of the Pacific, and a rather larger group from India; no one from the Muslim world except members of the ancient Eastern Churches; a handful from Sierra Leone and other stations on the coast of Africa, but no one from the interior; a fair-sized group from the West Indies, but (this being a Protestant dream) no one from Central or South America. The change wrought by a single century was astounding. In 1910 a few countries – Afghanistan, Tibet, Nepal – still remained obstinately closed to all missionary effort. Some remote regions had not yet been reached; certain others, such as northern Nigeria, were kept to all intents and purposes closed by the colonial powers. Otherwise, there were hardly any limits to the extent of the missionary enterprise. It stretched from China to Peru, and was at work both beyond the Arctic Circle and in the desolate and hostile wastes of Tierra del Fuego. Of course, within each great land mass there were areas that had not been entered and peoples that had not been touched, but with each year these were becoming fewer; the Christian faith was on the way to becoming literally a world-wide religion.

The primary barrier of language had been surmounted. Some languages in every known family of languages had been learned, and in many cases reduced to writing for the first time by the missionaries. No language had been found in which it was impossible to communicate the Gospel; in many cases a good deal of ingenuity had to be employed to supplement the deficiencies of those forms of speech in which there was no philosophical

3. See R. Rouse, 'William Carey's "Pleasing Dream"', in *International Review of Missions*, April 1949, pp. 181–92.

tradition, and Chinese was far from being the only language in which the rendering of the word 'God' caused controversy and disagreement. But in many languages, at first supposed to be poor and limited, fuller knowledge revealed an unexpected depth and range of expression. At the end of the eighteenth century the Bible had been translated in whole or in part into not more than seventy languages; at the end of the nineteenth, complete Bibles numbered more than 100, complete New Testaments another 120, and languages into which at least some part of the Bible had been rendered roughly 300 more. Owing to differing policies of missionary work the Roman Catholics had played little part in this tremendous effort of translation, which was almost wholly a Protestant achievement. Many of the early translations were rough-hewn and imperfect, in some cases laughably so; a great deal had to be redone, and perhaps Henry Martyn's Urdu version of 1810 is unique in being still the basis of the version current nearly two centuries after the translator's death. But the position of the missionary today, armed with grammar and dictionary, and building on earlier and more primitive versions, is wholly different from that of the pioneers, in many cases totally unversed in philological principles, who had to learn unwritten languages by ear on the well-worn principle of hit or miss.

To meet the demands of different situations, an almost infinite variety of missionary methods had been used.

The early missionaries were primarily preachers. As we have seen, Church and school, especially in the Protestant fields, marched closely hand in hand. The mud-and-thatch elementary school in the village grew over the years into the stately university. From the time of Alexander Duff in Calcutta (1830–48), higher education has been used not merely as a means of producing an educated Christian population, but in order to bring the Gospel to that intellectual élite which can hardly be reached by any other method. In most countries the missionaries have co-operated with the local system of education; in certain areas they have been led to create wholly independent universities of their own, such as the American University in Beirut, later no longer primarily a missionary institution. Special schools for the blind, for the deaf, and for the handicapped abound; this kind of work, previously unknown, has made a deep impression on non-Christians.

Already in the eighteenth century the Tranquebar mission had doctors, who however were not accredited by the sending authority in Denmark as missionaries in the full sense of the term. The doctor who was first and foremost a missionary, and used his medical skill as a means for proclaiming the Gospel in action, was in the main a product of the nineteenth century; the first such doctor missionary to reach India was John Thomas, the companion of William Carey. The American John Scudder, who arrived in Ceylon in 1819, and Peter Parker, who started work in China in 1835, were the pioneers of the more settled work which was typical of the nineteenth century. The first woman doctor in the service of the missions is believed to have been Dr Fanny Butler, who arrived in India in 1880. The small dispensary soon grew into the great and well-equipped modern hospital flanked by such auxiliaries as the refuge for lepers and the home for tubercular patients. The logical outcome of this work was the great teaching hospitals for the training of doctors and nurses at such centres as Vellore in South India and Ludhiana in the north.

Missions have run farms and agricultural institutions. They have developed industrial schools and taught every kind of handicraft. They have run printing-presses and publishing houses – the standard of work of the Methodist Press at Mysore was so high that for many years the Oxford University Press cut its costs by having many books printed in India. There was hardly an area of human activity which was not pressed into the service of the Gospel; even artist-missionaries, notable among them Bishop A. R. Tucker of Uganda and Lilias Trotter of Algiers, are to be reckoned in scores.[4]

One revolutionary change of the nineteenth century often escapes notice. Earlier missions had been almost exclusively a sphere of activity for men. Roman Catholic and Orthodox missionaries were in most cases celibate men, and the work of the sisters in Montreal (1639) was noted as an exception. The first Protestant missionaries were mostly married (Ziegenbalg at the beginning of his career was an exception, and Schwartz remained unmarried till the end of his days), and, if they went out unmarried, the missions undertook the grave responsibility of selecting and sending out partners for them; but most of these women were missionaries' wives rather than missionary wives, a distinction which is of the greatest importance. It was only in the middle of the nineteenth century that all the missions, Protestant and Roman Catholic alike, began to send out single women. When the proposal

4. The contribution of the artists of the younger Churches belongs almost wholly to a later period.

was made, it was met with strong opposition from such stalwarts as Bishop Daniel Wilson of Calcutta (1832–58), who remarked that such young women would be married off within the year and would be the source of endless troubles. Those who believed in the young women prevailed. By the end of our period women in the missions greatly outnumbered men. This is explicable, in the light of the much slower development of education for women and girls in the younger Churches, and in many countries by the prejudice against any other career for girls than that of marriage, but the disproportion in the ranks of the foreigners has not been altogether to the benefit of the work.

The success of the various missions has been curiously parallel in all the countries of the earth. Where Protestants have been able to start great movements, the Roman Catholics have profited by similar movements. Where the Roman Catholics have come up against impenetrable obstacles, the Protestants have been little more successful in overcoming the obstacles. But, looking back over the century and a quarter the results of which are being summarized in this chapter, it is possible to affirm that every race, every religion, every social level, and every form of human organization has yielded a number of converts to the Christian faith. From the 'higher' religions the yield has generally been small: resistance on intellectual, moral, traditional, social, and national grounds has been intense. But in every case the resistance has in a measure been overcome.

It was, naturally, among the poor and underprivileged, or in tribal societies without strongly developed religious systems of their own, that the successes of the missionaries were greatest. By the end of our period, both Roman Catholics and Anglicans had on their hands a full-scale movement among the intelligent and vigorous Baganda in Uganda. Most notable of all these peoples' movements were the so-called mass movements among the 'depressed classes' (now the 'scheduled castes') in many parts of India. In the Telugu country north of Madras, a million of these people entered the Churches in thirty years; Anglicans, Methodists, and Baptists were the principal beneficiaries of these movements, which still continue at the present time.

In one respect this success produced a revolutionary change. In earlier days the missionary had been everything. He lived in patriarchal fashion in the midst of a docile flock, every member of which he could know personally.

So the missionary became the patriarch, who was readily obeyed, and under whose leadership it was confidently believed that all would go well. Is it surprising that this position of the missionary was taken for granted and reflected in the order of the Church as this developed? The patriarchal structure of the Church was accepted as the only means by which its stability and its future could be safeguarded.[5]

With the immense increase in numbers brought about by the mass movements, this patriarchal relationship could no longer be maintained in the old way. Far more had to be done through 'the native agency'. It was, of course, possible for the missionary to wish still to be the dictator, to regard 'the native agency' as no more, in Dr Müller-Krüger's phrase, than 'his own extended arm', which moved merely according to the directives and the initiatives that came from above. But this could not go on for ever; the question of an independent indigenous ministry could not be for ever shelved. We have seen from time to time the efforts of the Roman Catholic missions to wrestle with this problem, and the partial solution reached in the Danish mission in the eighteenth century (see pp. 196–7). The great developments took plae in the second half of our period. As early as 1846 the great Welsh missionary John Thomas of Mengnanapuram in the Tinnevelly District of South India had successfully argued the case for the ordination of village catechists, who would not learn English or Greek. The work of the first six candidates, who were ordained in 1849, proved so successful that the principle was widely conceded as sound; by the end of our period, in a large number of missions of every conceivable ecclesiastical complexion the number of ordained nationals far exceeded the number of ordained foreigners.

But even ordained nationals can be kept in a position of tame subordination. The most important problem of all had yet to be faced. What was the missionary to do when surrounded by a large number of ordained colleagues in the field? The immediate and obvious answer is: 'Preach the Gospel.' This is still primary, and in a day in which more than half the people of the world have never so much as heard the name of Jesus Christ, this must remain central and obligatory. But, when the Gospel has been preached and some have heard and obeyed, what is to happen next? It is clear that the majority of missionaries in the nineteenth century took it for

5. Theodor Müller-Krüger in *Gemacht zu seinem Volk* (Centenary volume of the Batak Church, 1961), p. 33.

granted that they would be there for ever; converts were ignorant and backsliding was frequent; most of the national workers were on a lower level of education and competence than their missionary friends. All unnoticed, the mission had slipped into the position of the Church. Many missionaries went out with the best intentions of carrying out the declared intention of the London Missionary Society to preach the pure Gospel without tying it to any Western form of organization or polity, but they usually ended by producing a copy, faithful down to the minutest detail, of that form of the Christian faith to which they themselves were accustomed in their own country. For this the missionaries were not entirely to blame; converts are imitative, and it is often they who wish to have everything done in the way which is traditional in the Western Churches.

Missionaries in the nineteenth century had to some extent yielded to the colonial complex. Only Western man was wise and good, and members of other races, in so far as they became westernized, might share in this wisdom and goodness. But Western man was the leader, and would remain so for a very long time, perhaps for ever. When voices were raised in criticism of this accepted position, they were liable to be shouted down by an almost unanimous chorus of disapproval.[6] In 1914, the Roman Catholic Church had no bishop of non-European origin, except the four belonging to the Indian hierarchy created by Pope Leo XIII in 1887 and 1896 for the ancient Church of the Thomas Christians. When a young Belgian, Father Vincent Lebbe, raised the question whether the time had not come to create an indigenous episcopate in other countries, he was met almost everywhere by the view that, whereas the white race was capable of producing an unlimited supply of bishops, there was not a single man to be found in the yellow, red, brown, or black races capable of carrying the weight of the episcopate. Only the massive authority of Popes Pius XI and Pius XII, personally engaged, was sufficient, in the period following that which we are now studying, to crush this vocal and at times almost fanatical opposition.

But the question of the Church would not for ever remain unasked. What is a mission, and what is a Church? As early as

6. This led to the resignation of the Roman Catholic bishop in South India, de Marion Brésillac (1813–59), whom we shall meet later in connection with Roman Catholic missions in West Africa. See *Mgr de Marion Brésillac* (Foi Vivante, Paris, 1961), which contains a biography, and selections from the writings of de Marion Brésillac.

1854, Henry Venn, the prescient secretary of the Church Missionary Society in London, had spoken in terms of the aim of the mission as being the calling into existence of self-governing, self-supporting, and self-propagating Churches, and of the euthanasia of a mission. Once the mission has brought a Church into being, it may die out in that area; the missionaries may go on to the unevangelized regions, and leave the Church which they have brought into being to fulfil, under the guidance of the Holy Spirit, all the functions of a Church. Later experience has placed many question-marks against Henry Venn's formulation. Any such sharp separation between Church and mission as is implied in Venn's solution seems to lack theological foundation in the New Testament. And the first attempts to carry out the principles of Venn's dictum proved almost wholly disastrous. The establishment of the 'Native Pastorate' in Sierra Leone in 1860, with the complete withdrawal of the missionaries from participation in the affairs of the pastorate, inflicted on the Church a paralysis from which a whole century did not avail to deliver it. A similar attempt in Tinnevelly twenty years later would have proved equally disastrous, had not a new generation of missionaries put the clock back by taking over again the control and direction of a Church which had not yet attained the growth and maturity without which 'independence' is only a synonym for disintegration and decay.

Bishop A. R. Tucker of Uganda (1890–1908) drew very much nearer to the true solution of the problem. He envisaged a Church in which African and foreigner would work together in true brotherhood, and on a basis of genuine equality. For the most part missionaries of almost all the Churches were blind to this kind of possibility. The question of the Church had been raised. It was not to be answered till the succeeding period, and then not without dust and heat while delay had made inevitable controversy and contention which might have been avoided, had the doctrine of the Church been more clearly grasped by those whose business it was to call into being and to shepherd living Churches.

9

New Forces in Europe and America, 1792–1858

Books written in English have frequently spoken of William Carey (1761–1834) as 'the father of modern missions', and of the work that he brought into being as the first Protestant mission of modern times. Our earlier chapters have shown that this is a misunderstanding; Carey stood, and was conscious of standing, in a noble succession, as the heir of many pioneers in the past. Yet his work does represent a turning-point; it marks the entry of the English-speaking world on a large scale into the missionary enterprise – and it has been the English-speaking world which has provided four-fifths of the non-Roman missionaries from the days of Carey until the present time.[1]

Carey, who had turned Baptist at the age of eighteen, combined for a time the offices of village pastor and village cobbler. Visitors to his home noted the combination of the instruments of his humble trade, the beautiful flowers (Carey was always a passionate gardener) and the book which was always at his elbow. One of the first fruits of Carey's zeal for study was his treatise *An Enquiry into the Obligations of Christians to use Means for the Conversion of the Heathens* (1792).[2] The title indicates one of the difficulties with which Carey and those like-minded with him had to contend; the hyper-Calvinism of the day had convinced many that the conversion of the heathen would be the Lord's own work in his own time, and that nothing could be done by men to hasten it. Carey's answer is a patient, methodical survey of the world and of the whole history of Christian efforts to bring the Gospel to it. His mind is entirely free from the eschatological speculations of the pietists. Christ, he held, has a kingdom that is to be proclaimed in its power to the ends of the earth; it is the duty of all Christians to engage in the proclamation of this kingdom, whether the time allotted by God for the fulfilment of this purpose be long or short. The appeal of this pamphlet was reinforced by Carey's sermon to a group of

1. This chapter and the next deal with the Anglican and Protestant missions of the nineteenth century. The Roman Catholic and Orthodox missions are treated separately in Chapter 11.

2. A facsimile of the *Enquiry* was published in London (Baptist Missionary Society) in June 1942.

Baptist ministers at Nottingham on 31 May 1792; starting from the text Isaiah 54: 2–3, 'Lengthen thy cords, and strengthen thy stakes', he laid down his two great principles of action: Expect great things from God, attempt great things for God. Four months later the Baptist Missionary Society was formed. In June 1793 Carey left for India with his family as the Society's first missionary, and arrived in the Hooghly on 11 November of that year. The day of the English-speaking peoples in overseas missions had begun.

The moment of Carey's arrival in *India* was not propitious for the foundation of a mission. The East India Company, a commercial company which was in process of transforming itself into an empire and was by now the dominant power in India, was suspicious of missionaries and hostile to their entrance, not so much on religious grounds as from fear that the disturbance caused by the preaching of the Gospel might threaten their always uncertain control of their dominions. Carey and his party were, in fact, in the position of illegal immigrants, liable at any moment to deportation. This situation was met by the disappearance of the Carey family into the interior of the country, where the father worked as manager of an indigo plantation, but the mind of the mother became steadily more seriously unhinged and the children grew up as undisciplined ragamuffins. This exile gave Carey the opportunity to lay the foundations of his incomparable knowledge of the Bengali language, and at the end of five years he had in manuscript a complete translation of the New Testament in Bengali. This first venture, unhappily, was wholly unsuccessful: Carey was a self-taught man, with a notable but untrained gift for language. When tested, his translation was found to be unintelligible – the words were Bengali, but the idiom had not been mastered. With the indomitable courage and patience that were characteristic of him, Carey set to work to begin again from the beginning.

The situation was radically changed by the arrival in 1799 of a further group of missionaries, among them Joshua Marshman (1768–1837) the charity schoolmaster, and William Ward (1769–1823) the printer. The newcomers realized that their safety would lie in settling at Serampore, the tiny Danish colony sixteen miles from Calcutta. The Danes did not share the hostility of the British to missions; in Serampore missionaries would be free from the constant harassments and uncertainties of life on British Indian soil. A rather unwilling Carey was persuaded to come and join them, and so began one of the most famous partnerships in the whole history of the Christian Church, broken only by the death of Ward in 1823.

Carey was extraordinarily independent and modern in his outlook. He saw missionary work as a five-pronged advance, with equal attention directed to each of the five elements: (1) the widespread preaching of the Gospel by every possible method; (2) the support of the preaching by the distribution of the Bible in the languages of the country; (3) the establishment at the earliest possible moment of a Church; (4) a profound study of the background and thought of the non-Christian peoples; (5) the training at the earliest possible moment of an indigenous ministry.

In each of these five directions notable success was achieved.

1. As far as political conditions allowed, preaching tours were carried out in all directions, and as the work developed, missionaries were settled far afield – up the Ganges, in Orissa, and even as far away as Burma, where Carey's somewhat unstable son Felix was the pioneer, not with outstanding success.

2. The work for which the Serampore trio are specially remembered is the translation of the Scriptures into many of the main languages of the East, and this has to some extent overshadowed their many other merits. It was, indeed, a gigantic enterprise. In thirty years, six translations of the whole Bible were completed, Carey himself being responsible for Bengali, Sanskrit, and Marathi. To these were added twenty-three complete New Testaments, and some Bible portions in ten other languages. Not all these ventures were happy. Some of the 'languages' were no more than dialects and are no longer spoken. Dr Marshman spent fifteen years learning Chinese, and producing a translation of the New Testament – a notable piece of beautiful printing – but it was impossible that a translation produced outside China should meet the requirements of accuracy and idiomatic propriety. Even Carey's beloved Bengali New Testament, which he himself revised eight times, dying just after the completion of the eighth revision, was unable to hold its own and has been replaced by other versions.

3. One of the first acts of the missionaries on settling at Serampore was to form themselves into a Church on the Baptist model, and to elect a pastor. The pastor chosen was not Carey but Ward, described by one of those who knew the group as 'very much the best preacher at Serampore'. This meant that, when converts came, they were baptized into an existing Church, organized and settled in India, connected with the distant fellowship of Baptists in England but in no way under their control. At this point the

independent order showed its superiority to many others; Church and mission from the beginning formed an integrated whole.

4. Carey and his colleagues held strong views as to the exclusive claims of the Christian faith; the religions of the heathen were delusions of the devil. Yet they saw clearly that the missionary must understand not only the language but also the thought-world of those to whom the Gospel is to be preached. Carey's Sanskrit grammar, a beautifully printed work of 1,000 pages, was a memorable contribution. The time spent on the translation of much of the Rāmāyana into English was criticized by friends of the mission, but justified by Carey; and Ward's book on the manners and customs of the Hindus (1811) shows how far a foreigner could penetrate into the wholly unfamiliar world of Hindu thought and custom. Carey is held by the experts to have been the founder of prose literature in Bengali, a beautiful and flexible form of speech, in which all the earlier literature had been in a high poetic style, unintelligible to the ordinary reader.

5. From an early period in the history of the mission Carey had insisted on the need for competent and well-trained Indian fellow-workers. In 1805, in a statement of the principles on which they carried on their work, the missionaries affirmed that

another part of our work is the forming of our native brethren to usefulness, fostering every kind of genius, and cherishing every gift and grace in them; in this respect we can scarcely be too lavish of our attention to their improvement. It is only by means of native preachers we can hope for the universal spread of the Gospel through this immense continent.

A great step forward was taken with the opening at Serampore in 1819 of a 'College for the instruction of Asiatic, Christian, and other youth, in Eastern Literature and European Science'. This noble building, which still stands, is eloquent testimony to the width of Carey's outlook and the greatness of his Christian ambitions. The college opened with thirty-seven students, nineteen of whom were Christian and eighteen non-Christian. In 1827 the king of Denmark gave the college a charter, with the power to grant the degrees of Bachelor of Arts and Bachelor of Divinity. Under lesser men, who came later, the college did not fulfil the high hopes of its founders, but we shall meet it again in a different role at a much later stage of our history.[3]

3. A valuable survey of the entire history of the College is *The Story of Serampore and its College*, published at Serampore in 1961.

William Carey died on 9 June 1834.[4] As he lay dying, he remarked: 'After I am gone, brother Marshman will turn the cows into the garden.' His more solemn colleague replied with feeling: 'Far be it from me. Though I have not your botanical tastes, I shall consider the preservation of the garden in which you have taken so much delight as a sacred duty.' Marshman lived for another three years, the last survivor of a heroic epoch in missions, the consideration of which arouses in the mind of the student an equal measure of awe and inspiration.

During the time of the Serampore trio, the Church of England in India took on an entirely new aspect. We have referred before to the inadequacy, always in number and often in character, of the chaplains sent out by the East India Company. The change was due directly to the Evangelical Revival in England, and particularly to the influence of Charles Simeon, the great incumbent of Holy Trinity, Cambridge, who sent out his children to be 'princes in all lands'. The first in the new succession was the Reverend David Brown, who arrived in Calcutta in 1787, and who, though only in deacon's orders, gradually established himself as a great influence for good in a society which found nothing surprising in the remark that the 'luxury of a large seraglio was reserved for those who were high in the service and received large emoluments'. Brown was later joined by such men as Thomas Thomason, Daniel Corrie (later to be the first Bishop of Madras), and others who laboured with Charles Grant the civilian in India, and leaders such as William Wilberforce in London, for a change of attitude towards the new British dominion in India and the spiritual welfare of its peoples.

By far the most notable of the 'pious chaplains' was Henry Martyn, who arrived in Calcutta in 1806 and died in Persia on his way home to England in 1812 at the age of thirty-one. Martyn at first lived at Serampore, and Carey wrote of him that 'as the image or shadow of bigotry is not known among us here, we take sweet counsel together, and go to the house of God as friends'. Martyn threw himself at once and with enthusiasm into the projects of his friends for the translation of Scripture. But there was a difference.

4. By his orders nothing was inscribed on his tomb but his name, the dates of his birth and death, and two lines of an old hymn:

A wretched, poor, and helpless worm
On thy kind arms I fall.

They were all self-taught men, but Martyn had been Senior Wrangler at Cambridge, and had profited from the best philological training that the age could supply. He was at times rather sharply critical of the older men, and set himself a standard of scholarship which was beyond their reach. In seven brief years he had completed the New Testament in Urdu, a version which is still the basis of that which is in use today, had completed a thorough revision of the Persian, and was deeply launched on the revision of the Arabic. His early death was a heavy loss to the cause of Christ in India; his diary is one of the most precious treasures of Anglican devotion.

Friends of the Anglican cause in India had long been convinced that its establishment must be completed by the provision of a bishop. At last they were successful. The first bishop, Thomas Fanshaw Middleton, arrived in 1814. He was a good scholar, and a rather old-fashioned High Churchman. Brought up in familiarity with nothing but the English tradition of the parish and the parson, he was much perplexed by the missionaries (mostly Germans) of the Church Missionary Society who had recently arrived in Bengal. What was their status? 'I must either license them, or silence them', he wrote to a correspondent. But to what could itinerant evangelists without the vestige of a parish be licensed?

The great achievement of Middleton was the foundation of Bishop's College, Calcutta, for the training of young men for the ministry of the Church. Middleton brought out a remarkable man, William Hodge Mill, Fellow of Trinity College, Cambridge, and later Regius Professor of Hebrew (1848–53), to be the first principal of the college (1820–38).[5] But perhaps this grandiose undertaking was premature; the field from which candidates for the ministry could be drawn was too narrow, and a century was to pass before Bishop's College really began to accomplish the purpose for which Middleton had founded it.[6]

Middleton's successor was Reginald Heber (1783–1826), the greatest writer of English hymns since Charles Wesley. Heber was Bishop of Calcutta for barely three years, but perhaps no missionary has ever left on his surroundings so deep an impress of his personality in so short a time. Heber detested official formality:

5. Remarkable also in his descendants: Professor C. C. J. Webb was a grandson of Dr Mill.
6. This view is strengthened by the figures for ordination of Bishop's College students. In 1824–58, 43; 1859–70, 20; 1871–83, no record; 1883–9, 4.

To avoid the parade of a public entry into a station, he did not scruple to steal into it unperceived, mounted on a pony, with a light hat of Indian cork to shelter his head from the sun, and an umbrella in his hand.[7]

Very shortly after his arrival in India, he wrote affectionately to Carey and Marshman in favour of the union of the Churches:

Would to God, my honoured brethren, the time were arrived, when not only in heart and hope, but visibly, we shall be one fold, as well as under one shepherd . . . if a reunion of our churches could be effected, the harvest of the heathen would ere long be reaped, and the work of the Lord would advance among them with a celerity of which we have now no experience.

Heber was a century in advance of his time; the Baptist brethren were personally touched but theologically unmoved by this ecumenical approach.

The greatest of the early bishops of Calcutta was undoubtedly Daniel Wilson, who arrived in India in 1832 at the age of fifty-four, and ruled the see for twenty-five years. Tireless in vigour in spite of his age, he set himself to develop proper ministrations and education for those three classes in India on whom to so large an extent the reputation of the Christian faith must depend – the civil servants and others who came only for a period and planned to return to Europe; the soldiers of the two armies, that of the Company and that of the British Crown; and the Eurasians or Anglo-Indians, the people of mixed race, for whom it was hard to find a home in either world. As the British dominion in India grew, so, under the leadership of men like Wilson, grew the sense of Christian responsibility for its well-being. Among the best friends of the missionaries were the great Evangelical administrators and soldiers – Edwardes, Montgomery, Havelock, and the rest – who were there to carry into effect the great transition when in 1858 the British government took over from the East India Company the control of what by that time had become an immense empire.

The first great triumphs of the Gospel in India had been in the south, and to the south we must now return.

The first enterprise to attract our attention is the mission of help sent by the Church Missionary Society in 1816 to the ancient Church of the Thomas Christians. We left this Church at the

---

7. J. C. Marshman, *Life and Times of Carey, Marshman and Ward* (1859), Vol. 2, p. 293. Heber's chaplain was of opinion that the Bishop carried affability at times too far – even to the point of wearing white trousers in company.

Synod of Diamper in 1599, when the whole body was incorporated into the Church of Rome. It seemed for the moment that the whale had irremediably swallowed Jonah. But Jonah proved an uncomfortable tenant. The Syrians did not like the Jesuits, and they did not like the Portuguese; they constantly complained that the privileges and exemptions granted them at the synod were being infringed. At last in 1653 they gathered in indignation at the Koonen Cross in the churchyard at Mattancheri, and swore an oath to expel the Jesuits and to accept no ecclesiastical authority, other than that of their own archdeacon, until they should receive a bishop from the Eastern Church. It appears that the archdeacon was consecrated bishop with the title Mar Thoma I on 22 May 1653; in the absence of a bishop, twelve presbyters took part in the consecration, as Jerome tells us they used to do in the old days in the consecration of the patriarch of Alexandria.

For a time it seemed likely that the archdeacon would carry all before him. But the Roman Catholics worked hard, and managed to recover perhaps two-thirds of the Churches and Christians. When at last an Eastern bishop did arrive in 1665, it was already too late. The strange thing is that this bishop, Mar Gregorios, came not from the Nestorians in Mesopotamia but from the Monophysites at Diarbekir. But the Syrians were so pleased to have a bishop that they gladly accepted him, and were not greatly troubled by their move overnight from the extreme right to the extreme left in Christological doctrine. So the two Churches continued in not always happy rivalry. The power of the Portuguese steadily waned. When in 1663 the Dutch finally captured Cochin, they gave orders that all foreign priests and monks were to leave the country. Before he left, the last foreign bishop Joseph had consecrated the priest Parambil Chandy, commonly known by his Latin name of Alexander de Campo, a member of the same family as the archdeacon who had at one time actually been among the archdeacon's advisers, as the first Indian bishop for the Roman party. The two successions were carried on in a somewhat haphazard fashion, and this was the state of affairs when the ancient Church again emerged into the light of day at the beginning of the nineteenth century.

In 1816, at the suggestion of Colonel Munro, then Resident of Travancore, the Anglican Church Missionary Society sent a party of four missionaries to be at the service of the ancient Church, to assist in the training of its priests but not in any way to interfere in its inner life. The Syrians had long lived in isolation, and there was much to be done. The first group of missionaries followed strictly the injunctions which had been laid upon them. They founded what is now the Church Missionary Society's College in Kottayam. They made the first translation of the Bible into Malayalam, and printed it themselves (1829). But inevitably they assumed, or were accorded, a position of considerable authority or at least influence in the Church; also inevitably the Church, which had suffered so much in the past from foreigners, saw in their presence a menace to its own integrity. The accession in 1829 of a new Metropolitan, Mar Dionysius IV, and a certain impatience among the younger missionaries, led to an explosion. At a synod which met in 1836 at Mavelikkara, the official connection between the missionaries and the Church was broken off.

The missionaries, naturally but perhaps unwisely, stayed on to educate the Christians and to evangelize the non-Christians. A certain number of Syrians had become so much attached to the missionaries that they determined to follow them and to become Anglicans. This was not according to the wishes of the Church Missionary Society, the Madras Committee of which on 14 March 1836 placed on record its 'decided conviction that we ought to preserve their identity and not attempt to amalgamate them with the Church of England'. With this small group, matters had gone too far, and they were admitted to the Church of England. Some of them were ordained, and provided much of the leadership for what was later the diocese of Travancore and Cochin of the (Anglican) Church of India, Burma, and Ceylon; the first Indian bishop of this diocese, C. K. Jacob, belonged to one of the notable families of this group.

Although the most ardent friends of the missionaries had left the ancient Church, the reforming leaven was still at work within it under the leadership of a notable scholar, Abraham Malpān, Professor of Syriac in the College, who had learned from the missionaries to test all things by the Bible and had in consequence repudiated many of the ideas and ceremonies which had become customary in the Church. It was only a matter of time before another schism became inevitable; the moment arrived in 1889, when the reforming party was to all intents and purposes cast out of the Church, and had to launch out on the way of separate existence. Guided by the wise advice of Anglican missionaries, prominent among whom was Thomas Walker of Tinnevelly (1859–1912), the reforming party decided on this occasion not to become Anglicans, but to constitute themselves an independent

Indian Church commonly called the Mar Thoma Church of
Malabar, under the leadership of the one bishop, Mar Thomas
Athanasius, who was favourable to their cause.

In consequence of this further division, the ancient Syrian
Church now exists in no less than five branches: the Romo-Syrians
of the Syriac rite (actually in two divisions; there are also Christians of the Latin rite, the fruit of later missions); the 'Malankara'
(technically Monophysite and unreformed) Church; a small group
of Nestorians in the neighbourhood of Trichur; the Mar Thoma
(reformed) Syrian Church; and the Anglican diocese, which has
now become the Diocese of Central Travancore of the Church of
South India. It is sad that so many divisions have to be recorded;
yet, in spite of the divisions, the new life that has come into the
ancient Church, and the development in recent years of a vigorous
evangelistic spirit, make it necessary to recognize it as one of the
most significant forces in the life of the Churches in India in the
modern age.

In the meantime, on the other side of the western Ghats, the
Tinnevelly Church had also taken on new life. After the beginnings
of the mass movement recorded in an earlier chapter (p. 200), this
Church had been very much left to itself, under the care of Indian
pastors, most notable among them Satyanāthan,[8] and only very
rarely visited by missionaries. When one of the 'pious chaplains',
James Hough, later historian of the Church in India, arrived at
Palamcottah in 1816 as chaplain to the regiment stationed there,
he found the Church in a state of considerable disarray. Although
it was no part of his official duties, he set to work to pull things
together, and called in to his help the Church Missionary Society.

The Society sent down Charles T. E. Rhenius, a German who
had come through the Missionary Training Institution in Basel. A
better choice could not have been made. Rhenius was a good
scholar, who composed an excellent grammar of the Tamil language, and made a new translation of the New Testament. He was
also an outstanding organizer, and brought into existence the
system under which the Church was built up around the school,
the village schoolmaster being also the catechist responsible for the
conduct of the worship of the Church. The teacher-catechist
became the hero of Christian advance in India, as he has since been

8. The sermon preached by Satyanāthan at his ordination in 1790 was translated
into English, and published by the SPCK in London.

in Africa. From the start the work was largely self-supporting, and by the end of Rhenius's career the number of village centres under his care had grown to several hundreds. In 1829, the old work of the Society for Promoting Christian Knowledge was taken over by the Society for the Propagation of the Gospel, which thus again entered into the field of missions to non-Christians; the two agencies, CMS and SPG, worked together side by side, with occasional hints of rivalry and disagreement, but more generally in a spirit of harmonious co-operation.

After fifteen years of devoted service Rhenius was the cause of an unhappy schism. He had never received Anglican orders, and had followed the tradition under which the missionaries had themselves ordained Indian ministers as required. In 1835 the bishopric of Madras had been constituted, and the CMS indicated that for the future ordinations were to be carried out according to the Anglican tradition and in no other way. Rhenius, together with the colleagues who by now had joined him, felt unable to accept this ruling, and had to resign from the Society. Unfortunately, he decided to return to Tinnevelly, where out of personal loyalty to him a number of his old congregations decided to follow him into schism. He died in 1838, and peace was gradually restored. The Tinnevelly Church, forgetting this unhappy concluding episode, observes the memory of Rhenius with due honour as that of its second founder.

A second movement towards Christianity in the extreme south of India, this time on the Travancore side of the boundary, came into being through the witness of a remarkable man named Vedamānikkam, who belonged to almost the lowest stratum of Hindu society. In search of God, Vedamānikkam, accompanied by a nephew, made the long pilgrimage to the Hindu shrine at Chidambaram. Disappointed of the experience he had hoped for, he saw in a dream a venerable old man, who rebuked him for having come on a fruitless errand, and bade him return home. On the way the pilgrims stopped at Tanjore, were introduced by Christian relatives to the aged missionary Kohlhoff (the foster son of Christian Friedrich Schwartz), and were shortly afterwards baptized. Later Vedamānikkam invited W. T. Ringeltaube, who had come to India under the London Missionary Society, to visit his village of Mayiladi, where he promised him a ready hearing. Ringeltaube was in South Travancore from 1809 till 1815. His first converts were all from the depressed classes; but from 1810 onwards, many Nādārs – of the group which had yielded so many converts in Tinnevelly – came forward for baptism. An eccentric, lonely, generous man, Ringeltaube suffered at times from depression, and, though he had baptized nearly 1,000 people, he wondered whether anything worth while had been accomplished. But the foundations had been well and truly laid; the great Christian community which now makes up the diocese of Kanyākumari of the Church of South India is built upon the work of Ringeltaube.

A new period in the history of Indian missions begins with the arrival in 1830 of Alexander Duff (1806–78) of the Church of Scotland, whose term of service briefly overlapped that of Carey. Duff arrived with the conviction that the time had come to present the Gospel to the cultured sections of the community through higher education in English. His conviction was based on solid reasoning. He had the support of Raja Rām Mohun Roy (1772–1833), most notable of the early Indian reformers, and organizer of the syncretistic religious society the Brāhmo Samāj (1828), who knew English well, and had deeply studied the New Testament, though he never became a Christian. At the same time the British government was seriously concerned with the question of the medium of instruction in its schools – should it be English, or the classical languages of India? The matter was practically settled by the famous minute (1835) of T. B. Macaulay, the historian, at that time legal member of the Council in Calcutta.[9] Macaulay's contemptuous references to Indian wisdom, which he knew only in its corrupt Purānic form, have often been quoted. Less notice has been taken of his sincerely constructive proposals; the aim should be to create an intellectual élite, thoroughly at home in Western languages and sciences, and to encourage this élite to diffuse modern knowledge throughout the whole population. One part of this programme was carried out but not the other; the élite was created, but it lacked missionary spirit, and in point of fact the diffusion of useful knowledge was left almost exclusively to the missions. Duff had arrived at just the right time.

What later became the General Assembly's Institution was opened with five boys, but it soon grew to nearly 200. Duff's aims

9. This document, though constantly quoted, was for a long time practically inaccessible. It has now been reprinted in the admirable 'Renard' volume of selections from the works of Macaulay. It is a document which needs to be read as a whole and not in fragmentary selections.

were educational and evangelistic; both inside and outside the school he made friends with young Bengalis of leading families, who were beginning to be affected by the ferment of the times. As a result, between August 1832 and April 1833 four young men accepted the Christian faith and were baptized. Such a thing had never happened before, and the commotion was immense. For a time the whole work was threatened, but its merits were such that it gradually regained the confidence of the public, and the school went from strength to strength. Duff's converts were not numerous: thirty-three are recorded in the eighteen years of his work, but all were of sterling quality, and became the founders of some of the most notable Christian families in India. A considerable number became ordained ministers, among them Krishna Mohan Banerjee (Anglican), and Gopināth Nandi and Lāl Behāri Day (Presbyterians).

Duff's methods having proved so successful, it is not surprising that they were imitated in a number of other places, the lead in most cases being taken by the Scots. Thus in Bombay John Wilson in 1832 founded what was later to become Wilson College, to be followed in Madras in 1837 by Anderson and Braithwaite with 'The Institution', the ancestor of the Madras Christian College, and in 1844 by Stephen Hislop in Nagpur. Robert Noble, the first of the Anglicans to follow the pattern, in 1842 created, in Masulipatam in the Telugu country, the college which was later known by his name. In every case the experiences were much the same – a brief period of enthusiastic popularity; the conversion of one or two promising students; tumults and disturbances, legal cases and accusations; the emptying of the school; renewed popularity once the disturbances had passed. In one or two cases the converts were kidnapped and disappeared for ever. This, however, was the exception. Most of them lived to become outstanding Christians, and in many cases – like the first two Parsi converts in Bombay, Dhanjibhai Naoroji and Hormusji Pestonji – leading ministers of the Churches. As the converts were wholly rejected by their families, they had in many cases to grow up in the homes of the missionaries as their adopted sons. This was undesirable, as tending to an undue association of the Gospel with Western ways, but, Indian society being what it was, no other solution was possible at the time. The missionaries were bound to maintain their converts, until a means of livelihood could be found for them through which they could honourably support themselves.

In England the Evangelicals continued to press for the opening of India without restriction to missionary enterprise. This was achieved in 1833, with the renewal of the Company's Charter in that year. In consequence, from now on the picture of Christian effort in India becomes greatly diversified. Up till 1833 almost the whole of the Protestant work had been carried out by English societies – the Church Missionary Society, the London Missionary Society, and the Wesleyan Methodists, who started work in Ceylon in 1814 and from there spread to India. From 1833 onwards the forces of many nations began to enter the field.

The American Congregationalists (ABCFM) had made a small beginning in Bombay in 1813; they were able to settle in Madurai, the former home of Roberto Nobili, in 1835. Among the first missionaries was the doctor John Scudder, who founded in Arcot the work that was later transferred to the Reformed Church of America. Generation after generation of Scudders have served the Church in India; the name has become for ever memorable through the work of Dr Ida Scudder, founder of the great training centre for women (and later for men) doctors at Vellore. American Presbyterians came into the Punjāb in 1833, one of their early missionaries being Charles W. Forman, who served for forty years (1848–88), and gave his name to the great College of his Church in Lahore. Lutherans appeared in the south in 1841, and the Methodist Episcopal Church in the United Provinces in 1856.

Missionary interest in the continental Churches had been renewed as a result of the revivals of religion, and new societies began to enter the field. Two of these demand more than passing notice.

Basel, as we have seen, had supplied a number of missionaries to the Anglican CMS. In 1834 the Basel Mission, representing both Lutheran and Reformed elements in the continental Churches, began its own work on the west coast, with its great centre at Mangalore, north of the area of the ancient Syrian Churches. One of the first missionaries was Samuel Hebich (1803–68), who added a notable chapter to the story of the missionary eccentrics. Hebich preached a simple evangelical Gospel, and, though he never forgot his primary vocation as a missionary, his most outstanding successes were with the British officers of the regiments in his area. This is especially remarkable in view of his extremely limited command of the English language.[10] His methods were fantastic –

10. His careful colleague Dr Gundert worked out that he had a vocabulary of about 550 words.

and devastatingly effective; man after man yielded to his simple but ineluctable challenge, so much so that one regiment came to be generally known as 'Hebich's Own', an honour usually reserved for persons of royal descent. And these were no superficial conversions; Hebich's men remained devoted Christians to their dying day, and passed on a living faith to their descendants.[11]

The Basel Mission, more than most others, devoted itself to the economic advancement of the Christians, who came mainly from the destitute classes; Basel Mission tiles and Basel Mission textiles were famous throughout South India, until during the First World War the government formed the Commonwealth Trust to carry on the enterprises that had earlier been in the hands of the mission. There were dangers in this method: a mission which becomes a commercial concern may end by ceasing to be a mission. The spiritual integrity of the Basel Mission was, however, maintained throughout its history.

The Leipzig Lutheran mission entered South India in 1840, with a view to gathering the fragments that remained of the old Danish–Halle Mission, and extending the Lutheran witness. Almost at once this mission found itself engaged in fierce controversy. As we have seen more than once, missionaries from the beginning of time had been plagued and perplexed by the problem of caste. Was it to be regarded as a mere social distinction? Or was it fatally and irretrievably un-Christian? On the whole the missionaries had tended to look on it with a somewhat friendly eye, and to spare the susceptibilities of their high-caste converts. From time to time individuals would attempt to insist on a more rigid line, usually without success. Then in 1835 the formidable Bishop Daniel Wilson entered the lists with a strong pastoral letter in which he asserted that caste was 'eating as doth a cancer into the vitals of our infant Churches', and demanded that 'the distinction of caste must be abandoned, decidedly, immediately, and finally'. Dismay spread in the ranks of the higher-caste Christians, and, as the Leipzig Mission showed signs of being more tender towards caste feelings than others, many left the Anglican and other missions to find a new home, or in certain cases to rediscover an old home, in the Lutheran world.

11. Among them General Sir William Dobbie, the heroic Governor of Malta during the Second World War, and now Sir William's grandson Captain Ian Dobbie RE.

This account may have given the impression of a powerful and far-reaching enterprise, and, indeed, the extension within a short time had been memorable – the Church Missionary Society in its rapid advance across the northern plains had reached Amritsar in 1852, Peshawar on the north-west frontier in 1855. But, compared with the work to be done, the outlay of the Churches in men and material was almost contemptible. In 1851, the first year for which we have what appear to be reliable figures, there were in the whole of India 339 ordained missionaries belonging to nineteen societies; together with wives, this meant a striking force of about 600, in a country with a population of 150 million. Christians were reckoned at 91,092, of whom only 14,661 were communicants, but of these no less than 51,300 were in the Anglican missions in Tinnevelly and the LMS area of South Travancore, leaving less than 40,000 adherents for the whole of the rest of India.

On this small body the whirlwind of the Indian Mutiny fell in 1857 with unexpected and devastating fury. The policy of the government had, on the whole, been much less than favourable to missions; but the rapid extension of Christian work had given some substance to the rumours that plans were on foot forcibly to convert the whole population to Christianity. There is no evidence that the mutineers especially directed their violence against Christians or missionaries; these were simply caught up in the storm of hatred against all things Western. Fortunately the violence was limited almost wholly to the Ganges valley;[12] nor did it last long. As far as can be gathered, thirty-eight missionaries, chaplains, and members of their families died in the course of the outbreak. About twenty Indian Christian victims are recorded, but here there is less certainty about the numbers, which may have been far greater than is suggested by the record.

The Mutiny was a painful and tragic business. For many years it cast its shadow over the relations between Indian and European in the sub-continent, and it was long before the resentments were healed. But for the Christian cause it was no more than an episode; it was clear that the Gospel had come to stay, and that nothing could long impede its progress among the many peoples and languages of India.

12. The Memorial Hall in Madras is perhaps unique in being a memorial to something which did not happen – the south of India, where there had been earlier risings, remained tranquil throughout the whole period of the Mutiny.

Of *Japan* and *Korea* there is virtually nothing to say in this part of our survey. Japan remained hermetically sealed. The first Protestant missionary reached Korea only in 1865.[13] And in *China* progress was very much slower than in India.

As we have seen, China had decided to move back into, or perhaps to maintain unbroken, its proud isolation. It had rejected the Christian faith in its Roman Catholic form, and was not prepared to welcome any other. It was even forbidden to teach the Chinese language to any foreigner. Only in the Portuguese colony of Macao, and in a tiny strip of land in Canton, was it possible for a foreigner to reside at all.

It was in the face of such opposition that the first Protestant missionary to China, Robert Morrison (1782–1834), arrived at Canton in an American ship in September 1807. For a time he was compelled to live almost in hiding, but by 1809 his proficiency in the Chinese language was such that he was appointed translator to the East India Company. This gave him protection, a measure of security, and an income on which to live. For nearly twenty-five years Morrison was to hold on in this little corner, the only foothold which the European had been able legally to secure in the whole empire of China.

Fortunately, Morrison was a man of studious habits; his whole life was devoted to the extension of his knowledge of Chinese, that shoreless sea, and to the use of it for Christian purposes. In 1813 he had completed his translation of the New Testament; by 1819 the Old Testament had been added to it. His great dictionary of Chinese went far to establish the knowledge of that language on a scientific footing.[14] The first convert, Tsae A-Ko, was baptized on 16 July 1814 at 'a spring of water issuing from the foot of a lofty hill by the seaside, away from human observation'. Tsae died in 1818, faithful to the new way of life that he had adopted. During the rest of Morrison's time of service only ten further converts were baptized. But one ordination had taken place. Liang Fah, a printer won to the faith by William Milne who had arrived in 1813, was ordained to be an evangelist to his fellow-countrymen – apparently

13. See pp. 349–50 for a summary of the earlier history of the Roman Catholic Church in Korea.

14. It was Morrison's colleague Milne who gave the following description of the Chinese language: 'To acquire the Chinese is a work for men with bodies of brass, lungs of steel, heads of oak, hands of spring-steel, eyes of eagles, hearts of apostles, memories of angels, lives of Methuselah.'

the first Chinese to be ordained to the ministry in any Protestant Church.

Mainland China was almost inaccessible. But, then as now, a great many Chinese were living outside China, and Morrison was quick to perceive that here there were opportunities not merely to preach the Gospel to a certain number of Chinese, but also to prepare the way for the greater advance that might one day be possible. One of his great achievements was the foundation in 1818 of the Anglo-Chinese College in Malacca. Here, as in Carey's Serampore, the basis of learning was to be the Asian language, but those who were capable were to be instructed also in English and in Occidental Sciences. It was Morrison's hope that 'the light of science and revelation will, by means of this institution, peacefully and gradually shed their lustre on the Eastern limit of Asia and the islands of the rising sun'. This great venture was perhaps premature; it did not fulfil the high hopes of its founders. But it is recorded that between 1818 and 1833 forty of its students had completed the course and that fifteen of them had been baptized.

The opening of China to the Gospel was closely linked to the commercial and political pressures of the Western powers. In 1839 the tension reached a point at which war appeared to be the only answer. The immediate cause of the war was the British determination to secure the import of Indian opium into China, which the Chinese government wished to prevent. It is perhaps true, as two American writers remark, that

opium was not the real *cause*, but only the *occasion* of the war. The true cause lay in the conceited arrogance of the Chinese government, its utter contempt for treaty obligations entered into, the outrageous restrictions placed upon commerce, and the insulting and intolerable treatment of foreigners.[15]

Yet this is a period on which no Westerner can look back with equanimity. Protests in the West against the injustice of the action of the powers were not lacking; it would have been better if they had been louder and more unanimous.

The treaty of Nanking (1842) which brought the war to an end secured for the Westerner in China a number of advantages. Hong Kong was surrendered to the British, and became a British colony. Five 'treaty ports' – Canton, Amoy, Foochow, Ningpo, and

15. R. H. Glover and J. H. Kane, *The Progress of World-wide Missions* (2nd ed. 1960), p. 150.

Shanghai – were opened for the residence of foreigners. Under the principle of 'extra-territoriality', foreigners were guaranteed the right of trial under their own laws, and by the officials of their own country, not by the Chinese. Little was said in the treaty about religion, but it was clear that missionaries no less than merchants could take advantage of the privileges accorded to foreigners. On the whole, while deploring the war and doubting the wisdom of the treaty, missionaries took the view that what was deplorable in itself had been overruled by divine providence with a view to the opening up of China to the Gospel. This manifestation of Western aggressiveness was bitterly resented at the time by the Chinese, and the feelings which it aroused have never quite died away. That Christian work seemed so plainly to enter in the wake of gunboats and artillery was to be a permanent handicap to it in China.[16]

The response of Europe and America to the new opportunities was immediate. Almost every missionary society seemed ready to send workers to China, and almost all of them wished to be represented in all the six places which were open to residence. The LMS and the CMS both came in force,[17] to be followed by the Methodists and the Presbyterians; of the Americans, the Board of Commissioners (Congregationalist), the Presbyterians, the Baptists, the Methodists, and the Episcopalians were established within a few years of the signing of the treaty. As in the case of India, it is important not to exaggerate what was done. Missionaries were restricted in movement and few in numbers. Although there was no loss of life through persecution, the combination of an unfavourable climate and constant toil in the midst of anxiety took a heavy toll. Up to 1860 only 214 men missionaries of all the Protestant societies taken together had worked in China; of these forty-four had died in the field, and the average length of service was only seven years.

At first, the disadvantages of the presence of so many societies in so few places, and the consequent dangers of overlapping and rivalry, were not seriously felt. The cities were large. For a considerable period the main strength of the missionaries had to go into mastering the Chinese language and producing the beginnings of a Protestant Christian literature. All, including the

16. The most authoritative account of this period is Louis Wei Tsing-Tsing, *La Politique missionaire de la France en Chine 1842–1856* (Paris, 1960).

17. The SPG helped in the foundation of the bishopric of Victoria, Hong Kong, in 1849, but did not send missionaries to mainland China till 1863.

Anglicans, had come from the background of the various Evangelical revivals, and in spite of certain denominational differences found it possible to live and work fairly happily together.

The difficulty of missionary co-operation, even in a matter of the most central common interest, was however revealed in the progress of the revision of the Chinese Bible. In 1843 a sensible arrangement was reached by which the missionary body in each of the six occupied cities should be responsible for a part of the work. But before long problems of the kind that had convulsed the Roman Catholic mission raised their heads. How was the word 'God' to be rendered? Should it be *Shen* or *Shang Ti*? Or should the Catholic translation be followed, and *T'ien Chu* be used? And should the word 'baptize' be represented by a word which unmistakably implied immersion? When the New Testament was completed in 1850, the committee decided to leave the words 'God' and 'Spirit' untranslated, and to permit each society to print an edition filling in the blanks according to its choice. Then, again, was the aim to be literary elegance such as would appeal to the scholarly class, or the simplicity that would bring the Gospel within the reach of the wayfaring man? Differences of opinion resulted in two translations.

The style [of the earlier version completed in 1852] was of the kind to appeal to the Chinese scholar, but it sacrificed accuracy for literary grace and was too classical for the majority of the church members. The latter version, more exact in its translation and more easily comprehended by those of little education, but not having the literary elegance of the former, was completed in 1862.[18]

There was a tendency for missionaries to accept too easily the treaty restrictions, and to settle down to concentrated work in the cities, with a reduced awareness of the vast hinterland beyond. Three very different happenings in this early period opened wider perspectives before the Christian enterprise.

William Burns (1815–68), a Presbyterian,[19] had had a notable career as a revival preacher in England and Canada, before coming to China in his early thirties in 1847. Burns learned Chinese well, and was responsible for a translation of Bunyan's *Pilgrim's Progress* which proved highly acceptable. But, restless in spirit, he found it impossible to settle down to the routine work of a

18. K. S. Latourette, *A History of Christian Missions in China* (1928), pp. 262–3.
19. And a somewhat distant cousin of the writer of this book.

mission station, and was constantly engaged in journeys in the interior, mainly in the neighbourhood of Amoy, often alone, sometimes accompanied by one of the other missionaries who was prepared to defy convention and accept the risks attendant on travelling. There was little direct fruit from the work of Burns, but he had shown that travel in the interior, though hazardous, was not impossible for a European. Where he pointed the way, others were later to follow in large numbers.

To the decade between 1840 and 1850 belongs the tragi-comic history of Karl F. A. Gützlaff (1803–51), a missionary of the Netherlands Missionary Society from 1826 to 1828, and later independent, who may be variously judged as a saint, a crank, a visionary, a true pioneer, and a deluded fanatic. Gützlaff had done good work in Thailand, and had even briefly penetrated Korea in 1836. In the 1840s he elaborated a plan for the rapid penetration and evangelization of China by the Chinese themselves. Great enthusiasm was aroused by these plans on the continent of Europe, and both the Rhenish and the Basel Societies sent men to China to help Gützlaff in his work. By 1850 he had gathered round him several scores of Chinese workers, who were bringing in reports of journeys in every one of the eighteen provinces of China, with distribution of Scripture and the formation of groups of Chinese Christians. A fearful exposure was to follow. While Gützlaff was in Germany, one of his colleagues discovered that almost all of Gützlaff's Chinese workers were frauds – opium addicts and criminals. Few had travelled far from Hong Kong; money had been squandered, and there was nothing to show for it. On his return, Gützlaff set to work with untamed enthusiasm to cut his losses and to reorganize the work, but he died in 1851 with all his new projects unrealized.[20]

This was perhaps the worst of the not infrequent fiascos with which the history of missionary work is studded. But Gützlaff's work was not wholly in vain. He had made men aware of the 'eighteen provinces', and had brought two great societies into the work in China. One of his colleagues, Rudolf Lechler, served for more than fifty years, and was still in China when the twentieth century dawned. He died, full of years and honour, in 1908.

20. A very careful and satisfactory study of Gützlaff is H. Schlyter, *Karl Gützlaff als Missionar in China* (Lund-Copenhagen, 1946, with summary in English). Schlyter draws attention to the continued indebtedness of Hudson Taylor to the ideas of Gützlaff, and quotes the remark of Hudson Taylor that Gützlaff was 'the grandfather of the China Inland Mission', p. 301.

The T'ai P'ing rebellion is as much a matter of controversy as the work of Gützlaff, though for different reasons. Hung Hsiu-Ch'uan, a native of Kwangtung, had in 1836 received a number of Christian books from Liang Fah, the first ordained Chinese pastor of the Protestant missions. At the time he paid little attention to them, but in 1843 he came to be seriously interested in their contents, and a quasi-Christian movement began to come into being. In 1847 Hung spent some time with Issachar Roberts, one of the pioneers of the American Baptist Mission, and was being prepared for baptism, which however he did not actually receive. In the meantime, a society called the Worshippers of Shang-ti, the true God, had come into being; this was syncretistic in character, adopting some Christian practices, such as baptism, but knowing little of the true spirit of the Gospel.

Between 1848 and 1853 this apparently peaceful movement transformed itself into a liberation army, with the threefold object of ridding China of the Manchu domination, destroying idols, and extirpating the use of opium. On 19 March 1853 the great city of Nanking was stormed; the new dynasty of *T'ai P'ing* (Great Peace) was proclaimed, and Hung became *T'ai P'ing Wang*, King of the Great Peace. The weakness of the Manchus was grave, and for a time it seemed likely that they would collapse. But the weakness of the *T'ai P'ings* was also great; they were destroyers rather than creators, and had little idea of organizing or ruling their conquests. It was from the start only a matter of time before the movement disintegrated.

What was the West to think of this phenomenon? Many missionaries, impressed by the Christian elements in the movement, believed that it had come to stay, and that it might be the instrument for the opening of the whole of China to missionary work and for conversion on the largest scale. And indeed the borrowings were considerable and notable. The rebels had accepted the ten commandments, with their own interpretation; the seventh commandment was extended to cover a wide range of prohibitions, including the absolute condemnation of the use of opium. They practised baptism, and observed the Sabbath, though they seem to have had no knowledge of the Eucharist. Their doxology sounded quite orthodox in Christian ears:

> Praise God, the holy and heavenly Father,
>   Praise Jesus, the holy Lord and Saviour of the world.
> Praise the Holy Spirit, the sacred Spiritual Force [or Example].
>   Praise the three persons [who] United [constitute] one true Lord.

On the other hand, polygamy was permitted, and the remark of Hung's cousin that he 'often used to praise the doctrines of Christianity' but added that 'too much patience and humility do not suit our present times, for therewith it would be impossible to manage this perverted generation'[21] raises the question how far he had really understood the Spirit of Christ.

Until 1860 missionaries were able fairly freely to visit the rebels in their headquarters. All were impressed by the discipline of the *T'ai P'ings*, so different from the chaos that reigned in the armies of the Manchus. Many were convinced that, for all its imperfections of knowledge and practice, the movement contained a true Gospel seed. Griffith John of the LMS, who was in China from 1855 to 1912, wrote in 1860 that the *T'ai P'ings* had

created a vacuum not only in the temples but also in the hearts of the people which remains to be filled. This is the missionary's work . . . I fully believe that God is uprooting idolatry in this land through the insurgents, and that he will by means of them, in connexion with the foreign missionary, plant Christianity in its stead.

Others were from the start more doubtful. And in the end the verdict of history was adverse. The Manchus rallied their forces. In 1863 Captain Charles George Gordon appeared on the scene; under his ever-victorious leadership, the Chinese national armies quickly established mastery, and the kingdom of Great Peace vanished for ever from the earth. The cruel massacres of Manchus by the *T'ai P'ings* were now more than repaid by the counter-massacres carried out by the victors.

'Did ever Christendom have so golden an opportunity of winning a great heathen nation for Christ?' The question is asked by Dr Eugene Stock, the historian of the Church Missionary Society.[22] But did the golden opportunity ever in reality exist? Opinion today remains almost as much divided as it was a century ago. It is futile to speculate on might-have-beens. But the evidence seems to support the sober judgement of Professor Latourette:

At its close, as at its beginning, the *T'ai P'ing* movement was a Chinese sect, displaying some interesting results of contact with Christianity, but drawing most of its beliefs and characteristics from its Chinese environment and the erratic genius of its leaders. . . . Only a complete misunder-

21. Quoted in E. P. Boardman, *Christian Influence upon the Ideology of the Taiping Rebellion* (1952), p. 113.
22. Vol. II, p. 312.

standing of the message of the New Testament could have led to so great a travesty of the doctrines of Christ as that which existed at Nanking.[23]

The opportunity, if it ever existed, had been let slip. The Christian mission in China, after fifty years of work, had little to show in the way of tangible results. But it had well and truly dug itself in, and was ready to go on to wider and more exacting tasks.

Nothing is more characteristic of all the Protestant missions in China than their determination to have from the earliest possible date a fully ordained and responsible Chinese ministry. One of the first steps taken by the first English bishop in China, George Smith (consecrated 1849) of Victoria, Hong Kong, was to set up St Paul's College in Hong Kong for the training of Christian boys for the work of the Church. The first American bishop, William J. Boone (consecrated 1844), ordained his first deacon, Wang Chi, in September 1851, six years after the beginning of the mission in Shanghai. It was only twelve years later that the English bishop took similar action. This concentration on the indigenous ministry was of vital importance, and proved its worth a century later in the general collapse of missions in China.

South-east Asia is a region in which the dominant religions are Buddhism and Islam. Each of these has proved highly resistant to the Christian message, and where either of them prevails, Christian progress has been slow, difficult, and costly.

Thailand, a country of smiling, friendly people, professes Buddhism in perhaps the purest form in which it is to be found anywhere in the world today. The entry of the Gospel has proved correspondingly difficult.

Thailand has been in the main an American field. The Congregationalists arrived in 1831, the Baptists in 1833, and the Presbyterians in 1840. In 1849 the Congregationalists withdrew, after eighteen years of work in which they had not baptized a single Thai convert. Work proved a little easier among the Chinese. In the early days the missionaries had to endure every kind of hardship, not least among them the fiercely anti-foreign attitude of the king and the Buddhist priests. Matters improved in 1851 with the accession of King Mongkut, who was friendly to the missionaries. Still, it was only in 1859 that the Presbyterians baptized their first Thai convert, Nai Chune. In the meantime the translation of

23. op. cit., p. 298.

the New Testament into Siamese had been completed in 1843 by the Baptist John Taylor Jones.

Of *Malaya* at this time hardly anything is to be said. The foundation of Singapore by Sir Stamford Raffles in 1819 ensured the dominance of Britain in the area, and considerably diminished the importance of Malacca. As we have seen, Malaya had been valued by missionaries largely as a jumping-off place for China; as China was opened up, missionaries and institutions (notably the Anglo-Chinese College) were withdrawn to Hong Kong or to the coast of China; and by the middle of the century missionary effort in Malaya had dwindled to almost nothing.

Across the narrow waters, however, in *Borneo*, the picture was very different. James Brooke, who by an extraordinary series of chances had in 1842 become the 'White Rajah' of Sarawak, decided that he must have a mission. In 1847, largely by private subscription but with the help of the SPG, two missionaries were sent out, one of whom, Francis Thomas McDougall, doctor and priest in one, was to have a long and highly distinguished career. Difficulties, as always in pioneer work, were immense. The McDougalls lost five of their children one after the other. Converts were slow in coming. But in 1851 reinforcements arrived, and on 7 September of that year McDougall was able to admit the first five Church converts to Holy Communion.[24]

In 1851 the venerable Bishop of Calcutta, Daniel Wilson, after a visit to Kuching, wrote that 'there is no mission field on the face of the earth to be compared with Borneo'. In 1853 the SPG took over the responsibility for the mission. On 18 October 1855, McDougall was consecrated Bishop of Labuan, the tiny British colony in Borneo, to which the title Sarawak was later added by the rajah.[25] The work which had begun among the Chinese was extended to both the land and sea Dyaks, traditional head-hunters, who showed a surprising readiness to listen to the new Gospel.

24. McDougall had a varied and interesting life. In 1862, when he was sailing with Captain Brooke, the rajah's nephew, the ship was met by pirates, who greatly outnumbered the crew. McDougall incautiously mentioned in a letter to *The Times* that 'my double-barrelled Terry's breech-loader proved a most deadly weapon from its true shooting and certainty and rapidity of fire'; on which Bishop Tait of London remarked: 'When you next get into a similar encounter, you must get your wife to write about it'. How different the real Victorians were from the pale modern picture of them!

25. This was the first consecration of an Anglican bishop to take place in Asia. It is interesting that the third consecrator, with Wilson (Calcutta) and Corrie (Madras), was George Smith, the first Bishop of Victoria, Hong Kong.

In *Indonesia* the government-sponsored Church of the Netherlands East Indies went on its steady unimaginative way, ministering to the Dutch, to the increasing community of mixed origin, and
to the old Churches which had arisen in the previous centuries. But
early in the nineteenth century a new element came in with the
Netherlands Missionary Society, which like all the other continental missionary societies had grown out of a revival movement, and
came in with a more vigorous Gospel and a more dynamic
missionary purpose. It found its major field in the region of
Minahassa in the north of the island of Celebes. There its work was
so successful that before the end of the century the whole population had been Christianized. But in this area the colonial principle seems to have been all too firmly established, and little, if any,
independence was accorded to the Christians of Indonesian race.

The Dutch rulers were not averse from the preaching of the
Gospel to the simple and more animistic of the people under their
rule; when it came to the Muslims, their attitude was rather
different. What was all-important was peace and the quiet acceptance of the rule of the foreigner, and preaching to the Muslims
might 'involve a risk to beautiful rich Java, the chief source of
revenue from the East Indies'. Yet when at last, in 1849, the
missionary J. E. Jellesma was able to take up residence in East
Java, he found two remarkably diverse groups of Christians
already in existence in his area.

In 1811 a German pietist, Johannes Emde, settled in Surabaya
as a watchmaker. He had been told in Germany that there was no
winter in Java, and, as this seemed to him to contradict the promise
of Genesis 8 that winter and summer shall not fail, he concluded
that the only thing to do was to go to Indonesia and see for himself
what the situation really was. In Surabaya he married a Javanese
wife, and used the contacts which this brought him to preach the
Gospel as he understood it and to distribute portions of Scripture
in the Javanese language. In 1843 he was able to bring thirty-five
converted Muslims from the village of Wiung to the Dutch minister in Surabaya for baptism. 'Father Emde' had no understanding
of the significance of the ancient Javanese culture, and expected his
converts to accept western ways; but he had brought into existence
a living and convinced group of Christians.

Just about the same time Coenraad Laurens Coolen, who had
been for a time a servant of the Dutch government and had then
branched out as an independent planter, was creating another
Christian community on completely different lines. Coolen's

mother had been a Javanese lady of noble family. As a result he was exceedingly well aware of the ancient Javanese traditions, and of their importance in the life of the people. In consequence, he used entirely indigenous methods for the proclamation of the Gospel; and, as a Christian group grew up around him, he was so anxious that the converts should not lose their truly Javanese character that he would not permit any of them to be baptized.

It was at this point that Pastor Jellesma arrived on the scene. Which of the two groups was he to favour – the orthodox and pietistic group which had lost all interest in its own past, or the group which had retained much of the Javanese heritage but had neglected some things that ordinarily are regarded as an essential part of the Christian tradition? Wisely, he remained neutral, and settled at a third centre, Modjowarno, where it might be possible for him to combine the best insights of the two existing groups. To a large extent his hopes were realized; the East Javanese Church continued to manifest a highly independent spirit, depending for its expansion on the spontaneous efforts of lay evangelists. Nowhere else in the world have so many Muslims been won for the Christian faith. Indonesian Islam perhaps offers a more favourable soil for the Gospel than other forms of Islam; it has retained a great many animistic features from the Indonesian past, and is less fiercely dogmatic than Islam shows itself to be elsewhere. Nevertheless the achievement of conversion is remarkable, and would have been impossible without vigorous inner life and willingness for sacrifice on the part of the developing Church.

Very different was the situation in *Burma*. Here the coming together of a great missionary and an unexpectedly open door produced results far beyond anything that was to be seen elsewhere in this discouraging part of the world. Burma is in the main a Buddhist country, with its own vigorous Buddhist tradition. But it is a land of mountains and valleys, of impenetrable jungles and scattered peoples. At least 6 million – Kachins, Chins, Karens – belong to non-Buddhist peoples, each with its own language and its own animistic tradition. These were more ready than the Buddhists to hear the new tidings from the West.

The first Protestant missionary to settle in Burma, after an abortive attempt by Felix Carey, was the American pioneer Adoniram Judson (1788–1850).[26] Judson had been sent to India by the American Board, which is mainly supported by the Con-

26. Apparently Judson pronounced his name Adónirăm.

gregationalists. On the voyage, he set to work to prepare himself for his meeting with the English Baptists in Calcutta by reading up the baptismal question; to his surprise he found himself led to the conviction that the baptism of believers is the only proper fulfilment of the scriptural ordinance. He naturally resigned his connection with the American Board, and it was as a convinced Baptist that he arrived in Burma in July 1813.

Here he threw himself with unrestrained ardour into the learning of the Burmese language, of which he became in time an acknowledged master. Endless preaching in a *zayat*, constructed in Burmese style in a street in Rangoon, was his chosen means of communication with the people, but six years passed before Judson was able to baptize his first convert. As he himself said, winning a convert in those regions was 'like drawing the eye-tooth of a live tiger'. Work on the translation of the New Testament into Burmese was going on continuously throughout these years.

In 1824 Judson moved to Ava, the capital, and there followed the incident which made his name famous throughout the world. The first Anglo-Burmese war broke out, and although Judson was not British he came under suspicion as a foreigner and potential spy, and was incarcerated for seventeen months in a Burmese jail, under conditions of extreme squalor and suffering. Only the devoted ministrations of his wife, Ann Hasseltine Judson, who was allowed to visit him in the jail, kept him alive. When the war was over and the victory won, Mrs Judson died. Judson never really recovered from his sufferings. Till the end of his life he was liable to oscillate between serene Christian confidence and morbid introspection coupled with a depression that amounted almost to despair. But he never ceased to work; in 1834 the translation of the whole Bible into Burmese was complete, and at his death in 1850 he left behind an immense collection of materials for a dictionary; the English-Burmese section was ready for the press.

The great open door for the mission came through its contact with the Karens. When George Dana Boardman (1801–31) opened a new station at Tavoy, he was accompanied by Ko Tha Byn, the first Karen to become a Christian. Ko Tha Byn went everywhere among his own people, proclaiming his new faith, and found them ready to listen to him. The Karens, though illiterate and despised by the Burmese, were far from being an uncivilized people; and they had traditions which seem to have served as a real *praeparatio evangelica*. They knew of the Creator God, and had a story of the fall through which they had lost the favour of God and been reduced to this quasi-servile position. They believed also that in times past they had had a sacred book, which their fathers through carelessness had lost.[27] When a preacher came, bearing a sacred book and telling them that the God whose anger they had incurred had himself come to seek them in mercy in Jesus Christ, it seemed to them that their dreams and hopes had all been realized. Karens in their hundreds came forward to be instructed and to be baptized. Up to the end of the period dealt with in this chapter, the Baptists had it all to themselves except for the Roman Catholics; Burma was a Baptist country. In 1851 there were already more than 10,000 Church members in full standing, and this probably represented a Christian community of 30,000 people – a far higher proportion of the population than was at that time to be found in the Christian community in India.

Ceylon, as Sri Lanka was then known, is so near to India that it is natural to think of it as forming part of India. But in fact it is remarkably different in almost every way. Though it has today considerable Hindu, Muslim, and Christian minorities, the vast majority of the people are Buddhists; they are the heirs of a great Buddhist civilization, and the Buddhists claim that their language, Sinhalese, should be the sole national language of Ceylon.

We saw that, in the time of the Dutch occupation, many former Roman Catholics had become Protestants for not very reputable reasons. With the coming of the British in 1795, the Dutch Protestant movement almost wholly collapsed, most of the Christians being received back into the Roman Catholic Church which far outnumbers all the other Christian Churches in the island.

The coming of the British was followed by the arrival of a number of British missionary societies – the L M S in 1804 (till 1818 only), the Baptists in 1812, the Methodists in 1814, and the C M S in 1817. In the meantime, the American Board had entered Jaffna, the Tamil-speaking northern area of the island. The experience of all the missions was the same – widespread resistance, a few hard-won converts, a very slow but steady growth of the Church. As Buddhism became more self-conscious and better able to defend itself, even the small stream of converts tended to dry up. The missions rendered notable service through their educational

27. It must be mentioned, in the interests of scientific accuracy, that not all investigators are convinced of the reliability of early accounts of these Karen traditions.

institutions from the middle of the century onwards, to the Tamils from South India, who came in increasing numbers to work on the tea estates. But Ceylon to this day has remained a predominantly and obstinately Buddhist country.

For a part of the Christian enterprise that was numerically far more successful, we have to turn to another and very different island world – the *South Pacific*.

As we have seen, the narratives of the voyages of Captain Cook had aroused intense interest in the English-speaking world, and it was perfectly natural that on its foundation in 1795 the London Missionary Society should turn to the South Seas as a possible field for its activities. The first missionary party was sent out in September 1796.

It was known that the many and varied races inhabiting these islands were simple and primitive in their ways, and that many of their habits would be regarded as barbarous by European nations. But it seems that in 1796, and for long after, the missionaries were quite unprepared for what they would have to encounter. Some of these peoples are physically among the most beautiful in the world. Their sense of beauty is manifest in many splendid creations of primitive art.

These people maintained a sunny brightness of disposition, shared their goods with one another, practised unlimited hospitality, and in their best moments reached out toward something higher and better.[28]

But there were deep shadows on their life – ignorance, fear, and hatred, and a cruelty which regularly reached almost maniacal depths of bestiality. War was incessant and brutal. Cannibalism was common. One of the first missionaries to set foot on Fiji began his missionary career by gathering and burying the heads, hands, and feet of eighty victims who had been cooked and eaten.

Some knowledge of this, though far less than the full reality, had seeped through to Europe, and the conclusion had been reached that the preaching of the Gospel to such people was not likely to have much success, unless it was accompanied, or perhaps rather preceded, by a considerable period of the diffusion of civilization. In consequence, the great majority of the early missionaries in this area were artisans of one 'mystery' or another, and very few were ordained ministers. Such a method was plausible, but it was based on a misconception. There was some evidence that men and

28. F. H. L. Paton, *The Kingdom in the Pacific* (1913), pp. 15–16.

women of little education were less likely than others to be able to endure the hardships, the loneliness, and the temptations of a missionary life.

The first island on which the missionaries settled was Tahiti. One party went on to Tonga. The fate of this second party was typical of a great deal that happened in those early days. Of a party of ten, three were brutally murdered, one went native – a much commoner happening than is generally reflected in the edifying accounts of these early missions which are current – and the remaining six were picked up by a passing vessel and carried back to Australia. That for the moment was the end of the evangelization of Tonga. A similar sequence of events depleted the missionary force in Tahiti; at the end of the eighteenth century, there were only seven missionaries in the whole of the South Pacific.

But defeat was never more than temporary. Where some had gone out, others came in, and held fast until their cause triumphed.

Conditions in *Tahiti* were difficult, since the king, Pomare, a resolute idolater and cannibal, resisted all Christian influence; and his son, also Pomare, who succeeded him, seemed determined to follow in his ways. A startling change took place in 1812, when Pomare the younger decided to throw away his idols and to ask for baptism. Seven years later, in 1819, he was baptized in a huge church, which he himself had constructed, in the presence of 4,000 of his subjects. From then on, the position of the mission was secure; more than two generations were to pass before paganism was finally to disappear, but the end was in sight. In 1838 the complete Bible was published in Tahitian. In 1843 France took over the government of the islands; French displaced English, and the LMS wisely yielded to the Paris Society for Evangelical Missions, which has since cared for the souls of the islanders.

The work was seriously resumed in *Tonga* when the Methodist John Thomas, a blacksmith from Worcestershire, arrived to stay for twenty-five years. Here, as in so many islands, rapid progress was made only after the conversion of a leading chief. In 1830 Taufaahau of the island of Haabai was baptized and took the name of George. By 1839 George had made himself king of the whole Tonga group and promulgated a Christian code of laws for the islands. He died in 1893, being, as was believed, a hundred years old.

The most famous of all the pioneers in the South Seas was the Congregationalist John Williams, who was sent out by the LMS in 1817. He was assigned to Raiatea in the *Society Isles*, and also worked for some years as a pioneer on Rarotonga. But, as he himself said, he could not content himself 'within the narrow limits of a single reef'. He was the first to see clearly that the evangelization of the Pacific could be carried out only by Christians of the native races; hence his policy of placing native teachers, often with the slenderest of qualifications, on remote islands were they could hardly ever be visited by any missionary. By 1834 he was able to report that 'no group of islands, nor single island of importance, within 2,000 miles of Tahiti had been left unvisited'. On each island teachers were left. Naturally, there were some failures. But few marvels in Christian history can equal the faithfulness of these men and women, left behind among peoples of unknown speech and often in danger of their lives, to plant and build Churches out of their own limited stock of faith and knowledge, supported only by the invigorating power of the Holy Spirit and the prayers of their friends. Many watered the seed with their own blood; but the Churches grew, and far more widely than if reliance had been placed first and foremost on the European missionary.

Samoa provided a less eventful history than most of the other islands. The first approach seems to have been made by a Samoan who had learned the Gospel from the Methodists in Tonga. In 1830 John Williams entered, and left behind eight Tahitian teachers. When the first European missionaries came to reside, they found a Christian community of some 2,000 already in existence. Within a generation, the greater part of the population had become Christian. The Samoan Church well deserves the panegyric pronounced on it by an American church leader some forty years ago:

It is doubtful if there is another people on the face of the earth who, in proportion to their numbers, have given so many missionaries to the Church, or have paid so great a price in sacrifice and martyrdom. At home not only do they build and maintain all their own churches, schools, and other institutions, but they sustain their missionary guests as well. They regularly support the world-wide work of their Churches.[29]

In *Fiji* progress was more hardly won. The first contact with Christians, Tongans, seems to have come about in 1823. The first Methodist missionaries arrived in 1835. During the next ten years some converts were won, but hardly any impression seemed to have been made on the brutal and ferocious darkness of Fijian

29. H. P. Van Dusen, *They Found the Church There* (1945), p. 99.

paganism. Then in 1845 a great revival broke out; conversions were numerous, and progress was greatly furthered when the chief Thakombau, who had been the chief opponent of Christianity, surrendered and was baptized in 1854. What were the forces that lay behind these rapid conversions? The acute remarks of Professor Latourette on the subject of Fiji may be regarded as relevant to almost all the islands:

> The victory of Christians in warfare furthered the change of faith, for by the test of combat the Christian God had been proved more powerful than the old deities. Indeed, on at least one occasion victorious Christians gave the vanquished pagans the choice of death or conversion. One chief embraced Christianity because in a time of drought the prayers of non-Christian priests failed to bring relief but rain fell copiously during the Christian service on Sunday. The cures of disease wrought by missionaries and Christian teachers won some. A priest of the old cult ascribed his conversion to a dream in which his pagan god bowed to the earth before the Christian God.[30]

The work of missionaries in *Hawaii* has in late years received wide advertisement through Mr James Michener's interesting and highly picturesque account of them in his work under that title. The facts are, perhaps, less romantic than the picture. The missionaries, sent out by the American Board, arrived in 1820. The party of nearly twenty, including children, found to their astonishment that a considerable amount of Christian influence had preceded them; idols had been destroyed and a number of pagan customs abolished, and those who wished to restore them had been defeated in war. The arrival of the missionaries was well timed. Aided by a number of the chiefs who were favourable to their work, they made slow progress on the usual lines, opened schools, learned the language, translated part of the Bible. Then, in the Hawaiian group as in so many other islands, a great revival broke out; for good and ill, the methods followed were very much those of the Great Awakening in America, but serious efforts were made to avoid mere emotionalism and to test the sincerity of the converts. In the years 1839–41 more than 20,000 out of a population of about 100,000 were received into the Church. It is interesting to see how, in spite of his obvious prejudices against them, the missionaries gradually impose themselves on Mr Michener. In their utter devotion to the people, in such great achievements as the writing of the new code of laws for the Hawaiian people, he is compelled to recognize the undying service rendered by the Christian faith, even in its narrowest and least attractive form, to the maintenance of the life of a simple people threatened by the tides of western civilization. But he shows also that these services were in fact rendered to a dying people. A century after the arrival of the missionaries more than half the population of the islands was Japanese; only 9.3 per cent were pure Hawaiians, in numbers less than a quarter of those who had welcomed the missionaries a century before.

Of all the islands of the Pacific, the *New Hebrides* and the *Solomons* proved most resistant to Christian influences. In 1839 John Williams was able to place three Samoan teachers on the island of Tanna. But on 20 November of the same year he and his young companion Harris were set upon by the people of the island of Erromanga, clubbed and speared to death, and then dragged off to be cooked and eaten in a cannibal feast. Erromanga accounted for no less than five missionary martyrs, not to mention teachers of Polynesian race, and the evangelization of its people was completed only in the twentieth century.

Far away to the south, a branch of the Polynesian race had established itself in *New Zealand*. The Anglican chaplain in Sydney, Samuel Marsden, who had arrived in the Antipodes in 1794, had met Maoris in Australia, and, being deeply impressed by the dignity and intelligence of these people, was seized by the desire of starting a mission among them. Various hindrances delayed the project, but in 1814, with a missionary party which included craftsmen and mechanics, Marsden was at last able to reach New Zealand; on Christmas Day of that year he held at the Bay of Islands what is believed to have been the first Christian service ever to be held in the islands. The missionaries of the Church Missionary Society were rightly very cautious in giving baptism to inquirers; they suspected, and later found their suspicions justified, that some of those who seemed most anxious for baptism were really much less concerned about the state of their souls than about the possibility of acquiring firearms for use in their interminable wars. The first baptism took place in 1825.

Plans for European settlement in New Zealand were much debated in the second quarter of the nineteenth century. The missionaries were steadily opposed to them, believing that nothing but harm could come from the mixture of races in a small country. Fate was against them; British sovereignty was declared in 1840, and from that date onwards the influx of settlers was large. Today

New Zealand is a model of racial co-operation and harmony, but this happy state has been reached only after a tragic history of mistrust, bitterness, and war. Yet through it all the work of conversion went forward. The first Anglican Bishop of New Zealand, George Augustus Selwyn (1809–78), one of the most notable ecclesiastics of the century, remarked in a sermon preached in the second year of his episcopate (1842) that 'we see here a whole nation of pagans converted to the faith'. The good prelate was a little carried away by his enthusiasm; but in 1854 Sir George Grey, who had been governor of New Zealand, reported that all but 1 per cent of the Maori race had made profession of Christianity; and in 1835 Charles Darwin – in one of those commendations of missionary work that come rather surprisingly from his pen – wrote after a visit to the C M S station at Waimate: 'All this is very surprising when it is considered that five years ago nothing but the fern flourished here . . . The lesson of the missionary is the enchanter's wand.'

It is astonishing that from this period there is so little to record of Christian effort in the *Near and Middle East*, the heartlands of Islam. There were various exploratory journeys, notably those of that tough and much-enduring convert from Judaism the Reverend Joseph Wolff (1796–1862).[31] But there is little of a permanent character.

The American Board established work in *Turkey* in 1831. The Reverend William Goodell (1792–1867) settled in Constantinople, and the work gradually extended itself to other centres in Asia Minor and Armenia. Valuable educational work was undertaken, and is still carried on; but the main success of the work was not with Muslims but with adherents of the ancient Eastern Churches, and particularly the Armenians. Rather regretfully, and perhaps rather unwisely, the Americans were led to form a new denomination for those who had left their ancestral Church; the first evangelical congregation was formed in 1846, and the new denomination acquired legal recognition in 1850.

To *Egypt* the C M S sent a party of five missionaries in 1818. Two of them went on to *Ethiopia*, from which they were later expelled; the task of the remaining three was to co-operate with the Coptic Church, and to help it to adapt its life to the needs of the modern

---

31. For a brief account of Wolff's adventures, see W. T. Gidney, *The History of the London Society for Promoting Christianity among the Jews* (1908), pp. 101–22, 333–4.

world. This work proved unrewarding, and the mission was withdrawn in 1862. The United Presbyterians of the USA came in in 1854, and at once began to attract a number of the more intelligent Copts. Rightly or wrongly, they decided to found a rival Church, and their success has tended rather to the disruption than to the reconstitution of the ancient Church.

In *Syria* and the *Lebanon*, the pioneers were the American Board, followed by the American Presbyterians. The first missionaries of the American Board arrived in Beirut in 1823. In two fields notable work was done. The Bible was translated into modern Arabic. (It may be noted that the mission press was maintained from 1822 to 1833 in the British tranquillity of Malta, but was moved to Beirut in 1834.) The Syrian Protestant College began to attract students from a number of countries, and was destined to grow into the famous American University of Beirut (1920).

Henry Martyn had stayed one year in *Iran* on his final journey homewards in 1811, working on his Persian version of the New Testament, and had baptized one convert. Nothing more was done until Swiss missionaries of the Basel Mission settled in Tabriz in 1813, to be followed by the American Board, which opened a station at Urmia in 1835. The aim of the Basel missionaries was contact with the Muslims; as elsewhere, the Americans concentrated on the adherents of the ancient Eastern Churches, with exactly the same results as we have noted in Turkey and Egypt.

In *Palestine*, the pioneers were the Anglican Society for Work among the Jews.[32] This Society settled in Jerusalem in 1820, and in 1824 began in a simple way the medical work which was to develop in 1848 into its famous hospital. In 1851 the CMS also entered in.

This work was to lead to one of the strangest episodes of modern Church history. The authorities of Britain and Prussia agreed to found in Jerusalem a joint bishopric, of which the incumbent was always to be a bishop with Anglican episcopal consecration but whose appointment was to rest alternately with the Crowns of England and Prussia. There were political as well as religious factors at work: some authorities felt that the Russian protectorate of Orthodox Christians and the French protectorate of Roman Catholics had better be balanced by an Anglo-German protectorate of Protestants. The first bishop, Michael Solomon Alexander, a

32. The clumsy Victorian title the 'London Society for Promoting Christianity among the Jews' was superseded by the more attractive 'Church Mission to Jews', and quite recently has been changed again to 'The Church's Ministry among the Jews'.

converted Jewish rabbi, served only from 1842 to 1845. He was succeeded by Samuel Gobat, a French-speaking Swiss Protestant from the Jura, a brilliant linguist, who had served the CMS for some years in Ethiopia. Gobat proved to be a most controversial figure. He was violently accused of proselytizing activities among the Eastern Churches, and, though he explained that all that he had done was to accept certain Christians who had been driven out of their own Churches because of their interest in the Bible, feeling became so intense that the Archbishops of Canterbury, York, Dublin, and Armagh in 1853 took the unprecedented step of issuing a public declaration of their confidence in him. It is unlikely that Gobat, in his peculiar and difficult position, always acted with complete wisdom and prudence – on this much more objective study is needed than has as yet been carried out. But his educational work was a contribution of permanent value. In 1886 the Anglo-Prussian co-operation came to an end, and the bishopric (now archbishopric) in Jerusalem became a purely Anglican venture.[33]

Until the middle of the nineteenth century *Africa* remained, as it had been for centuries, the unknown and mysterious continent. By that time Europeans had mapped the whole of its coast-line, and for purposes of trade were holding on temerariously at a number of points. But that greatest ally of African independence, the mosquito, still held the white man at bay, and even caravans of explorers often found no more than an untimely death in the deserts and rain-forests of Africa. Nevertheless, the Christian forces were preparing themselves for the gigantic task of the assault, and feelers were being put forth from south and north, from east and west.

Sierra Leone on the west coast, where the hills rise to 2,700 feet and break a coast-line which is low and monotonous almost everywhere until broken again by the splendid mountains of the Cameroons, had been picked on by friends of the slaves as a home for those who had been freed, and a colony had been established. One of the early governors was the evangelical Zachary Macaulay, the silent father of the historian T. B. Macaulay, the greatest talker that the world has ever known. By 1846, 50,000 slaves had been

33. Professor E. Benz of Marburg, in his *Bischofsamt und apostolische Sukzession im deutschen Protestantismus* (Stuttgart, 1953), pp. 148–219, has very much that is interesting to say about the Jerusalem bishopric; but I think that much more work still needs to be done on this remarkable episode.

brought in: it was reckoned that they spoke 117 different languages, and inevitably they developed among themselves as their *lingua franca* the peculiar form of Africanized English known as Creole. They could not be said to be promising material; they have been described (by the German historian of missions Gustav Warneck) as

a confused mass, destitute of the slightest feeling of community, who lived in a state of constant conflict among themselves, and were dull, lazy, and in the last degree unchaste, besides being in bondage, without exception, to heathenish superstition.

The CMS sent out German missionaries to Sierra Leone in 1804. After some rather unsuccessful work among the Susu tribe on the Rio Pongas, the mission was transferred to the colony. The Methodists followed in 1811. In the early days the loss of life was terrible; in twenty years the CMS lost more than fifty men and women, yet recruits were always ready to take the places of those who had fallen. Gradually a stable work developed: the colony became a Christian land. It is only to be regretted that its Christianity has not proved expansive, and that the work of bringing the Gospel to the still pagan tribes of the protectorate has advanced only in so far as it has been undertaken by European and American missionaries.

In 1827 the CMS rendered an incomparable service to the whole of West Africa. It founded Fourah Bay College for the higher education of Africans; the first student entered on the roll was Samuel Adjai Crowther, whom we shall have occasion to meet again. The failure adequately to support and maintain this great institution (later affiliated to Durham University) reflects grave discredit on British Christianity. Yet, in spite of all the handicaps of inadequate staffing and miserable penury, Fourah Bay till the end of the nineteenth century and after educated the majority of those Africans who have made the history of English-speaking West Africa.

At this point mention must be made of yet another heroic and ill-starred venture. In 1851 Anglicans in the West Indies, where so much of the population is of Negro origin, decided to start their own mission in West Africa. Their choice fell upon the Rio Pongas, now in French territory, an insalubrious region, where the West Indian Negro showed little more ability than the white man to survive. The enterprise deserves mention, as one of the first attempts by a 'younger Church' to undertake missionary work on its own responsibility. But the Rio Pongas Mission has never fulfilled the high and generous hopes with which it was founded.

When the nineteenth century opened, Philip Quaque, the sole African clergyman of the Church of England, was still labouring at Cape Coast in what is now called *Ghana* (Gold Coast). But the Anglicans did not move forward from the bridgehead, and it fell to the Basel Mission and the Methodists to enter into this field.

Ghana had long had trading connections with Europe, but there was as yet no question of imperial occupation, and European settlement was almost confined to the coast. But an intensification of British activity in these waters resulted from Christian concern over the slave trade. In 1807 the trade had been abolished by act of the British Parliament, but other countries had not taken similar action and in order to make control of the traffic effective Britain for years maintained cruisers and gunboats on the west coast of Africa, in a continuous and often successful patrol. From these efforts resulted treaties with chiefs, then gradually a *de facto* occupation of the country, and finally annexation to the British Crown. But the process was very slow; at the time of which we are writing, the great inland independent kingdom of Ashanti, and still more the northern territories, were virtually unknown, and war between Ashanti and the coastal tribes continued until the end of the century.

In 1828 the Basel Mission, in association with the Danish trading interests on the coast, arrived to begin missionary work. After twelve years the mission seemed to have nothing to show for its efforts other than the graves of eight missionaries. But the sole survivor, Andreas Riis, refused to give up. Reinforcements arrived and survived. Notable work was done in education, and in the scientific study of the African languages. And, as in India, the Basel Mission devoted itself to agricultural and commercial developments. Cocoa was introduced and immediately flourished: Ghana proved to have the ideal climate for the production of cocoa, and by the end of the century was the largest producer in the world. The missionaries found Ghana divided, poor, ignorant, and racked by the slave trade. It was in no small measure due to their efforts that in 1957, when Ghana, first of the peoples of tropical Africa to emerge from colonial to national status, attained to full independence, it was united, rich, educated, and able to hold its own in the competitive world of western civilization.

The leading figure among the Methodists was Thomas Birch Freeman (1809–90). This remarkable man was the son of an African father and an English mother, born and brought up in England. Where others died, he survived; the climate, hard work, and disease seemed to have no lasting effects on his iron constitution. The Africans appear always to have thought of Freeman as a white man, but perhaps his origins gave him a natural affinity with them. By his friendliness, his courtesy, and his respect for their traditions and for the authority of their chiefs, he was able to win their confidence, and in some cases conversion followed on this confidence. Between 1838 and 1844 there was a steady growth in Church membership, and, true to the Methodist tradition, Freeman and his colleagues laid great stress on lay witness and on the spread of the faith among Africans by Africans who themselves had come to Christ.

Nigeria, as finally organized in 1900, is an immense country, four times the size of Great Britain, and the most populous of all the African nations. In the north were to be found the strong Muslim emirates. In east and west the people belonged to many tribes and spoke innumerable languages, some of Bantu and some of Sudanese type. Trade with Europe had existed for a long time, but it was not until 1851, with the occupation of Lagos by the British, that the first actual possession came into the hands of a European nation. Here, as so often, the Church was ahead of the political powers.

Christianity in Nigeria owed its origin to Sierra Leone. A number of the freed slaves made their way back to their place of origin in western Nigeria; they sent word to their missionary friends in Sierra Leone, and both the Anglicans and the Methodists responded.

In 1842 the Anglican Henry Townsend made his way to Abeokuta. In 1844 he returned with a party which included Samuel Crowther, to found a mission among the numerous and vigorous Yoruba people. Here, not long after his arrival, Crowther to his amazement recognized his own mother and sisters; they were among the first converts, and Crowther had the satisfaction of translating the baptism service into Yoruba for the baptism of his mother. The first conversions were followed by a period of intense, but happily short-lived, persecution at the hands of the local rulers; the converts held firm, and the Church began to grow. In 1853 David Hinderer and his wife were able to establish a station at Ibadan, greatest of African cities. In the meantime, the Methodists under the lead of T. B. Freeman had also arrived, and made Abeokuta their centre.

The problem of the Niger was not as perplexing as that of the Nile, but the determination of its course, by Mungo Park (1771–1806) and other explorers, was one of the great achievements of geographical discovery in the nineteenth century. Clearly this river held the key to vast and populous areas. Both Church and state were interested, and, when the government planned an expedition up the Niger, Crowther was among those who accompanied it. The CMS was already planning what became, in the period after 1858, its great mission on the Niger.

Still further east, in 1846 the United Presbyterian Church of Scotland began a mission in Calabar, that land of many rivers and many peoples. Hope Waddell, the pioneer of this group, had previously been a missionary in Jamaica. His first party included a Jamaican mulatto, and others of Negro blood later joined the mission. It is not always the case that the West Indian Negro makes a happy adaptation to work among his brethren in Africa; there are more important things than the colour of a man's skin, and the difference in outlook between Jamaican and West African is very wide. Yet members of the African race in the West Indies have in many cases rendered notable service in the building up of the African Church in Africa.

We turn now to the third Christian advance into Africa, that from the extreme south. As early as 1652 the Dutch had established a victualling station for their eastern fleet in what is now Cape Town. Gradually a considerable settlement of farmers and others grew up around the Dutch headquarters, and at the end of the eighteenth century the white population was reckoned at 21,000. Unlike West Africa, the south is a land in which the white man can settle and thrive; the eighteenth century could not foresee the terrible conflicts which would later arise between the black man and the white for dominance and possession of the land, but the seeds of dissension were being sown, and already the Dutch held strongly their characteristic view that it is the destiny of the white man to rule and that of the black man to obey.

A few efforts had been made by the Moravians to evangelize the African peoples of the south; but their first pioneer, Georg Schmidt, who arrived in 1737, was driven out by the Dutch in 1744, and the mission lapsed until 1792. When Moravians returned and founded their station of Genadendal, they were astonished and moved to meet a Hottentot woman who had been baptized by Schmidt half a century before, and still had a New Testament given to her by the missionary.

In 1795, in the course of the Napoleonic wars, the British took over the Cape, and, with the exception of a brief Dutch interlude, 'Cape Colony' remained until 1960 a part of the British Commonwealth of Nations. From the time of the British occupation, British Christians took a leading part in missionary work in the South, and to the racial clash between black and white was added the problem of a substantial difference between the attitudes of Dutch and British Christians respectively towards the black man.

The pioneer society was the London Missionary Society, which was born in the year of the British occupation of the Cape; the pioneer missionary was the Dutch physician John Theodore Vanderkemp. This man had had an unusual preparation for the work of a missionary. As a young student he had run away, in order to escape from the pious influences of his home, and had served for fifteen years as a dragoon. Later he completed his medical studies and practised for ten years as a doctor in Holland. When he was nearly fifty, he saw his wife and daughter drowned before his eyes in a boating accident. This personal tragedy drove him to a profound conversion and dedication to Christian witness; he offered his services to the LMS. His vigorous personality and dynamic faith seemed to outweigh the drawback of his age; he was accepted, and arrived in Cape Town in 1799.

Vanderkemp, with his three companions, had to face the problems of three different African peoples – the nomadic thieving Bushmen, an almost pygmy people, who have failed to hold their own against the spreading waves of western influence and have almost disappeared; the Hottentots, rather more civilized, and living in much closer contact with the white man; and the 'Kaffirs',[34] the masses of mainly Bantu peoples, vigorous, expansive, and warlike, who in their steady pressure southwards had reached the point at which they were bound to enter into conflict with the white man. Vanderkemp was deeply interested in the Bantu, and managed to make one long and adventurous journey among them; he was not able to stay long enough to secure any permanent results, but he seems to have left a profound impression on those whom he encountered. The main effort of the work was

34. 'Kaffir' is not really the name of any African people, though it was used for a considerable period of the Xhosa people. It is simply the Arabic word for 'unbeliever', and was used by the Muslim traders of the pagan African tribes with which they came into contact along the east coast of Africa.

concentrated on the Hottentots, for whom Vanderkemp created a city of refuge at Bethelsdorp about 400 miles east of Cape Town. Any attempt to defend the rights of the oppressed native races was certain to arouse the suspicions of the colonists, and Vanderkemp and his colleagues had many difficulties to face. Their relations with the colonists were not improved when Vanderkemp set the example – followed by two of his colleagues – of marrying an African wife (in his case apparently of Malagasy origin). However laudable as an example of 'identification', this method had practical drawbacks; in this particular case the hostility of the local white population to the mission was sensibly increased. Vanderkemp died in 1811. He had manifested many of the virtues of the pioneer; it was for others to supplement his work by greater gifts of prudence and pertinacity.

The second great figure of South African missions is undoubtedly John Philip. Philip, who arrived in 1820, was already forty-four years of age when he was appointed superintendent of the LMS missions in South Africa. He held the post for thirty years. Philip was an uncompromising supporter of the rights of the black man as against the white; he expressed plainly the conviction that, given the opportunities of education and training, the African would prove himself to be in every way the equal of the European. He and his friends had the ear of powerful supporters in England, and missionary influence is to be traced in many of the measures taken by the government during the years of Philip's ascendancy. What happened is still a matter of controversy. Unquestionably the policy of Philip and his supporters led many of the Boers to feel that life under the British was intolerable, and helped to bring about those massive treks through which the two northern states of the Orange Free State and the Transvaal came into being.

The third of our four great figures is Robert Moffat (1795–1883). Moffat was sent out by the LMS at the age of twenty-one, with little education and no formal theological training. Dr Richter rightly remarked of him that 'he is one of those in whom the vocation of a missionary has in outstanding degree manifested its power to produce great men and splendid characters'.[35] After a short apprenticeship, Moffat settled among the Bechuana at Kuruman, which was to be his home for forty-eight years. Here he created an oasis in the wilderness. In England he had been a

---

35. J. Richter, *Geschichte der evangelischen Mission in Afrika* (1922), p. 471.

gardener; now he brought the waters of the Kuruman river through a long irrigation canal to the borders of his dwelling.

But it was slow work to find the way into Bechuana minds and consciences. A revolution took place when Moffat was led to realize that the only key was the language of the people. For some years he had made use of Cape Dutch, which was understood by some of the men but by none of the women. When he resolved to make himself completely master of the Tswana language, the difficulties were formidable. This was an unwritten language, and Moffat was without philological training; he had first to catch the sounds, then to reduce them to writing, then to master a wholly unknown grammar, and finally to ascertain the extent to which the Tswana vocabulary was adequate to the purposes of Bible translation. All the difficulties were overcome; by 1857 the Bible translation had been completed, and seen through the press by Moffat himself at Kuruman. More important still, once the language had been learned, the attitude of the people towards him seemed completely to change; the Gospel began to take hold, something like a religious revival broke out, and the first baptisms took place in 1829.

Moffat's work had the weakness as well as the strength of greatness. In spite of his love for the Africans, he had little interest in the background of their thought, and left behind no treasure of anthropological observation. He underestimated their religious traditions,[36] and introduced unaltered the fervent evangelical Christianity of his own tradition, without considering the possibilities of its adaptation to an African world. His methods were always and increasingly patriarchal; he did not intend to suppress African initiative and independence, but it was noticed that Christians who lived at some distance from his authority were more vigorous and responsible than his immediate disciples. Yet Moffat's achievement was memorable. His stalwart figure stood for something; it had shown the Christians of Europe what could be achieved in Africa, and had convinced them that freedom, civilization, and conversion could go forward hand in hand among still simple peoples.

The fame of Moffat has been a little overshadowed by the superlative greatness of his friend and son-in-law David Livingstone (1813–73). Livingstone came from a hardy clan of Scotsmen, reared in poverty and godliness. He arrived in Africa in 1841, and

36. He believed that the Bechuana had no word for 'God'; in this, later and better acquaintance with the language has shown that he was mistaken.

for ten years served in the ordinary routine of missionary work. But he, like John Williams, was not a man to be held to one single reef; the mind and impulse of the explorer were in him, and he was always drawn on, in his own words, by 'the smoke of a thousand villages' that had never seen a missionary.

The first great journey which made him famous led him to the west coast in Angola, and then – because he would not desert the African carriers who had accompanied him – right across the continent to Quilimane on the east coast. He showed on this journey all the qualities of a great traveller. His manner with the Africans was so excellent, so patient, that he never had to use violence. His scientific and geographical observations were minutely accurate. He had opened the heart of Africa as it had never been opened before.

But Livingstone was at all times not only a traveller but also a missionary. His cause was the cause of the Gospel, and to that alone he looked for the transformation of the African peoples. In 1853, among the Makololo, he wrote that

I took thence a more intense disgust at heathenism than I had before, and formed a greatly elevated opinion of the latent effects of missions in the south, among tribes which are reported to have been as savage as the Makololo. The indirect benefits, which to a casual observer lie beneath the surface and are inappreciable, in reference to the probable wide diffusion of Christianity at some future time, are worth all the money and labour that have been expended to produce them.

His journal abounds in passages of almost mystical exaltation and devotion. Shortly before setting out on his great journey he wrote:

I will place no value on anything I have or may possess, except in relation to the kingdom of Christ. If anything will advance the interests of that kingdom, it shall be given away or kept, only as by giving or keeping of it I shall most promote the glory of Him to whom I owe all my hopes in time and eternity.

What moved him more than anything else was the slave trade. What he had seen of it, and of the desolation that it wrought, had burned into his mind the conviction that the righting of this wrong was the greatest duty laid on Europe and on the Churches. Just before leaving Linyanti on his long journey, he wrote to the directors of the LMS: 'Can the love of Christ not carry the missionary where the slave trade carries the trader?' And when, full of honours, he stood before the University of Cambridge on 4 December 1857, this thought was uppermost in his mind. His lecture was full of varied turns of thought; almost immediately after remarking

> You can hardly tell how pleasant it is to see the blooming cheeks of young ladies before me, after an absence of sixteen years from such delightful objects of contemplation,

he proceeded to his conclusion, in a shout which electrified his audience:

> I beg to direct your attention to Africa. I know that in a few years I shall be cut off in that country, which is now open. Do not let it be shut again! I go back to Africa to try to make an open path for commerce and Christianity. *Do you carry out the work which I have begun. I leave it with you.*

'Commerce and Christianity.' Was Livingstone, then, in reality simply a colonialist, a forerunner of those colonialist exploiters who made life in so many parts of Africa a horror and a nightmare? His words have been understood in that sense by some critics, but not by anyone who has taken the trouble to read what he said and to consider what he meant. The guilt of the white men on the west coast, and still more perhaps of the Arab on the east coast, in carrying on the slave trade, has been beyond all reckoning. But Livingstone had realized that the slave trade could not have been carried on at all apart from the African's own participation in it. When slave-raiding was the easiest, indeed the only, way of making oneself rich, the temptation was ever present to engage in those raids on weaker neighbours which made life perilous for the weak and defenceless over so much of the continent. Only if the Africans could be persuaded to engage in legitimate commerce, exchanging the products of their own fields and forests for those desirable things which the white man could supply, would the evil and destructive commerce be brought to an end.

His view may have been a simplification; the coming of Western commerce has not proved an unqualified blessing to the African, for not all those who have engaged in it have been inspired by the noble and altruistic motives of a Livingstone.

Livingstone and Moffat showed the way. They have had innumerable followers. Missions of all denominations – Anglicans, Methodists, Presbyterians, Lutherans of several branches, Plymouth Brethren, and others – have come in and have brought with them schools and model farms and seminaries, and all the appurtenances of modern missionary work. They have differed in their tenets and in their practices; almost all have been agreed in supporting the claim of the black man for freedom in his own country and the right to develop according to his own natural gifts, and in holding that only through the Gospel can the natural gifts of the African be developed to the point at which he can be genuinely a free man in his own country.

The fourth Christian thrust, that from the east, was slow in developing any major power.

As we saw, the Anglican missionaries were driven out of Ethiopia in 1838. One of them, Johann Ludwig Krapf (1810–56), took refuge in Aden, from there made his way to Zanzibar, and in 1844 was successful in establishing a station at Mombasa, the sea-port of Kenya. Two months later he was bereaved by the death of his wife and only child. In famous words, he wrote to the Church Missionary Society:

Tell our friends that in a lonely grave on the African coast there rests a member of the Mission. This is a sign that they have begun the struggle with this part of the world; and since the victories of the Church lead over the graves of many of her members, they may be the more convinced that the hour is approaching when you will be called to convert Africa, beginning from the East Coast.

In 1846 Krapf was joined by Johannes Rebmann, who held the fort, often almost alone, until 1874. The two made a number of remarkable journeys inland, in the course of which they discovered Mount Kenya and Mount Kilimanjaro, the highest peaks in Africa. An unbelieving world was not prepared to accept the fact of never-melting snow on the Equator, and high scientific authorities affirmed that the missionaries must have been deceived by the sun shining on limestone formations at a distance. The missionaries, being continentals, were unmoved, reckoning that they knew snow when they saw it.

Very little was achieved in these early years. Distance, the authority of the Sultan of Zanzibar, and the constant hostility of the Arabs, who did not wish their slaving operations in the interior to be exposed to the light of day, made it impossible for the missionaries to have more than transitory contacts with the fine and vigorous peoples of the plateau and the lake area. They were confined to the mixed population of the coast, which had been broken and demoralized by the Arabs and was not a promising soil for the Gospel. Their work was limited to the learning of Swahili and the translation of the New Testament into it, the care of the occasional convert – and waiting for a better day.

Madagascar is not infrequently treated as though it was a part of Africa. But in fact it is not, and is a world to itself. Its people are akin to the Malays, and the language which is spoken throughout the island, Malagasy, is not related to any African language. In the nineteenth century one of the tribes, the Hòvas, whose home was in the central plateau, had succeeded in bringing most of the island under their sway and imposing upon it a political as well as a linguistic unity.

We have noted the earlier and unsuccessful attempts to introduce Christianity into Madagascar. The work was taken up again by the LMS in 1818. In 1820 the pioneer David Jones, who had been left alone by the death of his colleagues and of his own wife and child, reached Antananarivo, the capital, and made contact with the king, Radama. Radama was not interested in Christianity, but, like so many other African princes, he saw in the missionaries the means of acquiring some of those good things of European life which have nothing to do with religion. He was prepared to favour the mission, and urged the LMS to send missionaries who were artisans in order to make the Malagasy people good workmen as well as good Christians.

Under this royal patronage things went well, and the first group of twenty-eight converts was baptized in 1831. But in 1835 Queen Ranavalona, the successor of Radama, took a completely different line, and ordered a violent persecution of the Christians. Her soldiers were told that they 'should seize every Christian they could find, and without trial bind them hand and foot, dig a pit on the spot, and then pour boiling water on them and bury them'. It is likely that hagiography has exaggerated the number of victims; persecution was spasmodic and fluctuating in its violence. Nevertheless it is probable that not less than 200 victims were actually put to death. In 1849 eighteen Christians were killed – fourteen hurled over a cliff, four burned alive; of these last an eyewitness recorded that

they prayed as long as they had life. Then they died, but softly, gently. Indeed, gentle was the going forth of their life, and astonished were all the people around them that beheld the burning of them.

Hundreds were sentenced to fines and floggings, and the loss of their official rank. The persecution did not finally die away till the death of the queen in 1861. When the new day came, out of the recesses of the forests there came men and women who had been wanderers and outcasts for years. They reappeared as if risen from the dead. Some bore the deep scars of chains and fetters; some, worn almost to skeletons by prolonged sufferings from hunger or fever, could scarcely drag themselves along the roads that led to the capital. Their brethren from the city went out to meet them, and to help them, and . . . as they saw their old loved city again, they sang the pilgrim song; 'When the Lord turned again the captivity of Zion we were like them that dream.'[37]

When a reckoning was made, it was found that the Christians were four times as many as they had been at the beginning of the persecution. How did it come about that so young a Church was able to maintain itself, without outside help, through a quarter of a century of persecution? The major factor was undoubtedly the possession of the New Testament in Malagasy. On this the Christians secretly fed their souls; this they passed on to others, in hand-written copies if the printed books were no longer available. There could hardly be more striking confirmation of the view held by almost all Protestant missionaries that the first duty of the missionary, after he has once learned the language, is to provide the people with the Word of God, 'without note or comment', in their own languages.[38]

This chapter must end with the description of one missionary venture on the western shores of the Atlantic, which, though in itself it ended in disaster, is memorable as an example of Christian endurance, and proved to be the inspiration for extensive and enduring achievement.

Much good work continued throughout the nineteenth century to be done in North America and the West Indies among the Indians and the Negro inhabitants of those regions. With the collapse of the Spanish and Portuguese empires in Latin America, that great area of the world was no longer, as it had been, the closed preserve of the Roman Catholic Church. Some Churches, such as the Anglican and Lutheran, set to work to follow their own people

37. *The Story of the L.M.S.*, pp. 353 f.

38. A footnote must summarize the later history of Christian Madagascar. After the peace, Madagascar became the great mission field of the Norwegians and of American Lutherans of Norwegian origin. In the north, Anglicans (first CMS, later SPG), the Paris Mission, and the Friends entered. The Roman Catholics built up anew what remained of their old missions. At the time of writing probably 40 per cent of the population of Madagascar is in some measure Christian.

and to provide spiritual ministrations for them in the great cities of South and Central America. Others considered the possibility of evangelistic work among nominal Roman Catholics – of this we shall have more to say in the next chapter. Yet others felt a vocation to preach to those remote and often very primitive peoples which in four centuries the Roman Catholic Church had never succeeded in reaching.

Allen Gardiner (1794–1850) felt called to Tierra del Fuego, and to the lonely Patagonians of that cold and desolate region, then reckoned by many as among the lowest and most degraded of the human species.

Gardiner had been from his boyhood an officer in the British Navy, and had reached the rank of Commander. Converted during one of his voyages, he was filled with love for men and a passionate desire for their salvation. At the age of forty he left the navy in order to devote himself wholly to religious work. His first attempt was in Natal, where he arrived in 1835. With wide vision he saw the possibility of a chain of mission stations stretching up the whole east coast of Africa as far as Zanzibar and beyond. But he was stronger in imagination than in execution. After a brief flirtation with the idea of a mission to New Guinea, his thoughts settled on South America. Attempts to undertake work in Paraguay and in Bolivia came to nothing through the opposition of the priests. And so Gardiner came to fix on Tierra del Fuego.

With six companions he started work in 1850. The ship with provisions failed to arrive, and during the winter on that inhospitable shore the whole party slowly died of starvation. But Gardiner wrote in his diary:

> Poor and weak as we are, our boat is a very Bethel to our souls, for we feel and know that God is here. Asleep or awake, I am, beyond the power of expression, happy.

When the bodies were later found, these words echoed around the world; the modern reader may well think of another naval officer, and of the noble words written in their diaries by Robert Falcon Scott and Edward Wilson as sixty years later they died in the Antarctic darkness.

The fruit of the sacrifice of Allen Gardiner and his friends was seen only long after, when in 1872 the first group of Tierra del Fuegans was baptized. And the best comment on the venture was, once again, that of Charles Darwin, who wrote to the South American Missionary Society:

The success of the Tierra del Fuego Mission is most wonderful, and charms me, as I always prophesied utter failure. It is a grand success. I shall feel proud if your committee think fit to elect me an honorary member of your society.

For reasons that will be made clear in the next chapter, the year 1858 may be taken as a watershed in the history of non-Roman missionary work. In sixty years, Protestant missions had entered a large number of countries, and most of the Churches of the Protestant world had become engaged in the enterprise. But we are still in the day of small things. The number of converts continued to be small. The loss in missionary personnel continued to be very high. Limited successes were matched by extensive failures. This chapter has, in fact, painted rather too rosy a picture, since from considerations of space enterprises which came to nothing have for the most part had to be passed over in silence. But the missionary force was there. Back-breaking work had given it its tools in language and Scripture. The sense of responsibility was growing in the nominally Christian lands. When new doors opened, as they opened on every hand in the following sixty years, the Churches showed that they were ready to take up the fresh responsibilities which the new day had brought with it.

10

The Heyday of Colonialism, 1858–1914

In 1858 Queen Victoria was thirty-nine years old. Gladstone was forty-nine; Lord Macaulay fifty-eight; Abraham Lincoln forty-five; Charles Darwin forty-nine; Charles Dickens forty-five. Pius IX was sixty-six; Cardinal Pecci, later Pope Leo XIII, was forty-eight; John Henry Newman fifty-seven; Samuel Wilberforce fifty-three; Ferdinand Christian Baur sixty-six; Dwight Lyman Moody twenty-one.

This list, to which many other names could be added, gives some indication of the extraordinary constellation of genius, talent, and power which existed in the middle of the nineteenth century, and may serve also as an indication of the confidence by which the Western world was animated, both in Church and State, at the opening of the period of its greatest influence. The foolish and unnecessary Crimean war had been brought to a satisfactory conclusion; the Indian Mutiny had been suppressed, with terrible deeds on both sides. Peace reigned almost unbroken for more than half a century. The whole world was open to Western commerce and exploitation, and at point after point Western man had demonstrated his military superiority to any enemy that had entered the field against him.[1] The day of Europe had come.

It is true that not everything could be entered on the credit side. The American Civil War was just over the horizon. Many social and industrial problems remained unsolved. The advances of Garibaldi and Victor Emmanuel were threatening to bring to an end a system with a history of a thousand years, through the abolition of that sovereignty of the Pope over the papal states which many Roman Catholics believed to be indispensable if the Pope was to maintain a rightful position in the world as well as in the Church. The publication in 1859 of Darwin's *Origin of Species*, and in 1860 of those *Essays and Reviews* in which critical views of the Bible were introduced to a public that was wholly unprepared for them, launched the Church on that period of controversy as to the truth of the Christian faith of which the end is not yet in sight. But

1. There were to be three notable exceptions to this rule in the second half of the century.

on the whole confidence was not gravely shaken. Those who live well over a century later, in a time of anxious questioning about everything, find it hard to enter into this mood of hopeful confidence, and are inclined rather resentfully to doubt whether there was ever any foundation for it.

The missionary enterprise of the Churches is always in a measure a reflection of their vigour, of their wealth, and of that power of conviction which finds its expression in self-sacrifice and a willingness for adventurous service. Precisely at the opening of the period of which we are speaking (1858–63), five events took place which may be taken as indicating in summary form the character of the period in the missionary history of the Protestant Churches that was to follow.

1. The first was the acceptance by the British people, through its government, of responsibility for rule and administration in India, and the end of the life of the East India Company as a quasi-sovereign power. The spirit of the new administration was set forth in the proclamation in which Queen Victoria accepted the new responsibility:

Firmly relying ourselves on the truth of Christianity, and acknowledging with gratitude the solace of religion, We disclaim alike the right and the desire to impose Our convictions on any of Our subjects. We declare it to be Our royal will and pleasure that none be in anywise favoured, none molested or disquieted by reason of their religious faith or observances, but that all shall alike enjoy the equal and impartial protection of the law . . . And it is Our further will that, so far as may be, Our subjects, of whatever race or creed, be freely and impartially admitted to offices in Our service, the duties of which they may be qualified by their education, ability and integrity, duly to discharge.[2]

This proclamation was intended to restore the confidence of Hindus and Muslims, but it was also a charter of liberty for Christians – they were henceforth to be free from the hostile prejudices and discrimination of which they had been the objects under the Company's régime.

2. The second war of the European powers with China had ended in 1858 with a series of treaties between China and the several European nations. There were some differences between the treaties, and certain doubts in the interpretation of them. But basically they were all the same: in addition to according permis-

2. The words in italics were added by the Queen herself to the original draft of the proclamation.

sion to foreigners to travel in the interior beyond the Treaty Ports (now increased to sixteen), they guaranteed toleration of Christianity and protection in the practice of their faith not only for missionaries but (either in so many words or by implication) for Chinese Christians also. Clearly the door had been opened wide for the peaceful penetration of China by the Christian forces, but those peaceful forces were entering with a hedge of all too warlike bayonets behind them.

3. The Second Evangelical Awakening, starting among laymen in America with an intense desire for individual and corporate prayer, crossed the Atlantic, and awoke revival in many areas, notably in northern Ireland. The new spiritual life into which many Christians entered found expression in a sense of responsibility for personal witness to Christ and for missionary service. A number of missionary societies were formed at this time, some of them reverting to that non-denominational pattern which had been the original ideal of the L M S; many of the older societies received new support, and an influx of recruits from among those who had been influenced by the revival.

4. In 1858 the first missionary of modern times, a Roman Catholic priest, entered Japan. In July 1853 an American squadron under Commodore Matthew C. Perry had anchored off Uraga in Tokyo Bay. A firm demand was made for relationships between the two countries, and in the following year the first simple agreement was drawn up; it provided for no more than humane treatment for shipwrecked sailors, fuelling rights for foreign ships, and the residence of an American agent in Japan. The first Resident (later minister) was Townsend Harris, a convinced and high-minded Episcopalian, who regularly held Christian services in his residence at Yedo. The barrier which had kept Japan aloof for more than two centuries was at last broken through; the Christian Churches were called to a new missionary task.

5. In 1857 David Livingstone published his *Missionary Travels and Researches in South Africa*. The enthusiasm generated by this precise, scientific, and at the same time warm and human narrative was very great. The Christian world was convinced that the time had come to resume the assault on Africa, and to press forward to the penetration of the very heart of the continent. One immediate fruit of Livingstone's appeal was the formation of the Universities' Mission to Central Africa; this brought into the work that Anglo-Catholic wing of the Anglican Church which

up to this point had had little to do with the work of missionary proclamation.

It would be possible to fill the whole of the rest of this chapter with a list of the missionary societies, groups, and organizations which came into being between 1859 and 1914. The effort put forth was so immense and varied that writer and reader alike are in danger of being submerged beneath a crushing weight of details. This can be avoided only by a severely selective method, in which the attempt is made to fasten on those things which were new, creative, and of permanent significance, and to give some impression of those beginnings and developments which prepared the way for the world Christian situation in which we find ourselves today. And, though the geographical method is a little mechanical, it proves itself to be in fact the best system for the organization of the abundant material that has to be considered.

We begin our survey with *Japan*. The renewal of contact between Japan and the West and the entry of the Christian mission were contemporaneous with, and in part the cause of, a revolution in the life of the country. Since the beginning of the seventeenth century Japan had been under the control of the Tokugawa Shogûns, the 'mayors of the palace', under whose protection the emperor maintained a somewhat shadowy existence. In 1867 a young man named Mutsuhito succeeded to the throne and as emperor took the name Meiji. He reigned till 1912. In the same year, 1867, the last of the Shogûns, Keiki, resigned. The Meiji era had begun; Japan was ready to face the new world. Devotion to the emperor as the visible god developed to the point of becoming a quasi-mystical religion – perhaps the most effective religion in what has been described as the land of the happy atheists – and with this went an intense and almost equally mystical patriotism and a sense of the destiny of Japan as the most highly favoured nation in the world.

The prospects for a Christian mission in Japan were far from favourable. Christianity was still a prohibited religion, punishable by death.[3] The early treaties had said nothing about the residence of missionaries in Japan; all that had been guaranteed in the treaty of 1858 was liberty for Americans to practise their religion on Japanese soil, and the right to erect suitable buildings for worship. If missionaries came in, they would be wholly dependent on the

3. The public notices affirming this were quietly removed in 1873.

capacity of an oriental government to look the other way; if they made converts, these would be liable to the severest penalties at any moment when the government thought fit to resume the policy of persecution. The penal laws were not, in fact, rescinded until the promulgation of the new Constitution in 1889. Article xxvIII of the Constitution reads: 'Japanese subjects, within the limits not prejudicial to peace and order, and not antagonistic to their duties as subjects, shall enjoy freedom of religious belief.' This somewhat ambiguously worded statement left room for considerable latitude of interpretation, but both missionaries and Japanese Christians hailed it as a charter of liberty.

In spite of the unpromising situation, four American missionary societies entered Japan between 1859 and 1869 – the Episcopalians, the Presbyterians, the Reformed, and the Free Baptists. Progress was slow. Most of the work of these early years consisted in learning the language, making a beginning with translations of the Bible, starting small and rather inconspicuous schools, and winning the confidence of a proud and suspicious people. Channing Williams, the first missionary of the Episcopal Church, and later a bishop, was able to baptize his first convert in 1866. James C. Ballagh of the Reformed Church, whose 'pre-eminence was in the field of Christian character, piety, prayer life, and most humble assiduity in service to anyone in need',[4] was able, on 10 March 1872, to baptize a group of nine young men. He immediately formed them into a Church, with two older Christians to guide them, and gave to this first organized Church the name *Kirisuto Ko Kwai*, the Church of Christ, a term often to be heard again in Christian history in Japan.

These were small beginnings. And, in point of fact, there has never been in Japan anything like a mass movement towards Christianity such as has promoted the rapid growth of the Church in other countries. The rugged individualism of the Japanese character seems to preclude the possibility. But in the history of the Church in Japan it is always the improbable which happens, and the most notable events of the earlier years are associated with the sudden and spontaneous development of group movements.

In 1871 a school was founded in Kumamoto, in western Japan, and put into the hands of Captain L. L. Janes, a graduate of West Point Military Academy in the United States. He ran his school on quasi-military lines, with strict discipline and long hours of work.

4. C. W. Iglehart, *A Century of Protestant Christianity in Japan* (1959), p. 35.

He did not directly teach Christianity, but such was his Christian influence that in 1876 thirty-five of his students climbed the hill of Hamaoka, and there took an oath of fealty to Jesus Christ. Christ was to be their Lord, with a view to the emancipation of their nation – an interesting blend of Christian faith and national feeling such as was to be characteristic of much Japanese Christianity in the years that were to come.

In 1876 the government, having decided to start an agricultural school at Sapporo in Hokkaido, the northern island of Japan, called in Dr W. S. Clark of the Massachusetts Agricultural College to head it for a year. Clark made no secret of his Christian profession and exercised such an influence that before the year was out the whole of the first class of fifteen students was applying for baptism. Even after Clark's departure, the Christian enthusiasm of these young men was such that they were able to lead to Christ all their successors in the second class.

Eight years later, a storm of revival struck Doshisha School in Kyoto. The spiritual excitement reached such a level that academic work had to be temporarily suspended. No less than 200 students were baptized; after this the excitement became less, and normal working could be resumed. This is an unexpected phenomenon. In Japan emotion tends to be rigidly hidden away under the calm, smooth surface of convention. Religion is a highly intellectual matter, relying on methods of persuasion rather than of emotion. Is it possible that, under the calm surface, fires are raging, and that at times the satisfaction of emotional needs through religion is to be welcomed rather than suppressed? On the whole, however, Japanese Christianity has remained intellectual and individual, and its history is largely that of the outstanding individuals who have influenced its course.

Undoubtedly the most notable figure in the early days was Shimeta Niishima, well known in the West as Joseph Hardy Neesima. As a young man, Neesima was deeply stirred by reading in a Christian textbook of God as the Creator of the universe. He decided to go to the West and make the acquaintance of the Christian religion in a Christian land. Although it was at that time illegal for any Japanese to leave the country, he managed in 1864 to make his escape from the northern port of Hakodate. In America he studied at Amherst College and Andover Theological Seminary, was baptized and ordained, and was accepted by the American Board as a missionary. On his return to Japan in 1874, his first aim was the foundation of a Christian college for higher education, in which the Gospel should be linked to all that was good in the ancient traditions. Through the help of influential friends he was able to secure land in Kyoto, not far from the palace, and Doshisha School (later Doshisha University) came into being. Without the support of American money and western colleagues Neesima would hardly have been able to carry on his work. But from the start this was an unmistakably Japanese school. Neesima was at the centre of everything, and brought into all the work something of the spirit of the *samurai*, the heroic class of Japan, without at any time infringing the central principle of loyalty to Christ. Neesima died in 1890, but others were there and ready to take up the work as he laid it down.

Kanzo Uchimura (1861–1931) had been one of the Sapporo Band; and, after the withdrawal of Dr Clark, became its leader. The group formed itself into a Church, having no connection with any denomination, with no guide except the Bible, and no regular pastor, though Uchimura was to all intents and purposes the pastor of the group. This was a good preparation for the work for which much later Uchimura became specially well known – the formation of the *Mukyōkai*, the 'non-Church' movement. Uchimura's formula was that 'the truly Christian temple has God's earth for a floor, and his sky for the ceiling; its altar is in the heart of the believer; its law is God's Word, and his Holy Spirit is its only pastor'. Uchimura was at pains to make clear that the term 'non-Church' is to be understood positively. The Japanese term *Mukyōkai* could be understood as meaning 'the movement that annihilates the Church'; this was far from being his intention.

Uchimura was a great Bible teacher; in later years he could draw a crowd of a thousand people to his Bible lectures in Tokyo. But such was his hostility to the idea of an organized Church that, if a group showed signs of forming itself into a Church under his leadership, he would dissolve the group and start all over again.

Mukyōkai may seem to be destructive, but it is really constructive. It seems to be awesome, but is really meek. It seems to wear the skin of a bear, but really has the heart of a lamb . . . We may seem to wear the mark of [the demon] *Hanuja*, but our main interest is to threaten those who pay attention only to exterior things in order to help them to see the interior things.[5]

The 1880s were a time of rapid growth for the Church in Japan. In 1882 there were 145 missionaries, and just under 5,000 Japanese

5. Quoted in C. Michalson, *Japanese Contributions to Christian Theology* (1960), p. 19.

Christians in association with the various Protestant Churches in Japan. By 1888, the number had grown to 451 missionaries, with 25,514 members. Among a people so filled with independent spirit and national pride, it was inevitable that the question of the organization of the Churches on a truly Japanese basis should early come to the fore.

One of those Japanese leaders who held most strongly the view that the foreigner must withdraw from leadership and that the Church must become genuinely Japanese was Masakisa Uemura. Uemura had been an early member of the Yokohama Band, and had been ordained in 1879 in the Presbyterian Church. He was convinced that the evangelization of Japan must develop from within, through the work and witness of Japanese themselves, and that it could not be greatly promoted by help received from abroad and in the main administered by foreigners. It was largely owing to the influence of such men that the first United Church of Christ in Japan, the *Nippon Kirisuto Itchi Kyokwai*, which brought into one the work of three Presbyterian missions, was formed in 1877. But Uemura was ill satisfied with the measure of independence that he enjoyed, even within this Church; in 1904 he withdrew, and founded the first independent theological seminary in Japan, the Tokyo Shingakusha.

The problems facing the Episcopal Churches were rather different from those affecting other missions. Missionaries had come in from America, Britain, and Canada, without planning and without mutual consultation. There was a good deal of overlapping and confusion; each of the three Churches was Anglican in origin, but each had developed certain traditions and characteristics of its own. Chaos was reduced to order largely through the work of Edward Bickersteth (1850–97), who had been a missionary in India, and in 1886 came to Japan as a bishop of the Church of England. In 1887, under the inspiration of Bickersteth, the three streams united in the *Nippon Sei Ko Kwai*, the Holy Catholic Church of Japan, which, while remaining firmly in the Anglican fellowship of Churches, claimed and claims to be an independent Japanese Church with full authority to organize its own life and to manage its own affairs. It is surprising that this Church hesitated so long over the consecration of Japanese bishops; it was not until 1922 that for the first time two Japanese priests were raised to the episcopate.

Christians have always been few in Japan, but their influence has been altogether out of proportion to their numbers. One notable sign of this was the 'Three Religions Conference' held on 25 February 1912. The three religions involved were not Shinto, Buddhism, and Confucianism, but Shinto, Buddhism, and Christianity. The vice-minister, who a few days before had announced the decision of the government to recognize Christianity as one of the religions of Japan, added that he hoped that Christianity would now 'step out of the narrow circles within which it is confined, and endeavour to conform to the national polity, and adapt itself to the national sentiments and customs, in order to ensure greater achievements'.

The resolution of the conference began with the following statement:

We acknowledge that the will of the government authorities, which led us to hold the conference of the representatives of *the three religions*, is to respect the authority of religion, which each possesses, to promote national morality, and to improve public discipline, without spoiling our original creeds, nor interfering with one another, and to maintain the honour of the Imperial Household and to contribute to the progress of the times.[6]

This public recognition filled a number of Christians with enthusiasm. But many of the wisest Japanese Christian leaders would have nothing to do with the 'Three Religions Movement'. What is the function of religion? Is it to be non-interfering, and to support a government in its ideas of progress? Every Japanese Christian was determined to be a patriot, and was convinced that national honour and stability could only be promoted by the spread of the Christian faith. But signs were not lacking that Japanese nationalism might take a form in which it would prove to be incompatible with Christian loyalty.

The burning issue was the nature of the Shinto shrines, and of acts of reverence performed at them. In 1911 the government issued an ordinance requiring of all schools attendance at the shrines and participation in the ceremonies. It was carefully explained that these ceremonies involved only 'veneration of ancestors', and therefore did not infringe the liberty of conscience guaranteed to all. Some Christian leaders, notably Dr S. Motoda, later one of the first Anglican bishops in Japan, felt that this was an acceptable interpretation; but the vast majority did not agree with him. And so the small and struggling Church in Japan was

---

6. The representation at the conference was thirteen Shintoists, fifty Buddhists, and seven Christians.

introduced to a problem of conscience which was to perplex it for the next forty-four years. It would be premature to say that even now a satisfactory solution has been found.

In *China*, the new-found liberty granted by the treaties encouraged rapid increase in Protestant work. Many new societies entered in, and the new freedom of movement made possible many things that could not be attempted under the old restrictions. Yet movement was carried out only within a very restricted area. In 1865, no Protestant missionary was to be seen in eleven of the eighteen provinces of China, and in the seven 'occupied' provinces the area of missionary penetration had not reached far from the coast, except for a number of stations in the Yangtze valley. A revolutionary change in the situation was brought about, as is so often the case, by the faith and conviction of one man.

James Hudson Taylor had come to China in 1854, at the age of twenty-one, under the Chinese Evangelization Society, a curiously incompetent body which almost wholly failed to meet its obligations, and after an inglorious career went into dissolution. In seven years Taylor learned Chinese, made long journeys in the company of William Burns, married, was led to resign from the Chinese Evangelization Society and to depend on God alone for everything, and, perhaps most important of all, to adopt Chinese dress as the most obvious method of self-identification with the Chinese people. These unconventional proceedings brought upon him the fierce and almost fanatical opposition of men and women who no less than Taylor were devoted servants of the cause.[7] In 1860 Taylor returned to England in ill-health, and there was no particular reason to suppose that he would ever see China again.

In England, however, Taylor did not cease to be interested in China, and to be burdened with a sense of the needs of the still unoccupied provinces. In 1865, unknown and without the support of any denomination, he was led to undertake single-handed the foundation of what for a time was the largest mission in the world, the China Inland Mission. At an early stage, he was led to lay down the principles of the mission, which were in many ways to differ from those currently in vogue in the other missions and Churches of the Protestant world:

7. J. C. Pollock in his *Hudson Taylor and Maria* (1962) brought out evidence of this hostility that had been carefully softened down in the official biography by Dr and Mrs Howard Taylor – a very great book, but, as we now see, in need of revision at a number of points.

1. The mission was to be interdenominational. Conservative in its theology, it would accept as missionaries any convinced Christians, of whatever denomination, if they could sign its simple doctrinal declaration.

2. A door was opened for those of little formal education. This was of great importance; missions were tending to become professional, and to have less place for pioneers of the type of Robert Moffat. It was good that one society was prepared to keep this door open; and cases were not lacking in which those who started with very little education grew to be notable scholars and sinologists.

3. The direction of the mission would be in China, not in England – a change of far-reaching significance. And the director would have full authority to direct. Like his contemporary William Booth, this young man calmly assumed to himself an almost papal authority. This sprang not from personal arrogance, but from the conviction that in such an enterprise rapid decision and flexible administration were necessary, and that no one else could supply them.

4. Missionaries would wear Chinese dress, and as far as possible identify themselves with the Chinese people.

5. The primary aim of the mission was always to be widespread evangelism. The shepherding of Churches and education could be undertaken, but not to such an extent as to hide or hinder the one central and commanding purpose.

Taylor had no lack of difficulties to contend with – failure in understanding both in China and at home, unfaithfulness on the part of some of his colleagues, misrepresentation as a result of difficulties with the Chinese authorities, ill-health, the death of his devoted wife in 1870. But almost from the start his success was sensational. Recruits crowded to his doors. Some had to be rejected, some were failures, but the majority held to their posts, and some proved to be outstandingly successful pioneer missionaries. By 1882, all the provinces had been visited, and missionaries were resident in all but three of them. Thirty years after its foundation, the mission had 641 missionaries drawn from many lands. Work had been begun among the aboriginal peoples in the far west of China. Missionaries were established in Sinkiang (Chinese Turkestan) and on the borders of Tibet.

Most of the early missionaries of the C I M had been drawn, like Taylor himself, from comparatively humble stations in life. Widespread interest was aroused when it was announced that seven Cambridge men of social, intellectual, or athletic distinction were about to give up everything and to go to China to join Hudson Taylor. One of the seven, D. E. Hoste, was to become the second director of the CIM. Another, W. W. Cassels (1858–1925), was in 1895 consecrated as the first Anglican bishop in western China. In nothing was Taylor's wisdom more remarkably seen than in his capacity to hold together his motley crew and to use their various gifts to the best advantage. Himself convinced that believers' baptism was the only true way of obedience to the Lord's command, he realized that Anglicans could not very well be put to work side by side with Baptists. A home was found for the Anglicans in Szechuan, where they could live in spiritual fellowship with their brethren of other persuasions and at the same time be free to maintain the traditions of their own Church.

Most of the converts of the CIM like the missionaries were of humble origin, but there were exceptions. One of the most notable of these was the Confucian scholar Pastor Hsi, who was brought to Christ in 1879 through the witness of David Hill, a Methodist and one of the most deeply loved of all the Protestant missionaries in China. Hsi had been an opium addict; having cured himself of the habit through his Christian faith, he did notable work in setting up refuges in which other victims could be cured through faith and prayer, as well as through the use of the appropriate medicines. Hsi worked in connection with the CIM but with almost unlimited personal independence.

The great service rendered by the CIM was that it demonstrated the possibility of residence in every corner of China. During the last third of the century, missionary societies of every conceivable kind, and other organizations such as the YMCA, extended themselves through the length and breadth of the land, and, though missionaries were never very many in relation to the total population, the occupation of China in outline was completed. Many missionaries did not agree with Hudson Taylor's methods, regarding his work as dangerously superficial; none, perhaps, remained completely untouched by the challenge of the mobility, the simplicity, and the devotion of the missionaries of the CIM.

A sharp distinction is to be noted between the policy of the CIM – which may be described as diffusion, the preaching of the Gospel to any who would listen – and the alternative policy of concentration. There were those who felt that in a country where the scholar is held in such veneration the appeal must be made in the first place to the scholar class, since converts from this class would be far more effective as missionaries to their own people than foreigners could ever be.

One of the outstanding champions of this point of view was Timothy Richard, a Welshman, a Baptist, and a product of the Second Evangelical Awakening. Richard arrived in China in 1870 and served for almost fifty years. He early developed a high regard for the best elements in Chinese civilization, and it became his aim not so much to convert individuals as so to penetrate the thought and mind of the rising intellectual class with Christian ideals, that in time the whole life of the country would undergo a thorough Christian transformation. A percipient colleague said of him: 'His seeming ambition amounts to this, that he wishes to serve all, but is conscious that he can only do so by serving the few – i.e. those in the highest places of authority and dignity.'[8]

Richard's chosen field of activity was with the Society for the Diffusion of Christian and General Knowledge among the Chinese. The inclusion of the word 'General' was highly character-istic. The aim of Richard was to diffuse every kind of useful information, in the belief that all knowledge is of God and can contribute to the work of salvation. Two periodicals, the *Wan Kwoh Kung Pao* ('Review of the Times'), general in character, and the *Tsung Hsi Kiao Hui Pao* ('Christian Review'), specifically for Chris-tians, were widely circulated and subjected to extensive borrowing by the rapidly developing independent press.

It followed naturally that Richard was also a warm supporter of the educational progress which was one of the outstanding features of the period between 1875 and 1914. From the beginning all missions had maintained elementary schools; the constant press-ure from the Chinese, who, as China became increasingly open to the West, wished to learn English and to put themselves abreast of modern knowledge, almost compelled a steady raising of stan-dards. A number of institutions called colleges had been founded; but the majority of these gave no instruction beyond the level of what would ordinarily be called a grammar school in Britain. It was the Americans, accustomed as they were to the very fluid system of universities and colleges that prevails in their country, who first became convinced that China must be provided with Christian institutions on a genuinely university level, to meet the

8. W. G. Walshe, Secretary of the Christian Literature Society, quoted in K. S. Latourette, *A History of Christian Missions in China*, p. 379, n. 1.

growing demand for higher education. The idea was at first far from welcome to mission boards and to the more conservative type of missionaries, and a good deal of resistance had to be overcome. But by the end of the century the Christian university was an essential part of the Christian scene in China. One of the earliest to be opened was the Episcopal foundation, St John's College in Shanghai. This was followed up by the Methodists in Nanking (1899), by the American Presbyterians in Canton (1893), and by the American Board at T'ung Chow, east of Peking. The university of Peking was incorporated, with an interdenominational board of managers, in 1890. At first numbers were everywhere small, and achievement moderate, but by 1896 it was reported that in Peking there were 125 students, and that the standards were those of colleges in the West.

At one point, the training of Chinese for the ministry, the work of all the missions seems to have stood still. As we have seen, the first Chinese minister had been ordained in the time of Morrison, and many Chinese had later been brought into the ministry. But for the most part their training had been elementary, and very few, if any, could stand on the same level of competence as their missionary friends. In 1876 it was reported that there were twenty theological schools, with 231 students: schools with an average of eleven students, and probably not more than two hard-worked missionary teachers with a less than comprehensive knowledge of Chinese, were not likely to attain to a high level of scholarship. St John's College, Shanghai, had a theological department, in which in 1880 there were thirteen students. In 1896 theological teaching in English was begun – in this the Episcopal Church seems to have been the pioneer. One or two Chinese had been sent overseas for study, but this was a method which on the whole was looked on with disfavour by the missionaries.

Numerically, the results of Protestant missions by the end of the nineteenth century were less than impressive. A body of about 1,500 missionaries, including wives, was established in 500 stations, almost all the provinces now having their quota. Around them they had gathered slightly less than half a million adherents, of whom rather more than 80,000 were communicants. But the missionaries were widely regarded – and feared – as the spearhead of Western penetration. And their activities, together with the rather more formidable approach of the Roman Catholics, were quite sufficient to arouse the anxieties of the more conservative sections of the population. Sooner or later there was bound to be an explosion.

The years 1895 to 1900 were marked by growing uncertainty and dismay. The foreign nations, among them Germany and Japan, were increasing their pressure on China, and a certain amount of Chinese territory had actually been occupied. There was a reforming and westernizing movement among the Chinese themselves countered by violent anti-foreign feeling. There were many grounds for the feelings of fear and dislike, and, as the missionaries were the largest and most widely dispersed body in China, it was naturally against them that the fiercest assaults, in thought and in action, were directed. The missionaries were not altogether free from blame. Some had been less than discreet in making use of the privileges assured to them under the treaties; some had shown an insensitive disregard of Chinese feelings with regard to propriety and order. Missionaries had been often in danger, but for more than half a century there had been an almost miraculous preservation of life. Now the protecting hand seemed to be withdrawn; from 1896 onwards a number of missionaries, mostly Roman Catholic, lost their lives in local tumults and disturbances.

Matters would probably not have become serious, had not the dowager empress, the 'Old Buddha', put herself at the head of the reactionary forces, and given open support to that violent movement the *I Ho Ch'üan*, the 'Righteous Harmony Fists', which very soon came to be called by Europeans the Boxer Movement. Everywhere the words *mieh yang*, 'destroy the foreigner', were to be heard. On 24 June 1900 an imperial decree ordering the killing of all foreigners was issued from Peking. In some areas the local authorities attempted to protect the alien. But in Peking itself the foreign legations were besieged for fifty-five days, and in many parts of the country chaos reigned supreme.

The exact number of Chinese Christians and missionaries, and of their dependants, who lost their lives in those months of carnage will never be exactly known. It is clear that the Roman Catholics lost far more heavily in Chinese Christians, and the Protestants far more heavily in foreigners. The most reliable figures suggest that 135 adults and fifty-three children among the Protestant foreigners died, a total of 188. No such loss had ever before been experienced in the whole history of Protestant missions. Hundreds of missionaries escaped, often under conditions of considerable hardship, to the coast. The Chinese Christians had to remain, and on them the hardest blow fell. Some failed to stand in the day of persecution, and apostatized. A great many stood firm, and died for or with their foreign friends in the effort to protect them.

The rising did not last long. In August a mixed force of the foreign powers, including Japan, fought its way through to Peking and relieved the legations. By the end of the year the country was prostrate at the feet of the conquerors, who were able to impose their own terms. These terms were harsh, and included compensation for loss of life and destruction of property, including mission property. This brought considerable perplexity to missions and Churches: how should damage be calculated, and through whom should the claims be made? The society that had suffered more heavily than any other was the CIM, just from the fact that its missionaries were so widely scattered in the interior. Hudson Taylor decided that nothing should be asked or claimed, in order to show to the Chinese the meekness and gentleness of Christ, 'not only not to enter any claim against the Chinese government, but to refrain from accepting compensation even if offered'. Few missions followed this example, but the later history suggests that the greater wisdom was that granted to Hudson Taylor. It is pleasant, however, to record that the first instalment paid to the United States was returned, to be built up into a fund for the education of Chinese, and that the payment of subsequent instalments was remitted.

In Christian circles there was little resentment against China and the Chinese. The one thought of most of the missionaries who had lost everything was to get back as soon as possible to their chosen work and their beloved people. New societies entered the field; old societies greatly strengthened their forces. At the end of our period, there were no less than 5,462 Protestant missionaries in the field, including the 1,652 wives of missionaries. The foreign force had more than quadrupled itself within twenty-five years.

The years following the Boxer rising and its débâcle were years of exceptional openness to the Christian message. Thousands of young Chinese were asking themselves the questions: How can China be regenerated? Where can the spiritual force be found to put new life into the vast body of the old empire? To many it seemed that there was only one answer: the West had good ideas, but the Christian Gospel alone would make it possible for these ideas to take effect in China. Thus it came about that in these years scores of Christian schools could record that every single student who had finished the course had been baptized before leaving school.

This rising Chinese Christianity had a somewhat exceptional character. It was little interested in the question of personal salvation. Not 'how can I be saved?' but 'how can China live anew?' – this was the burning question. It had little to do with the Churches. Most of these young people baptized in school or college had a very real loyalty to Christ and to his message; but many of them had never been in an ordinary church, had little interest in denominations, and had no idea of relating themselves to a worshipping congregation of people less educated than themselves. What they stood for was 'the Christian movement in China'. Ethically high-minded, socially conscious, ready for service, they had little awareness of the place and meaning of worship in the Christian life; they were more interested in the practical expression of Christian faith than in its inner development.

China was not allowed many years of peaceful development. Only ten years after the end of the Boxer troubles, the revolution broke out; the old régime came to an end, the emperor was dethroned, and a republic came into being. These events will be variously judged by posterity; the immediate results were not unfavourable to Christianity. It was well known that Sun Yat-sen, the provisional President, was a Christian; he had received much of his education from missionaries in Honolulu, and had been baptized in Hong Kong in 1884. One of the leading revolutionary generals, when asked to what he ascribed the success of the revolution, is recorded to have said:

To Christianity more than to any other single cause. Along with its ideals of religious freedom, it brings a knowledge of western political freedom, and along with these it inculcates everywhere a doctrine of universal love and peace. These ideals appeal to the Chinese; they largely caused the Revolution, and they largely determined its peaceful character.[9]

The general may have claimed too much. Christians were still a tiny minority in China, including the Roman Catholics not more than 1 per cent of the population. Yet they were an élite. Educated, alert, marked by integrity and resolution, with a clear idea of what they wanted to see accomplished, they were able to exercise an influence on the life of China far greater than their limited numbers

9. *China Mission Year Book*, 1913, p. 95, quoted by Latourette, op. cit., p. 610.

would suggest. And when the call came to take over leadership in the Church, they were found ready.

Korea, 'Chosen', the land of the morning calm, comes late into Christian history. Sandwiched between Japan and China, it does not belong to either of them. It has its own mysterious language, which is not akin to either Chinese or Japanese.[10] Its people, extraordinarily tough and sturdy, have learned from both, but have retained their own individual character. One who knew them extremely well wrote that 'they are not as phlegmatic as the Chinese nor as volatile as the Japanese . . . they are not slavishly bound by superstition, not as devoted to their old religions, not as faithful, perhaps, to the traditions of the past, as the Chinese, nor as initiative and ambitious as the Japanese'.[11] The religion of Korea is nominally Buddhism; but the older shamanism akin to that of the great Central Asian plain is still present not far below the surface, and manifests itself in the belief in and propitiation of evil spirits, which is perhaps in reality the religion of the average Korean.

A nineteenth-century Roman Catholic mission had been stamped out by persecution in 1864 and the following years, and the Hermit Kingdom had retreated into its own self-chosen isolation. But in 1882 a treaty with the United States changed the situation, and Korea followed Japan in opening its doors to the West. First in the field of missionary endeavour were the Northern Presbyterians and the Methodist Episcopal Church; in 1885 Horace Underwood and H. G. Appenzeller, both founders of families which have given a great many years of service to the Korean Churches, arrived to begin the work.

Korean Christians look back to the visit to Korea in 1890 of Dr John L. Nevius of Chefoo, China, as one of the turning-points of Christian work in their country. Dr Nevius was far ahead of his time in believing in the possibilities of an independent younger Church under the guidance of the Holy Spirit. In the spirit of prayer the missionaries in Korea were led to accept the 'Nevius method', and to make its four principles their guiding rule in the development of the work:

10. Korean is believed to belong to the Ural-Altaic family, and so to be akin to Turkish and Finnish.
11. H. G. Underwood, *The Call of Korea* (1908), pp. 45–6.

1. Each Christian should 'abide in the calling wherein he was found', support himself by his own work, and be a witness for Christ by life and word in his own neighbourhood.

2. Church methods and machinery should be developed only in so far as the Korean Church was able to take responsibility for the same.

3. The Church itself should call out for whole-time work those who seemed best qualified for it, and whom the Church was able to support.

4. Churches were to be built in native style, and by the Christians themselves from their own resources.

In order to fit the Christians for the work of witness great stress was laid on Bible teaching and study, and periods of intensive instruction were held every year.

The first converts were baptized in 1886; by 1894 the number had grown to 236. Then began the period of rapid progress. By 1910 there were nearly 30,000 communicants of the Presbyterian and Methodist Churches, with a much larger number of believers and adherents. A great revival, which began in 1906 and spread beyond Korea, renewed the vigour of the Church and kindled fresh evangelistic zeal. The fruits of the Nevius method were clearly to be seen in the character of the Church; there have been periods of tension between missionaries and Korean Christian leaders, but on the whole relationships based on mutual respect have been good; the Korean Christians have shown a spirit of independence which would not lie down under any kind of missionary domination, and were thereby prepared to hold on in faith in the periods of trouble which were to come on this sorely tried Church.

The Anglican mission of the SPG entered Korea in 1890, under the leadership of Bishop Corfe. Its strongly marked Anglo-Catholic character set it in sharp contrast to the free Protestantism of the American missions, and this new element, while not always understood or appreciated by those from other backgrounds, was undoubtedly of value in the growth of the Korean Churches. The Anglican mission has always been small by comparison with its great neighbours, but has held on its way. The third bishop, Mark Napier Trollope, consecrated in 1911, was determined that Anglican Christianity in Korea should stand in close relation to the traditional culture of the country; he built up a notable library of Korean books, and the most beautiful cathedral in the East stands as a memorial to his love of beautiful things and to his belief that only the best in every field is fitted for the expression of the Gospel.

Korea has always suffered from its propinquity to China and Japan. The Chinese and Japanese elements in the Korean language are evidence of the difficulty that Korea has experienced in maintaining the integrity of its own life and culture. From the time of the war between China and Japan in 1895, Japan had been able to establish its position as the paramount power in Korea; in 1910 the Korean Empire was brought to an end and the country was annexed to Japan. The independent spirit of the Korean Protestants made them natural allies of every movement for national independence, and therefore natural objects of the suspicion of the Japanese. In 1911, a considerable number were arrested, and accused of conspiring against the life of the Japanese governor-general; though the sentences passed by the lower court were reversed on appeal, suspicion in the Japanese mind was not allayed. This unfavourable attitude on the part of the authorities could not put an end to Christian growth, but it did set hindrances in its way, and the progress of the Church became much slower than it had been in the great days between 1890 and 1910.

A new field of activity for Protestant missions opened up when in 1898 the Americans drove the Spaniards out of the *Philippine Islands* and occupied the country. As we have seen, under Spanish influence almost the whole population had become Roman Catholic, and as long as the Spanish domination lasted no Protestant work or worship was allowed in the islands. But there was considerable discontent among the people. There had been for some time stirrings of national feeling, and this found expression, among other things, in a demand for more indigenous priests and for the appointment of Filipino bishops. These requests were disregarded by the Curia; and the result was the formation of the Philippine Independent Church under the leadership of Father Aglipay, a body which now claims about 7 per cent of the population of the islands and has inter-communion with the American branch and with one or two other Provinces of the Anglican Communion.

It was into this situation that the American Protestant missions entered – Presbyterians in 1899, Baptists in 1900, to be followed a little later by Methodists, and gradually by almost every colour in the spectrum of American religion. American Protestants have never had any inhibitions about missionary work in nominally Roman Catholic countries. In the Philippines they came in with the prestige of the conquering power and with the promise of a new freedom. There were plenty of discontented Roman Catholics and young people in search of a Western education. It was not long before strong Churches grew up in all the cities, and the work began to spread out into the countryside. Filipino Christians, like the Koreans, have shown a notable spirit of independence: the missionaries have been welcome friends and colleagues, but it has never been supposed that they were in any way masters of the Churches.

The Episcopal Mission, which arrived in 1902 under the leadership of Charles Henry Brent (1862–1929) – a Canadian who had become an American citizen, and was later to be the chief inspiring spirit in the Faith and Order movement – followed a different policy. Brent wished to remain on friendly terms with the Roman Catholics, and therefore directed the efforts of his missionaries to the as yet unevangelized folk in the mountains. Heroic pioneering work in the mountains of Luzon brought into being a living Church among the Igorots, and an attempt was made to approach the Moros, the Muslim peoples of the southern islands, who have maintained an almost unconquerable resistance to the Christian faith.[12]

South-east Asia was also the scene of certain new beginnings.

Of *Thailand* there is little to say except 'the mixture as before'. The strongest mission was that of the American Presbyterians, with their greatest success among the Laos in the north of the country and their strongest station at Chiengmai. Anglicans (SPG) started a small mission in 1903, and in the same year the British 'Churches of Christ' came in. But all the missions had the same experience – friendliness, good will, and an almost unalterable repugnance to the idea of conversion; the progress in all the Churches was very slow.

Under French influence, *Indo-China* had been almost a closed land to Protestants. But just at the end of our period, that great American inter-denominational body the Christian and Missionary Alliance was able to enter in – Swiss missionaries in *Laos* in 1902, and others in *Vietnam* and *Cambodia* in 1911.

In *Malaya*, the increasing numbers of Indians, who came in to do the heavy work and many of whom were Anglican Christians, drew in Anglican forces; among the immigrant Chinese the Anglicans,

12. The life of Bishop Brent has been written by Alexander C. Zabriskie; but there is room for a fuller and more scientific account of the work of a very great Christian leader.

Methodists, and Presbyterians strengthened their work. But the Muslim Malays, the original inhabitants, were almost untouched, and approach to them was made almost impossible by the attitude of the government.

By contrast, the mission in *North Borneo* and *Sarawak*, for which Dr Francis Thomas McDougall (1817–86) had been consecrated as bishop in 1855, was able to report considerable success, among both the primitive sea and land Dyaks and the immigrant Chinese in the towns.

In *Burma* the Baptists continued to make steady progress, still mostly among the non-Burmese peoples. Alongside them worked Methodists and Anglicans. The Anglican mission was started in 1853, after the conclusion of the second war between the Burmese and the British, and from 1860 was under the leadership of the immensely vigorous and dominating Dr J. E. Marks, whose educational work in Rangoon was of the highest value. The first bishop for Rangoon was consecrated in 1877.

It was in *Indonesia*, however, that greater progress was recorded than in any other country of South-east Asia. Religious awakening in Holland led to the formation of new missionary societies; and, with an almost mystical sense that God had given Indonesia to Holland as a Christian responsibility, almost all these missions devoted themselves to work in the island world. Once again it has to be noted that, from the point of view of numbers, no missions to Muslims have ever equalled the success of the Dutch missions in Indonesia. And in Celebes, in Timor, in Halmahera, and other island groups, large Churches were brought into being.

The most notable of all the achievements of this half century stands to the credit not of a Dutch but of a German missionary society – the Rhenish Mission, and its work among the Bataks of upland Sumatra.

The Bataks are a virile, vigorous people, now more than a million strong. When Christianity first reached them, just a century ago, Dutch rule had not penetrated the fastnesses of their hills. They had remained almost untouched by their Muslim neighbours to the south, and lived shut away from the world in a primitive state in which cannibalism was practised and internecine warfare between the tribes was the order of the day. The earliest attempts to approach them with the Gospel had not proved fortunate: in 1834 two missionaries of the American Board, Samuel Munson and Henry Lyman, tried to enter Batakland, but were killed and eaten by the inhabitants before they had been able to make even a beginning with missionary work.

In 1859 missionaries of the Rhenish society were driven out of Borneo by an uprising of the populace; looking for another field, they were inspired to turn to *Sumatra*, and settled there in 1861. In the following year they were joined by one of the most powerful missionaries of whom we have record anywhere – Ludwig Ingwer Nommensen (1834–1918). Nommensen, who was born in the island of Nordstrand in Schleswig-Holstein, at that time under the Danish Crown, was a man of sterling faith, indomitable resolution, and prophetic and poetic vision. At last in 1876 he was able to pay his first visit to the beautiful and at that time almost inaccessible lake Toba. On his return he wrote of what he had seen there in fact and in hope:

> Thou land on the shores of the lake, I hear the bells sound out everywhere across thee, I see thine inhabitants coming in crowds to thy Churches and thy schools. Where now stand only uncultivated hills, I see fair gardens and flourishing woods, and countless well-ordered villages of Christians. I see Batak teachers and pastors standing at the desk and in the pulpit to teach and preach . . . The sun has risen upon Batakland; who will prevent it from rising until its rays shine even upon the shores of lake Toba?

Nommensen lived to see this early prophecy fulfilled to the letter.[13]

The early beginnings were difficult. The life of the clan was so intense and intimate among the Bataks that little initiative was left to the individual. Those who became Christians lost all their rights to a share in the communal property, since they would no longer take part in the sacrifices to the spirits of the ancestors or contribute to the cost of them. They had to find new rice-fields and gardens in remote places. Missionaries have often been accused of unnecessarily separating Christians from the ordinary life of their people, but when converts have been cast out by their tribe, what is to be done? There seemed to be no remedy except that the missionaries should gather the little groups of the faithful into Christian villages.

The situation changed startlingly with the conversion of a number of chiefs; as in medieval Europe, the people were ready to follow almost without hesitation in the way that was pointed out to them by their leaders. What happened can be shown more clearly

13. It is greatly to be regretted that no life of Nommensen appears as yet to exist in English.

in figures than in words. In 1866, there were fifty-two Christians; in 1876, there were 2,056; in 1881, 7,500; in 1911, 103,525. All at once the missionaries were overwhelmed by a great people's movement, and had to face problems of church organization of which they had never dreamed. They had thought in terms of bringing individuals one by one into Churches of converted people; now they were faced by a 'people's Church', for which they had made no preparation.

In facing these two problems, the missionaries could count on four immense advantages. Although there were many clans and groups among the Bataks, they all belonged essentially to the same people, and, apart from slight local differences, they all recognized the same basic traditions and rules of society. They all spoke variations of the same language, in which, before many years had passed, a reliable translation of the Bible was available to them. Only one missionary society was at work in the region; the Roman Catholics had not yet entered, and the Bataks were free from the perplexities brought about by Western divisions. And as the Dutch government increasingly took control, it was prepared to help the educational work of the missions with generous subventions. Since, in most cases, the village teacher served also as a catechist, the rapid expansion of the work of the Church was to a large extent made possible by government money.

What use, then, was to be made of these advantages? At a very early date Nommensen and his companions had decided that this was to be a Batak, and not a purely Western, Church. This had not been the original concept: in the Church Order of 1866 we read that 'the congregations, in accordance with their confession, belong to the Evangelical Church as by law established in the Rhineland and Westphalia'; and pastors were required to pledge their loyalty to 'the canonical books of holy Scripture, interpreted in the light of the Augsburg Confession, Luther's Catechism, and the Heidelberg Catechism'. By the time that the new Church Order of 1881 came into being, a different spirit prevailed. The missionaries had learned that there was much which was good in the *adat*, the traditional law of the Bataks; there was to be no compromise with anything that was specifically pagan, but otherwise as far as possible nothing traditional was to be disturbed. From the beginning the missionaries had begun to train Batak colleagues for the ministry. In 1868 the first five trained evangelists were set apart for the work. In 1883 training of pastors was begun, and, when pastors were ordained, they were received into full spiritual equality with the missionaries. This contrasted favourably with the practice of the Dutch missionaries. These had been very slow to ordain Indonesians, and even when ordained the pastor in most cases had not the right to administer the sacraments: he remained hopelessly in the position of assistant to his European master. Notable in the Batak Church was the system of lay elders, under which men of experience in the congregations were entrusted with spiritual responsibility for a certain number of families.

All this sounded excellent on paper. Yet, in reality, the organization of the Church continued to be partriarchal. It could hardly be otherwise. At that stage of development the missionary was everything and everywhere. As Nommensen rightly said: 'If we sow with a view to the spiritual only, we shall never reap the whole man.' The missionary was the interpreter between the government and a puzzled and simple people. He was doctor and teacher, agricultural adviser and road surveyor, reconciler in conflicts, the wielder of discipline, and chancellor of the exchequer. Under the church constitution, every position of influence and authority in the Church was reserved for missionaries alone. Theoretically Nommensen and his colleagues were planning for a Batak Church, but it never seems to have occurred to them to look forward to and to plan for the realization of this excellent dream:

The leading position of the missionary in the growing Church is so much taken for granted that it is never even so much as called in question. It seems clear that Nommensen and his colleagues never even imagined that these churches for which they had cared could one day exist without missionaries, and in separation from the mother Church in Barmen. Apparently they were equally unable to take seriously the possibility that one day the colonial power would withdraw, and yield place to an Indonesian government. Certainly we must not accuse these missionaries of racial contempt or colonial outlook even when they seem to be naïvely and perfectly convinced that the natural position of the white man in these lands is that of master.[14]

This state of affairs survived the death of Nommensen in 1918, and still remained, modified but not radically altered, in 1940. The organization was admirably efficient; but till the end the missionaries seem to have been strangely unaware of the cry of the Bataks for equality and independence. It was almost with relief that the Church heard in 1940, on the invasion of Holland by

14. Theodor Müller-Krüger, in *Gemacht zu seinem Volk* (the Centenary Volume of the Batak Church, 1961), pp. 35–6.

Hitler's troops, that all the missionaries had been interned by the Dutch.

In the *South Pacific* the period under review was one of steady progress, with hazards and setbacks, yet still in many areas with the glow and brightness of the first period of pioneering.

In the unfriendly and dangerous *New Hebrides* John G. Paton, author of a famous autobiography, held on from 1858 till 1862, in almost daily danger of his life, on the wild island of Tanna. When his position there became quite untenable, he withdrew to the smaller island of Aniwa and laboured till he had seen the whole population of the island turn Christian.

Anglicans came comparatively late on the scene in these waters. George Augustus Selwyn, whom we have met as the first Bishop of New Zealand, found that through a clerical error in the Letters Patent of his appointment ('N' for 'S') he had been made bishop of an enormous area in the Pacific. Characteristically, he set to work to include this area in his sphere of operations: the Melanesian Mission came into being. Selwyn drew to his side John Coleridge Patteson (1827–71), who in 1861 was consecrated the first Bishop of Melanesia. Patteson was a man of great charm, intense humility, and Christian affection, and in addition a linguist who seemed to have a magical faculty for acquiring the many languages of his island world. The Anglican mission, the aim of which was to disturb as little as possible the manners and customs of the people, worked by the method of taking promising boys from many islands and bringing them together for training, first in New Zealand and later in Norfolk Island, with a view to their later becoming teachers in their own islands. In 1871 Patteson landed on the island of Nukapu in the Santa Cruz group, suspecting no harm. He was immediately set on and killed, and his body was placed in a canoe to drift back to the ship. It was found that five wounds had been made in the breast, on which a palm branch tied in five knots had been placed: Christians could not but be reminded of the five wounds of another innocent Victim. It was later learned that Patteson had been killed in vengeance for five of the islanders, who had been kidnapped and killed by rascally white traders. The death of the Bishop made a profound impression in England, and called forth a new wave of support for the work of the Church in the South Seas.[15]

15. The life of Patteson by Charlotte M. Yonge (1873) is among the best of Victorian biographies.

During this period *New Guinea* was added to the partly Christian countries of the world. New Guinea is the second largest island in the world, nearly four times as large as Great Britain. The centre is occupied by sharply serrated mountains, rising at points to 19,000 feet, and separated by deep and almost inaccessible valleys. These are inhabited by tribes speaking not less than 500 separate and distinct languages. The population may amount to 4 million. Many of the tribes are extremely small, with not more than a thousand members. They had lived isolated and in fear, since warfare was constant and cannibalism of a particularly brutal type was endemic. In most areas civilization had not advanced beyond the level of the stone age. In the scramble for territory in the nineteenth century the great island was divided up between Holland, Germany, and Britain (later Australia). But government control was little more than nominal; only the aeroplane has made possible the exploration of the remoter regions.

The first Protestants to arrive were the representatives, white and indigenous, of the LMS, who settled on the south coast in 1870. The Anglicans arrived on the north-east coast in 1891, to find themselves confronted by a band of warriors all with their spears at the ready. Happily the warriors agreed to trade; for 112 pounds of tobacco, ten tomahawks, a bundle of knives, beads, pipes, and a length of Turkey red cloth, the missionaries were able to purchase the land on which the cathedral was later built. The first bishop of New Guinea was consecrated in 1898. The Methodists arrived about the same time, and were assigned as their sphere the innumerable islands off the east coast of New Guinea.

In 1877 James Chalmers, who had already served for ten years in Rarotonga, arrived in New Guinea, to which he was to give nearly a quarter of a century of his life and which was to be inseparably associated with his name. Chalmers was one of the least conventional of missionaries,[16] able to make friends with men of every type and to command their respect. It was this that won the heart of Robert Louis Stevenson, and turned him from a hater of missionaries into a steadfast supporter of their work – with reservations: what commended Chalmers to Stevenson was that you would never have taken him for a missionary! In April 1901 Chalmers, with a young companion Oliver Tomkins, was on an

16. He was one of the first to abandon the long black coat and the stove-pipe hat which were the inseparable companions of the true Victorian missionary and which, alas, were adopted *con amore* by many of the native preachers.

exploratory trip near the mouth of the Fly river, where the people were particularly wild and inhospitable. The travellers had hardly landed when they were set upon, clubbed to death, cooked, and eaten.[17]

The Utrecht Missionary Union sent its first representatives into *Irian* (Western New Guinea) in 1861. Work was heartbreakingly difficult and progress heartbreakingly slow. At the end of the first twenty-five years of work there were only twenty believers; it was said that there were more missionary graves in Irian than Christians.

The Germans fared better. Their two societies, the Neuendettelsau Mission (of which the first worker, Johannes Flierl, arrived in 1886) and the Rhenish Mission (1887), also at the start suffered heavy losses and countless discouragements, but they held on, and at last the results began to come in. After thirteen years, the Neuendettelsau Mission baptized its first convert; the Rhenish Mission followed four years later.

But now the missionaries found themselves faced with the same problem as their brethren in Sumatra. The converts were not completely thrown out of tribal society; but they were regarded as no longer belonging to the tribe, and thus their power of witnessing to their faith was minimal. Under the influence of Christian Keysser, who had probably penetrated more deeply into the mind of the Papuan than any other European, the missionaries were led to try the experiment of 'tribal conversion'. Christian instruction was patiently continued for many years, until a whole tribe was ready to accept in principle the new ways and to put itself under instruction. Such conversion was not followed immediately by baptism; it was only the beginning of a further long process of instruction, and baptism would be accorded only to those whose fidelity had been carefully tried and tested. In that land of many tribes and tongues, almost all the work was done by native evangelists, many of them men of little education and very limited Christian knowledge, but their simple faith and their willingness to suffer for it told in the end. This heroic chapter in Christian missions has resulted in the existence of a Lutheran Church which at the time of writing numbers more than 200,000 members.

Missionaries have often been accused of destroying simple peoples by changing their age-long customs, and introducing such

17. The present (1963) Bishop of Bristol is in less danger than his uncle and namesake of coming to so untimely an end.

purely Western habits as the wearing of clothes. It has to be admitted that missionaries have made many mistakes, and have not always been wise in their handling of their converts. But on the whole the weight of evidence tells heavily against their critics. The missionaries from the start found themselves in bitter opposition to the white traders and exploiters, whose attitude was expressed by one of them to John G. Paton in the words 'our watchword is "Sweep these creatures away, and let white men occupy the soil"', and who, in pursuance of their aim, placed men sick of the measles on various islands in order to destroy the population through disease. Dr H. P. Van Dusen, in his book *They Found the Church There*, has collected a great many facts; all go to show that, in this new and competitive world, Christians had a better chance of survival than others; and that the combined efforts of government and missions gave new life to interesting and charming peoples which were in danger of dying out.

India, since 1858 a direct responsibility of the British government, now entered on a period of unexampled peace and progress. The successive British conquests had given to the country a unity which it had not known even in the great days of Asoka and Akbar. A succession of unusually able and high-minded government servants ruled impartially and for the benefit of all. The extension of the railways and the development of the 'Famine Code', one of the greatest achievements of civilized government in the modern world, gradually brought under control the ever-recurrent spectre of famine. Confidence was restored and trade again began to flourish.

What would be the attitude of the new government towards the Christian religion? On this question there was division in the ranks of the governors themselves. Those who were themselves earnest Christians (and they were many) felt that the government, while remaining faithful to the principle of non-interference, should make no concealment of the Christian principles that underlay its actions. Such men were in agreement with the utterance of Sir John Lawrence that 'Christian things done in a Christian way . . . will never alienate the heathen'. Others were much more cautious, and in fact interpreted 'non-interference' in a way highly unfavourable to Christian witness. This was shown in a curious little incident in May 1859. The Commissioner of Amritsar, Mr R. N. Cust, accompanied by some other high officials, had attended the baptism of six converts of the C M S mission in that city. Immediately a haughty note came from the government in Calcutta demanding an explanation. Sir Robert Montgomery (1809–87), the Lieutenant-Governor of the Punjāb, came vigorously to the defence of the liberty of the Christian man 'to attend on the religious ceremonies of his own Church, so long as the public service is in no way affected, or the principles of toleration compromised'.[18] No more was heard of the incident. But the controversy, of which it was a symptom, was never completely laid to rest.

At one point the action of the British authorities was entirely favourable to missions. In 1854 the government set forth an Educational Despatch in which, along with many other excellent proposals, it declared itself ready to give grants-in-aid to schools carried on by voluntary effort, provided that they accepted government inspection and guidance in respect to the secular part of their work. The right of managements to give such religious instruction to their pupils as they thought fitting was specifically recognized. Sir Charles Wood, the grandfather of the great viceroy Lord Irwin,[19] defending the proposals in a famous speech in the House of Commons, remarked:

I believe that by doing so we shall not weaken but strengthen our empire. But even if the reverse should be the case – even if the result should be the loss of that empire – it seems to me that this country will occupy a far better and prouder position in the history of the world, if by our agency a civilized and Christian empire should be established in India, than if we continued to rule over a people debased by ignorance and degraded by superstition.

It was open to any agency – Hindu, Christian, or secular – to take advantage of the aid proffered by the government; but naturally the missions, which had already done so much unaided for education, were the chief beneficiaries. Some voices were raised in warning – who sups with the government must have a long spoon – but almost every mission in India seized the opportunity with avidity. Schools on every level were multiplied with extreme rapidity, the government bearing about two-thirds of the cost, with the result that at the end of the century, though drawn in the main from the poorest classes, Christians were second to the Parsis alone

18. That sober work the *Dictionary of National Biography* adds a pleasant touch to our picture of Montgomery: 'His benevolence was recognized in the service in India by the nickname of "Pickwick".'

19. Sir Charles Wood became the first Viscount Halifax in 1866. His son, the second Viscount, was the great promoter of schemes for reunion between the Church of England and the Church of Rome. Lord Irwin succeeded his father as third Viscount in 1934.

in point of literacy in what was still for the most part an illiterate country, and the foundations had been laid of that large and prosperous Christian middle class which is one of the most noteworthy features of the Indian scene in the middle of the twentieth century.

Hindu society was on the whole prepared to accept, and even to welcome, the contributions of the missionaries. Non-Christian pupils were in a vast majority in almost all the schools. As we have seen, leading Hindu reformers such as Raja Rām Mohun Roy were prepared to lend their enthusiastic support to missionary projects. But, in the course of the next two generations, a different attitude began to develop. Thoughtful Hindus and Muslims came to feel, from their own point of view rightly, that the Gospel and Christian penetration, even apart from the problem of conversion, constituted a subtle threat to their whole way of life and to the age-long traditions of India. The ancient religions rallied their forces for defence, and gradually moved over from the defensive to the offensive.

One sign or portent of this change was the foundation of the Ārya Samāj by Swāmi Dayānand Sarasvati (1875). This was primarily a movement for the purification of Hinduism by a return to the simplicity of the Vedas, but it was also bitterly anti-Western and anti-Christian. One of its later activities was the movement for the reconversion to Hinduism of those members of the lower classes who had yielded to the persuasions of the missionaries.

In 1893 a young Bengali, Swāmi Vivēkānanda, spoke with memorable power at the Parliament of Religions held in that year in Chicago. His plea was for the mutual recognition of the spirituality of East and West; each had its own contribution to make; there should be fellowship in sympathy, but no attempt at proselytism. This was a cry that was to be increasingly heard – service but no proselytism, fellowship without aggression.

Missionaries were not insensitive to this propaganda, and a hitherto unknown uncertainty is to be found in their utterances in the closing years of our period. Scholarship was revealing the spiritual treasures of the ancient religions. A more liberal theology took a rather different view of the uniqueness of Christianity from that which had been current in earlier days. Missionaries were driven to reconsider their methods, and to ask again as to the purpose of their work. One of the most persuasive advocates of the new outlook was William Miller, the justly famous principal of what was now the Christian College in Madras. The Christian colleges in his day were no longer winning converts. Should their work, then, as some felt, be abandoned? Not at all, said Miller; the aim should not be the detachment of a small number of individuals from the mass, but a long term *praeparatio evangelica*, a deep penetration of the whole mind and thought of Hinduism, through which the way would be prepared for the ultimate triumph of Christianity on the largest possible scale.[20]

There continued to be conversions from the highest Hindu castes, and from among the Muslims, though perhaps they were even fewer than in earlier years. Three examples, from very different spheres and of very varied types, may be given.

Imad-ud-din was an earnest and scholarly Muslim who in 1854 had been present at a famous debate between C. G. Pfander, the noted scholar and controversialist, and a group of Muslim *moulvies*. Such was Imad-ud-din's reputation for learning that he was himself put up to preach against Dr Pfander. For years he was convinced that the answer to all his soul's needs was to be found in a purified Islam, and it was only after long struggles and inner agonies that he became convinced that for him the only answer was in Jesus Christ. His *Autobiography* opens with the words:

May the grace of our Lord Jesus Christ dwell on the whole world. The writer of this little Pamphlet became a Christian on the 29th of April, 1866, with the single object of obtaining salvation.

Imad-ud-din later won fame as preacher, author, and translator; in 1884 he was awarded the degree of Doctor of Divinity by the Archbishop of Canterbury – the first Indian ever to receive this distinction – in recognition of his services to Christian literature in India.

Nārāyan Vāman Tilak (1861–1919) was a Brahman of the straitest sect of the Marathi Chitpawan Brahmans. A highly intelligent young man with an intense interest in literature and poetry, he had no interest in Christianity, which he believed to be dangerous to the welfare of India. But one day an unknown and unnamed European gave him a copy of the New Testament, in the train in which they were travelling together, and asked him to read it. When he reached the fifth chapter of St Matthew's Gospel, Tilak found that he had the answer to innumerable problems which had perplexed him. He was baptized, and later was ordained a minister

20. At the Bangalore Missionary Conference of 1879, Miller made an eloquent plea on behalf of Christian education conceived in these terms.

of the Presbyterian Church. But no Church could really hold him. He was always independent, intensely critical of missionaries and Churches, eager that Indians should stand on their own feet and make their own contribution to the regeneration of India. His great gift was in poetry. Of his hundreds of hymns, many are included in the book of hymns used by the Marathi-speaking Churches, and some have found their way into English. At his death in 1919 he had made a greater contribution than any other Indian Christian up to his time to the presentation of the Gospel in literary form in an Indian language.

Ramābai (1858–1922) was the daughter of a Brahman scholar, a most unusual man who believed that girls as well as boys should be educated, and who taught Ramābai Sanskrit with such skill that in later life she was given the title *Pandita*, 'the learned', perhaps a unique honour for a woman. While in England in 1883 Ramābai (recently widowed) was led to ask for baptism, though her Christian faith and experience appear at that time to have been extremely limited. After her return to India she was brought into that deeper and heroic faith which led her to exploits such as no other Indian woman had ever undertaken. Her first concern was for the young and neglected widows who, under Hindu law, could never hope to marry again. This was extended later to the care of famine orphans. The multiple institution at Mukti ('deliverance'), through which hundreds of girls came to Christian faith, received help in staffing and in money from many quarters; but at the centre of everything, until her death in 1922, was the Pandita herself – a frail, indomitable figure, desiring nothing so much as to give all things and to endure all things for the sake of Christ.

These were the great ones in the land. As earlier, most of the progress of the Church was to be found among those who were little thought of by men, or who were excluded from all social privileges.

India is a land of many races. Successive waves of invasion have driven to the hills and jungles the weaker and aboriginal peoples who are to be found in their millions in almost every province of India. The process of absorbing these simple peoples into the Hindu caste system has been going on for centuries, but is still far from complete; and, just because they are animists and not Hindus, they are far more responsive than the Hindus to the hearing of the Gospel.

The experience of the Gossner Mission in *Bihar* is typical of many others. The first missionaries arrived in 1839, and in the course of the next twenty years occupied five stations in the Gangetic plain. There they worked faithfully but, like other missions, saw distressingly little result of their work. In 1845 some of the missionaries moved up into the highlands and settled in Ranchi, among the more backward 'Kolarian' peoples. Here in the hills there are three main groups – the Oraons, the Mundas, and the Hos[21] – each with its own language and customs. From 1850 onwards success came to the mission; by 1857, 900 converts had been baptized, and then each year brought an increasing number. The Gossner missionaries wisely related their work to the situation of the people; they wished to make them Christians within the order in which they lived, and not to transfer them to something entirely different. The later history of this mission is sad. A new generation of missionaries, coming out after 1860, found it difficult to work with its elders; and finally such an impossible situation was reached that three of the older generation asked to be admitted to the Church of England in India. After long hesitation and full investigation into the circumstances, Bishop Milman of Calcutta accepted the petition, and received and ordained the dissenting missionaries; in this way what is now the diocese of Chota Nagpur came into existence. At a later date Roman Catholics also entered this field, and the simple peoples were confronted with the full range of Christian divisions. But progress was not halted, and the fully independent Gossner Evangelical Lutheran Church, with 200,000 members, is a monument to the faithfulness of the early pioneers.

Not far away from the Kolarians live another great aboriginal people, the Santāls. Here many missions have been at work; that which has attracted the widest notice has been the Santāl Mission of the Northern Churches. This is due to the fame of the Norwegian Lars Olsen Skrefsrud (1840–1910), one of the most remarkable pioneer evangelists among simple people that India has ever seen. Skrefsrud's preparation for missionary work was unusual. Evil ways in youth led him to a four-year sentence in jail; there, under the influence of Christians who themselves had been influenced by the pietist movement associated with the name of Hans Nielsen Hauge (1771–1824), Skrefsrud underwent a complete conversion and decided to give himself to missionary work. Norway was not very ready to receive a jail-bird as a missionary, so in 1863 he went

21. There are competent articles on these, and on many other aboriginal peoples of India, in Hastings's *Encyclopaedia of Religion and Ethics*.

to India under the Gossner mission. In 1867 he separated himself from this mission and, in association with a Dane, H. P. Börresen, founded his own independent mission. Skrefsrud proved to have exceptional gifts for languages, and composed what is still the classic grammar of the Santāli language. His aim was to Christianize the people, making as little change as possible in their manner of life. By the time of his death in 1910 adherents of the Scandinavian mission were said to number 15,000. The problem of the Chinese rites repeated itself in the remote hills of Santālia: the missionaries of the various missions found it impossible to agree on the correct translation of the name of God, and, as they had no Pope to settle the matter for them, they were fain to go on in separation, using different translations of the Scriptures.

As early as 1841 the Welsh Calvinistic Methodists had been led to the *Khasi* hills in Assam. After fifty years they could count 2,147 communicants, and a total of about 10,000 Christians. In the jubilee year, 1891, the translation of the Bible was completed. From then on, progress was rapid; the whole life of the hills was transformed, and there were wide areas where the entire population was Christian. From 1892 onwards the Welsh extended their work to the *Lushai* hills, where the people are of Mongolian stock; there they were to encounter British Baptists moving in from another direction. From 1860 on, the American Baptists pressed even further into the north-eastern section of the province of Assam, and won converts among the Garos, the Abors, the Minis, and the head-hunting Nagas.

Limitations of space forbid reference to all the simple peoples who were reached by the Gospel, but room must be found for the smallest of all races, the *Todas*. This pastoral people, living more than 7,000 feet above the sea in the Nilgiri Hills and following the very ancient Indian custom of polyandry, when first discovered by the Europeans about a century and a half ago numbered roughly 1,000. As so often happens, contact with a more complex civilization threatened the very existence of the Todas; the number was reduced to barely half what it had been. In the 1880s Anglican missionaries in the hills began to be interested in the Todas; the first baptism took place about the turn of the century, and was followed rather slowly by other conversions. Strenuous remedial activity on the part of the government is just keeping the non-Christian Todas going; the Toda Christian habit of having anything from eight to twelve children per family seems to safeguard the Toda Christian community against any immediate danger of disappearance.[22]

One of India's gravest problems arises from the existence of the outcaste groups, now more politely referred to as 'the scheduled castes', who in many areas make up a fifth of the population. These fragments of older and pre-Aryan races live in a miserable state of isolation, not wholly without rights but with very few privileges, and condemned to a lifelong servitude in the exercise of crafts (leather-working, etc.) which by others are regarded as degrading. It is part of the mythology of missions that the missionaries turned naturally to the poor and degraded, among whom they would find less resistance to their message, and neglected the higher castes, but history shows that the exact opposite was the case. Almost every mission started with the attempt to reach the higher castes; when movements started among the poor, they were viewed with anxiety and a measure of embarrassment by the missionaries, who saw that their whole cause might be prejudiced by the influx of masses of ignorant and despised people.

We have seen that in South Travancore in the days of Ringel-taube a number of the very poor had come in. The great days of the 'mass movements' among the depressed classes came, however, in the period after 1870.

The American Baptist Mission had been working in the neighbourhood of Nellore in the *Telugu* area since 1840, with so little success that it had come to be known as the 'Lone Star Mission', and several proposals had been made for the abandonment of the work. Then the Reverend John E. Clough came in contact with a Mādiga named Yerraguntla Periah, of the village of Talla Kondapād some miles north-east of Ongole, who had been in touch with a missionary of the CMS in Ellore. As soon as Dr Clough arrived to open the station at Ongole, Periah appeared, asking for baptism; a visit to his village revealed that perhaps 200 people were believing in Jesus as a result of Periah's preaching. Dr Clough was very hesitant to baptize people living at such a distance from his station, but at length he agreed to do so. Hundreds and then thousands began to come in; 8,691 adults were baptized in six months in 1878, and by the end of 1882 the number of Church members in the area was 20,865.

22. This fascinating people has been the subject of one of the classics of anthropological research, *The Todas* by W. H. R. Rivers (1906), a work with more pages than Todas – 800 pages to 600 Todas.

Lutherans, Anglicans, Methodists, and others profited from the great movement in the Telugu area, which in thirty years brought a million people into the Church – not without the problems consequent on the addition to the Christian flock of such a mass of ignorance and illiteracy.

The beginnings of the movement among the Chuhras in the *Siālkot* district of the Punjāb were similar. In 1870 a highly unsatisfactory caste convert appeared at the Presbyterian mission house with a dark, lame Chuhra named Ditt, whom he claimed to have instructed in the Christian faith. Ditt wished to be baptized, and to remain in his own village carrying on his hereditary occupation of selling hides. The missionary was unwilling, believing that it was impossible for any man to stand as a Christian unless he came and lived in the mission compound. Ditt persisted, and was baptized. He had to endure considerable persecution, but held firm. Wherever his work took him, he bore witness to his faith. The message told. By 1900 half the Chuhras in the Siālkot district had been baptized, and by the end of our period almost the entire community had been brought in.

Between 1851 and 1901 the Protestant community in India had multiplied itself tenfold, and it was hardly possible any longer to disregard the question of the relationship which should exist between a foreign mission and a growing indigenous Church. Yet missionaries in this period seem to have been singularly blind to the changed situation. In most places they seem to have taken it for granted that missionary domination would continue for a very long time, and to have been almost wholly unaware of the new powers of leadership that were growing up within the Indian Church.

To the eternal credit of the Young Men's Christian Association, it must be recorded that much earlier than the Churches it recognized the possibilities of Indian leadership, and gave young men scope for the exercise of it. When at last in 1912 the Anglican Church made up its mind to the experiment of an Indian episcopate, the man chosen to be the first bishop, Vedanayakam Samuel Azariah (1874–1945), owed more to the YMCA than to the Church. The appointment was bitterly combated both by missionaries and by many Indian Christians, but Azariah grew steadily in spiritual stature and in authority, and was widely acclaimed in both East and West as a missionary statesman. At last Indian leadership was coming into its own.

In an earlier chapter we saw that there had been little to record in the *Middle and Near East*; and in fact Muslim lands have tended to be neglected by Christian missions in comparison with more productive fields. But the second half of the nineteenth century was marked by the beginning of a real encounter between the faith of Jesus Christ and the faith of Muhammad.

For centuries Christians had lived in considerable ignorance of the realities of Muslim faith. That ignorance was now at last dispelled by scholarship. One of the earliest works of Christian learning in this field was the *Mizan-al-Haqq*, 'Balance of Truth', of C. G. Pfander, which was completed in 1829 while its author was a missionary of the Basel Mission in Persia and adjoining countries.[23] This was a work of Christian controversy; for pure scholarship the palm must go to the *Life of Mahomet* in the light of the original sources by the devout Christian layman Sir William Muir (1821–1905), who had served the government in India for many years and had been lieutenant-governor of the Punjāb. Another of the services rendered by Muir was the discovery of the *Apology of Al-Kindi*, a defence of the Christian faith written in Baghdad in the ninth century by a learned Arab. With these and similar helps, missionaries were learning how to approach the Muslim in a broader and more tolerant spirit, and with an inner understanding of his faith such as earlier generations had lacked.

We have seen that some beginnings had been made in *Iran*. In the period we are now considering, the Anglicans entered this field in memorable circumstances. An Irish missionary, Robert Bruce, had spent ten years in the Punjāb among Muslims, and obtained permission to spend a year in Iran on his way back from furlough in Britain, in order to improve his knowledge of Persian and of Islam. One year was extended to two, and in 1871, just as Bruce was preparing to leave for India, nine Muslims with whom he had had much converse in Isfahan asked for baptism. Such an event was almost unknown in the Islamic world; it seemed clear that Bruce must stay. The Committee in England was not best pleased at having its hand forced in this way by the Holy Spirit, but it yielded to *force majeure*, and the Anglican mission in Iran became a reality. It has never been strong, but it has been faithful. Bruce wrote of his work:

23. On the circumstances in which this book was written, see E. Stock, *History of the Church Missionary Society*, Vol. II, p. 152.

I am not reaping the harvest; I scarcely claim to be sowing the seed; I am hardly ploughing the soil; *but I am gathering out the stones. That,* too, is missionary work; let it be supported by loving sympathy and fervent prayer.[24]

In 1894 the Iran mission was joined by a very unusual recruit. Edward Craig Stuart had gone to India under the C M S in 1850. Twenty-seven years later he was consecrated Bishop of Waiapu in New Zealand. After seventeen years of faithful work among settlers and Maoris, and at an age when most men would have felt fully justified in retiring, Stuart found life in New Zealand too comfortable and decided to give the closing years of his service to Iran. Since then there have been other deeply loved bishops in Persia; their work and witness reached a kind of climax when, on 25 April 1961, ninety years after the gathering of the first group of converts in Isfahan, the first Persian bishop of the Anglican Church, Hassan Barnabas Dehqani-Tafti, was consecrated to the episcopate.

Stuart was not the only bishop to return in old age to pioneer missionary work. In 1890 two men were travelling together down the Red Sea. Thomas Valpy French (1825–90) would have been distinguished in any career that he had chosen to follow. He had arrived in India in 1850 in the service of the Church Missionary Society, and in 1877 had been consecrated first Bishop of Lahore. In him zeal was not always matched with prudence, but it is fortunate for the Church that its greatest men are not always prudent. In his old age French decided on an apparently reckless and hopeless venture. He would go to Muscat in *Arabia*, and tackle Islam at its very heart. It was indeed a fantastic and unpromising scheme. French arrived in Muscat on 8 February 1891; on 14 May he was dead. His companion on the voyage was a young American of the Reformed Church, Samuel M. Zwemer, one of that group of pioneers who established the heroic mission of their Church in Arabia. French died in just over three months; Zwemer lived for more than sixty years, to be scholar, preacher, writer, evangelist, and apologist throughout the world of Christian missions to Muslims. At the great Tāmbaram Missionary Conference of 1938, the most moving of all the speeches was that of the veteran Dr Paul Harrison, who, having told the story of the five converts that the mission had won in fifty years, sat down with the quiet words: 'The Church in Arabia salutes you.'

24. Quoted by E. Stock, *History of the Church Missionary Society*, Vol. III, p. 125.

Egypt had come under British control in 1882; and from that time on Anglican work in the country was resumed. The CMS hospital in Old Cairo was the centre of evangelistic as well as of medical work. Egypt was one of the first countries to feel the influence of the new spirit that had come into the universities of the West, and had resulted in the formation of the Student Christian Movements, the Student Volunteer Missionary Union, and the World's Student Christian Federation.

One of the outstanding leaders of the British movement, Douglas Thornton, came to Cairo in 1899. His ardent temperament and burning zeal quickly wore him out and he died in 1907. His friend and successor, W. H. Temple Gairdner, became so great an expert in Arabic as to be able to compose in that language poems which were found worthy of publication. Both men worked on the principle of a frank, friendly, and courteous approach to Muslims, one of the main instruments of their service being the bilingual periodical *Orient and Occident*, which was used for the calm and temperate exposition of Christian truth in its relationship to Islam. Both men, and their successors, observed rigidly the Anglican principle of loyal service to the Coptic Church without interference with it. This resulted in warm friendship between the two Churches, and helped to build up that spirit which in later years made Cairo for a time the most ecumenical city in the world. Its Committee on Co-operation, presided over by a Roman Catholic bishop, included Copts and Evangelicals of various sorts, as well as Anglicans.[25]

North Africa has been an area much neglected by Protestant missions. The first in the field were the Anglican missionaries to the Jews, who started work in Tunis as long ago as 1829, and, after some interruptions, have carried it on steadily since 1860. This work was extended to Morocco in 1875. The only mission which works in all the four territories, *Morocco, Tunis, Algeria,* and *Libya,* is the interdenominational North Africa Mission, which, founded in 1882, has carried on for eighty years a work concerned more with sowing than with reaping. The quiet work of the Algiers Mission band attracted the genius of Lilias Trotter, whose artistic work had been admired by Ruskin when she was a girl, and whose books were illustrated by the sensitive and charming work of her own hands.

25. The Life of D. M. Thornton was written by W. H. T. Gairdner; that of Temple Gairdner of Cairo by Constance Padwick.

In 1858 David Livingstone still had fifteen years of life before him. In some ways his greatest days were already past. None of his later journeys equalled the splendour of the first, and he failed in the all-consuming ambition of his later years, the discovery of the sources of the Nile. But, when he died on 4 May 1873, on his knees, at Chitambo's village, he had rendered unequalled service to *Africa*: he had laid open its very heart, he had revealed the atrocities of the slave trade, he had directed the attention of the world to Africa. A year before he died he wrote these words:

All I can say in my loneliness is, may Heaven's rich blessing come down on everyone – American, English, or Turk – who will help to heal the open sore of the world.

The world would not forget. Christian forces would move forward, in what was now to become a five-pronged advance, until the whole surface of the continent had been explored and Christian influences brought to bear on every part of it.

Advance northwards from the *south* was continuous, though not with the continuity of an unbroken rhythm. Almost every Church, including the Dutch Reformed Church, became involved in the movement, but where missionaries could settle and what they could do depended on the manifold and changing circumstances of a period in which many things were changing all the time. Some promising ventures ended in disaster – sometimes because missionaries had been imprudent and had failed to make the necessary reconnaissance, but often because a change in the relations between the black man and the white wiped out a settlement or tribe overnight. And at all times missionaries were dependent on the favour or ill-will of the chiefs.

It is hard for the reader today to think himself back into the Africa of a century ago. The chieftainship has in most areas become an honorary or decorative function; the word of other authorities is law. Then the chief was omnipotent and the whole of African life revolved about him. Chiefs were of many kinds. There were the conquerors – almost as destructive in their way, but not on the same scale, as Genghis Khan or Tamerlane – who carved out for themselves an extensive but generally transitory empire. There were the wise and prudent statesmen who held their people together and guided them through the difficult period of the revolution brought about by the coming of the white man. There were those who were no more than local despots, cunning, arbitrary, and unscrupulous, of no importance beyond the limited area to which their words could reach. But in every case the chief's word was law; he had the power of life and death; and, though in many cases the elders were the repositories of the ancestral wisdom and the chief's power was not absolutely unlimited, the limits tended to be theoretical rather than effective. And, unless the chief gave his approval, no white man could hope to take up residence in his territory.

Various motives encouraged chiefs to permit the presence of missionaries among their people. Some were clever enough to recognize that a white man might be useful as a safeguard against the ever-encroaching menace of his fellow-countrymen. Others regarded him merely as a convenient milch-cow[26] from whom endless gifts and tribute could be extracted. Others again liked to have a tame missionary about the place as they might equally well have liked to have a tame elephant. But, whatever the motive, without the approval of the chief residence was impossible, and, even if residence was permitted, the acquisition of land on anything like a permanent tenure was always a matter of the utmost difficulty.

It will be convenient to arrange this part of our history around the personalities of three notable chiefs, of very different types.

Moshesh was the paramount chief of the *Basutos*, and as such had been recognized by the British government. The missionaries of the Paris Society (Société des Missions Évangéliques) had arrived as early as 1833 and had formed an excellent relationship with Moshesh, to whom E. Casalis served almost as a confidential counsellor. The Church began to grow. But difficulties multiplied. The non-Basuto inhabitants of the area were not altogether willing to accept the paramountcy of Moshesh; the last thing that the Boer farmers wanted was a strong African kingdom on their frontier; the British were steadily moving forward and extending their sovereignty northwards. Moshesh was threatened on every side. In 1858 the Boers invaded his country, and two of the mission stations were destroyed. But, through the strength of their own right arm and the mediation of the British, the Basutos were saved at that time from extinction.

It was at this juncture that the older missionaries withdrew, their place being taken by Adolphe Mabille and François Coillard

---

26. I first encountered this phrase in the writings of François Coillard, but no doubt it has been used by many others before and since.

(1834–1904). Many of the missionaries were fine men, but Coillard seemed to stand out above them all; his peculiar combination of patience, persistence, ability to understand the African, humour, and radiant sanctity made him one of the dominant figures on the African scene for forty years. It was he who succeeded to the place of Casalis as confidential adviser to Moshesh. For difficulties constantly broke out. In 1865 the Boers again invaded the country, and would almost certainly have destroyed it had not the British once again intervened and at the desire of Moshesh annexed the country to the British Empire. In 1884 Basutoland was granted the status of a protectorate, which it enjoyed for eighty years.

Moshesh had had dealings with the missionaries for thirty-six years. They had respected him, helped him, and even loved him. He had favoured and supported their work, and by 1872 there were more than 2,000 communicants, and many more believers, in the country. Yet Moshesh had never become a Christian; as chief he was committed to the old ways, and perhaps felt that his conversion would be the beginning of the disintegration of his people. But after the pacification of 1868 the missionaries found him much more open to the Christian message, and at last he announced that he had become a believer and asked for baptism. This was arranged; but he died, old and full of honours, on 11 March 1870, before the baptism had actually taken place. In the words of E. W. Smith: 'For the Basuto it was as if the sun had been blotted from the sky.'[27]

Coillard had laboured in Basutoland for nearly twenty years when it was decided that he should again become a pioneer and should attempt to open a mission on the *Zambezi* among the Barotse, who surprisingly spoke an only slightly divergent form of the language of the Basuto.

Here Coillard had to do with a very different chieftain, Lewanika. Lewanika had already been visited by the Scottish pioneer F. S. Arnot, whom he had liked, and was pleased by the prospect of having the French missionaries. But the process of settlement was long and tedious. To his surprise Coillard found that the procedure was democratic, and that in spite of the general permission given by Lewanika the presence of the missionaries must be approved also by the people. 'If you do not wish for them, fear not to say so, and they will return to their own home. Speak freely; now is your opportunity. Do not say that the king imposes

27. *The Mabilles of Basutoland* (1939), p. 185.

on you a thing you dislike. Speak!' And the chief himself was very far from inspiring the same confidence as Moshesh.

In 1888 Coillard wrote of him that 'there are great contradictions in this man. He is despotic, vindictive, and as cruel as possible, yet, with all that, has good sense, tact, generosity, and amiability. I could easily draw two portraits of him, which would have nothing in common. There is more than one Lewanika in the world.'

The missionaries found the Barotse much less civilized than the Basuto. Their own ranks were thinned by death. As everywhere, political complications and the problem of relations with the white men – eased by the acceptance of the Queen's protection in 1890 – darkened the sky. The attitude of the people towards the Christian message was ambivalent, and Coillard hesitated to baptize enquirers. Yet by degrees the influence began to penetrate. Lewanika introduced a number of beneficent reforms; in 1895 he omitted from his programme his annual state visit to the shrine of Mboho, the first Barotse king – an event which led Coillard to comment:

It was in his mind and in the eyes of the people a significant sign of the times, an indication that the old national customs were falling into desuetude, to give rights of citizenship to Christianity.[28]

When Coillard died in 1904, the outlook was still dark in many ways; but it was certain that the Church of Barotseland would 'take root downward and bear fruit upward'.

The greatest and deservedly most famous of all the African Christian chiefs was Khama Boikano of the Bamangwato in *Bechuanaland*. The first missionaries in this area were the Lutherans of the Hermannsburg Mission, who, not being British, were congenial to the Boers of the Transvaal Republic. On 6 May 1862 Khama, the eldest son of the chief Sekhome, was baptized on profession of faith by the missionary H. C. Schulenberg.[29] In 1865 Sekhome, when about to visit the camp of the young men being prepared for tribal initiation, was chagrined to discover that not one of his five sons was prepared to accompany him, as was customary on these occasions. Khama in particular was the object of his father's anger; he was driven out, and for a time kept under

---

28. *On the Threshold of Central Africa* (1897), p. 595.

29. After a short period, the Hermannsburg mission was replaced by the LMS, which was destined to be very closely associated with the destinies of Bechuanaland.

siege in a rocky fastness. But nothing would shake his Christian constancy, and in the end (1872) he succeeded to the chieftainship, which he was to hold for just over fifty years until his death in 1923.

To be a Christian and a chief is in Africa no easy thing: the dignity of a chief is measured by the number of his wives; he is officially the leader in the cult of the ancestors; he is the rainmaker of his people in time of drought. It is characteristic of Khama that, when the rain failed, he arranged for long and earnest services of intercession to be held in church, and himself took part in them. He was an almost fanatical campaigner against every form of alcoholic drink, imported or local, having seen the harm that drunkenness had caused among his people, and being convinced that the African had not yet reached the level of self-control which makes moderate drinking possible.

In 1885 Britain had declared a Protectorate over Bechuanaland up to the river Motopo; on 27 September 1892 it was announced that this was understood to include Khama's territory. In 1895 Cecil Rhodes, filled with ambitious plans for his great dominion in Central Africa, wished to include Bechuanaland in the domain administered by the British South Africa Company. To this Khama, who was happy under the protection of the Queen, objected, and his objection was supported by the London Mission. With two other chiefs Khama visited London and was received by Queen Victoria; his fine bearing and Christian character made a deep impression on all who met him. Nothing more was heard of the proposed transfer, and Rhodes – who was 'a good hater, violent when thwarted' – was duly incensed.

Khama's accession to the chieftainship was followed by the movement of a great many people into the Church. Yet there was always something ambiguous about this honoured and honourable Christian figure. He loved his people and was greatly concerned about their welfare; if loyalty to Christ and loyalty to his people ever came into conflict, to which side would he incline? Two sapient judgements on this man may help to make clear the dilemma which no Christian ruler in Africa can wholly escape. Dr N. Goodall writes:

For fifty years he was paramount chief of an important tribe. The son of a savage ancestry, he exercised among his own people the reforming leadership of a moral puritan, and dealt with modern governments with dignity and rectitude. More than any other African leader of his time, he compelled men, through his essential greatness, to recognize that 'protecting' Africans was not simply a matter of the strong protecting the weak; it was also a question of according the freedom and opportunity rightfully due to those who had their own distinctive contribution to make to the common weal.[30]

F. H. Hawkins, the Foreign Secretary of the LMS, who was in Bechuanaland in 1912, wrote:

He is a very astute man. Although no one can doubt the sincerity of his Christian profession, and his attachment to the Church at Serowe, the predominant consideration with him is the strengthening of the position of his tribe. I think there can be no doubt that it is his desire to play the Society, the Government, and the traders off against each other, with a view to the advancement of what he believes to be the interests of the tribe.[31]

These wise words give a living picture of the situation not only of Khama, but of many others who have been perplexed by the sometimes conflicting demands of a double loyalty.

In *West Africa*, the progress of discovery and the establishment of Western domination went hand in hand. The British government throughout showed extreme reluctance to annex any fresh territory or to accept any new imperial responsibilities. Only unwillingly, and under the pressure of an apparently irresistible series of events, was Nigeria declared in 1900 to be integrally a part of the British Empire. Spain and Portugal did not add to their traditional possessions. The French suffered no such inhibitions: their dreams of grandeur prompted them to take over everything in Africa that came within their reach; they were moved by a colonizing and civilizing passion to which there is hardly any parallel in human history. Germany had to be pacified, generously, with bits and pieces that were left.

The chaos produced by this imperial bargaining is well reflected in the Christian history of the *Cameroons*. Protestant history begins with the English Baptist Alfred Saker, who moved across from Fernando Po in 1858, and has to his credit the translation of the Bible into Douala (1872) and the first ascent of the Cameroons Mountain (13,500 feet) in the company, surprisingly, of Sir Richard Burton. When the Germans took over, it seemed wise to hand over the work to the Basel Mission, though not all the 'English Baptists' agreed to become 'Swiss Reformed'. Many of the

30. *A History of the London Missionary Society, 1895–1945* (1954), p. 259.
31. Quoted in N. Goodall, op. cit., p. 286.

older Christians in the Cameroons still speak German. But when in 1918 the French expelled the Germans, French became the common language, and the Basel Mission yielded to the Paris Society. Thus are Gospel and politics inextricably intertwined in Africa.

In 1864 the Church Missionary Society decided on a great new adventure – a purely African mission under an African bishop. We have already met Samuel Adjai Crowther (p. 259), the man who was chosen for this task. The consecration in Canterbury Cathedral of the freed slave boy as the first non-European bishop of the Anglican Communion aroused considerable enthusiasm.[32] Crowther was to work in Eastern Nigeria, principally on the river Niger, and was left a free hand in developing the work.

Crowther was sent off without any European help or support. He had to rely on Sierra Leonean helpers, not all of whom were well qualified or reliable. The Bishop had long been separated from his native country. He never learned an east-Nigerian language, and was dependent upon unsatisfactory interpreters. At the time of his consecration in 1864 he was already elderly,[33] and at his death in 1891 he was a very old man. Crowther was a faithful and pious Christian, and some good foundations were laid. The occupation of Bonny by his son Dandeson (later archdeacon) was the beginning of what is now the diocese of the Niger Delta. But when the old Bishop died things were found to be in a state of great confusion, and grave irregularities in the conduct of many of his helpers came to light. The Society reconstituted the mission as a joint African-European venture. There was strong feeling in Lagos, because Crowther's successor as bishop was not an African. Three successive European bishops followed over fifty years and in that period African assistant bishops served with great faithfulness, but only at the end of it was the full charge of a diocese again committed into the hands of an African bishop.

'On the 9th of August 1877, the 999th day from the date of our departure from Zanzibar, we prepared to greet the van of civilization.' So wrote Henry Morton Stanley just as he was about to conclude the tremendous journey, which was to solve the problem

---

32. The University of Oxford distinguished itself by giving Crowther the honorary degree of Doctor of Divinity. Fifty-six years later, Cambridge, for reasons inscrutable to the ordinary man, created the Indian Bishop Azariah honorary Doctor of Laws.

33. The date of his birth is unknown – it was probably not later than 1807.

of the Congo and with it the final mystery of the configuration of the interior of Africa. Speke, Burton, Grant, and Baker had discovered the sources of the Nile. Nile, Niger, Zambezi, and Congo – now all were reasonably well known. Where the explorer had penetrated, it was certain that the missionary would penetrate too; and the missionary would be followed by the trader, and the trader by the government official.

It had been a terrible journey.

The greatest danger [to quote Stanley again], an ever-recurring one, is that which we have to encounter each time the wild howling cannibal aborigines observe us. Indeed the sense of security is short-lived and our pleasure evanescent; but the sense of danger is always present and pervades our mind whether in our sleeping or our waking hours.[34]

Stanley was much less averse than Livingstone from firing upon Africans; but it is doubtful whether even Livingstone could have made his way through to the sea without having to fight for his life.

This was the unpromising region, a million square miles of it, the last great unknown area of the world, which that enterprising ruler Leopold II of the Belgians was to annex under the guise of the Congo Independent State and to rule as, in fact, his private property, until at last in 1909 personal rule passed over into the responsible sovereignty of the Belgian government.

Hardly had news of Stanley's achievement reached England, when evangelical forces were preparing to use the great river as the means of access to the heart of Africa. First in the field was the interdenominational and independent Livingstone Inland Mission. This was eager and adventurous but without the needed staying power, and soon passed out of the picture. Access to the interior was really secured in 1884, when the English Baptists reached the upper river, and placed a steamer on the thousand miles of navigable Congo between Stanley Pool and Stanley Falls. It was their strategy rapidly to set up a series of stations at intervals of about a hundred miles between these two points; by the end of the century this aim had almost been achieved. In the meantime the American Presbyterians, who had at first settled in the lowlands near the mouth of the river, also moved inland, and they in turn were followed by a host of other missions, mainly of American origin.

34. *Journal* for 6 February 1877; cited in H. M. Stanley, *Through the Dark Continent* (1878), Vol. II, 281.

No sooner had a settlement been effected, than the missionaries began to experience the difficulties of life in a tribal area. The last thing they desired was to create a new and separate Africa; yet again and again they found themselves the centre of a new settlement, made up of freed slave children, of men who for some reason had lost their identity with their tribe, of criminals fleeing from justice (murderers not excluded!), and of young men who wished to learn the skills which only the white man could teach. Willy-nilly, the missionary had become a chief. As Dan Crawford picturesquely expressed it:

Many a little Protestant Pope in the lonely bush is forced by his self-imposed isolation to be prophet, priest, and king rolled into one – really a very big duck he, in his own private pond. . . . Quite seriously, he is forced to be a bit of a policeman, muddled up in matters not even remotely in his sphere.[35]

The life in these settlements was orderly, diligent, and far superior to anything that the Africans could see in their own villages. Yet this was a ghetto existence, and the increasing separation of African Christians from their kind could become a grave obstacle to the spread of the Gospel in the Congo.

The great break-through took place when it became possible to send out African Christians to live as evangelists in the villages. At the start segregation had been inevitable and right. The man who lived in the unbroken tradition of tribal life was committed to customs which were incompatible with any degree of Christian conviction: when a chief died, slaves had to be buried with him; the wives of a dead man automatically passed into the possession of his brother. But the evangelist who had lived for a time in a mission village had established the necessary distance; he could now live in African society without being submerged by it. The system of village evangelists was developed everywhere in the Protestant missions, first, and with greatest success, at Luebo among the Baluba, the centre of the American Presbyterian Mission. The Kasai region is thickly populated. In 1904 Luebo already had forty out-stations, each provided with a literate evangelist. Church membership, which in 1904 stood at 3,000, by 1911 had increased to 7,000.

A different situation obtained in the *Katanga*, not far from the Rhodesian border, where the Scottish pioneer F. S. Arnot had been

35. *Thinking Black* (1912), pp. 324–5.

made welcome in 1886 by the powerful local tyrant Msiri (also spelt Msidi and Mushidi). Here and here alone in the Congo missionaries were able to establish themselves as the chief's white men, in constant attendance on his court. This situation had its drawbacks. Other white visitors to Katanga sharply criticized the attitude of the missionaries to the chief, and the helplessness to which it reduced them. Thus the English vice-consul Sharpe wrote in 1890:

The missionaries treat Msidi as a great king, do nothing without first asking his permission, are at his beck and call, almost his slaves; he sends for them continually for trivial things, and they meekly submit. They dared not come to see me on my arrival for several days, because Msidi told them not to come! They live like natives, on corn porridge, and occasionally stinking meat.

But in Africa patience tells. The day of the missionaries was yet to come. In 1890 Dan Crawford arrived, with others of the Plymouth Brethren persuasion, to begin a remarkable sojourn of twenty-two years in tropical Africa without a break. His attitude and his method are succinctly expressed in the title of his book, *Thinking Black, Twenty-two Years without a Break in the Long Grass of Central Africa* (1912). In a remarkable way Crawford managed to think himself into the African point of view, and so gained in a memorable degree the confidence of the Africans. As long as the tyrant Msiri lived, not much could be done; but the end of Msiri was to be sharp and sudden.

In December 1891 an expedition under Captain Stairs, who though British was in the service of the Belgian Compagnie du Katanga, arrived in Msiri's capital Bunkeya. In a hot dispute Captain Bodson, one of Stairs's assistants, shot the chief, and was immediately mortally wounded by Msiri's bodyguard. It is recorded that as he lay dying he murmured: 'Thank God, my death will not be in vain. I have delivered Africa from one of her most detestable tyrants.'

In the chaos that followed, and during the disturbed period that led up to the establishment of European rule, the perplexed and scattered people found in the missionaries their only friends. Thousands turned to them, and became open as never before to the message which the missionaries desired to impart. Crawford complained sadly that 'the stupid and mischievous notion has got currency that since Msiri's death *we* are the chiefs of the country'. The notion may have been stupid and mischievous, but it was none the less true. Crawford was *Konga Vantu*, the gatherer of the peoples, and he could not evade his new responsiblities. Eventually he led his people away from the scene of Msiri's exploits and infamies, and founded a new Christian city, Luanza, on the northern shore of Lake Mweru, where tribal differences were to be forgotten, and all were to live in fellowship as the children of one Father.

The penetration of Africa from the *east* has always proved particularly difficult. Apart from the natural obstacles the presence everywhere of the Arab slave trader set barriers in the way of any European penetration. Less than a century has passed since most of the peoples of East Africa first saw the face of a white man.

One of the first consequences of Livingstone's famous speech in Cambridge was the formation of the Universities Mission to Central Africa. Its first aim was penetration by way of the Zambezi to the highlands of the Shire, where Livingstone had assured the pioneers that living conditions would be favourable for white men, and that there was an open field for the preaching of the Gospel. Enthusiasm was unbounded. It was decided that, contrary to the former practice of Anglican missions, this mission should have a bishop at its head from the start; and Charles Frederick Mackenzie, a good and humble man, was consecrated in Cape Town on New Year's Day 1861 as bishop of an undefined diocese somewhere in Central Africa. On 7 February 1862 the party was at the mouth of the Zambezi.

Then everything went wrong. Livingstone showed his characteristic defects as an organizer, and his directions were not as clear as they might have been. The mission was ill served by its intermediaries. Without anyone to guide them as to African realities, the missionaries too soon became engaged in the complex business of freeing slaves (sometimes at the cost of violence) and in the internecine conflicts of local politics. In less than a year Mackenzie was dead, soon to be followed by others of the party. Mackenzie's successor as bishop, William George Tozer, an impatient man, wrote impatiently to Archbishop Gray in Cape Town that 'the Zambezi has proved in every way a miserable failure, and the selection of it for English missionary work can only be due to the blindest enthusiasm', and decided to withdraw the whole mission to Zanzibar. Livingstone was incensed at what he regarded as timorous and pusillanimous retreat. No doubt the plan *reculer pour mieux sauter* was in the circumstances wise; but the *sauter* took a very long time – not till twenty-four years after the death of Mackenzie did the steamer for which he had hoped sail the waters of Lake Nyasa. The worshipper in the cathedral on Likoma Island today may too easily forget the price paid by the pioneers; *tantae molis erat Romanam condere gentem*.[36]

The evangelization of the interior of East Africa on a large scale became possible only when the CMS in one heroic bound leaped over the intervening territories and landed in *Uganda*. The first white men to penetrate Uganda were the explorers Speke and Grant, who arrived in 1862, and made a favourable impression on King Mutesa, then about twenty-three years old:

I have not heard a white man tell a lie yet. Speke came here, behaved well, and went his way home with his brother Grant. They bought no slaves, and the time they were in Uganda they were very good.[37]

On 5 April 1875, Henry Morton Stanley arrived and was received by Mutesa. Finding that Islam had preceded him and was gaining strength, Stanley – still deeply under the influence of Livingstone, whom he had 'found' at Ujiji on 10 November 1871 – took upon him the unaccustomed role of a missionary, and set himself to impress on Mutesa's mind the truths of the Christian religion. He did more. He wrote a memorable letter, which appeared in the *Daily Telegraph* on 15 November 1875, appealing for missionaries. Generally it takes a long time for anything to happen in the Christian world, but on this occasion Victorian England reacted with its customary gigantic vigour. The first missionaries of the CMS were at Zanzibar on 26 June 1876; the advance guard reached Kampala on 30 June 1877 and were received by Mutesa two days later. In November 1878 the most famous of the pioneers, the Scottish engineer Alexander Mackay, arrived.

The missionaries found the Baganda a stalwart, intelligent, and lovable people. Although they had lived, until the arrival of the Arabs in 1844, almost completely isolated from the world, they had reached a high level of craftsmanship, and had worked out for themselves an ordered and effective social system. This is not to say that their civilization was perfect; it depended on the sacral power of the ruler, on whose arbitrary sway hardly any limits were

36. The history of this tragic year has been beautifully and movingly recorded by Owen Chadwick in *Mackenzie's Grave* (1959).

37. H. M. Stanley is the source of this report of Mutesa's words.

imposed. Mutesa was a shrewd and not unkindly man, yet hardly a day passed on which he did not doom one or more of his subjects to summary execution, and in the course of his life he acquired a larger collection of wives than any other human being of whom we have record. Standing already perplexed between the claims of the old African way of life, of Islam, of Anglican Christianity, Mutesa had to endure a fourth perplexity in the arrival of French Roman Catholic missionaries. The rivalries between the missionaries and the hatreds between their followers, culminating in a great civil war, form a grievous and highly unedifying chapter in missionary history. Peace returned only when the efforts of Captain (later Lord) Lugard (1858–1945), and of the friends of the mission in England, at last led to the establishment in 1894 of the British protectorate over the country, and its peaceable division into spheres of Protestant and Roman Catholic influence.

Both missions had their ups and downs. The first Anglican baptism, of five young men, took place on 18 March 1882. But on 9 October 1884 Mutesa died, and was succeeded by his eighteen-year-old son Mwanga; and then the trouble began. The Anglican bishop, James Hannington, made the mistake of attempting to enter Uganda from the east, through Busoga, the traditional approach of the enemy; this aroused the deepest suspicions of the Baganda, already inclined to think that the white men had come to eat their country. By orders of Mwanga the Bishop was speared to death on 29 October 1885, the very day on which Mackay finished the revision of St Matthew's Gospel in Luganda. Even earlier than this, Mwanga had turned in savage fury on some of his Christian subjects. This was not perhaps religious persecution in the strictest sense of the term. Mwanga had learned the practice of sodomy from the Arabs: the young converts of both missions had learned from their missionary friends that this would not do, and it was the refusal of these boys to make themselves available to the passions of their master that roused him to his paroxysms of fury – it was incredible that any African subject should resist his chief in anything. The first three martyrs were roasted over a slow fire on 30 January 1885. The greatest violence took place in May and June 1886, culminating in the burning in one great pyre of thirty-two young men. The exact number of the martyrs is not known; all witnesses bear testimony to the courage and serenity with which they met their death. One visitor at least, standing by the martyrs' cross a little way out of Kampala, has found himself more deeply moved than in any other place on earth; on that occasion the Bishop of the diocese of Uganda profoundly remarked: 'If it came to it, I think the Baganda would be ready to die for Christ today; it is living for him that they find difficult.'

Mwanga was banished. A railway was built from the coast. The country began to develop. The missions pulled themselves together. Converts began to come in, in hundreds and then in thousands. By March 1896 the Anglicans were able to record 6,905 baptized members of the Church, and over 50,000 'inquirers'.

Nothing is more remarkable in the early history of the Uganda Church than the evangelistic zeal by which its Christians were inspired. The kingdom of Buganda, the home of the Baganda,[38] had lived in anything but fellowship with its neighbouring kingdoms. But almost the first thing that the Baganda Christians realized was that the Gospel which was good for them was good also for everyone else. Baganda teachers were the pioneers in the kingdoms of Unyoro, Toro, and Koki. Most famous of all these pioneers was Apolo Kivebulaya, later canon of the cathedral in Kampala, the story of whose heroic witness and sufferings is a modern epic. From his westerly station in Toro, Apolo pressed on into the primeval forest, and won the confidence of the shy and dangerous pygmy people. His greatest achievement was the translation of St Mark's Gospel, apparently from the Lunyoro version, into the pygmy language; using his work, linguistic science was at last able to answer the question whether the pygmies had a language of their own.

Bishop Alfred Robert Tucker (1849–1914), who served the Church in Uganda from 1893 to 1911, faced with the great movement of peoples into the Church, very early began to concern himself with the problem of the emerging African Church. He was perhaps the very first missionary statesman to see clearly the true lineaments of a Church which should be everyman's Church, and in which national and foreigner should serve together on a basis of perfect spiritual equality. His plan for the Native Anglican Church, put forward in 1897, was to a large extent shattered by the inveterate opposition of the missionaries. As the number of missionaries increased they had dug themselves in, in a position of superiority, as rulers and directors; and they appear to have been incapable of the great imaginative effort involved in seeing themselves as servants of the local Church in real fellowship with

38. Each of whom, of course, is a Muganda, and speaks Luganda, and lives in what is now the independent land of Uganda, of which Buganda is a part.

Africans. Only a part of Tucker's vision could be realized during his time as Bishop of Uganda; for him, however, the vision never faded, and he was able to communicate it to others. It has become a permanent part of the structure of missionary thinking about the Church.

In the general distribution of the goods and persons of Africans among the European nations, the area now known as *Tanganyika* fell to the Germans, and naturally this colonial association provided an open door for German Lutheran missions. Their great work among the Chagga in the neighbourhood of Mount Kilimanjaro produced in time a prosperous, civilized, and almost wholly Christian people. But the CMS had long since had its station at Mpwapwa, a kind of coaching inn on the way to Uganda, and in course of time spread out widely on the plateau.

The southern and eastern parts of the country were the field of the UMCA. *Nyasaland* was divided between the UMCA and the Scots, the two great Presbyterian Churches of Scotland coming in with a wonderful array of enterprises – evangelistic, medical, educational, industrial, and agricultural, certainly among the best organized mission projects in the world (Blantyre 1877, Livingstonia 1881).[39]

The turn of *Kenya* came rather late. The Christianization of the densely populated lake region began when Mr (later Bishop) J. J. Willis sailed across the Victoria Nyanza from Uganda, and, in default of a church, held the first baptism under a tree at Maseno (1908). Anglicans spread inwards from the coast, accompanied by United Methodists and Presbyterians, and later by the Africa Inland Mission, the American Friends, the Salvation Army, and a great many other Christian bodies. Kenya, like the other East African territories, is now the home of great and rapidly growing African Churches.

It remains to look at one more of the great routes of access to the interior of Africa, the Nile. On 26 January 1885 General Charles George Gordon, isolated in Khartoum and abandoned too long through the pusillanimity of Gladstone's government, was speared to death by the exultant hosts of the Mahdi. The white man was long in coming back. It was not until 2 September 1898 that Sir

39. The joint work of the Free Church of Scotland, the United Presbyterians, and the Free Presbyterians had begun in 1876; after five years what became the permanent headquarters of the mission was chosen and given the name Livingstonia.

Herbert Kitchener won the battle of Omdurman and broke for ever the power of the successor of the Mahdi. Only a year later two CMS missionaries, Dr F. Harpur and the Reverend Llewellyn Gwynne, arrived to see what they could do. Not much was possible in Muslim Khartoum and its neighbourhood; the great opportunity came much further south, where the American Presbyterians were first in the field, to be followed shortly after by the CMS. Here the missionaries found themselves among the fine and untouched pagan tribes – the Dinkas, among whom a man less than six feet tall might be considered a dwarf; the Shilluk who spend long days happily dreaming of their cattle; the Bari; and many others. These peoples proved to be splendid material for Christian work. By 1914 the first-fruits of what have grown to be considerable Churches had been gathered in.

Bishop A. M. Gelsthorpe, who had served in Nigeria and was later Bishop of Khartoum, once explained the difference between East and West Africa in the following terms: in the West, the African's first picture of the white man was of someone who wanted to sell him gin; in the Sudan, his first impression of the white man was General Gordon. Gordon found a worthy successor in Llewellyn Gwynne (1863–1957), consecrated in 1908 to be Bishop of Khartoum. Gwynne was marked by the same fearlessness, the same utter integrity and Christian principle, the same resolute determination that justice must be done to all, and that there must be no distinction between black and brown and white.[40]

American Protestants, unlike most other Christians, have never had any hesitation over proselytizing work in nominally Roman Catholic countries, and treat such efforts as 'missions' without distinction from missions in non-Christian countries. Quite naturally, therefore, they have regarded Mexico, the Caribbean region, and South America as mission fields. Anglicans and Lutherans have in the main confined their efforts to those of their respective communions who have settled in Latin America. American Methodists, Presbyterians, Baptists, and others, in contrast, have come in, in large numbers, with the express purpose of 'converting' Roman Catholics. For this there is a measure of justification. Roman Catholic writers admit that the conversion of many of the aboriginal peoples was superficial in the extreme; and

40. The Life of Bishop Gwynne has been written by H. C. Jackson, *Pastor on the Nile* (1960).

in recent years the shortage of priests has been such that for many of the inhabitants there is extremely little chance of any real instruction in the tenets of the Roman Catholic faith.

It would be unprofitable to enumerate all the countries of this area, and the various Protestant bodies which work in them. Two countries, *Brazil* and *Colombia*, may be taken as specimens of the kind of thing that has happened.

In 1855 Dr Robert Kelley settled in Rio de Janeiro to begin an independent Congregational work under the title *Help for Brazil*, and managed to maintain himself for twenty years in the face of considerable and natural opposition from the local hierarchy. The American Methodists began work among the Brazilian population in 1876. The Presbyterians had come in 1859, and by 1888 were able to form the Presbyterian Church of Brazil. Their most notable achievement was the founding of the Mackenzie Institute in São Paulo, the only Protestant institution in South America to attain to university status. The Protestant Episcopal Church of the USA, diverging from the usual Anglican pattern, took up work in 1889 in the extreme south of the country. In 1898 Lucien Kinsolving was consecrated as bishop of what he intended to be an independent Brazilian episcopal Church. Unfortunately the authorities in the United States, tied to an inflexible and unimaginative system, reduced the Brazilian Church to dependent and colonial status, an anomaly which up till the time of writing has not been rectified.[41]

Colombia became independent of Spain in 1819, but it still retains a strong sense of its continuity with İberian culture. The non-European (Indian and Negro) elements in the population are smaller than in almost any other Latin American country. The hold of the Roman Catholic Church on the population is particularly strong. The first Protestant visitor appears to have been James Thompson, an agent of the British and Foreign Bible Society, who spent some time in the country in 1825. At first he received a warm welcome; but before long the hostility of the Roman Catholic authorities made it impossible for him to remain. In 1856 the Presbyterian Church of the USA arrived, and has carried on work ever since. Its educational programme has been notable, and, though the number of adherents has never been

41. The latest information is that plans are in hand for restoring to the Brazilian Church what it ought never to have lost, the status of an independent national Church within the Anglican family of Churches.

large, the work is vigorous and independent, and increasingly under Colombian leadership.

By the end of the period covered by this chapter, Protestant work had been established in all the republics of Central and South America, in Mexico, and in all the main islands of the Caribbean. But this was still the day of small things; in 1914 probably there were not more than 500,000 Protestants in the whole of this area of otherwise unbroken Roman Catholicism.

The Anglican South American Missionary Society, true to its policy of working only among non-Christians, extended its work widely among Indian peoples which the Roman Catholic Church had never reached.

With the Spanish conquest of *Chile*, the Araucanian Indians withdrew to the far south, a land of cold and rain. They were never conquered, and the Roman Catholic Church made only fitful attempts to follow them. The Anglicans came in, and for many years successfully carried on a work the value of which has been frequently commended by the government.

In *Paraguay* the same mission advanced into the Chaco, perhaps the least attractive area in the whole habitable earth. Even government agents feared to go among the untamed and violent Lenguas. In 1889 W. Barbrooke Grubb, a lay missionary, penetrated the area, made friends with the Indians, learned their language, and exercised so great an influence that he was given by the government of Paraguay itself the high-sounding title of *Pacificador de los Indios*. He reckoned that eleven years passed before he and his companions were fluent in the Lengua tongue, and seventeen years before the baptism of the first convert. In 1910 he was able to report that

where formerly it was dangerous for the white man to go without an armed party, anyone can now wander alone and unharmed, so far as any risk from the Indians may be apprehended, over a district rather larger than Ireland. From out a chaotic mass of savage heathenism we have now, by the aid of Divine power, the satisfaction of having admitted into the Church of Christ 149 Lenguas, and of this number there are no fewer than thirty-five communicants.

At the other end of the great American land mass lived the Eskimos, maintaining existence by restless ingenuity and skill in a climate in which those of other races would probably die within a week. The Eskimos of Canada were not an unknown people; but whereas, as we have seen, the Gospel had long been preached to the Eskimos of Greenland, no attempt seems to have been made in Canada till the CMS entered in, in 1876. The first missionary, Edmund Peck, had been a sailor – no bad preparation for the work that he had to do. His first station was Little Whale River on Hudson's Bay. In 1890 he started work at Blacklead Island in Cumberland Bay, and two years later on the far side of the Arctic Circle. Simultaneously approaches were being made to the Eskimos west of Hudson's Bay.

The most vivid pictures of life among the Eskimo come from the pen of Archibald Lang Fleming (1883–1953), later to be famous as 'Archibald the Arctic', the first Anglican bishop of the Arctic region.[42] His first winter in the north, 1909–10, was spent living in an igloo with two Eskimo families. His modest comment on this situation runs as follows:

Life in a crowded hut had many obvious disadvantages. The foetid atmosphere was sickening, and the acrid smoke from the blubber lamps was not an aromatic disinfectant, though when it caused us discomfort the hole in the roof was cleared and a better circulation of air was created . . . What Commander Peary wrote of Eskimo dwellings was true: 'A night in one of these igloos, with a family at home, is an offence to every civilized sense.'[43]

Far worse was to follow. The whole settlement at Kinguckjuak almost died of starvation. At the last possible moment for survival, the wind changed, the hunters were able to find walrus, and the danger passed away. Fleming comments:

because we had been so closely linked with the people in their days of strain and adversity, and because we had helped them to the limit of our own resources, we discovered a brotherhood of feeling and action which drew us together as nothing else could have done and made us feel an at-one-ness which we had not known before.[44]

In 1960 about 80 per cent of all the Eskimos in Canada were faithful Anglican Christians.

In 1910 the first World Missionary Conference was held at Edinburgh. This was not, in fact, the first but the fourth international assembly convened for the consideration of missionary affairs. It had been preceded by conferences in Liverpool (1860),

42. His book is called *Archibald the Arctic* (1957).
43. op. cit. p. 79.
44. op. cit. p. 83.

London (1885), and New York (1900). But Edinburgh 1910 surpassed all others in the meticulous care with which it had been prepared; in its character as an assembly for careful and scientific thought and not merely for the edification of the faithful and the expression of Christian enthusiasm; and in the steps which it took to secure the permanence of Christian co-operation in the future, to which further reference will have to be made in another context. More than 1,200 representatives had come together from all the world. It is to be noted that the Roman Catholic and Orthodox Churches took no part in the proceedings, that the delegates had come as representatives of missionary societies and not of Churches, and that only eighteen among them were from the younger Churches. Yet it was an impressive gathering, the like of which had never before been seen in Christian history.

The chairman of the conference was the American Methodist layman John Raleigh Mott (1865–1955), who, though he was never a missionary, was destined to play a leading part in all Protestant missionary affairs for fifty years. His name was associated with the slogan through which he had given inspiration to the Student Volunteer Movement for Foreign Missions in the 1880s and 1890s: 'The Evangelization of the World in this Generation.' This was still very much in the air at Edinburgh 1910. It attracted much enthusiastic support, and much criticism – mostly from those who had not taken the trouble to ascertain what the slogan meant. Gustav Warneck, the German founder of the science of missiology, persisted in supposing that it implied a rapid and superficial preaching of the Gospel in wide areas without time for the needed consolidation. Others, confusing evangelization with conversion, supposed that it represented a naïve American dream that the whole world could be made Christian in thirty years. A reference to the literature produced between 1885 and 1910 shows that all such criticism was misdirected.

The slogan was based on an unexceptionable theological principle – that each generation of Christians bears responsibility for the contemporary generation of non-Christians in the world, and that it is the business of each such generation of Christians to see to it, as far as lies within its power, that the Gospel is clearly preached to every single non-Christian in the same generation. This is a universal and permanent obligation; it applies to Christian witness both within what is commonly called Christendom and beyond it. If the principle is to be rejected, the New Testament must first be rewritten.

Secondly, in formulating his slogan Mott took into account the continually rising curve of missionary endeavour, and the hope that the curve might continue to rise similarly. He could point to a number of great achievements in the preceding century:

1. Though some countries, such as Tibet and Afghanistan, remained closed, missionaries had been able to find a footing in every part of the known world.

2. The back of the pioneer work had been broken. Languages had been learned and reduced to writing; all the main living languages of the world had by now received at least the New Testament.

3. Tropical medicine had solved most of the problems of disease, and made possible the prolonged residence of the white man even in the most unfavourable climates.

4. Every religion in the world had yielded some converts as a result of missionary preaching.

5. No race of men had been found which was incapable of understanding the Gospel, though some were more ready to receive it than others.

6. The missionary no longer stood alone; an increasing army of nationals stood ready to assist him.

7. The younger Churches were beginning to produce leaders at least the equals of the missionary in intellectual gifts and spiritual stature.

8. The Churches had become engaged, as never before, in the support of the missionary enterprise.

9. Financial support had kept pace with the rapid expansion of the work in every part of the world.

10. The universities of the West were producing a steady stream of men and women of the highest potential for missionary work.

11. The influence of the Christian Gospel was spreading far beyond the ranks of those who had actually accepted it.

12. Intransigent opposition to the Gospel seemed in many countries, such as China and Japan, finally to have broken down.

Comparison between the state of missions in 1810, in 1860, and in 1910 seemed to justify the hope that very rapid expansion might not be beyond the powers of the Western Churches. It was not unreasonable to expect that the strength of the Western missionary force might be trebled in thirty years, that the Church in many parts of the world would at least double itself within that period, and that the number of national Christian workers might multiply itself fourfold. A striking force of 45,000 missionaries, supported by ten times that number of national workers, would be a very far from negligible army.

All the dreams of Edinburgh 1910 have not been fulfilled. Yet, when we consider what has been achieved in spite of the disasters of two world wars, it is clear that the men and women of Edinburgh 1910 were not idle dreamers; they had both feet firmly planted on the ground.

But Edinburgh 1910 marked, more than was realized by most of those present at it, in many respects the end of an epoch. The Christian cause was to go forward through many bitter experiences of frustration, and many bright hopes would not be realized. The Protestant Christian forces of the world would never again assemble in quite such a spirit of high-hearted joy and confidence. But they were right to rejoice. After all, Professor K. S. Latourette had excellent grounds for giving the title 'The Great Century' to that period in the history of the Church which came to an end in 1914.

11

Rome, the Orthodox, and the World, 1815–1914

At the end of the eighteenth century we saw the Roman Catholic missions in a lamentable situation of decadence and almost collapse. The liquidation of the Jesuit Order had dealt them a deadly blow, and no resources were available to replace the more than 2,000 Jesuits who had had to leave their chosen work. Yet worse was to follow. The French Revolution had paralysed the French Church through outward hardship and inner dissension, making impossible the choosing and sending out of any missionaries. Napoleon occupied himself in harrying one unfortunate Pope, Pius VI (1717–99), to death, and alternately fascinating and infuriating another, Pius VII (1740–1823). It seemed impossible that the papacy should ever recover from this heartrending debility; weakness at the centre was reflected everywhere on the circumference. It is the astonishing fact that, when in 1805 Napoleon decided to reconstitute the three French missionary Orders, which like all other religious Orders had been dissolved, the Fathers of the Holy Spirit were not more than ten in number, the great Paris Society of Foreign Missions had only thirty-nine priests in its service, the Lazarists had thirty-three missionaries overseas, and there were also about forty Fathers of the Faith. The missionaries of the Paris Society were to fall as low as twenty-eight in 1832. It is said that at the end of the Napoleonic period there were not more than twenty missionary priests in the whole of India, supported by an Indian clergy which was inadequate in numbers and not always very reputable in character.[1]

This gloomy picture gives hardly an indication of the great new spiritual forces that were germinating below the surface, and were to manifest themselves gloriously in the course of the century. Napoleon ought to have known that it never pays to make martyrs. By humiliating the Pope, he had elevated the papacy. The sympathy of the world was drawn to the good old man, so cruelly harried from pillar to post by unsympathetic captors. And the

---

1. Mgr Delacroix gives the total number of European Roman Catholic priests at work at that time in all the missions of the world as about 300 (*Histoire universelle*, Vol. III, p. 170).

courteous insistence of Pius VII on maintaining his rights, though even so some thought that he had gone too far in making concessions to Napoleon, left an impression of sober and Christian dignity. Many circumstances in fact combined to restore the prestige of the papacy and to raise it to a height such as it had never attained before. The very fact that so many things had been destroyed added a halo of new sanctity and value to the things that had been left. In the harsh and unfriendly world that was developing all around them, Roman Catholics in every part of it tended to turn more and more to the Vatican and to the Pope, as to that centre which had been raised by providence above the storms and passions of human disputes. The papacy was at last able, gradually and cautiously, to move forward to that centralization of control which had always eluded it in the past. The charm and ability of the two great Popes, Pius IX and Leo XIII, whose long reigns (1846–78 and 1878–1903) between them covered more than the second half of the century, helped forward the process. Quite apart from the propaganda of passionate ultramontanes such as Louis Veuillot and Cardinal Manning, the nineteenth century was the century of ultramontanism. Even if the Vatican Council had not crowned the Pope with infallibility, irresistible forces of history would have raised him to a height of influence such as is not enjoyed by any other man on earth. In the course of this chapter we shall have occasion to note again and again the way in which the cause of missions was forwarded by the personal initiatives of the popes.

Almost the first act of Pius VII on returning to Rome (1814) was the re-establishment of the Jesuit Order by the Bull *Sollicitudo omnium Ecclesiarum*. Clement XIV had declared in his Bull of 1773 that no subsequent Pope should ever at any future date undo what he had done, but in point of fact no Pope has ever admitted any such limitation on his freedom through any action by a predecessor. The dissolution of 1773 had not brought the Order completely to an end. Jesuits had managed to maintain a partly open, partly surreptitious existence in Germany, Austria, and Poland; it was not long before they were able to bring together their scattered forces and to take up their work where they had laid it down in 1773. But in the modern world they never regained the power that they had before the French Revolution.

All the old Orders gradually reorganized themselves, and took up again their share of missionary labour. In addition, the nineteenth century was richer than any other in the formation of new Orders and Sisterhoods specially devoted to missionary work or prepared to devote a large part of their resources to it. Notable among them were the Oblates of the Blessed Virgin Mary Immaculate (1816), the Marists (1817), the Salesians of Don Bosco (1859), the Scheut Fathers (1862), and the White Fathers formed by Cardinal Lavigerie of Algiers for missionary work in Africa (1868). This list is very incomplete. There were also societies of secular priests, among which St Joseph's Society for Foreign Missions (commonly called the Mill Hill Fathers), partly Dutch and partly British (1866), is naturally of special interest to British people. And it is important not to forget such a lay fellowship as the Brothers of the Christian Schools, whose educational work in many lands has been of the highest merit.

One of the weaknesses of Roman Catholic missions in the past was that they had been highly professional affairs, mainly of interest to the religious Orders, and in very large measure dependent on the favour and financial support of rulers. From 1815 onwards, serious attempts were made to interest the laity, and to make ordinary Christians in the world feel that the work of missions was something in which they too were intimately concerned. The work in support of the Propagation of the Faith, first organized by Pauline Jaricot at Lyons in 1817, spread rapidly in many countries, and made available to the missions the contributions of innumerable humble people. To collect the pennies of the faithful was not enough; it was necessary also to instruct them and to solicit their prayers. The principal instrument here was a missionary periodical – *Annals of the Association for the Propagation of the Faith; a periodical selection from the letters of bishops and missionaries in both the old world and the new, and of all the documents relating to the missions and to the Association for the Propagation of the Faith.*[2] The first number appeared in 1822. The magazine was planned as a continuation of the *Curious and Edifying Letters* and the *New Edifying Letters* put forth by the Jesuits over many years. These letters had often proved more curious than edifying, and the relation they bear to facts is often highly problematic; indeed one of the problems of the critical historian of Roman Catholic missions is precisely the use to be made of these contemporary documents. The new magazine was to be less romantic, more factual, and was to cover

---

2. A reproduction of the title-page of the first bound volume lies before me as I write (*Hist. universelle*, Vol. III, back of p. 66). I have translated the long French title.

the work of all the missions and not only of the Jesuits. The work it accomplished over the years in educating its constituency was of the highest possible value.

Much time was needed for the rebuilding of missionary activity. European countries were short of priests and had few to spare. It took time for the new Orders to train their recruits and to get them into the field. Roman Catholic historians usually recognize that it was only under Gregory XVI (1831–46) that the work of renewal began to get under way on a large scale. Gregory looked far into the future; foreseeing the great expansion that was to come, he prepared the framework within which the missionaries would be able to work by creating a large number of bishoprics and prefectures in all parts of the world. For instance, he created the see of Algiers in 1838, and set up a vicariate for Madagascar in 1835, and another for the Cape of Good Hope in 1837. Four vicariates were set up in India, in face of the protests of the Portuguese. Although missionary work in Indonesia was forbidden, and there were in Java only three priests responsible for ministrations to the Dutch, Java became a prefecture in 1831 and a vicariate in 1842. Four vicariates were established in the Pacific, and, though Japan remained still closed and unapproachable, on 27 March 1846 Japan also became a vicariate. This represents only a selection from a much longer list. In many cases, such as those of Java and Japan, the hierarchical establishment represented no more than a framework and a hope; but sometimes the existence of the framework inspires the feeling that it ought to have something to frame, and hope is not always put to shame.

In *India*, in spite of the pessimistic estimate of the Abbé Dubois,[3] foundations still existed, and it was not necessary to begin all over again as though nothing had ever happened before. The Roman Catholic members among the Thomas Christians were where they had always been, with a considerable force of Indian priests. The Paravas of the Fisher Coast had remained faithful, though not well content with the Goanese priests who were ministering to them. Goa was still a great centre, though presenting a moral problem, as it had always done since the sixteenth century.

One of the difficulties that haunted the reconstruction of Roman Catholic work in India for more than a century was the existence of

3. See pp. 175–6 for an earlier reference to the Abbé Dubois.

the Padroado, the sole right of the Crown of Portugal to appoint for India bishops with territorial jurisdiction. There were four Portuguese dioceses – Goa, Cranganore, Cochin, and Mylapore near Madras. But Portugal had often failed to nominate bishops; Goa, the most important of all, was vacant from 1831 to 1843, Cranganore from 1777 to 1838, Cochin from 1778 to 1818, and Mylapore from 1807 to 1838. In this impossible situation, the Pope, as we have seen, had nominated a number of vicars apostolic to exercise the episcopate in India in his name, though technically without territorial jurisdiction. In 1838 he went further: in the Brief *Multa Praeclare* he suppressed the three southern sees, limited the jurisdiction of the Archbishop of Goa to the now tiny Portuguese possessions, and put all the rest of India under his own vicars apostolic. But at that time there were no diplomatic relationships between the Vatican and Portugal; the Bull was not communicated officially to the queen, or to the Portuguese authorities in India; the Portuguese clergy decided to treat the Bull as a forgery, and to have nothing whatever to do with the new masters whom the Vatican had imposed upon them.

This, too, was clearly an impossible situation. An attempt was made in 1843 to relieve it by the appointment to the see of Goa of Dr Silva Torres, a learned professor of the university of Coimbra. It was believed and hoped that the new Archbishop would pour oil on the troubled waters; instead, he chose to pour oil on the flames. The Pope had confused matters by issuing to Silva Torres two sets of apparently self-contradictory documents; this led the Archbishop to hold that by his appointment *Multa Praeclare* had been set in abeyance. On his arrival in India, he paid a visit to Bombay, went in solemn procession through the streets, and held confirmations and ordinations without any regard to the rights of the Vicar Apostolic Fortini, whom the Pope had sent to govern the Church in Bombay. He wrote passionately of the lies spread abroad by the vicars apostolic, and praised the faithfulness of the people to their old and true shepherds. In Goa he without delay ordained to the priesthood 600 (some authorities say 800, others 300) almost wholly untrained young men, and sent them out into the territories of the vicars apostolic in rebuttal of the charge that Portugal could not supply the priests of whom the Indian Church stood in need. At last, in December 1848, the Portuguese government agreed to the recall of Silva Torres; but the harm had been done – the Goanese schism was in existence, and like all schisms proved to be much easier to create than to heal.[4]

These strifes and contentions were bitter and harmful, but they did not altogether frustrate the development of the plans of Rome for the renewal of the Church in India. By 1859 sixteen vicariates were in existence in India, in addition to one in Burma and two in Ceylon. Various modifications of the relations with Portugal had brought about a certain measure of harmony. But no real improvement could take place until in 1886 Leo XIII decided to take the matter into his own hands and to create a regular ecclesiastical hierarchy for India. Certain far-reaching concessions were made to the feelings of Portugal. The Archbishop of Goa was given the title of Patriarch of the Indies in recognition of the services rendered by Portugal to the cause of Christ in India. The Padroado rights in relation to the four old Portuguese dioceses were maintained. And a 'double jurisdiction' was established, through which certain parishes, groups, and individuals living in the new dioceses were to remain under the jurisdiction of the Padroado bishoprics.[5] This Concordat was signed in August 1886. In the following month, Leo XIII created eight ecclesiastical provinces – Goa, Colombo, Pondicherry, Verapoly (in Travancore), Madras, Calcutta, Agra, and Bombay. In 1884 he had already called into existence the apostolic delegation, by means of which he would be able personally to control the affairs of the Church in India. The first apostolic delegate, Agliardi, was an Italian.

There were now more than twenty bishops in India; but every single one of them was a European. From 1845 onwards Rome had been impressing on its representatives in India the importance of the indigenous clergy, and the need to move rapidly forward in the training of Indian priests. These injunctions met with singularly little response. Bishops and others had had painful experiences with unworthy and irresponsible Goanese priests, and felt it necessary to be cautious. The Jesuit tradition, which once again was very strong in India, was, as we have seen, inclined to a similar

4. Thirty years ago the village of Manappādu in the Tinnevelly district was still divided between the two jurisdictions, Goanese and French. The feeling between them was so strong as to lead from time to time to exceedingly violent riots.

5. The extraordinary consequences of this are pointed out by M. Quéguiner (*Hist. universelle*, Vol. III, p. 220): a member of one of these communities could be ministered to only by a priest of his own diocese; in consequence, if he happened to die in a place where there was no such priest, it was impossible for the local priest to give him the last sacraments.

caution. And perhaps the Roman Catholic missionaries, like others, had come to share the general feeling of the superiority of western men, and to believe that the future of the Church would be safer if it was kept in their own hands. However that may be, a report sent in to Rome in 1862 by Mgr Charbonneau, the Vicar Apostolic of Mysore, had shown that at that time six of the vicariates – Vizagapatam, Hyderabad, Dacca, Calcutta, Patna, and Agra – had not a single Indian priest, and six others had no seminary for the preparation of priests. In the Serra, the land of the Thomas Christians, the situation was numerically very much better: there were 400 indigenous priests, but these were described as 'mediocre, ignorant, without piety and disobedient'. Forty of them were under suspension for irregularities. Only strong pressure from Rome brought about a change in the situation, and it was not till well on in the twentieth century that the number of Indian priests equalled, and then surpassed, that of the foreigners.[6]

In 1896 Leo XIII took a further step forward. In 1887 a separate hierarchy had been created for the Christians of the Syriac rite in Kērala, and this had been placed under the Congregation for Oriental Affairs, while the other dioceses were subject to the Propaganda, but the bishops were Europeans. In 1896, for the first time, all the three sees were filled by the appointment of Indians.

Most of the work of the Roman missions in India was of that quiet, patient, pastoral kind which in the end builds up a strong, coherent, and self-conscious Christian community, but in which there is little that is striking or outstanding to record. But in two directions the Roman Catholic Church in India launched out into what for it were new and unaccustomed fields.

It found itself suddenly faced with all the problems of a mass movement among aboriginal peoples. We have noted the success of the Lutherans and Anglicans among the tribal peoples of Chota Nagpur; the Roman Catholics entered only when these two missions were already well established, and secured their first converts in 1873. When the Flemish Jesuit Constant Lievens arrived in 1885, he found only a group of fifty-six Christians to care for. Lievens soon changed all that. He had noted with sympathy the distress of the tribal people, and the unsatisfactory nature of their relationship with their overlords, the Hindu *zamindars*. Taxes were

6. The latest report available to me shows that 61 per cent of the Roman Catholic priests in India are now Indian.

heavy and were ruthlessly exacted; as the Kols were mostly illiterate, it was very hard for them to know how much they ought to pay. When they had nothing wherewith to pay, they turned of necessity to the moneylenders, who lent at rates of interest of anything up to 100 per cent. Lievens decided to intervene, and to make himself the champion of the oppressed. He advised the peasants to pay as taxes only what they themselves judged to be right; when, as was inevitable, they were hauled into the lawcourts, he provided lawyers for them, and in many cases was able to defend them against the rapacity of their landlords. It is not surprising that the simple people came to regard this vigorous, at times almost violent, white man, riding about the hills on an elephant, as a saviour sent from heaven. Thousands left the Lutherans to join the Roman Catholic Church; thousands of pagans followed them. When Lievens, exhausted, returned to Europe in 1891, he left behind him a Church of 79,000 baptized Christians. His requirements of his catechumens were minimal; he relied on later teaching to bring them into line with more searching Christian requirements. His methods, however, were not always successful. In two villages his converts rose in revolt not only against their landlords but also against the government; in the subsequent legal proceedings, about a hundred of them were sentenced to imprisonment; and thousands of the newly converted, finding that their protector was not all-powerful, fell back into heathenism. But on the whole the work has stood, and at the time of writing the Roman Catholic Church has more Christians in Chota Nagpur than any other.[7]

From 1830 on, Protestant missions had engaged in higher education, and had produced a prosperous and often distinguished Christian middle class. What little the Roman Catholics had done in the way of education beyond the primary stage had been almost limited to seminaries for the training of future or possible priests. The Jesuits were the first to see that the Roman Catholics were in danger of putting themselves in a position of permanent social and educational inferiority to the Protestants, and that they must at once and vigorously enter into the new world of educational opportunity which had been opened up by the government's policy since 1860. In 1883 a college, originally founded in Negapatam in 1844, was moved to Trichinopoly, and almost at once began to

7. There is a very full account of the earlier phases of this work in H. Josson, SJ, *La Mission du Bengale occidental* (2 vols, Bruges, 1921).

attract a large number of students. Similar foundations followed at Madras, at Palamcottah, and in other centres. The government ruled that priests and nuns, who received a bare living allowance from the Church, might be entered for purposes of government grant at the figure of their 'commercial value' as teachers; this concession was, of course, of the greatest help financially to the Roman Catholic institutions. Conversions, as in the Protestant colleges, were few, but the Church was beginning to prepare that intellectual élite of which it would inevitably stand in need when the time came for the withdrawal of the foreign missionary.

One of the gravest weaknesses of Roman Catholicism in India was its extreme foreignness. As we have seen, all the higher members of the clergy were foreigners. Students for the priesthood learned Latin, and no attention was paid to the great heritage of the Hindu background. The foreigners developed in the Indian languages a curious Christian patois, sedulously copied by their adherents. Only here and there was a voice raised in defence of another way, and opposition to the current pattern could lead to tragic consequences.

A Bengali Brahman boy was born on 2 February 1861 in a village fifty miles north of Calcutta, and named Bhawāni Charan Banerji Upadhyāya. An eager student, particularly of philosophy, he flung himself into the search for truth, and came under various Christian influences. On 26 February 1891 he received baptism at the hands of an Anglican priest, without apparently any very clear idea of what he was doing. Six months later he transferred his allegiance to the Roman Catholic Church; at his second (conditional) baptism, he took the name Brahmabandhāv, which he understood as a Sanskrit translation of Theophilus, the beloved of God. Brahmabandhāv was a passionate Indian nationalist, and longed to deliver the Church from all those western swaddling clothes which hindered its development as the Indian representative of a universal Church. He was convinced that the Vedānta philosophy could be used as an introduction to Christianity without prejudice to Christian truth, and in his paper *Sophia* (founded 1894) attempted to show how this could be done. Among other things, he was eager to see an Indian hierarchy established, and was highly critical of the European priests for their failure to realize and to trust in the capacity of their Indian colleagues.

At first Brahmabandhāv attracted considerable sympathy among Roman Catholics of all races in India. But gradually sympathy changed to suspicion and suspicion to condemnation.

Brahmabandhāv had the mercurial temper of the Bengali; no doubt many of his ideas were erratic and his expression of them exaggerated. But it is hard not to think that with wiser handling his gifts might have been saved for the Church. To the end of his life, which came on 27 October 1907, he declared himself to be a faithful Christian, but he died outside the communion of his Church. He was a forerunner who has had many followers, more prudent and more prepared to wait. Yet it may be doubted whether even eighty years after his death the Roman Catholic Church in India has fully appreciated the significance of the problems which he raised.[8]

China had never been entirely deprived of the service of Roman Catholic missionaries. Throughout the times of persecution and repression a few had valiantly held on, in secret and often in danger of their lives. Roman Catholics constantly ran risks which the Protestants were not prepared to take, or perhaps did not feel it right to take, in view of the policies of their governments and of the fact that they had no groups of Chinese Christians to help by giving them hiding and protection. Four Roman Catholic missionaries are known to have been martyred in China between 1814 and 1840.

It was the treaties of 1844 and 1860 which gave to Roman Catholics, as to Protestants, the opportunity to enter in large numbers and to spread themselves throughout the eighteen provinces. In the course of the next fifty years, all the main Orders and societies entered – Jesuits, Franciscans and Dominicans, Augustinians, and many others, not to mention the Brothers of the Christian Schools; and, numerous as were the missionaries, the members of the Sisterhoods at work in China even surpassed them.

The relationship of the Roman Catholic missions to the government took on a very peculiar character. The Convention of 1860 entered into by China and France generally extended tolerance to Christianity in China; but the Chinese text went a good deal further than the French in its explanation of what tolerance was intended to mean. It affirmed among other things that it would be 'permitted to French missionaries to rent and purchase land in all the provinces, and to erect buildings thereon at pleasure'. The Chinese never admitted the validity of this clause, and it was the

---

8. A full and sympathetic account of Brahmabandhāv is given by Fr A. Väth, sj, *Im Kampfe mit der Zauberwelt des Hinduismus: Upadhyāya Brahmabandhāv und das Problem der Überwindung des höheren Hinduismus durch das Christentum* (Berlin and Bonn, 1928).

source of endless friction. It is typical, however, of the desire of France at this time to secure a dominant position in the affairs of China, and to make use of the missions to further that end. Napoleon III was at the height of his power in France; his position depended to a considerable extent on the support of the Church, and he was anxious to display himself as the Catholic sovereign *par excellence*, and as the protector of the Church throughout the world. In China he came very near to securing his aim.

From 1860 to 1888 all Roman Catholic missionaries carried a passport, delivered to them by the consular agents of France, and written in both French and Chinese. The Chinese text stated that the bearer was French, whatever his nationality may in reality have been. From 1888 onwards Germany and Italy reasserted the right to secure the protection of their own nationals. The missionaries tended to interpret rather liberally the terms of the treaty under which they worked, even in its Chinese form. They were entitled to secure the protection of their converts, if persecuted for their faith, but it was not always easy to be sure whether it was for his faith that the convert was being persecuted, or for some other and much more legitimate reason. Missionaries tended to interfere in lawsuits, and to use their influence with magistrates and others in favour of the Christians. Not unnaturally word began to get around that it was a good thing to have a missionary on your side, and to come under the broad wings of his protection. The cynical missionary soon learns that very few converts come with entirely unmixed motives and with a single eye to the glory of God – if they did they would hardly need to be converted. But it can hardly be doubted that the Roman Catholic method in China opened the door wide to those who came in for purely mercenary motives. Professor Latourette quotes with some amusement the remark of Mgr Faurie of Kweichow that 'it is worthy of remark that every one of the individuals who have been punished for reviling our religion have embraced with ardour the true faith on leaving prison'.[9] A fatal link was being forged between imperialistic penetration and the preaching of the Gospel.[10]

Building on their much longer tradition of life in China, the

9. *A History of Christian Missions in China*, p. 310.

10. In 1929 the Apostolic Delegate Mgr Costantini was on the point of arranging a convention directly between the Holy See and the Chinese government. Word of the project leaked out; even at that date French diplomacy was powerful enough to insist on a protectorate of Roman Catholic missions which had long outlived its usefulness, and the plan of Costantini had to be abandoned.

Roman Catholic missions grew more rapidly than those of the Protestant Churches. In 1890, it was reckoned that there were about half a million baptized believers in China; the number of foreign missionary priests was 639, and Chinese priests were 369. The last figure is remarkable, and reflects great credit on the missions which had brought about such a result in less than fifty years. But nemesis was preparing: if unsatisfactory methods are adopted, sooner or later a heavy price will have to be paid for their adoption.[11]

When the Boxer troubles broke out in 1900, all foreigners were in danger, but the anger of the nationalists was specially directed against the missionaries and against Chinese Christians, who were regarded as traitors to their country and running dogs of the alien. Chinese Christians were widely scattered throughout the country and particularly exposed to violence. In some places, such as Peking, where the number was large, Christians valiantly defended themselves, but elsewhere massacres were many and the loss of life was very great.

Considering the large number of Roman Catholic missionaries in China, their losses were remarkably light. No entirely reliable list has ever been drawn up, but the number of those violently slain appears to have amounted, subject to some uncertainties, to five bishops, thirty-one European priests, nine sisters, and two lay brothers. The fate of Mgr Hamer in the Ordos country in Mongolia was particularly tragic: he was captured after brave resistance, his fingers and toes were cut off and his feet nailed to boards, and thus the unhappy man was driven from village to village until he died. A number of missionaries made their escape from Mongolia into Siberia by travelling for forty-two days across the desert.

The losses endured by the Chinese Christians were very much heavier. The lowest figure suggested is 20,000; and 30,000 is probably nearer the mark.[12] Of these it is believed that about a hundred were priests.

But, with the Roman Catholics as with the Protestants, the

11. A careful study of the protectorate question, with quotations of original documents, is J. B. Sägmüller's 'Das französische Missionsprotektorat in der Levante und in China' in *Zeitschrift für Missionswissenschaft* (1913), pp. 118–33. At that time it was still possible to write very favourably of the help received by the missions through the protectorate.

12. This is the figure given by Dom C. Cary-Elwes, *China and the Cross* (1957), p. 222, the latest Roman Catholic source available to me.

Boxer incident was no more than an incident. The loss of life was terrible; the destruction of property was immense. But the Church has often been here before: the individual dies, the work goes on. Like the Protestants, the Roman Catholics were able to profit from the new spirit of openness in China; new Orders and societies entered, the work was reorganized and extended, and the number of Christians grew more rapidly than ever before. In 1900 there were 720,000 baptized believers; in twelve years these had almost doubled themselves, to 1,430,000. During the same period, priests had increased from 1,375 to 2,255. But the important thing here is that of these 2,255, only 1,421 were foreign, and 834 were Chinese.

But there was still no Chinese bishop; Gregory Lô had as yet no successor. Here we note once again the general conservatism of the Roman Catholic missionaries. They seem to have been quite content to dwell under the shadow of European protection, to accept their own position of leadership in the Church as of permanent divine appointment, and to regard the Chinese priests as having been trained only 'to assist the foreign missionaries in humble offices'.[13] But in this period we begin to hear one lone voice, soon to become a chorus, which speaks in very different tones. Father Vincent Lebbe, a Belgian Lazarist, soon after his arrival in China in 1902 had begun to feel that something was gravely wrong. Why should missionaries be protected? From whom are they to be protected? If the answer is 'from the Chinese', how will it ever be possible to win over a man from whom you wish to be protected? The only method is the total self-identification of oneself in love with those whom one desires to win. It might be Hudson Taylor speaking again. Lebbe saw the extent to which the Church in China was foreign; he was convinced that, if it was to do great things, it must become completely Chinese.[14] We shall hear much more of this in a later chapter.

Japan had remained firmly closed against all Christian penetration for more than two centuries. Roman Catholics had never given up the hope of finding their way back, but every attempt had been frustrated, and it was not until 1859, the year of the entry of the first Protestant missionaries, that the first Roman Catholic

13. The words are those of Pope Benedict XV in his great Encyclical *Maximum Illud* of 1919.

14. At a later date Lebbe himself carried this to the point of naturalization as a Chinese citizen.

missionary, Father Girard, was able to obtain a permit to reside in Tokyo. A little later others settled in Hakodate and Nagasaki, where Christianity had been so strong in Japan's Christian century.

Then followed a unique and most moving event – the rediscovery of the ancient Japanese Church. Some women approached the missionary Father (later Bishop) Petitjean, at first very cautiously and later with more confidence, and put to him questions that seemed to relate to the Virgin Mary and to the great 'king of the doctrine', the Pope. Questioning by the missionaries soon made it clear that these were indeed descendants of the ancient Church. Living in Nagasaki and Okuma and on the Goto islands, they had maintained the faith in secrecy through all the years of persecution. Their knowledge was somewhat clouded, as was natural, seeing that they had had no opportunities of instruction and that the literature available to them was minimal and seems to have included no part of the Scriptures. But they had kept the essentials of the faith. The organization of the secret community was almost the same in all the villages; there were usually two principal men, one of whom was the leader of the prayers on Sunday and ministered consolation to the dying, the other being the baptizer. There was considerable variation in the manner of administration of baptism.

Naturally these Christians, the most isolated in the world, were delighted again to have fellowship with that great Christian world of which they had heard but of which they knew almost nothing. But their reception into that fellowship was not unattended by difficulties. Naturally the French missionaries wished to bring their new friends into the full light of Tridentine orthodoxy. But the Japanese are a proud and sensitive people. These Christians had maintained their faith and their independence at great cost over a long period of time. They were not very ready to be ordered about by the foreigner. About 10,000 put themselves under the direction of the French missionaries; at least as large a number remained aloof.[15]

In 1865 Christianity was still a proscribed religion. The story of the Nagasaki remnant could not but come to the ears of the

15. In a most important communication to the *Neue Zeitschrift für Missionswissenschaft* (Vol. XI, 1955, pp. 69–70), Fr J. Van Hecken, C.I.C.M., made it known that there are still 30,000 of these crypto-Christians on the islands to the west of Kyushu, still maintaining their quasi-Christian faith and practices in total separation from the general life of the Christian Church.

authorities, who proceeded to take action. Between 1862 and 1870 about 4,000 of the Christians were arrested in the neighbourhood of Nagasaki and ordered to recant; on their refusal to do so, they were deported to distant regions, where the treatment meted out to them was so harsh that many of them died. In 1873, as we have seen, the attitude of the government towards Christianity became less harsh; persecution ceased, and peace reigned once more.

Encouraged by this successful beginning, and with memories of the past glories of Japanese Christianity, Roman Catholic missionaries seem to have hoped for rapid success in a Japan which was steadily opening itself to the world and becoming increasingly interested in Western ways of thinking. But their experience was the same as that of all the other missions; there has never been a mass movement, and each conversion has had to be individually and laboriously won. In 1891 Leo XIII constituted a full hierarchy for Japan, with the archbishopric at Tokyo and suffragan bishoprics of Nagasaki, Osaka, and Hakodate, but at that time there were no more than 44,500 Roman Christians in Japan. By 1910 the number had grown to 63,000, an increase of less than 50 per cent in twenty years. The first ordination of Japanese priests took place in 1883; in 1891 the number had risen to fifteen, and in 1910 to thirty-three.[16]

Korea has again and again proved the accuracy of its sobriquet 'the hermit kingdom'.

The beginnings of Roman Catholic Christianity in Korea form one of those romantic and almost incredible stories of which we have encountered a number in our journey through the centuries. About the year 1777, a group of Korean scholars set themselves to study a number of the Chinese treatises of Matthew Ricci, especially that called *True Principles concerning God*. They were so much interested that in 1783 they sent one of their number, Yi Seng Hun, to Peking, where he was baptized under the name of Peter. On his return Yi set himself to work to proclaim his new knowledge, and baptized a number of converts. Having no priest, the Koreans organized their own Church, with a bishop and priests, the celebration of Mass, the hearing of confessions, and all the other practices of the Catholic world – an astonishing example of lay Christianity creating and maintaining itself in a remote and inaccessible area. Closer contact with Peking revealed to these

16. For the consecration of the first Japanese bishop, see p. 389.

Christians their well-intentioned error; in 1794 a Chinese priest, James Ti-Yu, was sent to care for them and found 4,000 Christians ready to accept his ministrations. James was put to death in 1801. In 1836 and 1837 three European priests managed to arrive in Korea, but were caught and executed after only three years of service; yet the Church continued to grow in secret, and a number of missionaries were able to enter the country and to maintain themselves. It was reckoned that in 1866 there were 25,000 Christians. But in that year the worst of all the persecutions, political rather than strictly religious in character, broke out: two bishops, seven priests, and at least 8,000 Koreans perished. The Roman Catholic Church has never quite recovered from the blow, and its adherents today represent only a rather small minority of the Christian population of the country.

At the opening of the nineteenth century, the missions in *Indo-China* were perhaps the most flourishing in the whole of the Roman Catholic world. The work had had its ups and downs; but the faithfulness and effectiveness of the lay catechists had kept things going when priests and missionaries were few. The nineteenth century was to prove a time of torment. Here, as elsewhere, suspicion of Western man and fear of his colonializing tendencies helped to fan the hatred of his religion, and of its adherents as possible enemies within the camp. Two periods of especially fierce persecution are recorded, under Minh-Mang between 1833 and 1841, and under Tu-Duc between 1856 and 1862.

In 1833 the Emperor Minh-Mang issued a proclamation the tone of which very closely resembles that of the anti-Christian edicts in Japan two centuries earlier:

We order that all the adherents of this religion, from the mandarin down to the lowest of the people, are sincerely to abandon it, if they recognize and fear our power. . . . As for the places of worship and the houses of the priests, the mandarins are to see to it that they are razed to the ground; and for the future, if any of our subjects is found guilty of entering a church adhering to these abominable customs, they are to be punished with the utmost rigour, in order that this perverse religion may be stamped out in its very roots.

The first European martyr of this period was Father Isidore Gagelin, who was strangled on 17 October 1833. He was followed by nine others, who in the course of the next seven years died in prison or were violently put to death. In 1836 Minh-Mang had another idea; he sent crucifixes to the governors of the provinces, with orders that they were to be placed at the entrances to the towns in such a way that passers-by could not fail to tread on them:

Those who refuse to trample the cross under foot are to be beaten without mercy, tortured and put to death.

There was a period of relief between 1841 and 1847. The Church came out of its hiding, and under its courageous bishop, Mgr Retord, the Vicar Apostolic of western Tongking, boldly proclaimed its message. Vicariates were multiplied, and the Church gained in strength. But the relief did not last long. With the accession of Tu-Duc in 1847, persecution broke out again and continued with steadily increasing violence. In 1855 what was in effect an order of extermination was passed; large rewards were offered for the apprehension of priests, whether foreign or native. In order not to compromise their friends, the missionaries fled to the mountains and the forests; there, in 1858 Bishop Retord died in hiding, worn out with disease and privation.

The story of these sufferings gave Napoleon III, always eager to extend the power of France and its reputation as the protector of the faithful, the opportunity to intervene in Indo-China with armed force. An expedition was sent out in 1862, and this resulted in the occupation of the three provinces of Cochin-China, to which three others were added in 1867. The treaty of 1862 included a clause guaranteeing to Europeans and nationals alike liberty to profess and practise the Christian religion. This clause was completely disregarded by the authorities. It was a vicious circle. Christians had been persecuted through doubts as to their political reliability. The incursion of the French justified the worst fears of the rulers. In consequence, hatred of the Christians increased. Then, inevitably, France took further action in their defence. A final furious outburst of persecution in 1885 brought the tragedy to its close. France completed its occupation of the whole peninsula, divided it into the empire of Annam, the colony of Cochin-China, and the protectorates of Cambodia, Laos, and Tongking, and thus found itself for the next seventy years in possession of an empire which was an embarrassment rather than an advantage.

It is certain that 115 Indo-Chinese priests died as martyrs in the persecution. The number of Christians who perished is given as 300,000. We have seen reason to regard such figures as imaginative rather than accurate, but there can be no doubt that the sufferings were very severe, and for the most part heroically borne. The Church was shaken, but it was not exterminated. Given French protection and freedom to worship, it grew rapidly, and sixty years later Roman Catholics in the area were reckoned at a million and a half, $7\frac{1}{2}$ per cent of the population. By 1975 there were about 2 million Christians, and rooted into Asiatic culture as nowhere else in Asia.

In the rest of *South-east Asia* there were no results of such startling magnitude to show.

Thailand has always proved tenaciously resistant to Christian faith, and to religious resistance political suspicion has often been added. Thailand owes its continued independence rather to the mutual jealousy of Britain and France than to any intrinsic strength; and since most of the Roman Catholic missionaries have been French, they have found it hard to remain uninvolved in the political hurly-burly. In 1849 all the missionaries were ordered out of the country. The treaty of 1856 between France and Thailand gave the missionaries greater liberty; the work grew slowly, and the first priest of purely Siamese origin was ordained in 1880. But the majority of Christians – 36,000 in 1912 – were by race Chinese and not Siamese.

In *Burma* things went rather better. In 1856 the Paris Society was asked to take over the main responsibility for the work; the Vicar Apostolic, Mgr Bigandet, proved to be an outstanding scholar, one of the greatest western authorities on Burmese Buddhism, and also an excellent organizer. The Roman Catholic missions, like the Protestants, proved most successful among the non-Burman races; in 1912 they claimed about 90,000 adherents.

In *Malaya*, where the number of Christians in 1912 was given as 32,000, most of the Roman Catholics were of Chinese origin; Roman Catholics, like Protestants, had found no way of approaching the original Malay and Muslim population.

In *Indonesia*, where the Protestants had made such immense strides, Roman Catholics found it difficult to obtain a footing. In the half-century between 1809 and 1859, only thirty-three Roman Catholic priests reached Indonesia, and at the end of that period only seven were still active. Their field of work was mainly among the European residents. In 1847 the first Vicar Apostolic was deported by the government, which claimed the right to license priests and preachers, to determine the field of their work, and to exercise very strict supervision over them. It was only in 1859, when Flores and some neighbouring islands were ceded to the Dutch by the Portuguese, that the Roman Catholics found a real field for activity. There were Christians on these islands; by 1875 the missionaries had around them a flourishing Christian community of 14,000. In 1885 a station was opened in West Borneo, in 1886 in the Kei islands in the far east, and in Bencoolen in Sumatra. But in general progress was slow, and it was only in the twentieth century that Roman Catholicism in Indonesia had anything to show comparable to the great achievements of the Protestant missions.

The *South Pacific*, as we have seen, was one of the first, and numerically one of the most successful, of the fields of Protestant missionary work. The Roman Catholics entered comparatively late, and, inevitably, in a great many cases their work consisted not of preaching the Gospel to the heathen but of attempting to detach baptized Christians from the Churches to which they belonged.

This was not everywhere true. In a number of cases the Roman Catholic missionaries found a legitimate sphere of activity in totally unevangelized islands, and there, as elsewhere in the world, they proved themselves patient, resourceful, and heroic pioneers.

The island of *New Caledonia*, twice as large as Corsica, was first surveyed by the Marists as a mission field in 1843. Four years later the murder of a lay brother led them to withdraw, but in 1851 the work was resumed. An unexpected set of problems arose when France annexed the island and decided to convert it into a penal settlement. The discovery of the valuable minerals cobalt, chrome, and nickel led to an influx of prospectors and to the commercial exploitation of the islands; the indigenous population tended increasingly to be driven away into the mountainous and less fertile regions. Here was the classic case of the clash between an unsympathetic Western civilization and a primitive and helpless people. Christian missions, Protestant as well as Roman Catholic, were the only hope of the New Caledonian people. The struggle was long and arduous, but the ordination of the first New Caledonian priest, a little more than a century after the arrival of the first missionaries, is evidence of the stirring of new life in a people that had been threatened with extinction.

The attempt of the Marists to enter *Tonga* was for a long time prevented by the solid opposition of the Protestants, headed by the redoubtable King George. Foiled in their first attempt, the Fathers wisely concentrated on two islands which were still untouched by

Protestantism, *Wallis* and *Futuna*. Wallis was converted during the long ministry of a remarkable missionary, Mgr Bataillon. Futuna has also become a wholly Roman Catholic island. Its first missionary, Pierre Chanel, died as a martyr on 25 April 1841; he was canonized in 1954, and declared to be the patron saint of the whole of Oceania.

As early as 1848 Marist Fathers tried to settle on Woodlark Island at the eastern tip of *New Guinea*. But it was only in 1883 that settled work became possible in the islands, and only ten years later that German missionaries of the Society of the Divine Word set themselves to the difficult task of penetrating the mainland of New Guinea itself. The Australian government, which took over the control of Papua in 1894, decided to avoid rivalry between the missions by assigning to each boundaries which they might not pass. The Roman Catholics accordingly found themselves limited to a comparatively narrow stretch of the southern coast of the island, with no power to expand either to the east or to the west. Undeterred by the enormous difficulties of the task, they set themselves to penetrate into the wholly unknown and mountainous regions of the interior. The cost in human lives was immense; it is stated that eighty missionaries died within fifty years of the opening of the work.

For such efforts there can be nothing but praise. But the situation was otherwise on *Tahiti* and *Samoa* and *Fiji*, where the Protestants were already strongly established, and the inhabitants were in the main Christianized. Here the arrival of the Roman Catholics could mean nothing but rivalry, contention, and strain, and the humiliating display of Christian divisions before the eyes of simple and primitive peoples. And the Polynesians and Micronesians are not so stupid as not to see the advantages of being able to play off one mission against another. Even the tiny atolls of the *Gilbert* and *Ellice Isles*, which had been thoroughly evangelized by the LMS, were not spared; these too had to have their Roman Catholic mission.

In the *Middle East* and the Islamic countries, the concern of the Roman Church was not so much with missions to Muslims as with the attempt to create or to strengthen the Uniate Churches, those groups from the ancient Eastern patriarchates which at one time or another have entered into communion with the See of Rome. There are no less than seven groups which fall under this designation – the Armenians, the Syrian Orthodox (formerly Monophysite), the Melkites (Greek Orthodox), the Copts, the Ethiopians, the Assyrians (formerly Nestorian), and the Maronites.[17] The last of these groups, living mostly in the Lebanon and Syria, has been in communion with Rome since the twelfth century, though retaining certain independent characteristics in liturgy and organization as an Eastern Church. Each of the others has a long tradition of its own, each was intimately associated with the history, the language, and the culture of a people. At the time of the Crusades, Western influence had been strongly felt, but later there had been a reaction, and at the beginning of the nineteenth century the influence of Rome in these lands was inconsiderable. Throughout the century, assisted by the prestige and the influence of France, Roman missions moved heaven and earth to draw away the believers of these Churches from their own patriarchs, and into the allegiance of Rome, working through patriarchs of its own appointment.

The first representatives of Rome in this area were, naturally, all Latins. Some had little sympathy for the ancient Eastern traditions, and little understanding of the feelings of the people among whom they worked. They underestimated the tenacity of those traditions which they had so largely failed to understand. Even those Easterners who had become convinced of the advantages of union with Rome did not wish to be Westernized, Romanized, and Latinized; they wished to be, as they had always been, Eastern Christians and faithful inheritors of a tradition which (as they understood it) was as old as that of Rome itself. An improvement took place in 1862, when Pius IX set up a special department of the Propaganda to care for the affairs of the Uniate Churches. A further development took place under Benedict XV in 1917, when the Sacred Congregation for the Affairs of the Oriental Rite was set up, with the Pope himself as prefect. The threat of Latinization is always there, and is used as a reproach by the Eastern Orthodox against those who have defected to Rome. Not all Eastern Christians have been pleased at the appointment of Armenian and Syrian cardinals; the cardinalate is something that the Eastern Churches have never known, and some felt affronted rather than honoured by the choice of some of their members for this dignity. Some felt, equally, that in the latest form of Canon Law drawn up for them too much weight had been given to Western ideas, and too

17. Very useful and up-to-date information on all the Uniate Churches was brought together in *Le Monde non-chrétien*, no. 63, July–September 1962, pp. 115–66.

little to their own authentic traditions. Nevertheless, the attempt to make within the Roman Catholic world a place for the Eastern Churches in which they will really feel at home has not been unsuccessful.

Ethiopia, with its perhaps 3 million Christians,[18] which in its isolation has managed to maintain its independence, and to hold its own against the Muslims who have threatened its integrity for a thousand years, has attracted the attention of politicians and explorers, as well as of missionaries, for many years. The Scottish traveller James Bruce spent a considerable time in Ethiopia, towards the end of the eighteenth century, in his search for the sources of the Blue Nile; he was rewarded for the precise accuracy of his accounts of this extraordinary country by the general incredulity of the public and a wholly undeserved reputation as a charlatan.[19] Throughout the Middle Ages and after, Rome had made sporadic attempts to enter, none of which came to very much. The process was taken up again in 1839, when the Italian de Jacobis, a member of the Lazarist Order, managed to enter through the port of Massawa, and to establish a small group of 'converts' around him. But this was not to the taste of the suspicious Ethiopians; persecution broke out, in which one Ethiopian Lazarist, Ghebra Mikael, met his death. De Jacobis, now Vicar Apostolic, was imprisoned; and, though he managed to escape from his gaolers, he died of exhaustion on 30 July 1860. His colleague and consecrator Mgr (later Cardinal) W. Massaia (1809–89) was able to maintain himself for a longer time, mainly among the partly Hamitic and only very superficially Christianized Gallas. But having suffered a great deal through what Mgr Mulders described as 'exile, imprisonment, the destruction of mission stations, uprisings of the Protestants and of the schismatic Christians',[20] in 1877 he too was driven out.

Added to the dislike of the Coptic Christians for those who came in to disturb their ancient ways, ways which are unique in the whole of Christendom and seem to owe a good deal to Judaic as

18. It is extraordinarily difficult to give a figure. The number may be considerably higher; but in the absence of any reliable figure a conservative estimate is probably more prudent.

19. See an interesting account of Bruce and his work in Alan Moorehead's *The Blue Nile* (1962). One of the most remarkable fruits of Bruce's sojourn was the recovery of the Ethiopic Book of Enoch, which is of fundamental importance for the study of the background of the New Testament.

20. *Missionsgeschichte*, p. 413.

well as to Christian tradition, was the constant anxiety of the rulers
as to the intentions of the foreign powers. In 1868 the British sent
an expedition to overthrow and depose the Emperor Theodore,
who had imprisoned and ill-treated a number of foreigners, including two consular representatives and German and British missionaries. But a permanent occupation of the country was no part
of British policy, and the troops very soon withdrew. French and
Italian intentions were less clear. The Italians had established
themselves inland from the Red Sea in 1885, and had built up their
colony of Eritrea. An attempt to advance further was brought to an
end by the resounding defeat of Adowa in 1896. But Italy was only
biding its time. The invasion in 1935, in the days of Mussolini, was
temporarily successful; Italian control of the country was complete, and this roused hopes that the whole of the ancient Church
might be added to the Roman Catholic world. But reality and
dream were far from corresponding. With the liberation of
Ethiopia by the British in 1942, the ambitious Italian plans came
to a sorry end. For a number of years the University College in
Addis Ababa was under the direction of Canadian Jesuits; but
Roman Catholic hopes of the assimilation of the ancient Ethiopian
Church are further from fulfilment than they were a century ago.

At the end of the Napoleonic age Roman Catholic effort in *Africa*
had practically ceased, and the remains of the older missions were
few and far between. Roman Catholic historians attribute the first
renewal of African missions in the nineteenth century to the faith
and enterprise of a woman, Anne-Marie Javouhey (1779–1851),
who in 1805 had founded the Congregation of the Sisters of St
Joseph of Cluny, and in 1817 sent the first group of missionary
sisters to the Island of *Réunion* in the Indian Ocean. These were
followed by a party of sisters who went to *Senegal* in 1819; the first
ordination of Senegalese priests is recorded as having taken place
in 1840. A first attempt in *Liberia* was wholly unsuccessful. In 1841
Pius IX had created the vicariates of '*the two Guineas*' and *Mauritius*.
Mgr Barron, the first Vicar Apostolic, who came from
Philadelphia to follow up the first settlement of freed slaves in
Liberia, landed on 29 November 1843 with a party of seven priests
and three lay brothers. Within a few weeks eight out of the ten were
dead, and the mission was withdrawn.

These were only beginnings. In point of fact, the great Orders
and Societies which have devoted themselves to the evangelization
of Africa were founded at or after the middle of the nineteenth
century – the Fathers of the Holy Spirit in 1848, the Lyons Society

of African Missions in 1856,[21] the White Fathers in 1868, and the White Sisters in the following year.

The mention of the White Fathers brings us to their founder, the great Cardinal Lavigerie, Archbishop of Algiers, Apostolic Delegate for the western Sahara, and friend and champion of the slaves (1825–92). Lavigerie had become Bishop of Nancy in 1863. In 1866 Marshal MacMahon, the governor-general of Algeria, invi.ed him to become head of the Roman Catholic Church in North Africa; Lavigerie accepted, because 'he regarded Algeria as the open port of entry to a barbaric continent with 200 million inhabitants'. It is impossible to improve on the brief account of his character and aims given by Mgr Mulders:

When Lavigerie came to his difficult task in North Africa, he was equipped with an independent character, an indomitable will, a width of outlook gained through historical studies and apostolic journeys in the East, and a capacity for organization which had been developed in Rome and Nancy. In the following year he obtained religious liberty in Algeria, in face of the opposition of MacMahon and the government in Paris; so much so that there were thoughts of transferring this disturbing man to the archiepiscopal see of Lyons and the primacy of France. But Lavigerie did not allow himself to be drawn aside from his work, either by alluring titles of honour or by burdensome hindrances – he remained Archbishop of Algiers. . . . In his first Pastoral Letter he set out his programme plainly – first to turn Algeria into a Christian country, and then from it to let the light of faith stream out over the whole continent. To the Muslims he said expressly: 'I claim the right to love you as my children, even though you do not recognize me as your father.'[22]

Then came the foundation of the great Society of Missionaries of Africa, much more commonly known as the White Fathers, from the white cassock and mantle which form their uniform. The fathers are secular priests, together with lay brothers, who live together in community. They do not take the vows of the regular religious communities, but are bound by a solemn oath to lifelong work in the African missions and to obedience to their superiors. The fathers are among the best trained of Roman Catholic missionaries in Africa.[23]

21. The founder of the Society, Mgr de Marion Brésillac, had earlier been Vicar Apostolic of Coimbatore in South India, and had resigned his charge because of his failure to make any impression on the unshakeable conservatism of the other missionaries in the matter of the ordination of Indians to the priesthood.

22. A. Mulders, *Missionsgeschichte* (1960), p. 401.

23. An interesting, rather uncritical, account of the White Fathers is G. D. Kittler, *The White Fathers* (1957).

The first two attempts of the fathers to penetrate the Sahara were unsuccessful. In 1875 the Tuaregs of the desert undertook to conduct a party of missionaries to Timbuctoo, but murdered them all *en route*. The same fate befell a second party which made the attempt in 1881. The missionaries had to be withdrawn from the desert to the oases on its northern fringe, and their work had to be confined mainly to the manifestation of Christian love in action, since any direct preaching or witness was likely to stir up the fanaticism of their Muslim neighbours and to lead to trouble.

One of the chief concerns of Lavigerie was the slave trade. This had been widely ventilated in the English-speaking world through the writings of Livingstone and Stanley, and renewed attention was drawn to it later by the labours in the Sudan of Sir Samuel Baker and then of General Gordon. Continental countries were, perhaps, less well informed, and some at least among the rulers and administrators were of the opinion that the slave trade could not be eliminated at once, and that more harm than good would come from too hasty action. The Cardinal would have none of this; the strongest action must be taken by all the Christian powers, and the Pope himself must give a lead. Not all of Lavigerie's efforts were successful, but at two points public opinion was sufficiently alerted to stand in support of the forces of 'Christianity and civilization'.

In 1884 a Conference on Colonial Questions, at which all the main powers were represented, was convened in Berlin. In the invitation to the conference, Bismarck had expressly drawn attention to the responsibility of the powers 'to encourage missions and other enterprises which are likely to be of service in spreading useful knowledge'. One party hoped for a specific declaration of Christian purpose on the part of the powers, but, in view of the participation of Turkey in the conference, this was illusory, and the statements concerning religion had to be couched in such general terms as would cover Islam no less than Christianity. Nevertheless, what was gained was of considerable significance as a charter of freedom for all Christian missions in tropical Africa, and in particular in that new, strange, and anomalous state that was coming into existence in the Congo under the aegis of Leopold II, king of the Belgians. All the powers undertook to suppress slavery and in particular to take steps for the extermination of the traffic in slaves; they were to encourage all enterprises of a religious, scientific, or charitable character directed to the improvement and uplift of the Africans. Religious missions were to be the subject of special protection. No restriction or limitation was to be imposed on the free and public exercise of any form of worship; full liberty was guaranteed to all to set up buildings for religious purposes and to organize missions, without distinction of privilege as between different denominations. Some would have liked to go further; but the gains were great, and though Christianity was not specifically mentioned, it was likely that the Christian missions would be the ones to take the greatest advantage of these generous provisions.

In November 1889, largely as a result of the agitation carried on by Lavigerie, the Brussels Conference for the Abolition of the Slave Trade assembled. The General Act of the Conference was signed in July 1890; under it, for the first time, an international agreement for the abolition of the slave trade came into being. It was recognized that much would have to be done in the way of improving communications, and also that strongly fortified posts would have to be set up in the interior, both to prevent the capture of slaves and to protect the Christian missions. With this outcome of the conference Lavigerie could be well content.

One of his other plans did not meet with wide favour. So many missionaries were losing their lives before ever reaching the fields for which they were destined, that Lavigerie hit on the idea of developing from his own resources an armed 'militia of Christ' to travel with the caravans, to protect them from marauders, and to be the eventual founders of a Christian kingdom.[24] There were parts of the Sahara in which such action might have seemed not altogether inappropriate. But rather too many years had passed since the Crusades for this idea to find widespread favour, and, as the European powers extended and intensified their control, they were less and less willing to see someone else's quasi-military forces parading through their territories. The new Christian militia was never created.

Lavigerie's interest in slavery left a deep mark on the methods employed by Roman Catholic missions in tropical Africa. Shortly after his arrival in Algiers, the population was struck by an epidemic of cholera and typhus, followed by famine. Lavigerie gathered around him no less than 1,800 orphaned children who would otherwise have died, obtained permission to bring them up as Christians, and settled them in what were to become Christian villages. This experience led him to encourage others to follow the same methods elsewhere: slaves, especially children, could be bought and gathered in Christian settlements; these would form

24. See R. Oliver, *The Missionary Factor in East Africa* (1952), p. 48.

the nucleus for a growing Christian Church. As we have seen, Protestant missionaries had found themselves from time to time with freed slaves on their hands, but as far as possible they kept the numbers down. Roman Catholic missionaries, on the contrary, welcomed the opportunity to form these Christian enclaves, rapidly built them up to considerable numbers, and regarded them as the mainstay of their work. The 'reductions' in Paraguay in the eighteenth century offered a not-forgotten precedent.

One or two figures from the Congo will indicate the large numbers involved in this method. In 1897 the Scheut Fathers in Luluabourg were in charge of a population of 1,000; eight years later the Premonstratensians were caring for 1,600 abandoned children in two colonies, and a Jesuit colony at Kisantu sometimes had as many as 1,000 inhabitants.[25]

Life in such a *chrétienté* was on the whole very comfortable for the African. He had to keep the rules and to learn habits of order which were foreign to him, but in most cases adaptation proved not too difficult. On the other hand, the food supply was more plentiful than in the ordinary African village and there was medical care and other appurtenances of civilization for which daily labour was no unfair price to pay. Most of those in the *chrétientés*, whether children or freed slaves, had lost contact with tribal life and had nowhere else to go. Not unnaturally, in most cases they preferred to stay. But even the idyllic life of the *chrétienté* was not without its problems. Many of those who were brought in were very far indeed from being converts. They lied and stole and quarrelled. Discipline had to be maintained and, in the absence of any other lawful authority, it was the missionary who had to be head of the police force, lawyer, magistrate, and gaoler. When news reached Europe of the rigour of the discipline and the severity of the punishments imposed by the missionaries, there was a considerable outcry. In defence of the missionaries it can be said that they were only using and modifying methods which were familiar to the Africans from their own background, and that the punishments they inflicted were less arbitrary and less ferocious than those which were matters of everyday usage in the African tribe.

Roman Catholics, like Protestants, were aware of the dangers of

25. It was not only on the Congo that such methods were used. On 28 April 1886 Fr Poirier of the Society of African Missions wrote to his superior that while he had been ill Fr Zappa, the Italian, had bought thirty children for £310, which was far too much. (See J. M. Todd, *African Mission*, 1962, p. 120.) Too much money, or too much of a good thing? This was in central Nigeria.

this ghetto existence and of total separation from the ordinary life of the African peoples. Yet they felt it to be essential for the development of the Christian life of converts that they should have a measure of freedom from the temptations of tribal life. A Flemish Jesuit, Father Van Hencxthoven, is credited with the invention of a system which offered a middle way between isolation and absorption. This was the *ferme-chapelle*: from time to time a group was detached from the main station, and sent out to settle under the care of a catechist in the neighbourhood of a non-Christian village. Farming, handicraft, and the care of abandoned children made up the work of these settlements. In many cases the young men who had been brought up in a *ferme-chapelle* would return after marriage on a basis of permanence, and so a regular Christian village would grow up in close contact with the non-Christians, and exercising a profound influence on their way of life. This method proved so successful that by 1902 the Jesuits in one area alone were in charge of 250 *ferme-chapelles*, with a population of over 5,000 children.

Paternalism was perhaps the gravest weakness of all missionary work in the nineteenth century. If asked the direct question what they were aiming at, missionaries both Protestant and Roman Catholic would have replied that they were building an African Church which in time would be able to stand on its own feet and do without the help of missionaries; but this was regarded as belonging to so distant a future as not to come within the sphere of practical politics, and few missionaries were consciously or deliberately planning for a different state of affairs in which their own services would be no longer necessary:

The missionaries of the nineteenth century . . . were not half so ready as the Portuguese to give Africans ecclesiastical positions of responsibility and authority. They thought of Africans as children who needed protection, guidance, and training in order that one day in the distant future they might be fit for a place of responsibility in the Church. . . . The missionary was the father of his flock, and the day when he could become an elder brother, let alone a partner, seemed so distant that he very rarely considered it. . . . While he realized that at this stage he could do little without African help, he was convinced that the organization of this missionary outreach, and of the Christian communities it created, must still remain in his own hands. African converts were still his 'babes in Christ', and he expected them to need a very long training before they could be considered as mature Christians.[26]

26. Ruth Slade, *King Leopold's Congo* (1962), pp. 165, 169–70; at many points I am greatly indebted to this excellent book.

As we have seen, at an early date the pioneers of the new missions in Africa set themselves to the task of creating an African clergy. But in the early days disappointments were many, and the missionaries gradually seem to have slipped into acceptance of the idea that the time for an African priesthood had not yet come. In many areas education was only in its first beginnings. Celibacy, entirely unknown in a continent in which early and universal marriage was the rule, seemed to present an insuperable obstacle. Seminaries were few and often short-lived. In 1896 the Jesuits in the Congo area started a junior seminary at Kimuenza with five 'intelligent and pious' boys. Perhaps the boys proved to be less intelligent and pious than had been thought – after only three years the experiment was abandoned, and it was taken up again only in 1919. As a result, as late as 1923 only sixty-six African priests could be counted in the whole of tropical Africa, excluding Ethiopia but including Madagascar. The rapid extension of the African priesthood belongs only to the period after the Second World War.

A great many religious Orders, as well as secular priests and missionaries from almost every country in Christendom, have taken a share in the evangelization of Africa. As areas of the 'dark continent' have been successively explored and opened up, missionaries have been among the first to enter in and to take possession. Merely to enumerate them would take too much of the space available, and a bare list of the territories entered would be tedious and not highly illuminating. Only a rough survey can be given, with brief indications of those areas in which Roman Catholic work has been most highly successful.

As already noted, the first efforts of the White Fathers were directed towards the opening up of the Sahara. But the eyes of Cardinal Lavigerie were soon directed to a point beyond the desert wastes. Stanley had drawn attention to the kingdom of *Buganda*, with its unique strength and civilization. Lavigerie was a patriotic Frenchman as well as an ecclesiastical statesman of real stature; it seemed to him that the extension of French influence and Roman Catholic teaching could go forward together in an area which so far was outside the sphere of any of the European powers. When the news reached England that a French mission to Uganda was planned, Dr R. N. Cust, who had been Commissioner of Amritsar in India and was a great friend of the CMS in London, personally made the journey to Algiers to plead with Cardinal Lavigerie not to open a mission in Buganda, where the Anglicans were already at work, but to send his forces to one of the countless areas in Africa which were wholly untouched by the Gospel. The Cardinal would not listen; in fact his mission was already on the way, and he would not recall it.

Personal relationships between the Roman Catholic and Anglican missionaries were at times very good. It is pleasant to read in a letter from the Anglican Philip O'Flaherty, written on Christmas Day 1881:

Livinhac I love. He and I have many long walks, talking of the deep things of God – those delightful things that refresh the spirit. And O, the spirit needs to be refreshed in this dry parched land! We take a mutual pleasure in each other's company.[27]

Livinhac was later to be Bishop, and Lavigerie's successor as the Superior of the White Fathers. But others came in a less friendly spirit, and the tensions between the missionaries could not but be reflected in what can only be called hatred between their followers.

After the long period of persecutions, troubles, and war, to which reference has been made in another chapter, the country later known as the *Uganda* Protectorate was divided up among Protestant and Roman Catholic chieftains, as the best way of keeping the peace between them. Mgr Hirth, the French Bishop, had not secured the predominance of French influence in the country, nor had he been able seriously to weaken the Anglican mission. But he had obtained a free hand in a large territory and access to a responsive people. Missionaries poured in; the Roman Catholic faith began to take root, and this might be regarded as one of the most successful missions in the world. The French missionaries were not too well pleased when the Mill Hill Fathers were sent in to divide the work with the White Fathers;[28] once more European rivalries came from across the seas to perplex the minds of simple African Christians. Yet in 1962 nearly half the population of Uganda was Christian, Roman Catholics outnumbering other Christians by about two to one.

While one party of the White Fathers was travelling north into Buganda, another turned south in the direction of *Tanganyika*. This was the area which suffered most severely from the raids and cruelties of the Arab slave traders, some of whom, like the notorious Tippo Tib, had built themselves up almost to the position of

27. Quoted in J. V. Taylor, *The Growth of the Church in Buganda* (1958), p. 59, n. 4.
28. On the work of the Mill Hill Fathers, see H. P. Gale, *Uganda and the Mill Hill Fathers* (1959).

ruling-potentates. The missionaries had the utmost difficulty in obtaining a settlement anywhere. The situation became even more dangerous when it became clear that the Sultan of Zanzibar was setting the Arab leader Rumaliza to attack them. Relief came only with the extension of Belgian power from the west, and the gradual elimination of the Arabs and their ways, a process which was more or less complete by the turn of the century. Then the mission of Tanganyika began to flourish.

In 1889 Cardinal Lavigerie extended the sphere of the White Fathers to the area of *Nyasa*, hoping that the route to the hinterland through Mozambique would be shorter and safer than that through Zanzibar. In 1891 the other great society, the Fathers of the Holy Spirit, entered *Kenya* at Mombasa, and in 1899 reached Nairobi. Christians are not so numerous in Kenya as in Tanganyika and Uganda, and some northern areas have never as yet been evangelized.

In *South Africa* neither Boers nor Britons, with their hearty Protestant traditions, were particularly anxious to see the Roman Catholics among them. The story in this vast area is of slow, patient penetration in the face of at times considerable opposition. In numbers, both among Europeans and Africans, the Roman Catholics stand far behind the greater Protestant Churches. The one area in which they found an open door and an almost unhindered field of operations was *Basutoland*. Here, among the high mountains and the valleys, the great Moshesh made the first Roman Catholic missionaries welcome in 1862. It must be a matter of some regret that the Roman Catholics found it necessary to enter a small country of less than 20,000 square miles in which the French and Swiss Protestants had already been at work for thirty years and had made a deep impression on the whole life of the people. The comparative freedom enjoyed by Basutoland as a protectorate under British and not under South African sovereignty encouraged the Roman Catholics to regard this as a leading Church in South Africa. The acceptance of the Roman Catholic faith by the paramount chief Griffith was a further great encouragement to the Roman Catholic forces.

The relationships between Portugal and the Vatican have been variable and not infrequently stormy. But in general the Roman Catholic Church enjoyed a privileged position in the two great Portuguese territories of *Angola* and *Mozambique*. Portuguese methods of colonization differed from those of other European powers; the aim was to produce a small class of completely assimilated Africans, who would feel themselves to be in every respect Portuguese citizens. Less was done for the general uplift of the population than in other colonial territories. Protestant missions were not excluded – the United Church of Canada, among others, had done large and successful work in Angola – but they had to fight against various disabilities, and the government tended to view them with some suspicion as holding views on the rights of the African which were less in accord with the views of government than those of their Roman Catholic opposite numbers.[29] The Roman Catholic missionary enjoyed a special position, being regarded as a state functionary. Until 1908 all education was under the control of the Church. The old Portuguese mission had practically died out; the new mission of the Fathers of the Holy Spirit began its work in 1873. By 1890 it was claimed that a quarter of a million people, perhaps one eighth of the total population, was already Roman Catholic. The support of the government made conversion easy; but there were fewer signs than in other parts of Africa, that the faith had really taken deep root in the lives of Christian adherents, and the level of illiteracy was dangerously high, except among the Protestants.[30]

The approach to *West Africa* demanded of the Roman Catholics no less than of the Protestants tremendous sacrifices of life and health. In 1858 the young Mgr de Marion Brésillac, the founder of the Lyons Society for missions in Africa, was sent to *Sierra Leone* with three priests and one lay brother. Within a few weeks all five had died of yellow fever.[31] The work was resumed in 1861, *Dahomey* being this time chosen as the scene of operations. The initial

29. There were in 1962 about half a million Protestant Christians in Angola, a much smaller number in Mozambique. That their position was difficult was suggested by a diatribe, in the *Diario de Marina* of 10 July 1962, by Fr Alfredo Mendes (quoted in *The Times* of 12 July 1962), in which it was stated that American Protestant missionaries 'are worse than the communists, and more dangerous, with all their millions of dollars, because we can bar the admission of communists into Angola, while the Americans are allowed in, disguised as missionaries with Bibles under their arms . . . millions of dollars . . . which they spend, not in spreading the Gospel, but as a political investment to bring returns in due course to American financiers'.

30. On Roman Catholic missions in Portuguese Africa, see a useful summary in J. E. Duffy's *Portugal in Africa* (Pelican Books, 1962), pp. 171–5.

31. A very interesting account of de Marion Brésillac is given in J. M. Todd's *African Mission* (1962), pp. 12–38. It is pleasant to note that – no Roman Catholic priest being available, Fr Raymond being at death's door – such ministrations as were possible at the graveside were rendered by one of the Anglican missionaries in Freetown.

difficulties were gradually overcome, but in those days it was reckoned that the average period of service of a missionary was not more than three years. In 1862 the first missionaries arrived in *Lagos*. The tolerant attitude of the British government towards all forms of missionary service, and its willingness to help forward Christian educational work with generous financial subventions, was as encouraging to the Roman Catholics as to the Protestants. Their strongest hold is perhaps among the vigorous Ibo people of eastern *Nigeria*.

Perhaps the most successful of all the Roman Catholic missions in West Africa was that of the *Cameroons*. As this area was at the time under German rule, the work was first undertaken by German missionaries, to whom others were afterwards added. Large parts of the country had already been thoroughly evangelized by the American Presbyterians and the Basel Mission, and at first Roman Catholic advance was very slow; at the turn of the century only 2,500 Christians were recorded. But from that time on progress was rapid; with a missionary force outnumbering that of all the Protestants put together by four to one, Roman Catholics were able to establish themselves throughout the territory, in which certain areas gave the impression of being an entirely Christian country.

It is, however, to the *Congo* that we must look for the most spectacular of all Roman Catholic achievements in Africa. From the start the conditions were favourable. Leopold II of Belgium, who for thirty years exercised personal and complete control over the destiny of the Congo, was anxious to have the co-operation of Roman Catholic missionaries but was particularly anxious that they should be Belgian. The first to enter were the tireless White Fathers who, unlike the Protestants, entered from the east and from the area of the Great Lakes. The king was not too pleased at the arrival of so many Frenchmen in his dominions, but was placated when Cardinal Lavigerie arranged to recruit Belgians for his Society. Leopold, however, continued to press for further aid from Belgium. The Scheutists, whose society had been founded with a view to work in China, had rejected an approach made by the king in 1879, but in the end they agreed to co-operate, and sent out their first party in 1888. The vicariate of the Congo was created and placed under their direction. The Belgian Jesuits twice refused, but yielded in 1891 and took over the area of Kwango, which has ever since remained their field. With all these new forces arriving, it was possible for the Administrator-General of the

Congo State, as early as 1888, to write to the Belgian minister at the Vatican:

> Now Catholic work in the Congo is founded on a permanent basis. No more of the Portuguese patronage, no more interference from foreign missionaries; the new state is becoming Belgian from the religious point of view as it already is on the political side, and I hope we shall soon have an army of missionaries going to help found a new greater Belgium in that far-off land.[32]

The Roman Catholic authorities, no less than the communists, were aware of the significance of the Congo in the future development of Africa. A glance at the map shows why this is so. This immense territory of a million square miles lies at the very heart of the continent. In 1876 its wealth in copper and other minerals was hardly suspected; but it was known to be potentially rich in rubber and believed to be susceptible of almost unlimited development. If the Congo could be developed as a Christian nation, its influence on the whole life and future of Africa would be very great. Protestants had been first in the field; now it should be shown what the Roman Catholic Church could do in competition with them. The attitude of the authorities was not impartial. For a long period, the Roman Catholic missions alone could enjoy financial aid for education (which was granted to Protestants only when an anti-clerical minister for education in Belgium restored the equilibrium, rather through an inclination to injure the Roman Catholics than from a genuine desire to help the Protestants). Priests and nuns poured into the country. Every possible method was used to approach the people. The beginnings, here as elsewhere, were slow. In 1910 there were 191 priests, all foreigners, in the country, and about 100 sisters; baptized Christians were only 50,000 – though a vastly greater number were interested in the new religion. The landslide which brought perhaps a quarter of the country's population into the Church came only after the end of the First World War.

The general picture of Roman Catholic missions in the nineteenth century is one of abounding vitality and heroism. No one at the beginning of the century could possibly have imagined that this apparently moribund Church would produce from within itself these astonishing new manifestations of energy. In a great

32. Quoted in R. Slade, *King Leopold's Congo* (London, 1962), p. 147.

many areas Protestants had had a start of anything from thirty to fifty years. In some areas (though not in all) Roman Catholics, with government support, with apparently inexhaustible supplies of recruits, with a very flexible policy in regard to baptism, were able to rival, and in a number of cases to surpass, the Protestants, and to prepare the way for the rapid progress of the last fifty years.

One or two criticisms may be permitted. The association of the missions (in China, in the Belgian Congo, and elsewhere) with Western governments was certainly far closer than was wise or right. There was hardly a trace of ecumenical understanding or co-operation. We have referred with pleasure to certain examples of personal friendship, and indeed affection, between Roman and non-Roman missionaries, but these were the exception. Protestant and Roman Catholic missionaries could live for years in the same town and never exchange a word. It was taken for granted by the majority of Roman Catholics that the Protestants were the enemy. This attitude was succinctly set forth in a directive alleged to have been issued from the Propaganda in the early days of the Congo missions: 'The heretics are to be followed up and their efforts harassed and destroyed.' And the student is again and again amazed at the Westernness of the missions. Almost everywhere it seems to be taken for granted that the missionary period will go on for ever; the duty of the convert is clear – to trust in the superior wisdom of the white man and so to be conveyed without too much trouble in the safe bark of holy Church to the everlasting kingdom in heaven.

From the time of Peter the Great onwards, *Russia* had been striving, not without dust and heat, to become part of the Western world. The process of westernization was in part exceedingly unfavourable to the position of the Russian Orthodox Church. Liberal ideas streamed in from the world of Voltaire and the Encyclopedists and later from the world of revolutionary France. A concept of religious toleration quite incompatible with the claim of the Orthodox Church to be the Church of the whole Russian people came to be widely accepted. The Empress Catherine II set forth an Edict of Religious Freedom, in which for the first time liberty was granted to confessions other than the Orthodox Church to organize themselves as religious bodies. The Holy Synod of the Church published this edict, on 17 June 1773, with a preamble which justified it on the ground that Almighty God permits the existence of all kinds of beliefs, speech, and confessions and that, in accord with this divine will, it is the main purpose of her Majesty that love and amity should prevail among her subjects. The logical consequence of this is the end of missionary activity; instead the spiritual fathers of the Church are to see to it that no trouble arises through differences of opinion among the subjects of her Majesty, but that love, peace, and unity shall prevail among them. Among the manifestations of the weakening of Orthodox control are to be reckoned the spread of Western religious sects and the foundation of the Russian Bible Society in 1813.

The loss of missionary energy was followed by a widespread tendency to apostasy among the Christians who were the fruits of eighteenth-century Orthodox missions. The movement away from the Church started among those of Muslim origin but it was not long before it extended to those who had been brought in from the various pagan cults. Philaret Amphiteatrov, who was Archbishop of Kazan from 1826 to 1836, reports the number of apostates in his area as having been 299,314. Of the recently baptized Tartars, 13,058 out of 14,796 had fallen away; these had previously been Muslims. For those who had previously been pagans, the figures are as follows: of 350,818 Chuvashes, 233,500 had deserted the faith; of 66,650 Tchermisses, 45,096; of 4,866 Voticks, 4,409. Only the tribe of the Mordvins, who had been more completely Russified than the others, stood fast against the flood of unbelief. Even in the first days of the Islamic advance against Christianity, the figures of apostasy had never reached totals anything like this. The facts are so overwhelming as to amount to a grave condemnation of the whole Russian method of evangelism, through governmental pressure and favour without the kind of Christian teaching that could make conversion anything more than nominal.

The nineteenth century was a time of wonderful renewal in Orthodox piety and self-consciousness. Perhaps partly in response to the challenge of the West, Orthodoxy, and particularly Russian Orthodoxy, awoke to a new sense of its own special mission in the world. Orthodoxy was beginning to rediscover the treasures of its own historic past, in the theology of the great Greek Fathers of the Church and in its unique liturgical tradition. Prelates such as Philaret of Moscow (1782–1867, Metropolitan of Moscow 1821), theological thinkers such as Alexei Khomiakov (1804–60), great writers such as Fyodor Dostoevsky (1821–81), found in Orthodoxy their spiritual home, and built it up to new heights of grandeur. This inner renewal of the spirit of Orthodoxy found its expression in a renewal of missionary activity on a new and very much better basis.

It may be convenient to arrange this brief summary of Orthodox missionary activity around the names of three great missionaries.

Michael Jakovlevitch Glucharev was born in 1792, the son of a priest. As a student he rapidly distinguished himself by his abilities, and in particular by his gift for the acquisition of foreign languages. At the age of twenty-five he was already professor of Church history and the German language at the seminary of Ekaterinoslav. In those days his piety was marked more by the traits of German pietism and of mysticism in its later form than by the authentic tradition of Orthodoxy. But gradually he became dissatisfied with this type of religion, and sank more deeply into the expression of Christianity which was natural to one of his Russian background. In 1819 he became a monk, and took the name Makary – Makary Glucharev is in fact the name under which he is known to history. The scene of his lifework was to be the Altai plateau in Central Asia, where he was to be the Apostle of the Kalmucks of that region. This was a comfortless area in which to work:

The snow-covered heights of the Altai range made heavy demands on the missionary; pathless ridges with an average height of from 8,000 to 10,000 feet in height, valleys with dark lakes and marshy morasses, hot summers and exceedingly cold winters, made even travelling from place to place a torment.[33]

Makary knew enough of previous missionary history to be resolutely opposed to the methods that had hitherto been in use. He was willing to baptize candidates only after a long catechumenate during which they had received Christian instruction in their own language. And he constantly impressed on his fellow workers that baptism is the beginning of the process of conversion and not the end of it. Use must be made of every possible means to help the converts to live their lives genuinely as Christians. They must be encouraged to adopt a more settled way of life, taught agriculture and gardening, and helped to practise such handicrafts as are possible in the life of a village. The result of these principles is that Makary did not originate any mass movement; he is not recorded to have baptized more than 675 candidates in the course of fourteen years. But when, exhausted by the

33. J. Glazik, *Die russische-orthodoxe Heidenmission* (1954), p. 119.

labours and cares of his remote mission, he gave up the charge of it at the age of fifty and retired to a monastery, he left behind one Church, three schools, a hospital, and a number of Christian villages in which the Christian life was more than a name. Much more important than this, he had shown the Russian Church – at a crucial period of its development – what missionary work can really be.

One of the legacies of Makary to the Church was a book with the title *Thoughts on the Methods to be followed for a successful Dissemination of the Faith among Muhammadans, Jews, and Pagans in the Russian Empire*. Makary's concern was to interest the whole Russian people in the missionary responsibility which God had given it. But this is impossible unless a deep spiritual renewal of the people takes place. The only instrument for this is the diffusion of the Bible in its entirety among them (Makary himself made a translation of the Bible into Russian); from this alone is the necessary spiritual power to be derived. And, since a right understanding of the Bible presupposes a certain measure of literary culture, popular education is to be developed on the widest scale. The leaders of the Church in the period at which Makary was writing had not yet emerged from the stiff conservatism of the eighteenth century; most of what he said and wrote fell on deaf ears, and it was only much later that the significance of his work in the history of Orthodoxy came to be better appreciated.

There could hardly be a greater contrast than that between our first great figure and our second. John Veniaminov (1797–1879) was born, the son of a sexton, in the village of Anginskoe in the province of Irkutsk in the very heart of Siberia. Trained in the seminary of Irkutsk, he married the daughter of a priest, and in 1821 was ordained and installed as pastor of a city church in Irkutsk. In 1823 the Bishop Michael Burdakov asked the young priest to undertake the spiritual care of the Christians in the remote Aleutian Islands, where, as we have seen, the mission had dwindled away to almost nothing. Veniaminov, out of regard for his family responsibilities, refused, but, when the call was repeated, he finally gave way. The party left Irkutsk on 7 May 1823. After a journey which lasted fourteen months, they at last reached their goal – to find neither church nor parsonage awaiting them.

The Aleuts had all been baptized. When there was no priest, they baptized one another, or were baptized by Russian settlers in the vicinity. But they had had no missionary for thirty years, and in fact worshipped an unknown god. And their association with the Russians had introduced habits and diseases among them by which their very existence as a people was threatened. Veniaminov's first task was to build himself a house and church – a task in which the people could give little help, as they had no knowledge of handicraft. Then followed the learning of the language, the first simple translations, and the teaching of the faith. Veniaminov was astonished at the eagerness to hear the word of God:

> The most inexhaustible preacher might well be worn out before their attention and their eager desire to hear the Word of God begin to fail.

Veniaminov was not content with the pastoral care of one congregation. He passed from island to island, and in 1829 crossed to the American mainland at Nushagak, where he preached and baptized a number of converts. In 1834 he moved his headquarters to the island of Sitka. To this period belongs the composition of his most famous work, a simple book on the spiritual life called *A Guide to the Kingdom of Heaven*; this was later translated into Russian, and in 1848 also into German. In 1839 Veniaminov returned to Russia, where all doors and all hearts were open to him, and he received the highest commendation for his scientific as well as for his spiritual work. But his joy was darkened by the news of the death of his wife, whom he had left behind with his children in Irkutsk. This deprivation of family life, however, opened for him the way to another career. In 1840 he became a monk, taking the additional name of Innokenty; this step was soon followed by his elevation to the episcopate as bishop of an enormous eastern diocese which included the Aleutians, the Kurile islands, and the peninsula of Kamschatka.

The next thirty years saw a steady expansion of Veniaminov's vision and of the range of his responsibilities. He travelled everywhere in his vast diocese, even as far as the extreme north of Siberia, encouraging Christians, noting the good qualities even of the non-Christians – 'even unbaptized Koniaks and Tchukches have many good qualities and customs – hospitality, self-respect and regard for their good name, faithfulness to their pledged word, and readiness to help those who are in need without any expectation of reward' – and founding new mission stations. In 1850 he was raised to the dignity of archbishop, and in 1852 he arranged that the whole of the province of Yakutsk should be added to the area under his care; he transferred his own headquarters to

Yakutsk in order to make centralized administration possible. But this was not the end. Russia had been extending its power in the direction of the Amur river. In 1858 a great new province, extending as far as Manchuria and the Sea of Japan, was added to the Russian dominions. Veniaminov moved once again, this time to Blagoveshchenk, in order to supervise the spiritual occupation of the new lands.

When he is sixty-three years old, we meet him in Japan, two years later once more in Kamschatka, and five years later still in the interior of the Amur Province. At that time he was pondering plans for the extension of the work into Manchuria; he hoped to have missionaries qualified in medicine as well as in theology, in order to forestall the Roman Catholics, who were also moving in this direction. Lack of personnel and financial support made it impossible for these plans to be carried into effect.

At last, at the age of seventy, Veniaminov felt that the time had come to retire. He withdrew to a monastery in Russia – but not for long. It happened that just at that time Philaret Drozdov, the Metropolitan of Moscow, died; it was agreed by all that Innokenty Veniaminov was the right man to succeed him. So the aged prelate emerged from his retirement, to serve for eleven years as metropolitan of one of the greatest sees in the world. Here his aim was to expound the truth that missionary witness is a duty which is incumbent on the Church as a whole and on every member of it. He was instrumental in founding the Orthodox Missionary Society, which came into being on 25 January 1870. This late elevation was a strange conclusion to a remarkable career. As a French writer has remarked:

Veniaminov, born in the neighbourhood of Lake Baikal, and later Metropolitan of Moscow, stands as a symbol of an entirely new phase in the religious history of Russia. . . . At an earlier date, the Slavic peasant had descended from the Carpathians and extended his hold across Asia. Now he turns back to his own country; but now it is a new man who comes back, forged by the experiences of life in Siberia. . . . Tempered by the dangers, by the hardness of the climate, by their laborious studies, these priests came back to Russia, with their souls renewed, well-instructed and zealous.[34]

As we have seen, in 1860 Veniaminov was in Japan. There he encountered the third of our trio of great personalities, and two

34. Quoted in J. Glazik, *Die russische-orthodoxe Heidenmission*, p. 157, from *Missionaires*, Vol. x, 1945, p. 224.

men met who between them were to render almost a century of missionary service in the East.

Japan had been hesitantly opened to Russian residence in 1859. It was decided that Hakodate should be the dwelling-place of Russia's diplomatic representative in Japan, and with the recognition of diplomatic relations came also the right to enjoy the ministrations of a Russian priest. A student named Ivan Kasatkin offered himself for the post and was accepted. He was ordained priest, became a monk, and in religion took the name Nikolai. He arrived in Japan on 2 June 1861.

Nikolai stated long afterwards that he had come to Japan with the express intention of doing missionary work. But he had to proceed with great caution, since he had no missionary commission from his Church, and Christianity was still a prohibited religion in Japan. The first advice given him by Archbishop Veniaminov was that he should acquire a deep knowledge of the Chinese and Japanese languages; the first years were consumed in this difficult task. It was not until 1868 that Nikolai ventured to baptize his first three converts – Sawabe (a man of the Samurai class), the physician Sakai, and an otherwise unknown Urano.

In 1869 Nikolai returned to Russia, leaving a little flock of twelve baptized Christians and twenty-five catechumens. His representations were crowned with success; the Orthodox Mission was constituted, with a staff of one archimandrite, three hieromonks, and a catechist. Nikolai was raised to the dignity of archimandrite. When in 1873 the penal laws against Christianity were abrogated, Nikolai moved to Tokyo and occupied himself, among other things, with the building of the splendid cathedral, which was later to be severely damaged in the great earthquake of 1923. In 1880 he was consecrated bishop, and in 1906 he was given the title of archbishop.

Nikolai was determined from the start that this was to be an Orthodox mission to the Japanese people, entirely independent of the Russian state and its traditions. To this end, he laid it down in his instructions for the mission that from the earliest possible date promising young men should be selected with a view to training as catechists, the best among whom might later be ordained to the priesthood. Japan was to be evangelized by the Japanese. Lay people were to be drawn into the administration of the Church in a way that was almost unknown in other Orthodox Churches. A 'great Synod' was to be held once every two years, and attended by representatives from all the parishes; forty persons were present at the Synod of 1895, and this year was marked by the ordination to the priesthood of the first two converts, Paul Sawabe and John Sakai.

Priests were of two kinds. The so-called 'white' priests, who were in direct charge of the congregations, were married men who had received little training beyond what was necessary for carrying out their liturgical functions in church. The liturgy was celebrated throughout in Japanese, though the music followed the Russian tradition which is entirely alien to the Japanese understanding of music. The direction of the work was in the hands of the 'black' priests, the monks, whose training was very much more thorough. This distinction made possible a somewhat rapid development of the indigenous priesthood; the highest number reached appears to have been thirty-five in 1912. There was never a mass movement but the number of Christians continued over many years to increase by about 800 a year; thus there were 7,611 baptized Christians in 1882, 26,000 in 1900, and 34,782 in 1914. It had been the aim of Nikolai to attract the higher classes of society, in order to create the Christian élite through whom the work of Christianizing Japan could go rapidly forward, but in this he had less success than had been hoped for, and most of the Christians were drawn from the humbler ranks of society.

Naturally, the determination of Nikolai to identify himself with his Japanese friends was put to a severe test during the war between Japan and Russia in 1904–5. The attitude of the Japanese government was admirable. Missionaries were not disturbed in their work, and Russians living in Japan were protected against insult and assault. Nevertheless, national feelings will not be so easily quenched; and in the circumstances Nikolai's pastoral letter to his flock is a notable document:

Brothers and sisters, carry out all the duties that are demanded of you as loyal subjects in this situation. Pray to God that he may give victory to your imperial army; thank God for the victories that have been given; make sacrifices to meet the needs of the war. Those of you who are called to the field of battle must fight without regard for your own lives, not out of hatred against the enemy, but out of love for your own people. . . . But, in addition to our earthly fatherland, we have another, a heavenly fatherland. To this all men belong without distinction of nationality, since all men are equally children of the heavenly Father and brothers one of another. This our fatherland is the Church, in which . . . the children of the heavenly Father in very truth make up one family. It is for that reason, brothers and sisters, that I do not separate myself from you, but remain in your family as though it was my own.[35]

Nikolai lived to celebrate the golden jubilee of the beginning of his missionary work, and died not long after, on 16 February 1912. He left behind him a Church of 33,000 members in 266 congregations, with thirty-five Japanese priests, a hundred and six catechists, and eighty-two students in seminary. There were imperfections in the work, as there are in all missionary work. But when we consider the slow progress of all the other missions in Japan, with their far greater resources, the achievement of Nikolai stands out as very remarkable. He deserves the tribute paid to him by a distinguished missionary of another communion; Henry St George Tucker, later Presiding Bishop of the Episcopal Church in the United States, wrote of him that:

The rapid progress of the work of the Orthodox Church was due to the character and ability of their pioneer missionary, Father (afterwards Archbishop) Nikolai, the outstanding Christian missionary of the nineteenth century.[36]

Soon after the death of Nikolai, storms and tempests fell on the Orthodox Church in Japan. With the revolution of 1917 support was cut off, and the mission had difficulty in maintaining itself. Divisions in the Russian Church came to be reflected in divisions in the Church in Japan, with disastrous effects on its spiritual life. Today there is little to show for the noble work of the first great pioneer.

We have not attempted to depict all the missionary work of the Russian Church. There was a renewal of the mission in China, where the first Chinese priest was ordained in 1883. There were efforts in the Caucasus, and the continuation of work among the still non-Christian peoples of European Russia itself. The results make it questionable how far the missions had been conducted on the right lines, and how deep the Christian penetration into the life of the many and various peoples had been. In 1905 freedom of religion was decreed for all the inhabitants of the Empire. This was followed by relapses into Islam and paganism on such a scale as to suggest that the Christianization had been at best very superficial.

The monk Spiridon, who has left a lengthy and detailed record of

35. Quoted by F. Raeder in *Allgemeine Missionszeitschrift*, Vol. XXXII, 1905, p. 551: 'Die Missionstätigkeit der russischen orthodoxen Kirche'.

36. *The History of the Episcopal Church in Japan* (1928), p. 102.

his experiences in Siberia, gives us a rather gloomy picture of what he found. The missionaries were still following the ancient practice of using the influence of the state to further their work and to secure material advantages for their converts.

On one occasion [reports Spiridon] I went round the Buriat villages in the neighbourhood. . . . I entered a hut, and was received in a friendly fashion. I chatted of this and that, asked questions, and finally proposed that I should talk to them about God. . . . When I had ended, one old Buriat said to me: 'Religions are many, but there is only one God'. 'Zaschoi,' I replied, 'how nice it would be, if you were baptized.' 'I haven't stolen a horse,' he answered, 'why in the world should I be baptized?' I was deeply shaken. From his own point of view the old man was entirely in the right; under the rule of Bishop Melety [Yakimov] it was the custom to baptize all the rogues and swindlers and horsethieves. They asked for baptism, in order that as Christians they might be able to escape the penalty of their misdeeds.[37]

Later on he says:

As I came personally to know the Orochens, I found that, heathens before their baptism, they were still heathens after it, and are so till the present day. The fault, in my opinion, lies at the door of our missionaries. Their aim was not to enlighten these poor people, who lived without the light of Christ, nor to strengthen them in Christian living through the example of their own virtues, but simply to baptize as large a number of people as possible, and through the number of those whom they had baptized . . . to win the favour of their diocesan authorities.[38]

On one occasion, a lama spoke in such glowing terms of Christ – 'If all men were true Christians, they would find it impossible to sleep, they would be constantly awake from unutterable joy, and that would be heaven on earth' – that Spiridon asked him why he was not baptized.

The important thing [was the reply] is not baptism but the renewal of life. What good does it do you Russians that you call yourselves Christians? Excuse my frankness. You Russians do not know Christ, and you do not believe in him. You live in such a way that we uncultured folk flee from you, and fear you like the plague.[39]

This is not the whole of Orthodox missionary work; the imperfection of much of it is balanced by the heroic example of the

37. Spiridon, *Mes Missions en Sibérie* (Paris, 1950), p. 62.
38. ibid., pp. 65 f.
39. ibid., p. 67.

saints and the solid achievements that they have left behind. But it is good that Christians should hear and mark all that can be said from the other side. Our sharpest critics are often our best friends; and no reader of the New Testament need be surprised to learn that the work of God in the world goes forward in spite of the imperfections as well as because of the virtues of Christian believers.

12

From Mission to Church

Presumably all missionaries from the beginning have had it at the back of their minds that as a result of their labours Churches would sooner or later come into existence, and that these bodies must sooner or later acquire all the characteristics and qualities that are subsumed under the term 'Church'. But all too often they seem to have been hazy in their outlook, and hesitant about putting into force the experiments through which alone Churches can come into existence in regions where previously Churches were not to be found. And, strangely enough, it seems that missionaries in the nineteenth century had less Church-sense than their predecessors, and found it more difficult to imagine a state of affairs different from that which had grown up under their care and that of their predecessors. For this four reasons can be suggested.

The first new factor was the conquest of speed, and the ease of communication that resulted from it. The invention of the electric telegraph spoiled all. In the days of Carey, a year would ordinarily elapse between the posting of an important letter and the receipt of the answer. Naturally the missionary enjoyed almost complete freedom of action; he was compelled by force of circumstances to make his own decisions, right or wrong, in the light of the situation as he saw it. As communications improved and became more speedy, at every turn the missionary had to refer matters to his home board or committee. The man on the spot lost in importance. What he lost was gained by a distant body of men, the majority of whom had never visited the lands concerning the destinies of which they had to make so many decisions. The same phenomenon is to be observed in other spheres; the ambassador, the governor, the Indian civilian – each of these markedly changed his character as the century advanced.

Secondly, the great increase in missionary enthusiasm in the course of the century meant more missionaries and much greater continuity in the work. This had its excellent side, but it meant that few of the indigenous colleagues of the missionaries could work with such freedom as had been enjoyed by Andrew Ly or by

Satyanāthan. Continuity meant routine and rhythm; it was easy for the missionaries to be lulled into a sense that things would go on just as they were for a very long time, if not for ever.

In the third place, the doctrine of the Church played far less part in theology than it does today. The emphasis was on the Church as an administrative organization, as a corporation, rather than on the Church as the divine creation, the body of Christ. This was as true of the Roman Catholic Church as of any other. Father M. J. Congar, in a brilliant summary of dogmatic text-books about the Church much used in seminaries in the nineteenth century, tells us that

in the one treatise as in the other, the study of the nature of the Church is reduced to the study of its authority as judge in matters of controversy. These are treatises about the ecclesiastical or clerical structures of the Church. The only part that Christ plays in it is that of founder; the role of the Holy Spirit is to guarantee the final infallibility of the judgements passed by the Church and nothing else. Apart from a few pages at the beginning, where as part of the explanation of the various names by which the Church is called, a number of texts from the Bible are quoted, nothing whatever is said about the inner being of the Church.[1]

If the Church was no more than this, its emergence could well wait until other and more pressing tasks had been accomplished.

The gravest source of blindness or incomprehension was, however, the fact that the majority of Protestant missionaries had no strong sense of the Church at large. In most cases missions had been undertaken as the personal effort of devoted Christians, and not as the responsibility of the Churches as a whole. This was true even of the Roman Catholic Church. The pioneers in the work were the great religious Orders; we have seen something of the strenuous efforts that had to be put forth by the Propaganda and the Curia before what Rome regarded as a seemly measure of control over the various missions was arrived at. Ziegenbalg had been ordained by the Bishop of Zealand, but he was under the direction of the 'College' in Copenhagen, a body which was more responsible to the king than to the Church.

Separation between Church and mission was carried to the extreme possible limits in Germany, Holland, and Switzerland. In most cases the missionary had been trained in a special institution, where the studies were not on the same level of academic excellence

1. *L'Ecclésiologie au XIXᵉ siècle* (1960), p. 95.

as in the universities[2] and the examinations of which were not recognized by the Church. He was then ordained not by the Church but by the missionary society, to the office not of minister of the word and sacraments in the Church but of 'missionary', a theological concept unknown to the New Testament. When on leave, he could not preach in any church, since his ordination did not carry with it any right of ministry in his home country. He was simply the employee of a large concern in Europe, submissive to its directions, dependent on it for financial support, responsible to it and to it alone, without direct dependence on or responsibility to any church body. Naturally 'the mission' filled his thoughts and his horizon, and 'the Church' seemed to be a distant and not very important problem of the future.

Theoretically the Roman Catholic and the Anglican missionary should have been free from such perplexities. But their situation was less different from that of their colleagues than might have been supposed. In both cases the pioneer missionaries were sent ahead to carry out their labours without the help and direction of a bishop. This meant that they too were responsible to a missionary society in the West, the heads of which, however sympathetic, could not always be aware of the real needs of the work in the field and (though themselves churchmen) were acting to some extent independently of the central fellowship of the Church.

When bishops were provided for already-existing mission fields, the results were sometimes disturbing and startling. When in 1876 the young[3] and vigorous Reginald Stephen Copleston arrived in Ceylon as bishop, he set himself to reorganize the work of missionaries, chaplains, and others in relation to the bishop and the Church according to his own mind. His proposals were wholly inappropriate, and such as could have been thought up only by an Oxford dialectician. The resistance of the missionaries was strong, and as a result the Bishop withdrew from all of them the episcopal licence without which they could not officiate as clergymen. Deadlock was complete. In the end Archbishop Tait of Canterbury had to be called in to mediate. With endless patience he worked out a compromise which was acceptable to both sides. Copleston –

2. The same was true in England. The CMS had its famous institution at Islington, in which many notable men were trained.

3. His consecration as bishop had to be a little delayed, in order that he might reach the minimum canonical age of thirty. Copleston was the *fourth* Bishop of Colombo, the see having been formed in 1845; his actions brought out into the open tensions which had existed below the surface.

who apart from being an Oxford dialectician was a man of deep humility and spiritual power, a sincere and utterly devoted missionary – lived to become one of our outstanding authorities on Buddhism, and crowned a great career by eleven years of service (1902–13) as Bishop of Calcutta and Metropolitan of the Church of India.

This ancient controversy is revived only to make clear the kind of difficulties that can arise when a mission is not recognized from the beginning as being an instrument of the Church and nothing else. It is not surprising that for a number of years the CMS was suspicious of the bishops and all their ways, and that the missionaries tended to feel that their first loyalty, and that of their converts, was to the mission and not to the Church. The story of the leading Indian clergyman who came to London over a century ago, looked at St Paul's Cathedral, and asked whether it was a CMS church or an SPG church, is probably apocryphal; but an apocryphon, though not strictly true, can be *ben trovato*. It is clear that for many Christians in the younger Churches, the first and great Christian reality was 'the mission'. This was naturally identified with their friends the missionaries, with their way of doing things, their particular habits of worship, and even with national and political loyalties which were wholly irrelevant to the situation of the Indian or African Christian. Most Christians probably had some awareness of the existence of the world-wide Christian fellowship. But by a disastrous theological error, this reality was arrived at synthetically, by putting together the existence of Anglicans and Methodists and Baptists, instead of the other way round, the body of Christ being the great reality of which Anglicans and Methodists and Baptists were recognized to be fragmentary and very imperfect incorporations.

MISSIONARY ATTITUDES

This situation could not continue for ever. At quite an early date missionaries had begun to look forward to the emergence of the Church – the suggestion of 'an Indian Catholic Church' was put forward over a century ago, in 1862. What hindered progress was primarily the lack of any clear theological understanding of the nature of the Church.

It must not be supposed that missionaries were all the time resisting the passionate desire of their people for independence.

The vast majority of the Christians, never having experienced anything but the 'colonial' situation of missions, were fairly well content with its advantages, and had hardly an idea that it could be changed. And when the possibilities of change were put before them, many Christians of the younger Churches viewed the proposals with horror. When a delegation of the CMS visited Travancore in 1921, to plan greater independence for the Church, the representatives of the depressed-class element in the diocese, convinced that the exchange of missionary leadership for leadership by the Syrian element in the Church would be, if anything, worse than the replacement of King Log by King Stork, stated emphatically: 'We should, therefore, be protected for a hundred years more under the direct rule of foreign missionaries and bishops.' When, a generation ago, Dr Hendrik Kraemer – who perhaps did more than any other man to change the relationship between Churches and missions – was making his great journeys of inspection in Indonesia, he found the Christians painfully divided between a desire for greater independence and extreme anxiety with regard to their own capacity to undertake greater responsibilities than those that had already been granted to them. Was it really wise to disturb an old and well-established system which seemed on the whole to be working remarkably well?[4]

The movement for greater freedom for the younger Churches had, however, been steadily gaining in strength from the beginning of the twentieth century onwards. But the motives were in the main personal and national, rather than theological.

Missionaries were extraordinarily slow to recognize and trust the gifts of indigenous Christians. Even when ordained to the ministry, they were still regarded as no more than assistants to the missionary. In Indonesia the astonishing system prevailed that the Indonesian pastor could prepare candidates for baptism but the baptism had to await the occasional visit of the missionary. At the service the Indonesian pastor was allowed the notable dignity of holding the bowl containing the water for baptism. Change was resisted, on the ground that, if the local pastor were allowed to baptize, the effect would be not so much to enhance his prestige as to lower the value of the sacrament in the eyes of the faithful. Such being the case, it is not surprising that gifted and naturally

4. H. Kraemer, *From Mission-field to Independent Church: Report on a decisive decade in the growth of indigenous Churches in Indonesia* (1958). The journeys in question took place between 1926 and 1935.

ambitious young men hesitated to enter the service of the mission. So many new careers, better paid and offering greater independence, were opening before them in the secular world. If they felt led to Christian service, the YMCA offered far greater opportunities for real equality of status and treatment. So it was in the YMCA that two of the most notable Christians of the time, K. T. Paul in India and T. Z. Koo in China, found their field of operations.

With the rise of national feeling, the foreignness of the Church caused distress and anxiety to leaders in the younger Churches. The missionary was an alien, and had brought an alien faith. This was a hindrance to conversion; the suspicion was widespread that a Christian could not genuinely be a patriot. The direction of almost all missions and Churches was in the West. Financial control in the field was strictly in the hands of the missionaries. There was a growing feeling that all these things needed to be changed. Hence the emphasis on the *indigenous* Church. All these were well founded and legitimate aspirations, but they still dealt with what are really marginal considerations, and did not face the essential theological problem of the nature of the Church and of the relation between missions and the very existence of the Church.

LEADERSHIP IN YOUNGER CHURCHES[5]

A Church cannot become genuinely independent unless it has local leaders capable of replacing the missionary on every level of thought and activity. Lay leaders are indispensable, but much depends on the quality of the ordained ministry. Theological training is at the very heart of the life of a younger Church.

We have had occasion to allude from time to time to the policies and practices of missions with regard to the provision of an ordained ministry from among the Christians under their care. In some respects policy was more adventurous in the seventeenth and eighteenth centuries than it later became. And until the twentieth century hardly anywhere was there a carefully thought-out policy or an attempt to relate the work overseas to the standards demanded in the preparation of candidates for the ministry in Western countries.

5. It was about 1928 that the phrase 'younger Churches' became part of common missionary parlance. It is now a dated phrase.

Rash and hurried ordination of ill-chosen and ill-prepared candidates is always a mistake and leads on to disaster, as we have seen in connection with the scandal of the Goanese priests in India in the nineteenth century. But the reaction of excessive caution is equally to be deplored. Every single Church has at one time or another fallen into both these errors, but much more frequently into the latter than into the former.

It was only gradually that missions and Churches became aware that it was useless to talk about the development of indigenous Churches unless far more attention was paid to the training and development of the indigenous ministry. This was the burden of a larger number of directives and Encyclicals put out by the three great missionary-minded Popes, Benedict XV, Pius XI, and Pius XII, the effect of which was a revolution in the Roman Catholic world between 1915 and 1960 in the number and quality of indigenous priests, and in the facilities for their training. 'The Indigenous Ministry of the Church both ordained and lay' was one of the main subjects under discussion at the third World Missionary Conference, held at Tāmbaram (Madras) in 1938, the first of those conferences at which the representatives of the younger Churches were equal in number to those from the older Churches.[6]

In many areas the training given to ministers of the Gospel was gravely inadequate to prepare them for the burdens that they were destined to carry. In some cases a single missionary would gather around him a small group of disciples whom he would teach and train as best he might; though in such cases the intellectual level could hardly be more than elementary, the spiritual results were not rarely impressive. More often a group of three or four over-worked teachers, missionary and indigenous, would struggle to maintain a three-year course in theology with miserably inadequate facilities and with only a handful of books in the library. When teaching had to be given in an Asian or African language, the lack of any adequate Christian literature was painfully evident. The Tāmbaram Conference ordered an enquiry into this training and asked for a policy.

The Second World War broke out shortly after the end of the Tāmbaram Conference, and made immediate action difficult. Nevertheless, the Churches did pay attention to what they

6. And at which, by order of John R. Mott, half the delegates had to be under the age of thirty-five, a precedent which subsequent ecumenical conferences have failed to follow, to their own grave loss.

reported. A careful survey was made in India, on the basis of which Dr C. W. Ranson wrote an authoritative book, *The Christian Minister in India* (1946). A second survey, carried out by four groups of investigators, went through tropical Africa in the years 1950 to 1954; their researches were brought together in a second book of the greatest importance, *The Christian Ministry in Africa*, by Dr (later Bishop) B. G. M. Sundkler (1960). All this work has not gone without its results, particularly in the reduction of the number of theological teaching institutions, and the creation of strong central institutions in place of the many weak schools which previously existed. Thus, in South India, the formerly Anglican Theological College at Tirumaraiyur was recognized as the one centre of theological education for the whole Tamil-speaking area of the Church of South India. Anglicans, Methodists, and Presbyterians co-operate at Umuahia in Nigeria; Anglicans and Methodists at Immanuel College, Ibadan. In the Union of South Africa, careful plans worked out over a number of years resulted in the establishment of one single centre for theological education in which diverse churches work together on the lines of what has appropriately been called the 'miniature university'.[7] Trinity College, Singapore, was a joint enterprise of Anglicans, Methodists, and Presbyterians. Five Churches, among them the Waldensian, co-operate in the Evangelical Faculty in Buenos Aires.

A further stage in this development was reached when the plan for the theological education fund was accepted at the Assembly of the IMC held in Ghana in 1958. This had been made possible by the Sealantic Fund, under the control of the brothers Rockefeller, who had offered to provide 2 million dollars for theological education overseas if the mission boards would provide an equivalent amount.

Nine American mission boards supplied the amount required to balance the Sealantic offer. The offer was accepted. The Theological Education Fund Committee came into being. One of the notable achievements of the Committee was the calling into existence of a faculty of theology at Yaounde in the Cameroons; it was hoped that this higher school of theology might serve as the centre of training for those who would be the leaders in the rapidly growing Churches of French-speaking Africa.

7. 'A single college with a single faculty is composed of a number of separate hostels founded and maintained by the different Churches.' (*Tāmbaram Series*, Vol. IV, p. 208.)

THE INDIGENOUS EPISCOPATE

It is certain that the only way in which men and women can demonstrate their capacity for bearing responsibility is by being put into positions in which they must carry great responsibility and must stand alone. The central question in the younger Churches was whether those who had control of those Churches would commit the positions of highest authority and dignity in them to members of the non-European races.

We have noted in the appropriate contexts the early Roman Catholic experiments in creating an indigenous episcopate in India, China, and Africa, and the subsequent cautious withdrawal from this willingness to experiment. At the end of the nineteenth century almost the whole Roman Catholic world was convinced that the indigenous episcopate was a dream for a still far-distant future. There was one notable exception. Father Vincent Lebbe, whom we have twice met already in China (pp. 220 and 347), was of the opinion that the time had come, indeed had long since come, when this step forward ought to be taken, and that the indigenous hierarchy should at once be called into being. As a simple Lazarist, Father Lebbe could have had but little influence on affairs. But his views came to the notice of the rough and formidable Cardinal van Rossum, Prefect of Propaganda from 1918 to 1932, a Dutchman of whom it was written that 'his manner was generally cold, but he was not incapable of smiling', and that his character 'ordinarily reflected that of his people, accustomed to overcome through long patience and obstinate labour the difficulties that nature has accumulated on its territory'. It was the principal aim of Cardinal van Rossum to put into execution the liberating Encyclical of Benedict XV (*Maximum Illud*, 1919), in which the Pontiff lamented that

it is to be deplored that there are regions in which the Catholic faith has been introduced for centuries, without any indigenous clergy as yet to be found there except of a lower order; and that there are certain nations, which have long been illuminated by the faith, and have emerged from a savage state to such a degree of civilization that they possess men who excel in all the areas of the arts and sciences; and yet in several centuries have not managed to produce bishops to rule them, or priests capable of making a deep impression on their fellow-citizens.

Van Rossum turned to a quiet and studious Italian prelate, Celso Costantini (later Cardinal), and sent him to China as apostolic delegate, that is, as direct representative of the Pope with authority over all bishops and archbishops in the field. When

Costantini arrived in China in 1922, he had in his pocket the authorization for the choice of the first Chinese bishops. Yet, when this project was put before the heads of the missions in China, they replied that they had not a single man qualified to carry the heavy burden of the episcopate. Pius XI, known for the vigour of his views and for the power with which he carried them into effect, was not the man to be put off by such excuses; if the authorities in China did not know of Chinese priests suitable to become bishops, they must set to work to find them. The choice fell first on Father Philip Tchao, who had been a friend and colleague of Father Lebbe. Five others were quickly found, the Reverend Fathers Sun, Theng, Chen, Hu, and Ton. In order to mark the special solemnity of the occasion, the Pope called the six bishops-to-be to Rome, addressed them affectionately, and himself consecrated them in St Peter's (1926).

From this time on, progress in the development of the indigenous episcopate was extremely rapid. Already in 1923 Mgr Tiburtius Roche had been consecrated Bishop of the Fisher Coast in South India. In 1927 the first Japanese bishop, Mgr Hayusake, was consecrated. The first Annamite bishop came in 1933, the first Ceylonese also in 1933, the first Korean in 1937. In 1939 Pius XII held another great international consecration in Rome. Here, for the first time, was an African candidate, Mgr (after 1961 Archbishop) Kiwanuka from Uganda, and also the first Malagasy, Mgr Ramarosandratana; with them were a Chinese, Mgr Tien, and an Indian, Mgr Agnisami, as well as eight European or American candidates for scattered sees in different parts of the world. Many others have followed, notably in Indonesia, and in various areas of tropical Africa. More than once, in order to emphasize the truly international character of the Church, the Pope has appointed an African bishop to be the consecrator of a white colleague.[8] The number of indigenous bishops in Asia and Africa was stated in 1962 to be 69.[9]

8. The first case that has come to my notice is that of the consecration of Mgr Perrardin at Kabgayi in Ruanda, on Palm Sunday 1956, the consecrating bishop being Mgr Aloys Bigirumwami, a product of the White Fathers' mission.

9. This is the figure given by Fr Bernard Leeming in *World Christian Handbook*, 1962, p. 169, but this is almost certainly an underestimate. Gensichen, op. cit., p. 50, states that in 1959 there were 68 indigenous bishops in Asia and 25 in Africa. This is borne out by the statements in *Église Vivante*, September 1962, p. 217, that, of 68 bishops in India, 40 were already Indian; and p. 270, that in 1961 alone the number of African diocesan bishops had been increased by 15, either through new consecrations or through elevation of assistant bishops to diocesan status. The number is, of course, changing all the time.

For centuries the majority of the cardinals had been Italians and between 1523 and 1978 no one but an Italian sat on the throne of St Peter. It was Pius XII who took the decisive step of turning the Italian majority in the College of Cardinals into a minority, and of appointing to this high office bishops who were not of European origin. In 1945 no less than thirty-two new cardinals were named; among them were the Archbishop of Mozambique, Clemente Teodosio de Gouveia, Portuguese by race but the first cardinal in tropical Africa; Mgr Agagianian of the Latin Armenian Church, a favoured candidate for the papacy in 1958; and Mgr Tien, Archbishop of Peking. These were followed shortly afterwards by Mgr Valerian Gracias, Archbishop of Bombay. After them cardinals were appointed from the Philippines, Tanganyika, and a number of Latin American countries. There is no reason why the Pope should always be a European. Younger readers of this book may live to see an African Pope, reigning as a successor of those popes who took the decisive action by which the indigenous episcopate was called into being.

Before the end of the eighteenth century the SPCK in London was talking of the possibility of having in India suffragan bishops of Indian race, so that the Church should not depend on the fortuitous communication with Britain, which could at any time be interrupted by natural or human calamities.[10] We have referred to the first Anglican experiment with an African bishop and its unfortunate sequel. We have seen that Bishop Azariah was consecrated in India in 1912. The first appointment of a Chinese bishop was that of Archdeacon Sing as Assistant Bishop in Chekiang in 1918. The first two Japanese bishops were consecrated in 1922. There had been a steady succession of African assistant bishops in West Africa, of whom Bishop Oluwole was the most outstanding. There was a real danger that the tradition might be established that the European was always the diocesan bishop, and the national merely his assistant, really no more than an episcopal curate. In India the second and third bishops of Indian race, both men of the highest devotion, were assistants, Banerjea for Lahore and Tarafdar for Calcutta. When at length African bishops were consecrated in East Africa, they too were all in the position of assistants to European diocesans. There was, in fact, an accession of dignity but little, if any, accession of authority.

10. They spoke of suffragan bishops, because it was supposed at that time that diocesan bishops would be members of the House of Lords.

This could not continue. The bombshell came in 1940 when the Japanese bishops quite politely told their British, American, and Canadian colleagues that they must all resign and be replaced by Japanese bishops. Undoubtedly this was a wise step, however great the shock to Western feelings; the time had come when it was absolutely necessary for the Japanese Church to show that it was not an outlier of the West but a genuinely Japanese manifestation of the risen life of Jesus Christ.

For so small a Church to produce ten bishops put a heavy strain on its resources. Yet, if this change had not been made, it would have been far harder for the Church to hold together in the dark days of the Second World War, and to reconstitute itself in the new world of the postwar era.

A similar process had taken place in China. Almost all the Chinese bishops had been first elected as assistants to Westerners, but, having proved their ability, they succeeded to diocesan authority as the Western bishops withdrew.

In India progress was less rapid than might have been expected, but in a democratically organized Church, if the electors persist in thinking that a particular European is the man best qualified to fill the post, who can compel them to elect an Indian?[11] In Africa, also, the change came only rather later. Sierra Leone received its first African diocesan bishop only in 1962. The diocesan bishops in both Nigeria and East Africa are now African, but paradoxically at the election in 1961 of a new archbishop for West Africa, some of the Europeans voted for an African candidate, and some of the Africans voted for a European, Cecil Patterson, Bishop on the Niger. In the end it was the white man who became archbishop.[12]

The American Methodist Episcopal Church faced the problem of national leadership at a fairly early date, and not unnaturally first in Japan, where the pressure of national feeling was from the beginning particularly strong. The first Japanese bishop of this Church was Yoitsu Honda, who was appointed in 1907. Honda had been a member of the Yokohama group of early converts and had been baptized in 1878. Honda died in 1911, and was followed as bishop by Kogore Uzaki, who was present at the Jerusalem Conference of 1928. The time of India came rather later. The first

11. Just at the time of the writing of this chapter, the diocese of Bombay elected as its bishop the Rt Rev. Christopher Robinson, who had been for a number of years Bishop of Lucknow. But the diocesan bishops are now Indians.

12. The matter had to be referred to the Archbishop of Canterbury for final settlement.

Indian Methodist bishop, J. R. Chitambar, was appointed in 1930. Among those who have followed him, John Subhān, a convert from Islam, is well known from his autobiography *How a Sufi Found his Lord* (1942). All the Methodist bishops in India today are of Indian origin.

TOWARDS GENUINE INDEPENDENCE

These have been given as examples of a process that was going on in every part of the world, and affecting the missions of every Church. But behind the individuals stands the problem of the Church itself. As long as a link exists between a somewhat weak group of Christians in a mainly non-Christian country and a strong mission based in a nominally Christian country, can the alleged independence of the younger Church ever be anything more than a sham? One of the things that we have learned in the political situations of the twentieth century is to look behind appearances, and to identify the power structures by which the destinies of men and nations are really determined. In particular, it is always most necessary to ascertain the point at which financial control is exercised. It is possible to change the entire outward appearance of the fabric, and yet to leave the essential structures untouched.

The nettle was firmly grasped by one of the most brilliant and strongest bishops of modern times, Edward Harry Mansfield Waller (of Tinnevelly 1914–23, of Madras 1923–41). He insisted that in South India the two great Anglican societies, the CMS and the SPG, must lose their separate existence in such a way that the Church could become the very centre of Christian existence, and that the missionary from overseas from the very day that he landed should be, and should feel himself to be, a member, a servant, and a minister of the Indian Church, with no other national or ecclesiastical status whatever, as long as he remained in India. In an area where the traditions of the separate societies were deep-rooted, this was an outstanding achievement; in few areas has success been so decisive and so complete.[13]

13. Like many men of very quick intelligence, Waller did not always remember how long it takes to persuade ordinary men of the truth of what is self-evidently true. One result of his reorganization of the diocese of Tinnevelly was a schism, through which in 1925 about 7,000 people, many of them genuinely pious Christians, left the Church of their origins; after over sixty years the schism has not yet been completely healed.

For the *Roman Catholic Church* there was little difficulty, once the decision to move forward was made. In one area after another the territorial hierarchy was established; as soon as possible the number of indigenous bishops was increased, and the time came when the entire hierarchy of an area, including its head, was national. Territorial hierarchies (taking the place of the earlier rule of vicars apostolic) were created, for instance, for West Africa in 1950, for South Africa and for British East Africa in 1951, and for French Africa in 1955. All these hierarchies are part of the Latin Church, and their first task is to maintain the order of that Church as this is understood in Rome, with only certain possibilities of experiment within clearly defined limits. One of the links in the Roman Catholic system which makes possible a rapid development along these lines is the appointment of apostolic delegates. The apostolic delegate is the direct representative of the Pope for a certain large area – India, Indonesia, South Africa, or wherever it may be. He may not interfere in the detailed administration of the diocese, but he has the right to call general synods and conferences of bishops. It is his task to serve as the link between the Curia and the bishops, to send careful reports to Rome, and to keep a watchful eye on all that passes in his area. His authority is great; his influence, if he is careful to use it wisely, can be even greater. In cases where a government wishes to maintain diplomatic relations with the Vatican, the apostolic delegation may be raised to the dignity of a nunciature or an internunciature.

The *Anglican* system, while not dissimilar to the Roman, allows a good deal more independence to the developing local Church. Any four adjacent dioceses, subject to certain agreements, may constitute themselves an ecclesiastical province under their own elected archbishop. Such a province elects its own bishops, draws up its own constitution, canons, and rules, and may revise the Prayer Book as it wishes and deal with all matters concerning its inner life and its outward relationships. The Archbishop of Canterbury, apart from some residuary rights in the African provinces, has no authority in any independent province, though he may be and often is consulted on important matters of more than local interest. There is nothing to hold the provinces together except an intense and intangible loyalty. Each province knows that if it misuses its liberty, or goes beyond certain limits in the exercise of its independence, it is liable to lose a fellowship which it regards as extremely valuable. No coercion can be exercised by one on another, but the sense of belonging to a great world-wide body tends to lift the eyes of Anglicans above excessive preoccupation with their own local concerns.

The first independent province of the new type was New Zealand, formed in 1857 under the inspiration of the great Bishop Selwyn. We have noted in another chapter the beginnings of provincial organization in Japan. China followed in 1928, and India in 1930. In India the process was particularly complex, as the Church there was legally a part of the established Church of England, and it was found difficult to put asunder Church and State whom Henry VIII had so firmly joined together.[14] The turn of tropical Africa came rather later, with the provinces of West Africa (1956), East Africa (1958), and Uganda (1960). In 1957 an archbishopric was created in Jerusalem, with general responsibility for the countries of the Middle East. The Churches in Japan, China, and India already have nationals at their head.[15]

Many Churches were plagued by the problems of finance and property, and found it convenient to retain 'the mission' in existence even when 'the Church' had attained its independence. For instance, the German and Swedish *Lutherans* in South India brought into existence the Tamil Evangelical Lutheran Church, and provided it with a bishop.[16] But the bishop was not head of the Church of Swedish Mission, which was an entirely separate organization. In some cases, though not all, the division was made in such a way as to hand over pastoral and evangelistic work to 'the Church' while keeping the expensive institutions, schools, and hospitals in the hands of 'the mission'; with the result that the Church was not interested in the institutions, and the institutions tended to feel but little sense of responsibility to the Church.

In some cases the definition of a younger Church was so narrowly drawn as to make it almost impossible for a foreigner to be either a member or a minister of it. In this case, missionaries were reduced to a state of complete paralysis, since as foreigners

14. This is one of the few processes of devolution of which we have a full and completely reliable account by one who took part in it. See C. J. Grimes, *Towards an Indian Church* (1946). I have not noted here the dates of the formation of the mainly English-speaking provinces.

15. The election of the second national Metropolitan of the Church of India, Pakistan, Burma, and Ceylon in 1962 was interesting, in that Dr Lakdasa de Mel, who then became Bishop of Calcutta, was Ceylonese and therefore technically a foreigner in India.

16. The first Indian bishop of this Church, Dr Rajah B. Manikam, was consecrated in Tranquebar in 1956, during the celebration of the 250th anniversary of the arrival of Ziegenbalg and Plütschau in 1706.

they were unable to work within the Church, and as churchmen they were unwilling to work outside it because they did not wish to set up a parallel and possibly rival organization. Cases are on record in which missionaries who desired to break through this deadlock by taking service as ministers of the younger Church were informed that they were fully at liberty to do so, but that they would automatically lose all their pension rights in their home Church, through the labours of which the younger Church had come into being.

In certain cases the independence of the younger Church was brought about, or at least accompanied by, the total disappearance of the missionaries. We have seen that, until the death of L. I. Nommensen and after, hardly any preparation for independence had been given to the Batak Church in Sumatra. Until the outbreak of the Second World War, the devoted and efficient German missionaries had retained strict control over almost every detail of the life of the Church. Then suddenly all the missionaries without exception were interned. The Church was left completely on its own, and had to take over immense responsibilities for which it had been very imperfectly trained. It need hardly be said that a time of considerable disorder followed, but the Batak Church held together, and emerged from the time of trouble with a firm resolution never again to admit any foreigner to a position of control or authority in the Church.

PROBLEMS OF THE CHURCH

The tension between the local and the universal is a permanent part of the perplexities of the Church in its pilgrimage through time. Can there be such a thing as an indigenous or national Church? And, if so, what should its character be? And how is it to be related to the universal and unchangeable realities of the Christian tradition?

Missionaries of certain traditions within the Christian world have held very firmly that their business was not to impose upon Indians and Africans a particular form of Christian doctrine, still less a developed form of Church order, but to sow a seed which, falling into alien soil, would grow according to the law of its own being into forms never previously seen in the Christian world. This point of view was admirably stated by a Congregational missionary in China in 1919:

The other conception of the Church is simply that of a spontaneous, natural fellowship of believers, whose outward form and inward growth are alike to be determined by the indwelling Spirit of Christ. Our task as missionaries is not to establish an institution, but to teach a way of life – not merely individual life, but corporate life in Christ. Such a Church has no material basis. What is sown is a living seed. We believe it will grow because we believe in the gift of the indwelling Spirit. The outward form and organization will be the outcome of inward, spiritual need, and is not introduced merely because there is such and such an ecclesiastical system in the West.[17]

Many missionaries set out with this ideal. In practice it was found to be unworkable, for two reasons. In the first place, the first conversions do not usually come for ten or twelve years. During that time the interested observers have become perfectly familiar with the externals of Christian worship. If they are in an Anglican area, they know that Christians kneel for prayer; naturally it has never occurred to anyone to tell them that the Orthodox Churches stand for prayer. The convert is imitative; he wants to do things exactly in what he conceives to be the proper Christian pattern and in no other way. Secondly, the convert has literally thousands of questions on what he may and may not do in countless situations; he can no more be expected to work out for himself the answer to all these questions from the New Testament than he can be expected to work out the theorem of Pythagoras for himself. He demands answers, and will not be put off. Nowhere is this development more clear than in the Church of the island of Bali. The founder of the Church, Dr Hendrik Kraemer, was determined that from the beginning this was to be the Church of the people and not of the missionaries. The result has been seen in a most laudable and satisfactory spirit of independence. But in all its inner and outward life the Balinese Church is more like the Dutch Reformed Church than the Dutch Reformed Church is like itself. It manifests hardly a trace of the wonderful art and culture of that most beautiful island.

Some missionaries have been highly content with this docile dependence of the Christians on the Westerner and his ways. Others have been interested from the beginning in the background of their people and the local culture, and have perhaps been more concerned than the local people that a bridge should be built between the old ways and the new. In recent years this has been a major preoccupation of all those who have thought deeply about the mission of the Church.

At an earlier stage we have considered the wise words of the Propaganda to the vicars apostolic whom it was sending out to the Far East. At the beginning of this century the Roman Church began again to take an interest in the creative capacities of those who had been won for the faith:

Where the Gospel is preached in any new lands, it should not destroy or extinguish whatever its people possess that is naturally good, just, or beautiful. For when the Church calls people to a higher culture and a better way of life under the inspiration of the Christian religion, she does not act like one who recklessly fells and uproots a thriving forest. No, she grafts good stock upon the wild, that it may bear a crop of more delicious fruit.

So Pope Pius XII, in the Encyclical *Evangelii Praecones* of 1951. What are these good things in the old which must be preserved through the grafting on to them of the new? A distinguished French Jesuit, with the verve of his nation, draws us an exciting picture of the possibilities:

The day the African world is christianized, one can foresee a prodigious sacramental and liturgical development, a religious art, a return to the sacred dance, which is now foreign to us. . . . I cannot conceive how Africans could praise God without dancing, for the dance is so much part of their being that it is an integral part of their civilization. Through them we should discover once again the liturgical meaning of the sacred dance. This would have disconcerting consequences for us. How could we impose the Roman Mass on them – this silent Mass, so admirably western, so sober, so inward, so discreet, so reserved, wherein the mightiest religious feelings find expression in perfect decorum?[18]

What, if anything, hinders the development of this spontaneous adaptation of the old to the new? Resistance comes primarily from the converts themselves, and from their reluctance to have anything to do with the world from which they have emerged. Only in rare cases does the convert regard his former religion as a preparation for the new. The old world was a world of evil in which he was imprisoned, and from which he was delivered by the power of

18. Jean Daniélou, SJ, *The Salvation of the Nations* (Sheed and Ward, 1949), p. 39. The priests of the Ethiopian Church do dance rhythmically as they sing in church; this is moving and exciting for the beholder, but would cause comment in Westminster Abbey.

Christ. The last thing that he wishes is to turn back in any way to be associated with that which to him is evil through and through. And, after all, he is the only man who knows; he has lived in that world, and knows better than anyone else its lights and shadows. If his reaction to that world is wholly negative, who has the right to condemn him? This may not be the last word on the relation between Christian faith and that which has come before it, but it may well be a transitional word which is worthy of all respect.

This attitude meets us so constantly, and in so many parts of the world, that there can be no doubt that it is spontaneous and not simply due to prejudices inculcated by the missionaries. The resistance is most striking, perhaps, in the field of music. Some years ago young people in the Church of Bali began to set Christian words to the old traditional tunes. The elders were profoundly shocked; it was impossible for them to dissociate the tunes from their origins, and all that they conveyed was wholly unedifying. It was decided that the songs might be sung in informal gatherings of Christians, but that they could form no part of the regular and official worship of the Church. The same is true of architecture. Missionaries have developed a feeling that churches should be built more on the lines of traditional architecture, and less as imitations of Western models. But when in India certain churches were built to look somewhat like Hindu temples, the general feeling of the Christians was wholly hostile. In the first place, a Hindu temple is not built for corporate worship; secondly, what goes on in a Hindu temple is, according to the judgement of many Indian Christians, wholly incompatible with what the Christian wishes to express in his worship of the one true God. A temple should look like a temple, a mosque like a mosque, and a church like a church; if looking like a church means looking like a pale imitation of Western nineteenth-century Gothic, that may be a pity, but for the moment there is no more to be said – from the point of view of the conservative Indian Christian.

Clearly this should not be the last word. If races and nations are part of the plan of God for his world, the Gospel must work so creatively as to find its expression variously along the lines of the outlook and experiences of the different races and nations. But time must be allowed for this. The old non-Christian past must sink below the horizon. That which has come from the West must be so absorbed and assimilated that it can be transformed and re-expressed in categories different from those of the world of its origin. But this is the work of generations, not of years.

Some encouraging beginnings have been made. Especially in Africa, both South and West, the African artistic genius began to find its own idiom for the expression of Christian truth in painting and sculpture. The pale white Christ of traditional Western art was being replaced by a figure that the African could recognize as his own. The churches in South India have had for a century and a half the tradition of the writing of Christian lyrics in Indian metres to be sung to Eastern tunes.[19] We have already met the great Marathi hymn-writer Nārāyan Vāman Tilak. The high-caste Tamil convert H. A. Krishna Pillai in the early years of this century produced in his *Rakshanaya Yāthrikam* an Indian version of the *Pilgrim's Progress* in epic form which (though too difficult for the ordinary reader) is recognized as conforming to all the canons of classical Tamil poetry.[20]

The West looks eagerly to the East for new insights into Christian theology. A century ago the great Bishop Westcott of Durham expressed the opinion that the definitive commentary on St John's Gospel would come from India, with its background of mystical insight. But so far very little has come back in answer to this expectation. The West has done its work too well; the trained theologians of the younger Churches have been so conditioned by the effort of mastering western theology that they have little to offer in the way of native and original understanding. Younger Church leaders are aware of the problem. At the time of the Tāmbaram Conference a group of Christian thinkers, some of them converts from Hinduism, put out a book called *Re-thinking Christianity in India* (1938). The book is not in itself outstanding; rethinking is not achieved merely by substituting Sanskrit words for appropriate words of Greek origin. The effort was, however, most significant as evidence of the striving of the younger Churches for genuine self-expression. The work of Dr P. D. Devānandan, as an interpreter of Christ to the Hindu, and of the Hindu to the Christian, is of the highest value.[21] The National Christian Council of India has its Theological Commission, and a suggestive book, *The Theological*

19. The first church register of the cathedral in Palamcottah, dating from 1780, includes the name of the great singer Vedanāyaka Sāstriar, at that time a boy of about twelve years old.

20. It is to be noted that both these famous poets were adult converts. The difficulty of creative and original work seems to be much greater for those who have been brought up from birth as Christians.

21. See especially his principal work *The Concept of Māyā* (1952). Since writing these words I have learned with sorrow of the death of my deeply-valued friend.

Task in India (1960), has been published. From Japan come the beginnings of authentic and original utterance.[22] But these are as yet small beginnings.

TOWARDS CHRISTIAN UNITY

Renewed attention to the doctrine of the Church could not but raise the fundamental question of its unity. Less harm was caused by Christian divisions than might have been expected. Hinduism and Islam are both religions of innumerable – and sometimes mutually excommunicating – sects. They did not expect of Christianity a unity which they did not possess themselves. To the tribesman in New Guinea it did not seem out of the way that the Dutch tribesman should do things rather differently from the German tribesman. But this mitigation of the evil could not be accepted as justification for continuing in division. The history of Protestant missions in the twentieth century is the history of steady progress in the direction of unity.

Throughout their whole history, Protestant missions have experienced in countless ways the benefits of *co-operation*. What has brought them together more than anything else has been fellowship in the work of the translation of the Bible. From its inception in 1804 the British and Foreign Bible Society was ecumenical in constitution, in outlook, and in purpose. This excellent attitude has constantly been reflected in the field. In many areas, missionary translators have not always found it possible to agree as amicably as the translators of the Septuagint are mythically alleged to have done; but they have acknowledged themselves bound by a common loyalty to the Word of God and to the truths revealed in it.

The growing sense of mutual responsibility found expression in a whole series of conferences of missionaries in the various major areas of the world: India from 1835 onwards; Japan from 1872; China from 1877 and Latin America only after 1910.

It must be noted that all these were in the strictest sense of the term 'missionary conferences'. Those who attended them were almost to a man foreigners in the lands where they worked; there

---

22. On which see Carl Michalson, *Japanese Contributions to Christian Theology* (1960), a careful study of a number of recent and contemporary Japanese theological thinkers.

was a certain awareness of the growing Church, but almost everything was discussed from the foreign point of view. Nationals were not excluded, but those who were present had come as guests rather than members, and exercised a minimum of influence on the course of the proceedings.

One result of all these conferences was the establishment of the principle of the Comity of Missions. At the start Protestant missions had tumbled in higgledy-piggledy, without any plan or consultation. The resulting confusions were endless. Gradually it became plain that a delimitation of territories, and a gentleman's agreement among the missions not to work in the territory where another mission was already established, would greatly help to clear up the situation. Agreements entered into were generally kept, and a rather seemly patchwork quilt replaced the rags of earlier disorder.[23] There were, of course, absurdities and limitations. Some missions did not enter into or accept the validity of such agreements.[24] It could hardly be thought reasonable that the inhabitant of a village on one side of a small stream should be baptized not merely as a Lutheran but as a Danish Lutheran, and that his cousin on the other side of the stream should become a member of the American Dutch Reformed Church. Geography, not conviction, became the basis for denominational allegiance. But on the whole the system worked well, as long as Indian Christians were content to stay where they were. With the growth of education, however, Christians, like other Indians, began to wander far and wide in search of work, and might land in a place where there was no Church of their own denomination. With the opening up of the tea estates in the hills, thousands of families went off for prolonged periods of work. What was to happen? Should the denominations follow their own sheep wherever they were? Or should the sheep find temporary refuge in alien folds? On the whole, Lutheran and Anglican shepherds followed the sheep; Free Churchmen regarded folds as interchangeable. But, in any case, it became clear that comity was no solution, and could not be more than a palliative in a situation which in itself was indefensible.

23. It is interesting to note, however, that at the London Conference of 1888 feeling waxed very sultry over alleged breaches of the rules of comity.

24. It is clear from what has been written earlier that the Roman Catholic Church has never been party to any such agreement.

This was the situation when the great Edinburgh Conference of 1910 took place. This brought into being a new era, which may be called the era of *Councils*.

It had long been clear to the wisest heads that co-operation on the local or national level must lead to international co-operation, and that what was happening in the various mission fields must sooner or later be reflected in the West. As early as 1888 Gustav Warneck, the great German theorist of missions, had put forward, in a remarkable paper read at the London Missionary Conference of that year, a comprehensive plan for a General Missionary Conference to be held every ten years, and for a Central Committee to hold things together between the conferences:

> To give the Central Committee a sound basis, Missionary Conferences should be formed in every Protestant nation, to include all existing Evangelical Missionary Societies of that nation, and elect deputies to represent them on the Central Committee.

The duties of the proposed committee, including the initiation of united action, were outlined, and the paper concluded:

> That we must learn to look upon Missions as a *common cause* . . . to kindle a missionary *corps d'esprit* . . . to accustom ourselves to a *solidarity of missionary interests*, and to place in the foreground the *vital* truths of the Gospel common to us all.[25]

Warneck was a prophet born out of due time. His views were so far in advance of those commonly held in missionary circles in that day, that in the absorbingly interesting and revealing discussion on the subject of comity[26] no reference at all was made to his proposals. But Warneck, as a true prophet, had correctly discerned the signs of the times; the next generation was the period in which Conferences of Missionary Societies were formed in almost all the lands of the sending Churches.

This was the background of the Edinburgh Conference of 1910. The greatest of all the achievements of that Conference was the bringing into existence of the first permanent instrument of international Christian co-operation outside the Roman Catholic Church. The vision of Warneck was at last to be realized. It is hard

25. Quoted in W. R. Hogg, *Ecumenical Foundations* (1952), p. 44. This book admirably surveys all the material relevant to this section of our study.

26. In the course of which the Bishop of Nelson, New Zealand, made some astonishing remarks about Presbyterian bishops and the possibility of double ordination for some missionaries.

to believe that up to this date no such instrument existed, but the mutual suspicion of the missions was such, and their safeguarding of their own autonomy so jealous, that even in 1910 the coming into existence of the Continuation Committee of the Conference must be regarded as something of a miracle.

The war intervened, and it was not until 1921 that the International Missionary Council was formally constituted, with Dr John R. Mott as chairman and Dr J. H. Oldham as secretary. The two great architects of the conference thus became the two great architects of the council. But there were certain advantages in this delay. In the West the council was based on the co-operative conferences of missionary societies; it needed the support of similar co-operative bodies in the mission fields, and as yet no such bodies existed. Perhaps the greatest of all the services rendered by Dr Mott was the journey in the East, between 11 November 1912 and 11 April 1913, during which he convened and presided over no less than twenty-one conferences and was instrumental in bringing into existence what gradually grew into the National Christian Councils of Japan, Korea, China, and India.[27]

At last the missions in the various countries had a common point of reference, an instrument for common action if they so desired, a regular meeting-place, and a body that on occasion could act on behalf of the missions and Churches in relation to governments. One of the most effective of all the councils was the National Missionary Council (later National Christian Council) of *India*, *Burma*, and *Ceylon*. Its action at one particular crisis may serve to illustrate the kind of service that the councils have continuously rendered. Hardly had the council been constituted when the First World War broke upon the nations. Gradually all the German missionaries were interned, and the council was faced with the responsibility for carrying on the work of these not inconsiderable missions. Through its wise and conciliatory actions, Churches were kept in being, and the continuity of the work was maintained. Specially notable was the service rendered by Foss Westcott, Bishop of Chota Nagpur (later of Calcutta), who exercised the oversight of the German (Gossner) mission in his area for four years without the smallest attempt to turn Lutherans into

27. Mott himself took this view of the work of those months. In 1945 he remarked to Dr Richey Hogg: 'My first and greatest service to the International Missionary Council was to bring about the formation of the National Christian Councils.' (*Ecumenical Foundations*, p. 156.)

Anglicans, and, when at length the German missionaries were allowed to return, handed the work back to them intact.

The council method having proved itself, the number of councils continued steadily to grow. One difficulty, however, was that councils tended to be created for smaller and smaller areas. One of the most successful councils was that of *Kenya*, which managed to draw together all the non-Roman missions and Churches in Kenya.[28] But *Tanganyika* had a separate council, and there was no single body which could operate on behalf of East Africa as a whole. Clearly the council method has its limitations; the next period of development was marked by the tendency towards regional organizations.

REGIONAL ORGANIZATION

The starting-point of the new movement was a conference held at Manila in January 1948, at which leaders of the East Asian Churches from *Japan* to *Pakistan* were for the first time brought together.[29] It was at once evident that these leaders had never met one another before, and had no common point of view. Their connections had been with Europe and America, and no lines of communication had ever been established in Asia. The first step was the setting-up of the East Asia Secretariat, a joint enterprise of the IMC and the World Council of Churches, to serve as liaison between the Churches, and to create those lines of communication which had hitherto been so conspicuously lacking. The first secretary, Dr R. B. Manikam, was so successful in this task that within ten years the Churches were ready for another forward move. At conferences held at Prapat (*Sumatra*) in 1957 and at Kuala Lumpur (*Malaya*) in 1959, the East Asia Christian Conference was brought into being as a standing organization of the Churches in the area, with officers and a secretariat. It is notable that *Australia* and *New Zealand* were invited to send representatives, and that a New Zealander, the Reverend Alan Brash, was appointed to the secretariat.

Where Asia had begun, *Africa* was soon to follow after. The first

28. At the price of being unable to affiliate with the IMC, to which some of the missions were unalterably opposed.

29. Only two foreigners were present at the conference, Dr J. W. Decker representing the IMC and Bishop Stephen Neill representing the World Council of Churches.

All-Africa Christian Conference was held at Ibadan, *Nigeria*, in February 1958. This was the first All-Africa Conference ever to be held, the Church at this point having gone ahead of the state. Representatives were present from all the African countries, with the exception of the small Spanish colonies. One hindrance to common action was found in the lack of a common language. English, French, and Portuguese had to be used as official languages. But this conference, too, set up a continuation committee to prepare the second conference, held at Makerere College, Uganda, in April 1963, and as a result Africa south of the Sahara grew into a region of the Christian Churches with its own permanent organization.

The value of the regional organization was at once apparent. There are certain great issues which cannot be dealt with on the basis of a single country, however large. Four issues which at once present themselves are the attitude of the Christian faith towards the now resurgent non-Christian religions; higher theological training; the advance of Islam in Africa; and the action required of Christians in regions of rapid social change.[30]

A council, in the current sense of the term, is an entirely new phenomenon in the Christian world, as to the theological and ecclesiastical significance of which we are still uncertain.[31] But, even before the national and regional councils had got into full working order, and in spite of the notable services they rendered, it became clear to many that such loose and flexible organizations could not provide the final answer to the search for effective and united Christian action in the modern world. There could be no answer short of the corporate union of the Churches.

ORGANIC UNION

The search for corporate union, though never wholly forgotten in the history of the Church, has taken on new and more urgent aspects in the twentieth century. There is the undoubted fact that the Church is more gravely threatened today than it has been for a

---

30. On the last of these, see the two books put out by the World Council of Churches – W. de Vries, *Man in Rapid Social Change* (1961), and P. Abrecht, *The Churches and Rapid Social Change* (1961).

31. This point is made by H. P. Van Dusen in his ecumenical survey *One Great Ground of Hope* (1961), pp. 60 ff., 127 ff.

thousand years, and that, in face of these menaces from without, division is a grave source of weakness. The practical argument in favour of union, based on overlapping and rivalry in the mission field and on the need for concentration of forces, became increasingly powerful with the growth of the Church and the increase in the number of agencies at work. The plaint from the younger Churches themselves, resentful of 'divisions for which we were not responsible, and which we do not desire to maintain', became ever more plangent.[32] But the really effective impetus behind the movement for unity was simply the theological rediscovery of the nature and doctrine of the Church; at about the same time it became evident to a number of thinkers in very varied communions that the spiritual unity of the Church is not sufficiently represented unless it finds its expression in an outward and visible unity.

Already more than a century ago seers in India were beholding afar off the vision of a single Catholic Church in India. But this was regarded as an eschatological expectation for a very distant time, and little was done to transform it into practical reality. The history of Christian union is the history of the twentieth century.

The first notable union was that of the Congregationalists and Presbyterians in *South India*, to form the South India United Church in 1908. This body had certain features which are characteristic of federations rather than of Churches. The formation of it does not seem to have been preceded by deep theological consideration of the differences in confession and Church order. Much freedom in liturgy and organization was left to the eight councils (one in northern Ceylon) of which the Church was made up. Yet those who lived in that Church maintained emphatically that it was a Church and much more than a loose federation, and it certainly helped to prepare the way for the greater union that was to follow.

The Edinburgh Conference of 1910 set in motion echoes throughout the whole of the Christian world, and the subject of unity, though not directly dealt with by the conference, was one of those that inevitably came to the fore. One result was seen in the series of conferences held at Kikuyu in *Kenya* between missionaries of the Anglican, Presbyterian, and Methodist persuasions with a

---

32. Younger Church statements on the need for union were read at almost all the great ecumenical conferences, notably at Jerusalem 1928 and Tāmbaram 1938.

view to closer union. One of these conferences in 1913 let loose an explosion, the precipitating cause of which was nothing more terrible than a service of Holy Communion at which non-Anglican missionaries were invited by the bishops present to take part in the reception of the sacrament. The passionate storm of protest from certain quarters, and the equally passionate storm of support from others, made plain both the intensity of the feeling engendered in favour of Christian unity, and the intensity of the opposition that any scheme of Church union must expect to encounter. The Kikuyu plans died away amid the fumes of the First World War, and Kenya still awaits its united Church, but the episode was of great value by reason of the education that it gave to countless thoughtful people in the Church.

The Church of Christ in *China* came into existence in 1927, on the basis of a simple confession of faith in Jesus Christ as revealed in the Scriptures, and brought together a wide range of Protestant Churches and missions, though without the adhesion of Lutherans or Anglicans. China is so large, and Christians were so scattered, that each region in point of fact continued to act very much as it had always acted. Yet the synods of the Church were experiences of a real and growing unity, and the undertaking of corporate missionary work in several areas, including that of the aboriginal peoples of the south-west of China, was a further bond of fellowship.

In *Japan*, as we saw, it was government pressure rather than an inner sense of spiritual need that led to the formation of the Church of Christ in Japan (*Nippon Kirisuto Kyodan*) in 1940. There was a danger, after the war, that the unity would be completely dissolved into its constituent parts. This has not happened; though some have departed, Methodists, Congregationalists, and some Presbyterians have held together. The Church has put forth a confession of faith far more definite than anything that it was able to produce during the war. A rather similar situation arose in the *Philippine Republic*. From 1900 onwards American missions proliferated. There, as in Japan, it was the desire of the Japanese during the occupation to have a smaller number of bodies to deal with that led to a large measure of Protestant amalgamation, and so union was promoted for pragmatic rather than for theological reasons. Various permutations and combinations took place, but the United Church of Christ in the Philippines, formed in 1948 out of Methodists, Presbyterians, and other Protestant elements, looked destined to survive and to grow. In 1962 it was credited with nearly 300,000 members, and it is considerably the largest of all the Protestant bodies in the Philippines.[33]

It is time to turn to the broadest, the most controversial, and in some ways the most successful of all the unions of Churches which have come about in the last fifty years – that which was achieved in *South India* in 1947 after twenty-eight years of hard labour. The Churches concerned were the Anglicans, the Methodists – though not including the Americans, who were more concerned with union in the north – the Presbyterians, the Congregationalists, and the Basel Mission Church (of Swiss and German origin). For the first time in history it was found possible to bring together episcopal and non-episcopal elements in a single Church. The task was not easy: those engaged in the discussions came again and again to the point of feeling that they could go no further, but faith and patience, and an overwhelming sense of obligation to the whole Church throughout the world, held them fast until the end.

The scheme as finally adopted expressed an unusual combination of definiteness with freedom. No attempt was made to draw up a comprehensive 'Confession of Faith' on the continental model, but a great deal of carefully thought out and precisely expressed theology – on such subjects as the nature of the sacraments and the ministry, and the role of the laity in the Church – is to be found scattered through the Scheme of Union. It was agreed that much liturgical freedom should be allowed to the Churches, until such time as the Church of South India itself should agree as a whole on its own liturgical expression. The most original feature of the scheme was an interim period of thirty years during which the union would be gradually brought to its completeness, and the ministry would be unified on the basis of ordinations in which bishops and presbyters would join in laying hands on candidates put forward by the congregations. This plan was criticized by some as a compromise in which essential elements of the Church's faith were in danger of being lost, hailed by others as the divinely inspired means through which an insoluble problem at last reached solution.

Those responsible for the planning of the Church of South India were aware that what they were doing would be intelligible only if seen as part of a great world-wide movement which was already in being, and to the furtherance of which the existence of the CSI

33. This Church is episcopal, but makes no claim to the historic succession of the episcopate.

would itself constitute a rousing summons. The stability shown by the CSI and the effects that it produced in various directions are evidence that they were not mistaken in their understanding of the situation.

The CSI itself engaged in discussions with the *Baptists* and the *Lutherans*. The former for the time being came to nothing. The latter, after many hindrances and frustrations, won through to the point of agreement; unless some unexpected happening puts new difficulties in the way, it seems certain that Lutherans whose Churches have their origins in Germany, Sweden, Denmark, and the United States will in the course of the next few years find a new home in fellowship with others who have always been their geographical neighbours but have previously been separated from them by ecclesiastical allegiance.[34]

Both in *North India* and in *Ceylon* plans of union were worked out which in most of the essentials have followed the path in which the Church of South India was the pioneer. Both, however, have had to face new problems through participation of the Baptists in the discussion; an ingenious plan of permitting both baptism of infants and baptism of believers, with confirmation at an appropriate stage for both, attempted simultaneously to safeguard the particular witness which the Baptists feel it their duty to maintain and to do justice to the view of those who feel that baptism of infants is in accordance with the mind of Christ. In order to avoid the difficulties felt by some over the interim period as provided in South India, and the coexistence within one Church of different types of ministry, a further ingenious proposal was put forward to make possible the unification of all existing ministries, through a ceremony of the laying-on of hands at the time of the formation of the union. Enthusiastically welcomed by many, and warmly commended by the Lambeth Conference of Anglican Bishops in 1958, this solution ran into unexpected difficulties, and it is not yet certain whether the union of all the Churches can be brought about on the basis of these proposals.

In *Nigeria*, Anglicans, Methodists, and Presbyterians had been for a long time drawing nearer to one another and in the end had put forward a scheme which at almost every point corresponded to

34. Reliable information on the discussions between the Church of South India and the Lutherans is provided by S. Estborn in *The Lutheran World*, October 1962, pp. 493–502.

that which was the basis of union in South India. Anglican pressure led Nigeria to consider modifications in the direction of Ceylon and North India. For a time it seemed doubtful whether the revised scheme would prove acceptable to the Churches, but the United Church of Nigeria came into being in December 1965.

It is clear that the movement for organic union is still in progress, and that its effects are being felt in many parts of the world. It is possible, however, that it is becoming rather less strong; the reason for this may be that much of the attention of the Churches has been concentrated on a rather different area of the unitive movement of the century.

MISSIONS AND THE ECUMENICAL MOVEMENT

The World Missionary Conference held at Edinburgh in 1910 is the starting-point of the modern ecumenical movement in all its forms. It was there that Charles Henry Brent, missionary Bishop in the Philippines, saw the vision which led directly to the Faith and Order Movement and to the first World Conference on Faith and Order held at Lausanne in 1927. The parallel movement, known as Life and Work, which held its first great conference at Stockholm in 1925, while arising less directly out of Edinburgh 1910, had many connections with it both in thought and in membership. But inevitably the various branches of what was from the beginning a single movement tended to develop in rather different directions. Faith and Order and Life and Work both became steadily more ecclesiastical – the Churches began to take a direct interest in the work, and those who came to the great conferences came increasingly as official delegates of the Churches. The International Missionary Council could not, and did not, change its constitution as a fellowship of missionary societies and of councils which were not in any sense of the word Churches.

But from an early date it was clear that this dichotomy could not continue for ever. There was a considerable overlap in personnel. Dr J. H. Oldham, who had won fame as the organizer of the Edinburgh Conference, was also the chief organizer of the Life and Work Conference held at Oxford in 1937 on 'Church, Community, and State'. William Temple (Bishop of Manchester 1921–9, Archbishop of York 1929–42, Archbishop of Canterbury 1942–4) had been present at Lausanne in 1927, was a delegate to Jerusalem in 1928, and was the principal architect of the message of that conference; he became chairman of the Continuation Committee of Life and Work, presided over the Faith and Order Conference in Edinburgh, 1937, and was present also at the Oxford Conference of 1937. Furthermore, there was an increasing sense that all problems must from henceforth be considered on the world-wide scale, and that the distinction between 'Home' and 'Foreign' was rapidly becoming an anachronism. Life and Work had been driven to consider problems of theology. The voice of the younger Churches was heard loud and clear at Lausanne 1927 and at Edinburgh 1937. Thus it seemed quite natural that when, in 1937, proposals for a World Council of Churches were brought forward and accepted in principle by the two conferences of that year, notice of the plans was sent to the International Missionary Council. The Tāmbaram Conference of 1938 took notice of them with favour and approval, though under its own constitution it could not directly take part in the plans for a council which from the start was to be a Council of Churches, and in which no other body would have membership.

The years between 1946 and 1961 were a period of steadily increasing co-operation between the two great bodies. 1946 saw the establishment of the first joint enterprise, the Commission of the Churches on International Affairs. This was followed by the creation of a Joint Committee, by the official declaration that each body was 'in association' with the other, by the incorporation of the study apparatus of the IMC into the Study Department of the WCC, by the creation of the East Asia Secretariat as a joint enterprise of both, and by co-operation in a host of other ways. This outward movement towards close association was furthered by a psychological consideration of the utmost significance – the dislike of the younger Churches for the word 'mission' and for everything associated with it, and their enthusiasm for the World Council. However unjust and unreasonable this may seem, it was clear that by 1948 the younger Churches had come to think of 'mission' almost exclusively in terms of Western aggression and financial domination, and of the missionary as the representative of alien and undesired control. In a Church organization they could feel the new and stimulating breath of equality; missionary organization seemed to speak of a permanent situation of inferiority and dependence. At the start the World Council was heavily Western; but this could be regarded as no more than a passing phase, a curable disease; and, in point of fact, the voice of the younger Churches was heard with ever-increasing force in both the open debates and the most confidential consultations of the World Council.

It was clear that amalgamation of the two organizations could not be for ever delayed. The problems arising from the differing constitutions were formidable, but the genius of the planners rose to the occasion; it was proposed that the IMC itself should enter the World Council as its Division of World Mission and Evangelism, but that a Commission should be formed through which bodies which were not Churches could retain their association with the IMC in its new form.

The process of amalgamation was not achieved without difficulty. When the proposals were put before the IMC Assembly in Ghana in 1958, the strength of the opposition became evident. The Orthodox Churches were unhappy, since they could not dissociate the idea of mission from that of proselytism – not unnaturally, since they had suffered so bitterly from the aggression of both Roman Catholics and Protestants in their own countries. The extreme conservatives, who had from the start regarded the World Council with the profoundest suspicion, were naturally unwilling to move into any closer association with it. Some held that the World Council had never shown the slightest interest in world evangelization, and that the cause was much more likely to be prejudiced than furthered by amalgamation with it. Yet others held that the World Council was already too large and top-heavy for effective working, and that, if two such organizations were brought together, they would tend to be paralysed by their own weight. But it was clear that feeling in the younger Churches was overwhelmingly in favour of the 'integration'. The crucial assembly of the World Council of Churches was postponed from 1960 to 1961 in order to give one more year for preparation and interpretation, and so the stage was set.

On Sunday 19 November 1961, at the Third Assembly of the World Council of Churches in New Delhi, the various resolutions leading up to integration were read, and the proposal of the Central Committee of the World Council of Churches was placed before the Assembly by the President, Archbishop Iakovos of the Greek Orthodox Church in the United States of America. The resolution was accepted without opposition. Archbishop Iakovos then solemnly declared that the two Councils were now united in one single organization, which would henceforth bear the name 'The World Council of Churches'.

This decision might in the end prove to be no more than a

change in outward organization. But, if the Churches knew what they were doing on this occasion, the event could be epoch-making in the history of the Church. In all periods from the beginning 'missions' have tended to be an adventure of inspired individuals, of religious Orders, of private societies, of groups of 'friends of missions'. Only rarely have they engaged the attention and the wholehearted support of Christian denominations. In some they have been strenuously opposed; in others harshly criticized, usually left ill-supported and half-starved. If the Churches knew what they were doing at New Delhi, they committed themselves to a revolution in their theology, in their understanding of the nature of the Church, in the organization of their manpower, in the distribution of their financial resources. Time will show how far fair words will be successful in translating themselves into heroic enterprises.

13

Yesterday and Today, 1914 and After

WESTERN ADVANCE AND NATIONAL REACTION

Again and again in our survey we have seen Christianity striving not to be a European religion. But on the whole its attempts were far from successful. Whether we like it or not, it is the historic fact that the great expansion of Christianity coincided in time with the world-wide and explosive expansion of Europe that followed on the Renaissance; that the colonizing powers were the Christian powers; that a whole variety of compromising relationships existed between missionaries and governments; and that in the main Christianity was carried forward on the wave of Western prestige and power.

Every conceivable attitude towards this situation was taken up by both governments and missionaries. We have seen Portuguese and Russian authorities in the closest alliance with missionary forces, and using all the powers of government to propagate at least the externals of the Gospel. We have seen the Dutch using the enticements of political privilege to subvert Roman Catholics and to convert non-Christians. We have seen the East India Company jealously attempting to keep every missionary out of its territories, and a British government making it plain that missionaries would be less than welcome in the mainly Muslim Northern Territories of Nigeria. Some missionaries felt so strongly the drawbacks of this colonial entanglement that, like the Belgian Father Lebbe, they went so far as to become naturalized citizens of the countries in which they worked. Others served as dutiful agents of their governments, sometimes being vested, like Livingstone, with consular powers, and in one or two cases rising to ambassadorial rank.[1] A great many, to their own distress and to the perplexity of their friends and fellow countrymen in government service, found themselves in the strongest possible opposition to their own governments in such matters as forced labour in Kenya.[2]

1. The last American ambassador to China before the communist triumph, Dr Leighton Stuart, was a former missionary.

2. In the period of development after the First World War, the Anglican archdeacon was one of the strongest critics and opponents of the government's policies.

In a great many cases missionaries welcomed the advance of the West, believing that it could bring peace to warring peoples and such blessings as the abolition of the slave trade and the establishment of justice for those who were too weak to secure it for themselves. Nationals were sorely perplexed. Many of them welcomed the West because of certain good things that it could give to their peoples. But often they recognized that the West was both deliverer and destroyer, and that therefore the white man was necessarily both friend and foe. Converts were usually from the classes that gained most from the advent of the West, and therefore for them the sense of deliverance was particularly strong. But it was quite certain that, if one day they should awake from the sleep of acquiescence, the missionary too would come to be regarded as both friend and foe. And all the time the wisest spirits had seen that this period of the greatness of the West could not be more than temporary, and that in the end a heavy price might have to be paid for alliances based on something other than obedience to the word of God.

The first sign of change came with the war between Japan and Russia in 1904–5 and the decisive defeat of Russia by Japan. For the first time Asia had successfully answered back. Most people in the West failed to read aright the signs of the times. Russia had made itself a great power in the nineteenth century, but many in western Europe still had the feeling that Russia was hardly European – a vast, medieval, and only partly civilized power. Japan, on the contrary, had made a successful bid for recognition as a modern nation. In 1902 Britain had concluded an alliance with Japan, and had held the ring while Japan concluded her affair with Russia. Japan was the new boy in the school, but so far regarded with approval as a slightly unusual but highly promising pupil. There had certainly been a reorientation of power; there seemed no reason to regard it as a revolution. Minds moved otherwise in Asia. News of the Japanese victories reverberated round the continent and were hailed with the excited astonishment of novelty. Today Japan and Russia; tomorrow, perhaps . . . but the sentence was generally left unconcluded.

What 1904–5 had begun, 1914–18 concluded. The European nations, with their loud-voiced claims to a monopoly of Christianity and civilization, had rushed blindly and confusedly into a civil war which was to leave them economically impoverished and without a shred of virtue. The Boer war, by a tacit agreement between the combatants, had been fought as a white man's war;

others had not been armed. In the First World War it was otherwise: Indian, African, and Japanese troops took part, with great distinction, against white men. On the whole they dutifully followed the behests of their rulers; but here and there there was lingering resentment that so many thousands of Indians and Africans had been drawn into quarrels which were not theirs. The Second World War only finished off what the first had already accomplished. The moral pretensions of the West were shown to be a sham; 'Christendom' was exposed as being no more than a myth. It was no longer possible to speak of 'the Christian West'.

Awakening to reality is always a painful process. We may think that the Christian realism in which we live is in the end far more conducive to real Christian witness than the euphoria which reigned up till the time of the First World War; but the first blasts of this reality were cold indeed to the Churches – and to their missionaries, and to those who had put their trust in them.

The Russian revolution of 1917 was a new and perplexing factor in the situation. A great new anti-Christian force had been let loose upon the world, a force with which for the future the Churches would have to reckon. News of bitter persecution and of the murder of the royal family set up a tremor of indignation and disgust throughout the Western world. But this first negative reaction began to give way to a certain anxious self-questioning, which continues till the present day. Were the Marxists not in part right? Was not the colonial epoch in reality a period of shame rather than of glory for the Western world?

The natural consequence of all this was the awakening of the ideals and passions of nationalism among the peoples of Asia and Africa. Nationalism is a strange phenomenon. At its best, it expresses a man's sense of loyalty and deep indebtedness to the country and people that have brought him forth. But this can easily slip over into a narrow and arrogant intolerance, and a contempt for the members of other and less favoured nations. If the state is deified and becomes the final and unquestioned authority in all the areas of man's life, then the way is opened to idolatry and blasphemy against God; any nonconformist minority is regarded as having no real ground for its existence at all; conformity or extermination are the alternatives. It was already clear that the new nationalism in Asia and Africa and elsewhere was exposed to all these dangers. It awakened high and noble sentiments in the minds of many who were previously asleep: it called forth devotion and the spirit of self-sacrifice, and inspired some of the most high-minded and admirable characters of this century. But what gave this new nationalism its special character was that it was basically a reaction against the West, against foreign and colonial dominance, and therefore – in a measure, and in certain cases – against that religion which came in with the West and was regarded by some as one of those destroying acids that corrupted the substance of national life and character.

Nationalism is still in the heyday of successful self-assertion in the till-recently colonial world. But as a matter of fact it goes back quite a long way in history, and it is not possible to fix an exact date for its beginning. In Japan it may be thought to coincide with the beginning of the Meiji era. In India, a convenient starting-point is the first meeting of the Indian National Congress in 1885, as a sequel to the first steps taken by the viceroy Lord Ripon to associate Indians with local self-government in their own country. Educated Indians were beginning to feel that they could do things on their own:

The new class perceived that the administration as a whole was against them, but they also felt that a strong tide of opinion in Britain was on their side. They were deeply impressed by the results of organized agitation. . . . The first meeting was held in Bombay in December 1885. It comprised only seventy members, who qualified by paying a small fee, and consisted mainly of lawyers, journalists, and schoolmasters. They were nervous and diffident. They seemed, in that first session, almost more concerned with insisting on their loyalty and the blessings of British rule than calling for progress and reform. But a start had been made, a call, if rather a muted one, had been sounded. It was from these modest beginnings that the Indian political giant of the twentieth century grew.[3]

MISSIONARY UNCERTAINTIES

At the same time the mind and temper of the Christian Churches was becoming afflicted by a new kind of uncertainty. There had been little discussion of theology at the Edinburgh Conference of 1910. There had seemed to be little need for it, when all were at one on all the fundamentals. All were agreed that Jesus Christ the Son of God was the final and decisive Word of God to men; that in Him alone is the certainty of salvation given to men; that this Gospel must be preached to every living human soul, to whom God has

---

3. P. Spear, *India: A Modern History* (1961), pp. 308–9.

given the freedom to accept or to reject and who must stand by that acceptance or rejection on the last day. The delegates differed somewhat in their attitude towards the non-Christian religions, but all were agreed that, as the lordship of Christ came to be recognized, these other religions would disappear in their present form – the time would come when Shiva and Vishnu would have no more worshippers than Zeus and Apollo have today. Expression of these views might differ a little in detail; it cannot be questioned that in 1910 there was practical unanimity with regard to the substance of them.

But in these years of rapid missionary expansion, a very different Gospel had been growing up and taking hold of the minds of a great many Christians, especially in America. The liberal was not by any means so sure that Jesus Christ was the *last* Word of God to man.[4] He was repelled by the exclusive claim to salvation through Christ alone. He tended to take a much more favourable view of the other religions than his more conservative colleagues, and to look forward to some kind of synthesis of religions rather than to the disappearance of any of them. The real enemy is secularism. Adherents of all the great religions should stand together in defence of the spiritual reality of man's life. There should be no hostility between them, the spirit of proselytism being replaced by the willingness to learn from one another.

This point of view was strongly represented at the second of the great World Missionary Conferences, held at Jerusalem in 1928. It is strange to contrast the confident tone of the Edinburgh pronouncements with the almost hesitant accents of what was said at Jerusalem. Clearly a comprehensive change was taking place in theological climate, in attitudes to other religions, and in the understanding of the missionary task. The most striking expression of the new point of view is to be found, however, not in the Jerusalem reports but in the Report of the (American) Laymen's Foreign Missions Enquiry, entitled *Rethinking Missions* (1932).[5] The Commission had travelled widely in Asia and Africa on behalf of the American missionary societies, and its factual reports are full of valuable observations and insights. The controversial elements

4. The first and perhaps the ablest expression of this view is *Die Absolutheit des Christentums und die Religionsgeschichte*, by the famous German scholar Ernst Troeltsch (1901). Troeltsch speaks of the Gospel as 'the highest point until now', and of the 'relative absoluteness' of Christianity. Can paradox go further?

5. The full title is *Rethinking Missions: A Layman's Enquiry after One Hundred Years*, by The Commission of Appraisal, William Ernest Hocking, Chairman.

are concentrated in the summary just referred to, which was in the main the handiwork of the eminent philosopher W. E. Hocking. The point of view here expressed was as different as could be imagined from that of the earlier missionaries. The report distinguishes between temporary and permanent elements in the function of a missionary. The task of the missionary today, it was maintained, is to see the best in other religions, to help the adherents of those religions to discover, or to rediscover, all that is best in their own traditions, to co-operate with the most active and vigorous elements in the other traditions in social reform and in the purification of religious expression. The aim should not be conversion – the drawing of members of one religious faith over into another – or an attempt to establish a Christian monopoly. Co-operation is to replace aggression. The ultimate aim, in so far as any can be descried, is the emergence of the various religions out of their isolation into a world fellowship in which each will find its appropriate place.[6]

Almost before this liberal view had had time to find formulated expression, the reaction against it had set in. A number of missionaries, mostly of continental origin, had come under the influence of the theology of Karl Barth, with its strenuous repudiation of liberalism in all its forms. Yet it has proved impossible to go back to the earlier point of view; and the kind of propaganda on behalf of missions which was acceptable in the nineteenth century now makes little appeal in the more cultivated and thoughtful circles in the Church. Western man had learned how much there was in his colonial record of which he had to be ashamed. He was much less sure than he had been of the uniqueness and finality of the Christian Gospel, and of his right to impose on the heirs of other great traditions what might prove to be, after all, no more than a Western myth. Tolerance was coming to be the most popular of all virtues, and conversion to be regarded as but one phenomenon of religious experience.

NEW PATTERNS IN MISSIONARY SERVICE

While the traditional Churches, or some of them, wondered for the first time whether they had been less than understanding of the

6. Professor Hocking restated and amplified these views with charm and persuasive power in his later book, *The Coming World Civilization* (1956).

faiths, and even the superstitions, which they sought to replace, the opportunities grew astonishingly. Africa at last was open, and a continent of naturally religious peoples who looked for a higher faith. Latin America was open, and for social reasons Christianity assumed a key importance. The number of missionaries, Roman Catholic and Protestant, grew steadily and in places astonishingly. Cardinal Lavigerie's White Fathers were essential to the missionary work of the Roman Catholic Church in Africa. Between 1939 and 1959, the number of White Fathers grew remarkably, until in 1967 it reached 3,621 (3,061 priests and 560 brothers). The Missionary Society at Mill Hill reached its top point in 1968, with 1,211 missionaries.

In both the Roman Catholic and the Protestant Churches, the United States appeared as a sending country. Until quite recent times America itself had been regarded as a mission field; Roman Catholics were comparatively few, and belonged almost entirely to the poorer strata of the population. Few priests were produced locally, and the American Church was so dependent on Ireland as to have the reputation in the Roman Catholic world of being no more than an Irish colony. Gradually the situation changed completely. In 1908 the Pope withdrew the United States from the jurisdiction of the Propaganda, thus indicating that it was no longer a mission field. In 1911 the archbishops approved the plans for a national seminary for foreign missions, the Catholic Foreign Missionary Society of America, with its headquarters at Maryknoll, New York. The initiative in this matter was taken by James A. Walsh, who became the director of the new institution. In 1920 sanction was given for the formation of the Foreign Mission Sisters of St Dominic, also with headquarters at Maryknoll. In 1918 the first party of 'Maryknollers', young priests trained in the most modern ideas of missionary work – and with an interest in sport and art and other things such as might have caused St Francis Xavier to raise his eyebrows incredulously – left for China to take up work in southern Kwangtung and eastern Kwangsi. The first party of six sisters followed in 1921. Maryknoll is still a small concern: in 1956 it had only 464 priests in the lands under the direction of the Propaganda (as contrasted with 5,000 Jesuits and 4,000 Franciscans) and 463 sisters. But Maryknoll was more significant than these numbers suggest.[7]

7. For an interesting, rather uncritical, account of the work of the Maryknoll Mission, see G. D. Kittler, *The Maryknoll Fathers* (1961).

On the Protestant side, also, the number of missionaries tended steadily to increase. But the increase was partial and patchy, and a careful analysis of the figures would amount to a dissection of the whole movement of theological and ecclesiastical development in the Protestant world in this century. In 1958 that reliable authority the Missionary Research Library in New York estimated the number of Protestant missionaries in the world at 43,000 – at least a fourfold increase since the beginning of the century. When the figures are looked at rather more closely, five significant facts emerge:

1. Of these missionaries no less than 27,733 (in 1958) were from the United States of America. What in the Roman Catholic world was described as a small river had already become a flood in the Protestant world. This is beyond question the American century. The increasing dominance of the United States in the political affairs of the world is reflected in the vigour, generosity, and vision of the American Churches in the field of Christian missions.

2. The most rapid developments were in the direction of the non-denominational society. The missions connected with the great historic Churches remained stationary; or, if they grew, could not show growth comparable in its rapidity to that of the other type of missionary society.[8] As an example we may mention the Sudan Interior Mission, founded in 1901 as a venture of faith by the Canadian Rowland S. Bingham. This mission drew its workers mainly from the 'Bible Belt', the traditionally conservative area of the midwest of the United States. It professed a simple biblical theology, held to an extreme free Church type of polity, and in recent years committed itself to a more definitely Baptist point of view. The first station of the SIM was at Patiqi in Nigeria, 500 miles up the Niger river among the Nupe tribe. It is probably the largest single Protestant missionary organization in the world, and spread its operations – evangelistic, medical, and literary – across the very heart of Africa.

3. The emergence of the Pentecostalist Churches and their missions was among the most startling phenomena of the Church history of the twentieth century. Most Pentecostal groups – they are many, and each is only loosely related to the others – derive from holiness movements, and these in their turn from the revival

8. An exception is the work of the Southern Baptists, which in increase in range and numbers and in vigour of policy is second to no other in the world. In some areas Southern Baptist missionaries have found it possible to work in close fellowship with missionaries of other Christian persuasions.

movements, mainly among the Methodists, by which religious life in the United States was diversified in the nineteenth century. As their name implies, all these groups lay special stress on the doctrine of the Holy Spirit and in varying degree on the phenomenon of *glossalalia*, 'speaking with tongues'. In certain countries the Pentecostalists entered areas in which other Churches were working and were a source of painful and unnecessary divisions. Elsewhere they devoted themselves to work among non-Christians, and with notable success; they appear to have a special gift for making the Christian message audible where human misery is at its worst. Statistics show that their successes were lower in rural districts than in towns. Many Pentecostal groups were at work in Latin America; it is said that in Chile and Brazil their membership was larger than that of all the other evangelical groups put together. Other areas could not show such striking results, yet in Kenya, Uganda, and Tanganyika the Pentecostal Assemblies of Canada claimed that their membership increased from 55,000 in 1957 to 90,000 in 1961.

4. The great historic Churches of the continent of Europe, and particularly the Churches of Germany, were making far less than a proportionate contribution to the work of Christian witness in the world. It is easy to see why this is so. The Hitler régime began in 1933. From that year onwards the Churches in Germany were torn by the conflicts and uncertainties of that time of difficulty and hardship. The missions were increasingly cut off from financial support and from the coming of new recruits. The war followed and brought with it the internment and repatriation of the majority of German missionaries. In the years that followed the collapse of 1945 the German Churches, busied with the innumerable demands made upon them by the tasks of their own reconstruction, were in no position to undertake extensive work abroad.

5. After the independence of India and Africa from colonial rule the number of foreign missionaries fell. This was partly because the sending countries had fewer qualified men or women who volunteered to go. But much more it came from the feeling in the new independent countries that foreign missionaries were a political force from a foreign power and their influence must be restrained or abolished. It also came from the feeling of young Churches and their best western advisers that, whether or not they yet possessed quite as many well-trained leaders as they would like, they must take the responsibility for leadership in their own Churches.

The results of this movement against 'the missionary', as a

representative of a foreign people, varied very much. In certain states which underwent violent coups or civil war the missionary was no longer safe. Intolerant governments sometimes expelled all or most of the foreign missionaries. Burma expelled nearly 375 in 1966, of whom 234 were Roman Catholics and fifty-six American Baptists.

Burundi expelled some missionaries during the civil war of 1972–3, while Maoist China had expelled all its missionaries in 1951. More than a thousand clergy or pastors were ejected from Castro's Cuba between 1958 and 1961, and some foreign missionaries from the Congo (Brazzaville) in 1964–5. Most of the Spanish priests in Equatorial Guinea were expelled shortly before independence in 1968. Guinea expelled all its foreign missionaries in 1967 and only eight Guinean priests were left to carry the burden of the Church amid a population dominantly Muslim. In Haiti the tyrant Duvalier expelled some twenty-five missionaries in 1959–64 but foreign clergy still remained dominant in the Churches. India was more reluctant to give visas to foreigners, but continued to act with a certain liberality, and the number of expatriate clergy diminished (1968–70) only from 6,420 to 4,903. In May 1971, forty-eight White Fathers left Mozambique in protest against the colonialist policy of the Portuguese government, and after Independence in 1975 President Machel expelled other foreign missionaries. Nigeria expelled some missionaries in 1970. The tyrant Idi Amin in Uganda forced fifty-eight missionaries to leave (of whom fifty-five were Roman Catholic) in 1972. A lot of foreign clergy had to leave South Vietnam when the South fell to the armies of the North in 1975. Zaïre expelled large numbers of foreigners in 1975.

It will be seen from the above that many countries still needed expatriate clergy, often in large numbers, whether for their churches or for their schools and higher education. In some countries the numbers of foreign clergy rose sharply during this period. Countries like Namibia, Guatemala, and Honduras could raise so few clergy from their own people that they could not do without an increase in the foreigners. A government like that of Kenya was wise enough to know that expatriate missionaries were no threat whatever to the independence of the country, that they were invaluable to education as well as to the Churches and that they helped the influx of foreign aid – and was very glad that many of them should remain.

The strangest moment in this whole development was when

after the Second World War the proconsul in Japan, General MacArthur, asked for 1,000 missionaries to come to Japan.

THE SUCCESS OF CHRISTIAN MISSIONS

For all the elements of disturbance, conflict, and chaos that have been let loose upon the world since 1914, and in spite of the extermination of Christian work through communist persecution in certain areas such as Central Asia, missions and Churches made unexampled progress in the period now under review.

The missionary 'occupation' carried out between 1792 and 1914 was so extensive and so effective that, in dealing with the period subsequent to 1914, it is only rarely possible to speak of absolutely fresh beginnings of Christian work in countries which prior to that date had had no contact whatever with the preaching of the Gospel.

In *Afghanistan* no preaching of any kind to Muslims is permitted. It is possible occasionally to meet an Afghan Christian who was won for Christ through personal contact with a foreigner or with one of the missions that work on the frontiers of the country. But no such convert could possibly live in his own land – the penalty for apostasy is still likely to be death.

Tibet, always a closed land, was doubly closed through its subjection to the communist yoke. But the Moravian Mission was at work at Leh in Ladakh from 1857. In 1955, two men of Tibetan race and language, though of Indian political allegiance, were ordained to the ministry of the Church. The whole Bible was translated into Tibetan; the Bible Society report for 1954 informs us that the greater part of the first edition of 1,000 copies went into Tibet, and was studied by the monks.

Nepal remained the only Hindu kingdom in the world, and closed to Christian missions. In 1950 it agreed to receive missionaries for educational and medical purposes only. With only slight delay, advantage was taken of this opportunity. In 1953 Roman Catholics opened a hospital in Katmandu. In 1954 the United Mission to Nepal was formed with the co-operation of no less than seventeen different Churches and mission boards. The main emphasis of the work is medical. Change of religion is not permitted. But if missionary work is permitted, is it really possible to forbid or to prevent conversion? This is a problem to which the government of Nepal, in consultation with the missions, will have to direct its attention in the coming years.[9]

If not much can be said about the opening up of Christian work in countries not previously touched, the strengthening and extension of the hold of the missions on almost every country in the world could be recorded at great length. It is in this period that we discern the beginnings of the landslide through which in many parts of the world hundreds turned into thousands and thousands into millions. A few examples may be given to indicate the strength of the Christian movement, and the acceleration in conversions once the initial difficulties were overcome. We noted that in 1911 the Batak Church in Sumatra claimed 103,528 baptized Christians; in 1941 this had risen to 380,000, and, though no accurate and up-to-date statistics are available, it was believed that this number doubled in the next twenty years. Between 1921 and 1931 (the last year in which reliable census figures were available), the Christian population of India increased by 32 per cent, as against a general increase of 10 per cent; Protestant missions recorded gains of 45 per cent, Roman Catholics of 16 per cent. In one year, the Anglican diocese on the Niger (now divided into three) baptized 11,000 adults in an area where now more than half the population claims to be Christian. In 1914 there may have been half a million evangelical Christians in Latin America; in 1960 they numbered at least 7 million, and perhaps many more.

THE FAR EAST

We now turn to survey very rapidly the main areas of the Church's ministry outside Europe and North America.

In *Japan*, the Christian missions continued to pursue an even course for a quarter of a century, marked by slow but steady progress, and an increasing concentration of both missionaries and Churches in the cities. Vigorous and individual evangelistic effort on the part of such leaders as Toyohiko Kagawa (1888–1960), combined in his case with vigorous witness on social questions, attracted attention from time to time, and the sale of Kagawa's

9. In point of fact, conversion took place, and a number of Nepalese were baptized. This tiny Church at once suffered through a period of repression which is hard to distinguish from persecution.

books, especially his novel *Before the Dawn*, was immense. But no great number of conversions took place through these methods; it was individual witness to individuals that seemed to be the chosen method of advance in this nation of individualists, in which religious feeling does not seem to have been at any time particularly strong.

The inflamed patriotism which preceded and led up to the entry of Japan into the Second World War not unnaturally brought the Church into many difficulties. Every Japanese Christian was a Japanese patriot, but it is impossible for any Christian to forget that he is also a member of a world-wide fellowship; the Christian is naturally the target for the suspicions of any totalitarian power. From 1940 on, the work of the foreign missionary became increasingly difficult and restricted. In that year, under the Religious Bodies Law, the government tried to bring about an amalgamation of all the Protestant bodies, from motives of obvious practical convenience. Some groups – such as one part of the *Nippon Sei Ko Kwai*, the Anglican Church in Japan, and the Holiness Church – stayed out. In consequence they suffered dissolution as legal bodies; pastors and other leaders suffered bonds and imprisonment, and in one or two cases death. Most of the others yielded to the government's desire, and the *Nippon Kirisuto Kyodan*, the Church of Christ of Japan, came into existence. This was the largest single Christian body in the country, and tried to take seriously its task of bearing constructive Christian witness in a difficult time.

With the military collapse of Japan in 1945, all the government's wartime rules fell to the ground. The moral and spiritual shock of the defeat was incalculably severe; in revulsion against the system that had brought them to such disaster many Japanese seemed prepared to accept the American way of life entire, and the Christian Gospel as part of it. It was thought that out of this mixture of frustration and hope a great Christian movement might develop. In this expectation almost every mission under the sun pressed into Japan, and by 1963 the figures showed more than 4,000 foreign Protestant workers in the country, almost all from America. As is characteristic of Protestant effort, this cataract arrived for the most part without mutual consultation and without planning. Almost all the new missions, like their predecessors, settled in the cities; and for all that the number of workers was so large, the evangelization of rural Japan hardly began. Moreover, the expected landslide never took place; the Japanese soon began to be occupied with their economic reconstruction to the almost total exclusion of everything else, and the rather superficial religious interest of the immediate post-war years soon died away. Baptisms were more numerous than before, perhaps twice as many as had been recorded annually in the years before the war. But it seems that in Japan, as always except in the days of the *daimyos*, progress comes through individual conversion and in no other way.

It is probable that in 1963 Christians in Japan numbered about three quarters of a million, in a nation of 90 million, Protestants outnumbering Roman Catholics by about two to one. But the influence of Christianity was far greater than this figure would lead one to suppose. Christians are a highly educated community, and members of the Church are to be found everywhere in positions of great influence. Also a great many who do not call themselves Christians are far more deeply influenced by the ethics and principles of the Gospel than by anything else. Some would be prepared to put the number of those who in this sense at least are Christians as high as between 2 and 3 million.

It was not long before the high hopes associated with the revolution of 1911 in *China* faded away into nothing or worse than nothing. The revolutionaries had broken up one régime, but it was soon clear that they had little to put in its place and were totally unable to control the country. China fell into the hands of contending warlords. The increasing chaos was accompanied by a steady growth in anti-foreign feeling. The fact of being a foreigner did, up till 1926, confer a certain measure of protection, but the murder of missionaries was not an uncommon event – as Professor K. S. Latourette drily remarks:

> Being a missionary now in many parts of China was an extra hazardous occupation, and being a Christian did not carry as much immunity from attack as in the first years after the Boxer uprising.[10]

By 1927 five-eighths of the missionary force had been withdrawn from the interior of the country. It seemed that the ultimate day of trial for the Christian cause in China had come.

The gradual emergence of the Kuomintang as the strongest power in China, and of Chiang Kai Shek, its leader, as the *de facto* ruler of increasingly large areas in the country, gave a period of

10. *A History of Christian Missions in China*, p. 818.

respite. In 1930, Chiang declared himself a Christian and was baptized; there is no reason to doubt the sincerity of this action, though some have entertained questions as to the depth of the conversion involved.

In spite of the uncertainties of life, the Christian cause continued to make progress. Thoughtful young men and women still seemed to themselves to find in the Christian way the answer to China's social and moral problems, and so were led to accept Christian baptism rather than the logical and ruthless answers given by the Marxists, who throughout this period were attempting to obtain a stranglehold on the life and thought of China. In two successive years the Protestant missions reported a 10 per cent increase in membership. And though many of the converts were of lowly origin, among them were also to be found men and women of stature who were to enter into positions of leadership and power. At the time of the final collapse of Free China, several of the cabinet ministers in the government of Chiang Kai Shek were Christian men of the highest integrity and capacity.

The time of respite came to an end with the Japanese invasion in 1937. Though technically Japan never declared war on China, in point of fact a state of war existed from 1937 to 1945. The sufferings of the country were intense. The ruthlessness of Japanese methods brought grave losses to Christians as to others, in the destruction of mission property, in the deaths of many Chinese Christians, and in the overthrow of much promising work. Yet this time too gave new opportunities of Christian service. Mission compounds were opened to the thousands of refugees and wounded, who were able to receive at least the minimum needed for sustenance and rudimentary medical care. Missionaries, along with their Chinese Christian friends, retreated before the advancing armies. Many Christian schools and colleges started a new existence in western China, beyond the furthest reach of the Japanese; here the work of preparing for a better day through education and Christian teaching went forward, and students continued to be baptized, both in mission colleges and in those for which the government was responsible.

In 1945 the Japanese were at last thrown out. The Christian forces emerged from exile, and set to work everywhere to reconstruct, to restore, and to renew. But no sooner had one enemy been overcome than another appeared on a not very distant horizon. The communists had only been waiting for the chance which now presented itself. It is too soon to assess realistically the situation which confronted them. The friends of Chiang Kai Shek maintain that only time was needed for the economic and social recovery of the country; his enemies affirm that the Kuomintang government wholly lacked foresight and efficiency, and that, through the failure of Chiang Kai Shek to deal with the less desirable elements in it, corruption had eaten so deeply into its vitals that the situation had become hopeless. Be that as it may, the resistance of the Kuomintang troops was sporadic and fitful; the communists armed themselves with the munitions sent in by the Americans and all too easily captured and won victory after victory. Yet the end, when it came, came suddenly and unexpectedly. On 1 October 1949 the People's Democratic Republic of China was proclaimed in Peking; Chiang Kai Shek and his supporters fled to Taiwan (Formosa).

What were missionaries and Chinese Christians to do? Many Chinese Christians accepted the communist victory with relief if not with alacrity. They had lost all faith in the Kuomintang régime; they felt new hope and promise in the air. Missionaries viewed the future with graver apprehension; they were under no illusions as to communism and the kind of world that it was out to create. But their allegiance was to China (or rather to Christ in China) and not to any particular political régime; they prepared to make the best of the situation and to stay on. The high-water mark of the Protestant missionary body in China had been reached in 1925, when there were 8,158 missionaries in the country. The number had steadily decreased, but in 1949 there were still 4,062 Protestant missionaries in China, and 5,682 non-Chinese Roman Catholic priests and nuns. Missionaries knew that they would be subject to many restrictions, and that they would live under constant suspicion; all this they were prepared to accept, if only they might continue to serve the people.

It very soon became clear not only that the missionaries would be allowed to do nothing, but that their continued presence in the country would bring danger to their Chinese friends. In 1951 the government expelled such missionaries as remained. A few westerners were killed; a larger number suffered longer or shorter periods of prison and solitary confinement, together with 'brainwashing'. It is believed that the last Protestant missionary to leave China was Miss Helen Willis of the Plymouth Brethren, who was brought out in April 1959. At that time there were still a few foreign Roman Catholics in China, but these were all in prison. The hostility of the Vatican to communism made Roman Catholicism anathema to the communists, and it is probable that the fate of

Roman Catholics was harder than that of their Protestant colleagues, who were able more easily to adapt themselves to the new régime.

The Chinese Christian found himself in a situation of grave perplexity. If interest in the West was to be regarded as a crime, then every Chinese Christian was automatically a criminal. The Gospel had come to him from the West. He was often sharply and almost hysterically critical of his Western friends, but he loved them and had been convinced of the purity of their motives in coming to China. Now he was assured that Christian missions had been simply a part of the cultural aggression of the West against the East,[11] and that through his share in that cultural aggression he had been a traitor to his country. He was no longer sure of himself. Nothing in all this history is more painful than the denunciation of missionaries by Chinese friends whom they had trusted; it is evidence of the agony of mind through which Chinese Christians passed.

'Now we can be ourselves.' This remark of a Chinese Christian leader probably represents accurately the feelings of a great many Christians in that country; the presence of the foreigner, and all that he represented in the way of Western dominance and financial control, had always been an embarrassment. Now that he was gone, the Christians could set to work to bring into existence a genuinely Chinese Church according to their own understanding of the term.[12] Some of the leaders – notably Dr Wu Yao-tsung, and Bishop K. H. Ting, who was long resident in the West in the service of the Student Christian Federation – came out quite openly 'on the side of the revolution', and all Chinese Christians knew that they could exist only if they were politically beyond suspicion. The losses were heavy. All educational, medical, and social work was taken out of the hands of the Church. Church buildings were not at once confiscated; services could be maintained, and the regular work of the Church carried on. Four theological schools were open for the training of candidates for the ministry. The baptism of converts was not impossible. For some

11. A leading Chinese Christian, Dr Wu Yao-tsung, spoke contemptuously of the attempt of the Western missions to reorient themselves in the light of the needs and demands of the younger Churches; from his point of view the Western missionary cause is so hopelessly linked to capitalism and colonialism as to be incapable of improvement.

12. It is interesting that there seems to have been no strong movement towards Church Union in China since the time of the communist victory.

time the Christians in China were completely cut off from direct contact with their friends in other countries, but gradually the bamboo curtain lifted a little. A number of parties of Christians – Quakers, a group from Australia, Professor Walter Freytag of the University of Hamburg – were able to spend some time in China and to talk with considerable freedom to their friends, though it was found that some periods and some problems were better left untouched. The main impression from these discussions was that the Chinese Christians were convinced that they now enjoyed greater freedom than they had ever had before to make a truly Christian witness to China, and that, in spite of all the political differences, which they made no attempt to conceal or to minimize, they wished to be regarded as standing within the world-wide fellowship of the Christian Church, and desired the help and the prayers of their fellow Christians.

From 1958 onwards it was possible to remark a change in the situation. Between 1957 and 1963 the state allowed the formation of a Constitutional Catholic Church, that is, a Church separated from the Vatican. Forty-five bishops were elected and consecrated. In 1964 government forbade the teaching of religion to anyone under the age of eighteen. But during 1966–7 the Cultural Revolution prompted bands of young thugs, protected by the state, to go round China smashing churches and mosques, and this pogrom obliterated or drove underground what little Christianity remained. The Constitutional Catholic Church vanished like everything else. During the 1970s a faint relaxation of the state's grip could be seen, and after Chairman Mao's death in 1976 it grew less faint. In 1981 there was evidence of rapid Christian growth among the young, but the whole episode of 1949–80 was a Christian disaster of the first magnitude. In 1949 there were perhaps 3¼ million Chinese Roman Catholics, but by 1981 there were probably only something over 100,000 who dared to profess, and this decline marked the Protestant communities.

There was one consolation. Many of the refugees from Mao's persecution headed for *Hong Kong*. There the Chinese Christian congregations flowered remarkably, during the 1950s and 1960s; less remarkably during the 1970s, as the refugees no longer came in such numbers.

With the arrival of Chiang Kai Shek and his hosts in *Taiwan* (Formosa), the Christian situation in that most beautiful of islands changed overnight.

Until 1949, apart from a small Roman Catholic mission, Taiwan had been a Presbyterian island – Canadians in the north, English in the south.[13] Numerical progress had never been rapid, but Formosan Christians were well on the way to creating solid, well-established and independent Christian communities. Shortly before the Second World War a remarkable Christian movement had begun among the aboriginal and non-Christian peoples in the mountains, Tayels, Amis, and others; during the Second World War, when no missionaries were at liberty to carry on their work, and any penetration of the mountain region by the Gospel was most strongly resisted by the Japanese, the movement continued to grow and to develop without any external aid.[14]

Then came the deluge. Many of those who accompanied the Generalissimo were Christians, and brought with them their own particular form of the Christian faith. Missions which had lost their field of work in China, and were looking for new fields of activity for their missionaries, naturally cast their eyes in the direction of Taiwan. About 1962 Roman Catholic priests appeared to number 682, of whom no less than 527 were foreigners. The Protestants had rather fewer – 411 ordained ministers, of whom only 150 were foreigners. But these were divided up among no less than forty-nine different bodies and Churches, and even the expert in missionary affairs might be perplexed to identify exactly the Glad Tidings Temple Missionary Society, the True Jesus Church, and the Suomen Lähetysseura. As is usual in the Protestant world, these many missions seem to have come in without mutual consultation or planning, and the first idea of most of them appeared to have been to establish themselves in Taipeh, the capital. It was right and natural that provision should be made for the spiritual welfare of the Christians, who are now several times as numerous as they were in 1948.[15] In this period there was danger of Christians becoming identified with a political programme because Taiwan was supported by so many as a possible base for a future political and military reconquest of mainland China. But all ten of

13. The union of the northern and southern synods into one fully independent Church took place in 1956; the number of adherents in 1981 was perhaps in the neighbourhood of 150,000.

14. A careful critical account of this remarkable movement has appeared in German: G. F. Vicedom, *Ein Volk findet Gott* (1962). No English translation has as yet been made.

15. The latest figure available indicates that there are now 1¼ million Christians in the island, out of a population of more than 8 million; the Presbyterian Church is by far the largest of the Protestant Churches.

the mountain tribes were rapidly turning into Christian tribes during the 1960s and 1970s. The Taiwan denominations were usually hostile to the World Council of Churches because of its openness of mind towards mainland China.

In *Korea* under Japanese domination the position of the Korean Christians was bound to be painful and uncertain. The mere fact that all Churches (except the Roman) used the Korean language in worship and propagated literature in Korean was enough to bring suspicion on Christians as Korean nationalists in a rather thin disguise. As this is what most of them were, it cannot be said that from the Japanese point of view the Japanese suspicions were wholly unfounded. In March 1919 many Christians took part in a rising aimed at the recovery of independence; reprisals were correspondingly severe. It was reported that by the end of the year forty-seven members of the Presbyterian Church alone had been done to death, and that a very large number were still in prison. A rather more tolerant period followed. Yet Korean Christians were all the time harassed, like Christians in Japan, by the vexed question of the Shinto ceremonies, and of the veneration to be paid to the portrait of the emperor. In 1939 all missionaries were ordered out of the country, and as soon as Japan entered the war the Church entered once again on a period of repression, varying a little from time to time in harshness and intensity. Yet all the time the Churches continued to grow.

The end of the Second World War brought about the unnecessary and irrational division of the country into North and South at the 38th Parallel; what had been intended only as a military stand-fast line was allowed to become a cause of permanent division.

When missionaries were allowed again to enter Korea, none were permitted to go to the North. Very little is known of what has happened to the Church in that region, but from the tales of refugees it seems likely that not much has been allowed to survive.

In the South the recovery after the war was almost miraculous. Christians came out of hiding, churches were full, missionaries were made welcome, and every form of Christian activity was resumed. But only a brief five years of grace were given: on 25 June 1950 the invasion of South Korea by the North began.

In the three dreadful years of war that followed, South Korea was saved for the civilized world, but at a terrible price. The destruction of property was immense; the loss of life was heavy, and the burden of refugees insupportable. The ending of the war on 21 July 1953 did not lead to the reunification of the country or to political stability. In North Korea many Christians were murdered during the war, and many fled South from 1953, for North Korea was a country closed to religion. Some Christians continued to meet secretly in North Korea but in 1957 ten of their leaders were executed. In South Korea the refugees from the North and then the growth of the Churches produced an astonishing increase in the number of Christians. Probably there were in 1981 some 8 million Christians, about a quarter of the population, a higher proportion than in any other country of Asia except the largely Christian Philippines. The dictatorship established in South Korea in 1972 led to Christian protests against acts of the régime and to the expulsion of some foreign missionaries and the arrest of some progressive priests and laity.

In the Island World, from the *Philippines* through *New Guinea* to *Hawaii*, the years between 1914 and 1939 were a time of quiet and unspectacular progress. Without any very sensational movement, the number of Christians in the area doubled itself. Of an ever-increasing number of islands it could be said that they had been entirely Christianized, though this did not always mean that the Christianity practised on them was of a very high order. In certain areas such as some of the Solomon Islands resistance to the Gospel continued to be fierce and obstinate, but this was the exception. These years were, for example, the time of rapid progress in that Lutheran Mission in New Guinea of which we have already written. The battle for survival had been won; at last it was clear that the tendency to depopulation and disappearance had been overcome, and almost everywhere the population had begun to increase again. What was not so clear was whether the combined forces of wise and usually generous colonial government and the expanding influence of missionary work from the West would together avail to guard the Pacific peoples against the corrupting influences of that civilization which Western man was so eager to spread abroad among them.

In this unstable situation the Japanese hurricane burst upon the islands. Many missionaries were killed, many others interned or driven out. In some areas it became a question whether the presence of the missionaries would be of advantage to the local Christians or the reverse – whether the consolation to be derived from their presence and advice would be outweighed by the increased danger to their flocks which would certainly result if they continued to harbour the white man. Most of the Anglican missionaries in New Guinea decided to stay. Their bishop, Philip Strong (elected Archbishop of Brisbane in October 1962), had written to them:

We must endeavour to carry on our work in all circumstances, no matter what the cost may be to any of us individually. God expects this of us. The Church at home, which sent us out, will surely expect it. The universal Church expects it . . . The people whom we serve expect it of us. We could never hold up our faces again if, for our own safety, we all forsook him and fled, when the shadows of the passion began to gather around him in his spiritual and mystical body, the Church in Papua.[16]

Within a few months eight of the missionaries were murdered by Japanese soldiers.

After the war the pace of conversion to Christianity quickened. By 1966 92 per cent of the population professed Christianity, Lutherans being the largest denomination. The Churches were still heavily dependent on foreign pastors. In 1970 the Roman Catholic Church had fifteen indigenous priests and 475 others, though it was growing very rapidly in numbers of converts.

Almost the whole of the indigenous *Fijian* population is Christian, and for the most part Methodist. But today Fijians are in a minority in their own country. In the later years of the nineteenth century Indians were brought in to work as indentured labourers on the plantations; they have stayed and multiplied, and now outnumber their hosts. Here, missions found as difficult a field as in India itself; Indian Christians were few, and as yet no effective means has been found to break through a steady and determined resistance. This must be reckoned as one of the major missionary problems of the Pacific area, and in particular as a missionary task for the Christian Churches in India.

Another problem – this can be paralleled in Africa and other areas where Christianization has been rapid – is the tendency for the resurgence of pagan ideas, often in partly Christian dress. New Guinea and other areas have been troubled by that strange phenomenon, the Cargo cult:

Basically the Cargo cult represents an attempt to accept western civilization and to make use of it – on the Papuan's own terms. . . . The

16. Quoted in H. P. Van Dusen, *They Found the Church There* (1945), p. 32.

question that lies at the root of the Cargo cult in New Guinea is this: How does it come about that the white man is so astonishingly rich, when he is not seen to work particularly hard? His ships go on and on bringing him goods without measure . . . The white man is never seen to pay for these things: apparently he gets them all free. They are sent out from inexhaustible storehouses which belong to a higher power. There is a connection between the wealth of the white man and his religion. The white man through the missionaries has passed on the Gospel to the Papuan; but he has not passed on to him the secret of access to all this wealth. The Papuans must, therefore, somehow or other discover this secret for themselves.[17]

This is the confusion which Western men – missionary and trader, tourist and government official – have produced.

In *South-east Asia*, the tides of war brought many startling changes, and the growth of nationalism, culminating in independence for eight new nations, together with the aggressive revival of the ancient non-Christian religions, has brought the Churches into an entirely new situation.

After the Japanese flood had receded *Indonesia* passed through a long period of uncertainty which has not yet come to an end. On 28 December 1949 the Republic of Indonesia became independent, and the three centuries and more of Dutch rule came to an end. In some areas, such as Celebes and Ambon, the new political authorities would have been happy to work with Dutch advisers, and the Churches would have been happy to have once again the help of Dutch missionaries. This did not fit in with the plans of the ruling group in Java for a strictly centralized government, and for the extinction of everything that could recall the time of Dutch ascendancy. The anti-Dutch feeling was so strong that the great majority of those Dutch missionaries who had been able to return were compelled to withdraw, and the Churches have been largely left to themselves.

Indonesia is a country with a largely Muslim population. It has not officially declared itself a Muslim state; yet questions of

17. G. F. Vicedom, *Church and People in New Guinea* (World Christian Books no. 38, 1961), pp. 59 ff. G. Höltke quotes a letter of the Roman Catholic Bishop of Alexishafen, stating that Papuans believed that the riches of the white men were due to the fact that one white man had offered his life as a sacrifice for the general well-being. In 1961 a Papuan persuaded another man to kill him (it was intended that this should take place during Mass), and the deed was actually done. But the secret of the white men's *magic combination of numbers* was not discovered.

religious affiliation do play a considerable part in political affairs and public life. The constitution proclaims religious liberty. After 1966 strong movements of conversion to both Catholics and Protestants were recorded. Revivalist movements were strong. Perhaps 2½ million 'converts' came after 1966 from persons who were not Muslim by conviction but had been counted as 'Muslim' by censuses. South-west of Sumatra are islands, the Mentawai, where religion was animism not untouched by immorality. In 1954 Indonesia suppressed the religion and ordered all the inhabitants to be either Muslim or Christian – and by 'Christian' they counted only Protestants, though after 1970, Roman Catholics also. In 1982 there were 15,000 Protestants, 12,000 Catholics and a very few thousand Muslims. The 17 million Christians in all Indonesia (11 per cent of the population) were determined to play their part in the life of the nation. A number of them were elected to Parliament.

Burma, on becoming an independent nation, decided to withdraw from the British Commonwealth of Nations and to launch out on its own. Its tendency was increasingly in the direction of the identification of the national life with the Buddhist tradition. This was not welcome to the non-Burmese peoples, who had always been animists rather than Buddhists. The Karens, a large number of whom are Christians, would have preferred to have an independent state of their own. This was not permitted; the will of the majority prevailed, and Burma retains its unity within the frontiers of pre-war days.

In 1961 Buddhism was declared the state religion of Burma, and a further step was taken to make effective in all walks of life the succinct statement that whatever is Burmese is Buddhist, and whatever is Buddhist is Burmese. The constitution defends religious freedom, and Christians enjoy the right to worship, and, within limits, to proclaim their faith. But this was not regarded as inconsistent with the granting of special privileges to Buddhism,

18. This was quite clearly expressed some years ago by the attorney-general of Burma, U Chan Htoon: 'We are of the firm conviction that the time has come for us to make everyone in the country live according to the Teachings of the Buddha. All aspects of national life, including the civilization, culture, literature, law, and customs, etc. of all the indigenous people of Burma, have risen from and still have their root in Buddhism.' Quoted in A. C. Bouquet: *The Christian Faith and non-Christian Religions* (1958), p. 289. The new military government has not maintained the affirmation that Buddhism is the state religion of Burma.

and the encouragement of one religion at the expense of all others.[18] The Sixth Buddhist Council was held in Rangoon from May 1954 to May 1956, and drew world-wide attention to Burma as one of the centres of the Buddhist renaissance.

Christians in Burma were strong and well established, among Karens, Chins, and Kachens. The largest denomination was the Baptist, descended from Adoniram Judson (see p. 248). A 1981 calculation reckoned some 2 million Christians in Burma, more than 30 million Buddhists, and over a million Muslims. But it was not certain how well the Churches could maintain their education and their ministry in the political predicament of Burma. They lost all their schools and hospitals in a nationalization of 1965.

In *Sri Lanka* Christians represented about 8 per cent of the population but the political divisions of the island made Buddhism seem the unifying force, and in 1972 it became the state religion. The Buddhist government pressed the minorities – religions (Hindu, Muslim, Christian)[18] and languages (Tamil and English). They took over almost all the Christian schools. The growth of Christian numbers did not quite stop but it was slower than the growth of the population, and also than the growth of Buddhists and Muslims. In 1966 the government abolished Sunday as a day of rest but restored it six years later.

In *India* between 1914 and the present day, as in the period just before, one of the most notable features was the steady growth and increase in the mass movements among the depressed classes.

When Vedanayakam Samuel Azariah was consecrated in 1912 as the first Indian Bishop of the Anglican Church in India, he found himself in charge of a large area in which a mass movement was in progress. This he guided with consummate skill through thirty years, helped by the support of a number of exceptionally able and self-effacing European missionaries. Throughout the whole period the number of baptisms averaged 3,000 a year. Azariah followed the practice that had been familiar to him in his own boyhood days in Tinnevelly; as soon as possible, village workers who had approved themselves as catechists were brought forward, and, in spite of defective general and theological education, were ordained to the priesthood of the Church. Educational standards were steadily raised, and by the end of his time Azariah

18. See footnote on p. 437.

was ordaining men who were graduates both in arts and in theology.

The policy of the Methodists in the adjoining area of *Medak*, where their great pioneer was the Reverend Charles Posnett, was rather different. Holding that there should be as little disparity as possible between the European and the Indian minister, they admitted to ordination only those who had received full theological training. As a result, fifty years after the beginning of the movement their missionaries still outnumbered their Indian ministers. To meet the urgent need for sacramental ministrations in the villages, the Methodists began to give an annual licence to certain of the senior lay catechists in the villages to administer the Lord's Supper; these men were known as pastors, but were not ordained through the laying-on of hands. This temporary solution of a pastoral problem was to cause considerable difficulty in the plans for closer union with Churches of a different tradition.

Many missionaries and many leading Indian Christians looked with considerable disfavour on these movements among the depressed classes. With great labour the missions had built up a Christian middle class, and had made Christianity almost acceptable in most areas of society. It was felt that the flooding of the Church by streams of these simple and generally despised people must have the result of strengthening the opinion, already widely held in India, that Christianity is a religion only for the poor and uncultured, and that thus it would hinder rather than help the aim of the full evangelization of India.

Supporters of the older forms of missionary work were highly critical of 'mass-conversion'. In such conditions, it was maintained, there can be no question of individual decision, the only way in which true believers can be added to the Church; everything must begin on the level of mere conformity, and is not likely to rise to any higher level. Furthermore, it was maintained that, owing to the caste stratification of Indian society, even if the depressed class groups in India became Christians to the last man this would have no effect on the higher castes, and the mere accumulation of numbers would prove gravely deceptive.

No one can deny that there is some force in these arguments; but none of them is conclusive. In two outstanding books, *Christian Mass Movements in India* (1933) and *Christ's Way to India's Heart* (1938), Bishop J. W. Pickett of the Methodist Church showed, first, that an overwhelming percentage of India's Christians owe their origins to group movements in the villages and, secondly, that for India, where individual decision is so much less developed than in the West, group movements are to be expected, and to be accepted as the natural way of the movement of the Spirit of God. Of course individual conversion must remain the aim, but this is much more likely to occur and to bear permanent fruit within the framework of a family and a community which has already been in part Christianized. Later experience proved false the expectation that the higher castes would remain unaffected by what happened to their social inferiors. Imperfect as their conversion might be, the change in the demeanour and the habits of out-caste Christians in the Telugu area was so startling that in a number of cases their high-caste neighbours came to inquire what power it might be that had produced such unexpected results, and to put themselves under Christian instruction.

The trouble about all mass movements is that sooner or later they cease to move. It seems to be a law of nature that in course of time inertia will reassert itself. But in the case of the Indian mass movements there was also the simple external fact that in no case were the forces supplied by the Western Churches adequate to secure the necessary continuity in the work and the after-care that is so urgently needed by simple and illiterate Christians. Experience shows that intensive pastoral care must be supplied during a period of thirty years before a Christian community of this kind can be regarded as stable. In hardly any case was this possible. As a result, far too much came to be taken for granted; it was assumed, mistakenly, that the sons and grandsons, who had not shared the experiences of the first converts and the persecutions that almost invariably followed upon their decision to become Christians, would follow loyally in the same steps. In many cases failure in pastoral care resulted in the existence of masses of baptized heathens, and, when once a movement has run down in this way, it is very difficult to get it started again.

From a very early date the Indian Churches have produced a number of exceptionally gifted ministers. But these were the exceptions. It came to be felt by many in the Churches that the time had come when it should be possible to supply to candidates for the ministry in India a training hardly differing in academic excellence from that enjoyed by their missionary friends from the West. The first steps were taken in South India, where the number of Christians is much greater than in other regions. In 1910 the United Theological College came into existence at Bangalore. It was fortunate in having as its first principal the distinguished Dane, L. P. Larsen (d. 1940). An excellent Tamil scholar, a thoughtful preacher, a well-read theologian, a man of God, Larsen was qualified as few others to impress on the rising generation of Indian students the highest ideals of the ministry. A few years later steps were taken to bring Carey's Serampore back to its original purpose and to make use of that clause in the old Danish charter, never yet used, which authorized the College to confer the degree of Bachelor of Divinity. Since that time Serampore served, on the model of London University, as the organizing and examining centre for theological work in India; colleges in the most distant parts of India could be affiliated to it for the degrees of BD and LTh, and thus a practical uniformity of syllabuses, methods, and standards grew up. Almost contemporaneously Bishop's College, Calcutta, which had sunk to being no more than a hostel for university students, was brought back to its proper function of theological training. Rather later, the American Methodists created Leonard College, Jabalpur, and the American Lutherans their centre at Rajahmundry. India was thus supplied with five centres in which students who had already taken a degree in arts could go on to the serious study of theology.

Complaints had long been heard among Indian Christians as to the foreignness of Christianity in India, but little had been done to remedy this defect. One man more than any other showed to this generation what Christianity could be in a purely Indian guise and dress. Before his baptism in 1905 Sundar Singh had been a Sikh. Although he started to prepare for the Anglican ministry, he never completed the course, and instead launched out on the life of an Indian sādhu, with saffron robe and extreme simplicity of life, attached to no Church and at the service of all. His bearded figure, radiant smile, and homely figures of speech became widely known in many countries. Sundar Singh disappeared in Tibet in 1929, and left no successor; others who called themselves Christian sādhus failed to reveal like gifts with the one whom they claimed as their master. But the āshram movement, which in many ways is trying to acclimatize the Gospel in India, may be held to have arisen under the inspiration of the sādhu's example. The term āshram is rather loosely used of any group of men and women who, living together in community, observe the rules of simplicity of life and of devoted service to their neighbours. The Christukula Āshram at Tiruppattur, run for many years by two doctors (the Tamil Jesudāson and the Scot Forrester-Paton), and the Vidivelli

Āshram, Sāyamalai, where Miss Joy Solomon and Miss M. Frost gave many years of utterly self-sacrificing service to village women, may be cited as examples of what an āshram can be and do. The growth of Christian āshrams was remarkable. They adopted an Indian life-style, and founded retreats of silence and contemplation.

Up to 1914 hardly any Indian Christians took an interest in politics. Living a little isolated from the rest of the population, they were on the whole highly content with British rule, which had brought them peace, justice, and prosperity on a scale never previously imagined. All that they wished was that the days of the good Queen Victoria might go on for ever. When a new period of Indian national agitation began with the return of M. K. Gāndhi from South Africa in 1915, most Indian Christians strongly disapproved of the actions and policy of the Indian National Congress. Gāndhi's known interest in the teaching of the New Testament encouraged many hundreds of young Hindus, who would not otherwise have done so, to read the Gospels; yet at the same time his policy of telling Hindus that they could have all the good things of Christianity without ceasing to be Hindus was perhaps the strongest factor in limiting the spread of Christianity among educated Hindus in this period.

By 1930 it was clear that the isolation of Christians from the general life of India could not continue much longer. Educated Christians did not like to be told that they were no better than foreigners in India so long as they continued to be 'the running dogs of imperialism'. Some enthusiastically, others reluctantly, joined the Congress party; quite a number went to gaol during the various movements of civil disobedience. When it became clear that India would before long become independent, Christians no less than others braced themselves to face the great change and prepared to play an active part in the political life of the independent nation.

For a number of years missionaries had been told by candid Indian friends that, though perhaps themselves unconscious of it, they were actuated by imperialistic motives and were no true servants of India. This is the kind of accusation which it is impossible to refute; missionaries held their tongues and suffered in silence. When independence came, not one single missionary of any Church resigned from the work; all simply remained and prepared to carry on with their work in the new situation. Some of them believed that independence had come too soon, and that it might have come in better ways, but they were prepared to accept the fact, and to show that Christianity is not tied to any particular political tradition or organization.

The policy of Mahātma Gāndhi and Mr Nehru had progressively alienated the Muslims. When in 1947, the British Labour Government was prepared to make an offer of independence, it was clear that the only alternatives were delayed independence with a united country, or a divided country with immediate independence. It was the latter solution that was chosen by Gāndhi and his lieutenants.

The formation of the two separate nations of *India* and *Pakistan* may have been necessary, but it brought down in ruins the structure of unity which, from the coming of Babur more than four centuries before, had been steadily built up by the Moguls and the British in India. And the beginning of independence was marked by the most terrible massacres recorded in modern history: at least three quarters of a million people lost their lives in a few weeks. It was this dreadful time that gave the Christians their first opportunity to prove clearly their value to their country. The feeling between Hindus and Muslims was so intense that there was no situation in which either could be of service to the other. Christians, being neutral, could come in with doctors and nurses and social aid, and give help to those who were in need without distinction of race or religion. The cry could never again be raised that Christians were second-class citizens.

Politically the separation of India and Pakistan is complete. Only the Churches (Roman Catholic, Anglican, and some others) maintained their integrity across the borders, and served in a measure as a link between two nations whose failure to reach understanding was a source of anxiety to all their friends. Yet, inevitably, the course of events and the situation of Christians developed differently in the two countries.

India declared itself to be a secular democratic republic, observing strict neutrality in the matter of religion. The constitution of the country includes a generous provision for religious liberty, inserted at the instance of the Christian minority. There was no open discrimination against Christians, and India's first minister of health was a highly distinguished Christian lady, the Rājkumari Amrit Kaur. But the situation of Christians is less than completely comfortable. There were naturally differences of opinion among non-Christians as to the existence and value of the Christian community in India. The first Prime Minister, Mr Jawaharlāl Nehru, held the view that religion has done nothing but harm in the history of the world, and would gladly have seen its complete disappearance. But as long as he was Prime Minister the constitution was strictly observed; as he himself pointed out, Christianity had been in India far too long to be regarded as a foreign religion. Not all share this tolerant view. The extreme Hindus think of India as Hindustān, the land of the Hindus, and are not willing that others should share in equal rights as citizens. The evil tradition of identifying religions with political communities still persists, and some are radically opposed to all 'conversion' as a weakening of the Hindu community. Some years after independence, complaints of improper methods used by missionaries led to the appointment of a commission in the Central Provinces, and the publication of the so-called Nyōgi Report. It was not difficult for the Christian forces to show that this report was wholly uncritical and that most of the charges made in it were flimsy, unsubstantiated, or exaggerated. Nevertheless the fact that it was written indicated that in the future things might be less easy for Christians than they had been in the past.

The government of India was a little less than generous in the matter of granting visas to missionaries who wished to enter India, since it desired to keep under control the number both of missionaries and of missions at work in the country. It was necessary for missionaries and Indian Christians to be circumspect and prudent in their actions, and to avoid every possibility of suspicion that conversions are due to force and fraud. Yet vast tracts of education and medical work were left in the hands of the Churches, and opportunities for quiet evangelism were many. There were some complaints of discrimination against members of the depressed classes who became Christians in such matters as government aid for the education of their children; but it cannot be said that there was any general policy of discrimination against Christians as such. In the main, freedom to worship, to teach, and to witness have been retained. What more could Christians ask?

In *Pakistan* the government was less liberal, and this was partly because the Muslim religion was more dominant than the Hindu religion in India. In India the Christians, though located mostly in the south, made some 3½ per cent of the population. In Pakistan they made about 1½ per cent. Pakistan became independent in 1947 and declared itself an Islamic republic in 1956. The origin of its being was religious. Though freedom for all was guaranteed, it was made clear that only Muslims could expect to enjoy to the full the privileges of citizenship. In the intervening years Pakistan has had its own internal problems. It was not long before tension developed between the Ulemā – the Muslim religious leaders, who desired that everything should be worked out in terms of the Shari'ath, the traditional Muslim code of law – and the Western-trained statesmen, who had different and broader ideas of demo-cratic liberty. Under the dictatorship which came into being in 1958 the word 'Muslim' was dropped from the official title of the state, and this is significant. Yet in Pakistan Christians are no more than a tolerated minority; they find it hard to maintain themselves, and, as in other Muslim lands, feel that the weight of public opinion is heavily against them. The government liked to control the Christian institutions to prevent proselytism. Some mem-bers of the ruling élite evidently felt that Christianity should be suppressed. But the constitution, in this matter, was just main-tained to ensure the basic rights of Christians.

THE WORLD OF ISLAM

Pakistan is our natural point of transition to the mainly Muslim countries of the *Near East* and *Middle East*. No part of the world has suffered more severely from the shocks and changes of this century. The First World War and the defeat of Turkey marked the end of the Muslim dream of world domination. The *Dar-ul-Islam*, the world of Islam, had never fallen into such low estate. The colonial powers were at its very heart, in Egypt and Syria and Iraq; Muslims who lived under the rule of European powers were far more numerous than those who lived under Muslim governments.

In two areas Muslim Turkey was very hard on historic bodies of Christians. Islamic nationalism meant, in massacres from 1877 to 1915, the almost total destruction of the large and historic body of Armenian Christians (who survived only under the protection of Russia in Soviet Armenia, or in Western exile) and (in the Greek–Turkish war of 1922) a disaster for, though not the total destruction of, the large and important Greek Orthodox Churches of Turkey, which descended from the historic Byzantine Churches.

After the Second World War Morocco, Tunis, Libya, Egypt, the Sudan, Syria, Iraq, Pakistan, and Indonesia became independent. Oil, the chief riches of a world economy, was most plentifully found in the States of Arabia, as well as in Iraq and Iran and Libya. The Islamic bloc carried no small weight in the Assembly of the United Nations.

The newly independent Islamic states varied greatly in their attitude to Christians. Westernized governments in Muslim states often behaved fairly, as in Syria, Tunis, Indonesia, Jordan, and Egypt. Iranian nationalism under Ayatollah Khomeini was very hard on every sort of minority including Christians, who, however, were not numerous. Mauretania and Morocco were closed to Christianity but had hardly been opened except to expatriates.

These decades were marked by a far more sympathetic attitude to Islam among Christian thinkers, and an attempt to find common ground. There was no agreement between Christianity and Islam but there were areas of common concern – the existence of God, revelation, the duty and the destiny of man – which ought to make dialogue possible. This point of view will be familiar to readers of the books of Kenneth Cragg, its most notable expositor.[19] His books are only part of an approach in which free and open discussion was welcomed to a degree which had hardly been possible for centuries.

The effects of Christian missions on Islam are far more considerable than the actual number of converts would suggest. Nowhere was this more clearly seen than in modern presentations of the person of Muhammad. At point after point the figure was subtly Christianized until the desert ruler of Arabia became much more like the Carpenter of Nazareth than earlier students would ever have supposed to be possible. Of this new and in many ways attractive presentation of the Prophet, one Christian scholar has written:

The Muslim who accepted his religion from these [modernist] writers might hold his head high, even when confronting western Europe. His religion, point by point, is proved the finest in the world as judged by the most modern standards. The Prophet whom he adores is the supreme character of all history. The Muslim might well be proud, and confident. The spirit of his religion, he found, is the highest liberal ideals, put here in contemporary and glowing terms.[20]

19. A. K. Cragg, *The Call of the Minaret* (1956) and *Sandals at the Mosque* (1959). His approach may be summed up in the words: 'If we would in the end bespeak an adequate Muslim awareness of Christ, we must essay an adequate Christian awareness of Islam.'

20. W. Cantwell Smith, *Modern Islam in India* (1943), pp. 44–5. It should be added that Professor H. A. R. Gibb, who also quotes this passage, comments on it:

The deep, though not always enlightened interest of Muslims in the story of Jesus Christ can hardly fail to lead to better understanding between Muslim and Christian.

The great new fact in the Islamic world was the existence of the state of Israel. This is no place to enlarge upon the searing flames of hatred that have been let loose by this phenomenon; but the whole equilibrium of the area was upset and one new element of conflict added to a part of the world which was never noted for its peacefulness. Christians held diverse views of the new state. Some regarded it as a merely political entity without religious significance. Others looked upon it as the fulfilment of Old Testament prophecy. In the Arab lands feeling is so strong that it is scarcely possible to use the term Israel as a synonym for the people of God in the Old Testament. Such an atmosphere is hardly favourable to Christianity. Most of the Christians in Israel belong to the Roman Catholic and Eastern Churches and are Arab by race. These enjoy a measure of religious liberty. But Christians of Hebrew origin are extremely few, and are regarded with deep suspicion as traitors; any attempt to bring Christian influence to bear on Jews is regarded as intolerable. Nevertheless, certain Christian bodies – Roman Catholic, Anglican, Lutheran, and others – have managed to maintain themselves in Israel; there is a 'presence' of the Church in the country, even though its witness must be given in silence rather than through speech.

The quiet and steady work of the missions in *Egypt* was brought to disruption in 1956, through the sorry episode of the British, French, and Israeli invasion of the area of the Suez Canal. All British missionaries, including the Anglican Bishop, were expelled, and much of the work came to an abrupt end. The American missions were, of course, less gravely affected, and American missionaries did their best to keep things going, but the damage to much of the work was irreparable. Egyptian Christians who were Protestants were few. The crisis threw them on their own resources and brought out a quite unexpected strength. Meanwhile the wave of Islamic nationalism, though it affected educated Egypt far less than it affected Iran or Libya, brought under pressure the Coptic

'The liberal modernists have achieved this result at a serious cost. Not only have they discarded or distorted vital elements in the personality of Muhammad (thereby, in my opinion, inflicting a grave injury upon the historical structure of Islam) but, by their disregard of all objective standards of investigation and of historical truth, they have debauched the intellectual insight and integrity of their fellow-Muslims.' (*Modern Trends in Islam*, 1947, p. 77.)

Church in Egypt. The Copts make the largest body of Christians in any mainly Muslim state, or in all the Arab world. The pressure caused them to lose to Islam several thousand Copts a year. Early in 1977 mobs attacked Coptic churches and priests, but were stopped by government.

One of the Islamic countries that was most violently caught up in the whirlwind of change is the *Sudan*. On 1 January 1956 the Sudan became an independent republic after rather more than fifty years of Anglo-Egyptian rule. This involved the subjection to Muslim control of a large number of non-Muslim tribes in the south; some of them were wholly pagan, but among many others the Gospel had taken firm hold. The change was not by any means to the mind of the peoples of the south, and one of the first consequences of independence was a rebellion, repressed, with the probable loss (1963–72) of a million lives, many of them Christian. The plans of the government, rightly concerned for the unity of the country, involve if not the Islamization of the south, at least its Arabization. Arabic was imposed as the language of communication and education. All Western missionaries, of whatever confession, were expelled from the country, on the charge of involvement in political affairs, and the Churches were left to carry on, under very grave difficulties, from their own resources. Fortunately the missions had early started on the training and ordination of African ministers; with the consecration of two African assistant bishops the form of the Anglican Church was complete.

AFRICA

The Sudan is the natural point of access to our next main area, *Africa*. Here, too, change went forward at a pace that a generation ago no living man could possibly have foreseen. Country after country became independent. The transformation of the British, French, and Belgian empires brought into existence a host of African states, jealous of their independence, uncertain of themselves, vocal, unwilling to commit themselves to either East or West in the struggle for the freedom of the world. The magnitude of the experiment is expressed in the fact that twenty-six countries attained self-government in less than fifteen years.[21] Nigeria, the

21. Six of these are in the Muslim north, and do not belong to the tropical Africa which is the subject of this section.

largest in population of these African states, has rather more than 40 million inhabitants, nearly a fifth of the population of Africa. Every state has at least a Christian minority; and most African political leaders, with the exception of the Muslim leaders in northern Nigeria, are at least nominal Christians.

An encouraging feature in this rapid growth was that so much of it was the work not of the missionary but of the Africans themselves.

One of the most remarkable movements in the whole history of Christianity in Africa is that associated with the 'Prophet Harris' – William Wadé Harris, an Episcopal Christian from Liberia, who after experiencing a deep inner conversion and a sense of being called by the Holy Spirit to special mission, began about 1914 to appear in the French colony of the Ivory Coast and to preach with great power to the simple animistic people. Although a man of little education, Harris is described by a contemporary observer, Captain Marty, as 'an impressive figure, adorned with a white beard, of tall stature, clothed in white, his head enturbaned with a cloth of the same colour, wearing a black stole; in his hand a high cross and on his belt a calabash, containing dried seeds, which he shakes to keep rhythm for his hymns'.[22] The heart of his simple Gospel concerned belief in one God, the abandoning and destruction of fetishes, the observance of Sunday as a day of rest, and the prohibition of adultery. Those who came under his influence and accepted his teaching were baptized. Harris bade them build churches in their villages, stressed the incomparable importance of the Word of God, and bade them wait for the teachers who would come later, and give them the fuller instruction which he had no time to give. After a brief ministry, he withdrew to his own country, and, having been refused readmission by the French authorities, was seen no more.

Almost ten years after his departure, missionaries of the English Methodist Society came in to follow up the work. They found that, though many of those baptized by Harris had fallen away, something like 45,000 simple people remained faithful to what they had understood of his teaching. They were eager to receive the missionaries and to learn the teaching of the Book, which they possessed but could not understand, since in many cases it was in

22. Quoted in W. J. Platt, *An African Prophet* (1934), p. 59. At the time of his appearance in the Ivory Coast, Harris appears to have been about sixty years old.

English. What followed was the more normal history of the building up of a mission, with all its lights and shadows, but the romance of its beginnings can never be entirely forgotten.

Harris is of the essential type of the African prophet. Later in this chapter we shall meet others of the same family, though with a very different message. What was the secret of Harris's power? It may be called hypnotic, or otherwise psychologically explained. But such explanations do not carry us very far. His hearers felt that the power of the unseen God was with him. They heard and obeyed; in isolation and ignorance they held fast to the simple elements that he had taught them. Somehow Harris was able to speak directly to the souls of his people, as the French Roman Catholic priests who were in the area had never succeeded in doing.

Statistics are more difficult to come by in Africa than elsewhere, and must always be treated with caution. In 1963 it was claimed that Protestants in Africa south of the Sahara numbered about 19 million and Roman Catholics 26 million. Like most Christian figures these seemed to be considerably inflated, and in any case they included the considerable white population in the Union of South Africa and Zimbabwe. A sober estimate would perhaps be that African Protestant Christians numbered then about 15 million and Roman Catholics about 22 million in the whole of Africa, excluding the Muslim north. If the total population was 200 million, another reasonable estimate, Christians made up more than one-sixth of the whole. This is an astonishing result, when it is remembered that in most areas it is the achievement of little more than a century of missionary work, and that over the greater part of the continent rapid advance began barely half a century ago. There is no sign as yet that Christian progress is slowing down. It must be borne in mind that census figures, where they are available, are considerably higher than those handed in by the Churches; this means that in many areas every person who has received any education at all is registering himself as a Christian, though in many cases his contact with the actual teaching of the Churches may have been no more than minimal. But when all sober deductions have been made, it remains true that Christian progress in Africa is one of the massive realities of our time.

No Christian, however, is likely to be complacent about the situation in Africa. The stability of the Churches is threatened from three different sides.

In the first place, Islam is a great reality in the scene. It has been rightly said that five forces are contending for the soul of Africa today – the old African tradition, sheer materialism, communism, Islam, and Christianity – and that it is not yet clear in whose hands the future is to lie.

Islam is a power, and there is no doubt that it is spreading rapidly. Although it has no organized missionary society, it has shown and shows great penetrative power; because it presents itself as an African religion and makes fewer demands on pagan man for change than does Christianity, it can take hold of the life of a whole tribe and refashion it within a very short time. Unfortunately no precise information appears to be available as to the direction and the effectiveness of its thrusts.

For the *World Christian Encyclopaedia* of 1982 a survey was undertaken of rates of growth in population and in the different forms of religion between 1970 and 1980. Naturally the statistics are often unreliable. But they show the virtual certainty that in all Africa south of the Sahara both Christians and Muslims were growing in percentage terms faster than the population, at the expense of animism, tribal religions, etc., and in most, though not all, areas, Christian numbers grew faster than Muslim, sometimes much faster. Only occasionally – the northern part of Cameroon, for example – was Muslim growth faster. In certain denominations, much of the growth of Christianity happened not in traditional Churches from Europe – though in certain areas traditional Churches expanded rapidly – but in indigenous Churches. These were often charismatic, though they might not use that word: they knew less, and cared less, about the historic doctrines of Christendom, and sometimes they were happy to tolerate or even propagate survivals from animism or tribal religion. Their services were long or very long. They almost all had healing missions, and this healing was central to the cult. They were concerned also with protection from the devil or wicked spirits. They often used dance and music as a form of shared communication. They looked to the Holy Spirit as God's force and messenger and their charismatic experience might be marked by violent movements of the body or by speaking with tongues. Usually their sacraments were infrequent. The Bible was a best seller, and was frequently quoted or commented upon. Some communities practised public confession, even of adultery or theft. The sermon would be likely to make little distinction between the sacred and the secular, between religious truth and non-religious truth. It might impart knowledge of agricultural method if the speaker was so moved.

One curious feature so far unexplained is the difference by area. In Ghana, for example, the indigenous Churches grew with extraordinary speed, until by 1980 they perhaps numbered 30 per cent of the Christian people in Ghana. Yet there are also huge areas of Africa where they do not exist.

One so far unsolved problem is that of polygamy. What is to be the attitude of the Church to an ancient custom which is well-nigh universal in tropical Africa? Almost all the Churches which have come in from the West took the line that monogamy is part of the biblical revelation with regard to the nature of man, and that no compromise with any other form of social organization is possible. Some of the early missionaries insisted that those who wished to become Christians must put away all their wives except the first. But this was found to lead to grave social disorganization and to a situation of intolerable moral disorder; in addition, it was the cause of lasting resentment against the Church in the minds of the children of the women who were put away. It therefore seemed better to allow the polygamous family of the first generation to hold together, and to permit the baptism of a woman who is the wife of only one husband, while keeping in the status of catechumen the man who is the husband of more than one wife. This apparently illogical procedure was that which seemed to work out best, though it led to the strange situation in many Churches that the number of baptized women far surpasses that of the baptized men. Some Churches permitted the baptism of the polygamous husband in the first generation only; but apparently the distinction between first and second generations was much clearer to the missionaries than to the members of the Church, and this led to a variety of confusions. No solution which is free from all objection has presented itself.

In the meantime, there was rather strong reaction even among African Christians in favour of polygamy as the natural form of the African family. Almost all Africans are convinced that women in Africa greatly outnumber men, though this view is not confirmed by the figures in any place in which an accurate census has been taken. Polygamy is partly a matter of prestige – traditionally, the greater the chief the greater the number of the wives by whom he has been served – and partly a matter of economic necessity. In a land where agriculture is women's work, the acquisition of a new piece of land by the prosperous farmer has almost automatically led to the acquisition of a new wife to work it. Practically, the Churches failed to make their own rule effective. From some areas it was reported that, though every chief was technically a Christian, not one among them was in good standing in the Church. While this book was being written, the visitation of one parish in East Africa revealed the fact that all the Christian families, with the exception of four, were as a matter of fact polygamous. The attitude of the Churches was that though this has so far been a losing battle, it is a battle that has to be fought. Many Africans asked whether this was really the case. Is not monogamy simply a European pattern which the missionaries introduced because it was familiar to them? Has the time come when the Churches should recognize that Africa is not Europe, and should prepare themselves for a radical reconsideration of what they have been inclined to consider fundamental principles? It is hard to see how any Church which takes the New Testament as its standard can make any concession to this kind of argument.

In part this demand for a reassessment of African values was good and necessary. But much of what reasserts itself is the primeval African past and that ancient world which the Christian could only describe as darkness. African philosophy was most intimately associated with the belief in 'forces', unseen powers, which may be good or may be maleficent.[23] The witch-doctor and 'medicine', in the broadest sense of that term, played an enormous part in African life, and acceptance of Christian faith in many cases failed to eradicate this ancient structure of thought. Some of the survivals in the use of charms and fetishes are comparatively harmless, though indefensible by Christian standards. But more than once the Churches in widely separated areas were disturbed by outbreaks of ritual murder. To certain parts of the human anatomy special magical potency is attributed: to have its full effectiveness, the part must be taken from the body of a freshly-killed victim; murder, when it takes place, is not usually prompted by hatred of the particular victim chosen, but by the unfortunate necessity of obtaining what is required for magical purposes. A Western society which is plagued by sporadic outbreaks of satanism has little right to criticize the African societies in which such things occur. The underlying cause in both cases seems to be the same – some strange deep instinct in the heart of man which if suppressed and kept hidden in the darkness may acquire compulsive strength and force its way out to these very disturbing

23. See P. Tempels, *La Philosophie bantoue* (1945; Eng. trans., *Bantu Philosophy*, 1959).

exhibitions of its power. In every time of revival in Africa, confessions of participation in the works of darkness on the part of most respected members of the Churches have brought horror, as well as relief, to those who have been concerned in them.

The indigenous Churches vary much in type and in the causes of their origin. Some are recognizable as schisms from Western missions and Churches; here the cause may be a desire for greater self-expression on the part of the African, or may be nothing more than the harsh exercise of Church discipline by the European missionary in one particular case. Other Churches are genuinely independent, in that they seem to have come into existence without any sense of conflict with a particular Western cause. Some are tender to such African traditions as polygamy; but it would be a grave mistake to class them all together as manifestations of laxity, and of a desire to escape from the more rigid traditions of the Western Churches. Almost all have a revivalist strain. Most of these Churches worked out new and strange ritualistic patterns of their own, partly by borrowing from the West elements which have not in every case been correctly understood, partly by the development of genuinely African traditions. Many have high-sounding titles and pretensions. Much of this may appear to the Western observer as either comic or repellent. But such an attitude is wholly unjustified; this phenomenon must be approached by the white man with humility, with sympathy, and in certain cases with admiration.[24]

For at the heart of this whole movement, directly or indirectly, will be found the sin of the white man against the black. It is because of the failure of the white man to make the Church a home for the black man that the latter has been fain to have a Church of his own, and to seek Christ outside the official Churches. Bishop Sundkler quotes from the book *I am Black* in the following terms:

Do you not understand that Jesus is not the God of the Black man? I found that out when I came to this big city of the White people. At home there was one White man, the Preacher, and many Black people, but there was no talk of Black people or of White people. The writings spoke only of

24. Our best authority for this whole movement is still B. G. M. Sundkler (lately Bishop of Bukoba, Tanganyika), *Bantu Prophets in South Africa* (second edition 1961), to which can now be added C. G. Baëta, *Prophetism in Ghana* (1962), a study of the 'spiritual churches' in Ghana; and H. J. Margull, *Aufbruch zur Zukunft* (1962), a study of the Cargo cult in the South Pacific, of the Kimbangu cult in the Congo, and of a number of Bantu prophet-movements.

men. . . . Here are many White men, and Jesus is their God only. Here there are great houses built for him . . . but I cannot go into these houses of the White men's God.[25]

So the black man turns in on himself, to find his own fellowship and his own Christ. Beginnings of discontent in the Protestant Churches in Africa were observable a century ago. But the starting-point of the modern situation may perhaps be traced back to the year 1892, when the Wesleyan minister Mangena M. Mokone seceded from the Church of his ordination, and set up in Johannesburg 'the Ethiopian Church'. The name is significant. Mokone's interest was far from being purely tribal. He was dreaming of a great African Church under African leadership. Naturally his movement had no connection with the geographical Ethiopia, which at that time was still generally known in the West as Abyssinia; the name was almost certainly drawn from Psalm 68; verse 31: 'Ethiopia shall soon stretch out her hands unto God.' But it is also true that the ancient Christian kingdom of the Lion of Judah, which has maintained its independence through all the centuries, and the Christianity of which is not derived from any European source, has exercised an almost magnetic power on the minds of countless African leaders.

Inevitably in such movements the personality of the individual leader plays a major part; and almost all the initiators of the movements are of the 'prophet type'. These men passed through a period of deep religious crisis, felt themselves called by dreams or visions, believed themselves to be filled with the Holy Spirit, and then set out to preach and often to heal. Sundkler gives us as example the Zulu prophet Isaiah Shembe (1870–1935), who exercised a wider influence than any other Zulu of modern times. Shembe experienced a number of dramatic visions, which led him among other things to give up the four wives whom he had married as a young man. In 1906 he was baptized in the African Native Baptist Church, but soon set out upon his own and chose for the centre of his work Ekuphakameni, 'the high and elevated place'. Ekuphakameni recurs again and again in the hymns of the Nazarite Church:

> Ye all who thirst
> Come ye to Ekuphakameni,
> Ye will drink freely
> From the springs of water.

25. Op. cit., p. 280, quoting Ray Williams, *I am Black*, p. 205.

By a transition perfectly natural to the African mind, the rejoicings over the splendour of Ekuphakameni 'are, without warning, transposed into a higher key and suddenly you find yourself, not eighteen miles north of Durban, but in heaven and Eden and Paradise'. And if we have an earthly Zion, is it not possible, by an equally natural transition, that we may have also a Christ on earth? Nothing is plainer than the tendency for the Bantu prophet to become also the black Christ. The white Jesus seems so remote and unfeeling; here is one whom we can see and know and touch. So we have no cause to be surprised when an African woman says:

Jesus! Him we have only seen in photos! But I know Shembe, and believe in him. He is the one who created heaven and earth; he is God for us black people.

Here the danger-line is crossed. In every form of Christianity Jesus of Nazareth is the central figure. Any form of religion in which he has been extruded from that central place is no longer Christianity but something else. And thus it comes about that the Christian observer of the independent African Churches, however sympathetic, is bound to regard some of them as a danger to Christianity, not because they threaten the dominance of the white man and the sacredness of Western traditions, but because they – or some of them – are a threat to something that is at the very heart of the Gospel itself. Bishop Sundkler, that most sympathetic of observers, noting the existence of a so-called 'Zulu Shaka Church', writes:

It is significant that here the pagan Zulu king[26] turns into a Bantu Church Father. *The syncretistic sect becomes the bridge over which Africans are brought back to heathenism* – a viewpoint which stresses the seriousness of the whole situation. It can be shown how individuals and groups have passed step by step from a Mission Church to an Ethiopian Church, and from the Ethiopians to the Zionists, and how at last via the bridge of nativistic Zionism they have returned to the African animism from where they once started.[27]

The only answer, if answer is the right word, to the Ethiopian-Zionist Independent movement is the revival and renewal of the Churches in Africa in such a way as to give satisfaction to all the legitimate demands of the African Christian for freedom, self-

26. Shaka or Chaka was the first (and murderous) Zulu leader, who was murdered by his brother Dingaan in 1828.
27. op. cit., p. 297.

expression, and self-government. The most notable thing about the great revival in East Africa – the movement of the Bālokale, 'the saved ones' – which could so easily have broken away and formed a new independent sect, is that it has remained within the organized Churches. Though of missionary origin (in the field of the CMS in Ruanda-Urundi), the movement[28] rapidly took hold in the African Churches, and spread to Uganda, Kenya, and Tanganyika. It had the usual characteristics of a revival – a profound sense of sinfulness, confession, the assurance of forgiveness, and a strong missionary urge. The danger of the movement was its self-righteousness, its tendency to condemn and criticize, and to judge that all who did not immediately accept the movement and all its shibboleths could not have had any genuine Christian experience. The great hero of this period was Bishop C. E. Stuart of Uganda, who, in the face of unparalleled and almost unimaginable provocation, refused to be provoked; and, when any roughness or impatience on his part would certainly have resulted in a schism, by sheer patience and temperate goodness maintained the unity of the Church.

If the movement can develop theological depth in proportion to its intensity, it may prove a great creative force throughout the Churches of East Africa.

The third and gravest danger to the African Churches is the increasing alienation from them of the intellectual élite, and particularly of the political leadership in the newly emerging countries.

In any time of crisis and rapid change, the Church is placed in a difficulty. Its task is to be the home and friend of everybody without distinction. The demand is often made that it should identify itself with one particular party or movement. In many cases it is the most advanced and revolutionary party that makes the loudest claims; not unnaturally, since it identifies its own plans and policies with the well-being of the whole people, in which the Church also claims to be specially interested. Any failure on the part of the Church to respond is attributed, not to the resolute determination it has shown, at least in some areas, to be the Church of the whole people and not of a political party, but to its involvement in the colonial situation, and to a greater concern for the defence of its own interests than for progress and freedom. It has to be admitted that the Church and its leaders have often failed

28. See M. A. C. Warren, *Revival: An Enquiry* (1954).

to discern the signs of the times, partly through sheer conservatism, and partly through preoccupation with more immediate tasks. A missionary or an African teacher whose salary is mainly or entirely provided by the government can hardly claim to be an independent agent; and this may bring painful consequences if at any time there is a serious clash between the plans of government and the will of a majority of the people. With the attainment of independence the situation is likely to right itself, but only on condition that the Church deliberately trains itself to be alert to the movements of the human spirit in times and areas of rapid social change.

For the problem of intellectual alienation, no other cause need be sought than the gap between the generations, which is wider in Africa than almost anywhere else in the world. Throughout Africa, the parents in the Church are for the most part converts of the first generation; their children are at home in the modern world of telephones and racing cars. Naturally the majority of the pastors are simple men, faithful and diligent but theologically not highly trained, and often unaware of the questions that are surging through the minds of the younger people in the Church.[29]

The danger in this is that educated Africans may come to think that Christianity is a stage that can be passed through and left behind. Pagan animism belongs to the childhood of the individual and the race; Christianity is on the Sunday-school level of adolescence. The future belongs to the mature man, who is able to understand it in terms of material progress and advancement, and needs no fitful and uncertain ray from heaven to guide him on an already well-lighted and very earthly way. Of the forces competing for the soul of Africa today, materialism is perhaps the strongest and the most dangerous. It falls with devastating force on a people which in the past has been profoundly religious, which has never known a separation between sacred and profane such as is now accepted in the West, and whose life in the past has been touched at every point by religious observance. The problem is not limited to Africa, though perhaps more acute here than elsewhere.

It is not to be supposed that governments and missions were unaware of this problem, or had done nothing to meet it. Notable examples of attempts to create a genuine élite under Christian auspices can be quoted from many regions. As long ago as 1924, an

29. On all this, see B. G. M. Sundkler, *The Christian Ministry in Africa* (1960; paper-back edition, abridged, 1962).

imaginative governor of the Gold Coast (now Ghana) brought into existence Achimota, a school which it was intended should grow into a college, and bring the best of Western knowledge and Christian ideals to bear upon the African intelligence. The members of the staff of Achimota were not missionaries but civil servants. But they were all – Roman Catholics, Anglicans, and others – actuated by the Christian motive of service. It was the aim of the first principal, A. G. Fraser, who had previously seen missionary service in Uganda and Ceylon, that Achimota should prepare Christian leadership for an eventually independent nation. With this in view he persuaded J. K. Aggrey (d. 1927), who had been born in the Gold Coast but had lived for many years in the United States, to return to his own country as vice-principal of the new school. Aggrey was outstanding as an interpreter between men of different race and colour, and as a passionate expounder of faith in true human equality in Christ.

The newly independent countries were left with weak economies. Times of drought or slump or vast rise in oil prices could drive their people towards desperation, or even starvation. Nowhere did they inherit a political tradition of long standing.

The problem of any state, not only a new state, is the control of men with guns, the army and the police. This is especially true of new states without an accepted tradition of a constitution. In all the poor Spanish and Portuguese independent states of Latin America, one military government followed another, one *coup* the next. Between March 1957 and April 1985 there were sixty-three successful *coups d'état* in African states. Only eighteen states out of fifty-one had no military *coup* in these years. Ghana and Benin each suffered five, Nigeria and the Sudan four. The *coup* in Uganda of July 1985 was the one hundred and fortieth violent *coup* in Africa since independence started. In 1985 only twenty-three out of fifty-one states were ruled by the army, but because Nigeria was one of them as many Africans were under military rule as were not. All the black states but Kenya were ruled either by the army or by a one-party system. The instability of democratic governments was due to rapid growth in population and rapid growth of cities at the same time as economic decline – conditions under which no government could obtain the people's blessing.

So many *coups* threw up leaders of every variety, from humane and responsible men to blood-thirsty despots and torturers. Sometimes civil war ensued. Civil war and tyranny had devastating consequences in young Churches: civil war always meant a breakdown in public authority and was usually accompanied by massacre. In the very Christian state of Burundi (population 4¼ million; Roman Catholics 73.2 per cent; Protestants 4.9 per cent; Islam 1 per cent; originally a German colony, seized by Belgium 1916, ruled by Belgian mandate 1923, independent 1962, first army *coup* 1962), the civil war of 1972–3 saw the massacre of 4,000 Tutsis and then 150,000 Hutus including eighteen priests and more than 2,000 catechists in Catholic schools. The devastation in the Churches was greater because foreign missionaries were expelled and some 100,000 Hutus fled as refugees to neighbouring lands. In Equatorial Guinea (population 339,000; Roman Catholics 81 per cent, the largest percentage of baptized Roman Catholics in any state in Africa; formerly ruled by Spain; independent 1968) tens of thousands were murdered after independence, and by 1973 only twenty priests were in service. President Macias was a militant atheist who murdered 150 Liberal-minded Christians in prison, prohibited religious education, Christian names and religious funerals. All priests and pastors were ordered to read at services: 'Never without Macias. All for Macias.' Naturally his own career was ended by assassination (1979).

The tyrant Idi Amin in Uganda was a Nubian Muslim whose régime gravely damaged the Christian majority of the country, including the murder of the Anglican Archbishop Luwum (1977). Such despotic careers were exceptional but were not the only such careers in the new states. Even in Nigeria during the civil war of 1967–70 there was mass killing of Christians in the Muslim north of the country, consequent emigration of most Christians, and the turning of northern Nigeria into an almost entirely Muslim country.

But most of the states continued with a mixture of that tension and liberality which had marked their predecessors.

In poverty and economic decline the doctrine of Marxism might attract. Its attraction was sometimes increased, as in Ethiopia, by the hope of Russian money. A few African rulers were drawn to the anti-religious side of Russian Marxism, but Marxist doctrines had far less success in Africa than in Asia or Latin America. Ethiopia acquired a doctrinaire Marxist–Leninist dictatorship (1977) which maltreated but nevertheless respected the Ethiopian Church. (It forcibly retired eight bishops and tried to force new bishops on the Church.) The Congo (Brazzaville) proclaimed itself Marxist–Leninist in 1968 but hardly began to pressurize the

Churches till after their Cardinal Biayenda was assassinated in March 1977. Benin declared itself Marxist in 1974 but its government went on broadcasting Catholic and Protestant services, for here the Christian population was rising very fast. Angola became Marxist in 1977 and started a stream of anti-Christian propaganda, and Mozambique also had Frelimo rulers attracted to Marxism (1975).

Marxist, or so-called Marxist, states of independent Africa were rare. For most, the doctrine had little attraction. The African peoples, as a whole, were far too 'naturally religious' for materialism to stand a chance.

The political difficulties of young states within a constitutional tradition were made far worse by the decline in the world economy. Civil conflict invariably produced difficulty and often danger for Churches, not only in Africa. These problems, which were those of entire societies and not just of Churches, were by far the gravest which the Church in Africa needed to face, and they troubled the historic Churches more than the indigenous Churches because the historic Churches cared about historic Christianity. They knew that they were part of Christendom, and had an internationalist outlook which was suspect to any nationalist soldier who seized power with a few tanks. While Africa outside the Muslim north grew steadily, and in places rapidly, more Christian in profession, its honoured roll of Christian martyrs lengthened every year. And since the African religious mind was so alive, the religious leader might in many circumstances become a political leader. In 1984 Desmond Tutu was elected Bishop of Johannesburg and thereby became the most weighty African churchman in the world. As such he could not help but be a leader in the political campaign against the apartheid laws enforced by the South African state.

Church leaders in Africa (as we shall see later, in Latin America, and even in the United States) had to ask themselves unfamiliar questions: a Christian pastor has a mission of peace – what is his duty when the people for whom he is responsible revolt against oppression? Was his duty the non-resistance preached by Martin Luther King (assassinated 4 April 1968) or Gāndhi, or did he 'lose' his people if he failed to stand up for justice with them, if necessary violently? Was it his duty to invite martyrdom if his people were subjected to tyranny? In black Africa, in Latin America, and even in black suburbs in the United States, Christian leaders were forced by events into an agonizing moral predicament.

Despite martyrdom and persecution and moral doubt, some

leaders of the African Churches had a vision of a future black Africa, largely Christianized, and able one day to bring into the historic Christian tradition a wealth of spiritual and moral insights which would recall the European tradition to the better things in its past and lead it onwards, as though the Christian apprehension, and new facets of Christian thought or life, were inherent in Africa's destiny. Desmond Tutu expressed the message of African Christianity thus: Africans find the classical arguments for the existence of God 'an interesting cerebral game' (by whites), 'because Africa taught us so long ago that life without belief in a supreme being was just too absurd to contemplate'; they approach the awesomeness of the transcendent with excitement while some of their contemporaries find even the word God an embarrassment; and they insist that material and spiritual, secular and sacred, are all of one piece.

The most potent influence [he said] for the development of an *African* Christian theology came because Christianity came swathed in Western garb . . . Christianity to be truly African must be incarnated in Africa. It must speak in tones that strike a responsive chord in the African heart and must convict the African of his peculiar African sinfulness. It must not provide him with answers to questions he has never asked.

And yet Tutu simultaneously worried that African theology as he observed it offered little but 'disengagement', from the world in the face of *coups*, military rule, poverty and disease.

When African leaders talked in this way, the idea of mission had changed. A missionary was still needed, but only Africans, perhaps, could show Africans the faith in the African context. The idea of the European missionary, which lies at the heart of so much of this book, faded as the social and religious context changed. As a North American missionary described the change, 'We used to be rather superior people handing on a pearl of great price, to people who might or might not want it. Now we have become the servants of the people digging for the pearl.'

LATIN AMERICA

The continent was once called 'the only Christian continent in the Third World'. Probably between 80 and 90 per cent of its inhabitants south of the United States were baptized Catholics. And yet it was a continent which the Christian Churches felt needed mission, not as a poor Christian Europe needs mission but as a not-yet-Christian East needs mission. Probably a higher proportion of Christian ministers were foreigners than in Africa or India.

Latin America is constantly spoken of as a unity; and for this there are certain grounds. There is the common background of Iberian culture, both Spanish and Portuguese. There is the common history of four centuries. There is the common factor of the revolutionary wars in the early nineteenth century through which political independence was secured. There is the republican organization which nominally prevails in all the Latin American countries, and a certain similarity in the oscillations between advanced liberal democracy and dictatorship by which almost all have been affected. In many of the countries poverty and illiteracy are major problems.

Yet within these similarities there are also major differences. In Colombia the Spanish tradition is strong. By contrast Peru, Bolivia, and Paraguay are largely Indian countries. Chile is perhaps the most European of all – it is typical that one of the most honoured names in Chile is that of the liberator O'Higgins. Argentina is more cosmopolitan: the common language is Spanish, but a great many prominent Argentinians have Italian names. The railways were built by British capital; the main commercial contacts are now with the United States; and education follows the lines of the French positivist tradition. Brazil is a melting-pot of nations – Indian, Negro, Portuguese, German, Japanese, and many more.

The Latin American states witnessed two extraordinary developments in Christian mission.

1. *The Roman Catholic Church.* Since the conquests of the sixteenth century the Church was part of the established order of things, except in those days of the nineteenth and early twentieth centuries when anti-clerical revolutionaries persecuted it, as in Mexico of 1926–35 (the time powerfully illustrated by Graham Greene's novel *The Power and the Glory*, when some 300 priests were martyred). In some states Catholicism was officially the religion of the state, in others not, but whichever it was, and whether or not the practice of Sunday Mass was followed by a large percentage of the people, Catholicism had become part of the structure of society. In Mexico the old anti-clerical laws lay among the statutes into the second half of the twentieth century, but were almost unused. Only in Uruguay were atheist anti-clericals still powerful in politics. Everywhere the reverence of the people for the cult, the saint, the

image, or the local priest could be seen by every observer. The cult might contain elements drawn from other sources than Catholicism: that of the Virgin of Guadalupe was one of the strongest religious forces among the Mexican people. Although it had a long history and the highest patronage, since the first vision to an Indian in 1531, the cult contained for some of its followers more than a pure devotion to the Virgin. In Bolivia the Catholic religion inherited something, at least in the remote country, from pre-Catholic cults, and produced a 'folk-Catholicism', and likewise in that part of Ecuador which lay high in the mountains.

The Roman Catholic Church used to be the conservative force of society. But, historically, this was true rather of the higher clergy than of the lower. In the revolutionary wars of the age of the French Revolution, when Latin America freed itself from Spanish rule, the country priests were often leaders of the people against the Spanish.

Therefore the Latin American Churches had two political traditions: a hierarchy which sustained government and state, and in return won the patronage of government and state for the Church; and lowly priests who shared the discontents of the people, saw how their lot might be improved and to this end did not shrink from political action. But lowly priests were often poor, ill educated, and at the mercy of their superiors.

Latin America never produced enough indigenous clergy. Vast populations had very few priests to administer the sacraments. In 1970 Nicaragua had one priest for 8,300 Catholics. In Mexico, the majority of the clergy in modern times are nationals; in Panama (1970) 221 expatriates and forty-four indigenous; in Guatemala most of the pastors were foreign, though Roman Catholicism is the religion of the State. In Latin America as a whole about half the clergy were foreigners; usually from Europe or North America. And in certain countries, Peru above all (1901: 82 per cent of priests Peruvian; 1970: 39 per cent of priests Peruvian), the number of indigenous clergy was falling steadily during the twentieth century, and the percentage of foreign clergy rising rapidly. Important to Latin American mission was the closing of China to foreign missionaries in 1949. North American missionary effort, in men and women and money, could be and was diverted into Latin America. At the time when the African and Indian Church leaderships became African and Indian, Latin America became more and more influenced by the foreigners.

The foreign clergy were much less dependent on the bishops.

They had stipends often paid by a missionary society. They did not need the approval of the hierarchy, or at least, if they earned disapprobation, they had an option not open to the indigenous clergy: they could go home.

In this way, the foreign priest of the twentieth century quite often became a force for change, and therefore a political threat to the local magnates. He was necessary. The Church, desperate for priests, could not exist without his help. But he had an education, which did not always fit the axioms long prevailing in Latin America. He might have acquired ideas of justice and equality as part of a Christian state. And incipient industrialization, the growth of cities, the flight of peasants to cities, were producing poverty and suffering on a scale which Europe and North America, with their modern welfare provisions and much higher incomes, seemed to have left behind. The Churches with their few priests looked incapable of coping with the crisis of society.

To the university student, or the few, though increasing, members of the bourgeoisie, the alternative seemed to be either the oppressive military dictatorships which alone had a chance of securing public order, or a Marxist type of revolution, especially after 1959, when Fidel Castro succeeded with a Marxist revolution in Cuba. The dominant power of the continent, the United States, feared communism as the organ of Russia. Therefore the policy of the United States sometimes meant support for military despots, as the less bad alternative for Latin America, and many Latin American bishops or churchmen agreed with this verdict. The Church must therefore stand on the side of the present arrangements of society. The old function of the Church, to maintain society at peace, revived strongly. In Puerto Rico, for example, the Church was the firmest force in the state for discouraging change. In Argentina the state looked to the Church to help secure order and in 1966 the government dedicated the country to the Immaculate Heart of Mary. In Honduras (1969) it was the government that placed the army under the protection of the Virgin of Suyapa and made every part of the army render her public homage.

This was not the attitude of many foreign priests, who came in with ideas of democracy and found themselves among an oppressed peasantry. Nor was it the attitude of some indigenous priests, especially if they had been educated abroad.

The experience of Cuba did not encourage all Roman Catholic leaders to imagine that even a more humane Marxist state was good for the Church. After 1959 in Cuba the profession of atheism and agnosticism grew steadily. The practice of Sunday Mass fell rapidly, indeed catastrophically. By 1980 perhaps only 1 per cent of the Catholic people in some dioceses attended Sunday Mass. One priest to 39,175 people (1969) was not a ratio which made sacraments plentiful. And all this happened without serious persecution except the expulsion of many foreign clergy. The situation had the advantage that the Cuban Church seemed to have freed itself from the reputation of being always with the possessor against the oppressed.

But as the social situation worsened in some states, civil war threatened or broke out, between a military government determined on public order and a peasantry led by radical bourgeois who were sometimes priests and were accused by the government of being Marxists because this was thought to be the only alternative to what existed. No one could imagine the then Indian peasantry of Latin America turning quickly into a viable form of social democracy.

One wing of the Church became a radical influence in society. This was very much encouraged by the new open-mindedness of the popes between 1961 and 1967, John XXIII (*Mater et Magistra*, 1961; *Pacem in Terris*, 1963) and Paul VI (*De Populorum Progressu*, 1967). The occasional young priest, of whom Camillo Torres was the most celebrated (he was a graduate of Louvain, killed in an exchange of fire with the Colombian army in 1966), joined the guerrillas with the object of overthrowing reactionary government by violence, but this was a type of extremism which the Churches as a whole could not countenance. The important change was that the radicals were no longer hot-headed curates. They included bishops and archbishops – Dom Helder Camara of Recife, Romero of El Salvador, Pedro Casaldaliga, Bishop of the Amazon, Proano of Riobamba in Ecuador, a stalwart defender of the Indians' rights, from whose house in August 1976 an entire synod of seventeen Latin American bishops was arrested and deported. Some despotic governments, from Guatemala to Argentina, kept order by the murder or torture of political dissidents. Bishops had a vocation to protest: some of them went further than protesting against such breaches of elementary morality and criticized the structure of society which made such crises possible, thus linking themselves with the political radicals.

The idea of mission had always been individual, the bringing of a soul to God, and this is how it remained. But in the Latin America of the twentieth century, it became, as never before elsewhere, linked to a political end: the creation of a just society.

In countries with a vast Catholic majority, Catholic traditions held to the union of Church and state, and in several Latin American states that union continued, either formally or without formal sanction in law, but nevertheless effectively. Yet the consequence of the ferment was a standing apart of Church and state. The Church wished not to be repudiated because of any association with dictatorships which trampled on human rights, and some of its leaders wanted to be freer to criticize government. State authorities no longer saw the Church as a reliable force for the harmonies of society and for law and order. They resented the incoming foreign missionaries with liberal ideas. Since they regarded all critics as 'Marxist' they accused the more radical Church leaders of being Marxist, and a few of the more extreme radical priests took up parts of a Marxist philosophy of the poor. In Nicaragua after 1975 some Catholic leaders were deeply committed to the idea of a Marxist government, and three priests were members of the Cabinet.

Therefore the Churches of Latin America were increasingly divided. Conservative bishops and middle-class laity on the one side disliked the encouragement to violence by a Church of peace and otherworldliness. They saw in such an encouragement only the incitement to useless shedding of blood in which the police were bound to win and which afforded every excuse for the maintenance of the police state. The more radical bishops, many foreign missionaries, some of the middle class and many of the poor, believed that Christianity is inseparable from human rights and freedom; Churches and church people had a religious duty as well as a moral obligation to stand up for human rights, and to seek to overthrow any government which denied such freedoms. These divisions in the Church would be painful beyond experience. Archbishop Romero of El Salvador denounced inhumanity from the pulpit for three years (1977–80) and did not hesitate to bring it home to his government, police, and army. His own suffragan bishops when in Rome denounced him as a Marxist. On 24 March 1980 he was shot dead while saying a funeral mass at a hospital chapel. The evidence showed a connection between his assailant and the military, but only one out of five Salvadoran bishops wished, or dared, to be present at his funeral.

The tensions, social divisions, innate violence of society and old feudal traditions meant that a Christian social democracy was impossible in Latin America. Chile had a democratic tradition and tried it (it had a Christian Socialist party) but the experiment was manifestly collapsing before it was ended in brutal violence in 1973. Prosperous states – Venezuela with its oil, Costa Rica, at times even Mexico – could make a showing at a Catholic social democratic state, but even here the radical tension which was often a class tension and the underlying violence disturbed the equilibrium of the society and its Church from time to time.

In 1968 the Latin American bishops met at the Conference of Medellín in Colombia, and Pope Paul VI came to the meeting. This council was a landmark in the history of the Latin American Churches. It publicly and formally identified the Church with the quest for a just society, and so encouraged Christian radicals all over Latin America. It was like the coming-of-age of the Latin American Churches. As African Christianity realized simultaneously that it was not merely a shadow of European Christianity, Medellín made Latin America realize that they were not simply dependents of European Catholicism, but were themselves the biggest Catholic population in the world and had their own contribution to make to the common inheritance of Christianity. The conference denounced injustice and 'institutionalized violence'; it removed the doctrine of obedience to governments, stated in Romans 13, as a ban on all fights against tyranny. It held that there are cases where revolution is a morally legitimate act for Christians, and it pointed to the concern for the poor as at the heart of the Church's evangelical mission.

The vile persecutions of some Churches in Africa by a few dictators was paralleled in Latin America. Between 1964 and 1978 some 260 foreign missionaries were expelled by the Latin American states; thirty-five bishops were arrested, two were killed, two disappeared; 455 priests were arrested and forty-one were killed, six of them while fighting like Torres with the guerrillas. In May 1977 there were threats to shoot all the forty-seven foreign Jesuits working inside San Salvador, for the Jesuits had encouraged peasants to occupy unused land.

The sense of danger to the Churches – and the fear that they were leading some of their better people to martyrdom – caused a reaction against the free speech of Medellín. In 1972 the Latin American bishops elected a strong conservative as the secretary of their conference. When Pope John Paul II came to the Puebla (Mexico) Conference of Latin American Bishops (1979) he spoke strongly for the poor. He also spoke strongly for freedom, for the right to life, for the right to life's necessities. He denounced torture and abduction. He spoke against a too-worldly involvement of Christians in politics and in violence, and against the portrayal of Christ as a revolutionary in politics, as 'the subversive of Nazareth'. He condemned 'ideological systems' adopted to help the Church mission. Despite an inaccurate report that he condemned 'liberation theologians', this utterance did not discourage the radicals.

One of the key words at the Synod of Medellín was liberation. The year before, in 1967, at the stimulus of the noble bishop, Dom Helder Camara, seventeen bishops of the Third World of whom nine were Latin American, defined revolution in gentle terms, as 'a breach with a system which no more guarantees the common good, and the creation of a new order more calculated to achieve it'.

In July 1968 the Peruvian professor Gustavo Gutierrez (born at Lima 1928, university degrees from Louvain and Lyons) gave a lecture at Chimbote. He defined faith as 'opting for the poor by means of a search for a better society'.

The idea of 'liberation theology' was felt by some radicals as almost like a Pentecost, a new leading of the divine Spirit. The movement agreed that theology starts with a commitment to the poor and oppressed against every form of injustice. The first act of theology is engagement. Its members tended to push academic theology aside as an irrelevance, and to set practical theology as the task; that is, to ask not what the Bible said to the age when it was written, but what it says in a contemporary crisis of oppression.

The Peruvian bishops published a document condemning liberation theology as a perversion of Christianity, and other bishops, not only in Peru, feared the links of some of its practitioners with Marxism. Pope John Paul II spoke out against it when he went to Lima in 1985. Gutierrez was accused by some of being 'a red priest', and indeed some of its lesser practitioners were crude in their thinking. But Gutierrez himself, and the best among his colleagues (Leonardo Boff, who was in trouble with the Vatican in 1985, Jon Sobrino, Ronaldo Muñoz) were not crude. A soul, they held, cannot have a spiritual life unless it has a minimum of physical comfort. There is no Christian life which is not spiritual life, and therefore the Christian life is dependent on social conditions. Thus, without a commitment to the poor there is no Christian life. Unlike Torres, Gutierrez totally rejected killing.

Father Cardenal, one of the priests who was a cabinet minister in the Marxist Nicaraguan government, said, 'Every authentic revolutionary prefers non-violence to violence, but he does not always have the freedom to choose.'

Liberation theology seemed too partisan, too little of a quest for the truth of God, to satisfy the European or North American tradition of Christian thought. In Africa and Asia it awoke some echoes. An Ecumenical Association of Third World Theologians was created, with two bishops and a Catholic priest from Sri Lanka in the lead. In January 1979 a Sri Lankan Conference took up all the themes of the Latin Americans as the key to faith and evangelism in modern societies. The language of their declaration implied that authentic Christians must be socialists. 'We do not back violence unconditionally but very often it cannot be avoided.' 'The theology of the so-called theologians is only authentic if it is grounded in the history and struggle of the poor and the oppressed.'

The divisions of opinion over these matters caused tense debates at the 1980 meeting of the World Council of Churches in Melbourne, especially over selective attitudes to liberation – if the conference was willing to say something about liberation in South Africa and Salvador, ought it to say something about Afghanistan? Such a proposal was impossible for the Russian delegates and so split the conference.

2. *Protestants in Latin America*. While these dramatic events occurred in the Church of the majority, almost equally dramatic events occurred among the Protestants of Latin America.

Very conservative and simple Catholic peasants had either hardly or never encountered Protestants. The entry of North American missionaries during the twentieth century could produce violence: they were often revivalist, and their methods were undiplomatic, and sometimes they did not mince their words about Catholicism. In addition, they held opinions about democracy which did not agree with military governments. They were eyed as though they were almost as bad as communists.

Between 1948 and 1956 the history of Colombia was marred by violent outbreaks against Protestants, in which seventy-eight victims lost their lives, forty-seven churches and chapels were destroyed, and 200 schools were closed. Two-thirds of the country was declared mission territory in which only the Roman Catholic Church might work. After 1963 the atmosphere grew more tolerant. The Protestant communities began to grow fast, especially in slums and shanty towns, but they remained relatively few in a dominantly Catholic country.

But elsewhere in parts of Latin America, Protestant growth was astonishing. A Roman Catholic estimate of 1962 spoke of 1,000 people a day leaving the Roman Catholic Church and joining one or other of the Protestant bodies. This estimate concealed the truth that Latin America was a continent of mission; that though so many were baptized Catholic, few ever practised Catholicism. Paraguay was in baptism a totally Catholic country but half of all babies were born out of wedlock. For obvious reasons some of the military governments preferred to have the Catholic hierarchy weaker, and therefore put no obstacles in the way of Protestant expansion. And some of the methods, parallel to the methods used in African indigenous churches – revival, dance, drums, healing, teetotalism – were found to be what the Latin American poor needed likewise. In Brazil many were of African descent, and the conditions making for African indigenous Churches were also present in Brazil. The expansion of Protestantism was far greater in the new cities and their slums than in the old peasant country-side, and the strongest of the Protestant denominations was the Pentecostalists (see p. 421).

They did not like the word Protestant. They claimed that European differences of the sixteenth century were no concern of theirs. They used of themselves the word evangelical, *evangelicos*.

The statistics showed amazingly rapid growth; but not every-where, because in some areas, for still unexplained reasons, no evangelical groups appeared. In Chile, formerly an almost exclus-ively Catholic country, and still a more practising Catholic country than most in Latin America, the Evangelicals by the 1980s had reached 1¼ million adherents. Mexican Pentecostalists grew fast. In Guatemala, where the Catholic Church was desperately short of priests, and where almost all clergy and bishops were foreign, and where 2 million Indians were untouched by anything Catholic except baptism, the Evangelicals had reached 6 per cent by the 1980s, and the Pentecostalists were their leaders. Here, also, the government deported foreign priests who protested at its despotic acts, and although the Cardinal reaffirmed support for the régime, the state saw small reason to discourage the work of the Evangeli-cals. In Marxist Cuba the Pentecostalists were the strongest of the Protestant groups, and had overflowing churches with many young people. In Bolivia the Pentecostalists were less successful – it was the country with the slowest rate of urbanization – and the

Seventh Day Adventists were the most numerous of the evangelical groups. In Brazil, uniquely in Latin America, a Protestant, Geisel, became President (1974). The Evangelicals in Brazil rose from 2.6 per cent of the population in 1940 to 5.2 per cent in 1970. The Pentecostalists were the most rapid in their increase, but Seventh Day Adventists also grew fast. (One extraordinary feature of Brazil was the success of the Roman Catholic Church among the large Japanese community of more than a million: by the end of the 1970s there were twice as many Japanese Catholics in Brazil as in Japan.) But Brazil also saw in this modern period an expansion of spiritism and regression to former cults. Roman Catholic attendance at Mass remained very high, but the country suffered a calamitous shortage of priests and the government discouraged foreign missionaries. In Guyana, where Hindus were many, Roman Catholics increased faster in percentage terms than the population; but that was not true of the Evangelicals.

In Haiti there existed the largest number of Protestants in the Caribbean – nearly a fifth of the population – but all denominations grew rapidly, including the majority Roman Catholic Church which was strongly marked by the charismatic movement. Foreign missionaries were still, during the 1970s, in the leadership. The control of the Churches by an unpleasant régime, that of Doc Duvalier, led to periodic expulsions of missionaries, and in 1960 the banishment of the Archbishop.

The new attitudes within the Roman Catholic Churches were of great importance, and this development of evangelical faith in South and Central America was at least of equal importance. It was hardly possible to take part in the life and worship of these Churches without realizing that here was something potentially different from anything that was produced by the Christian Churches in other parts of the world. Latin America, like Africa and India, now carried weight within Christendom.

Conclusion

In the twentieth century, for the first time, there was in the world a universal religion – the Christian religion. Christianity acclimatized itself in every continent and in almost every country. In many areas that hold might be precarious, and its numbers small, yet in country after country the Christians evinced the power to be a dynamic minority. It took root, not as a foreign import, but as the Church of the countries in which it dwells.

At a time when Churches were declining, at least in numbers, in many of their historic European homes, the statistics of Christian expansion were still extraordinary. This was partly a factor of birthrate. Christianity was expanding faster in most of those countries where the population was still expanding fastest, like Africa and Latin America and parts of South Asia. Repeated condemnations of contraception by the popes (especially the encyclical *Humanae vitae*, July 1968, by Paul VI) had less to do with this than the general inability of simpler folk to acquire the means of birth control or even to understand why it might be desirable. In Europe and North America Roman Catholics began in large numbers to use methods of birth control whatever popes or bishops might say. But in Africa, or Latin America, the restraint on the growth of Christian population was far more likely to come from calamities, such as famine in the world's belt south of the Sahara, especially a devastation of the historic Ethiopian Church by a combination of famine in 1984–5 and the hostile inefficiency of an unpleasant military dictatorship; or by civil war, which the guns of the twentieth century often turned into massacres, as in Ruanda-Burundi, Idi Amin's Uganda, or the Christian population in the southern Sudan. If it were not for the inability of Africa to feed its poorest areas, and the inability or reluctance of the rest of the world to help with enough food and medicine, the Christian population of the world would be growing even faster.

Some hostile critics argued that this vast Christian expansion was nothing but the accompaniment, and hangover, of European power, military and industrial, in Asia and Africa and would certainly decline, fail, and perhaps vanish as Europe declined and European influence in Asia and Africa returned to nothing. There was some evidence in favour of this thesis. Christianity in China suffered a disaster when the Westerners were thrown out by Chairman Mao. French control of Indo-China enabled the building up of a large Vietnamese Catholic population. When the French were ejected, Western influence was maintained for some years by American military intervention in the Vietnam war, and the Church continued, more or less, to prosper. When the Americans were thrown out, communist rule from North Vietnam was soon a disaster for, though not at all the total destruction of, the Catholic Church in Vietnam. In Burma the sense of identity between the ruling Burmese and Buddhism was soon a disaster for, though not at all the total destruction of, Christianity in Burma. We have seen the effect of reviving nationalism in Turkey and Egypt.

But in other parts of the world events proved that there was no necessary connection between European political power and Christian expansion. Decolonization in Africa was accompanied by the most extraordinary Christian expansion of modern times.

Meanwhile, the historic Churches in Europe were not prospering, at least in numbers of those who entered churches to pray. In Western liberal Europe there was a growing shortage of priests and ministers. This was partly because the Roman Catholic rule of celibacy for priests produced a scarcity of ordinands in countries like France and Holland, but more because the coming into existence of modern welfare states transferred much welfare to government agencies with taxpayers' money instead of charitable money, and so deprived Christian ministers of a weighty part of their historic function in society; partly because the intellectual climate about religion was disturbing to the young intellectual; and partly because a welfare state had to be accompanied by a measure of inflation. Inflation hurt all old endowments, and therefore all Churches suffered a creeping loss of the wherewithal to pay ministers a living wage, a loss made up only in part by the increased giving of the faithful. All the great missionary bodies, Catholic or Protestant, had fewer missionaries in 1985 than in 1960.

The Church in Russia had been associated with the tsarist régime. Karl Marx taught his followers that religion was the opium of the people. From 1918 the Russian Orthodox Church suffered bitterly from indiscriminate persecution meted out to everything that belonged to the past. One estimate is that in the early years of the Bolshevik régime twenty-seven bishops and 1,290 priests were done to death (some Western estimates were far higher). Christian faith was the object of a continuous barrage of attack from the anti-God movement; religion was held up to ridicule as outworn and unscientific; the practising Christian fell under the odium of political unreliability. There is little doubt that the more convinced communists expected religion to disappear within a generation. That the Churches survived at all under such a hostile régime – especially that of Stalin in the later 1920s and the 1930s – is evidence of their toughness. That they managed in a measure even to flourish is a miracle. But the Second World War made Stalin realize that he needed the loyalty of the people and that here the Churches could help. The Russian dioceses were provided with bishops where they did not already have them. Seminaries for the training of priests were reopened. The Baptists, and in the former Baltic States the Lutherans and Roman Catholics, shared in the increased freedom, but it was a limited freedom, and liable to sudden acts of tyranny.

In all the Balkan area, excluding Greece, the end of the Second World War brought communist régimes, all but two of them satellites of Russia. In Albania, a country partly Muslim, partly Roman Catholic, partly Orthodox, the government of Enver Hoxha was as nasty and irreligious a government as that of President Macias in Equatorial Guinea, which was the least civilized government in Africa. In all the others, Christianity and nationality were to some extent entangled. In Bulgaria and Romania all the historic buildings were churches or monasteries. The continued flourishing of Christianity under communist régimes – because it was necessary to the people – was true above all in Poland where the Second World War had been a calamity for both Polish Jews and Polish Protestants, and where Catholicism and Polish nationality went hand in hand. The religious aspect of communist Poland was given a new impetus when Pope John Paul II, a Pole, was elected in 1978, the first non-Italian Pope since 1523.

East Germany made a special case because the people were mostly Protestants. Except for the Baptists and Lutherans in Russia and some Reformed and Lutherans in Hungary and Romania, they were the only Protestant Churches under communist rule. Tension between government and Church was continuous. But Church life continued with vigour, and some East German Christians hold that opposition and hardship gave to

Christian faith a depth and purity often lacking in outwardly more favoured lands.

We saw what happened in Marxist Cuba, and certain of the African republics which professed Marxist principles.

One of the events of 1961 was the adhesion of the Orthodox Churches of Russia, Romania, Bulgaria, and Poland to the World Council of Churches. Until they came in, the word World in the phrase World Council was optimistic rather than real.

In Asia, outside communist China, the Church was still advancing in certain areas – parts of Indonesia, part of South India, countries for Chinese refugees like Formosa and Hong Kong, South Korea as a home for North Korean refugees. It was losing heavily in Vietnam and Cambodia, though the numbers of Cambodian Christians was very small anyway. Christians everywhere accepted the new independent régimes. They felt no conflict of loyalties. In many of the Asian countries there was little restriction on freedom of action.

Yet on the whole the Churches in Asia were engaged in a holding action, not an advance. The old religions of Asia pulled themselves together, recovered their spiritual inheritance, realized that they had things to offer the world. They seemed to be making themselves and their adherents even more impervious to the Christian Gospel.

Latin America and Africa both gave grounds for encouragement. The change in the Churches of Central and South America was startling. This growth was accompanied by every sort of political trouble, by martyrdom and murder, courage and compromise, but for the first time Latin American Christianity became a mighty force in world Christianity. The Roman Catholic Church there awoke to a new sense of its Christian responsibility, and the growth of the evangelical Churches was startling. But the political predicaments of Latin America looked as far as ever from finding a solution, and the Churches seemed destined to endure more spiritual travail as the states looked destined to endure social tension.

In Africa the twentieth century was the Christian century. No more is necessary than to take a look at the map of Africa as it was in 1886 and a map which shows the extent of Christian penetration in Africa in 1986. Much of the work might be superficial. The influence of Islam grew likewise. The political, racial, and economic problems looked, and sometimes were, insurmountable, but overall, the twentieth century in Africa has seen the consolidation of Christianity in the continent.

A thousand years ago, in the unbroken darkness of the tenth century in Western Europe, it must have seemed most unlikely that the Church would ever find the way to new greatness; in fact thoughtful Christians were of the opinion that the excessive evils of the times were a sign that the second coming of Christ was just around the corner. But what followed was not the second coming of Christ but the first great renaissance of Europe, with Anselm as its principal thinker, and Norman architecture as its massive and memorable outward expression.

The cool and rational eighteenth century was hardly a promising seed-bed for Christian growth; but out of it came a greater outburst of Christian missionary enterprise than had been seen in all the centuries before. There is no reason to suppose that it cannot be so today. But such renewals do not come automatically; they come only as the fruit of deliberate penitence, self-dedication, and hope. And the starting-point of all these is ruthless realism as to the situation in which the Church actually finds itself.

When Churches of the West were rich and their countries powerful, when the missionary impulse reawoke after 1790, it was natural for Western Churches to be 'sending' Churches and the other countries to be only on the receiving end. It could not have been otherwise. With the existence of a universal Church a new period dawned. The terms 'sending' and 'receiving' lost much of their meaning. Quickly the terms 'older Churches' and 'younger Churches' grew out of date. At the Second Vatican Council the black bishops of Africa contributed to the debates with mellow wisdom. Christians everywhere had the same work; to present Christian faith and life in the world, Western, Eastern, or Southern, which has its doubts, hostilities, and rival philosophies of life.

The age of missions ended. The age of mission began.

It was still different in different societies. To be a Christian in a half-Christian or post-Christian society, even in an officially anti-Christian but formerly Christian society like Russia, is not the same task as to be a Christian in an area which has never heard the Gospel before, in a speech which was never used there before, in a society where the organization was never touched by Christian principles. A third of the people in the world, perhaps, have not yet heard the name of Jesus Christ, and another third, perhaps, have never heard the Gospel presented in such a way as both to be intelligible and to make a claim on their personal lives. There is plenty still to be done.

In this narration we have not tried at any point to conceal the weakness of human endeavour – the sinfulness and pettiness of the agents, the blind selfishness of the Churches, the niggardliness of the support that they have given to the work of the Gospel, the mistakes that have been made, the treacheries, the catastrophes, the crimes by which the record is sullied. And yet the Church is there today, the Body of Christ in every land, the great miracle of history, in which the living God himself through his Holy Spirit is pleased to dwell.

The splendour of the purpose of God is such that it far surpasses the power of human imagining:

According to his good pleasure which he hath purposed in himself: that in the dispensation of the fullness of times he might gather together in one all things in Christ, both which are in heaven, and which are on earth; even in him: in whom also we have obtained an inheritance, being predestinated according to the purpose of him who worketh all things after the counsel of his own will: that we should be to the praise of his glory, who first trusted in Christ . . . and hath put all things under his feet, and gave him to be the head over all things to the Church, which is his body, the fullness of him that filleth all in all. (Eph. 1:9–12, 22–23).

When Paul looked out on the mystery of this purpose, and on the first stages of its fulfilment, he was moved to cry out in astonishment:

O the depth of the riches both of the wisdom and knowledge of God! how unsearchable are his judgements and his ways past finding out! For who hath known the mind of the Lord? or who hath been his counsellor? or who hath first given to him, and it shall be recompensed unto him again? For of him, and through him, and to him, are all things: to whom be glory for ever. Amen. (Rom. 11:33–36).

Bibliography

The literature is enormous, and only a small selection can be given by way of introduction to further study. For the most part this bibliography is confined to books in English; books in languages other than English are included only if they contain information which is not anywhere readily available in English. Almost all the books mentioned have bibliographies which will serve to guide those who wish to make more detailed studies of particular subjects.

I. GENERAL

i Only one book covers the whole of the field with which we have been concerned in this history of Christian Missions: K. S. Latourette's *A History of the Expansion of Christianity* (7 vols., London, 1937–45).

Latourette handles temperately, charitably, and with immense erudition every part of Christian expansion – Roman Catholic, Protestant, and Orthodox. It is baffling to his successors that, when we think we have made some specially bright discovery of our own, we nearly always find that he has been there before us.

Latourette's *Christianity in a Revolutionary Age* (5 vols., New York, 1957–61), Vols. III and V deal with Christianity outside Europe.

Next to Latourette in range and thoroughness is the four-volume composite work, edited by Mgr S. Delacroix: *Histoire Universelle des Missions Catholiques* (Paris, 1956). This, like most composite works, is uneven, and too much repetition has been allowed by the editor. But it contains much material not readily available elsewhere, has splendid illustrations, and does recognize the existence of Protestant missions.

C. H. Robinson: *A History of Christian Missions* (London, 1915) is for its period a very good piece of work and still valuable, though naturally at some points out of date.

R. H. Glover and J. H. Kane: *The Progress of World-wide Missions* (New York, revised edition 1960) is indispensable. Of the handbook type, it contains an amazing amount of reliable and up-to-date information about missionary societies, countries, and Churches.

Successive editions of the *World Christian Handbook* (London, 1949, 1952, 1957, 1962) contain a great deal of valuable material. Unfortunately the statistics in the 1962 edition have been so badly compiled as to be almost worthless. Now indispensable is *The World Christian Encyclopedia* (ed. D. B. Barrett, Oxford, 1982).

See also:

S. C. Neill (ed.) and others, *The Concise Dictionary of the Christian World Mission* (Guildford, 1970).

Those who can read German should turn to the extensive work of Julius Richter, who was Professor of Missions at Berlin and died in 1940:

J. Richter: *Allgemeine evangelische Missionsgeschichte* (1906–32). (1) *Indische Missionsgeschichte* (2nd very much improved ed. 1924. Eng. trans. of first ed. *A History of Missions in India*). (2) *Die ev. Mission in Fernen und Südost Asien, Australien, Amerika*. (3) *Geschichte der ev. Mission in Afrika*. (4) *Das Werden der chr. Kirchen in China*. (5) *Die ev. Mission in Niederländisch-Indien*. (6) *Mission und Evangelisation im Orient* (2nd ed. 1930. Eng. trans. of first ed. *A History of Protestant Missions in the Near East*, Edinburgh, 1910)

Richter was a tremendous toiler, and much of his work is still of value. But, as his titles imply, he was concerned only with Protestant *missions*: he had very little sense of the Church. And his work is marred in a number of places by a very strong anti-British prejudice which he is at no pains to conceal.

The classic work of J. Schmidlin: *Die katholischen Missionen* (1926; Eng. trans., with some additions, *Catholic Missionary History*, Techny, Ill., 1933) has now been superseded by A. Mulders: *Missiegeschiedenis* (Bussum, 1957; German trans. *Missionsgeschichte; die Ausbreitung des katholischen Glaubens*, 1960; not yet, I think, in English) which is balanced, factual, and notably accurate; but of course deals only with Roman Catholic missionary work.

Two volumes in the *Twentieth Century Encyclopedia of Catholicism* give a broad general survey of Roman Catholicism in the modern world:

R. P. Millot (tr. J. Holland Smith): *Missions in the World Today* (New York, 1961)

B. de Vaulx (tr. R. F. Trevalt): *History of the Missions* (New York, 1961)

H. W. Gensichen, in the chapter contributed by him to the handbook *Die Kirche in ihrer Geschichte* (edited by K. D. Schmidt and E. Wolf) on *Missionsgeschichte der neueren Zeit* (Göttingen, 1961) has brought together in sixty-two pages a wealth of concentrated information and bibliographical material, especially relating to periodicals, which is of the highest value. But this is a book for experts rather than for the ordinary reader.

K. B. Westman's *Den Kristna Missionens Historia* (Stockholm, 1960; German trans. by H. von Sicard, *Geschichte der Christlichen Mission*, Munich, 1962) proved invaluable in the checking of facts and dates.

It used to be very difficult to get satisfactory information about the missions of the Orthodox Churches. For the Russian Church the difficulty has been finally removed, for those who can read German, by two splendid books, factual, scientific, and complete:

J. Glazik: *Die russisch-orthodoxe Heidenmission seit Peter dem Grossen* (1954)
   Die Islammission der russisch-orthodoxen Kirche (1959)

S. Bolshakoff: *The Foreign Missions of the Russian Orthodox Church* (London, 1943) lacks the precision and complete reliability of the work of Glazik.

Three very useful, though also very brief, books should be mentioned here:

E. A. Payne: *The Growth of the World Church* (London, 1955)
J. Foster: *Beginning from Jerusalem* (World Christian Books, no. 10, London, 1956)
   To all Nations (World Christian Books, no. 35, London, 1960)

A recent survey of the world Christian situation is provided by a *Festschrift* presented to Professor K. S. Latourette: W. Harr (ed.): *Frontiers of the Christian Mission since 1938* (New York, 1962)

A useful chronological summary of the important events and dates in missionary history is provided by

T. Ohm: *Wichtige Daten der Missionsgeschichte* (2nd ed. 1961; also French trans. Tournai-Paris, 1961)

As a practical and useful bibliography of missionary subjects, *A Critical Bibliography of Missiology* (ed. L. Vriens OFM, A. Disch OFM, and J. Wils, Nijmegen, 1960) can be recommended.

ii Among the innumerable *missionary periodicals*, seven stand out as being of exceptional value, and indispensable to the advanced student:

The International Review of Missions (London, 1921–). The annual surveys (till 1969), and the classified bibliography, are an incomparable boon to anyone engaged in missionary research. *Église Vivante* (Louvain, 1949–). Roman Catholic, but broadly ecumenical, and with specially valuable reviews of books of all kinds and in many languages. *Evangelische Missions-Zeitschrift* (Stuttgart, 1940–4; 1949–). Edited for many years by my predecessor in the Chair of Missions at Hamburg, Walter Freytag, and marked by German thoroughness and a genuinely ecumenical width of vision.

Evangelische Missionsmagazin gives the Swiss and South German point of view on missionary work.

Het Missiewerk (formerly edited by Mgr A. Mulders at Nijmegen) gives, for those who can read Dutch, sober factual material as well as studies in missionary method and practice.

The two German Roman Catholic periodicals: *Zeitschrift für Missionswissenschaft und Religionswissenschaft* and *Neue Zeitschrift für Missionswissenschaft* give the results of detailed research on a wide range of missionary problems.

iii The *histories of the great missionary societies* are a valuable source for information of all kinds, which needs sometimes to be critically checked against other sources – the writers sometimes conceal things that ought to be known.

The best of these histories is

E. Stock: *History of the Church Missionary Society* (3 vols., London, 1899; Vol. 4, London, 1916)

Also valuable are:

G. G. Findlay and W. W. Holdsworth: *The History of the Wesleyan Methodist Missionary Society* (5 vols., London, 1921–4)

R. Lovett: *The History of the London Missionary Society 1795–1895* (2 vols., London, 1899). And especially the continuation of it:

N. Goodall: *A History of the London Missionary Society, 1895–1945* (Oxford, 1954)

W. Canton: *The History of the British and Foreign Bible Society* (5 vols., London, 1904–10)

H. P. Thompson: *Into All Lands: The History of the Society for the Propagation of the Gospel in Foreign Parts 1701–1900* (London, 1951)

E. G. K. Hewat: *Vision and Achievement 1796–1956. A History of the Foreign Missions of the Churches United in the Church of Scotland* (London, 1960)

G. Hewitt: *The Problems of Success (the Church Missionary Society 1910–42*, Vol. 1) (London, 1971)

Almost every society has its history, and the list could be indefinitely prolonged, especially if the Roman Catholic records, such as A. Launay's *Histoire Générale de la Société des Missions Étrangères* (3 vols., Paris, 1894), and records of the continental missionary societies, such as W. Schlatter's *Geschichte der Basler Mission 1815–1915* (3 vols., Basel, 1916; vol. 4, 1964) are included.

On the American side, a comprehensive study is W. C. Barclay (ed.): *History of Methodist Missions* (New York, 1945–; to be completed in six volumes).

Recent additions to the long list of American histories are:

F. F. Goodsell: *Ye Shall be my Witnesses* (Boston, Mass., 1959) on the work of the American Board of Commissioners for Foreign Missions.

S. H. Swenson: *Foundations for Tomorrow: A Century of Progress in Augustana World Missions* (Minneapolis, 1960)

R. G. Torbet: *Venture of Faith: The Story of the American Baptist Foreign Mission Society and the Women's American Baptist Foreign Missionary Society* (Philadelphia, 1955)

On *Missions to the Jews*, for the English reader
W. T. Gidney: *The History of the London Society for Promoting Christianity amongst the Jews* (London, 1908) gives a comprehensive account of Anglican work up to the date of publication.

The best general introductions to the subject are

G. Hedenquist (ed.): *The Church and the Jewish People* (London, 1952)
A. R. Eckhardt: *Christianity and the Children of Israel* (New York, 1948)

iv On the *theory of missions*, the classic work is that by Gustav Warneck, who is commonly regarded as the founder of the science of missiology.

G. Warneck: *Evangelische Missionslehre: Ein missionstheoretiker Versuch* (5 vols., 2nd ed., Gotha, 1897–1903). All later writers have borrowed much directly or indirectly from Warneck.

On the Roman Catholic side, the older work of Schmidlin has now been replaced by

A. Mulders: *Inleiding tot de Missien Wetenschap* (Bussum, 1900), and
A. V. Seumois, o m s: *Introduction à la Missiologie* (Schöneck-Beckenried, 1952)

To these must now be added the immense work (927 pages): T. Ohm, o s b: *Machet zu Jüngern alle Völker* (Freiburg im Breisgau, 1962) which is particularly valuable through its innumerable quotations from writers of all Christian confessions and of none.

On the Protestant side, the field for the moment is held by

J. H. Bavinck: *Inleiding in de Zendings-Wetenschap* (Kampen, 1954; Eng. trans. *An Introduction to the Science of Missions*, Philadelphia, 1960)

But mention should also be made of

H. Lindsell: *Missionary Principles and Practice* (Westwood, n j, 1955)

British writers on the whole are not theorists, and such comprehensive studies are not common. A great deal can be learned from the many writings of Canon M. A. C. Warren, and notably:

M. A. C. Warren: *The Christian Mission* (London, 1953)

Certain aspects of the theory of missions were vividly treated by one of the prophets of the modern understanding of the Church:

R. Allen: *Missionary Methods, St Paul's or Ours?* (London, 1st ed. 1912, 5th ed. 1960)
    The Spontaneous Expansion of the Church (London, 1st ed. 1927, 3rd ed. 1956)
    The Ministry of the Spirit (ed. D. M. Paton, London, 1960)

And somewhat in the same line:

D. R. McGavran: *The Bridges of God* (London, 1955)
    How Churches Grow (London, 1959)

v On the vexed, and now much discussed, question of the *theology of mission*, it is best to start with:

N. Goodall: *Missions under the Cross* (London, 1953) the report of the Missionary Conference at Willingen, Germany, 1952.

A brief study is

W. Anderson: *Towards a Theology of Mission* (London, 1955)

The much more ambitious book:

G. H. Anderson (ed.): *The Theology of the Christian Mission* (London, 1961), a collection of essays by twenty-five eminent theologians and others, reveals more than anything else the theological confusion which prevails in the ranks of the ecumenically-minded Churches, as against the massive simplicity of the approach of the Roman Catholics and the extreme evangelicals.

Here should be noted also the study of H. Boer:

Pentecost and Missions (2nd ed., London, 1961),

and two books commissioned by the World Council of Churches:

J. Blauw: *The Missionary Nature of the Church* (London, 1962)
D. T. Niles: *The Mission of God and the Missionary Enterprise of the Church* (London, 1962)

vi On the question of *Christianity and the other faiths*, the literature is endless; but the following represent the diversity of points of view as to the right approach of Christians to the ethnic faiths:

W. E. Hocking: *Re-thinking Missions* (New York & London, 1932)
H. Kraemer: *The Christian Message in a non-Christian World* (London, 1938)
Religion and the Christian Faith (London, 1956)
World Cultures and World Religions: the Coming Dialogue (London, 1960)
Why Christianity of all Religions? (London, 1962)
E. C. Dewick: *The Christian Attitude to Other Religions* (Cambridge, 1953)
A. C. Bouquet: *The Christian Faith and non-Christian Religions* (London, 1958)
S. C. Neill: *Christian Faith and Other Faiths* (Oxford, 1961)

And, more generally:

R. C. Zaehner (ed.): *The Concise Encyclopaedia of Living Faiths* (London, 1959)

vii On the *growth and development of younger Churches*, the only general study so far is

P. Beyerhaus: *Die Selbstständigkeit der jungen Kirchen als missionarisches Problem* (1956; shortened English translation, 1964)

but see also:

M. L. Hodges: *The Indigenous Church* (Springfield, Mo., 1953)

A splendid beginning has been made in the *World Mission Studies* of the International Missionary Council, of which the following have so far appeared:

J. V. Taylor: *The Growth of the Church in Buganda* (London, 1958)
J. V. Taylor and D. Lehmann: *Christians of the Copperbelt* (London, 1961), both of which, though dealing only with one limited region, raise many questions that are relevant to the whole problem of the growth and independence of younger Churches.

viii On *colonialism* and the involvement of missions in the politics of western powers:

D. M. Paton: *Christian Missions and the Judgement of God* (London, 1953) should not be overlooked.

In this same field, basic reading for all Christians is:

K. M. Panikkar: *Asia and Western Dominance* (London, 1953) in which the sections on missions, though often ignorant and often unfair, represent accurately the attitude of a cultured Asian who has studied the Christian faith and rejected it.

A Roman Catholic summary of the problem of the reaction of the non-Christian world to missions is:

T. Ohm: *Asia looks at Western Christianity* (Eng. trans. New York, 1959)

In this connection, the question of the missionary motive is significant. Here the best introduction is:

J. Van den Berg: *Constrained by Jesus' Love: An Inquiry into the Motives of the Missionary Awakening in Great Britain in the Period between 1689 and 1815* (Kampen, 1956)

ix Basic for the history of the development of the missionary movement in its ecumenical phase are the reports of the great missionary conferences:

(1) [Edinburgh] *World Missionary Conference 1910* (9 vols.). (The best and most impressive of the whole series.)

See also:

W. H. T. Gairdner: *'Edinburgh 1910': An Account and Interpretation of the World Missionary Conference* (Edinburgh and London, 1910)

(2) *The Jerusalem Series: Report of the Jerusalem Meeting of the International Missionary Council, March 24th–April 8th 1928* (8 vols., Oxford, 1928)

(3) *Tāmbaram-Madras Series: International Missionary Council Meeting at Tāmbaram, Madras, December 12th to 29th 1938* (7 vols., Oxford, 1939)

(4) [Whitby 1947] C. W. Ranson (ed.): *Renewal and Advance: Christian Witness in a Revolutionary World* (London, 1948)

See also:

K. S. Latourette and W. R. Hogg: *To-morrow is Here: A Survey of the World-wide Mission and Work of the Christian Church* (London and New York, 1948)

(5) [Willingen 1952] N. Goodall (ed.): *Missions Under the Cross: Addresses at Willingen . . . with Statements issued by the Meeting* (London, 1953)

See also:

C. Northcott: *Christian World Mission* (London, 1952)

(6) [Ghana 1958] R. K. Orchard (ed.): *The Ghana Assembly of the International Missionary Council, 28th December to 8th January 1958* (London, 1958)

(7) [New Delhi 1961] W. A. Visser't Hooft (ed.): *The New Delhi Report: The Third Assembly of the World Council of Churches* (London, 1961)

See also:

K. Slack: *Despatch from New Delhi* (London, 1962)

The books which cover the whole movement are:

R. Rouse and S. C. Neill (eds.): *A History of the Ecumenical Movement 1517–1948* (London, 1954)

H. E. Fey: *A History of the Ecumenical Movement 1948–68* (London, 1970)

W. R. Hogg: *Ecumenical Foundations: A History of the International Missionary Council and its Nineteenth Century Background* (New York, 1952)

See also:

N. Goodall: *The Ecumenical Movement* (London, 1961)

S. McC. Cavert: *On the Road to Christian Unity* (New York, 1961)

x On the movement for *Christian Union* there are innumerable works of only ephemeral significance and unfortunately very few genuinely scientific studies. Together with the *History of the Ecumenical Movement 1517–1948* already referred to, the student may be directed to the following books, and especially to the bibliographies with which most of them are provided:

S. C. Neill: *Towards Church Union 1937–1952* (London, 1952), a general survey of all movements for Church Union in the period under review.

Studies of various aspects of the Church Union movement in the lands of the younger Churches are to be found in:

S. C. Neill: *Christian Partnership* (London, 1948)

J. E. L. Newbigin: *The Reunion of the Church* (2nd ed., London, 1958)

D. T. Niles: *The Temple of Christ in Ceylon* (London, 1948)

H. P. Van Dusen: *One Great Ground of Hope* (New York, 1961) with an excellent chronological table of notable events in the progress of the movement.

B. G. M. Sundkler: *The Church of South India* (London, 1954) with an exceptionally full and valuable bibliography.

xi On the *training of the ministry* in the lands of the younger Churches much work has been done in recent years. The only general survey so far is:

Yorke Allen, Jr: *A Seminary Survey* (New York, 1960), which covers the work of the Roman Catholic, Orthodox, Anglican and Protestant Churches; but, unfortunately, is not entirely reliable.

On the Roman Catholic side, the pioneer work is:

A. Huonder: *Der einheimische Klerus in den Heidenländern* (Freiburg i. Br., 1909)

See also:

J. Beckmann, SMB (ed.): *Der einheimische Klerus in Geschichte und Gegenwart* (Schöneck-Beckenreid, 1950), a series of essays of unequal value on theological training in various countries.

On the non-Roman side, in addition to a number of careful surveys not published for general circulation, we have two classic surveys:

C. W. Ranson: *The Christian Minister in India* (London, 1952)
B. G. M. Sundkler: *The Christian Ministry in Africa* (London, 1960)

xii The last general missionary atlas was that published in New York in 1925: *World Missionary Atlas* (ed.: H. P. Beech and C. H. Fahs), in connection with the Jerusalem Missionary Conference of 1928. An atlas of this kind is now out of date, and it is unlikely that another of the same type will be published

For purposes of ready reference:

R. S. Dell: *An Atlas of Christian History* (London, 1960) can be strongly recommended, but it does not provide the material needed for detailed study.

II. BY CONTINENTS AND COUNTRIES

A. The Far East

i JAPAN

HISTORIES
C. R. Boxer: *The Christian Century in Japan, 1549–1650* (Cambridge, 1951). Thorough and completely reliable.
O. Cary: *A History of Christianity in Japan* (2 vols., Chicago, 1909)

W. T. Thomas: *Protestant Beginnings in Japan: The First Decades 1859–89* (Rutland, Vt., 1959)

C. W. Iglehart: *A Century of Protestant Christianity in Japan* (Rutland, Vt., 1959). Full of information but, as its name indicates, only on the Protestant side.

J. Jennes, CSCM: *History of the Catholic Church in Japan, 1529–1873* (Tokyo, 1959)

H. St G. Tucker: *History of the Episcopal Church in Japan* (New York, 1938)

R. H. Drummond: *A History of Christianity in Japan* (Grand Rapids, 1971)

BIOGRAPHIES

W. Axling: *Kagawa* (London, 1932)

N. Ebizawa (ed.): *Japanese Witnesses for Christ* (World Christian Books, no. 20, London, 1957). Sketches of five leaders in the Church by Japanese writers.

R. P. Jennings: *Jesus, Japan and Kanzo Uchimura* (Tokyo, 1959)

J. Trout: *Kagawa, Japanese Prophet* (World Christian Books, no. 30, London, 1959). A brief biography, with selections from Kagawa's writings.

Uchimura Kanzo: *The Diary of a Japanese Convert* (Chicago, 1895)

STUDIES

R. G. Hammer: *Japan's Religious Ferment* (London, 1962)

C. Michalson: *Japanese Contributions to Christian Theology* (Philadelphia, 1960)

ii KOREA

HISTORIES

The Catholic Church in Korea (Hong Kong, 1924)

A. Choi: *L'Érection du premier Vicariat apostolique et les origines du Catholicisme en Korée 1592–1837* (Schöneck-Beckenried, 1961)

G. C. Paik: *The History of Protestant Missions in Korea 1832–1910* (Pyeng Yang, 1929)

T. S. Soltun: *Korea, the Hermit Nation and its response to Christianity* (London, 1932)

M. N. Trollope: *The Church in Corea* (London, 1915). An Anglican survey.

BIOGRAPHY

C. Trollope: *Mark Napier Trollope, Bishop in Corea 1911–1930* (London, 1936)

STUDIES

C. A. Clark: *The Korean Church and the Nevius Methods* (New York, 1930). Deals only with the Presbyterian Church.

J. C. Nevius: *The Planting and Development of Missionary Churches* (1958; reprint of the original edition of 1890)

iii CHINA

HISTORIES

K. S. Latourette: *A History of Christian Missions in China* (London, 1929). This first great work of Professor Latourette shows the same qualities of thoroughness, balance, and charity by which all his later works are marked. Extraordinarily complete up to 1928, and can be supplemented by the relevant sections in the same writer's *Christianity in an Age of Revolution*, Vol. III (1961), pp. 431–45.

C. Cary-Elwes: *China and the Cross: A Survey of Missionary History* (London, 1957). Mainly Roman Catholic, but with a brief notice of non-Roman missions.

Successive volumes of the *China Mission Year Book* are of exceptional value for missionary history.

Of historical interest are

D. MacGillivray (ed.): *A Century of Protestant Missions in China: Being the Centenary Conference Historical Volume* (Shanghai, 1907)

A. E. Glover: *A Thousand Miles of Miracle in China* (new ed. London, 1957). Stories of missionaries and Chinese Christians at the time of the Boxer troubles.

BIOGRAPHIES

M. Broomhall: *Robert Morrison, Master Builder* (London, 1924)

V. Cronin: *The Wise Man from the West* (London, 2nd ed., 1959). A popular, not wholly reliable life of Matthew Ricci, by a Roman Catholic journalist.

J. C. Pollock: *Hudson Taylor and Maria* (London, 1962)

L. Sharman: *Sun Yat-sen: His Life and its Meaning. A Critical Biography* (New York, 1934)

W. E. Soothill: *Timothy Richard of China* (London, 1924)

J. Leighton Stuart: *Fifty Years in China* (New York, 1954). Reminiscences by the last United States ambassador to China before the collapse of 1949.

Dr and Mrs Howard Taylor: *Hudson Taylor and the China Inland Mission* (London, 1919)

Hudson Taylor in Early Years (London, 1920)

Memoirs of the Life and Labours of Robert Morrison (2 vols., London 1839)

Mrs Howard Taylor: *Pastor Hsi: One of China's Christians* (London, 12th ed., 1908)

STUDIES

P. A. Cohen: *China and Christianity: the Missionary Movement and the Growth of Chinese Anti-foreignism* (1963)

E. Holt: *The Opium Wars in China* (London, 1964)

F. R. Jones: *The Church in Communist China* (New York, 1962)

J. Krahl, SJ: *China Missions in Crisis: Bishop Laimbeckhoven and his Times, 1738–1787* (Rome, 1964) (see p. 174)

P. A. Varg: *Missionaries, Diplomats and Chinese: The American Protestant Missionary Movement in China, 1890–1952* (Princeton, 1958). Unfriendly, and at times naïve.

Two earlier studies:

C. N. Moody: *The Heathen Heart* (London, 1912)
The Mind of the Early Converts (London, 1920) are still valuable and stimulating.

Information on events and movements in China since the communist revolution has to be sought in various periodicals. The annual survey in the *International Review of Missions* gives reliable information, but the news is as yet too fragmentary for any general survey to be possible.

For *Formosa* the classic work on the earlier period is:

W. Campbell: *Formosa under the Dutch: Described from Contemporary Records* (London, 1903)

On the problems of Formosa, see

Lai En-Tse: 'The Task of a Church Historian in Formosa' in *South-East Asia Journal of Theology*, April 1962, pp. 42–50

On the movement among the aboriginal peoples of Formosa, the following can be recommended:

E. Band: *He Brought Them Out* (London, 1945)

J. Whiteborn and E. Band: *He Led Them On* (London, 1955)

G. F. Vicedom: *Ein Volk findet Gott* (Stuttgart, 1962)

iv SOUTH-EAST ASIA

As an introduction to the study of this area,

B. Harrison: *South-east Asia: A Short History* (London, 1954), which includes a well-chosen bibliography of books relating to each of the countries surveyed, can be warmly recommended.

For the general Christian history of this area see the histories (notably Richter) listed above.

R. B. Manikam and L. T. Thomas: *The Church in South-east Asia* (New York, 1956) is valuable as a brief, general survey.

(a) The Philippines

H. de la Costa, SJ: *The Jesuits in the Philippines 1581–1768* (Harvard, 1961)
The South-East Asia Journal of Theology devotes the whole of its issue of July

1962 to the Philippines, and, in addition to articles, contains reviews of three important books dealing with the troubled period at the turn of this century:

P. S. de Achútegui, sj, and M. A. Bernard: *Religious Revolution in the Philippines. The Life and Church of Gregorio Aglipay 1860–1960* (Manila, 1961)

I. R. Rodriguez, osa: *Gregorio Aglipay y los Origenes de la Iglesia Filipina Independiente 1895–1917* (2 vols., Madrid, 1960)

L. B. Whittemore: *Struggle for Freedom, History of the Philippine Independent Church* (Greenwich, Conn., 1961)

The first two Roman Catholic and highly critical; the third Episcopalian and highly favourable.

On the Protestant side:

C. Osias and A. Lorenzana: *Evangelical Christianity in the Philippines* (Dayton, 1931)

J. B. Rodgers: *Forty Years in the Philippines: A History of the Philippine Mission of the Presbyterian Church in the United States of America* (New York, 1940)

F. C. Laubach: *The People of the Philippines: Their Spiritual Progress and Preparation for Spiritual Leadership in the Far East* (New York, 1925)

H. C. Stuntz: *The Philippines and the Far East* (New York, 1939)

W. N. Roberts: *The Filipino Church* (New York, 1936)

On the movement for Christian unity in the Philippines, see E. C. Sobrepeña: *That They May be One* (Manila, 1955)

(b) Thailand

G. B. McFarland (ed.): *Historical Sketch of Protestant Missions in Siam* (Bangkok, 1928)

K. E. Wells: *A History of Protestant Work in Thailand* (Bangkok, 1958)

I. Kuhn: *Ascent to the Tribes: Pioneering in North Thailand* (London, 1956).
Gives an account of the work opened up on the borderland between Thailand and Laos.

(c) Indonesia

Almost all the literature is in Dutch or German.

A history of the Churches in Indonesia has been prepared (in Indonesian) by Dr T. Müller-Krüger; it is hoped that versions in German and English may be made available before long.

The classic work on the Protestant Church in Indonesia is:

C. W. Th. Baron van Boetzelaer van Dubbeldam: *De Protestantsche Kerk im Nederlandsch-Indië: Haar Ontwikkeling van 1620–1939* (The Hague, 1947)

His other great work is

De Gereformeerde Kerken in Nederland en de zending in Oost Indië in de dagen der Oost-Indische Compagnié (Utrecht, 1906)

There seems to be as yet no English life of Nommensen; there are a number in German, of which mention may be made of:

J. Warneck: *D. Ludwig I. Nommensen, Ein Lebensbild* (Barmen, 3rd ed., 1928)

H. Kraemer: *From Mission Field to Independent Church: Report on a decisive decade in the growth of indigenous Churches in Indonesia* (London, 1958) is a classic on the transition period in missionary history; the reports contained in it were written between 1926 and 1935.

For the Batak Church, much valuable material is contained in the centenary volume,

H. de Kleine (ed.): . . . *Gemacht zu seinem Volk* (Wuppertal Barmen, 1961)

For Bali, the two indispensable books are:

H. Kraemer: *De Strijd over Bali en de Zending* (Amsterdam, 1938).
J. L. Swellengrebel: *Kerk en Tempel op Bali* (The Hague, 1948) by one of the experts of the Netherlands Bible Society; a beautifully illustrated volume.

The survey by A. McLeish (ed.): *The Netherland Indies* (London, 1935) is still of value.

(d) Burma

Apart from the general histories, much is to be learned from biographies, among which naturally those of Judson have pride of place.
The irreplaceable original biography is:

Francis Wayland: *Memoir of the Life and Labours of the Rev. Adoniram Judson D.D.* (2 vols., Boston, 1853)
For a more popular modern life, see:

C. Anderson: *To the Golden Shore, The Life of Adoniram Judson* (Boston, 1956)

A recent life of George Dana Boardman, the apostle of the Karens, is:

J. C. Robbins: *Boardman of Burma* (Philadelphia, 1940)

For the work of the Anglican Churches, see:

W. C. B. Purser: *Christian Missions in Burma* (London, 1911), which is excellent up to the date of publication.

B. The Pacific

Apart from Richter, as above, there seems to be no general history.
Of unique importance historically is:

J. Davies: *The History of the Tahitian Mission 1799–1830* (ed. C. W. Newbury, Cambridge, 1961) a contemporary and authentic account.

C. E. Fox: *Lord of the Southern Isles, being the Story of the Anglican Mission in Melanesia, 1849–1949* (London, 1958) contains much of value, especially on the Anglican side.

For information on recent developments, turn to:

Beyond the Reef, Records of the Conference of Churches and Missions in the Pacific, Malua Theological College, Western Samoa, 22 April–4 May 1961 (London, 1961)

BIOGRAPHIES

Much can be learned from the denominational histories, especially that of the London Missionary Society. Beyond these, reference must be made to the biographies, of which the following is a selection:

C. Butler OSB: *The Life and Times of Bishop Ullathorne* (2 vols., London, 1926). Ullathorne was in Australia 1832–40, as Vicar-General of the Roman Catholic Mission there.

L. Creighton: *Life of G. A. Selwyn D.D., Bishop of New Zealand and Lichfield* (London, 1923)

J. R. Elder (ed.): *The Letters and Journals of Samuel Marsden 1765–1838* (Dunedin, 1932)

J. Farrow: *Damien the Leper* (London, 1937)

J. Flierl: *Forty-five years in New Guinea* (Eng. trans. of 2nd ed., Columbus, Ohio, 1931)

E. C. Hawley: *The Introduction of Christianity into the Hawaiian Islands* (Brattleboro, 1932)

R. Lovett: *James Chalmers, his Autobiography and Letters* (London, 1902)

C. Northcott: *John Williams Sails On* (London, 1939)

J. B. Marsden: *Memoirs of the Life and Labours of the Rev. Samuel Marsden of Paramatta* (London, n.d.)

J. G. Paton: *An Autobiography* (original edition, London, 1889; many times reprinted)

E. Prout: *Memoirs of the Life of the Rev. John Williams* (London, 1843)

H. W. Tucker: *Memoir of the Life and Episcopate of George Augustus Selwyn D.D.* (2 vols., London, 1879)

C. M. Yonge: *The Life of Bishop Patteson* (London, 2nd ed. 1878)

STUDIES

H. P. Van Dusen: *They Found the Church There* (London, 1945). Very delightfully brings together evidence from war-time of the effect of missions on the Pacific peoples.

A. A. Koskinen: *Missionary Influence as a Political Factor in the Pacific Islands* (Helsinki, 1953). An indispensable survey.

G. F. Vicedom: *Church and People in New Guinea* (World Christian Books no. 38, London, 1961) is an able and up-to-date study of the problems of Church and mission among primitive peoples.

C. India and Pakistan

HISTORIES

Apart from Richter as listed above, see:

C. B. Firth: *An Introduction to Indian Church History* (Madras, 1961). Though short, this is a balanced and scholarly piece of work, though unfortunately it is fuller and better on the earlier than on the later period.

P. Thomas: *Christians and Christianity in India and Pakistan* (Allen & Unwin, 1954). By an Indian Christian, this account is unfortunately uncritical and not wholly reliable.

E. Chatterton: *A History of the Church of England in India* (London, 1924)

BIOGRAPHIES

A. J. Appasamy: *Sundar Singh* (London, 1958)
H. Birks: *The Life and Correspondence of Thomas Valpy French, First Bishop of Lahore* (2 vols., London, 1895)
J. Brodrick, sj: *Saint Francis Xavier* (London, 1927)
S. P. Carey: *William Carey* (London, 1925)
V. Cronin: *A Pearl to India: the Life of Robert de Nobili* (London, 1959)
C. E. Gardner: *Life of Father Goreh* (London, 1900)
C. Graham: *Azariah of Dornakal* (London, 1947)
N. Macnicol: *Pandita Ramabai* (Calcutta, 1926)
J. C. Marshman: *The Life and Times of Carey, Marshman and Ward* (London, 1859)
C. E. Padwick: *Henry Martyn: Confessor of the Faith* (London, 1922)
W. Paton: *Alexander Duff, Pioneer of Missionary Education* (London, 1922)
H. Pearson: *Memoirs and Correspondence of C. F. Schwartz* (2 vols., London, 1833)
O. Hodne: *Lars O. Skrefsrud* (Oslo, 1966)
G. Smith: *The Life of Alexander Duff* (London, 1879)
    The Life of John Wilson (London, 1878)
G. Smith: *Henry Martyn* (London, 1892)
G. Smith: *Bishop Heber* (London, 1895)
G. N. Thomssen: *Samuel Hebich of India* (Cuttack, 1905)
L. Tilak (tr. by E. J. Inkster): *I Follow After* (O U P, India, 1900) (the life of Nārāyan Vāman Tilak)
L. Tilak: *From Brahma to Christ* (World Christian Books no. 9, London, 1956)

D. C. Wilson: *Dr Ida: the Story of Dr Ida Scudder of Vellore* (New York, 1959)
Fr G. Schurhammer's great life, *Francis Xavier: his life, his times* (Eng. trans., 4 vols., Rome, 1973–82) is fundamental.

STUDIES

L. W. Brown: *The Indian Christians of St Thomas* (Cambridge, 1956)
E. R. Hull: *Bombay Mission-History with a Special Study of the Padroado Question* (Bombay, n.d.)
K. Ingham: *Reformers in India 1793–1833* (Cambridge, 1956)
H. Josson sj: *La Mission du Bengale Occidentale* (2 vols., Bruges, 1921). Recounts the triumphs of Fr Lievens in Chota Nagpur.
E. Maclagan: *The Jesuits and the Great Mogul* (London, 1932)
A. I. Mayhew: *The Education of India* (London, 1926)
A. I. Mayhew: *Christianity and the Government of India* (London, 1929)
R. D. Paul: *Chosen Vessels: Lives of Ten Indian Christian Pastors of the Eighteenth and Nineteenth Centuries* (Christian Students' Library no. 25, Madras, 1961)
J. W. Pickett: *Christian Mass Movements in India* (Nashville, 1933)
J. W. Pickett: *Christ's Way to India's Heart* (Livingstone Press, 1938)
M. A. Sherring: *The Indian Church during the Great Rebellion* (London, 1859)
B. G. M. Sundkler: *The Church of South India* (London, 1954)
E. Cardinal Tisserant: *Eastern Christianity in India* (Eng. trans. from French, London, 1957)
O. Wolff: *Mahatma und Christus* (Berlin, 1955). A critical study of M. K. Gāndhi and his relationship to the Christian faith.

D. The Middle East

The only general history appears to be Richter, as above.

For books on Islam, see the bibliographies to the books listed in I, vi, *Christianity and the Other Faiths*.

There are also many books dealing with the problems of Christianity in relation to Islam, and of Christian missions among Muslims. Notable among these are the long series of works by S. M. Zwemer, and also the writings of W. W. Cash (missionary in Egypt, and later Bishop of Worcester). Note also especially two books by Kenneth Cragg: *The Call of the Minaret* (London, 1956) and *Sandals at the Mosque* (London, 1959).

BIOGRAPHIES

Anon: *Samuel Gobat, Bishop of Jerusalem: His Life and Work* (London, 1884)
R. Bazin: *Charles de Foucauld, Hermit and Explorer* (Eng. trans. 2nd ed., London, 1931)
H. B. Dehqani-Tafti: *Design of my World* (World Christian Books no. 28, London, 1959)

W. H. T. Gairdner: *D. M. Thornton* (London, 1908)

W. P. Livingstone: *A Galilee Doctor, Being a Sketch of the Career of Dr D. W. Torrance of Tiberias* (New York and London, n.d.)

C. E. Padwick: *Temple Gairdner of Cairo* (London, 1929)

B. A. F. Pigott: *I Lilias Trotter . . . Founder of the Algiers Mission Band* (London, n.d.)

C. C. Rice: *Mary Bird in Persia* (London, 1916)

J. Robson: *Ian Keith-Falconer of Arabia* (London, n.d.)

R. Voillaume: *Seeds of the Desert: The Legacy of Charles de Foucauld* (Eng. trans. London, 1955)

STUDIES

J. T. Addison: *The Christian Approach to the Moslem: A Historical Study* (New York, 1942)

P. W. Harrison: *Doctor in Arabia* (New York, 1940)

H. H. Jessup: *Fifty-three Years in Syria* (2 vols., Chicago, 1910)

J. Rutherford and E. H. Glenny: *The Gospel in North Africa* (London, 1900)

S. M. Zwemer: *Arabia, the Cradle of Islam* (London, 1892)

E. Africa

HISTORIES

Here, in addition to Richter, as above, we are fortunate in having

C. P. Groves: *The Planting of Christianity in Africa* (4 vols., London, 1948–58). This is full, careful, reliable, and complete, though not always very inspiring.

For South and Central Africa,

J. Du Plessis: *A History of Christian Missions in South Africa* (London, 1911); *The Evangelization of Pagan Africa: A History of Christian Missions to the Pagan Tribes of Central Africa* (Cape Town and Johannesburg, 1930), are authoritative.

BIOGRAPHIES

E. C. Dawson: *James Hannington: A History of his Life and Work, 1847–1885* (London, 1886). The first of many lives, and one of the best missionary biographies ever written.

H. L. Demmens: *George Grenfell: Pioneer in Congo* (London, 1922)

P. Hinchliff: *J. W. Colenso, Bishop of Natal* (London, 1960)

H. Johnston: *George Grenfell and the Congo* (London, 1908)

W. P. Livingstone: *Mary Slessor of Calabar* (London, 1916)

W. P. Livingstone: *Laws of Livingstonia* (London, 1921)

C. Northcott: *Robert Moffat: Pioneer in Africa, 1817–1870* (London, 1961)

M. Perham: *Lugard: The Years of Adventure* (London, 1956)
  Lugard: The Years of Authority (London, 1960)

W. J. Platt: *An African Prophet* (London, 1934). A popular study of 'The Prophet Harris' and his work on the Ivory Coast.

R. Oliver: *Sir Harry Johnston and the Scramble for Africa* (London, 1957)

G. Seaver: *David Livingstone: His Life and Letters* (London, 1957)

G. Seaver: *Albert Schweitzer, The Man and his Mind* (London, 5th ed. 1955) with which compare Schweitzer's own book *My Life and Thought* (London, 3rd ed. 1933)

A. P. Shepherd: *Tucker of Uganda, Artist and Apostle 1849–1914* (London, 1929)

E. Shillito: *François Coillard: a Wayfaring Man* (London, 1923)

E. W. Smith: *Aggrey of Africa* (London, 1929)

E. W. Smith: *Robert Moffat: One of God's Gardeners* (London, 1923)

F. D. Walker: *Thomas Birch Freeman: The Son of an African* (London, 1929)

W. F. Ward: *Fraser of Trinity and Achimota* (Oxford, 1965)

STUDIES

C. G. Baeta: *Christianity in Tropical Africa* (Oxford, 1968)

D. B. Barrett: *Schism and Renewal* (Oxford, 1968)

F. Coillard: *On the Threshold of Central Africa* (Eng. trans. New York and London, 1903)

R. Coupland: *The Exploitation of East Africa* (London, 1939)

R. Coupland: *East Africa and its Invaders* (London, 1938)

R. S. Foster: *The Sierra Leone Church* (London, 1961)

G. M. Haliburton: *The Prophet Harris* (Harlow, 1971)

A. Hastings: *Church and Mission in Modern Africa* (London, 1967)

N. Q. King: *Christians and Muslims in Africa* (London, 1971)

Z. Marsh (ed.): *East Africa through Contemporary Records* (London, 1961)

J. S. Mbiti: *An Introduction to African Religion* (London, 1975)

R. Oliver: *The Missionary Factor in East Africa* (London, 1952)

A. Phillips (ed.): *Survey of African Marriage and Family Life* (London, 1953)

R. M. Slade: *English-Speaking Missions in the Congo Independent State 1878–1908* (Brussels, 1959)
  King Leopold's Congo: Aspects of the Development of Race Relations in the Congo (London, 1962)

E. W. Smith: *The Golden Stool* (London, 1926)

B. G. M. Sundkler: *Bantu Prophets in South Africa* (2nd ed. London, 1961)

J. M. Todd: *African Mission* (London, 1962)

J. B. Webster: *The African Churches among the Yoruba 1888–1922* (Oxford, 1964)

F. B. Welbourn: *East African Rebels: A Study of some Independent Churches* (London, 1961)

F. The Americas and the West Indies

For North America, we now have a valuable survey of early missionary work:

W. Kellaway: *The New England Company 1649–1776: Missionary Society to the American Indians* (London, 1961)

For the United States and the British West Indies, the records of the SPG (see H. P. Thompson: *Into All Lands*) contain much information.

Francis Parkman's great series of volumes on *France and England in the New World* (1865–92) contains immense and now largely forgotten riches about the early period ('Parkman was the first great literary author who really understood the Indian's character and motives' – *Encyclopaedia Britannica*).

There is a large literature on Las Casas and the struggle on behalf of the Indians in the *Caribbean* and *Mexico*. A useful and brief study in English is to be found in:

D. Jenks: *Six Great Missionaries* (London, 1930) pp. 10–40. In the same book Jenks has a chapter on Jean de Brébeuf, the apostle of the Hurons, pp. 146–73.

Much more thorough and scientific are:

L. Hanke: *The Spanish Struggle for Justice in the Conquest of America* (Philadelphia, 1949)
Bartolomé de las Casas (The Hague, 1951)
Aristotle and the American Indians (London, 1959)

There is also a large literature on the Jesuits and their work in Paraguay. A popular account in English is:

R. B. Cunninghame Graham: *A Vanished Arcadia* (new ed. London, 1924)

A good summary account with extensive bibliography is:

A. Huonder, in *Catholic Encyclopaedia* Vol. XII, pp. 688–700.

For Central and South America in modern times it is difficult to present a general picture. There are twenty countries, each different from all the rest.

The series of surveys carried out thirty years ago by the World Dominion Press, though out of date in detail, contain information which is not easily available elsewhere. The best of the series is:

E. Braga and K. G. Grubb: *The Republic of Brazil: A Survey of the Religious Situation* (London, 1932)

See also

K. G. Grubb: *The Northern Republics of South America, Ecuador, Colombia and Venezuela* (london, 1931)

Religion in Central America (London, 1937)

W. E. Browning: *The River Plate Republics: A Survey of the Religious, Economic and Social Conditions in Argentina, Paraguay and Uruguay* (London, 1928)

W. E. Browning, J. Ritchie, and K. G. Grubb: *The West Coast Republics of South America, Chile, Peru, and Bolivia* (London, 1930)

F. C. Macdonald: *Bishop Stirling of the Falklands* (London, 1929)

J. W. Marsh and W. H. Stirling: *The Story of Commander Allen Gardiner, R.N., with Sketches of Missionary Work in South America* (London, 2nd ed. 1868)

On the relation between Church and state, the standard work is

J. C. Mecham: *Church and State in Latin America: A History of Politico-Ecclesiastical Relations* (Chapel Hill, 1934)

On the movement of Liberation theology in Latin America:

Trevor Beeson and Jenny Pearce: *A Vision of Hope: the Churches and Change in Latin America* (London, 1984)

Leonardo Boff: *Jesus Christ Liberator* (Eng. trans. New York, 1978)

P. Erdozain: *Archbishop Romero* (New York, 1981)

P. Lernoux: *The Struggle for Human Rights in Latin America* (Harmondsworth, 1982)

Index